Library of Congress Control Number: 2008936813

Printed in China.
ISBN: 978-0-7643-3229-6

We are interested in hearing from authors with book ideas on related topics.

Published by Schiffer Publishing Ltd.
4880 Lower Valley Road
Atglen, PA 19310
Phone: (610) 593-1777
FAX: (610) 593-2002
E-mail: Info@schifferbooks.com.
Visit our web site at: www.schifferbooks.com
Please write for a free catalog.
This book may be purchased from the publisher.
Please include $5.00 postage.
Try your bookstore first.

In Europe, Schiffer books are distributed by:
Bushwood Books
6 Marksbury Avenue
Kew Gardens
Surrey TW9 4JF, England
Phone: 44 (0) 20 8392-8585
FAX: 44 (0) 20 8392-9876
E-mail: Info@bushwoodbooks.co.uk.
Visit our website at: www.bushwoodbooks.co.uk
Free postage in the UK. Europe: air mail at cost.
Try your bookstore first.

Table of Contents

INTRODUCTION AND ACKNOWLEDGMENTS

This book, the first in a series that will provide a detailed examination of US Navy aerospace projects from the 1920s through the 1960s, tells the story of some of the most radical attack aircraft ever designed to operate from an aircraft carrier. These incredible projects were developed in the 1948-1949 time period to equip the USS *United States*, an immense 65,000-ton vessel that was to have been the core of the Navy's nascent long range nuclear attack capability. The ship itself was a substantial departure from traditional carrier design, being a flush-deck configuration without an island or other obstructions, permitting the operation of aircraft of unprecedented size and weight. The Bureau of Aeronautics (BuAer) drew up specifications for two classes of attack aircraft to equip this mighty ship: the Class VA, Long Range Heavy Attack and Class VA, Long Range Special Attack.

The majority of America's legendary aircraft companies submitted proposals to the subsequent competitions: Convair, Curtiss-Wright, Douglas, Fairchild, Lockheed, Martin, North American, Northrop and Republic. The submissions varied widely in appearance, ranging from Douglas's relatively compact and conservative Model 593-2 to their exotic Model 1186 series, a group of studies inspired by the X-3 Stiletto featuring a small parasite aircraft mounted atop a gigantic missile. In all, at least 35 major proposals were submitted, along with dozens of alternate configuration studies. These studies are emblematic of an exciting period of innovation and risk taking in the aerospace industry that has yet to be surpassed.

Unfortunately, the Navy's hopes for the USS *United States* and its new classes of attack aircraft were rudely dashed on April 23, 1949 when the aircraft carrier was cancelled by Secretary of Defense Louis A. Johnson. Johnson was a close ally of the Air Force, which had long been opposed to the new supercarrier due to the threat it represented to the Air Force's monopoly on strategic nuclear bombardment. The cancellation caused the immediate resignation of John Sullivan, Secretary of the Navy, and later sparked the infamous "Revolt of the Admirals" that cost the job of Admiral Louis Denfeld, Chief of Naval Operations.

Of the two classes of attack aircraft conceived to operate from the carrier, only the Heavy Attack class survived its cancellation, though in a much reduced form. The winner of that competition, the Douglas Model 593-8, would be built as the A3D Skywarrior. Ed Heinemann, chief aircraft designer at the company, had wisely included a study for a smaller and lighter aircraft than required by the specification in Douglas's original proposal, allowing it to operate from existing carriers. Whether the Navy ever declared a formal winner to the Special Attack competition remains unknown; in any case, none of the radical designs prepared for it ever left the drawing board. The Air Force's victory over the Navy proved to be short-lived; in the 1950s, escalating Cold War tensions led to the development of the *Forrestal* class supercarrier, a 75,000 ton vessel with an air wing of 80-100 jet aircraft that would include the nuclear-capable Skywarrior.

This book focuses primarily on the aircraft proposals connected with the USS *United States*; for those interested in the development of the ship itself and the political circumstances surrounding it, I highly recommend both *Revolt of the Admirals: The Fight for Naval Aviation, 1945-50* by Jeffrey G. Barlow and *U.S. Aircraft Carriers: An Illustrated Design History* by Norman Friedman. These books provided invaluable background for the opening and concluding chapters of this book and should be on the shelves of any serious student of US naval aviation. At the time of writing, a detailed design history of the flush-deck carrier, on the order of Conway's *Anatomy of the Ship* series, has yet to be written; I highly encourage a ship specialist to undertake one, as it is a fascinating subject with ample surviving primary documentation begging to be explored.

I am grateful to Barry Zerby at the National Archives for helping me navigate the vast holdings of that remarkable institution. I am also indebted to Lowell Ford for graciously lending me his rolls of Northrop microfilm containing so many unusual tailless aircraft projects. Special thanks to my wife Yvanne for tolerating yet another ambitious book project and helping me see it to its conclusion. This book is dedicated to her and our daughter Verity, born in February of this year.

Jared A. Zichek
San Diego, California
April 2008

CHAPTER 1 — Carrier Aviation vs. the Strategic Air Offensive

In the final years of World War II, the US Navy carrier force achieved historic victories against Japan, decimating its land-based air power and shore targets on Japanese-held territory. The exceptional performance of US Navy carrier aviation challenged the conventional wisdom that land-based aircraft were inherently superior to their carrier-based counterparts. The US Navy's performance in WW II proved that carrier aviation could be a powerful offensive force, as long as it was part of a larger, balanced force. The Army Air Force, on the other hand, believed strategic bombing to be the superior method of attack. These strong differences in doctrine between the services would prove to be a source of great conflict in the years immediately following WW II.

Conflicting Doctrines

The Army Air Force's doctrine was based in part on the writings of Brigadier General Billy Mitchell and General Giulio Douhet. Mitchell asserted that Army aviation had to achieve air dominance through the employment of pursuit aircraft; this was followed by a sustained bombing campaign against the enemy. Douhet stressed the primacy of the bomber even further, recommending precision aerial bombardment against the enemy's airports, supply bases, and centers of production; if these bombing attacks were sufficiently powerful and rapid, the enemy's war effort and morale would quickly collapse. He opposed generalized attacks on urban areas and believed that bomber formations did not require pursuit escort; "the bomber would always get through." These premises held sway with the AAF during the 1930s, only to be shaken by the crucible of aerial combat over Germany in WW II. The supremacy of unescorted bomber formations was brutally discredited in early daylight raids over Europe, in which the Eighth Air Force suffered massive losses against defending Luftwaffe fighters. Only with the arrival of long-range escort fighters such as the P-51D in 1944 were the losses reduced and the effectiveness of the raids improved. Despite a heavy bombing campaign in the final sixteen months of war, in which German aircraft factories, air bases, oil production facilities, ball-bearing plants, and motor transport factories were relentlessly pounded, German resistance did not collapse. Surrender did not occur until Allied armies overran German territory and subdued the country in the traditional way.

Strategic bombardment in the European Theater was a mixed success, the results failing to measure up to promises of AAF doctrine. Air Force bombers failed to deliver a knockout blow, with few of the attacks on principal target systems succeeding in putting these systems completely out of action. High-altitude precision bombing proved to be less precise and effective than predicted; the bombing accuracy of heavy bomber formations was often mediocre and target systems required repeated attacks before being destroyed or disabled. The initial stages of the AAF's involvement in the Pacific Theater were similar, with B-29s launching high-altitude, daylight, precision bombing operations from Chengdu, China and the Marianas against Japan's principal target systems, achieving only moderate success in the latter half of 1944. In early March 1945, Major General Curtis E. LeMay reversed policy, ordering B-29 bomb groups to undertake massive low-level incendiary strikes on Japanese urban areas. These raids proved more successful, and incendiary area bombing became the preferred method of the AAF to destroy Japan's will to resist. This departure from precision bombing marked a notable shift in AAF doctrine.

However, even area bombing proved incapable of ending the war in the Pacific. Despite having half of its urban areas burned down by the beginning of August 1945, Japan continued to fight on. It took the destruction of Hiroshima and Nagasaki with atomic weapons, along with the entry of the USSR into the Pacific War, for the Japanese government to surrender. Despite the questionable effectiveness of AAF strategic bombardment doctrine during WW II, senior Air Force leadership did not see it as flawed. Instead, Generals Arnold and Spatz blamed the failure of the doctrine on inadequate resources and the "foolish" diversion of AAF assets to support land and naval campaigns. For these men, the atomic bomb held the promise of overcoming the limitations of strategic bombardment demonstrated in WW II.

Like the AAF, the Navy experienced serious losses in the opening months of fighting during WW II. The nadir was likely the sinking of the aircraft carrier Hornet in late 1942, which left the Navy with a single operational carrier in Pacific. It wasn't until 1943-1944 that the Navy began receiving large numbers of new Essex class carriers and Independence class light carriers; truly effective carrier-based fighter aircraft became available in mid-1943 with the introduction of the F6F Hellcat and the improved F4U Corsair. These elements became part of a Fast Carrier Attack Force led by Vice Admiral Marc A. Mitscher, which would go on to achieve great successes against the Japanese. With a large number of fast carriers at his disposal, Mitscher was able to employ several multicarrier task groups as the offensive striking components of his force. These carriers were able to operate within range of Japan's land-based air power in the final years of the war without loss of a single Essex-class ship due to improvements in radar-assisted fighter direction and ship damage control enabled.

By the end of the war, the Navy's carrier air doctrine had evolved to encompass several fundamental beliefs. Foremost was the belief that carriers had to be capable of launching limited offensive strikes against selected land targets in the opening stages of a conflict in order to maintain control of seas. It was paramount that enemy submarines be destroyed in their pens, along with land-based aircraft positioned to threaten the carrier task force. The Air Force did not disagree with this objective, though it believed that the mission could be more efficiently accomplished with its strategic land-based bombers.

Unification and an Independent Air Force

The movement to unify the War and Navy Departments went back to the 1920s, when Billy Mitchell called for an overall Department of National Defense, under which a separate air arm with authority over naval aviation was one of its main components. The Navy effectively opposed this attempt to strip it of its air power, and subsequently remained wary of similar Army proposals for economy and centralization. In late 1943, Army Chief of Staff General George C. Marshall submitted a paper to the Joint Chiefs of

Staff (JCS) raising the issue again. The Navy opposed unification on several grounds, its strongest objection being to the proposed independent air component, which threatened to completely absorb carrier aviation or markedly reduce its funding. The Army supported a single defense department in order to preserve funding for their ground forces in the postwar competition for dollars, assuming that the department's powerful chief of staff would look beyond narrow service interests and be more equitable in the distribution of funds. The Army Air Force supported unification to achieve independence from the Army. Separate service status would enable the Air Force to fight for funding on the same footing as the Army and Navy, becoming their coequal.

In early 1946, Congress drafted new unification legislation. In March, AAF Commanding General Carl A. Spaatz sought control over all land-based aviation, including aircraft in the ASW, maritime reconnaissance, and shipping protection roles. By October, the AAF was attempting to influence the JCS to restrict funding for Navy land-based aircraft in the FY 1948 budget. In November, the AAF accused the Navy of trying to set up a strategic air force of its own, usurping the role of the Air Force; this was linked to the Navy's insistence on procuring long range, land-based aircraft, such as the Lockheed P2V Neptune. Based on Spaatz's arguments, the budget director cancelled the Navy procurement request for land-based aircraft in December. It took an urgent letter from Secretary of the Navy James Forrestal to President Truman on January 13, 1947 to reverse the decision.

The AAF public relations campaign to increase public and congressional support for an independent Air Force had begun in the closing months of WW II. In this campaign, the AAF claimed that air power had become the nation's dominant military force and that the Air Force, as the only true exponent of air power, was the preeminent line of defense for the continental United States. Equipped with the atomic bomb, the AAF could both defend the US against air attack and launch an early atomic counteroffensive. Strategic bombardment remained the most important function of an air force. Superior Air Force public relations would do great damage to Navy interests throughout the early postwar period; the Navy's PR efforts were quite amateurish in comparison.

On July 26, 1947, the National Security Act of 1947 was signed into law, creating a National Military Establishment composed of the Army, Navy, and Air Force and coordinated by the Secretary of Defense. The Navy's conflict with the Army and Air Force over roles, missions, and most importantly budgets intensified. By 1948, the Navy realized that the very existence of its carrier aviation force was under threat from the Air Force. It began expressing skepticism of the vaunted strategic air power of the Air Force in meetings within the National Military Establishment, but did not engage in a counter-public relations campaign of its own. The Navy was hampered by its Secretary, John Sullivan, who refused to fight back against the Air Force, as he saw a public fight with the service as harmful to the spirit of unification encouraged by Secretary of Defense James Forrestal. The Air Force had no such reservations, and the Navy gradually lost much of the public and congressional support it had held throughout the war years and in the first years of peace.

Atomic Weapons and the Strategic Air Command

In the immediate postwar period, the atomic bomb remained an extremely expensive weapon in terms of both critical materials and industrial effort, resulting in its limited availability. Thus, it was primarily considered as a strategic weapon of destruction against concentrated urban and industrial areas vital to the war effort of an enemy nation. It was generally not viewed as a tactical weapon suitable for employment against ground forces or naval forces at sea, given the widely dispersed nature of these targets.

In 1946, the Strategic Air Command (SAC) was established to conduct long range offensive operations in any part of world using the atomic bomb and other advanced weapons. At the time, the Air Force only had a handful of B-29s modified to carry the atomic bomb, along with six trained Air Force weaponeers to man them. Air Force planning did not incorporate a real understanding of the atomic bomb's potential; there were no programs directed to exploit the technology, and no airplanes in research and development that could take full advantage of the atomic weapon. Despite exaggerated Air Force claims to the contrary, SAC was a "hollow threat" from 1946 to 1948, with a command poorly trained and ill-prepared for its mission. Equipped with increasingly obsolescent B-29s and B-50s, it was incapable of attacking most significant Soviet urban-industrial targets on round-trip missions. Thus was born the idea of a "one-shot" operation of retaliation, in which the bombers would perform one-way missions into the Soviet Union, sacrificing both planes and crews to hit targets deep within the country's interior.

Initially, the Air Force stressed avoiding attacks against enemy population centers, instead targeting specific systems vital to enemy's war-making capacity, such as industrial systems, enemy military power, and ports and harbors. However, Air Force analysts came to believe that even the complete and total destruction of these systems would still allow the enemy to fight on for at least a year. By early 1947, the AAF's Air War Plans Division began to emphasize atomic attacks against large industrial centers as well as enemy governmental control centers, communications and population. This evolved to the point where Air Force planners began advocating atomic attacks against Soviet cities rather than specific industrial target systems. It was during this period that the concept of "bonus damage" was developed, in which an atomic attack on an urban-industrial area would destroy not only the intended industrial targets but also kill or incapacitate a large percentage of the population working or residing nearby. This grim strategy was necessitated by the small size of the US atomic stockpile. The primary objective of SAC's emergency war plan became the annihilation of selected urban industrial populations, with industrial targets becoming incidental.

In early October 1948, Secretary of Defense Forrestal began to doubt the effectiveness of the Air Force's proposed strategic air offensive after particularly acrimonious debates within the JCS over the FY 1950 budget. Admiral Louis Denfeld expressed his skepticism of the USAF's "one-shot" war, while Army Chief of Staff Omar Bradley objected to severely cutting Army and Navy budgets to pay for the strategic air offensive, which amounted to putting all the eggs in one basket. Even Air Force Vice Chief of Staff Muir S. Fairchild admitted that he was uncertain that the US could mount a full scale strategic air offensive from Britain, a key aspect of the plan. The USSR would likely put the UK out of the war immediately, eliminating one of its two major enemies and denying the other the use of its most critical forward base.

On October 19, Curtis LeMay became SAC's commanding general. He was brought in to fix the troubled organization, which suffered from terrible combat readiness and serious staff, supply and administrative problems. LeMay quickly realized that only a priority effort from the top of the USAF to adequately fund SAC would allow him to build up his command's capabilities sufficiently to carry out its responsibilities. This meant that the Air Force had to get a larger share of the budget at the expense of the other services. In the meantime, LeMay deceived Secretary Forrestal, convincing him over the course of several meetings that SAC could drive home attacks on targets in Russia. It actually wouldn't be till the early 1950s that SAC would become the nation's preeminent atomic deterrent force and be capable of such operations. USAF leadership believed that atomic and conventional attacks by SAC could disrupt Soviet industry, undermine its will to resist, and eventually disarm its armed forces. The Air Force argued that the US could not afford the high cost of recruiting and maintaining large conventional ground forces to counter the Red Army and that US naval forces would be of little utility in war against a major continental power lacking significant naval forces. These arguments gained increasing traction in the face of Navy passivity.

Atomic Weapons and the Navy

Surprisingly, the Navy possessed more technical knowledge of the atomic bomb than the Air Force, as several naval officers had been heavily involved in the Manhattan Project from its earliest days. The Navy's primary problem was how to integrate the weapon into the fleet, since both the Mk I "Little Boy" and Mk III "Fat Man" were too bulky and heavy to be carried in existing Navy carrier-based aircraft.

Navy leaders believed in the necessity of launching an early strategic air offensive, though they were skeptical that it would rapidly bring the war to a successful conclusion. They recognized the importance of using ground forces to hold Western Europe against Soviet attack, to maintain the Mediterranean line of communications and to secure oil-producing areas in the Mideast. These objectives were not obtainable by air attacks on the Soviet heartland, and all required the presence of significant naval forces to establish and hold the essential sea and air lines of communication to Europe and Africa. The Navy planned to use carrier task forces, operating in forward areas such as the Mediterranean and Norwegian Sea, as power projection forces. Carriers air assets would be used not only to strike Soviet naval and air targets, but also to provide air support for the ground campaign.

In 1946, the North American XAJ-1 heavy attack aircraft was under development; it was later modified to carry the 10,300 lb Mk III atomic bomb. At the same time, the flush-deck aircraft carrier, which did not have a conventional island and was designed to operate much larger, longer-range attack aircraft, was undergoing design study. Air Force leaders considered Navy efforts to ready its forces for delivering limited, long-range atomic attacks as an unwarranted infringement on their service's primary role and mission. In fact, the Navy had no interest in usurping the Air Force's responsibility for strategic air warfare; its pursuit of a long-range atomic attack capability was influenced by its negative assessment of the effectiveness of the Air Force's proposed strategic air offensive in the early postwar period.

The Navy objected to the massive destruction of Soviet urban-industrial areas because of the cost of the resources expended, which could be better applied against specific target systems. Navy planners also opposed the infliction of massive casualties on the enemy's civilian population; only collateral civilian casualties incurred in carrying out the minimum targeting necessary to accomplish the mission was justified. However, the Navy did see value in employing Air Force and Navy offensive air assets together in precision attacks against vital enemy target complexes best suited to their respective capabilities.

The Air Force plan was based on long range flights made by slow flying bombers operating without escort deep into the heart of the USSR. These bombers could not protect themselves against the newest Russian jet interceptors and likely would have suffered high operational losses. At one point, it was proposed that the Air Force and Navy cooperate on a development program for supersonic long-range bombers with ceilings above 40,000 ft; the Air Force displayed little interest in the idea. Studies performed by the Navy Strategic Plans Division in 1947 showed that the limited, long-range atomic attack force proposed by the Navy was as an augmentation of Air Force capabilities, not a replacement for land-based strategic bombing.

Nonetheless, Air Force opposition to the Navy's use of atomic weapons and its role in strategic bombing gathered force in early 1948. It viewed the continued development of carrier aviation as a threat and considered aircraft carriers to be obsolescent and highly vulnerable platforms in the postwar era. Air Force officers did not see the value of carriers in the Mediterranean, and did not believe that the Navy could reach significant portions of the Soviet Union's interior. To the Air Force, the real military worth of carriers came in the time bought as the carriers were sunk (estimated to be a few weeks), allowing more capable land-based air power to arrive in theater - a cynical view indeed!

On March 11, 1948, a meeting of Service Chiefs and Operations Deputies at Key West, Florida was held to address the controversy over roles and missions. The resulting Key West agreement gave the Air Force the primary function of strategic air warfare, while the Navy was tasked with supporting the overall air campaign as directed by the JCS. The key points of contention were how "strategic" would be interpreted and whether the Navy could strike inland targets in connection with their campaign. The Air Force finally agreed to recognize the right of the Navy to procure the weapons the service considered essential to its function, though the Navy would not be allowed to function as a separate strategic air force. The Navy was also permitted to attack inland targets, such as enemy airfields, and it was allowed to use the atomic bomb. Unfortunately, no written transcript of the Key West meeting was made, each service having its own interpretation of what had been agreed to; this would prove to be a source of friction later on.

In August 1948, Forrestal held a meeting with the JCS and Operations Deputies in Newport, Rhode Island. In this conference, the Air Force was assigned the role of interim executive agent of the Armed Forces Special Weapons Project (AFSWP), an interservice training and support organization responsible for the handling and assembly of atomic weapons released to military custody by the Atomic Energy Committee. The Navy's right to participate in both tactical and strategic atomic bombing was reaffirmed. Nonetheless, the service had to constantly fight to maintain its role in atomic warfare planning and operations throughout the remainder of the decade.

The Flush-Deck Carrier and the Large Carrier-Based Attack Aircraft

In the spring of 1945, the Navy Bureau of Aeronautics (BuAer) began investigating the potential of large, carrier-based bombers and a new type of aircraft carrier to operate them. BuAer initially looked at aircraft capable of carrying 8,000 to 12,000 lb bomb loads. In December of 1945, BuAer conducted a series of design studies to determine whether increases in range and bomb size would be possible in carrier-based aircraft in the foreseeable future through technological advances; Admiral Salada presented these studies in a memo to the CNO on December 11, 1945. In the following table titled "BuAer's New Categories of Bombing Aircraft," the Category B type would become the AJ-1 Savage:

	A	B	C
Gross weight, fully loaded (lbs)	30,000	45,000	100,000
Gross weight, landing (lbs)	20,000	30,000	65,000
Bomb size (lbs)	8,000[1]	8,000[1]	8,000[1]
Maximum speed/altitiude (mph/ft)	362/sea level	500/35,000	500/35,000
Combat radius (nm)	300	1,000	2,000

[1]12,000 lb bomb could not be carried without sacrificing fuel/range

The decision to develop a new, larger type of carrier was led within OPNAV by DCNO (Air) Vice Admiral Marc Mitscher, who had been the Commander of Task Force 58 during battles near the Philippines in 1944. Due to the short combat radius of Navy aircraft, Mitscher had been forced to operate his carrier forces close to the enemy shoreline in order to attack Japanese air bases that posed a threat to the fleet. This resulted in continuous air attack by the Japanese on the carriers, causing extensive damage to the vessels, the aircraft and casualties among the crew. This harrowing combat experience underscored the need for longer range fighter and attack aircraft, along with larger carriers to operate them. Mitscher was a supporter of the unorthodox flush-deck carrier, as he believed that this design would facilitate the Navy's transition to all-weather operations. In mid-January 1946, Mitscher was succeeded by Admiral Arthur Radford; he would come to play a primary role in the construction of the new carrier over the next two years, believing it to be essential for the operation of large reconnaissance aircraft as well as large attack planes and fighters.

The flush-deck carrier was designed to have a flight deck completely free of vertical obstructions, which allowed much larger aircraft to be operated from the deck of the ship. The island on existing carriers imposed considerable limits on the size of aircraft that could be safely launched and recovered. The deletion of the carrier island was a source of some controversy within the naval aviation community; it was concluded that the operational viability of the flush-deck carrier could only be determined by the construction and evaluation of a ship.

National Archives, RG 341

Artist's impression of the USS *United States* (CVA-58), the Navy's 65,000 ton flush-deck aircraft carrier, released to the press on October 6, 1948. Though the basic design and major characteristics of the ship had been fixed, the location of certain structures, such as the stacks, elevators and the telescopic bridge, was still under study. The ship appears to be carrying Lockheed P2V Neptunes and McDonnell F2H-1 Banshees.

In early January 1946, Admiral Mitscher recommended a design study of a new carrier class along with 100,000 lb bombers to equip it. The carrier study was approved on January 23, 1946, with the bomber study being approved two weeks thereafter. The Ship Characteristics Board (SCB) began the carrier study using the BuAer Aviation Design Research no. 42 (ADR-42) aircraft design study as a basis, which weighted 90,000 lbs (100,000 lbs fully loaded). ADR-42 was used for planning purposes until early 1948, being subsequently replaced by the ADR-62, and then by the ADR-64. Unfortunately, the author has been unable to locate any drawings or photos of these studies for inclusion in this chapter, though they are believed to have been fairly conventional designs for the period.

The Bureau of Ships (BuShips) began drafting a carrier study designated the CVB-X, basing its estimates on the Lockheed P2V patrol aircraft, which at the time was the Navy's largest land-based bomber. The CVB-X study was completed on May 20, 1946; the ship had a standard displacement of 69,200 tons, a trial displacement of 82,000 tons, an overall length of 1,190 ft, and a beam of 130 ft. The maximum width of the flight deck was 132 ft, which enabled the carrier to operate 24 ADR-42 attack aircraft. The CVB-X lacked a hangar deck, requiring that the aircraft remain on the flight deck for all maintenance and storage. In this form, the CVB-X was a specialized single-purpose carrier, designed solely for conducting atomic warfare with 100,000 lb long-range attack aircraft. There was no need for a hangar to store additional aircraft such as defensive fighters, which were to be provided by other carriers in the task force. CVB-X would have required the accompaniment of at least two other carriers. No sacrifice of the ship's basic characteristics was considered to also equip it with fighters.

The initial design was not a true flush-deck carrier, as BuShips was concerned that the complete deletion of the island would cause problems in the control of the ship, as well as the removal of stack gases from the power plant. The CVB-X was therefore equipped with a small island featuring navigation, flag and communication bridges as well as uptakes for the stack gases. This truncated island was nonetheless opposed by aviators, who were concerned that it would reduce the effective width of the flight deck and restrict the size of future attack aircraft. In addition, due to the immaturity of the ADR-42 aircraft study, there was insufficient data for planning details of ship construction, such as the strength of the flight deck. Due to these factors, the CVB-X (now redesignated as the Project 6A carrier) was not included in the FY 1948 shipbuilding program, being funded instead as a design study.

The design of BuAer's ADR-42 study continued to progress; by late 1946, it had evolved into a swept-wing aircraft with a length of 87 ft, a height of 32 ft (28 ft with tail folded), and a wing span of 110 ft. The wings folded for stowage, and the aircraft was powered by four De Laval turbine engines located in nacelles under the wings. The top speed of the ADR-42 was 440 kts at 40,000 ft, the cruising speed exceeding 350 kts, and the combat radius was 2,000 nm.

The design of the flush-deck carrier also continued to evolve. On February 13, 1947, the SCB produced a tentative set of characteristics for the Project 6A carrier. The carrier now had a hangar deck of sufficient clearance to accept the largest aircraft of the air group, which consisted of a) 12-18 ADR-45A attack aircraft (a smaller 57,000 lb, 750 nm radius plane) and 54 McDonnell XF2D-1 fighters, or b) 12 ADR-42 attack aircraft and 54 XF2D-1s.

On August 22, the SCB sent its revised flush-deck carrier study to the CNO for approval. The Project 6A carrier was to have an estimated length (at the waterline) of 1,000 ft and a beam of 125 ft, with a standard displacement of 60,000 tons. The size of the carrier's air group had increased to a total of 18 ADR-42 attack aircraft and 80 XF2D-1 fighters, with the option of substituting 27 ADR-45A attack aircraft for the 18 ADR-42s. These carrier characteristics were approved by the CNO on September 2, 1947. The Project 6A was assigned priority 2 under the FY 1949 Shipbuilding and Conversion Program, which was subsequently approved by the Secretary of the Navy on September 3.

In May of 1948, the Navy testified before Congress in support of its FY 1949 program. CNO Denfeld stated that the 6A carrier had received the approval of the JCS, the

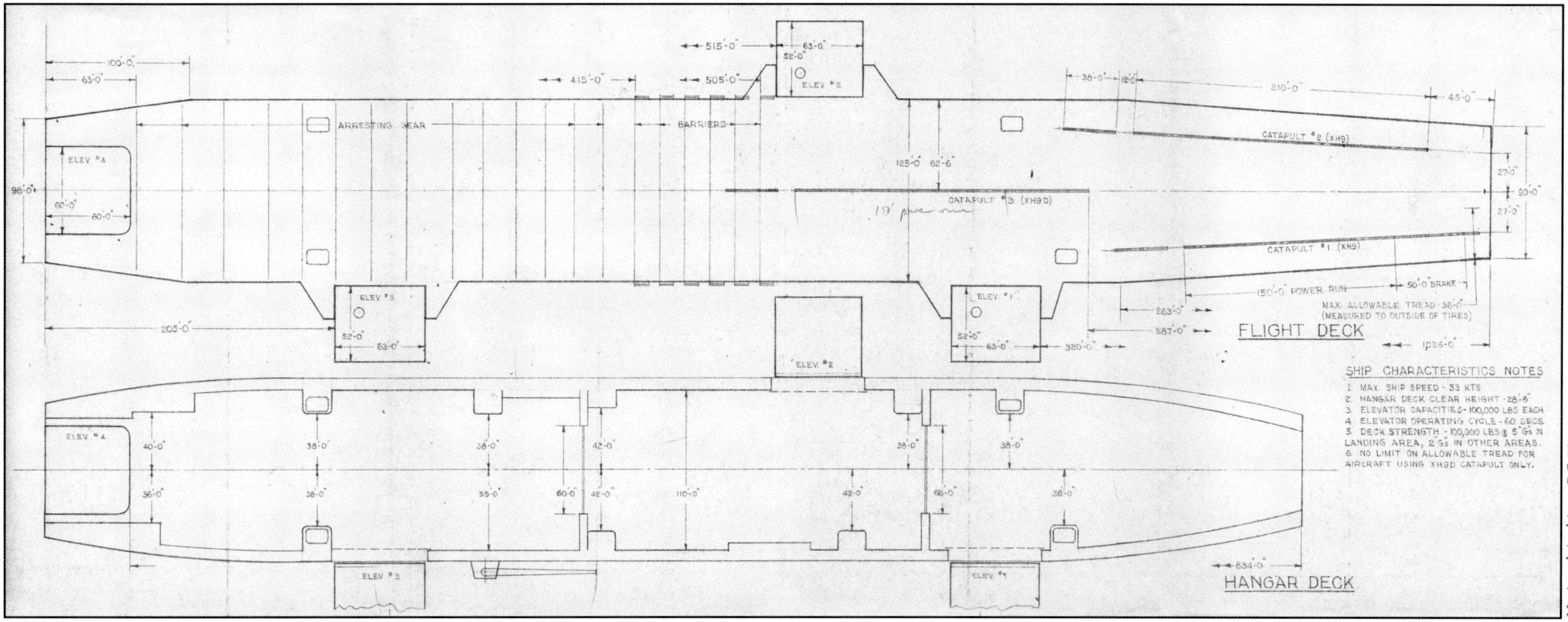

National Archives, RG 72

Plan view of the flush-deck carrier showing the flight and hangar decks as they stood in August of 1948; this drawing was sent along with OS-111 and OS-115 to aid manufacturers in the design and spotting of their proposed aircraft. Note the complete absence of the carrier island, which enabled the vessel to operate much larger aircraft than was possible with existing carriers.

Secretary of Defense and the President. This was not entirely true, as the JCS had not been consulted because the Secretary of the Navy felt that the approval of other defense agencies was unnecessary. This decision was reversed on May 26, when a presentation of the 6A carrier was made to the JCS; three of the four members approved, with only the Air Force objecting.

The Navy originally planned to build four Project 6A carriers, spreading out their construction over FY 1949 through FY 1952. All four were expected to be operational by FY 1955, providing the long-range offensive core of four carrier task groups. However, Secretary Sullivan told a subcommittee of the Senate Appropriations Committee that the first 6A carrier would be a prototype only, with no others being constructed until it had been completed and tested. This lack of coordination with OPNAV killed the program of building 4 ships. Sullivan's testimony reflected the view held by Forrestal that the Navy support for the flush-deck carrier could only be maintained by presenting it as an experimental design that would undergo thorough evaluation before any others were requested. Congress authorized the construction of the Project 6A carrier as part of the FY 1949 program; the initial money for its construction was appropriated on June 24, 1948. On July 22, the carrier's name was changed again, becoming the CVA (Heavy Aircraft Carrier); the first carrier was designated the CVA-58 USS *United States.*

Earlier on July 20, in correspondence with the CNO regarding stowage of aircraft engine parts aboard the Project 6A carrier, the Chief of BuAer mentioned a change in the aircraft complements planned for the ship. Complement A consisted of 80 F2H-1s and 18 ADR-62s, while Complement B consisted of 18 ADR-62s and 21 ADR-280s. The ADR-62 was powered by two XT-44 turboprops and one XJ-40 jet engine, while the ADR-280 was powered by two XT-38 turboprops and two J-46 jet engines. As with the previous ADR studies, no drawings or photos of these designs have thus far been located.

The Long Range Carrier-Based Bomber vs. the Strategic Land-Based Bomber

At the time the Navy was proceeding with the development of its flush-deck carrier, the USAF was committed to the Convair B-36 Peacemaker, an increasingly obsolescent wartime design with serious flaws. It was slow, expensive, lacked the range to hit key targets in Europe and Asia, and was moderately armed, leaving it vulnerable to the newest Soviet jet interceptors. Furthermore, the huge bomber suffered from serious developmental problems and delays. Nonetheless, it was the only intercontinental bomber available that could enter service in the near term; the more promising Boeing XB-52 was still on the drawing board. SAC was becoming concerned over the increasing vulnerability of overseas bases required for operating the shorter-ranged B-29 and B-50 bombers. The B-36 became a critical interim bomber to enable SAC to carry out the strategic air offensive. The USAF consistently underplayed the problems of the B-36 while overstating its capabilities to sell it to the public and Congress. Opponents in the Navy often challenged these exaggerated claims in letters to the editors of major newspapers.

As concerned as the Air Force was about the vulnerability of its bombers and bases to the Soviets, it was equally concerned about the Navy's ambitious new flush-deck carrier and long range carrier-based attack aircraft. In 1948, the Air Force conducted several studies comparing the estimated capabilities of the new Navy bombers against existing and future Air Force land-based bombers to gauge their relative effectiveness. These studies, summarized below, provide a great deal of information on the Navy's internal ADR studies for a long range carrier-based attack aircraft.

The first known study was described in a memo to General Craigie from J.S. Holtoner, Colonel, US Air Force, Chief, Aircraft Branch, dated February 19, 1948. On the previous day, Major W.D. Brady and Captain L.R. Standifer of the Aircraft Branch had discussed with Captain J. Murphy, Captain Brunton, and Commander R. Woodhall of BuAer the development of the Navy ADR-62 and the flush-deck carrier.

ADR-62 represented a preliminary Navy study for a long range, carrier-based attack aircraft prepared by its own engineers. At the time, the Navy had 6 to 7 possible designs of which 3 looked promising, according to Captain Murphy. The military characteristics for this airplane were essentially as follows:

Gross Weight:	100,000 lbs
Combat Radius:	1,700 nm minimum (2,000 nm desired)
Maximum Speed:	450 kts for a 100 nm run to target, and 100 nm from target
Cruise Speed:	Estimated approximately 355 kts
Takeoff:	Approximately 700 ft into a 25 kt wind. This was an unassisted free roll takeoff, no JATO/catapult/arresting gear
Bombing Altitude:	40,000 ft
Bomb Bay:	To take the same special envelope as specified for the new USAF medium bomber
Load Factors:	3 over target; 4 to 5 for landing
Crew:	5
Armament:	Twin 20 mm tail guns only; some of this type of aircraft were to have been used as escort and would have had all-around armament and no bomb load
Equipment:	Radar bombing equipment with optical sight as standby; radar gun laying for tail turret

It was estimated that this aircraft would have been powered by 2 turboprop engines backed up by turbojets for takeoff and high speed. As the ADR-62 was carrier-based, its development depended upon the construction of a large carrier, the Project 6A. The main characteristics of this carrier included:

a. No superstructure.
b. Carrier deck approximately 1,000 ft long. This was just about equivalent to the overall length of the carrier.
c. Gross weight was estimated to be approximately 70,000 to 80,000 tons.
d. Estimated range was 12,000 miles at 20 kts. However, range seemed to be of no concern as the carrier could have been refueled from a tanker flotilla.
e. Maximum speed was 33 kts. Economic cruise speed was estimated at 15 kts.
f. The carrier deck had two 200,000 lb catapults, two 60,000 to 100,000 lb catapults, two 60,000 lb elevators, one 100,000 lb elevator, and a ramp to below deck using an endless chain arrangement for moving aircraft.
g. The carrier had the capacity to handle the following combination of aircraft:
   1. 18 ADR-62s, 80 F2H-1 Banshees

2. 18 ADR-62s, 21 1,215 nm escort fighters (design study by BuAer)
3. 18 ADR-62s, 21 F2H-1s, 18 1,215 nm escort fighters
4. 24 ADR-62s
5. 64 1,215 nm escort fighters

The question of what sort of a Task Force was to be made up around the subject carrier was discussed. Captain Murphy stated that a Task Force consisted of one or more Task Groups. His personal opinion of the composition of a task group using the big carrier was:

1 Carrier, Project 6A type
1 Carrier, Midway Class
2 Carriers, CV9 Class
Antiaircraft screen consisting of 4 or 5 cruisers
12 destroyers

This was just one possible combination, the combination probably being dependent upon the circumstances of the situation. (A General Luedecke later indicated that the Navy was considering a much larger task force of four 80,000 ton carriers, twelve Midway class carriers, etc.)

It was estimated by Captain Murphy that approximately 4½ years were required to equip 1 Squadron with ADR type aircraft, and that the aircraft development needed to be pushed vigorously to be ready at the same time the carrier was finished.

Colonel Holtoner also noted that neither the ADR-62 nor the Project 6A carrier had progressed beyond the very preliminary design stage. Design criteria had not yet been submitted to the contractors for proposal estimates. In spite of this, Captain Murphy indicated that it was his belief that the Joint Chiefs of Staff and the President approved the two projects.

On March 4, 1948, the Air Force's Office Aircraft Laboratory at the Air Materiel Command produced the *Memorandum Report on Carrier Based Bomber.* This report, written by Harold S. Brown, summarized the results of an analytical preliminary design study of a carrier based bomber; this study was prepared at the request of the Chief of the Aircraft Laboratory.

This study was made according to the military characteristics set forth by the Navy for a carrier based bomber. In this study, the design gross weight was limited to 100,000 lbs; with this weight, a takeoff wing loading of 100 lbs per sq ft was used.

There were three distinct versions of this study:

a. Design No. 1 used solely the Allison T-38 type turboprop power plants. Two nacelles were used with three units in each nacelle.
b. Design No. 2 used the same arrangement of the Allison T-38s plus one Westinghouse J-34 turbojet in the fuselage as a booster.
c. Design No. 3 was the same as Design No. 2, except that a Navy method of combat radius calculation whereby rendezvous high speed run, reserve, etc. were considered.

In Design Nos. 1 and 2, the Air Force definition of combat radius being three-eighths the range was employed. The only armament used in these designs was a two-gun 20 mm tail turret. The medium bomber bomb bay envelope accommodated a 10,000 lb bomb. Inasmuch as the USAF study had to be prepared in a limited time, the design data used were extracted from a large number of the Aircraft Laboratory's medium bomber studies, summarized in the following table:

Comparative Table of Performance

	Design No. 1	Design No. 2	Design No. 3	ADR-62
Gross Weight - lbs.	100,000	100,000	100,000	100,000
Power Plants	(6) T-38	(6) T-38 (1) J-34	(6) T-38 (1) J-34	Turbo-Props + Turbo-Jets
Radius - Nautical Miles	1,737	1,600	1,737*	1,700
Ave. V_{cr} - Knots	381	381	381	360
V_{max} at Target Wt. - Knots	424	435	435	450
Service Ceiling - ft.	41,000	41,000	41,000	Over 40,000
Take-Off (No JATO)				
No Wind - ft.	3,400	3,400	3,400	
25 Knot - ft.	2,700	2,700	2,700	
Catapult - ft.	700	700	700	700

* Navy type combat problem.

National Archives, RG 341

Brown also performed a preliminary comparison between the ADR-62 and the XB-52; the latter was still in the preliminary design stage and may have still been configured as a turboprop at the time. Key cost figures had not yet been determined:

	XB-52	Carrier-Based Bomber
High Speed (kts)	435	450
Armament	Tail turret only (twin 20 mm guns or four 50 cal)	Tail turret only (twin 20 mm guns)
Cost/Unit (based on cost for 100 units)	$5,903,800	$1,951,320
Cost to deliver 100 bombs in 10 days (includes cost of carrier, escort vessels, number of personnel)	-	-
Cost of Air Base	-	-
Block Speed (kts)	435 kts (average) for 1,738 nm to and from target	450 kts for 100 nm to and from target
Cruise Speed (kts)	420 kts (average)	355 kts

Brown concluded that the Design No. 1, using solely Allison T-38s, could attain a combat radius of 1,737 nm (2,000 statute miles) at an average cruising speed of 381 kts (440 mph); it had a high speed of 424 kts (490 mph).

Design No. 2 using the Allison T-38 plus a Westinghouse J-34 as a booster could attain a combat radius of 1,600 nm (1,850 statute miles) at an average cruising speed of 381 kts (440 mph); however, the high speed increased to 435 kts (500 mph).

Employing a Navy method of combat radius calculation whereby rendezvous, high speed run, reserve, etc. where considered separately, Design No. 3 had a radius of 1,737 nm (2,000 statute miles) at an average cruising speed of 381 kts (440 mph); it had a high speed of 435 kts (500 mph).

The takeoff requirement of 700 ft in a 25 kt wind required auxiliary means such as JATO or catapult. Approximately 50,000 lbs of additional thrust was necessary to meet the takeoff requirements with JATO.

The end of the report was generally inconclusive, with Brown recommending that the report be used in the study of carrier-based versus land-based bombers for long range bombing missions. He believed that the Navy's ADR-62 bomber was possible of attainment and was feasible.

On April 27, a copy of the study was forwarded to the Director, Research and Development, Deputy Chief of Staff, Materiel, USAF in Washington DC from Wright Patterson. The memo that accompanied the report noted that to indicate the relative cost of a 100,000 lb carrier-based bomber and the XB-52, cost estimates were made based on the XB-45 as representative of a 100,000 lb airplane and the XB-52 representative of a 280,000 to 300,000 lb airplane. The estimated performance of the XB-52 vis-à-vis the 100,000 lb carrier-based bomber assumed that all of the detailed requirements then specified for the XB-52 would be met, and that certain pending changes would be made which reduced weight.

On May 20, the report was forwarded to the Office, Director of Plans and Operations, Brigadier General C.S. Picher by Colonel J.W. Sessums, Deputy Director of Research and Development, Office, Deputy Chief of Staff, Materiel, USAF. Colonel Sessums noted that approximately 50,000 lbs of assisted takeoff over a 700 ft run in a 25 kt wind was needed to get the airplane off. It was understood that existing Navy cable catapults could produce about 100,000 lbs assist over a 90 ft run.

On June 3, Colonel Holtoner sent an updated memo to General Craigie titled *Naval Project for a 100,000 lb 1,700 Nautical Mile Combat Radius, 500 Knots Per Hour Carrier Based Bomber*. The Naval Design Research Branch had further developed and completed its study for a 100,000 lb, 1,700 nm combat radius, 500 kt carrier-based bomber. The study was now designated "Project 64," and it represented the Navy's entrance into heavy, carrier-borne aircraft. Their research personnel were favorably impressed with the study and had presented it to the Chief of Naval Operations for approval. The go-ahead for writing MCs was being withheld pending Congressional approval of the large new carrier on which the aircraft would serve.

The study showed that the following performance was expected from a 100,000 lb aircraft using two J-40 engines:

Combat Radius	1,700 nm
Cruise Speed	490 kts
Combat Speed	510 kts at 45,000 ft (in a block 100 nm to/from target)
Takeoff Distance	7,400 ft (no assist at 100,000 lbs gross weight)
Weight Empty	43,000 lbs
Crew	3

The trend in heavy carrier-based aircraft was toward no defensive armament whatsoever. This was a necessary compromise to reduce the weight to enable launching and secure range and speed. The need for a similar aircraft to accompany the bomber, armed but not carrying bombs, was also contemplated.

Operational Specifications 111 and 115

By August of 1948, support for the construction of the flush-deck carrier appeared firm, while the internal BuAer ADR studies had matured to the point that BuAer felt it was time to approach manufacturers and undertake the development of actual aircraft. BuAer established two classes of attack aircraft to operate from the USS *United States*: the Class VA, Long Range Heavy Attack and the Class VA, Long Range Special Attack. The former is described in Operation Specification 111 (OS-111), discussed in the following chapter. It called for a high performance near-term attack capability that was within the current state of the art. The Special Attack class is described in OS-115, discussed in Chapter 11. This specification called for a high speed long range attack capability that pushed the technical envelope; the proposals it generated are covered in Chapters 12 through 16. The OS-111 and OS-115 designs ranged from the relatively conventional to the outright bizarre, ranking as some of the most interesting aircraft ever proposed for carrier operation.

CHAPTER 2 — *Outline Specification 111*

The Bureau of Aeronautics sent out a Request for Proposal (RFP) for a Model Long Range Heavy Attack Airplane on August 16, 1948 to the nation's major aircraft manufacturers; enclosed with this letter was Outline Specification OS-111 and various supporting documents to aid in the preparation of the proposals. BuAer invited the companies to submit design studies and informal estimates of cost and first flight dates for the design and construction of an experimental long range heavy attack airplane in accordance with the specification. Given the importance of the project, BuAer demanded that the companies observe a very strict interpretation of the confidential classification; access to information on the project was limited to personnel directly concerned. For those companies that submitted proposals, they had to be in accordance with specification SR-65D and include the weight empty; maximum speed in level flight, at a combat altitude of 40,000 ft; and power off stalling speed, landing condition. The companies had to be willing to guarantee these figures.

BuAer requested that the design and cost proposals be submitted assuming the construction of two flight articles and one static test article, fabrication of the static test article to precede the fabrication of the two flight articles, the latter to be complete in all respects. The cost proposals were to consider the use of government furnished power plants.

BuAer anticipated that fiscal considerations would necessitate the award of any resulting contract on a phase basis, the initial commitment covering only Phase I. Therefore, it was requested that in addition to the cost quotation covering the complete proposal and the supporting cost breakdown, a further breakdown into the following phases be submitted:

- Phase I — Preliminary design through mock-up and including those items covered in document SR-6J.
- Phase II — Design and construction of static test and flight articles and including those items covered in SR-6J and also all ground tests required prior to release for first flight.
- Phase III — Flight testing, correction of defects including BIS changes and demonstrations.

At the time of writing, BuAer intended to authorize commencement of each phase according to the following schedule:

- Phase I — Between December 1948 and March 1949.
- Phase II — Between July and December 1949.
- Phase III — Between July and December 1950.

The bureau wanted an informal quotation from the manufacturers and intended that any resulting contract be placed on a negotiated basis. In selecting the manufacturer to receive the contract, BuAer would give consideration to all relevant factors including price. In this regard, it preferred that the contractor submit a fixed price quotation with cost breakdown for the entire project. However, if the contractor favored CPFF, both types of quotations were to be submitted.

No government financing in the form of advance payments or loans was to be furnished. If progress payments were requested, the proposal had to state this and indicate the amount of such payments and the basis upon which it was desired that such payments be made. Progress payments would not be made in excess of the value of the work done prior to payment; no additional capital facilities or equipment were to be financed by the government.

BuAer requested that the engineering proposal be submitted to its Attack Design Branch by November 22, 1948, and the cost proposal by December 6, 1948. Companies not interested in the design competition were to advise BuAer as such and return the supporting specifications and other documents.

The RFP did not commit the government to pay any costs incurred in the submission of the quotations or in making the necessary studies or designs for the preparation thereof, nor to procure, or contract for the services or materials for which quotations were requested.

Outline Specification for a Class VA Airplane, Carrier-Based Landplane - July 1948

The outline specification covered the essential requirements for the design of a long range carrier-based heavy attack aircraft. The primary mission of the airplane was the execution of a high altitude horizontal bombing attack with large bombs and special weapons (i.e., atomic bombs) at a point not less than 1,700 nm from the point of takeoff. The bomb load for general design considerations was 10,000 lbs. The airplane was to take off from and land on the deck of a carrier or an ordinary landing field. The catapult could be used alone or in conjunction with JATO.

Characteristics The maximum gross weight of the airplane was not to exceed 100,000 lbs. It was emphasized, however, that the lightest and smallest airplane possible within the parameters of the specification was desired. Performance desired was as follows, in order of importance as listed:

Performance Characteristic	Attack (10,000 lb. Bomb Load)
Cruise Speed	Mach .85
Maximum Speed at Basic Flight Design Gross Weight	Mach .9
Combat Altitude at Basic Flight Design Gross Weight	40,000 ft or higher
Rate of Climb at Sea Level at End of Deck or after Expenditure of JATO	500 ft/min (Navy standard hot day)
Stalling Speed without Power at Sea Level at Design Gross Weight	not more than 115 kts (landing condition)
Combat Radius at Maximum Takeoff Gross Weight	1,700 nm

BuAer noted that should the aerodynamic and weight effects of the tail armament preclude attainment of specified performance, minimum reductions in combat radius would be acceptable if required to maintain other performance values.

General Requirements The size of the airplane was limited by the following:

1. It had to be possible to move one airplane past another on a 125 ft. wide carrier flight deck when both aircraft had their wings spread and with tip tanks affixed. One aircraft could be placed at an angle to the ship center line and the wings, tail or nose could overhang the flight deck if necessary to accomplish the bypass. However, the clearance had to be such that the passing airplane could clear the other without the necessity of backing and repositioning either aircraft during the passing. In no case could the outboard wheel be placed any closer than 12 inches to any deck edge.
2. Maximum folded span was 58 ft.
3. Maximum height over any part of the airplane with wings folded not to be greater than 27'6".
4. The airplane was to be designed for catapulting from a double XH9 catapult; JATO could be employed if necessary.
5. The airplane had to fit on the elevators of a Project 6A carrier for rapid movement from the flight deck to the hangar deck and vice versa.

Provision was to be made for a pilot and co-pilot/navigator in a pressurized cabin; a bomber radar operator in a pressurized area forward of the bomb bay; and access to the bomb bay from the cockpit in flight. Pressure in the pressurized area could be broken during access to the bomb bay. Consideration was to be given to providing reasonably safe emergency egress for the crewmen under conditions of high speed and possibly uncontrolled flight.

The airplane was to contain provisions for folding the outer wing panels, and vertical tail as necessary to meet dimensional requirements. A bomb bay was to be provided capable of accommodating a 10,000 atomic bomb.

Concerning armament, a government-furnished, power operated, uninhabited, AGL turret system Aero X11E, containing two 20mm, M-24 guns was to be installed. Provision was to be made external to the turret for all components including 500 rounds of ammunition per gun, and the APG 25 radar. Total weight of all defensive armament and controls was limited to 1,600 lbs.

A bomb director AN/APB-2 (Mk V) including modified AP-31 radar was to be installed. Space provision was to be made for an antenna dish having a swept hemispherical volume of 40 inches diameter in the nose of the airplane.

Consideration was to be given to expeditious handling of the airplane on deck. BuAer indicated that it would entertain proposals for specific items of special power deck handling equipment.

The Navy would go on to receive at least 8 proposals from 7 manufacturers (the El Segundo and Santa Monica divisions of Douglas each submitting separate designs) for the Class VA competition. These fascinating proposals are covered in the following 8 chapters.

CONFIDENTIAL

GUARANTEED ENGINE RATINGS ACCEPTABLE TO THE BUREAU OF AERONAUTICS - EFFECTIVE 19 July 1948

ENGINE Turbo-jets	RATING SEA LEVEL STATIC Thrust Dry/Wet Dry//Afterburning	ESTIMATED DATE AVAILABLE FOR PROTOTYPE FLIGHT	SOURCE OF POWER PLANT DATA
XJ33-A-27	5853/6500	April 1949	Allison Spec. No. 275-A 18 February 1948
XJ33-A-29	5600//7500	July 1949	Allison Spec. No. 271 19 December 1947
XJ34-WE-32 (C-8)	3500 3370//4900	October 1949	(WEC Spec. No. WAGT-X24C10-2-A (24 March 1948 and WEC ltr. (3055 dtd. 2 July 1948
J35-A-17	4900/5600	December 1948	Allison Spec. No. 267-A 12 December 1947
XJ40-WE-4	6800	December 1949	(WEC Spec. WAGT-X40E2-2 dtd.
XJ40-WE-6	7500	July 1950	(15 April 1948 and curves dtd. 11 June 1948
XJ40-WE-8	7310//10900	December 1950	Curves 333,-337 to 341 and -297-1.
XJ40-WE-10	8100 7920//11750	July 1952	(WEC Bid Spec. WAGT-X40E8-2 (15 March 1948
XJ42-P-6	5000/5750	January 1949	P & W Spec. N-1603 dated 9 September 1947
XJ46-WE-2 (C-10)	4200 4080//6100	February 1951	(WEC Spec. WAGT-X24C10-2A dated (24 March 1948 & WEC ltr. 3055 (dated 2 July 1948
XJ47-GE-(c)	5400/6200		(GE ltr. 3-411 RES:dlt dated
(d)	5200//7000	December 1949	(11 May 1948
XJ48-P-2	6250/7000	October 1949	P & W Spec. N-1607 dated 15 April 1948

National Archives, RG 72

Table showing the turbojet engines available for consideration to manufacturers in the Class VA Heavy Attack competition; due to its relatively high performance, the Westinghouse XJ40-WE-10 would prove to be the most popular choice.

CONFIDENTIAL

GUARANTEED ENGINE RATINGS ACCEPTABLE TO THE BUREAU OF AERONAUTICS - EFFECTIVE 19 July 1948

ENGINE Turbo-Props	RATING SEA LEVEL STATIC SHP/THRUST	ESTIMATED DATE AVAILABLE FOR PROTOTYPE FLIGHT	SOURCE OF POWER PLANT DATA
XT34-P	4900/1380	December 1950	P & W Preliminary Spec. N-3507 dtd. 6 April 1948
XT35-W	8900/1590	January 1950	WAC Preliminary Spec. AC-135 dtd. 5 November 1947
XT38-A	3535/537	November 1951	Allison Spec. 273-A dtd. 19 April 1948
XT40-A	7070/1075	November 1951	Allison Spec. 272-A dtd. 19 April 1948
XT48-P	9800/2760	September 1951	P & W Preliminary Spec. N-3508 dtd. April 6, 1948
XT44-A	10605/1612	November 1952	Allison Spec. 274-A dtd. 19 April 1948

National Archives, RG 72

A variety of turboprop engines were also permitted for consideration. While these were superior to the turbojets in terms of fuel consumption and range, their inability to meet the maximum speed requirement of OS-111 caused most of the manufacturers to drop them from consideration early on, with the notable exception of Lockheed.

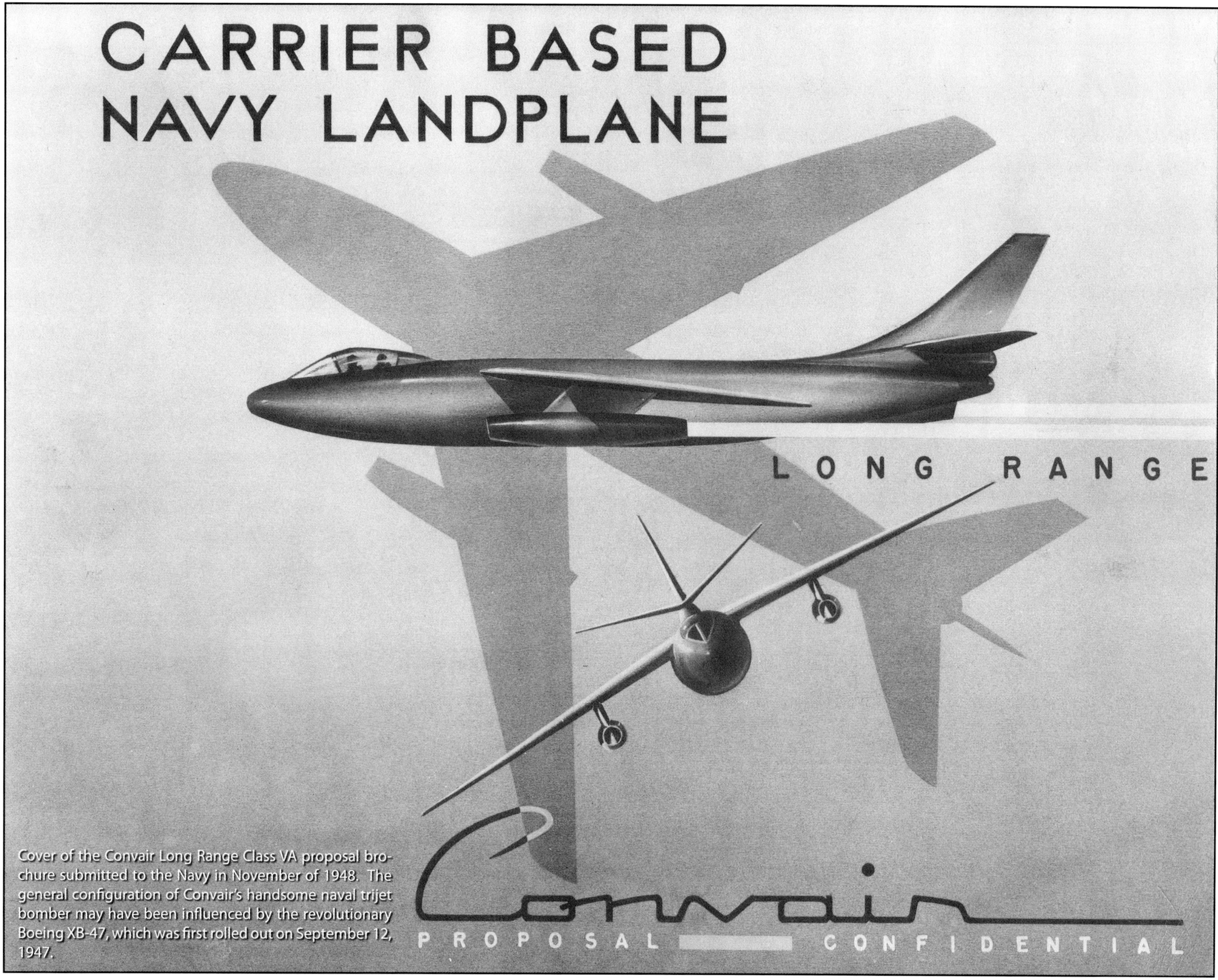

Cover of the Convair Long Range Class VA proposal brochure submitted to the Navy in November of 1948. The general configuration of Convair's handsome naval trijet bomber may have been influenced by the revolutionary Boeing XB-47, which was first rolled out on September 12, 1947.

National Archives, RG 72

CHAPTER 3 — *Convair Carrier Based Landplane Class VA - Long Range*

Artist's impression of Convair's clean and modern Class VA aircraft in climb; except for the trijet configuration, it was among the more conventional designs in the competition.

National Archives, RG 72

Convair's proposal was designated the "Carrier Based Landplane Class VA - Long Range;" no internal model number appears to have been assigned. As per OS-111, the principle mission of the airplane was high altitude horizontal bombing attack with large bombs and special weapons. The airplane was a three-place carrier-based landplane having a swept-back high wing and swept-back tail surfaces. The airplane structure was of riveted aluminum alloy construction.

Double-slotted flaps and retractable slats were provided, along with power-operated wing folding. The landing gear was of the bicycle type with outriggers; it was fully retractable. The bomb bay was equipped with doors which retracted into the fuselage. The control system was power-operated through mechanical linkage and incorporated means for emergency operation.

The crew compartment was pressurized and ejectable seats were provided. Passage to the bomb bay was permitted during unpressurized flight. Flak suits and curtains afforded protection for the crew.

Design Analysis

In its design analysis, Convair asserted that for the range of cruising and high speed required, a swept thin wing offered a practical solution in delaying drag divergence due to compressibility. Studies of several sweep angles and wing thicknesses for a representative taper and aspect ratio showed 40° of sweep and 10% thickness to be a practical selection considering both structural stiffness and stalling characteristics. Computation of the fuel requirements for the required combat radius and of the wing and tail weights for a series of aspect ratios determined that the optimum was a takeoff wing loading of approximately 110 lb/sq ft and an aspect ratio of 7.

An analysis of the effect of taper ratio indicated that the gross weight was reduced with increase in taper up to the highest taper investigated of 6:1. Published experimental data on the stalling characteristics of swept wings are limited to tapers of approximately 2:1; however, theoretical calculations indicated that satisfactory stalling characteristics were obtainable up to at least 4:1 taper with some indication that as high as 6:1 might be made to work. Limited time dictated selection of the 4:1 taper and a wind tunnel model of this wing was built and tested. The resulting test data showed encouraging results and substantiated earlier theoretical analyses.

Analysis of turbojet and turboprop power plants available for the design favored the former. The best turbojet was the XJ40-WE-10, which was selected on the basis of specific fuel consumption and thrust ratings. Studies of two-engine and three-engine designs definitely favored the two-engine arrangement; however, the power of the XJ-40 was insufficient, even considering advanced ratings, to meet the required performance with two engines. Three engines ensured high performance, particularly with respect to hot day climb at takeoff, and high altitude climb with normal power. Also, sufficient power was available to reach cruising altitudes where optimum lift-drag ratios were attainable with powers in the region of lowest specific fuel consumption.

A three-engine arrangement was therefore selected. Future engine developments such as the WAC TJ-6 turbojet would give a two-engine design with performance equaling the existing design with three XJ-40 engines. The basic design incorporated wing mounted nacelles on pylons. An arrangement with nacelles at the wing-fuselage juncture was also drafted. Insufficient data was available to determine the relative merits of these two arrangements. It was expected that wind tunnel tests of these nacelles plus corresponding weight studies would dictate the best arrangement for construction of the airplane.

General Description

The airplane had a sweptback wing and tail and was powered by three Westinghouse XJ40-WE-10 turbojets. Two of the engines were located in nacelles suspended on pylons below the wing, thus providing efficient intake ducts, an uninterrupted flap arrangement, and a clear area for the jet blast. The third engine was located in the aft portion of the fuselage with semi-flush intake ducts, each located on the lower sides of the fuselage. The jet outlet was below the tail turret.

The flight deck was pressurized to 4.0 PSI and accommodated a three man crew consisting of the pilot, co-pilot/navigator, and the bomber/radar operator. The bubble canopy and a panel in the top of the fuselage could be jettisoned and all three crew members were provided with ejectable seats for emergency escape.

The pilot and co-pilot had excellent visibility though the canopy, which was provided with a V-type windshield made of flat plate glass to prevent distortion.

The bomber/radar operator actuated the bomb director and tail turret controls installed at his position. A passageway was provided along the left side of the flight section for interchangeability of the crew, and for access to the bomb bay in flight when non-pressurized.

The bomb bay was located approximately in the center of the fuselage and had an envelope of 60 x 66 x 192 inches, as specified to accommodate various bomb loads. The bomb bay doors, which were pneumatically actuated for rapid operation, rotated on support arms at each end of the bay. They operated completely internally to ensure that bombing accuracy was not reduced and the airplane was not damaged by buffeting during bomb release. Provisions were made for use of a "single-lug" bomb shackle and the bombs could be loaded from the deck as indicated, without the necessity of pit-loading. Controls, electrical, hydraulic, and other equipment was located in the sides of the fuselage and was readily accessible for servicing from the deck through the open bomb bay.

The defensive armament consisted of a remote controlled tail turret containing two 20mm M-24 guns with 500 rounds of ammunition per gun in separate containers. The ammunition containers were pre-loaded and hoisted into place by means of a standard hoist, through a readily removable access door in the bottom of the fuselage. Radar operated gun laying equipment for this turret was controlled by the bomber/radar operator located forward in the flight section.

The total fuel capacity of 7,440 gals was distributed between the wing and fuselage. PBY type integral tanks in the wing center section contained 1,680 gals and in the fuselage two bladder cells (400 gals) and four self-sealing cells (5,360 gals) provided the remainder. The wing skin averaged .4 inches thick in the integral tank area and would consequently provide a measure of bullet protection. Large access doors were provided for all self-sealing cells to allow fuel cell removal and replacement without the necessity of collapsing the cells.

The landing gear was of the bicycle type with fore and aft units located in the fuselage and small outrigger units housed in the nacelles. The nose wheel was steerable for maneuvering. The main gear wheels were readily replaceable by jacking up the landing gear slightly to remove one or both wheels.

Location of the nacelles on pylons below the wing permitted service and maintenance of the engines and the "outrigger" gear from the deck, without the use of platforms or stands. Servicing of the engine accessories could be accomplished through the outrigger gear wheel well between the engine air ducts. Quick engine change was readily accomplished by means of portable ground equipment.

Alternate Configurations

On November 17, 1948, Convair prepared report ZP-48-4004, titled "Miscellaneous Design Studies – Carrier Based Landplane Class VA – Long Range." This report included data from preliminary studies that were made in the selection of the design for the basic proposal. Early layout studies showed distinct advantages for a twin-engine arrangement; however, the best available turbojet (the XJ40-WE-10) had insufficient power

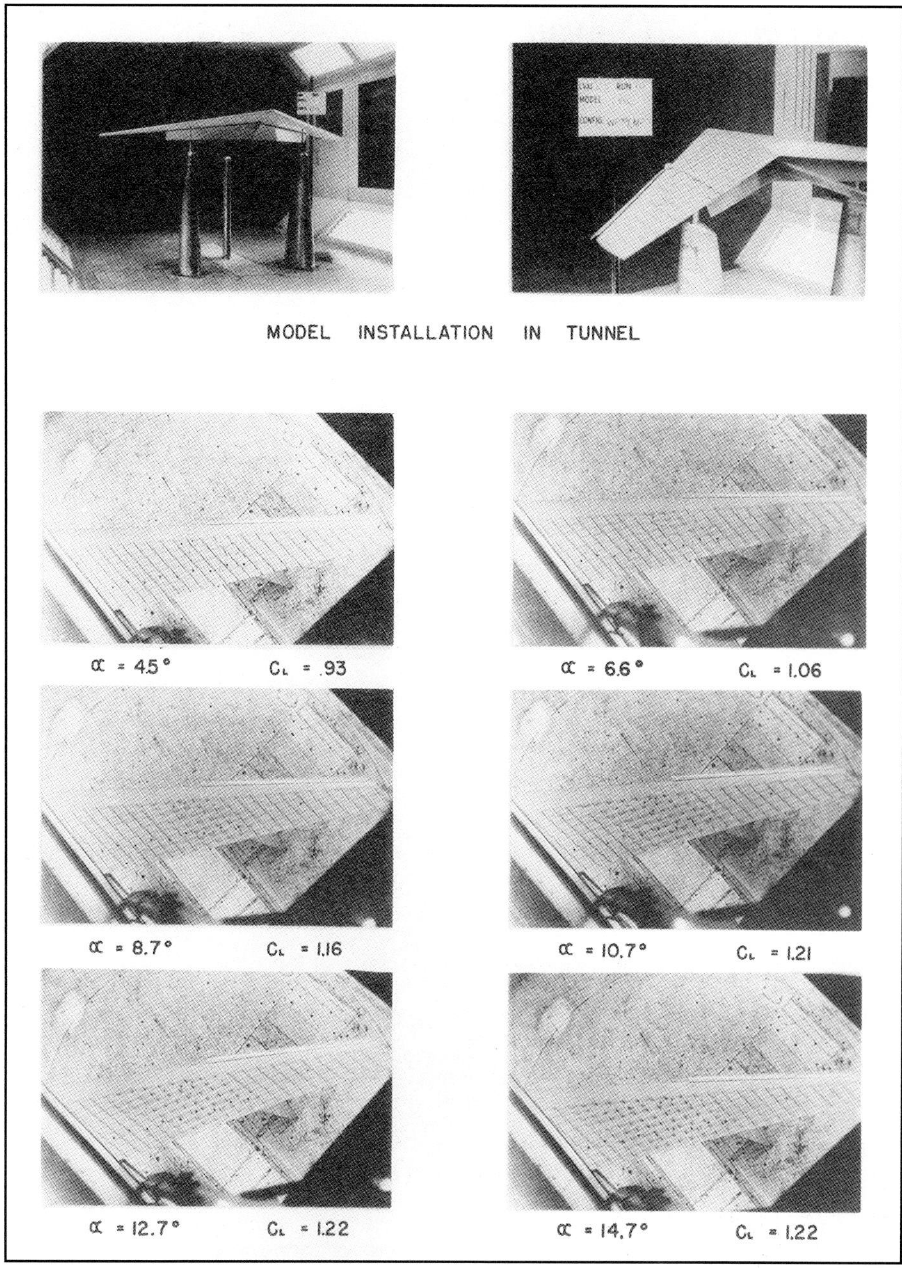

National Archives, RG 72

Convair performed several wind tunnel tests to establish the ideal wing sweep and airfoil; a wing of 4:1 taper ratio was selected due to encouraging test results and time constraints.

event with advanced ratings to give the required performance with the fuel necessary for the range. The three engine arrangement of the basic proposal ensured good climb at takeoff and at altitude and gave sufficient power to cruise at best lift to drag ratio and lowest specific fuel consumption.

In order to investigate the future possibilities of this design, higher powered engines (not included in the authorized list of OS-111) were studied. The Wright Aero Corp. TJ-6 turbojet (available July 1951, according to WAC Specification AC-141) had on the order of 25% more power than the XJ40-WE-10 with approximately the same weight and size. Convair claimed that use of this power plant in a two-engine arrangement would meet or exceed all of the OS-111 requirements.

MISSION AND DESCRIPTION

THE PRINCIPAL MISSION OF THIS AIRPLANE IS HIGH ALTITUDE HORIZONTAL BOMBING ATTACK WITH LARGE BOMBS AND SPECIAL WEAPONS.

THIS AIRPLANE IS A THREE-PLACE CARRIER-BASED LANDPLANE HAVING A SWEPT-BACK HIGH WING AND SWEPT-BACK TAIL SURFACES. THE AIRPLANE STRUCTURE IS OF RIVETED ALUMINUM ALLOY CONSTRUCTION.

DOUBLE-SLOTTED FLAPS AND RETRACTABLE SLATS ARE PROVIDED. POWER-OPERATED WING FOLDING IS PROVIDED. THE LANDING GEAR IS OF THE BICYCLE TYPE WITH OUTRIGGERS AND IS FULLY RETRACTABLE. THE BOMB BAY IS EQUIPPED WITH DOORS WHICH RETRACT INTO THE FUSELAGE. THE CONTROL SYSTEM IS POWER-OPERATED THROUGH MECHANICAL LINKAGE AND INCORPORATES MEANS FOR EMERGENCY OPERATION.

THE CREW COMPARTMENT IS PRESSURIZED AND EJECTABLE SEATS ARE PROVIDED. PASSAGE TO BOMB BAY IS PERMITTED DURING UNPRESSURIZED FLIGHT.

FLAK SUITS AND CURTAINS AFFORD PROTECTION FOR THE CREW.

DIMENSIONS

SPAN:	
WINGS EXTENDED	79'-2"
WINGS FOLDED	50'-4"
HEIGHT OVER TAIL	24'-4"
MAXIMUM LENGTH	88'-4"
TAIL SPAN	28'-4"
FLAP SPAN (% WING SPAN)	55%
WING AREA	900 SQ.FT.
TREAD (OUTRIGGER WHEELS)	31'-0"

WEIGHTS

LOADING	GROSS-LBS	L.F.*
EMPTY	44,170	-
BASIC	44,490	-
DESIGN	80,200	2.67
COMBAT	64,675	3.5
MAX.T.O.	100,000**	2.25
MAX.LAND.	80,200	-

** LIMITED BY SPEC.OS-111
* LIMIT MANEUVER LOAD FACTORS

FUEL AND OIL

LOCATION	TYPE	GALS.
FUSELAGE	SELF-SEALING	5360
FUSELAGE	BLADDER	400
WING	INTEGRAL	1680
	TOTAL	7440

AVIATION GASOLINE

OIL

OIL SYSTEMS AND RESERVOIRS INTEGRAL WITH ENGINES. A TOTAL OF 20 GALLONS IS ALLOWED.

ELECTRONICS

AN/APN-22 RADAR ALTIMETER
AN/ARC-19 VHF TRANS-REC.
AN/APB-2 RADAR BOMB DIR. (MK5)
AN/ART-13 MHF TRANSMITTER
AN/ARR-15 MHF RECEIVER
AN/ARR-12A NAVIGATION REC
AN/APX-6 IFF
AN/AIC-4 INTERPHONE (3-PLACE)
AN/ARC-15 RANGE RECEIVER
AN/APN-4 LORAN (PROV. ONLY)

POWER PLANT

THREE XJ40-WE-10 WESTINGHOUSE TURBO-JET ENGINES.

TWO JATO UNITS

RATINGS

TURBO-JET ENGINE RATINGS CONFORM TO WEC BID SPEC. WAGT-X40E8-2, 3-15-48, AS MODIFIED BY NAVAER REPORT 1045.

JATO UNITS
33,000 LBS. THRUST EACH FOR 4 SECONDS.

ORDNANCE

GUNS:
TAIL TURRET
2-M-24 20MM GUNS
1000 ROUNDS AMMO.

BOMBS:
10,000 LB. BOMB LOAD ENVELOPE 16 FT. IN LENGTH, 66 INCHES HIGH AND 60 INCHES WIDE INCLUDING FALL CLEARANCES.

National Archives, RG 72

Excerpt from the Standard Aircraft Characteristics charts submitted by Convair to BuAer as part of its Class VA proposal. This packet of charts, which was generally 4-10 pages in length, provided a condensed summary of the proposal for circulation among BuAer's various branches for evaluation.

PERFORMANCE DATA *

GROSS WEIGHT	LB.	100,000
FUEL	LB.	44,000
BOMBS	LB.	10,000
BASIC FLIGHT DES. GROSS WEIGHT	LB.	80,200
BASIC LANDING DES. GR. WT.	LB.	63,600
HIGH SPEED WITH MIL. RATING FLIGHT DES. G.W. @ 40,000 FT. ALT.	KNOTS	540(M .94)
AVERAGE CRUISING AIRSPEED ON COMBAT PROBLEM	KNOTS	490(M .85)
COMBAT RADIUS (PROB. NO.A-3 AT 35000 FT. TO 47500 FT. ALT. WITH 40000' ALT. 100 MILE FROM TARGET)	N.MI.	1,700
RATE OF CLIMB @ S.L. AFTER EXPENDITURE OF JATO (NAVY STANDARD HOT DAY) WITH GEAR AND FLAPS EXTENDED	FT/MIN.	950
STALLING SPEED @ DESIGN LANDING WEIGHT	KNOTS	110
RATE OF CLIMB WITH NORMAL RATING - FLIGHT DES. G.W. @ 40000 FT.	FT/MIN.	900
SERVICE CEILING WITH NORMAL RATING - FLIGHT DES. G.W. 300 FT/MIN. RATE OF CLIMB	FT.	42,300
SERVICE CEILING WITH NORMAL RATING - ONE NACELLE INOPERATIVE - FLIGHT DES.G.W. 300 FT/MIN. RATE OF CLIMB	FT.	30,700
TAKE-OFF OVER 50 FT. OBSTACLE ON PAVED RUNWAY (TWO 4AS-33000 JATO)	FT.	3,460
LANDING DISTANCE OVER 50 FT. OBSTACLE ON PAVED RUNWAY (BASIC LANDING DES. G.W.)	FT.	4,225

*BASED ON ADVANCE ENGINE RATINGS PER DR REPORT 1045.

AIRCRAFT DIMENSIONAL DATA

WING		
AREA	SQ.FT.	900
SPAN (TOTAL)	FT.IN.	79'2"
SPAN (FOLDED)	FT.IN	50'4"
ROOT CHORD	FT.IN.	18'2"
TIP CHORD	FT.IN.	4'6.5"
MEAN AERODYNAMIC CHORD	IN.	152.6
AIRFOIL SECTION	NACA	63-010 MOD.
WING INCIDENCE	DEG.	4.5
SWEEPBACK (.25C)	DEG.	40
DIHEDRAL (CHORD PLANE)		0
ASPECT RATIO		7
TAPER RATIO		4:1
HORIZONTAL TAIL		
AREA	SQ.FT.	200
SPAN	FT.IN.	28'4"
SECTION	NACA	63-009 MOD.
INCIDENCE	DEG.	3°
ASPECT RATIO		4
VERTICAL TAIL		
AREA	SQ.FT.	100
ASPECT RATIO		1.5
SECTION	NACA	63-012 MOD.

National Archives, RG 72

Table summarizing the key performance and dimensional characteristics of Convair's basic Long Range Class VA design.

PERFORMANCE SUMMARY

		Two WAC TJ-6 Turbojets	Two West. XJ40-WE-10 Turbojets
Gross Weight	lb.	100,000	100,000
fuel	lb.	48,380	48,180
bomb	lb.	10,000	10,000
Basic Flight Design G.W.	lb.	78,200	78,300
Basic Landing Design G.W.	lb.	61,000	61,100
High Speed with Mil. Rating - Flight Design G.W. @ 40000 ft. Alt.	knots	530 (M=.92)	500 (M=.87)
Average Cruising Airspeed on Combat Problem	knots	490 (M=.85)	490 (M=.85)
Combat Radius (Problem A-3)	Naut.Mi.	1,700	1,600
Combat Altitude @ Flight Design G.W.	ft.	40,000	32,500
Rate of Climb @ Sea Level after expenditure of Take-off Jato (Navy Standard Hot Day) with gear retracted	ft/min.	675	200
Stalling Speed @ Basic Landing Design G.W.	knots	108	108
Engine Rating - Take-off @ 0 Knots & S.L.	lb.	11,000 (per WAC Spec AC-141)	8,900 (per DR-1045)

National Archives, RG 72

Performance summary of a future twin engine variant showing the superiority of the Wright Aero TJ-6 over the XJ40-WE-10. Drawings of this alternate design are shown on page 29.

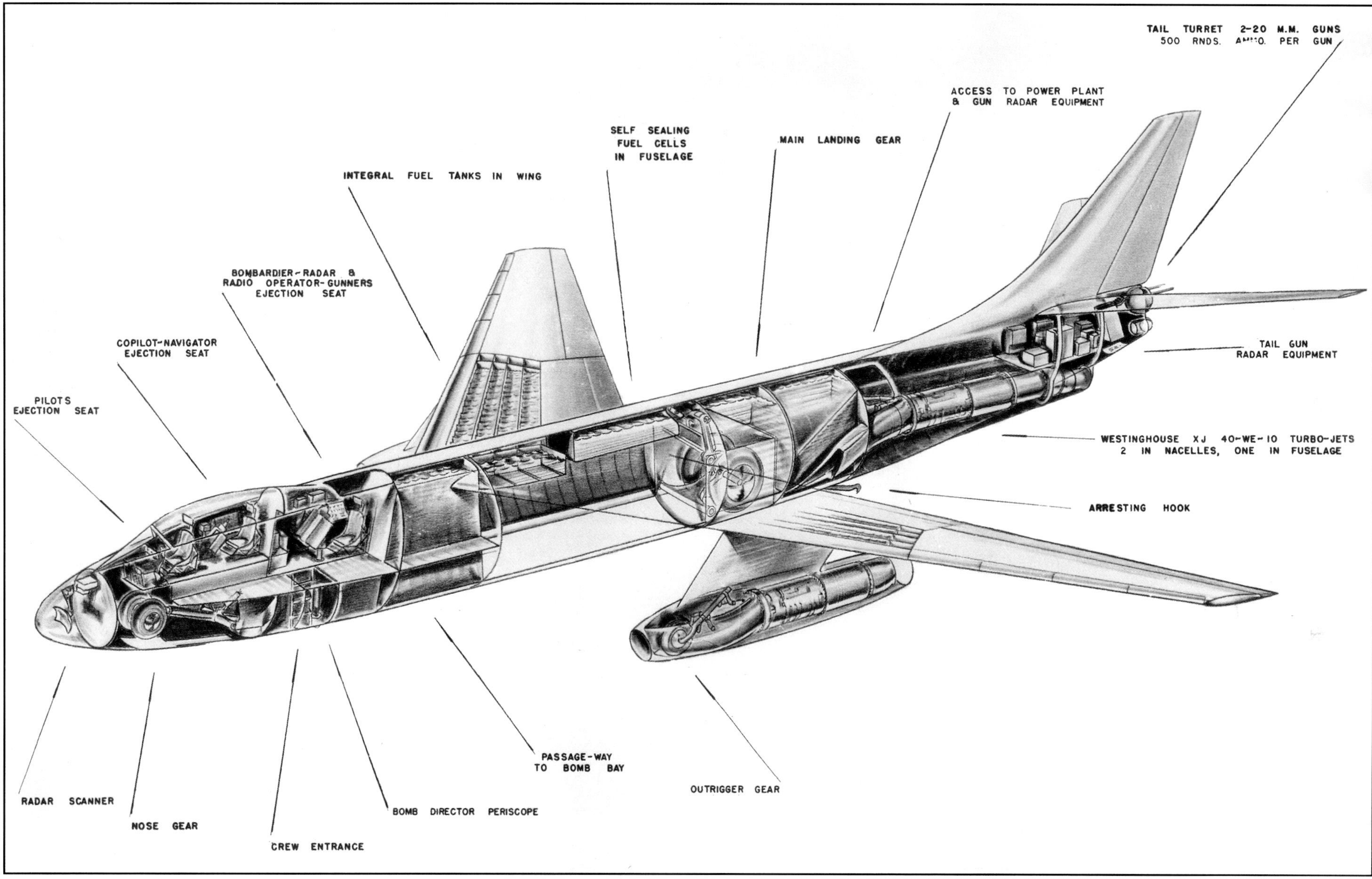

National Archives, RG 72

Perspective cutaway illustration showing the major internal components of Convair's VA proposal; note the recessed side air inlets for the central turbojet installed in the aft fuselage.

Next Page

Extracts from the Convair proposal brochure showing carrier spotting; bomb and ammunition loading; landing gear servicing; and engine access provisions. The company put considerable thought and effort into making its Class VA proposal suitable for the unique challenges of operating in a maritime environment.

National Archives, RG 72

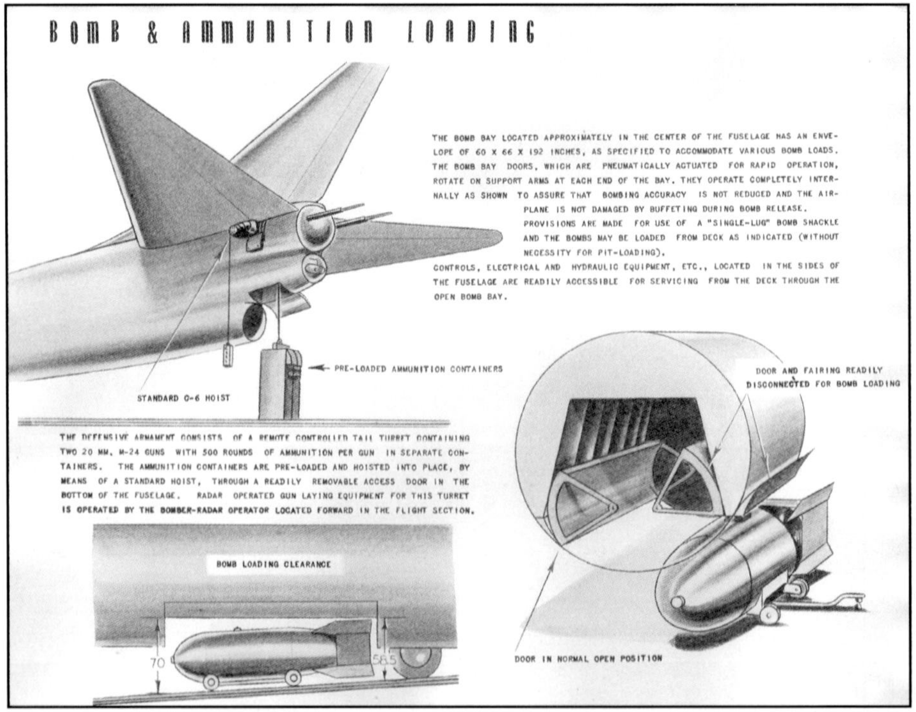

National Archives, RG 72

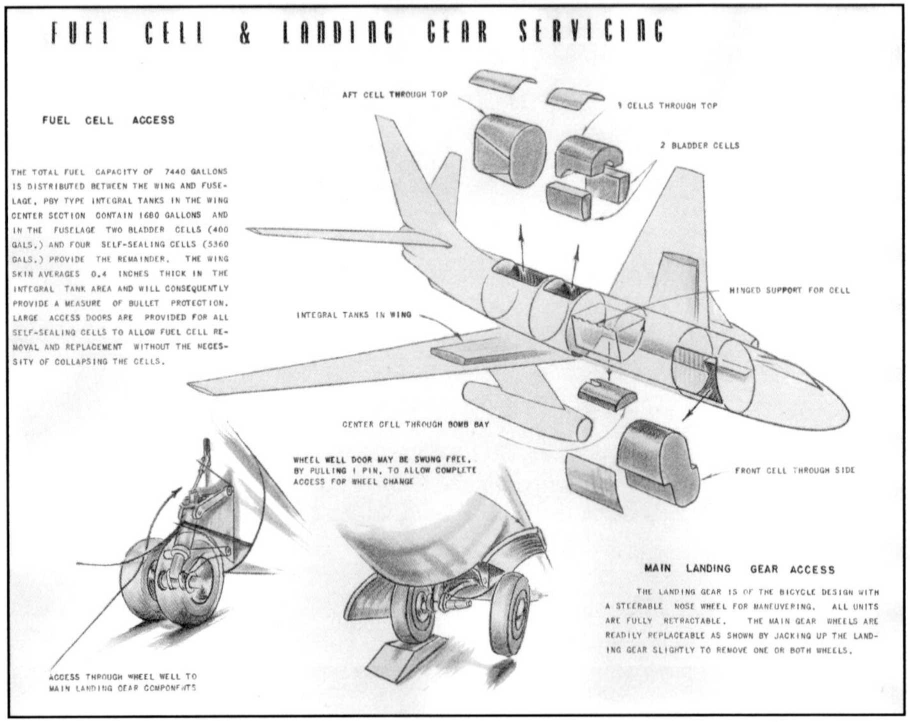

National Archives, RG 72

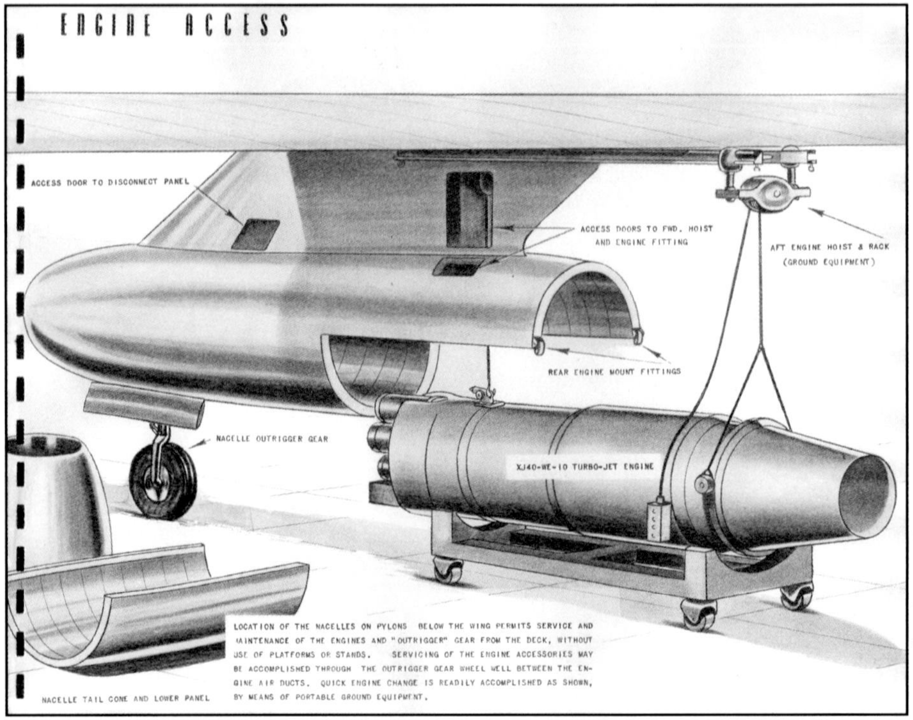

National Archives, RG 72

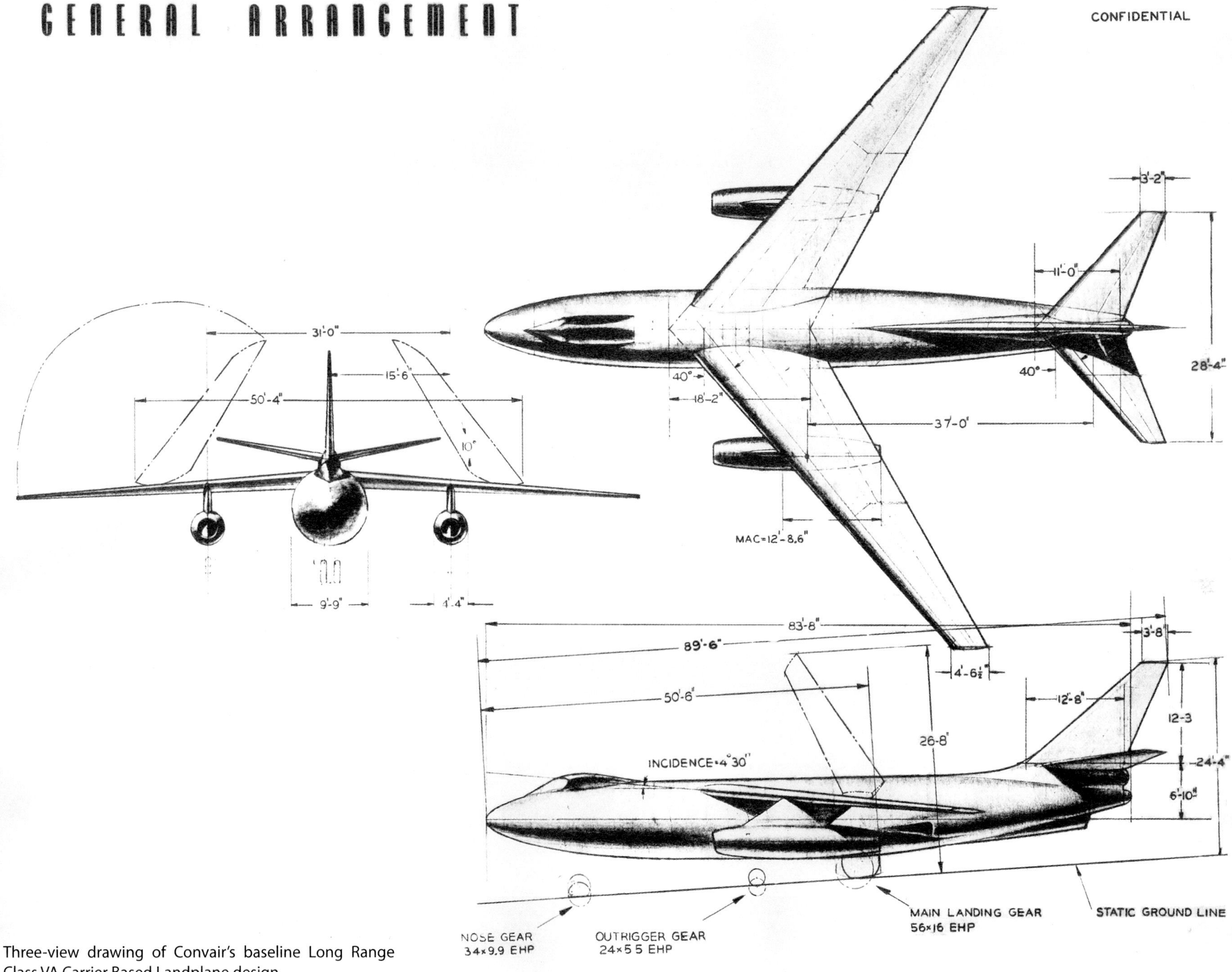

Three-view drawing of Convair's baseline Long Range Class VA Carrier Based Landplane design.

National Archives, RG 72

Convair went as far as producing a desktop model of its Long Range Class VA proposal. It appears to be painted Glossy Sea Blue overall and features a handsome articulated base to display the model from various angles, as shown in this photo and those on the pages 19-20.

National Archives, RG 72

National Archives, RG 72

National Archives, RG 72

National Archives, RG 72

National Archives, RG 72

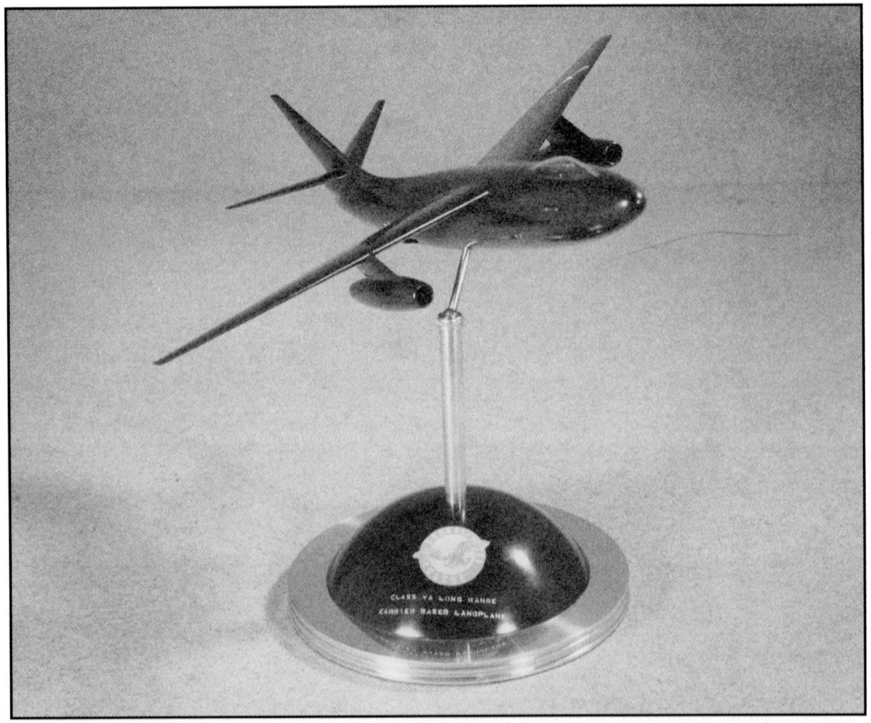

National Archives, RG 72

National Archives, RG 72

National Archives, RG 72

National Archives, RG 72

Left: Inboard plan and profile drawing of the Convair Class VA proposal. The company submitted a very comprehensive set of blueprints documenting the major design features of both this and their Special Attack proposal, covered in Chapter 12.

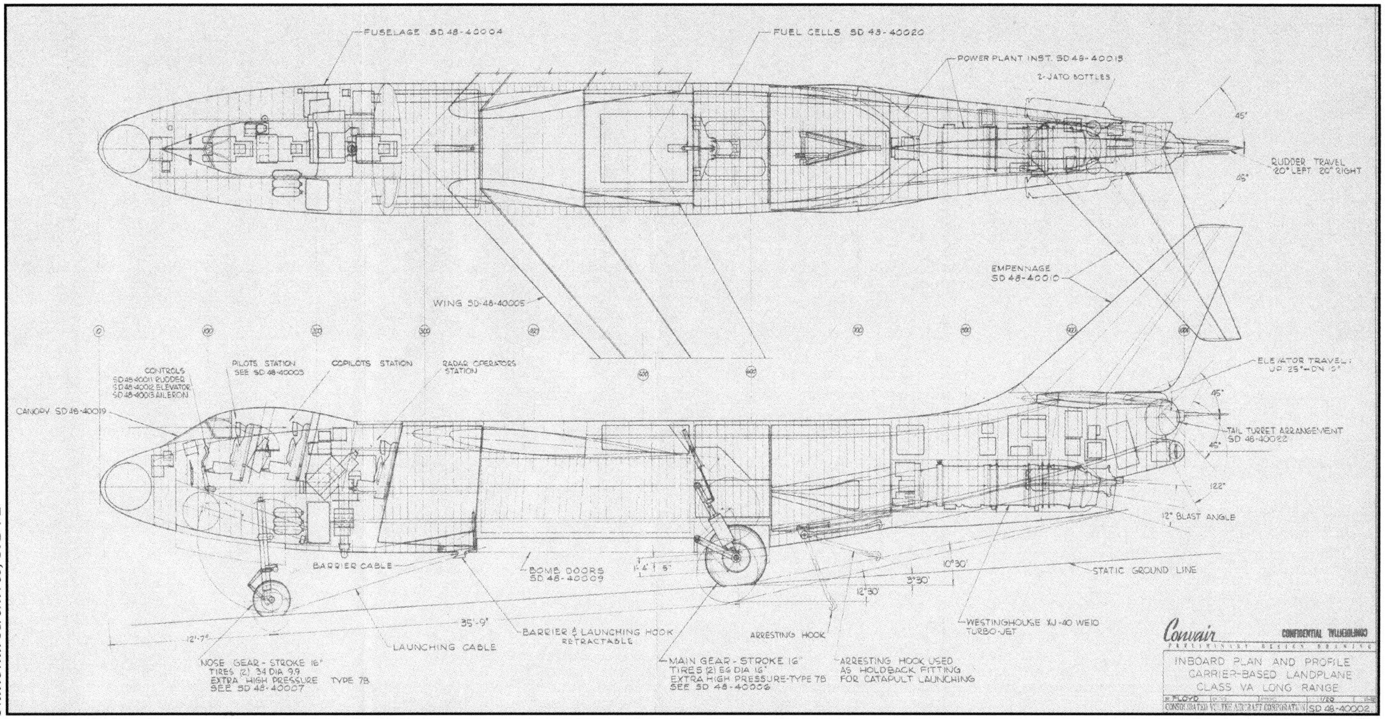

National Archives, RG 72

Below: Detail drawings of the flight deck, which was pressurized to 4.0 PSI and accommodated a three man crew consisting of the pilot, co-pilot/navigator, and bomber/radar operator.

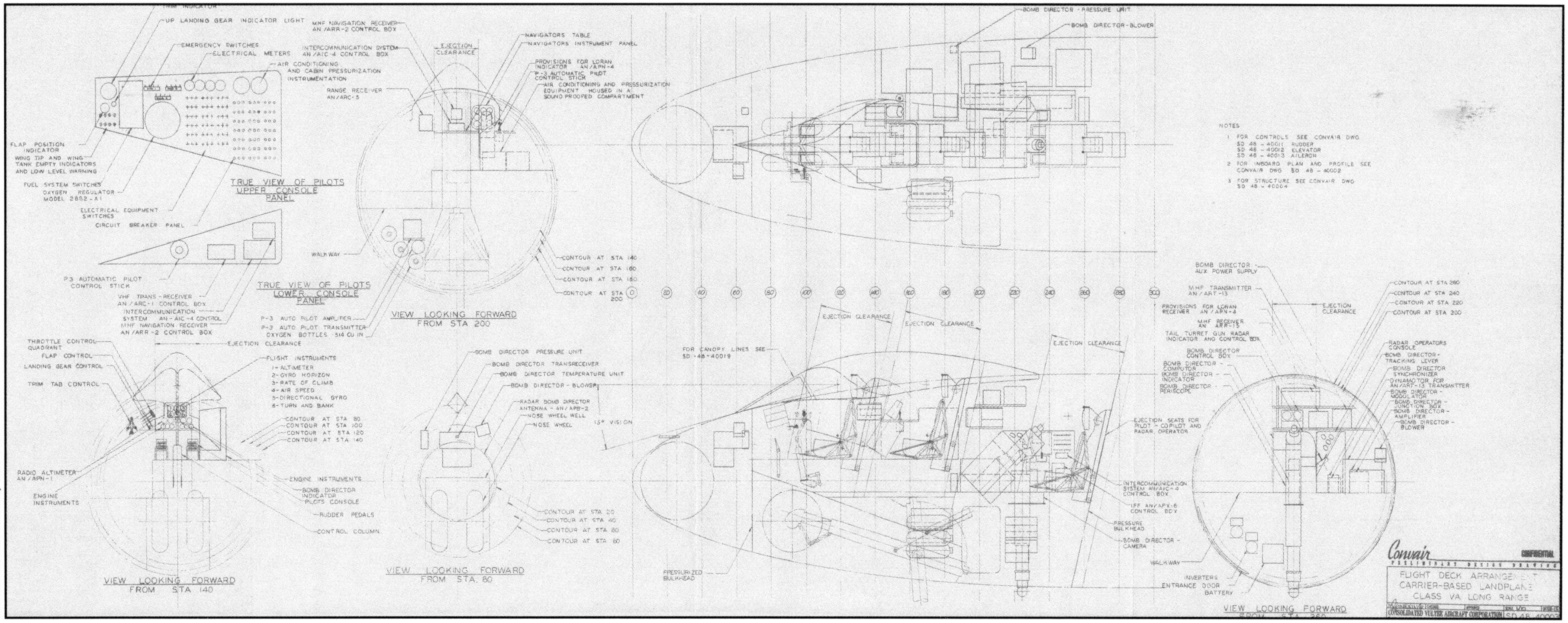

National Archives, RG 72

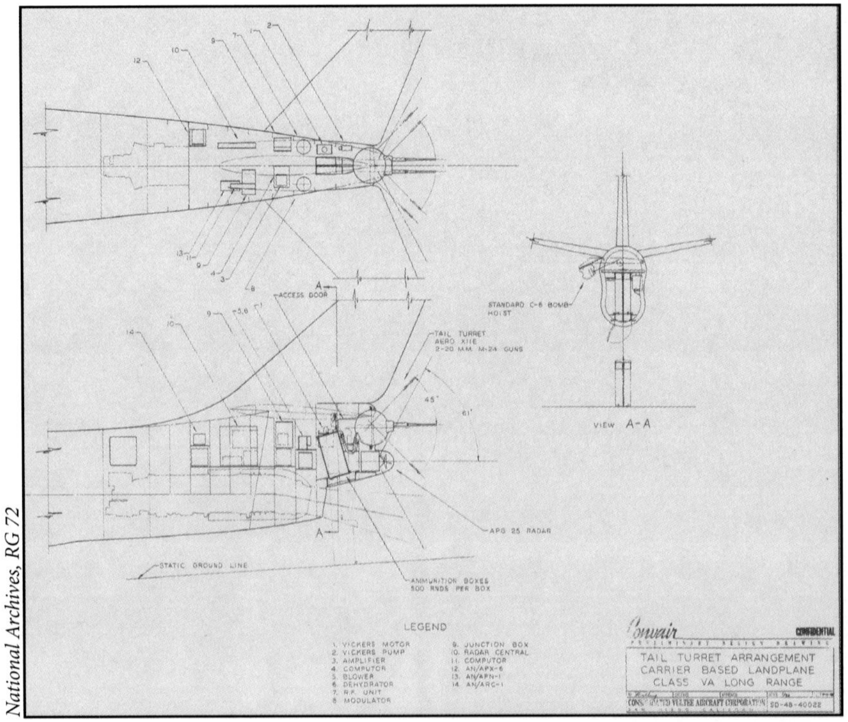

National Archives, RG 72

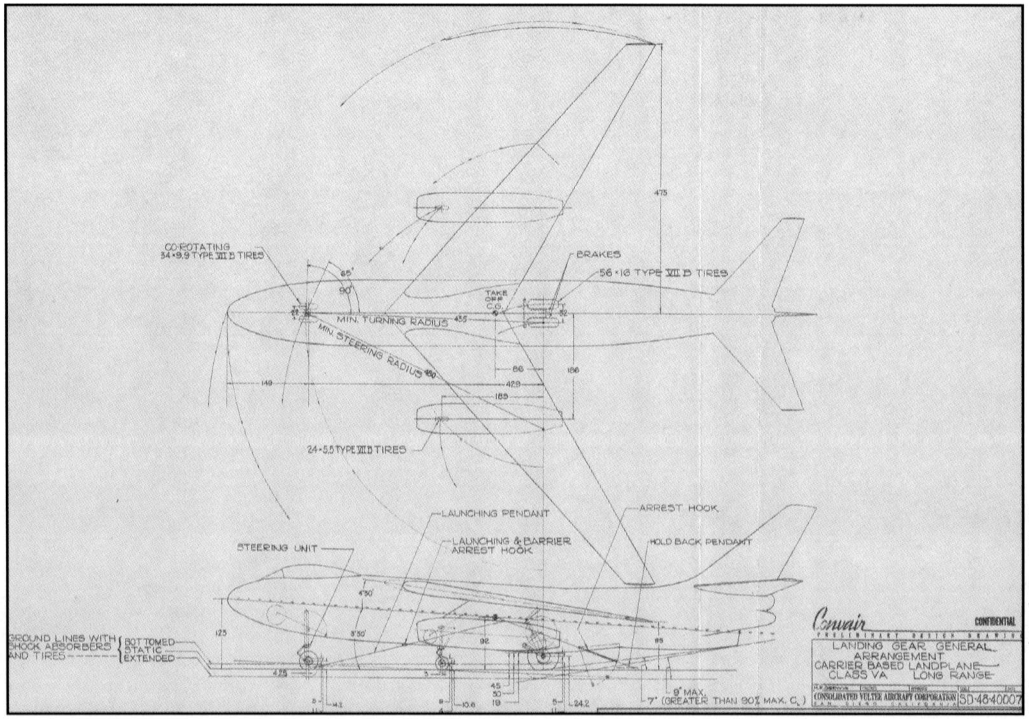

National Archives, RG 72

Upper Left: Detail drawings of the Aero X11E remote control tail turret equipped with two 20 mm M-24 guns.

Upper Right: Blueprint of the landing gear arrangement, which consisted of a pair of center line bicycle main gear and a pair of small outrigger gear mounted in the engine nacelles.

Right: The basic fuselage structure of the Convair Class VA aircraft.

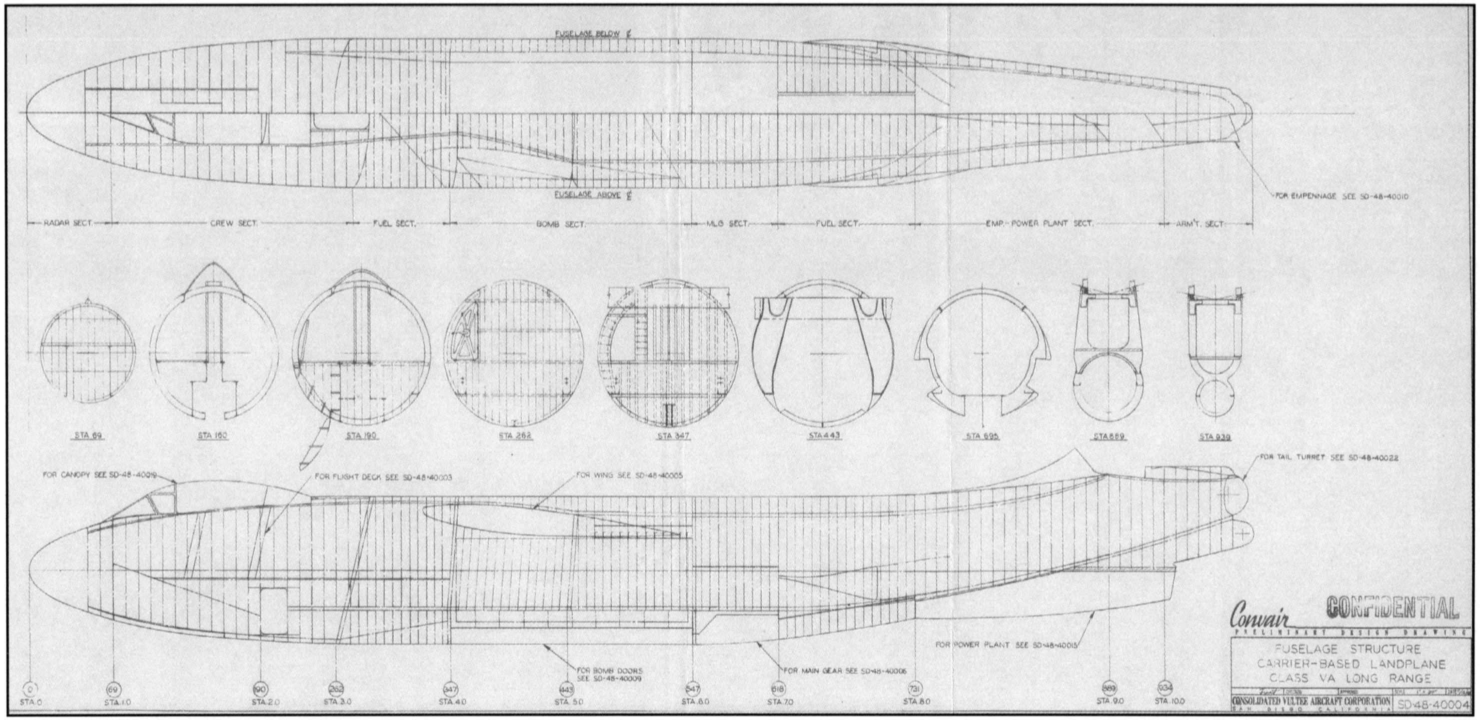

National Archives, RG 72

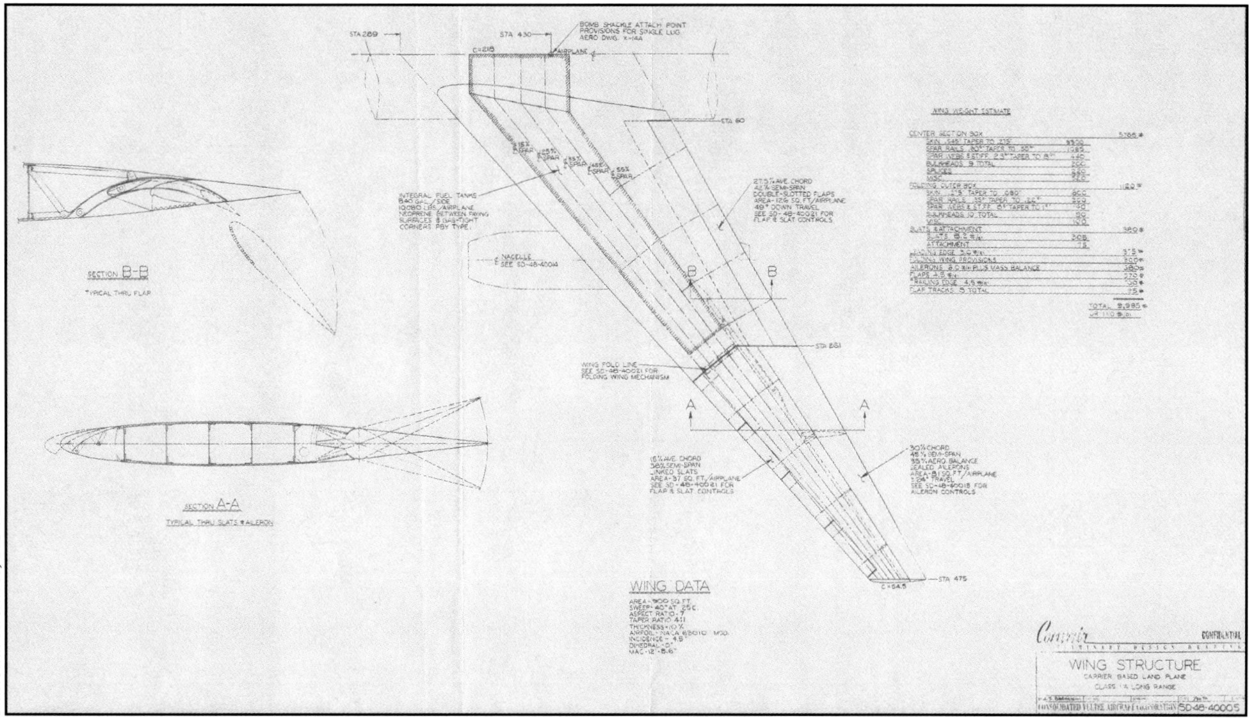

National Archives, RG 72

Left: Blueprint depicting the aircraft's wing structure and control surface arrangement.

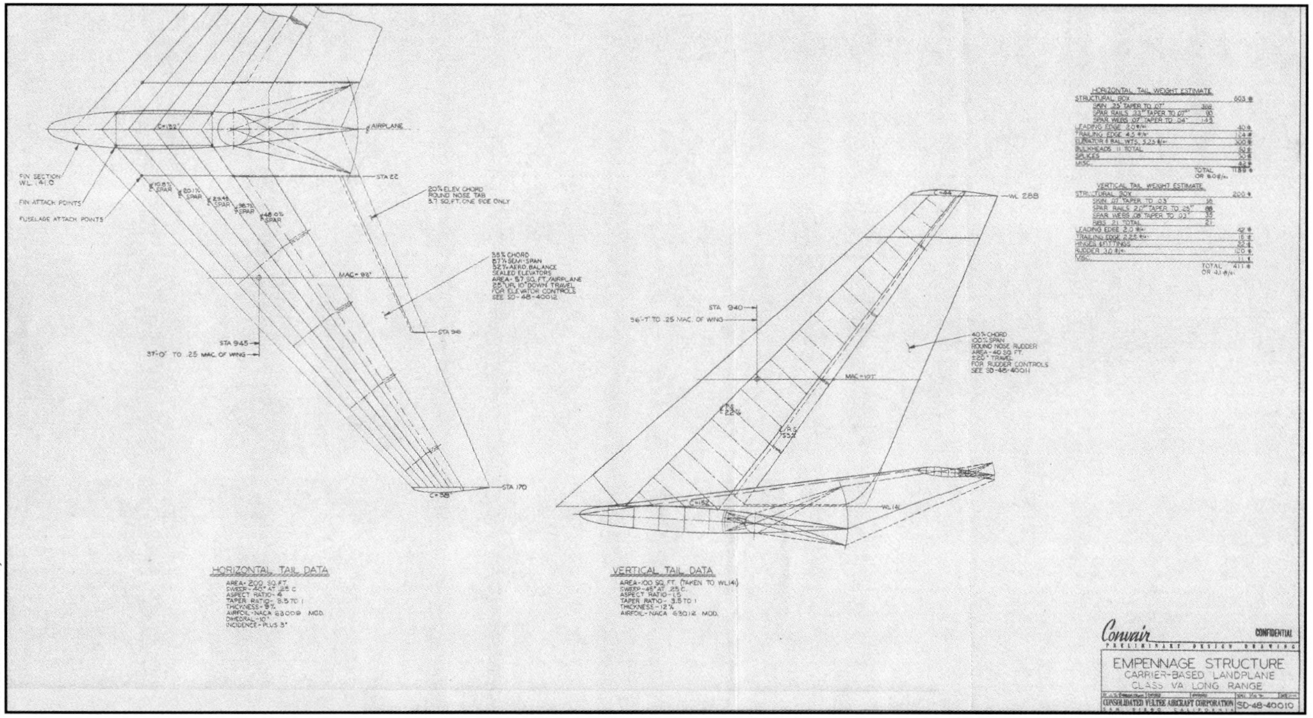

National Archives, RG 72

Left: Blueprint of the empennage structure.

Next Page

Upper Left: Detail drawing of the aft main gear, which retracted vertically into the fuselage. The bicycle arrangement saved considerable weight over a more conventional tricycle type gear.

Upper Right: Blueprint of the bomb bay door installation. The pneumatically actuated doors rotated on support arms at each end of the bay, operating completely internally to ensure a high degree of bombing accuracy and minimize buffeting during bomb release.

Bottom: Diagram of the proposed aircraft's auxiliary wing controls.

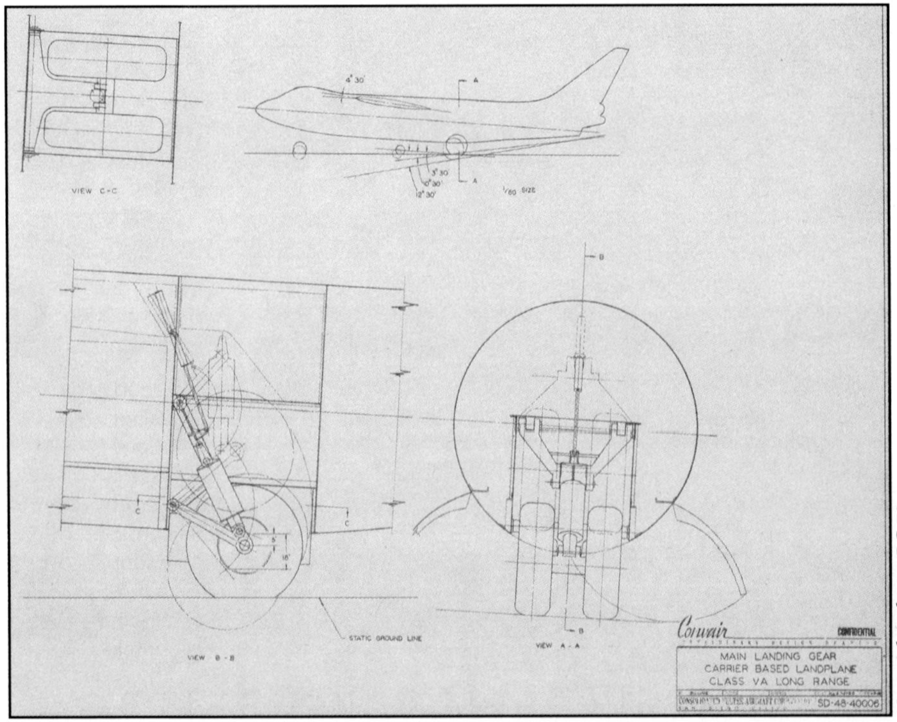

National Archives, RG 72

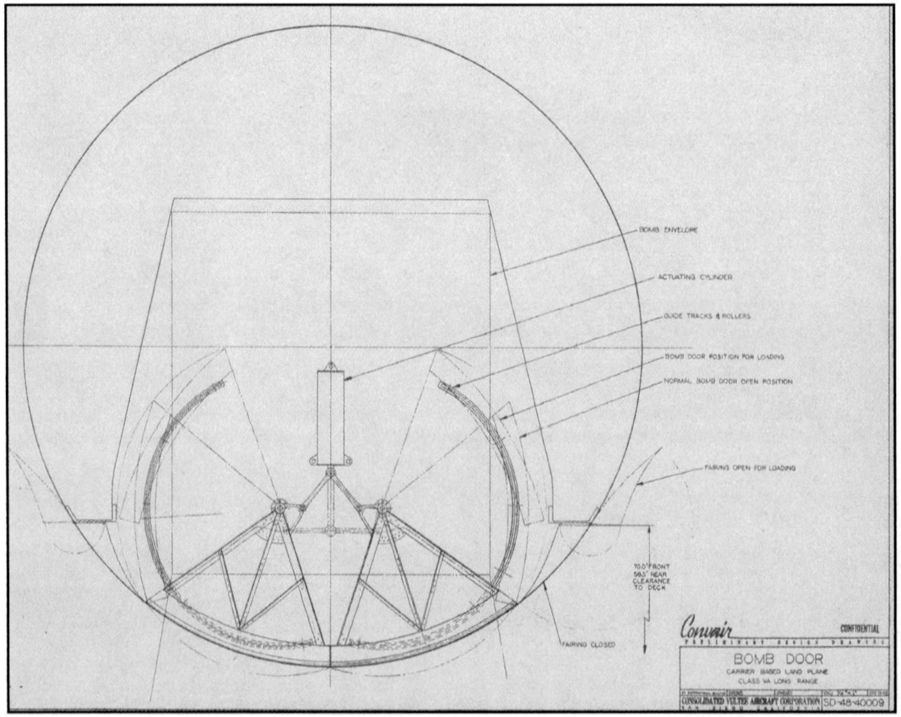

National Archives, RG 72

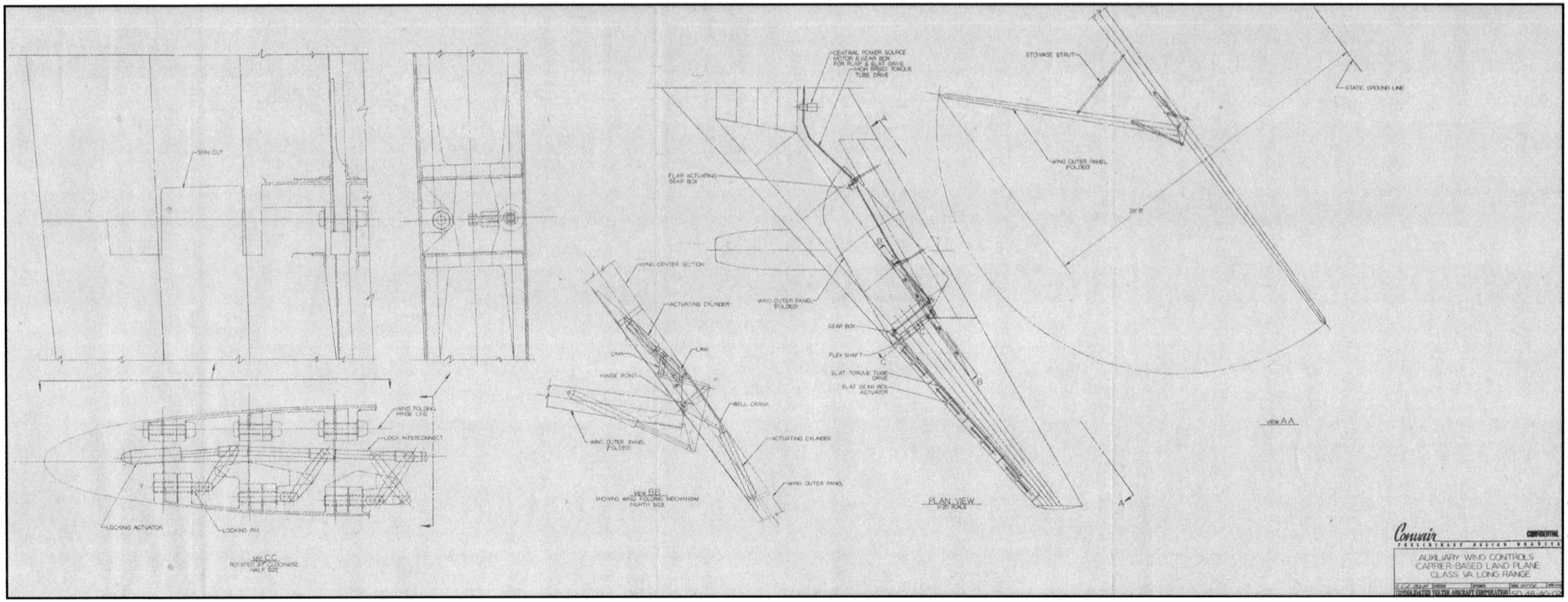

National Archives, RG 72

Left: Blueprint of the Westinghouse XJ40-WE-10 engine nacelle installation. Placement of nacelles on pylons below the wing permitted service and maintenance of the engines and the "outrigger" gear from the deck, without the use of platforms or stands.

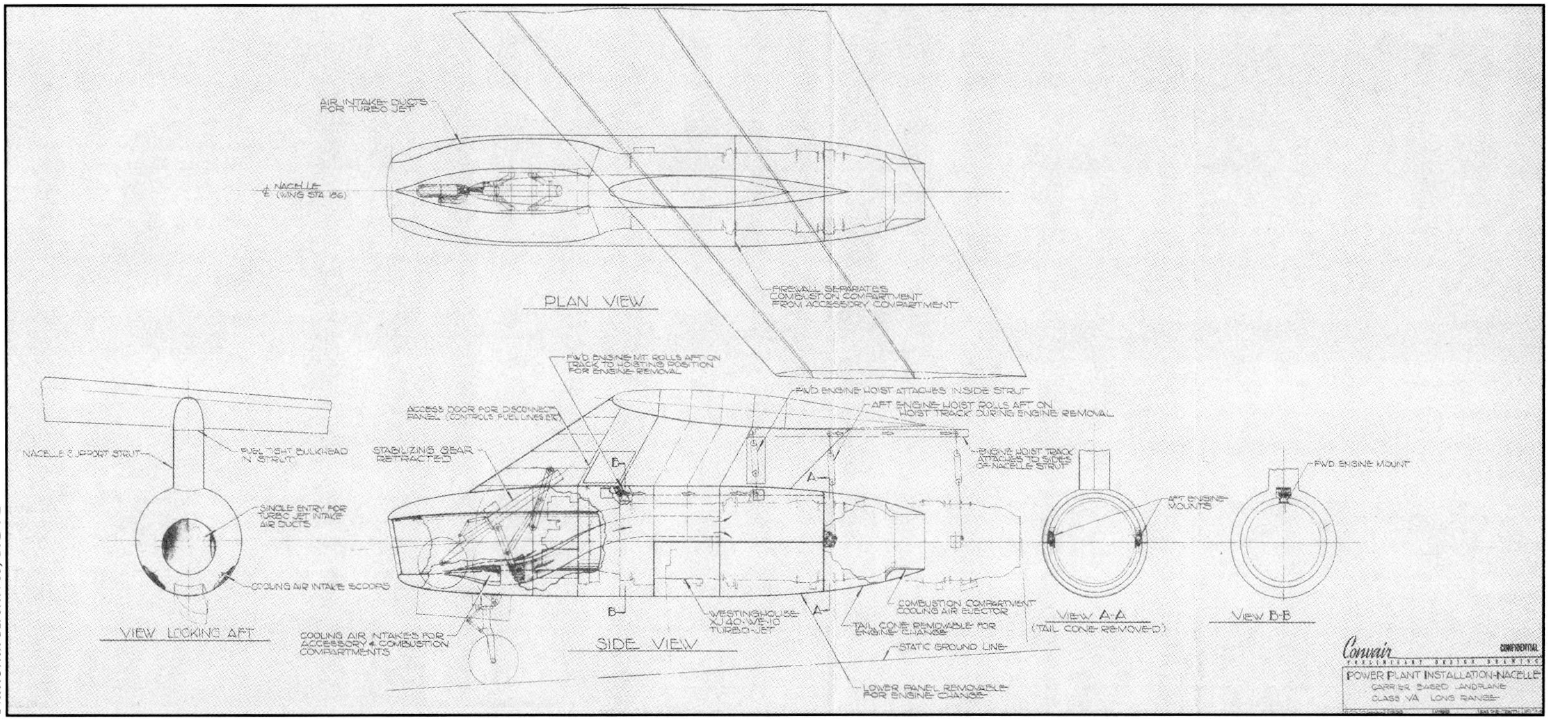

National Archives, RG 72

Below Left: A third XJ-40 jet engine was installed in the aft fuselage of the Convair Class VA aircraft due to a lack of sufficiently powerful engines for a more conventional twin engine configuration. Air was provided to the engine by semi-flush air scoops with boundary layer intake slots mounted on either side of the fuselage.

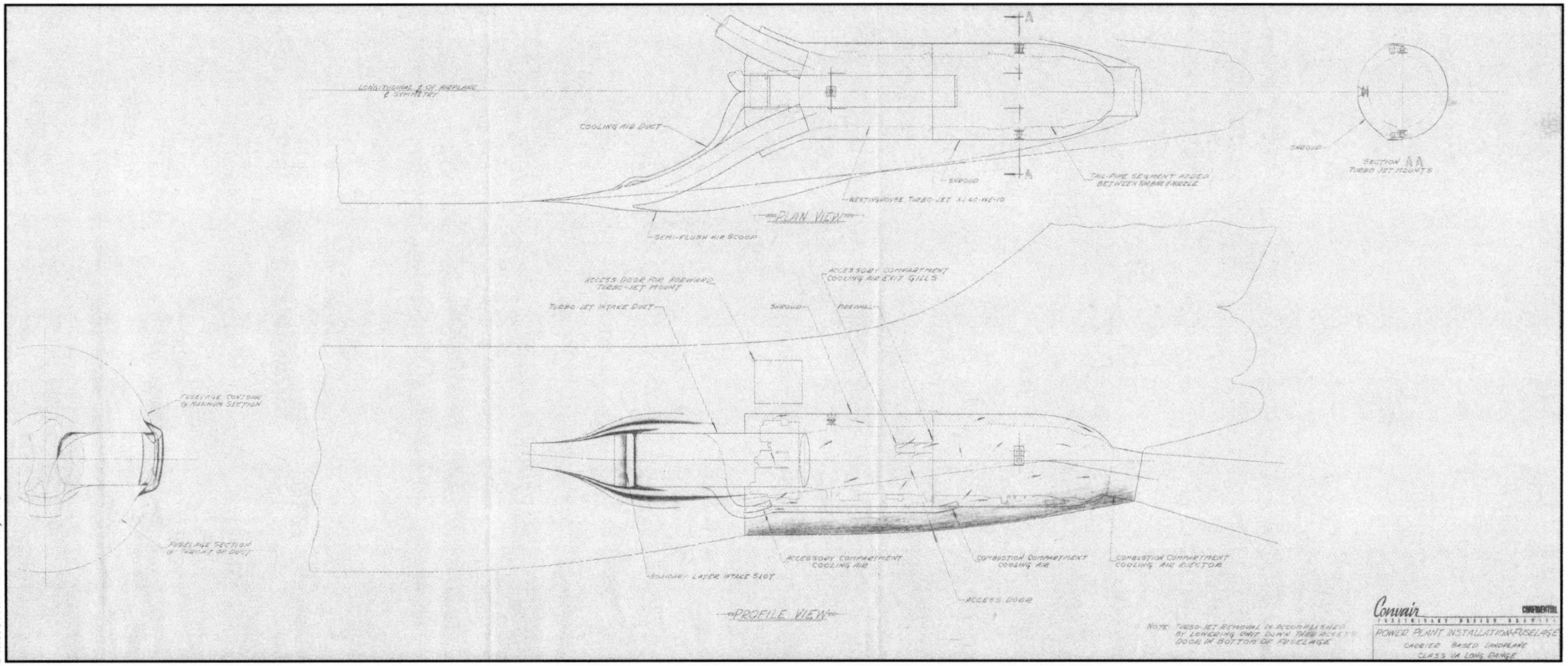

National Archives, RG 72

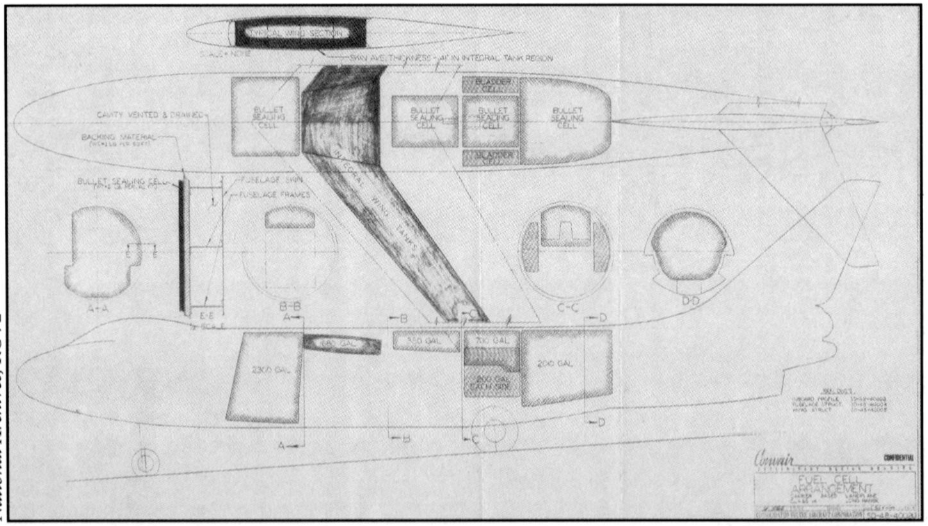

National Archives, RG 72

Diagram of the fuel cell arrangement, which held 7,440 gals distributed between the wing and fuselage. The wing center section featured PBY type integral tanks with a capacity of 1,680 gals, while the fuselage contained two bladder cells (400 gals) and four self-sealing cells (5,360 gals).

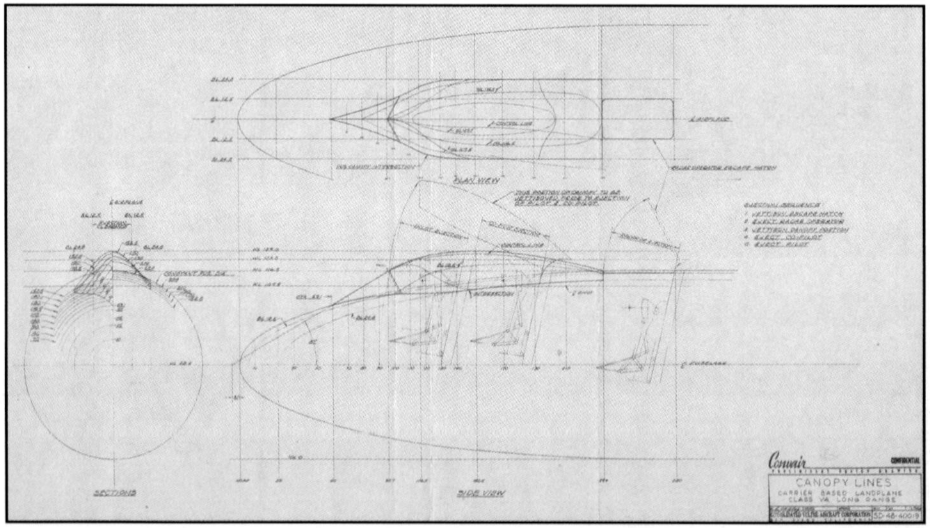

National Archives, RG 72

Canopy lines of the Convair Long Range Class VA proposal. The canopy featured a V-type windshield made of flat plate glass to prevent distortion. The bubble canopy and a panel in the top of the fuselage could be jettisoned to provide emergency egress for all three crew members, who were equipped with ejection seats.

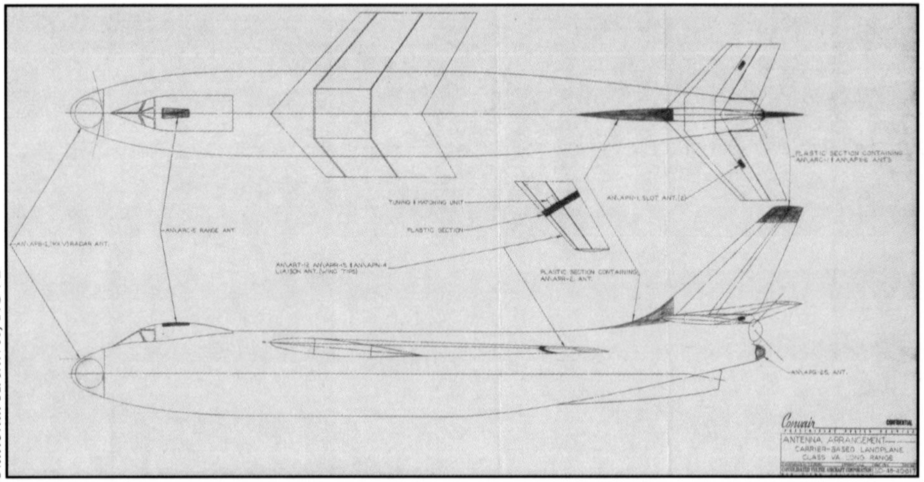

National Archives, RG 72

Diagram of the Convair Long Range Class VA antenna arrangement, which was entirely flush-mounted to reduce drag.

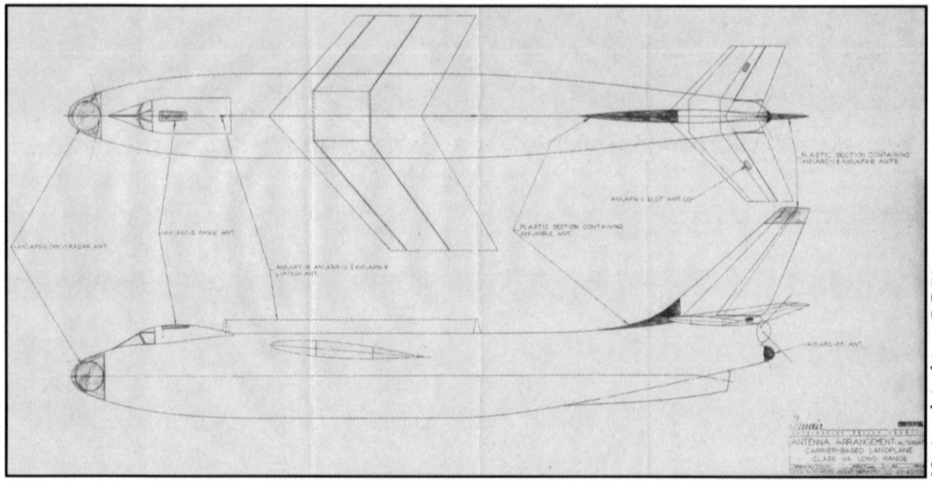

National Archives, RG 72

Convair also submitted an alternate antenna arrangement with an external wire running on top of the fuselage for the AN/ART-13, AN/ARR-15 and AN/APN-4 liaison antenna.

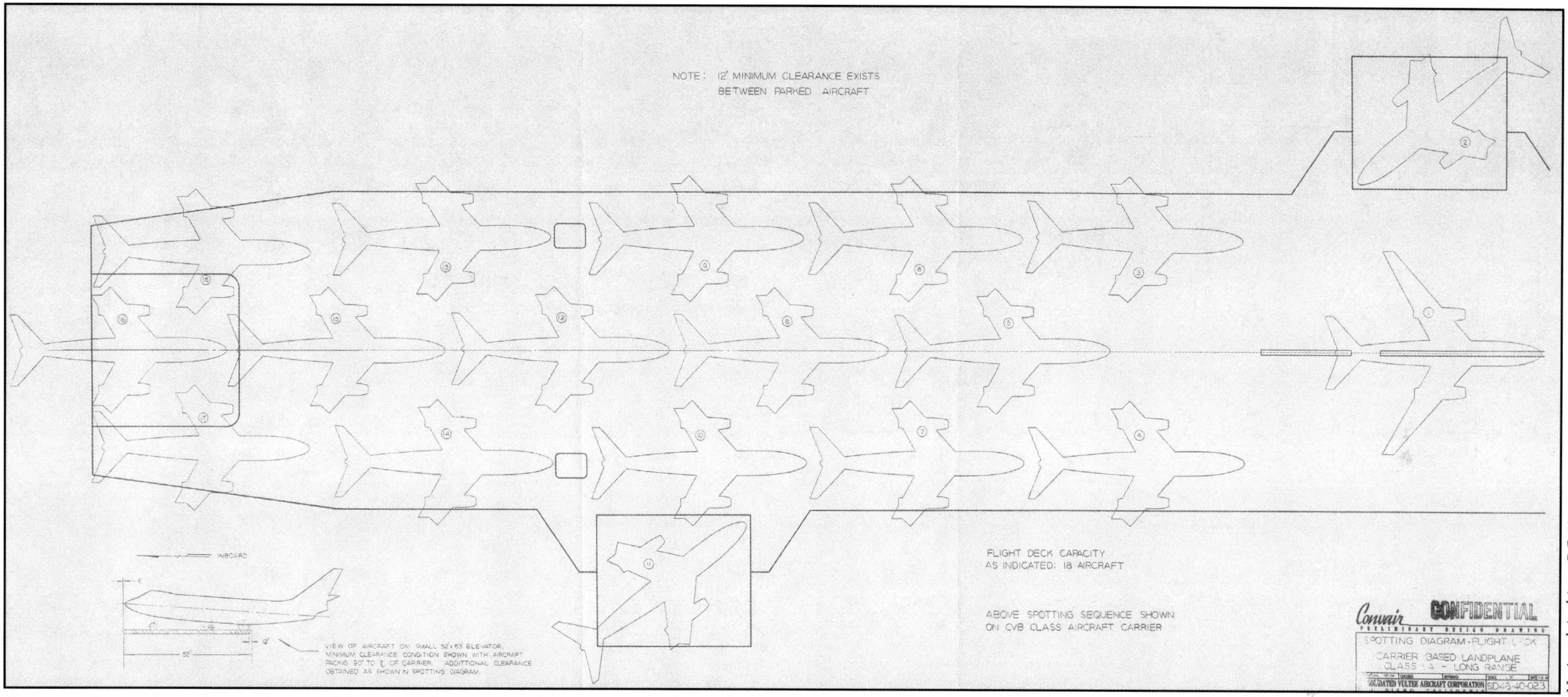

National Archives, RG 72

Above: Carrier spotting diagram for the flight deck of a CVB class aircraft carrier, which could accommodate a maximum of 18 Convair Long Range Class VA aircraft.

Below: Twenty of Convair's Class VA aircraft could fit on the hangar deck of the same carrier.

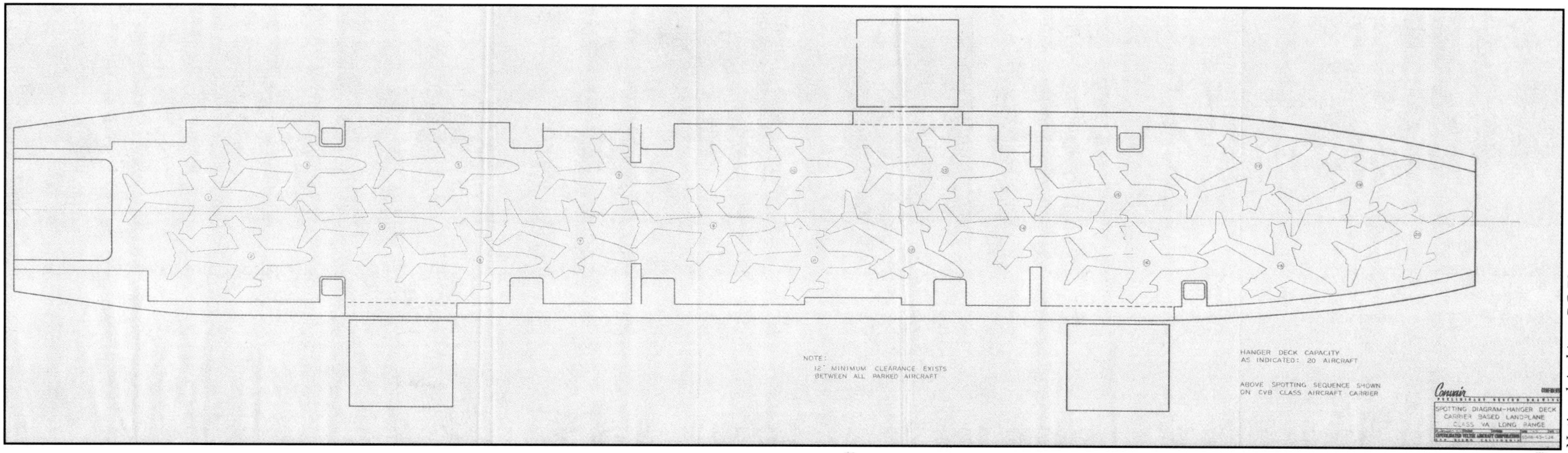

National Archives, RG 72

Right: Diagram showing the breakdown of the Convair Class VA's major subassemblies.

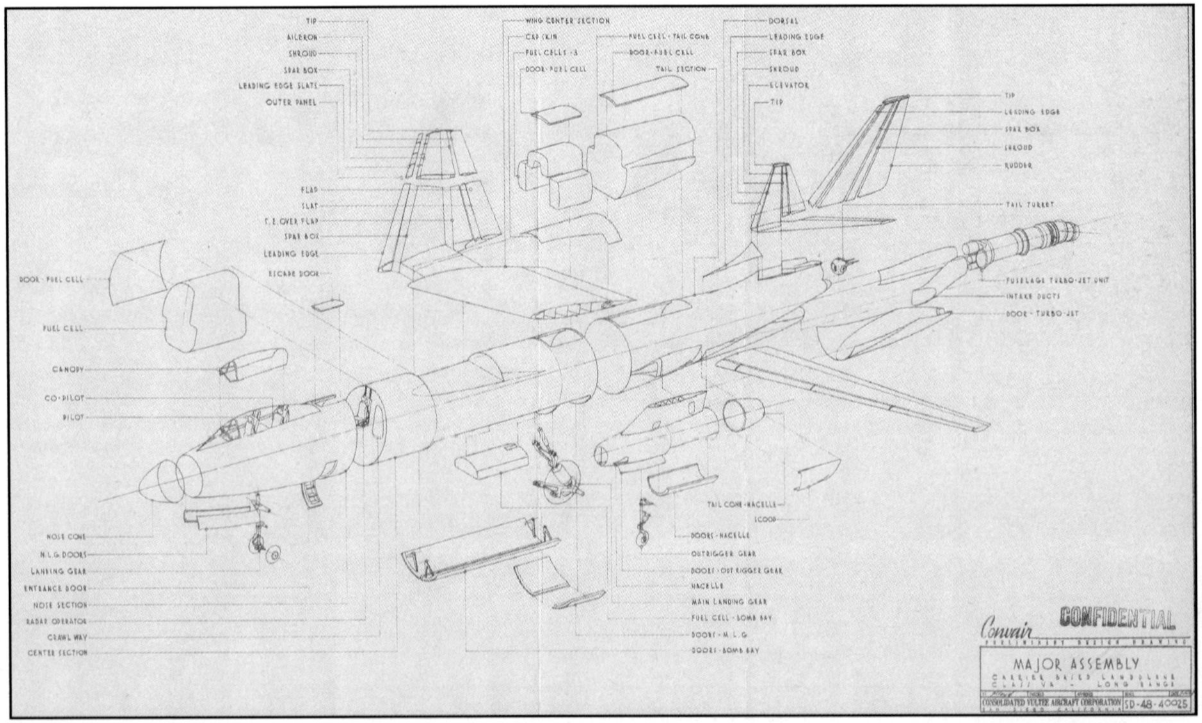

National Archives, RG 72

Below: Illustration of the proposed production procedure.

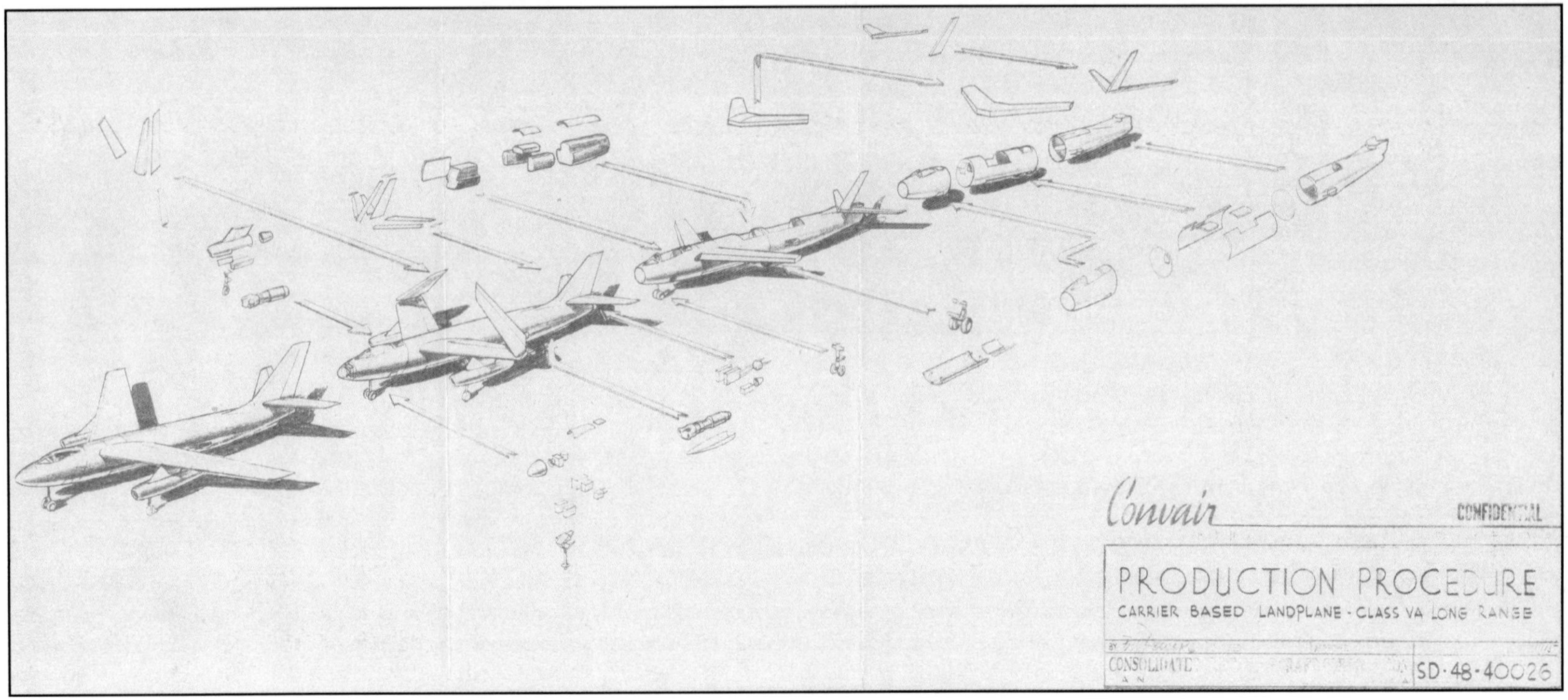

National Archives, RG 72

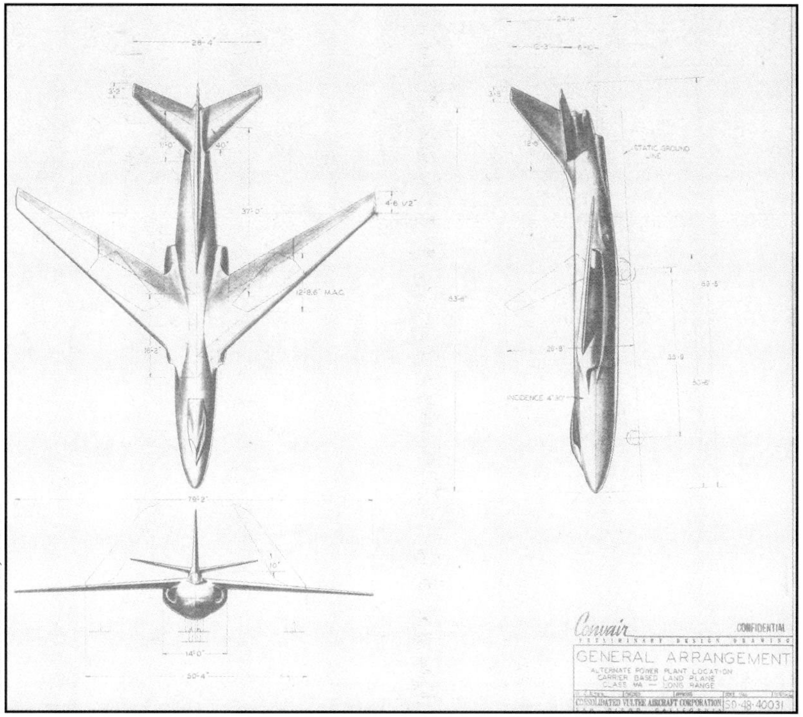

National Archives, RG 72

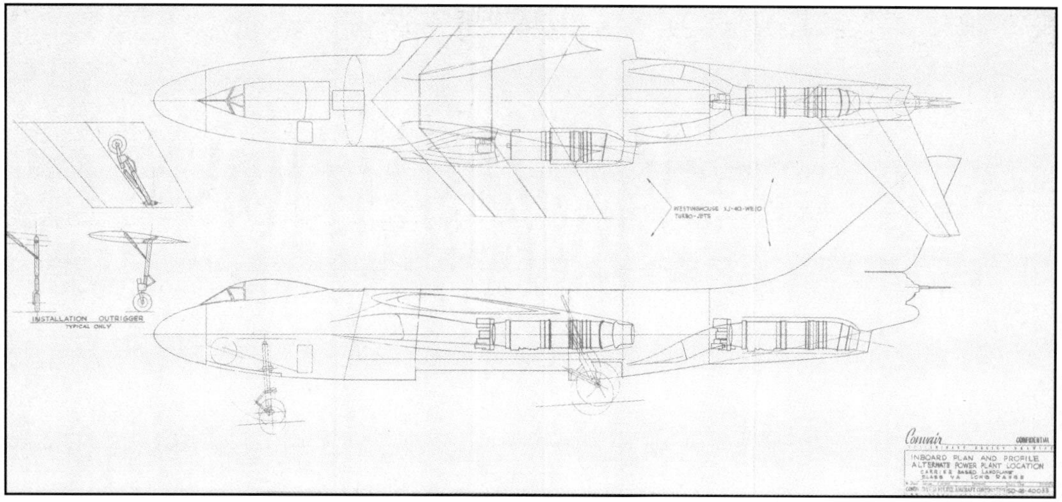

National Archives, RG 72

Left & Above: Three-view and inboard profile of the Convair Long Range Class VA proposal with an alternate engine arrangement, in which two Westinghouse XJ40-WE-10 turbojets were placed on the fuselage below the wing roots. While this arrangement probably contributed less drag than the wing-mounted nacelles of the baseline design, it also made engine servicing and maintenance more difficult.

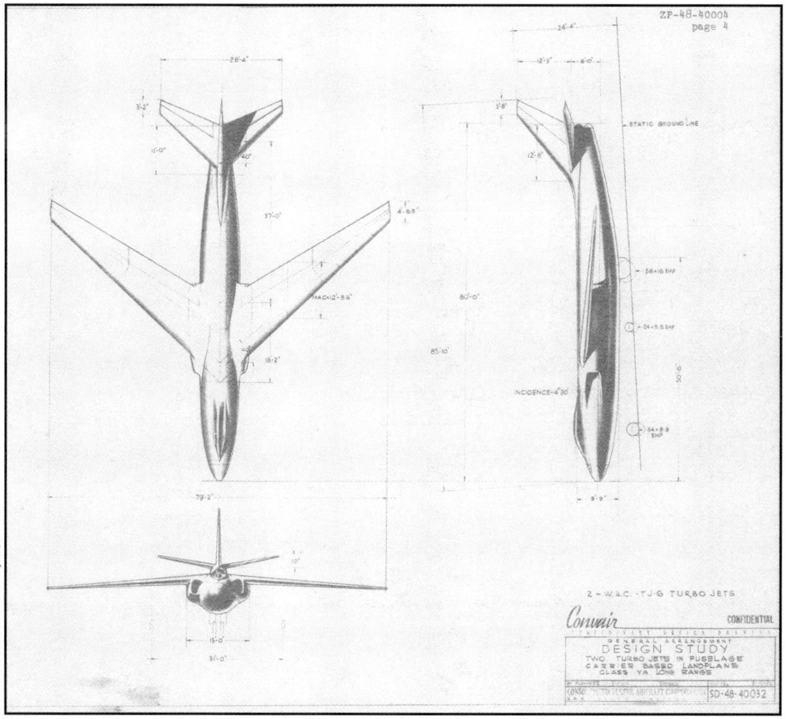

National Archives, RG 72

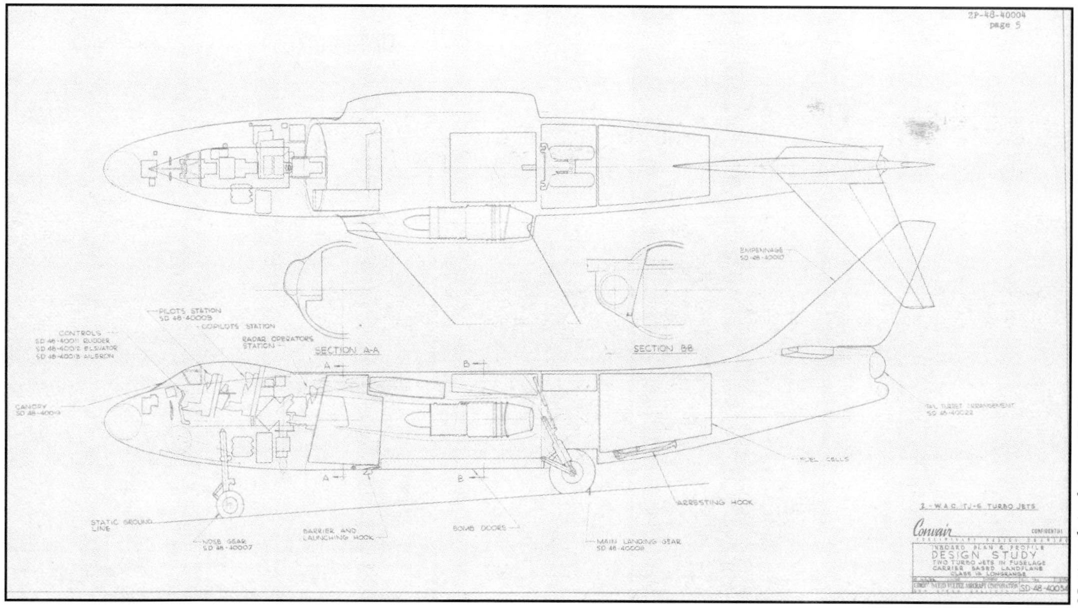

National Archives, RG 72

Left & Above: Three-view and inboard profile of a future variant equipped with a pair of WAC TJ-6 turbojets mounted below the wing roots on the fuselage. On paper, this study offered performance equaling that of the existing trijet design.

CHAPTER 4 — *Curtiss-Wright P-558*

Curtiss-Wright's submission to the Class VA heavy attack competition was designated the P-558. Desperate for a contract win in the face of a declining business base, the company appears to have put a great deal of effort into its proposal. Curtiss-Wright claimed that the P-558 design met or exceeded the requirements of OS-111, utilizing power plants capable of prototype flight by 1953. Using power plants scheduled for prototype flight by 1952, however, resulted in all requirements being met or exceeded except with respect to maximum range.

It became apparent during Curtiss's investigation of this aircraft that no design utilizing the power plants specified by OS-111 could completely meet the desired maximum gross weight and maximum range requirements simultaneously without severe deviation from other desired operational characteristics. An airplane which met the maximum range requirements would weigh considerably more than the desired 100,000 lbs, whereas an airplane having a gross weight of less than 100,000 lbs would be deficient in range.

However, since the issuance of OS-111, weight and performance data for the TJ-7 turbo-jet engine had been presented by Wright Aeronautical Corporation to the government and Curtiss. The performance characteristics of this engine, estimated to be capable of prototype flight by 1953, were such that it permitted the design of an airplane which would meet all requirements of OS-111.

Curtiss proposed an airplane with a normal takeoff gross weight of 87,000 lbs without external fuel tankage, and of 94,150 lbs with external fuel, which exceeded the requirements of OS-111 when powered with TJ-7 engines. This same airplane, when powered by XJ40-WE-10 engines without external fuel, met all requirements except maximum range, which was listed in OS-111 as being the most acceptable for deviation.

Wright Aeronautical Corporation had also presented a specification for a turbo-jet engine, designated the TJ-6, estimated as being capable of prototype flight by 1952, which enabled this same airplane to meet al specified requirements at a takeoff gross weight with external fuel of 84,000 lbs.

Furthermore, Curtiss proposed an innovative "package" flight refueling unit which could be installed in the bomb bay of the basic VA airplane with no other modifications to permit its use as a tanker for refueling other VA airplanes. Curtiss presented an analysis which showed that by this method of flight refueling the range of the VA airplane using XJ-40 engines may be extended to or beyond that required by OS-111.

Curtiss expected that with the existing rate of engine development and improvement, by the time these airplanes were in production, power plants would be developed which would enable the P-558 to exceed the desired maximum range and to exceed the other desired performance characteristics, at a normal takeoff gross weight of 87,000 lbs with no external fuel load. Provision of water injection and use of compressor bleed burning, provisions contemplated for the TJ-6 and TJ-7 engines, would reduce the JATO required for takeoff. Curtiss proposed that advantage be taken of this favorable trend in engine development to reduce the maximum gross weight for takeoff, and recommended the 87,000 lb gross weight, twin-engined P-558. Prior to production, all the desired performance could be demonstrated on prototype airplanes utilizing then available engines.

National Archives, RG 72

Artist's impression of the Curtiss-Wright P-558 flying over a flush-deck carrier. Unlike several of its competitors, Curtiss did not place the aircraft's engines under the wing on pylon-mounted pods, locating them instead on the fuselage at the wing roots. This left the P-558's high aspect ratio swept wing clean and uncluttered, but made engine maintenance difficult.

An important feature of the proposed aircraft was its ability to takeoff from the carrier deck in a training configuration (i.e. 40% of internal fuel aboard and no bomb) without the aid of JATO, with either the XJ-40 or TJ-7 engine installations. This fuel

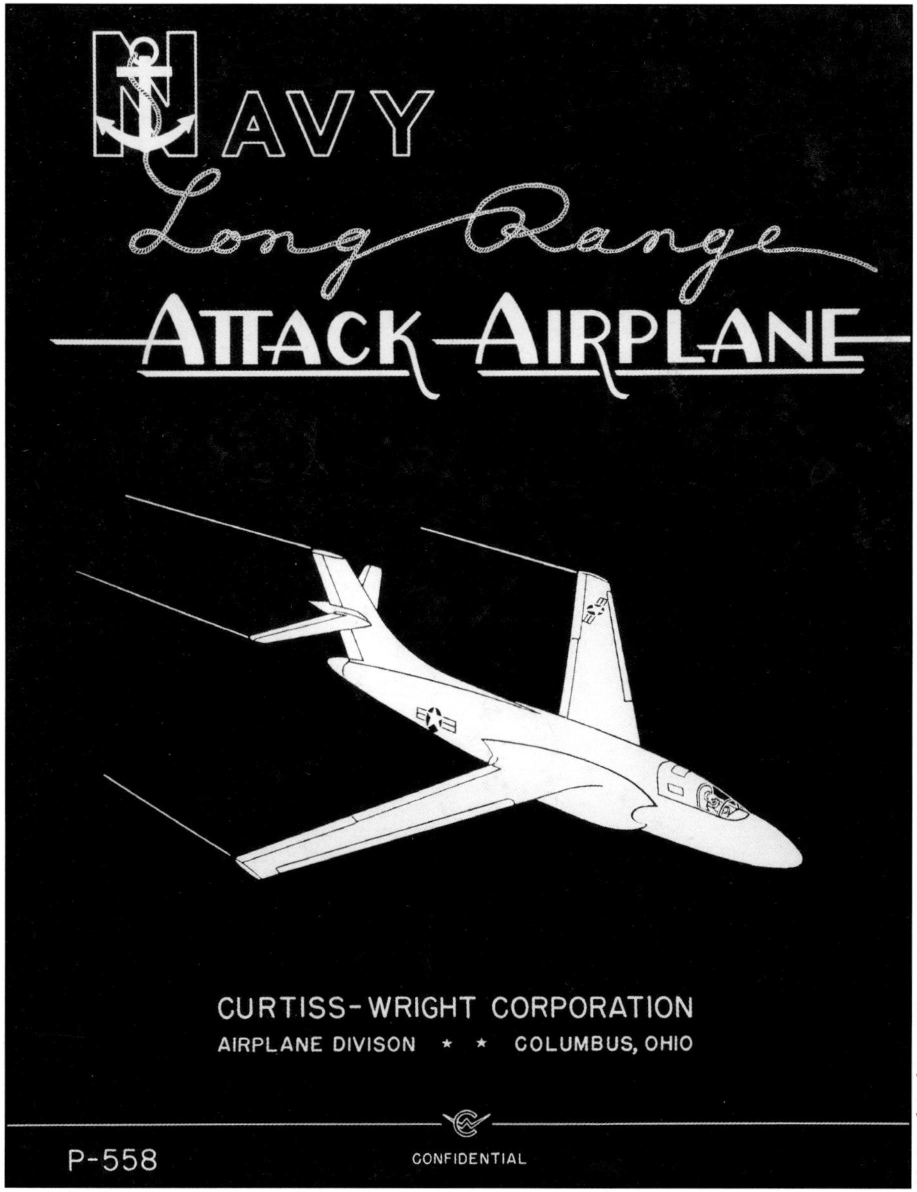

National Archives, RG 72

Cover to the Curtiss-Wright proposal brochure for its handsome P-558 Class VA design; the perspective of the drawing appears slightly off, but otherwise conveys the general look of the aircraft reasonably well.

load permitted four training takeoffs and landings without refueling, assuming a training schedule as outlined in Curtiss's proposal.

Power Plant

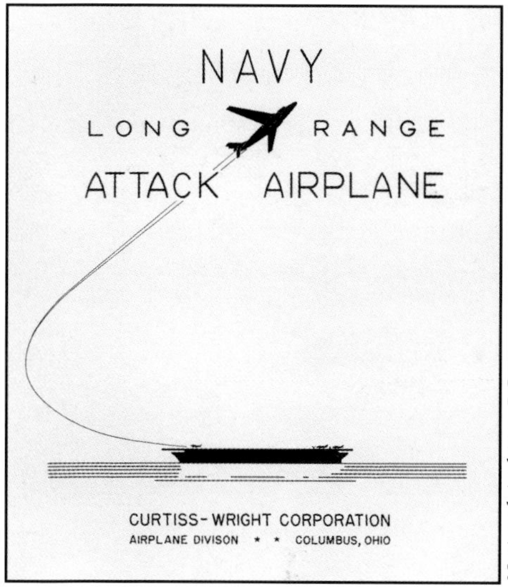

National Archives, RG 72

Stylized illustration of the Curtiss-Wright P-558 taking off from a carrier on the brochure's frontispiece, a nice example of aeronautical graphic design from period.

The power plant installation consisted of two turbojet engines, one located under each wing root and partially submerged within the fuselage. This location afforded minimum nacelle drag, minimum wing interference, good single engine stability and control, reduced duct losses, and provided ready access to the engines for routine maintenance.

The nacelles allowed interchangeability of the XJ-40, the WAC TJ-6 and TJ-7 engines. As required by OS-111, the basic design of the airplane was predicated upon the use of the anticipated performance ratings of the XJ-40 engine as presented by BuAer, and basic proposal data were based upon the characteristics of the engine. It was expected that the prototype airplane would be temporarily powered by XJ-40 turbojets, and corresponding airplane performance data were presented. The design of the airplane allowed ultimate installation of turbojets of the WAC TJ-6 or TJ-7 types, and performance data herein presented showed the advantages accruing from the use of these engines.

The fuel system arrangement was so designed as to allow single-point refueling at the rate of 500 gallons per minute to permit rapid flight refueling, in addition to two-point refueling at the rate of 150 gallons per minute per refueling point, as required by OS-111. Droppable wing tanks were proposed for maximum range operation with TJ-6 and TJ-7 engines.

Armament

Armament consisted of a bomb bay arrangement as required in OS-111 and a government-furnished 20 mm two-gun automatic tail turret controlled through an unrestricted 90° field of fire by means of APG 25 radar equipment. Electronic, navigation and bombing control apparatus were carried as required by the special tactical bombing duty expected of this aircraft. An expendable bomb bay closure and hinged internal doors which closed immediately behind the bomb after it was dropped were proposed as means of obtaining the quickest possible opening and subsequent closure of the bomb bay in order that the bomb bay be dropped at Mach 0.9 with minimum effect on airplane stability and control. Alternate types of internally housed bomb doors could be provided depending upon the ultimate bomb loading desired.

PERFORMANCE SUMMARY

ENGINE MODEL DESIGNATION	XJ-40	TJ-6	TJ-7	TJ-7	MINIMUM REQUIREMENTS OS-111
NUMBER OF ENGINES	TWO	TWO	TWO	TWO	
V-MAX. AT 40,000 FT. AT (MAX. T.O. GR. WT. MINUS 45% TOTAL FUEL - *Knots*	517	529	534	532	517
Mach No.	0.90	0.920	0.928	0.925	0.9
COMBAT RADIUS AT MAX. T.O. GR. WT. 0.85 MACH NO. AVG. CRUISE SPEED *Nautical Miles*	1367	1711	1570	1823	1700
S.L. STALLING SPEED AT NORMAL GR. WT. MINUS 60% INTERNAL FUEL & BOMB *Knots*	115	115	115	115	115
RATE OF CLIMB AT END OF DECK, NAVY STD. HOT DAY, MAX. T.O. GR. WT. (FLAPS & GEAR DOWN) *Ft./Min.*	500	500	779	500	500
RATE OF CLIMB AFTER RAISING FLAPS & GEAR, NAVY STD. HOT DAY, MAX. T.O. GR. WT. *Ft./Min.*	1955	2240	2980	2640	---
JATO THRUST REQUIRED FOR T.O. *Pounds* / *for Sec.*	55000 / 4	76000 / 4	55000 / 4	70000 / 4	---
plus *Pounds* / *for Sec.*	3300 / 20	2500 / 20	0	0	---
MAX. T.O. GR. WT. (INCLUDING EXTERNAL FUEL, MINUS JATO WEIGHT) *Pounds*	87000	96000	87000	94050	100,000
NORMAL GR. WT. T.O. GR WT. MINUS EXTERNAL FUEL & TANKS) *Pounds*	87000	87000	87000	87000	---
INTERNAL FUEL - *Pounds*	33450	33450	33100	33100	---
EXTERNAL FUEL - *Pounds*	0	8400	0	6550	---

National Archives, RG 72

Table summarizing potential performance of the P-558 with various engine installations. Curtiss-Wright lobbied heavily in the proposal for the Navy to alter the requirements and use its Wright TJ-6 (later designated J61) or TJ-7 (J59) jet engines, both of which were immature designs that would ultimately be cancelled.

Wing and Empennage

A wing with a sweep back angle of 40° and a thickness ratio of 11%, together with horizontal and vertical tail surfaces with thickness ratios of 10% and with 40° and 35° sweep back angles respectively were selected to enable the airplane to exceed the desired maximum Mach number of 0.9 without lift divergence or excessive compressibility drag rise as well as assure favorable control characteristics at limit dive speeds of Mach 0.9 plus 60 knots. The relatively long distance from the airplane center of gravity (CG) to the tail center of pressure (CP) in proportion to the length of the wing mean aerodynamic chord (MAC) resulted in favorable control characteristics and relatively light control loads. An aspect ratio of 8.0 was selected for the wing, resulting from an extensive study concerning the effect of aspect ratio on wing structure and range. Satisfactory landing stall speeds were obtained by use of leading edge flaps synchronized with single slotted trailing edge flaps. The 81 ft wing span permitted two airplanes to pass side-by-side on the carrier deck with the wings spread and with the outrigger wheels spotted as specified.

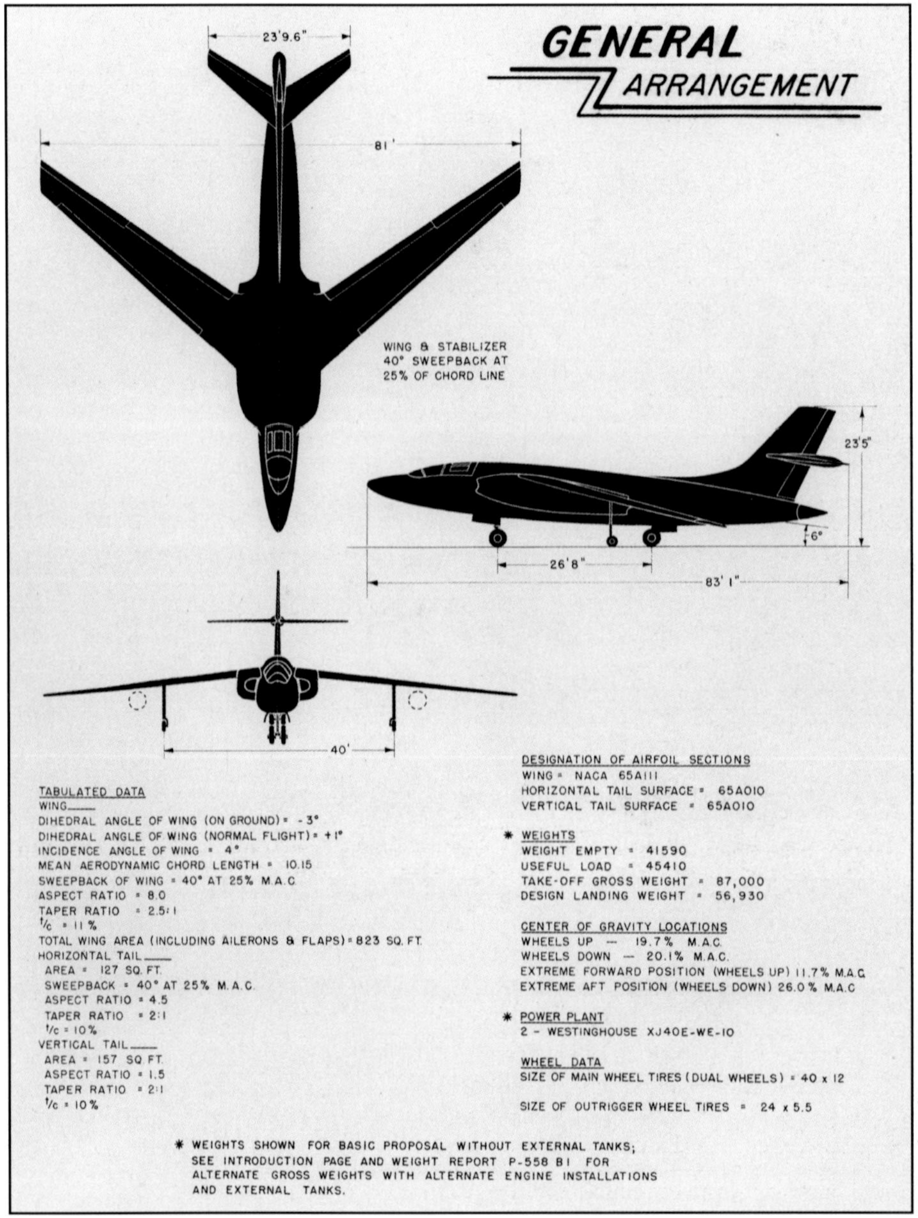

National Archives, RG 72

Basic general arrangement drawing and specifications of the P-558. Like Convair, Curtiss-Wright chose a bicycle landing gear to reduce weight and maintain a clean wing.

Landing Gear

A bicycle type main landing gear, retractable into the fuselage, with outrigger stabilizing wheels, folding into the wing panels, was proposed to maintain the cleanest possible

TACTICAL RANGE DATA

	XJ-40-WE-10 ENGINES RATED PER DR-1045 (NO EXTERNAL FUEL)				TJ-7 ENGINES (NO EXTERNAL FUEL)			
	TIME HOURS	DISTANCE NAUTICAL MILES	ALTITUDE FEET	FUEL CONSUMED POUNDS	TIME HOURS	DISTANCE NAUTICAL MILES	ALTITUDE FEET	FUEL CONSUMED POUNDS
WARM-UP & TAKE-OFF	.083	0	SEA LEVEL	1,093	.083	0	SEA LEVEL	1,350
CLIMB	.358	151	S. L. TO 36,000	3,941	.210	92	S. L. TO 39,500	2,783
CRUISE OUT	2.380	1,166	36,000 TO 39,700	13,220	2.912	1,428	39,500 TO 43,400	13,980
BOMBING RUN	.192	100	39,700	1,300	.187	100	43,400	1,303
CLIMB	.040	19	39,700 TO 42,500	258	.047	22	43,400 TO 47,800	272
CRUISE BACK	2.650	1,298	42,500 TO 46,600	10,293	3.059	1,498	47,800 TO 51,900	10,102
TOTAL	5.703	2,734		30,105	6,498	3,140		29,790
	SPECIFIED FUEL RESERVE			3,345	SPECIFIED FUEL RESERVE			3,310
	SPECIFIED FUEL CAPACITY			33,450	SPECIFIED FUEL CAPACITY			33,100

National Archives, RG 72

swept-back wing, and to reduce landing gear weight.

Crew Arrangement

The copilot and bombardier-navigator seats were located side-by-side at a station immediately aft of the pilot. Aisle space and equipment were arranged such that all crew members could communicate directly with each other, or exchange stations in an emergency. Careful attention was given to crew comfort, heating, ventilation and pressuriza-

TACTICAL RANGE DATA

	TJ-6 ENGINES (WITH EXTERNAL FUEL)				TJ-7 ENGINES (WITH EXTERNAL FUEL)			
	TIME HOURS	DISTANCE NAUTICAL MILES	ALTITUDE FEET	FUEL CONSUMED POUNDS	TIME HOURS	DISTANCE NAUTICAL MILES	ALTITUDE FEET	FUEL CONSUMED POUNDS
WARM-UP & TAKE-OFF	.083	0	SEA LEVEL	1,350	.083	0	SEA LEVEL	1,350
CLIMB	.256	100	S. L. TO 35,000	3,790	.198	86	S. L. TO 35,000	2,890
CRUISE OUT WITH EXTERNAL TANKS	.440	215	35,000 TO 35,830	3,260	.351	172	35,000 TO 35,620	2,310
CRUISE OUT WITHOUT EXTERNAL TANKS	2.755	1,346	35,830 TO 39,970	15,751	3.093	1,515	35,620 TO 39,800	15,806
BOMBING RUN	.187	100	39,970	1,420	.186	100	39,800	1,538
CLIMB	.076	33	39,970 TO 46,800	500	.068	36	39,800 TO 47,200	490
CRUISE BACK	3.332	1,628	46,800 TO 51,700	12,434	3.552	1,737	47,200 TO 51,700	11,956
TOTAL	7,129	3,422		38,505	7.531	3,646		36,340
	SPECIFIED FUEL RESERVE			3,345	SPECIFIED FUEL RESERVE			3,310
	SPECIFIED FUEL CAPACITY			41,850	SPECIFIED FUEL CAPACITY			39,650

National Archives, RG 72

Upper Left & Above: These charts present estimated performance figures at various stages in a typical attack mission for the P-558 with different engines and with/without external fuel tanks. While the Wright TJ-7 offered superior overall performance, it was not available within the time frame desired by the Navy. Thus, it was proposed to initially use the Westinghouse XJ-40 and then upgrade the power plants when the TJ-7 became available.

tion. Ejection seats were provided for all members of the crew for emergency egress. An access tunnel to the bomb bay was entered by means of a door located between the seats of the bombardier-navigator and the copilot.

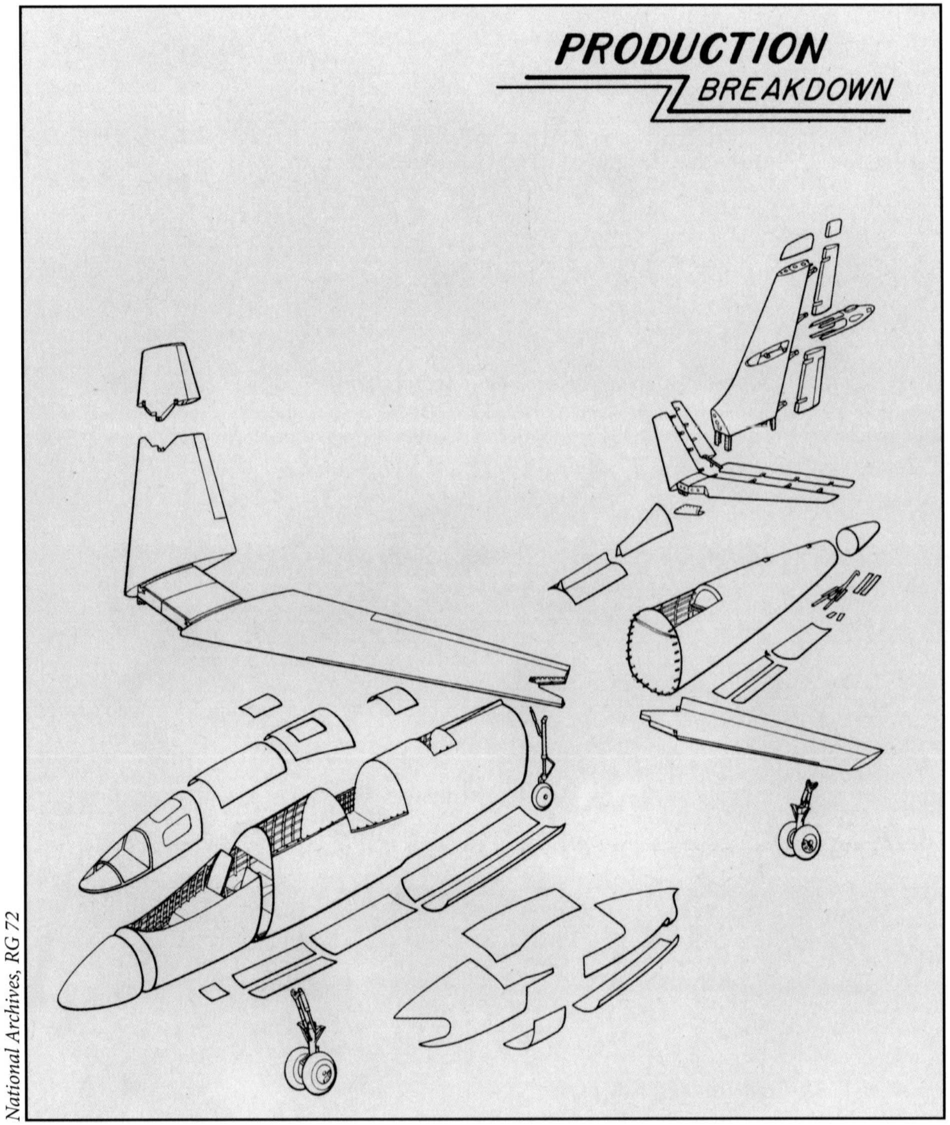

National Archives, RG 72

P-558 production breakdown showing the aircraft's major subassemblies.

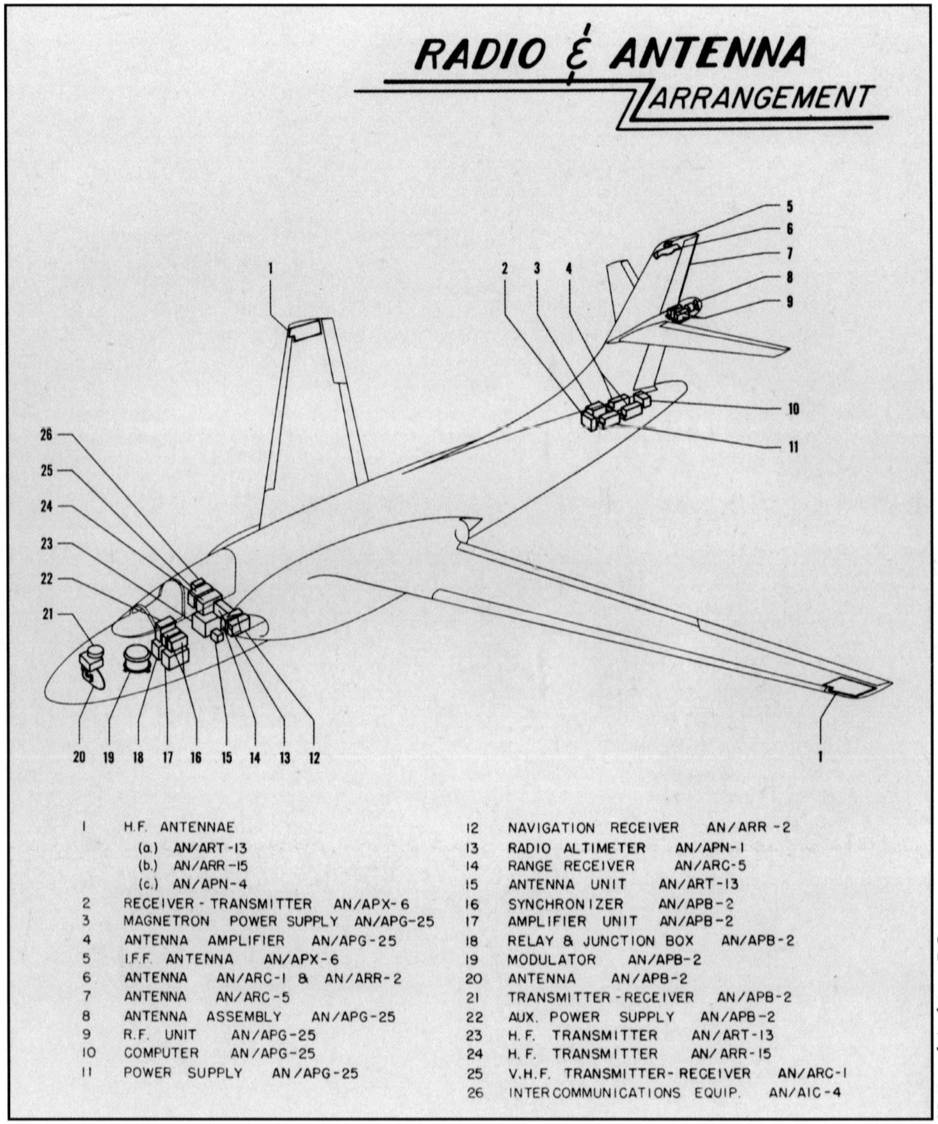

National Archives, RG 72

Diagram of the P-558's radio and antenna arrangement.

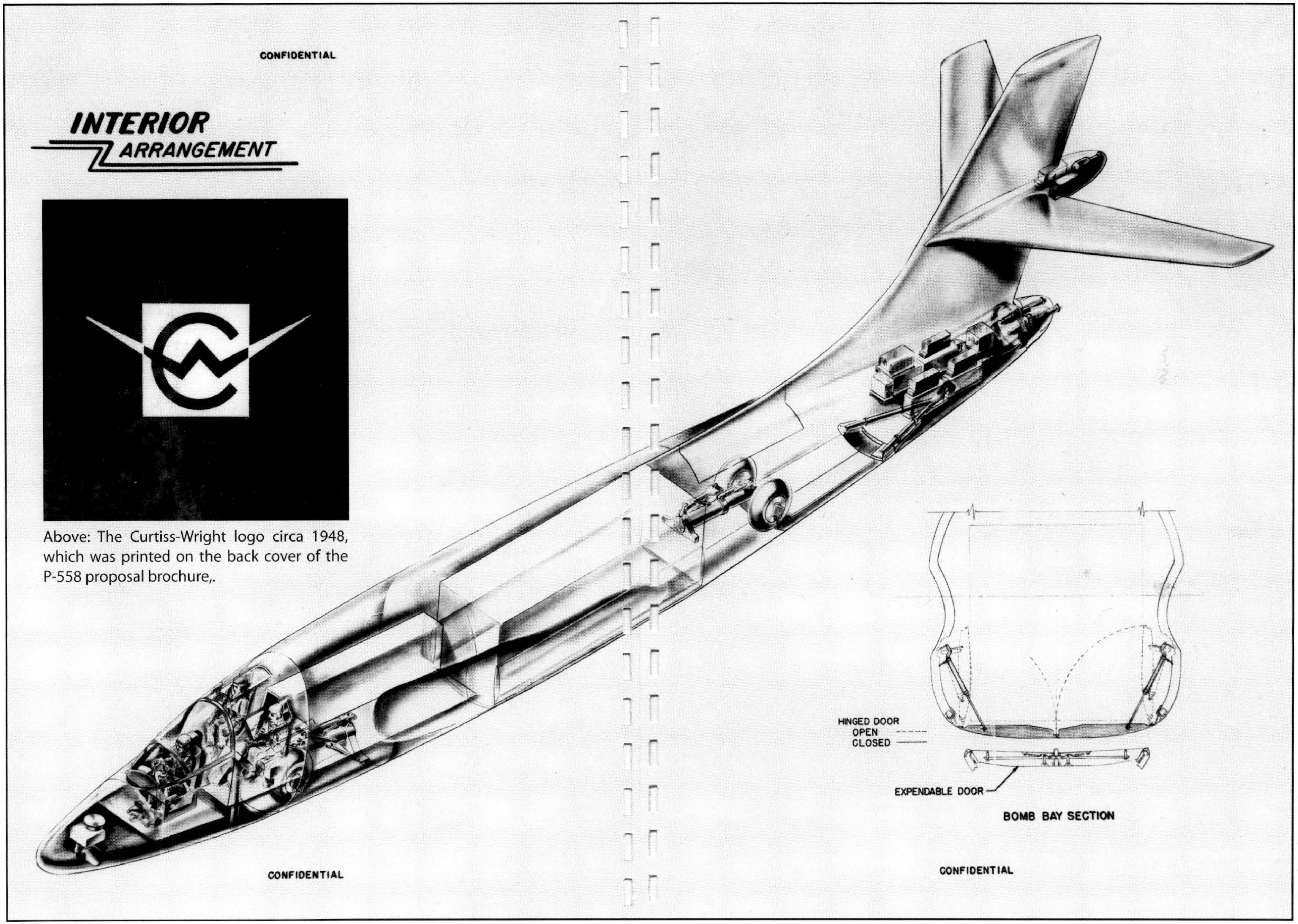

Above: The Curtiss-Wright logo circa 1948, which was printed on the back cover of the P-558 proposal brochure,.

National Archives, RG 72

Overhead perspective view of the Curtiss P-558's internal arrangement, along with a sectional drawing of its bomb bay. The bomb bay closure was expendable and hinged internal doors closed immediately behind the bomb after it was dropped at Mach 0.9 to minimize drag.

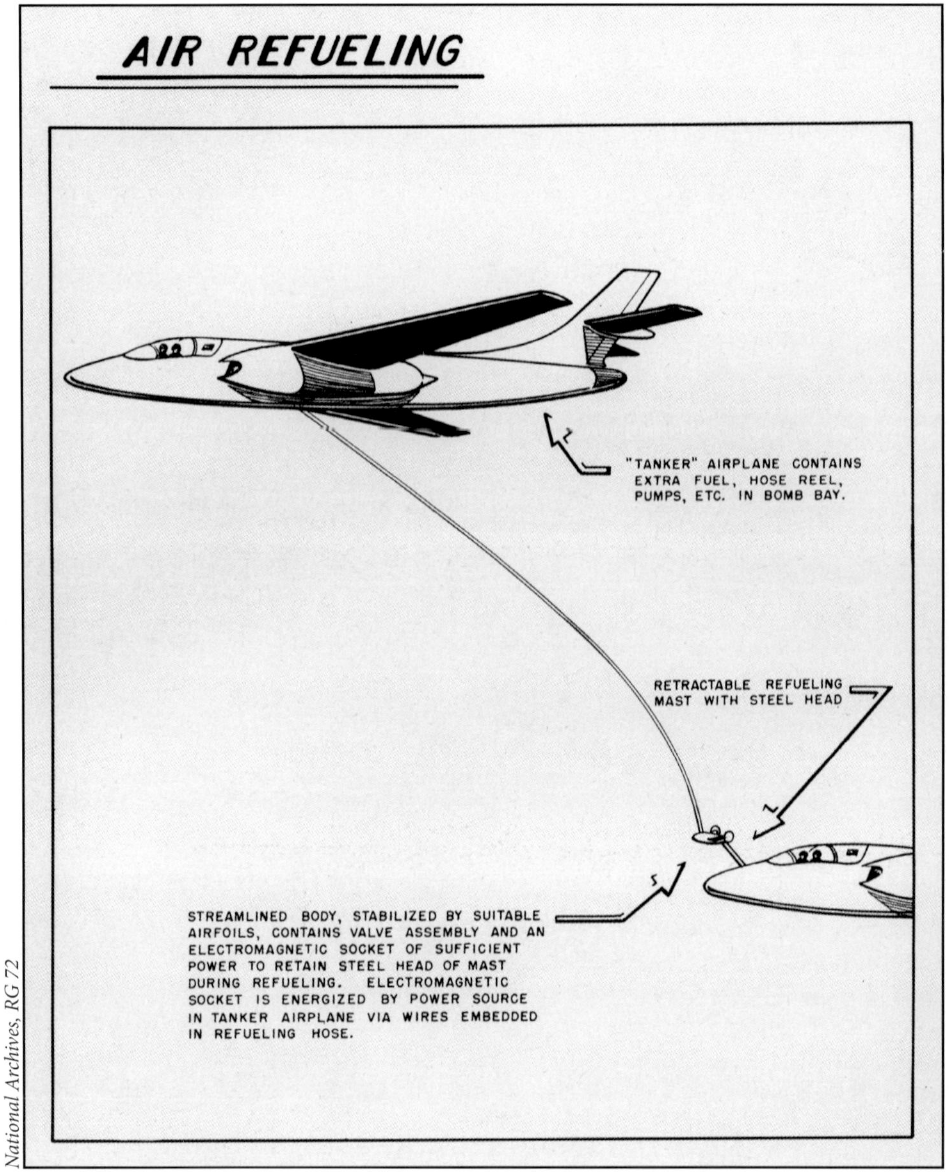

National Archives, RG 72

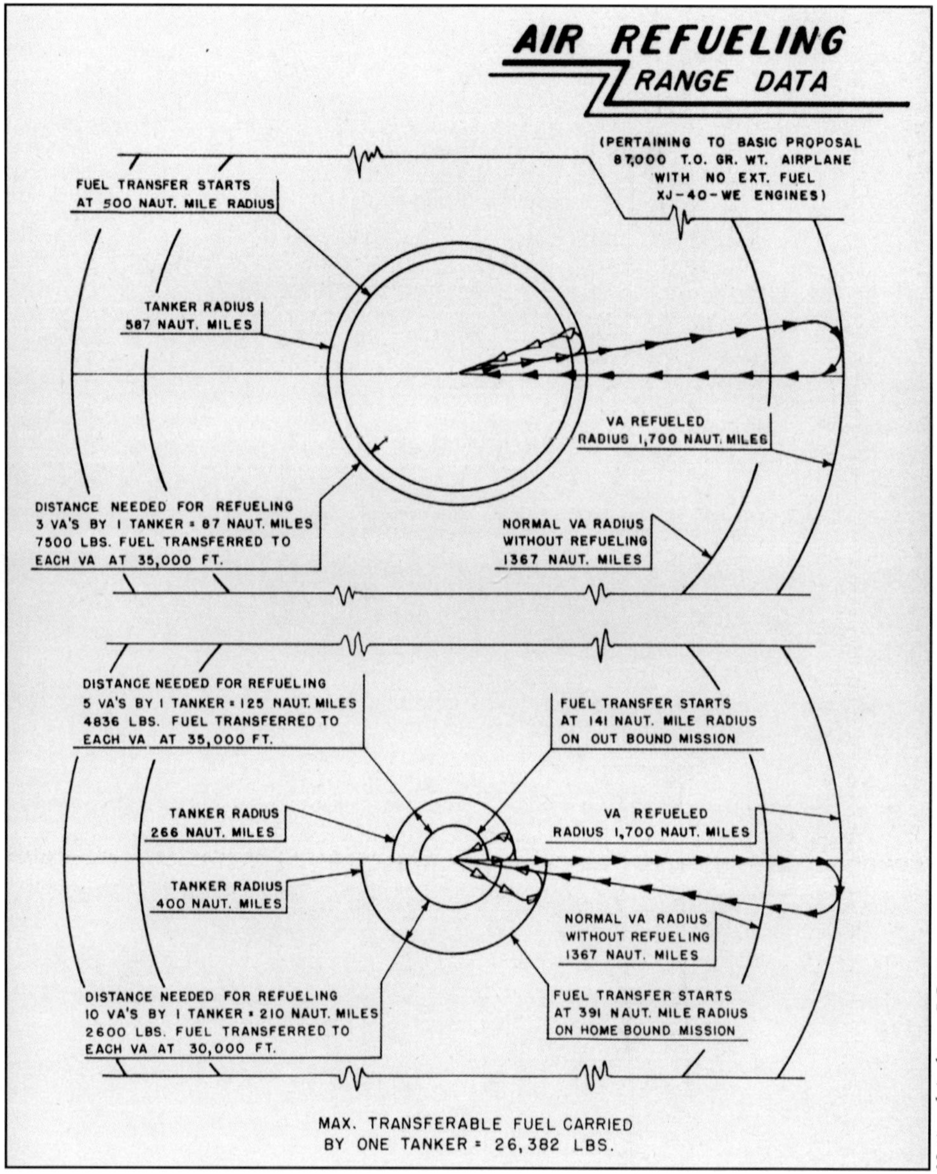

National Archives, RG 72

Curtiss was one of the few manufacturers far-sighted enough to propose aerial refueling for its heavy attack proposal. A "package" flight refueling unit could be installed in the bomb bay of the basic P-558 airplane with no other modifications to permit its use as a tanker for refueling other heavy attack aircraft. This had the potential of extending the useful range of the aircraft beyond the challenging requirements of OS-111. Air-to-air buddy refueling would become a vital component of naval air operations in the decades to follow.

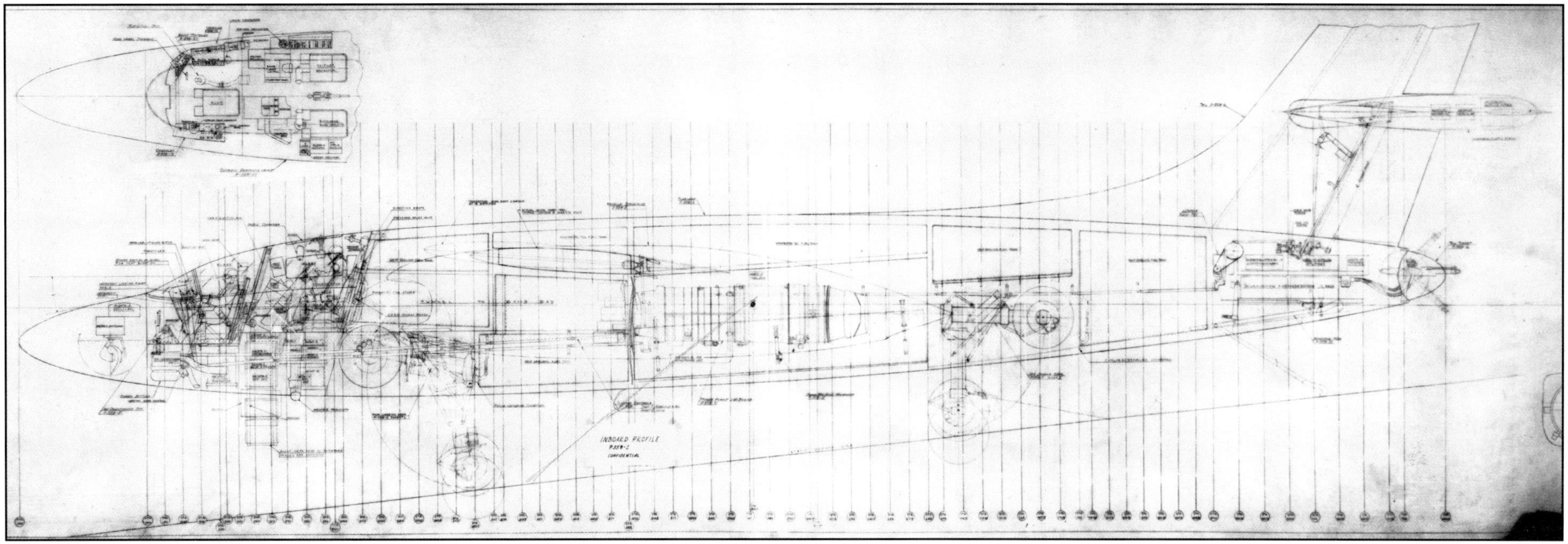

National Archives, RG 72

Above: Inboard profile of the Curtiss P-558 Class VA proposal.

Below: P-558 station diagram and fuselage structure.

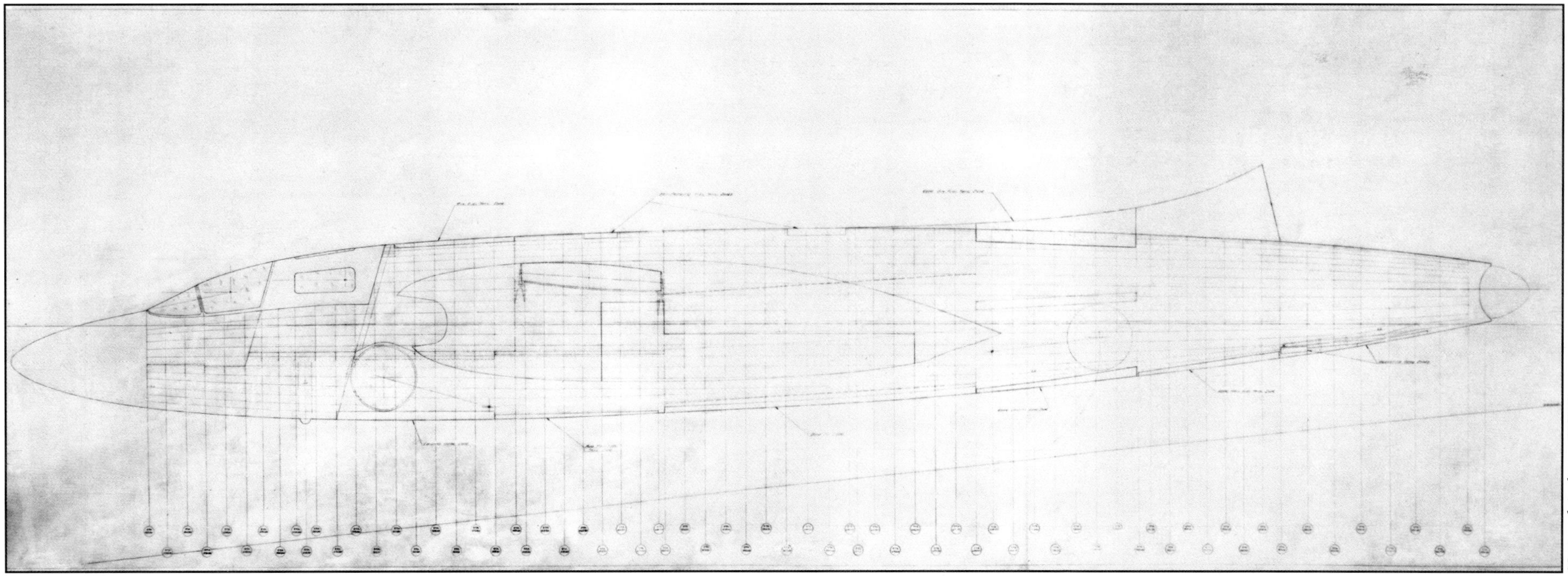

National Archives, RG 72

Right: Blueprint of the P-558 wing structure. The wings were foldable for carrier stowage and the outrigger gear retracted flush into the wing, which was swept back at an angle of 40° and had an 8.0 aspect ratio. It featured leading edge flaps synchronized with single slotted trailing edge flaps to provide satisfactory landing stall speeds. For its proposal, Curtiss photographed the P-558 blueprints and reduced them to fit a standard page; the wrinkles apparent in some of these drawings were present in the original images and are not the result of poor digital scanning.

Below: Detail drawings of the empennage structure. The horizontal and vertical tail surfaces had thickness ratios of 10% and sweep back angles of 40° and 35°, respectively. This cruciform arrangement was likely adopted to keep the tail out of the engines' slipstream and minimize interference drag with the wing.

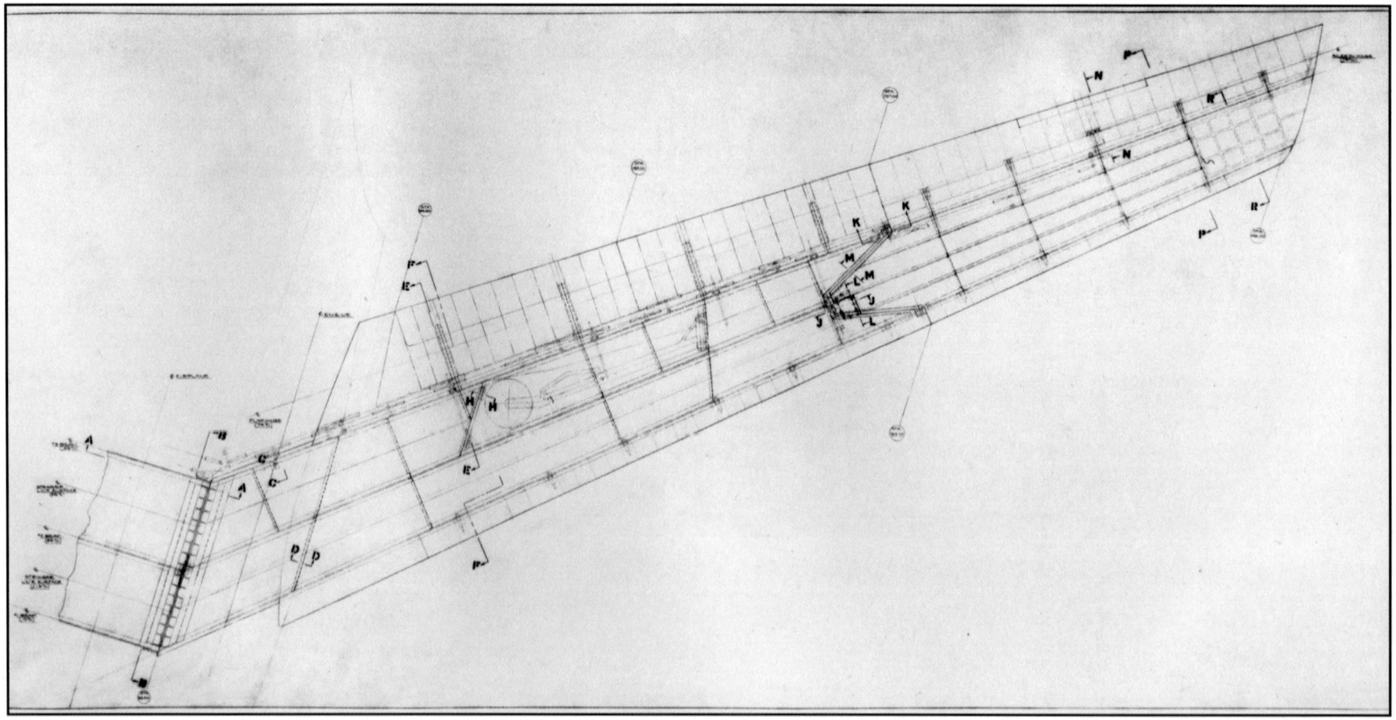

National Archives, RG 72

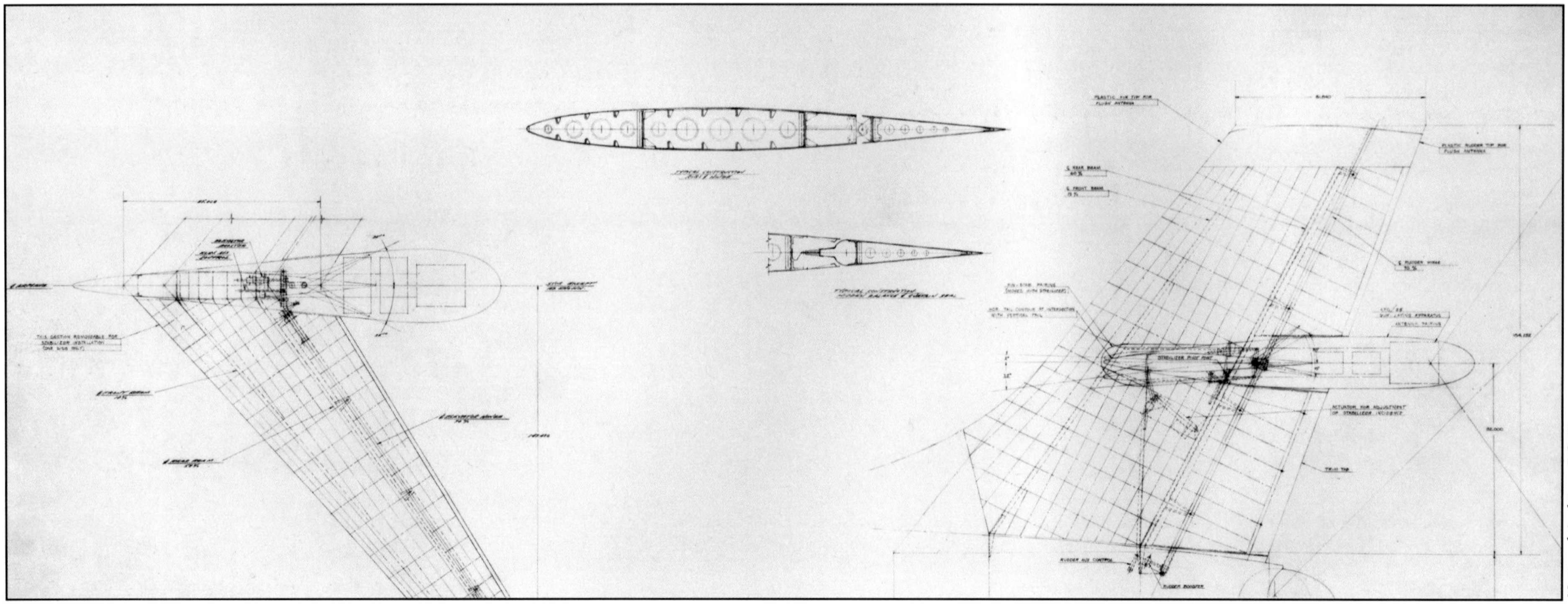

National Archives, RG 72

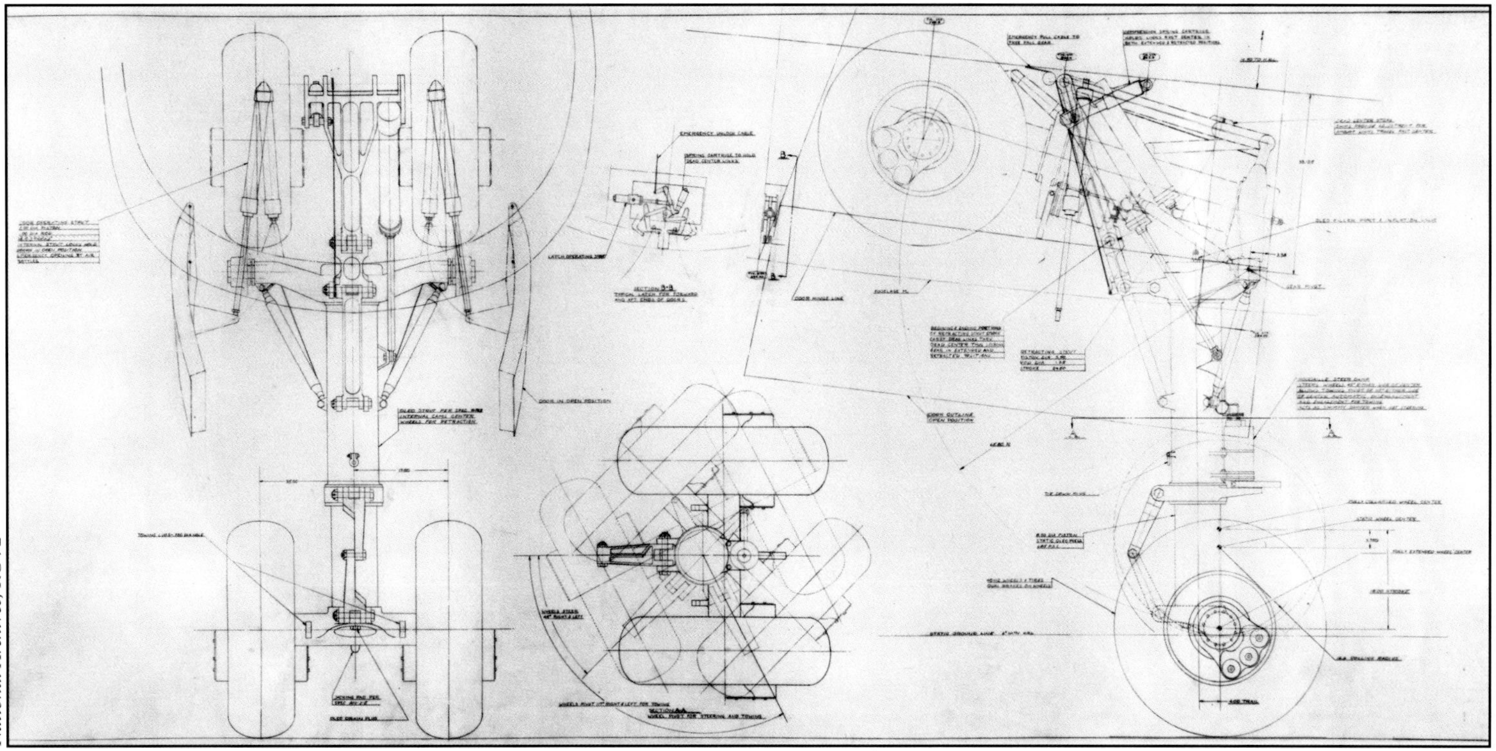

National Archives, RG 72

Left: The forward center line main gear of the P-558's bicycle landing gear, which retracted forwards into the fuselage.

Below: Diagram of the P-558 control system.

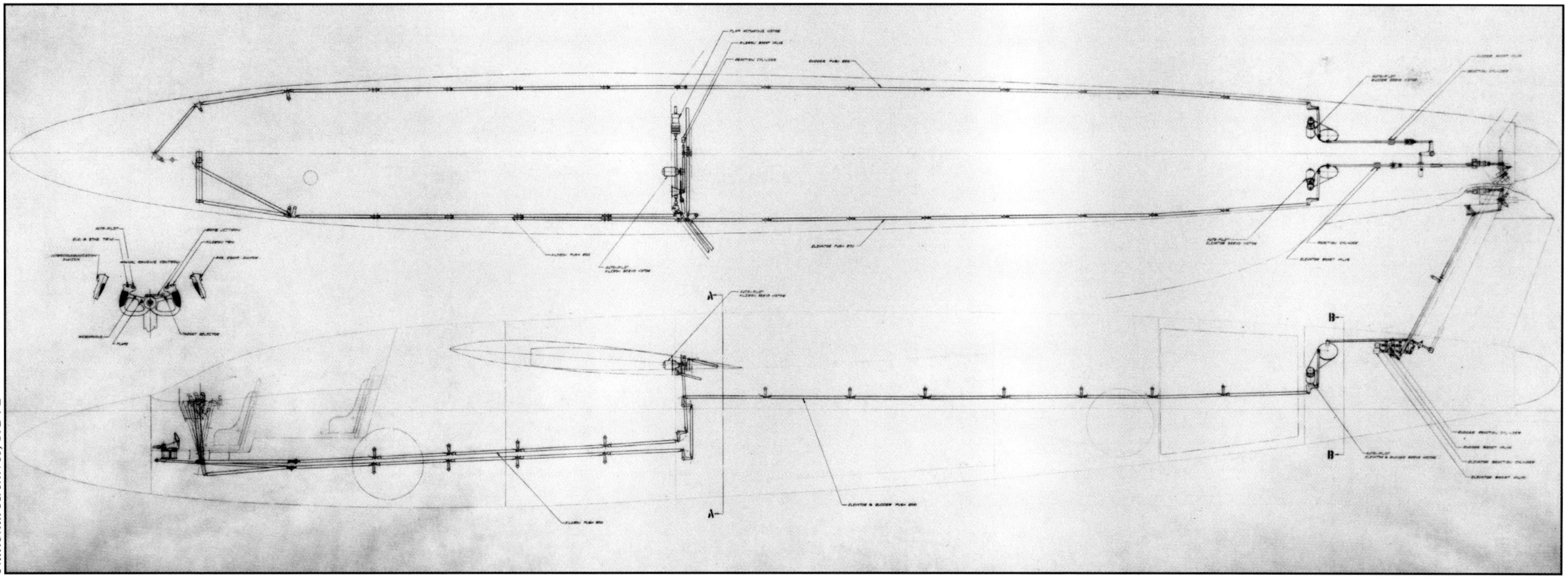

National Archives, RG 72

Right: Blueprint of the wing control system.

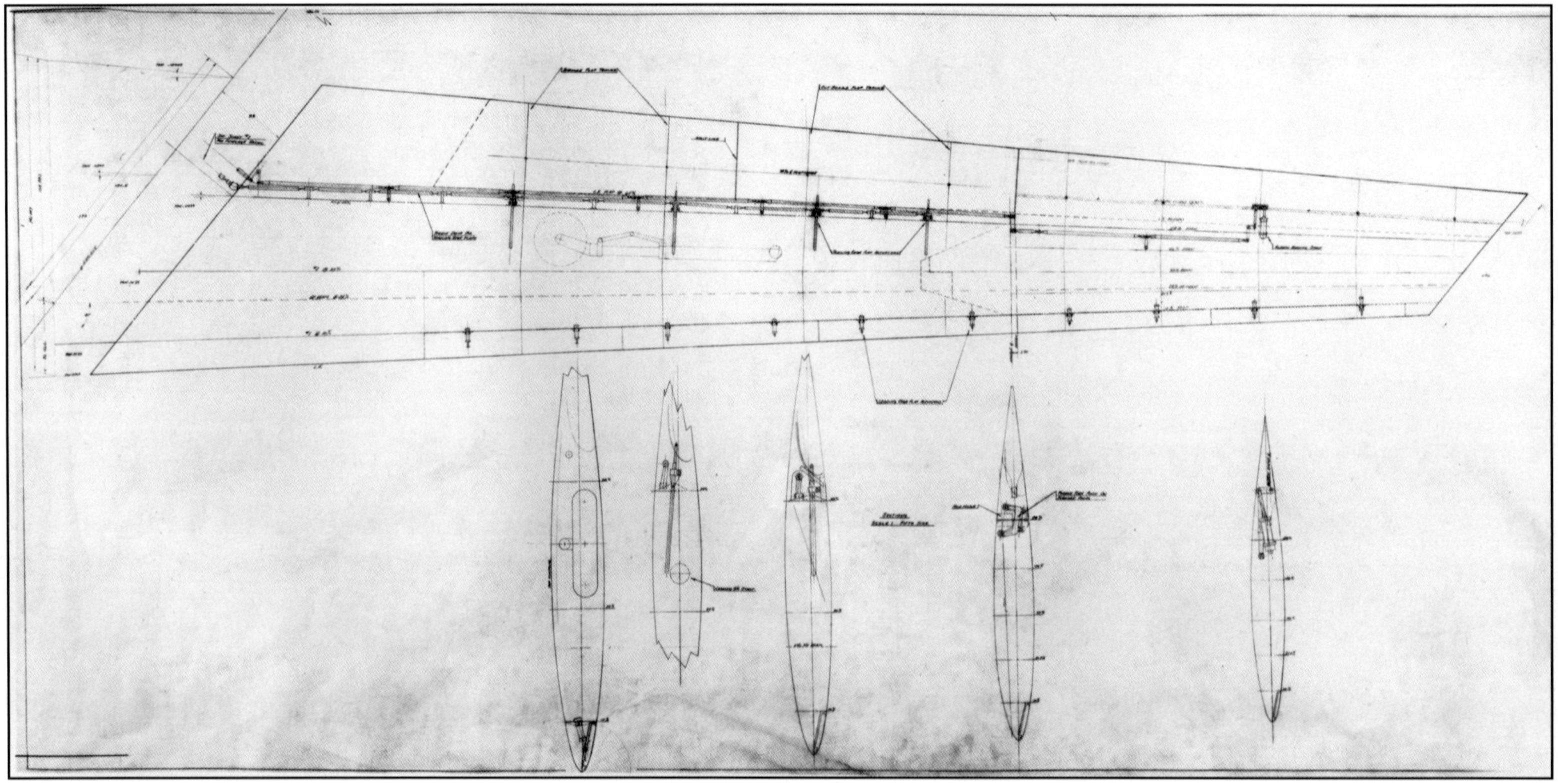

National Archives, RG 72

Below Left: Nacelle arrangement drawings showing the installation of the Westinghouse XJ40-WE-10 turbojet.

Below Right: Nacelle arrangement drawings showing the installation of the future WAC TJ-7 turbojet.

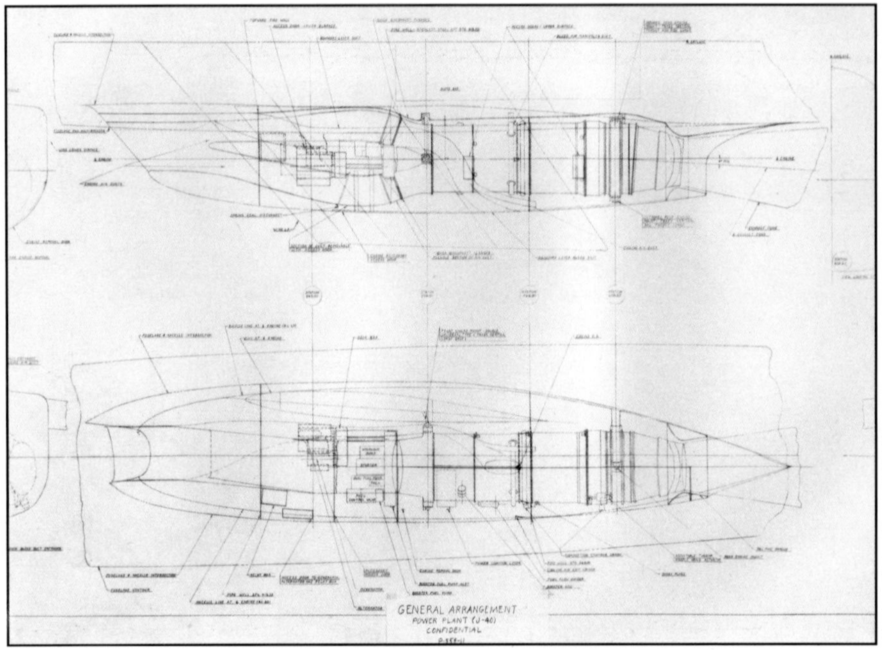

National Archives, RG 72

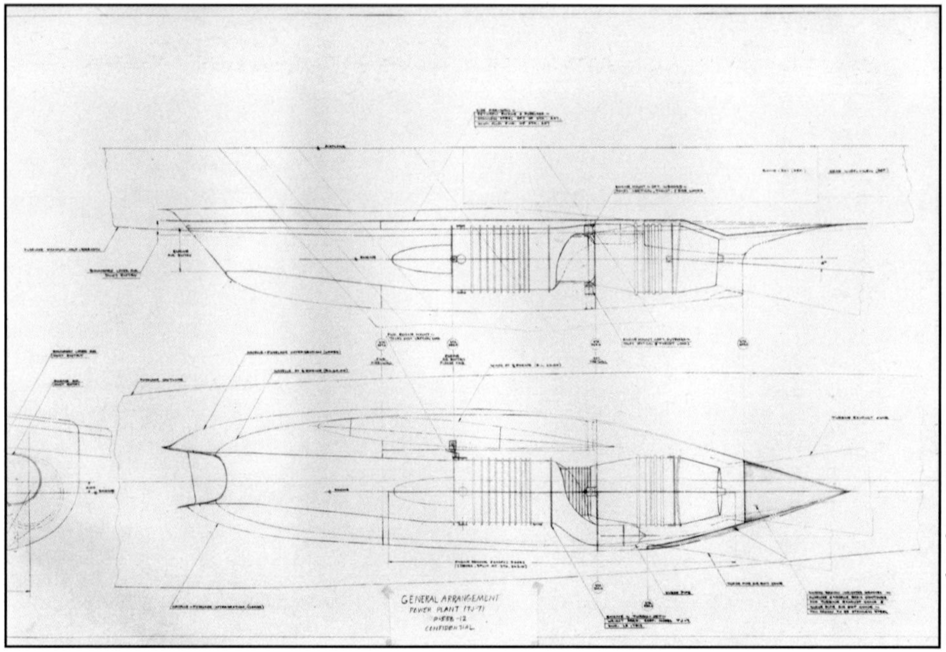

National Archives, RG 72

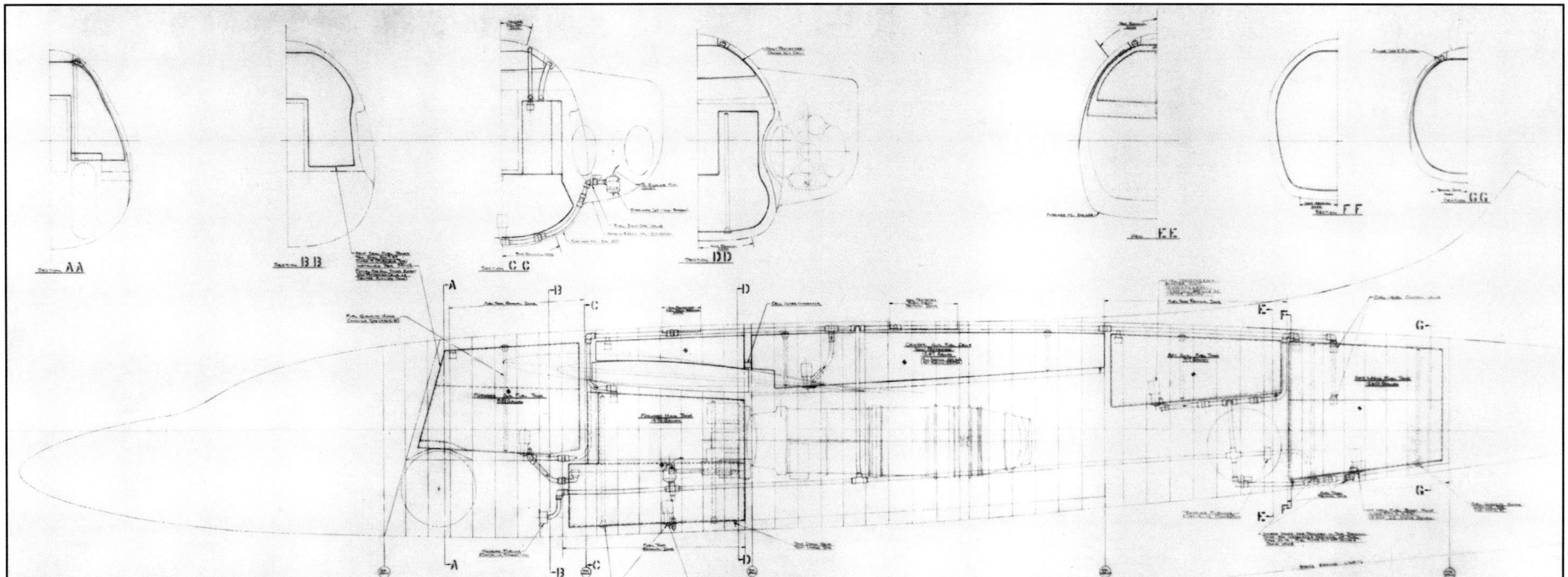

Detail drawing of the P-558's fuel system.

National Archives, RG 72

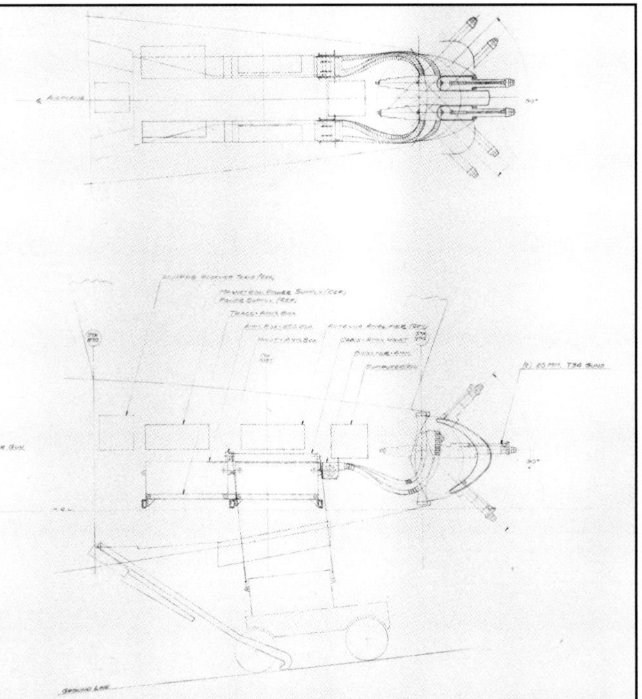

The 20 mm two-gun automatic tail turret installation, which had an unrestricted 90° field of fire.

National Archives, RG 72

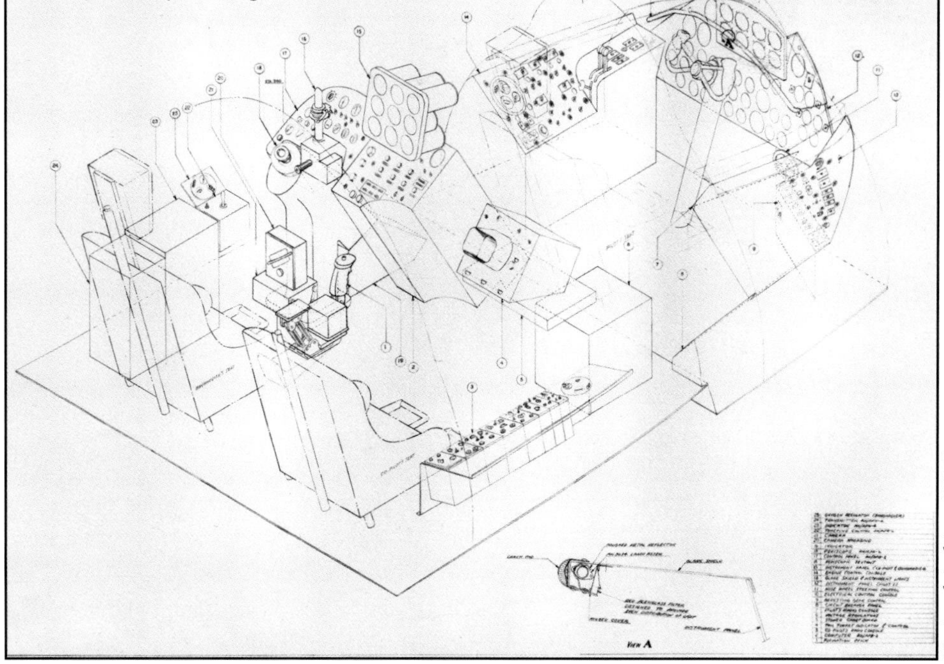

The P-558 cockpit arrangement.

National Archives, RG 72

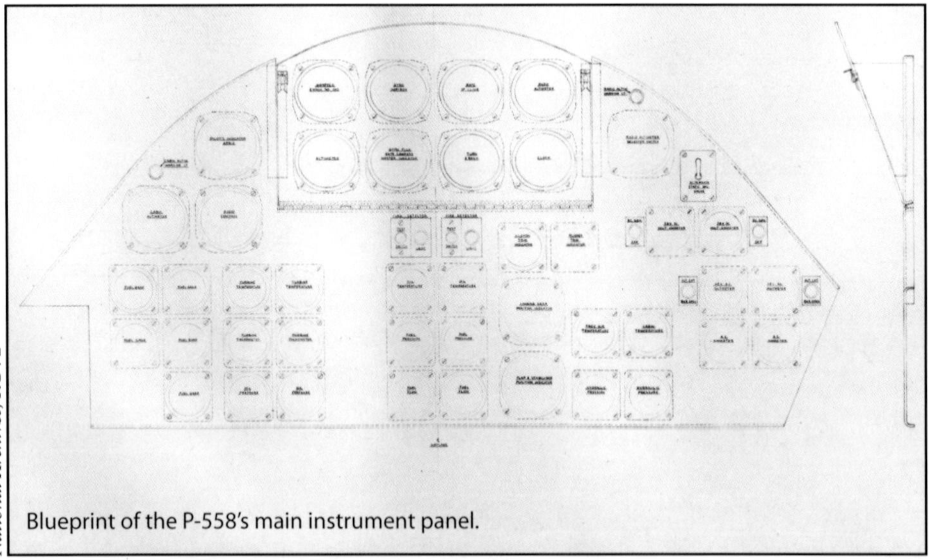

Blueprint of the P-558's main instrument panel.

National Archives, RG 72

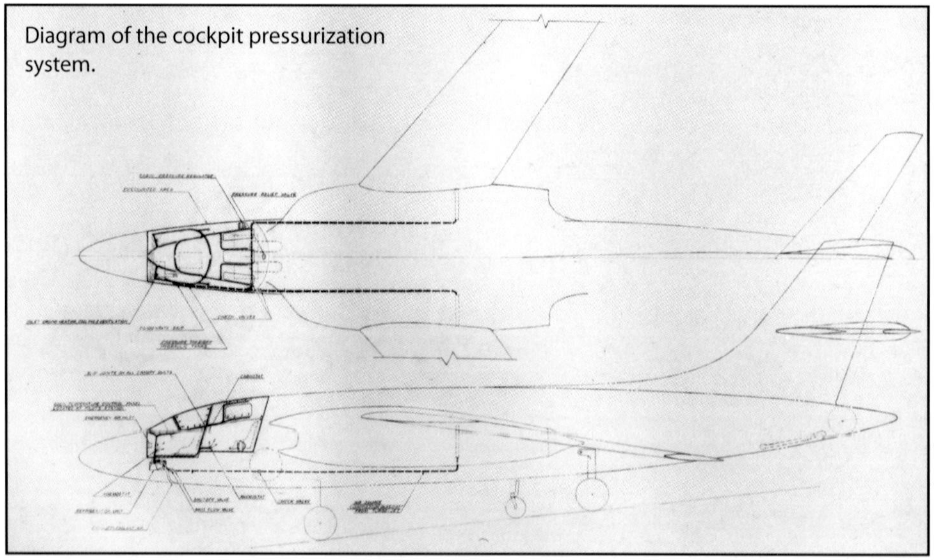

Diagram of the cockpit pressurization system.

National Archives, RG 72

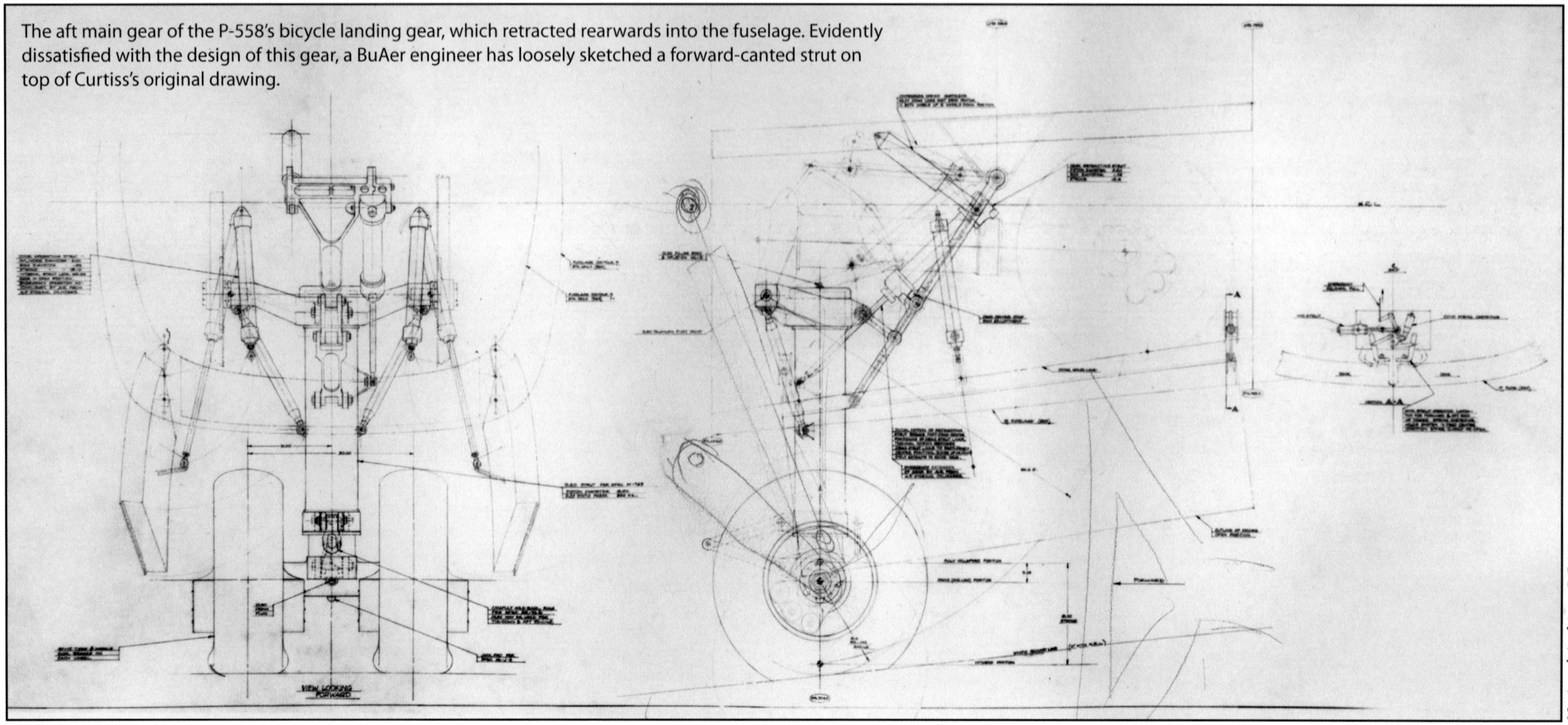

The aft main gear of the P-558's bicycle landing gear, which retracted rearwards into the fuselage. Evidently dissatisfied with the design of this gear, a BuAer engineer has loosely sketched a forward-canted strut on top of Curtiss's original drawing.

National Archives, RG 72

Left & Below: Blueprints of the P-558 arresting gear, which consisted of a combination retracting strut and shock absorber.

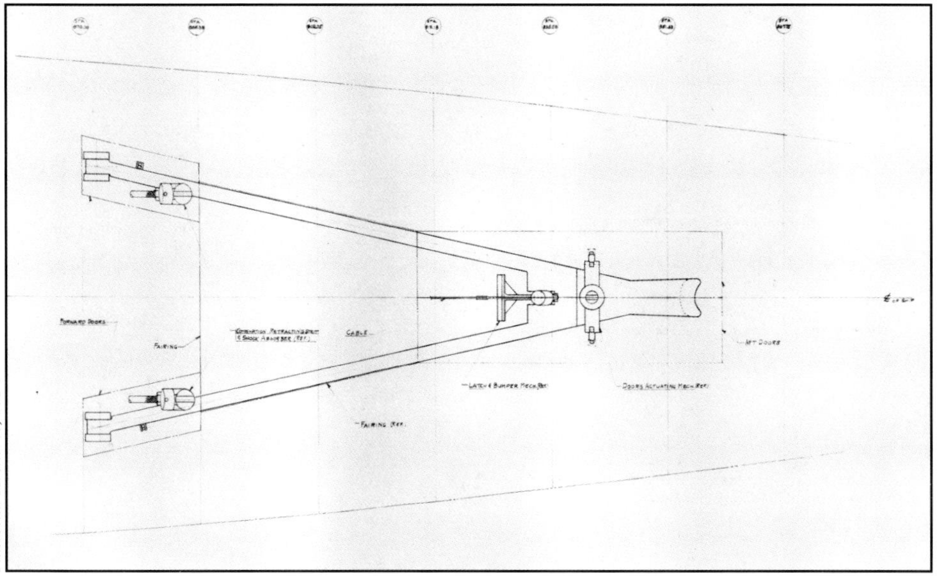

National Archives, RG 72

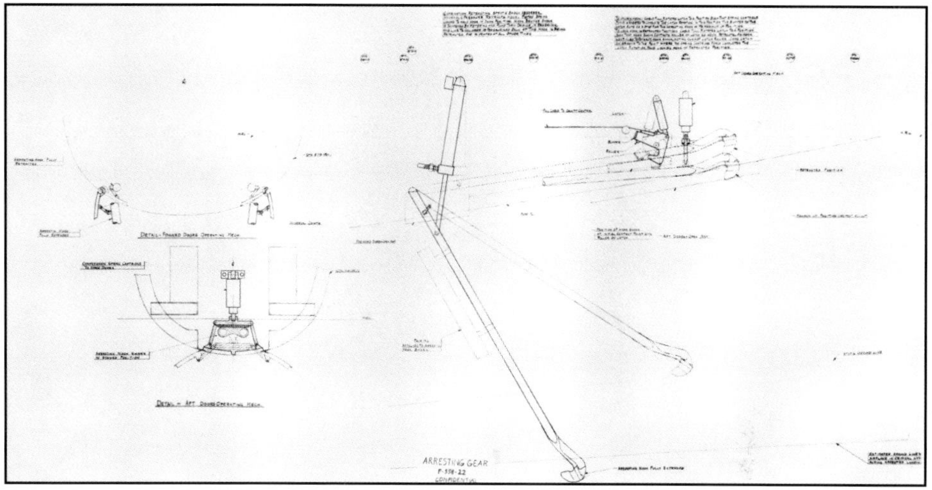

National Archives, RG 72

This carrier spotting diagram shows that 15 P-558s could be accommodated on the flight deck of CVB class carrier.

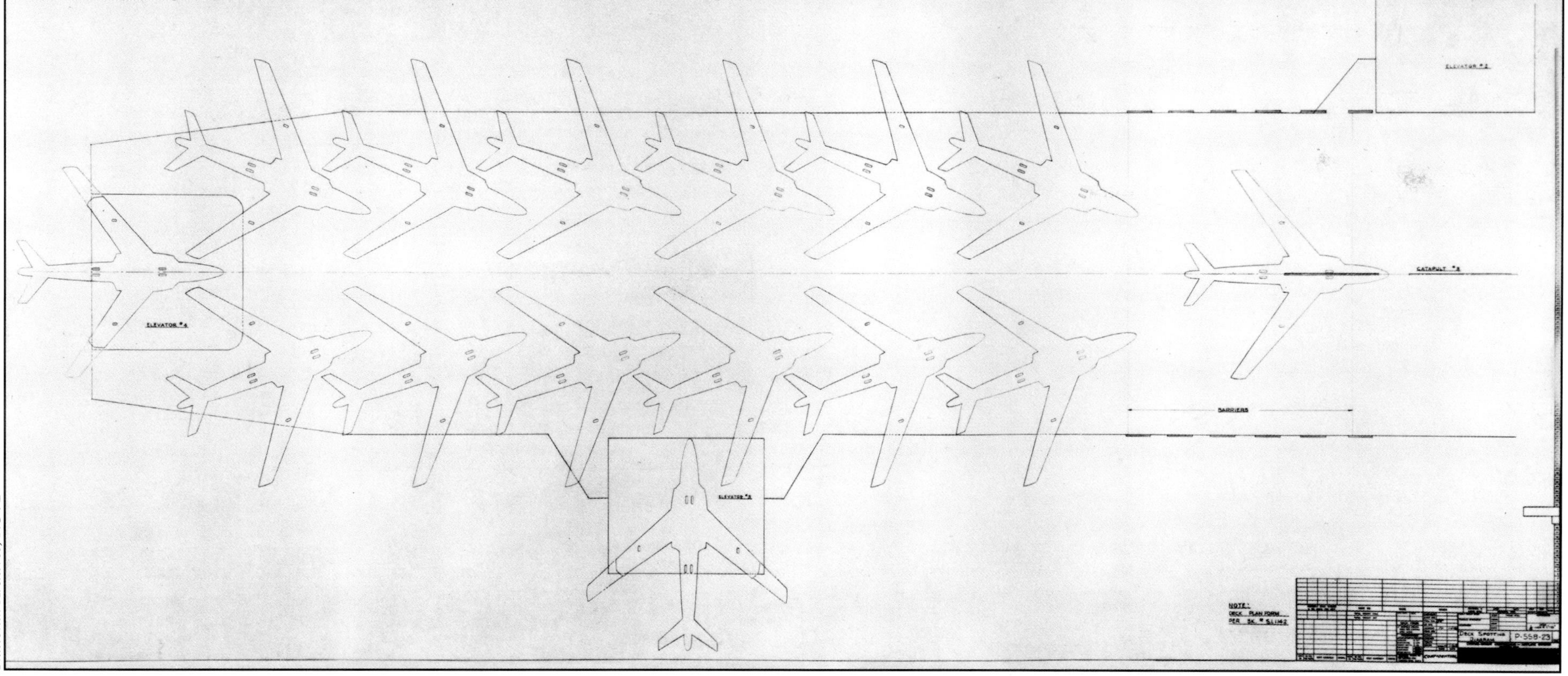

National Archives, RG 72

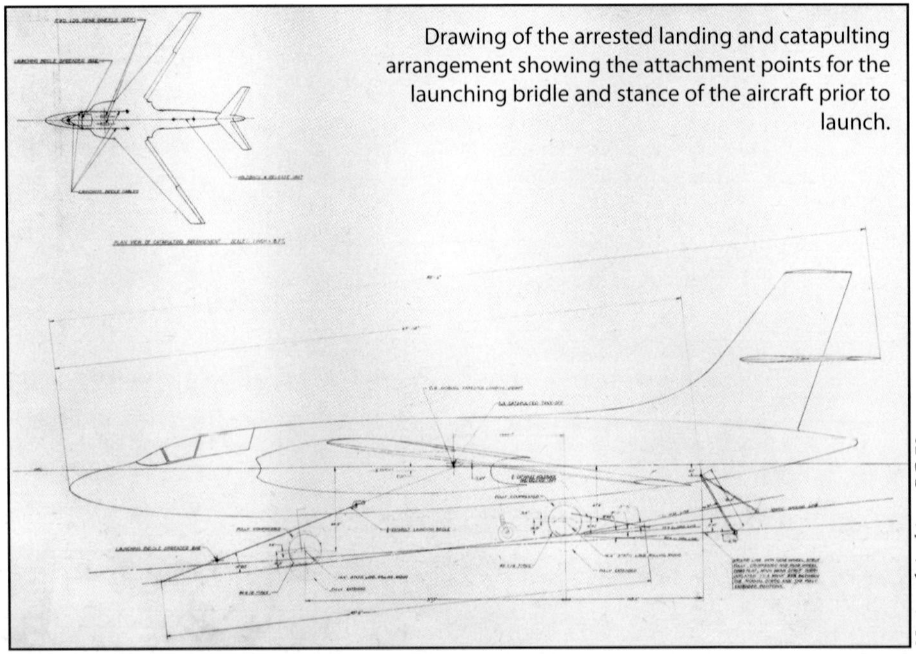

Drawing of the arrested landing and catapulting arrangement showing the attachment points for the launching bridle and stance of the aircraft prior to launch.

National Archives, RG 72

Below & Right: Standard Aircraft Characteristics charts for the Curtiss-Wright P-558 equipped with XJ-40, TJ-6, and TJ-7 turbojet engines.

XJ-40-WE-10 ENGINES (GUARANTEED RATINGS)

MISSION AND DESCRIPTION

THIS AIRCRAFT IS A TWIN ENGINE (TURBO JET) CARRIER-BASED, VA CLASS, BOMBER, DESIGNED PRIMARILY TO CARRY OUT HIGH ALTITUDE HORIZONTAL BOMBING ATTACKS. PRIMARY EMPHASIS HAS BEEN PLACED ON ACHIEVING MINIMUM SIZE AND GROSS WEIGHT, HIGH CRUISE SPEEDS (MACH NO.+.85), HIGH V MAX (MACH NO.+0.9), TOGETHER WITH MAXIMUM COMBAT RADIUS.

THE DESIGN OF THE AIRCRAFT HAS BEEN BASED ON THE REQUIREMENTS OF BUREAU OF AERO TYPE SPEC. OS-111 DATED JULY 1948.

WEIGHTS

	LBS.
WGT. EMPTY	41,590
BASIC	87,000
L. F.	2.25
DESIGN	87,000
L. F.	2.25
COMBAT	71,950
L. F.	2.72
MAX. T. O. (LESS JATO)	87,000
L. F.	2.25
DESIGN LANDING	56,930
EMERG. LANDING	71,950

FUEL AND OIL

TOTAL FUEL-GALS.	5,575
NO. OF TANKS	6
SELF-SEALING TANKS-GALS.	4,328
EXTERNAL TANKS-GALS.	—

OIL

OIL CAPACITY-GALS. 6

POWER PLANT

NO. & MODEL — 2 NAVY XJ40-WE-10
MFG. — WESTINGHOUSE ELEC. & MFG. COMPANY

RATINGS

SEA LEVEL STATIC RATINGS PER W. E. C. SPEC. WAGT X40 E8-2 OF 15 MARCH 1948

RATINGS	LBS. THRUST	R. P. M.
MILITARY	8,100	7,260
NORMAL	7,300	7,260
CRUISE (1)	5,400	7,260
CRUISE (2)	4,300	7,260
IDLE	495	3,000

ORDNANCE

1 TAIL TURRET AGL AERO XIIE

2 20MM T-34 GUNS
500 RDS. PER GUN
90° COVERAGE

1 SPECIAL BOMB LOAD AS REQ'D BY BUREAU OF AERO TYPE SPEC. OS-111

WEIGHT 10,000 LBS.

DIMENSIONS

NO. OF CREW	3
OVERALL WIDTH	81'-0"
OVERALL LENGTH	83'-1"
OVERALL HEIGHT	23'-5"
WHEEL TREAD	40'-0"
TAIL WIDTH	23'-9.6"

ELECTRONICS

1	AN/APX-6	REC.-TRANSMITTER
1	AN/APG-25	R. F. UNIT
1	AN/APG-25	COMPUTER
1	AN/ARR-2	NAVIGATION REC.
1	AN/APN-1	RADIO ALTIMETER
1	AN/ARC-5	RANGE RECEIVER
1	AN/APB-2	TRANSMITTER-REC.
1	AN/ART-13	H. F. TRANSMITTER
1	AN/ARR-15	H. F. TRANSMITTER
1	AN/ARC-1	V.H.F. TRANS.-REC.
1	AN/AIC-4	INTERCOM. EQUIP.

National Archives, RG 72

MISSION AND DESCRIPTION

THIS AIRCRAFT IS A TWIN ENGINE (TURBO JET) CARRIER-BASED, VA CLASS, BOMBER, DESIGNED PRIMARILY TO CARRY OUT HIGH ALTITUDE HORIZONTAL BOMBING ATTACKS. PRIMARY EMPHASIS HAS BEEN PLACED ON ACHIEVING MINIMUM SIZE AND GROSS WEIGHT, HIGH CRUISE SPEEDS (MACH NO.+.85), HIGH V MAX (MACH NO.+0.9), TOGETHER WITH MAXIMUM COMBAT RADIUS.

THE DESIGN OF THE AIRCRAFT HAS BEEN BASED ON THE REQUIREMENTS OF BUREAU OF AERO TYPE SPEC. OS-111 DATED JULY 1948.

WEIGHTS

	LBS.
WGT. EMPTY	41,590
BASIC	87,000
L. F.	2.25
DESIGN	96,000
L. F.	2.04
COMBAT	76,567
L. F.	2.56 *
MAX. T. O. (LESS JATO)	96,000
L. F.	2.04
DESIGN LANDING	60,290
EMERG. LANDING	76,567

* DEVIATION IS TAKEN SINCE THIS FIGURE IS HIGHER THAN MAXIMUM ATTAINABLE LOAD FACTOR AT COMBAT ALTITUDE.

FUEL AND OIL

TOTAL FUEL-GALS	6,975
NO. OF TANKS	8
SELF-SEALING TANKS-GALS.	4,328
EXTERNAL TANKS-GALS.	1,400

OIL

CAPACITY-GALS. - 6

POWER PLANT

NO. & MODEL — 2 WRIGHT AERO MODEL TJ-6
MFG. — WRIGHT AERO CORP.

RATINGS

SEA LEVEL STATIC RATINGS PER W. A. C. SPEC. AC-141-A OF 3 NOVEMBER 1948

RATING	DESIGN JET THRUST/LBS.	R. P. M.
T. O. & MILITARY	11,000	6,600
NORMAL	10,000	6,600
CRUISE 80% NORMAL	8,000	6,600
CRUISE 60% NORMAL	6,000	6,310

ORDNANCE

1 TAIL TURRET AGL AERO XIIE

2 20MM T-34 GUNS
500 RDS. PER GUN
90° COVERAGE

1 SPECIAL BOMB LOAD AS REQ'D. BY BUREAU OF AERO TYPE SPEC. OS-111

WEIGHT 10,000 LBS.

DIMENSIONS

NO. OF CREW	3
OVERALL WIDTH	81'-0"
OVERALL LENGTH	83'-1"
OVERALL HEIGHT	23'-5"
WHEEL TREAD	40'-0"
TAIL WIDTH	23'-9.6"

ELECTRONICS

1	AN/APX-6	REC.-TRANSMITTER
1	AN/APG-25	R. F. UNIT
1	AN/APG-25	COMPUTER
1	AN/ARR-2	NAVIGATION REC.
1	AN/APN-1	RADIO ALTIMETER
1	AN/ARC-5	RANGE RECEIVER
1	AN/APB-2	TRANSMITTER-REC.
1	AN/ART-13	H. F. TRANSMITTER
1	AN/ARR-15	H. F. TRANSMITTER
1	AN/ARC-1	V.H.F. TRANS.-REC.
1	AN/AIC-4	INTERCOM. EQUIP.

National Archives, RG 72

MISSION AND DESCRIPTION

THIS AIRCRAFT IS A TWIN ENGINE (TURBO JET) CARRIER-BASED, VA CLASS, BOMBER, DESIGNED PRIMARILY TO CARRY OUT HIGH ALTITUDE HORIZONTAL BOMBING ATTACKS. PRIMARY EMPHASIS HAS BEEN PLACED ON ACHIEVING MINIMUM SIZE AND GROSS WEIGHT, HIGH CRUISE SPEEDS (MACH NO.+.85), HIGH V MAX (MACH NO.+0.9), TOGETHER WITH MAXIMUM COMBAT RADIUS.

THE DESIGN OF THE AIRCRAFT HAS BEEN BASED ON THE REQUIREMENTS OF BUREAU OF AERO TYPE SPEC. OS-111 DATED JULY 1948.

WEIGHTS

	11A-LBS.	11C-LBS.
WGT. EMPTY	41,940	41,940
BASIC	87,000	87,000
L. F.	2.25	2.25
DESIGN	87,000	94,050
L. F.	2.25	2.08
COMBAT	72,105	75,707
L. F.	2.71	2.58 *
MAX. T. O. (LESS JATO)	87,000	94,050
L. F.	2.25	2.08
DESIGN LANDING	57,140	59,760
EMERG. LANDING	72,105	75,707

* DEVIATION IS TAKEN SINCE THIS FIGURE IS HIGHER THAN MAXIMUM ATTAINABLE LOAD FACTOR AT COMBAT ALTITUDE.

FUEL AND OIL

	11 A	11 C
TOTAL FUEL	5,517	6,608
NO. OF TANKS	6	8
SELF-SEALING TANKS-GALS.	4,328	4,328
EXTERNAL TANKS GALS.	-	1,092

OIL

CAPACITY-GALS.	6	6

POWER PLANT

NO. & MODEL — 2 WRIGHT AERO MODEL TJ-7
MFG. — WRIGHT AERO CORP.

RATINGS

SEA LEVEL STATIC RATINGS PER W. A. C. SPEC. AC-142 OF 1 SEPTEMBER 1948

RATINGS	DESIGN JET THRUST/LBS.	R. P. M.
T. O. & MILITARY	12,000	6,600
NORMAL	10,000	6,600
CRUISE 80% NORMAL	8,000	6,600
CRUISE 60% NORMAL	6,000	6,170

ORDNANCE

1 TAIL TURRET AGL AERO XIIE

2 20MM T-34 GUNS
500 RDS. PER GUN
90° COVERAGE

1 SPECIAL BOMB LOAD AS REQ'D. BY BUREAU OF AERO TYPE SPEC. OS-111

WEIGHT 10,000 LBS.

DIMENSIONS

NO. OF CREW	3
OVERALL WIDTH	81'-0"
OVERALL LENGTH	83'-1"
OVERALL HEIGHT	23'-5"
WHEEL TREAD	40'-0"
TAIL WIDTH	23'-9.6"

ELECTRONICS

1	AN/APX-6	REC.-TRANSMITTER
1	AN/APG-25	R. F. UNIT
1	AN/APG-25	COMPUTER
1	AN/ARR-2	NAVIGATION REC.
1	AN/APN-1	RADIO ALTIMETER
1	AN/ARC-5	RANGE RECEIVER
1	AN/APB-2	TRANSMITTER-REC.
1	AN/ART-13	H. F. TRANSMITTER
1	AN/ARR-15	H. F. TRANSMITTER
1	AN/ARC-1	V.H.F. TRANS.-REC.
1	AN/AIC-4	INTERCOM. EQUIP.

National Archives, RG 72

National Archives, RG 72

Artist's impression of the Douglas Model 593, which was designed closely to the requirements of OS-111 and had a takeoff weight of 87,500 lbs. The original was painted by the legendary R.G. Smith, the talented Douglas engineer and aviation artist.

CHAPTER 5 — *Douglas El Segundo Model 593*

Unique among the manufacturers that participated in the Class VA competition, Douglas internally divided its efforts and submitted two separate proposals. The El Segundo division of Douglas submitted the Model 593, which is covered in this chapter, while the Santa Monica division submitted the Model 1181, covered in the following chapter. This was an interesting strategy - Douglas management may have felt that submitting two separate proposals increased the probability of winning the competition, though there was the obvious danger of dividing engineering resources and producing two weak offerings to the Navy. The El Segundo division was fortunate to have Chief Engineer Ed Heinemann managing its proposal effort, who would go on to become a legend in the aerospace industry.

In its Model 593 proposal, Douglas asserted that the problem of carrying a 10,000 lb bomb 1,700 miles, as requested by the bid specification, could be met with a turbojet-powered carrier-based airplane. Preliminary studies were also made of turboprop-powered aircraft, which had some advantage in combat radius, particularly at reduced speeds. The turboprop studies were dropped at an early stage, however, due to uncertain propeller characteristics at high Mach numbers which, together with the longer engine, reduction gear and propeller development time, indicated that turboprop airplanes based on existing knowledge had considerably poorer potential than turbojet-powered arrangements.

From the performance summary below, as well as the turret discussion that follows, it could be seen that a tail turret of the type specified accounted for a weight increase of approximately 6,500 lbs for an airplane of this type (12,250 lbs if engines and wheels were reduced proportionately), or a loss of approximately 123 nm combat radius. A turret was included in the basic engineering proposal designated Model 593, but omitted from an alternate of the basic proposal designated Model 593-1. The gross weight for these two airplanes hand been held at a constant of 87,500 lbs and the equivalent of the turret weight added to the alternate 593-1 design in the form of fuel. An increase in gross weight above 87,500 lbs with a turret was not recommended with the power available. Adding another engine increased the gross weight considerably over 100,000 lbs.

As a result of the alarming increases in development and manufacturing costs that were particularly aggravated by the tendency of airplanes to increase in size and complexity, an additional proposal designated the Model 593-2 was included. The purpose of this study was to show that if the weight of the bomb carried was reduced to 4,000 lbs, the diameter to 24 inches, and the number of crew was reduced from 3 to 2 with the elimination of corresponding equipment, it was possible to develop a 40,000 lb airplane powered with smaller engines that was capable of approximately the same performance as the larger airplane, with a resultant cost of approximately half of the larger airplane and greatly improved catapulting, deck handling, spotting, maintenance and general utility.

As a result of these studies, Douglas strongly recommended that consideration be given to the installation of tail warning equipment in lieu of the tail turret specified. The company strongly recommended selection of its smaller 40,000 lb 593-2 airplane

PERFORMANCE COMPARISON

Model		593			593-1			593-2
Bomb Load	(lb)	10,000			10,000			4,000
Turret		ONE TAIL TURRET			NO TURRET			NO TURRET
Wing Area	(sq.ft)	920			920			420
Span	(ft)	80.33			80.33			54.15
Aspect Ratio		7.0			7.0			7.0
Wing Thickness in Line of Flight	(%)	9			9			9
Engines		2-XJ40 (FUTURE ESTIMATE)	2-XJ40-WE-12 (SPECIFICATION)		2-XJ40 (FUTURE ESTIMATE)	2-XJ40-WE-12 (SPECIFICATION)		2-XJ46-WE-2 (SPECIFICATION)
S.L. Static Rating	(lb)	2x9125	2x8100		2x9125	2x8100		2x4200
Loading Condition		NORMAL	NORMAL	OVERLOAD*	NORMAL	NORMAL	OVERLOAD*	NORMAL
Take-off Weight (Without JATO)	(lb)	87,500	87,500	92,740	87,500	87,500	92,740	40,000
Fuel	(lb)	37,800	37,800	42,600	39,384	39,384	44,184	18,200
Combat Weight (T.O. Wt. less 45% Fuel)	(lb)	70,490	70,490	73,130	69,777	69,777	72,417	31,810
V_{max} S.L. Combat Wt. ø	(knots/Mach No.)	565/.85	540/.82	540/.82	568/.86	542/.82	542/.82	560/.85
V_{max} 40,000' Combat Wt. ø	(knots/Mach No.)	517/.90	501/.87	497/.86	518/.90	502/.87	499/.87	515/.90
V_{stall} at Take-off Weight	(knots)	134.5	134.5	138.5	134.5	134.5	138.5	134.6
V_{stall} at Landing Weight	(knots)	106.5	106.5	108.9	105.5	105.5	107.9	106.6
Max. R/C at S. L. at T.O. Weight ø	(fpm)	3230	2770	2540	3250	2840	2570	3490
Combat Radius (A-3 Problem)	(naut.mi.)	1615	1562	1711	1738	1686	1847	1528
Cruising Speed	(Mach No.)	.85	.85	.85	.85	.85	.85	.85
Altitude at Target	(ft)	40,700	38,000	37,400	41,200	38,600	38,000	40,300
Operation from 6A Carrier with Double XH9 Catapult								
1) JATO required for take-off in 25 kn wind								
Standard Day	(lb)	12,200	14,500	38,000	12,200	14,500	38,000	5,500
90°F Day	(lb)	35,300	37,000	66,400	36,300	37,200	66,400	16,000
2) Wind required for take-off without JATO								
Standard Day	(knots)	27.7	30.8	40.5	27.7	30.8	40.5	27.7
90°F Day	(knots)	34.9	49.7		34.9	49.7		32.5
Operation from CVB Carrier With Double H4-1 Catapult								
1) JATO required for take-off in 25 kn wind								
Standard Day	(lb)	38,700			38,700			
2) Wind required for take-off without JATO								
Standard Day	(knots)	55.5			55.5			
Operation from CV9 Carrier with Double XH8 Catapult								
1) JATO required for take-off in 25 kn wind								
Standard day	(lb)							6400
90°F Day	(lb)							17200
2) Wind required for take-off without JATO								
Standard Day	(knots)							31.7
90°F Day	(knots)							37.1

ø Military Thrust
* Overload with 2-400 gal. external droppable tanks

Performance comparison of the three Douglas El Segundo designs submitted in the Class VA competition. While the Model 593-2 was generally the least impressive, it was a smaller and more practical aircraft that could operate from CV9 class carriers, unlike its larger and heavier cousins.

National Archives, RG 72

arrangement, which was made possible with the reduction of the bomb size to 4,000 lbs. Douglas believed that the magnitude of the problem of developing airplanes for the new larger carriers and/or reconversions of smaller carriers, training preparations and the many problems connected with such an operation warranted the development of a special bomb for that purpose. It was unofficially understood by the company that such a bomb development was within the realm of possibility.

The Model 593

Performance Models 593 and 593-1 were powered by the Westinghouse XJ40-WE-12 turbojet. Two cases were presented – one using the advanced rating of 9,125 lbs static thrust, and the other using specification performance. The power plant for the Model 593-2 was the XJ46-WE-2.

The normal gross weight for Models 593 and 593-1 was 87,500 lbs. It was shown that by overloading them with two 400 gallon drop tanks, the combat radius could be increased to 1,711 and 1,847 nm, respectively. In spite of the small size of Model 593-2, it had a combat radius of 1,528 nm with full internal fuel.

As allowed by OS-111, takeoff performance was calculated at or near maximum lift coefficient, but in all cases the takeoff rate of climb was at least 500 ft per minute. If a margin was desired between stalling speed and speed at the end of the deck, it could be provided by allowing additional wind or JATO as required.

Structural Arrangement The fuselage structure was conventional in all respects. The wing structure was unique, with rigidity being the important consideration in all design decisions. Considerable work was done by Douglas to ensure that an optimum apportionment of structural weight was attained for both rigidity and strength requirements. In an aircraft of this size, speed and strength class, rigidity was considered to be of paramount importance; only by a proper distribution of structural weight could it be obtained economically.

The wing was designed using tapered skin and spanwise stabilizing "pillow" doublers supported between pillows by bulkheads with 24 to 36 inch spacing. In such a design, the skin doubler acted with the skin to resist shear deformation. The result was that the shear rigidity of the cover skin was increased over normal skin stiffener construction as much as 80% for the same outer skin thickness. In addition to this gain in rigidity, the skin and supporting pillows were designed to resist the wing bending loads. The bending material, which normally was in large spar caps or spanwise stiffeners, was distributed into the cover skin and pillows. Since this type of construction required a heavier outer skin, the torsional stiffness was further increased by as much as 50% in addition to the 80% already realized. The increases in rigidity were obtained at a possible net saving in wing structure weight.

If desired, the vertical tail could be made to fold to permit stowage below decks on the CVB class carriers. Provision for heat deicing of the wing slat, the leading edge of the wing, and the leading edge of the tail surfaces was incorporated by the use of chordwise pillows.

Landing Gear, Catapult and Arresting Hook A conventional taildragger landing gear was selected by Douglas, as it was considered most suitable for carrier operations. Moreover, it permitted stowage below decks on the Project 6A carrier without folding the vertical tail; and in the case of the CVB carriers only part of the vertical tail had to be folded.

The tail wheel location was chosen so as to permit handling of the airplane in either the fore or aft direction on the 60 ft elevators. The landing gear was designed to retract in 5 seconds to improve rate of climb after takeoff.

Surface Controls A wheel type control was provided in order to ensure satisfactory forces with power boost inoperative. Power boost was incorporated on all surfaces. In this connection it was intended to incorporate the power boost, auto-pilot servo and control surface damper in a single unit for each control surface. It was estimated that approximately 100 lbs of weight could be saved by using this system as compared to the conventional system, which required separate units for these three functions.

Armament Space was provided to carry a 10,000 lb bomb. The clearance envelope deviated slightly from the dimensions shown in OS-111, but satisfied the requirements of the Air Force's bomb bay for a 10,000 lb bomb. Snap action bomb doors were provided which permitted opening the doors, dropping the bomb, and closing the doors in a period of 3.5 seconds so as to minimize the effects of buffeting. The after corner of the bomb bay had been rounded off in order to reduce disruption to the aerodynamics. Provisions were made for the 20 mm two gun tail turret.

Power Plant Installation External power plants were chosen in order to obtain maximum ram recovery, minimize tail pipe losses, provide superior accessibility and to permit flexibility in the choice of alternate engines. Douglas selected the Westinghouse XJ40-WE-12 engine as the primary power plant, though Wright Aeronautical Company TJ-6 turbojets could be installed by changing only the nacelle details, depending on the availability of these engines.

The fuel system incorporated four tanks connected to a common sump in the fuselage above the bomb bay. The fuel was transferred from the left hand wing tank, through the aft fuselage tank to the sump; and from the right hand wing tank through the forward fuselage tank to the sump by engine pressure. From there it was supplied to either or both engines through two fuel valves. With this system it was not necessary to shut off engine pressure when the wing tanks were exhausted. The only controls required by the pilot were an on-off fuel switch for each engine.

The wing tanks contained fuel only for the first 800 miles of the combat radius and were not bullet proof. Fuel could be drained from all tanks during level flight and climb attitudes. The sump tank was of 650 gal capacity and always had sufficient fuel to supply the engines during dives. All tanks were connected with large manifolds for single point refueling at the rate of 600 gals per minute. It was estimated that refueling could be accomplished in approximately 10 minutes.

JATO provisions were also incorporated in the Model 593. It was considered that 12 seconds of JATO were necessary. This allowed 2 seconds to ensure that both JATO bottles were operating prior to catapult launching, 3 seconds during the catapult and deck run, 5 seconds to retract the landing gear, and a 2 second margin.

Electronics All of the equipment was conveniently located to the operators. The equipment that was not controlled by the operators was located forward of the cockpit in a compartment where it could be cooled by the outlet to the to the cockpit cooling system. All antennas were flush except the single antenna for the low frequency APN-4, ARR-15 and ART-13 units. This antenna was a wire that could be heated to prevent ice formation.

The Model 593-1

This model was identical to the Model 593, except that the 1,975 lb tail turret and related equipment was deleted and replaced by 320 lbs of tail warning radar, a window (chaff) dispenser and 1,655 lbs of fuel and tankage. The drawings shown for the previous Model 593 were applicable to this model.

The Model 593-2

The Model 593-2 was a small 40,000 lb airplane designed to carry a 4,000 lb bomb, a crew of 2, and reduced weight of radio, radar and bombing equipment.

Engine Selection (All Models)

Selection Preliminary studies, confined to the power plants and ratings allowed by the bid specification, determined that the XJ-40 engine was best suited to this application. This power plant had the lowest specific fuel consumption and the greatest potential development of any engine considered.

Description The power plant installations in the Douglas proposals were ideally located from the standpoint of obtaining maximum practicable performance out of the engines. The underslung nacelles had very short, constant area intake ducts and the tailpipe and nozzles were those supplied with the engine. Although the estimated inlet duct losses were almost so small as to be negligible, their effect, together with the effects of compressor air bleed and accessory power extraction on the power plant performance, had been estimated and used in the airplane performance calculations.

Performance The airplane design was based on a "Future Estimate" of the performance of the XJ-40 engine in accordance with recommendations by the Aviation Design Research branch of BuAer. The guaranteed performance was calculated using the XJ40-WE-12 engine performance of the Westinghouse Bid Specification WAGT XJ40-WE-10. Although the "Future Estimate" performance by BuAer showed an increase in specific fuel consumption with altitudes above 35,000 ft, the specific fuel consumption in the study by Douglas was assumed not to change under these conditions. The reasons for this assumption were:

1. A higher compression ratio engine was assumed.
2. The XJ40-WE-12 engine did not show this characteristic.
3. Discussions with Westinghouse indicated that on the basis of their more recent combustion experiments, there was no reason to expect that the fuel consumption would increase appreciably until altitudes in excess of 60,000 ft were obtained.

A 90 lb weight allowance over that predicted by BuAer was made for an increase in compression ratio of the "Future Estimate" XJ-40 engine.

Future Development Douglas compared the sea level static performance of various suitable engines against the estimated date of availability of prototype engines. Nominally, all of the engines examined were of the same physical size and weight. From this study, Douglas drew the following conclusions:

1. The "Future Estimate" XJ-40 thrust apparently could be significantly increased by developments incorporated in the design of the Wright engines (i.e., higher temperatures, compression ratios and airflow).
2. If the Wright engines reached a satisfactory stage of development at the time they were needed for the production airplanes, they could be substituted for the XJ-40 engines with a resulting improvement in performance.

The range characteristics of the proposed aircraft were directly affected by improvements in specific fuel consumption. It was encouraging and an incentive to note that, according to the information received from an overseas representative, a British manufacturer was developing an engine with 9% lower (and eventually 27% lower) specific fuel consumption values than obtained from the "Future Estimate" XJ-40 engine in the design cruise condition.

Turret Considerations

The effects of eliminating equipment items in the Model 593 airplane wherever possible resulted in appreciable savings in overall gross weight. The complete impact of such savings was not immediately apparent, but a simple example indicated the severe penalty to be paid when nonessential weight was added to aircraft of this type.

The important consideration was not the initial increment of unessential weight; it was the overall increase in weight required to absorb the initial increment that had to be considered most important. Douglas labeled the ratio of the initial increment in weight to the increase in overall gross weight the "Aircraft Growth Factor," which determined the real penalty to be paid for adding weight to the aircraft. The value of the Growth Factor was fixed by the items of performance which had to be held constant.

The growth factor of the Model 593 airplane was 7.4 if all performance characteristics remained fixed. Since it was not possible to vary the actual power plant smoothly as performance required, the Growth Factor was reduced to 4.3, but high speed and climb performance varied while combat radius and takeoff speed were held constant. Another variable which did not change smoothly was the landing gear wheel assembly. If the landing gear wheel weight was held fixed, the Growth Factor was reduced to 3.92.

The initial weight reduction possible by removing the tail turret from the Model 593 airplane and replacing it with a tail warning device and a window (chaff) dispenser was 1,655 lbs. The 1,655 lbs could be removed with several different results:

1. 1,655 lbs of fuel/tanks could be added to increase Combat Radius 123 nm.
2. Size and weight could be reduced in three ways:
   a. For fixed performance the weight would decrease 12,250 lbs.
   b. For improved speed and climb performance the same engines would be retained and the weight decrease would be 7,110 lbs.
   c. For fixed engines and landing wheel assemblies, the speed and climb performance and landing wheel life would be improved, but the weight decrease would only be 6,500 lbs.

It was felt that 12,250 lbs, which was the true cost of the turret, was a heavy price to pay for the protection afforded by two automatically operated 20 mm guns in the bomber's tail turret.

The Model 593 and 593-1 airplanes were designed specifically to operate from the Project 6A carrier. It was possible with minor revisions to the airplane – folding the vertical tail – to operate either of these airplanes from a modified CVB carrier under different conditions. The primary assumption was that the two H4-1 catapult runs be connected in parallel and shifted from the existing bow locations to a position just forward of the aft elevator. Since there was no increase in catapult energy requirements, Douglas did not consider such a shift in catapult runs out of the question. It would have also been necessary to use a double Mark V arresting gear for arrested landings. With these carrier modifications, it was possible to operate the 593 or 593-1 airplane from a CVB carrier or a Navy Standard Day Carrier within certain restrictions.

It was apparent that, if the full radius was to be obtained on a standard day with double H4-1 catapults, JATO thrust was the more reasonable of the two systems for operating these airplanes from a CVB carrier. The JATO thrust required for a full radius was such that the weight of the JATO units was only about 10% of the total fuel load of the aircraft. The price was relatively low compared to the possible gain in utility and operational effectiveness.

Douglas noted that one Project 6A carrier could handle ten Model 593 aircraft successfully, while three CVB carriers could each handle ten Model 593s. If it was necessary to build three aircraft for every one operating from a carrier, the full utility of the Model 593 airplanes could be realized from one 6A carrier only if 30 aircraft were built. Similarly, if it was possible to operate Model 593 airplanes from CVB class carriers, these aircraft would be operated at full effectiveness only if 120 were built. The ratio of the cost of building four times as many aircraft was not four to one; it was probably closer to 2 ½ to one. The simple consideration of quantity of aircraft and manufacturing cost gave an effectiveness to cost ratio of 4 to 2 ½, or 1.6 to 1. Thus, on a basis of quantity of aircraft alone, the unit value of the aircraft had increased 60%. There were, of course, further considerations which indicated additional advantages to be gained from multiple carrier operation.

Advantages of Multiple Carrier Operation

Douglas presented very basic reasoning to illustrate the advantages of operating aircraft from more than one carrier. Consider solely the problem of enemy detection of the carriers. Assuming that the search system of the enemy was capable of such coverage, the chances of finding any one carrier were one in ten. Therefore, the chances that the enemy would know the position of a single carrier capable of completing a given mission with the full element of surprise was also one in ten.

If four carriers operated together, the chances of the enemy knowing the positions of all of the carriers were still one in ten. If, however, the carriers separated into two independent groups of two, and each group operated independently of the other, the chances of the enemy finding at least two carriers were 19 in 100; but the chances of the enemy finding all four carriers were 1 in 100. If the units separated into four independently operating carriers, the chances of the enemy finding at least one carrier were about 34 in 100, the chances of his finding at least two separate carriers were about 5.2 in 100, the chances of his finding at least three of the four carriers were 3.7 in 1,000, and the chances of his finding all four carriers were 1 in 10,000.

This search problem clearly showed the relative value of one or four independently operated carriers. The cost to effectiveness ratio had further indicated the relative value of quantity of aircraft. The certain gains made possible clearly revealed the reason for designing the 593 airplane to operate from the CVB carriers as well as the 6A carrier.

The penalty of folding the vertical tail was only about 3 to 4 nm combat radius. It was feasible then to operate the Model 593 airplane successfully from CVB carriers without seriously compromising the individual aircraft utility, but with substantial gains in overall effectiveness for relatively small increment costs.

The same reasoning led to consideration of a smaller version of the Model 593, the Model 593-2 airplane. This airplane had been designed to operate from 6A, CVB and CV9 class carriers. Since there were about 20 carriers from which this aircraft could be successfully operated, the search problem alone was evidence of the relative worth of such an airplane.

The search reasoning was clear-cut. It further served to accentuate the point that weapons should not be restricted to operations from a single base of any kind. It was quite possible that the neutralization of any base could eliminate its effectiveness as surely as if it had been annihilated. Douglas felt, therefore, that the search solution was indicative of the relative worth of the combined weapons, for if any carrier could be kept under observation it could be easily neutralized and inhibited in its activity with respect to strategy, tactics and the associated element of surprise.

It was evident that if full effectiveness was to be realized in the employment of large aircraft, such aircraft had to be able to operate from as many carriers as possible. JATO had, of course, provided an interim system for operating large aircraft from carriers. The important direction in which steps had to be taken was toward improved carrier catapult capacities.

Carrier Catapult Capacity

The Model 593 airplane wing/tail arrangement and size were fixed by catapult end speed and stability and control requirements. If the catapult end speed were increased to be consistent with the landing speed limitations, the end speed have been about 145 knots instead of 129 knots. Such an increase reduced the aircraft gross weight for a 1,700 mile radius with a 10,000 lb bomb load to 65,100 lbs. The striking reduction in gross weight of 22,400 lbs was definitely possible if complete account was taken for all variable structure and equipment items in this aircraft.

Conclusion

In view of the aforementioned discussion, Douglas concluded that the Model 593 type aircraft was able to operate from as many carriers as possible to justify and warrant the expense of such a project. The most feasible solution to the carrier operation problem was to improve the catapults of the CV9, CVB and even the 6A carriers. It was concluded that a catapult having an end speed of 150 knots at a maximum capacity of 100,000 lbs should be developed, along with a suitable arresting gear, to maintain a consistent rate of carrier, catapult, arresting gear and aircraft progress. Douglas's gamble to offer a smaller and somewhat less capable aircraft than specified in OS-111 that could operate from the Navy's existing inventory of aircraft carriers would prove to be a brilliant and lucrative decision for the company.

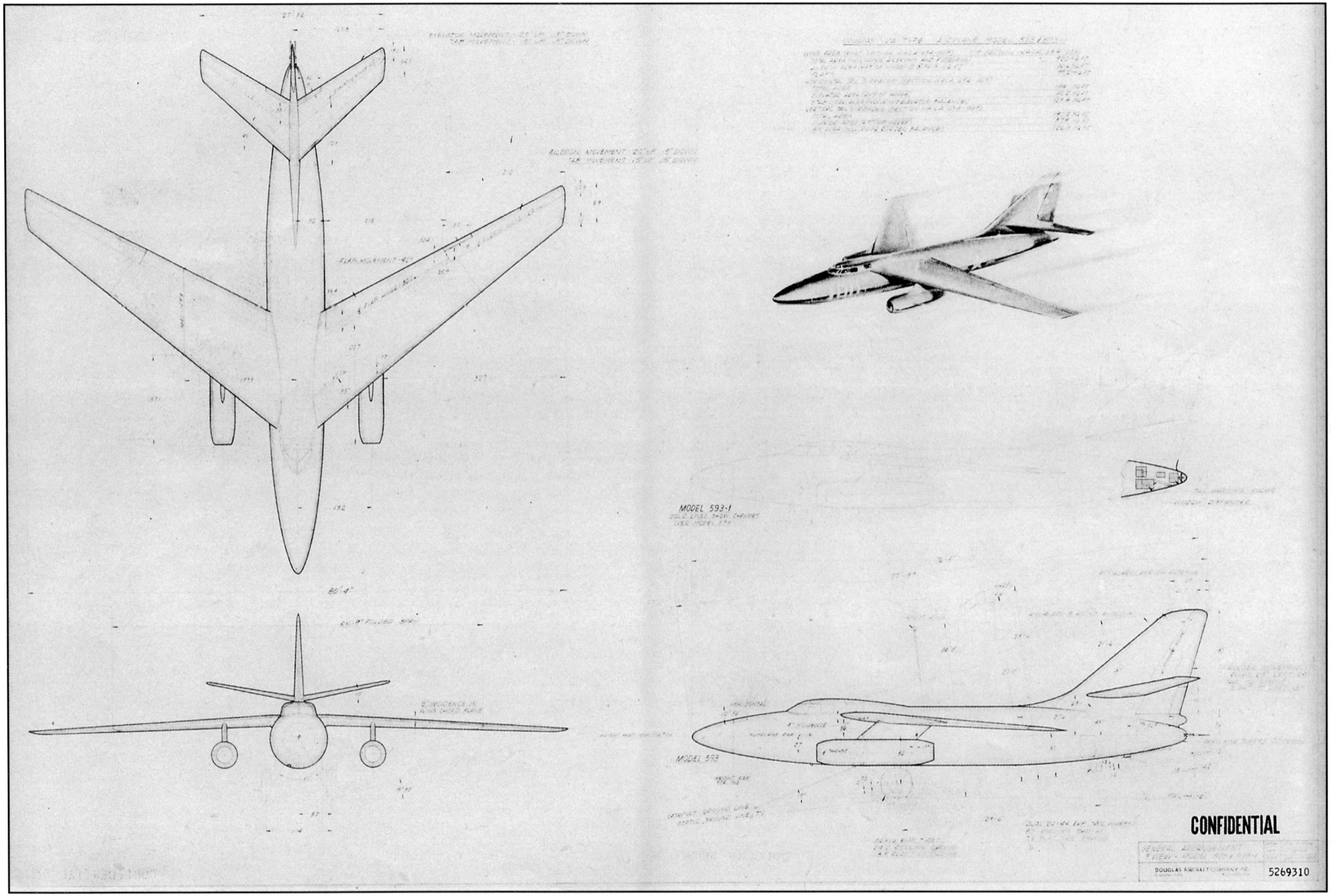

National Archives, RG 72

General arrangement drawing of the Douglas Model 593, with a side view of the Model 593-1. The latter differed from the baseline design in the deletion of the tail turret and substitution of a tail warning radar with "window" (a chaff dispenser), reducing weight by 655 lbs and improving overall performance.

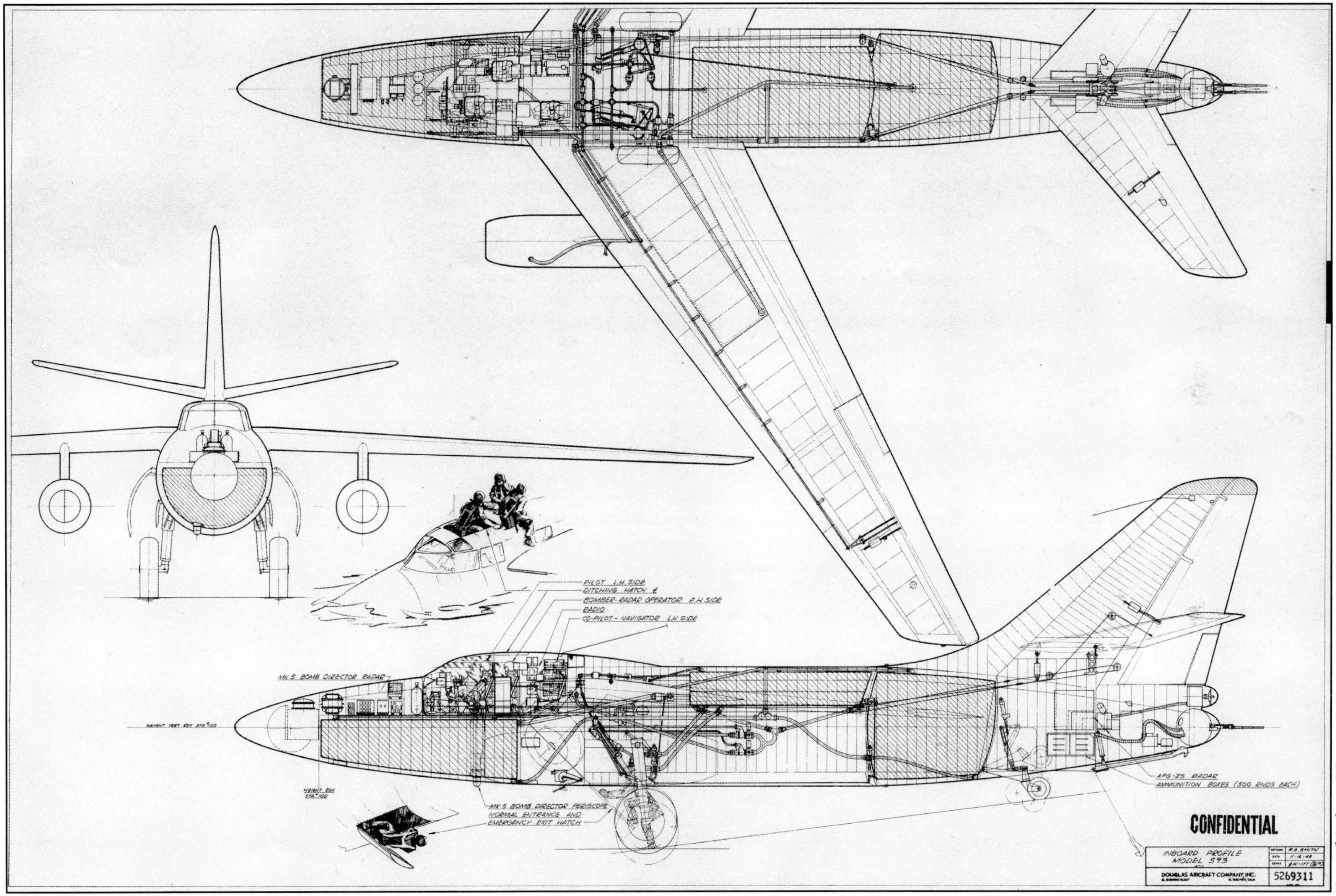

National Archives, RG 72

As can be seen in this inboard profile of the Douglas Model 593, the pilot and bomber-radar operator were located side by side, while the navigator was placed aft of the pilot. An escape chute was provided through the floor of the cockpit. Access to the bomb bay was provided through the escape chute. An openable hatch was shown on the top of the cockpit which could be left open during carrier approaches and was intended to be used for ditching, as shown in the thumbnail illustration.

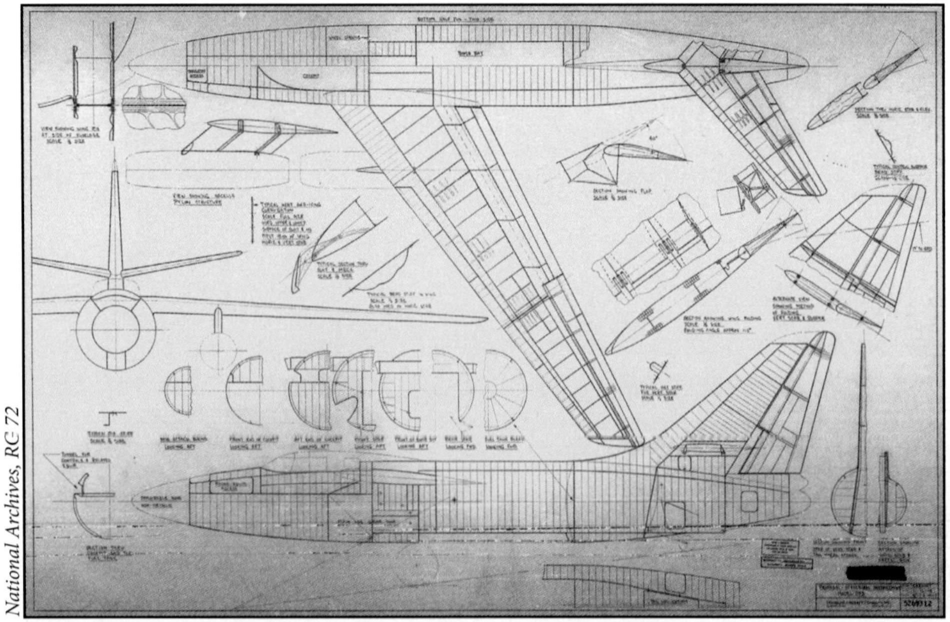

National Archives, RC 72

Above: Structural arrangement drawing of the Douglas Model 593.

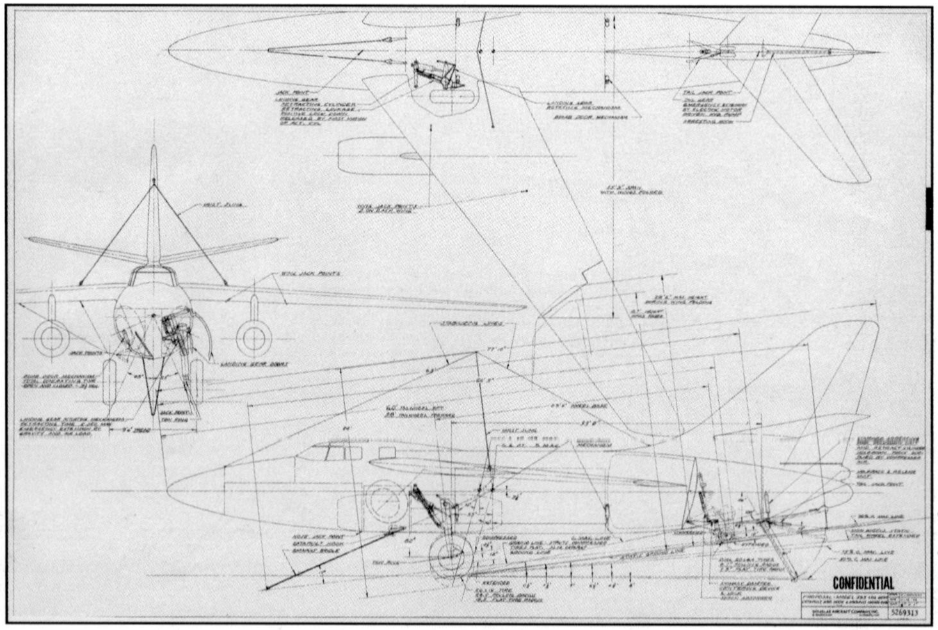

National Archives, RG 72

Above: Blueprint depicting the landing gear, catapult arresting hook and ground handling provisions for the Model 593. Unique among the proposals in the Class VA competition, Douglas chose an anachronistic tail dragger configuration for its big jet.

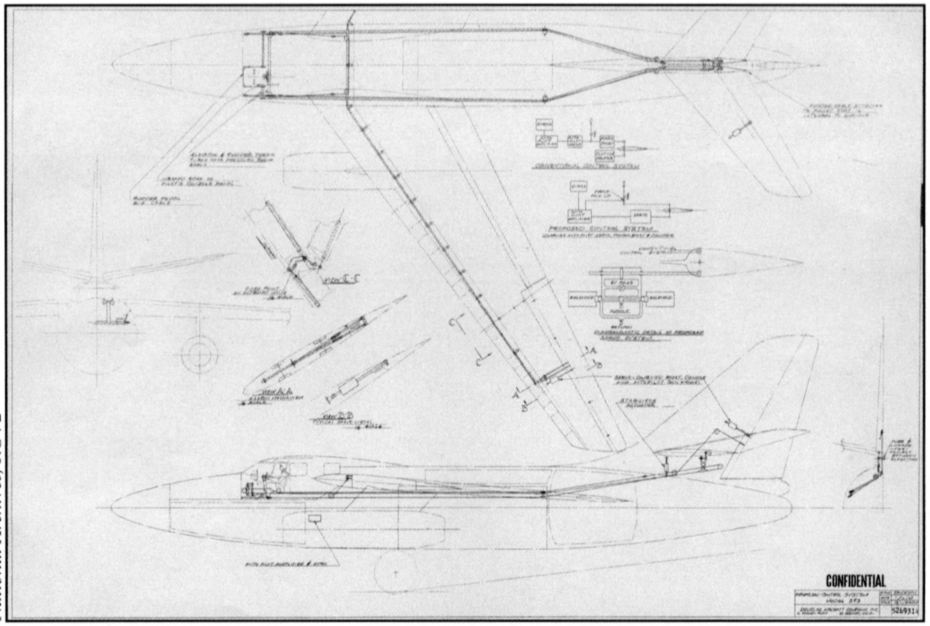

National Archives, RG 72

Above: Diagram of the Model 593 control system. Douglas proposed incorporating the power boost, auto-pilot servo and control surface damper in a single unit for each control surface, saving approximately 100 lbs of weight as compared to a conventional system.

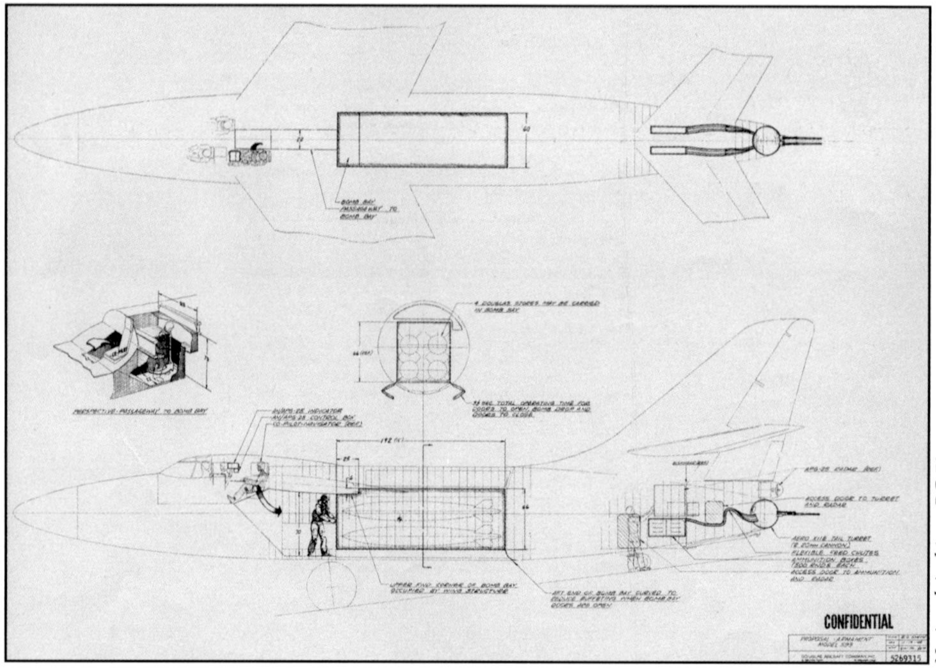

National Archives, RG 72

Above: The Model 593 armament consisted of a large bomb bay and an Aero XIIE tail turret.

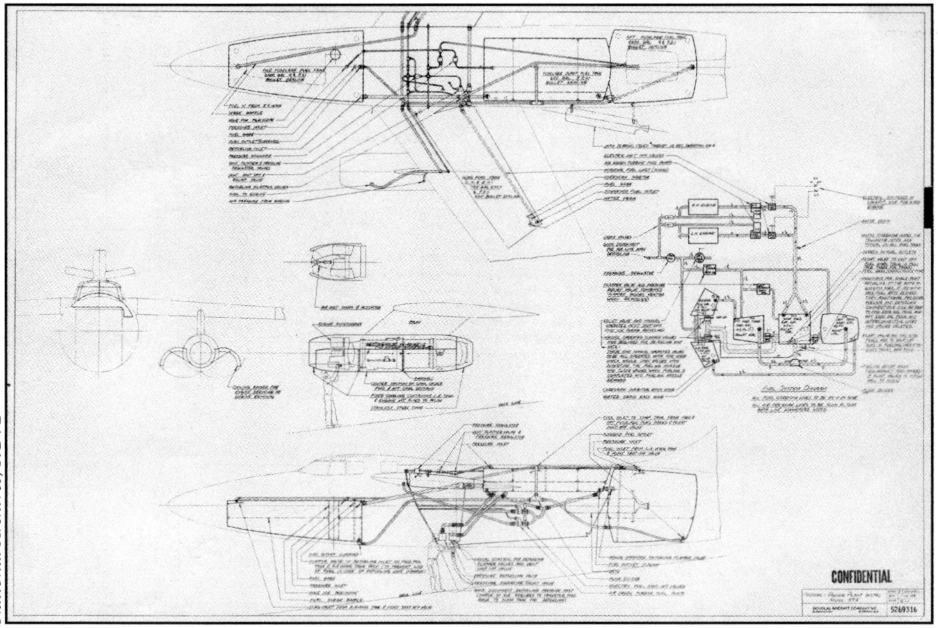

National Archives, RG 72

Above: The Douglas Model 593's power plant and fuel system installation. Douglas mounted the turbojets externally in order to obtain maximum ram recovery, minimize tail pipe losses, provide superior accessibility, and to permit flexibility in the choice of alternate engines.

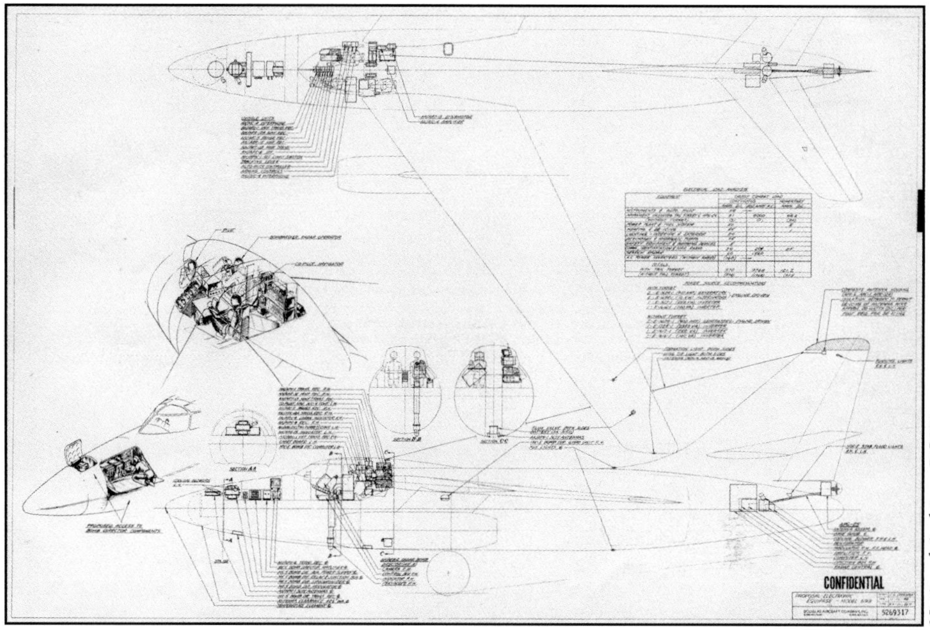

National Archives, RG 72

Above: Blueprint of the Model 593 electronic equipage and crew accommodations. Douglas endeavored to conveniently locate the equipment for the operators; equipment not directly controlled by the operators was located forward of the cockpit in a cooled compartment.

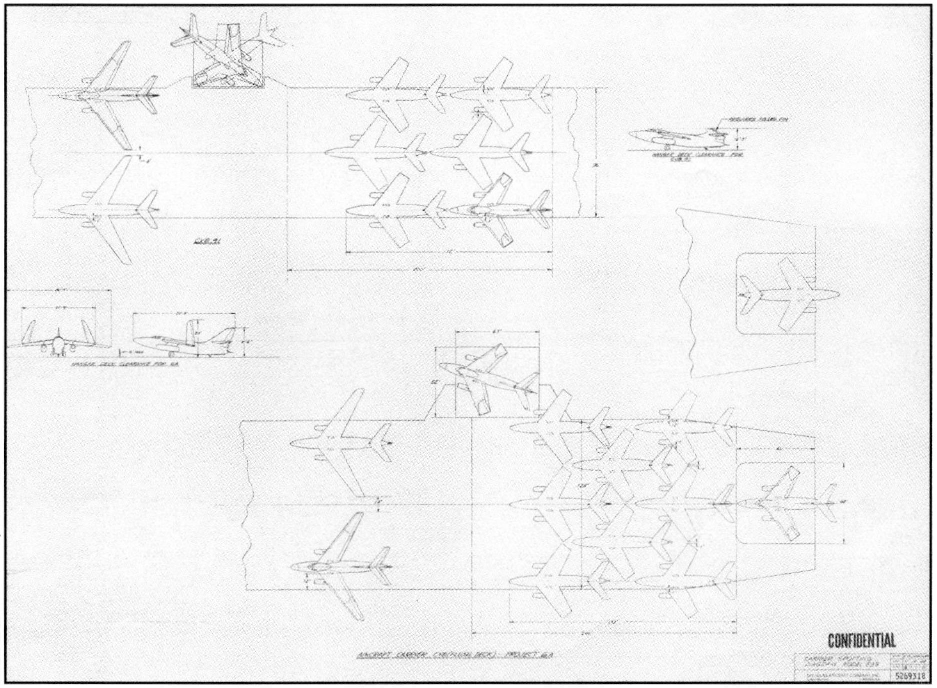

National Archives, RG 72

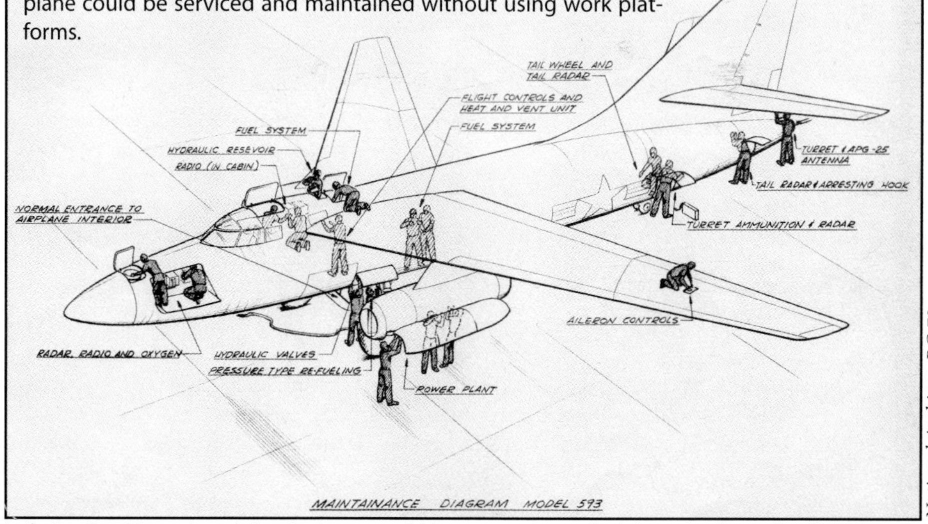

Douglas designed the Model 593 so that the majority of the airplane could be serviced and maintained without using work platforms.

National Archives, RG 72

Left: On the 6A carrier, eight airplanes could be spotted in a deck length of 172 ft. The airplane could be handled readily on the stern or deck-edge elevators. On the CVB-41 carriers, six airplanes could be spotted in a deck space of 96 and 172 ft. The airplane could be handled on the deck-edge elevator.

R.G. Smith's painting of the Douglas Model 593-2, a small 40,000 lb airplane designed to carry a 4,000 lb bomb, a crew of 2, and a reduced weight of radio, radar and bombing equipment. This deviated substantially from OS-111 requirements, but resulted in a more versatile and economical attack aircraft that could operate from the Navy's entire fleet of carriers.

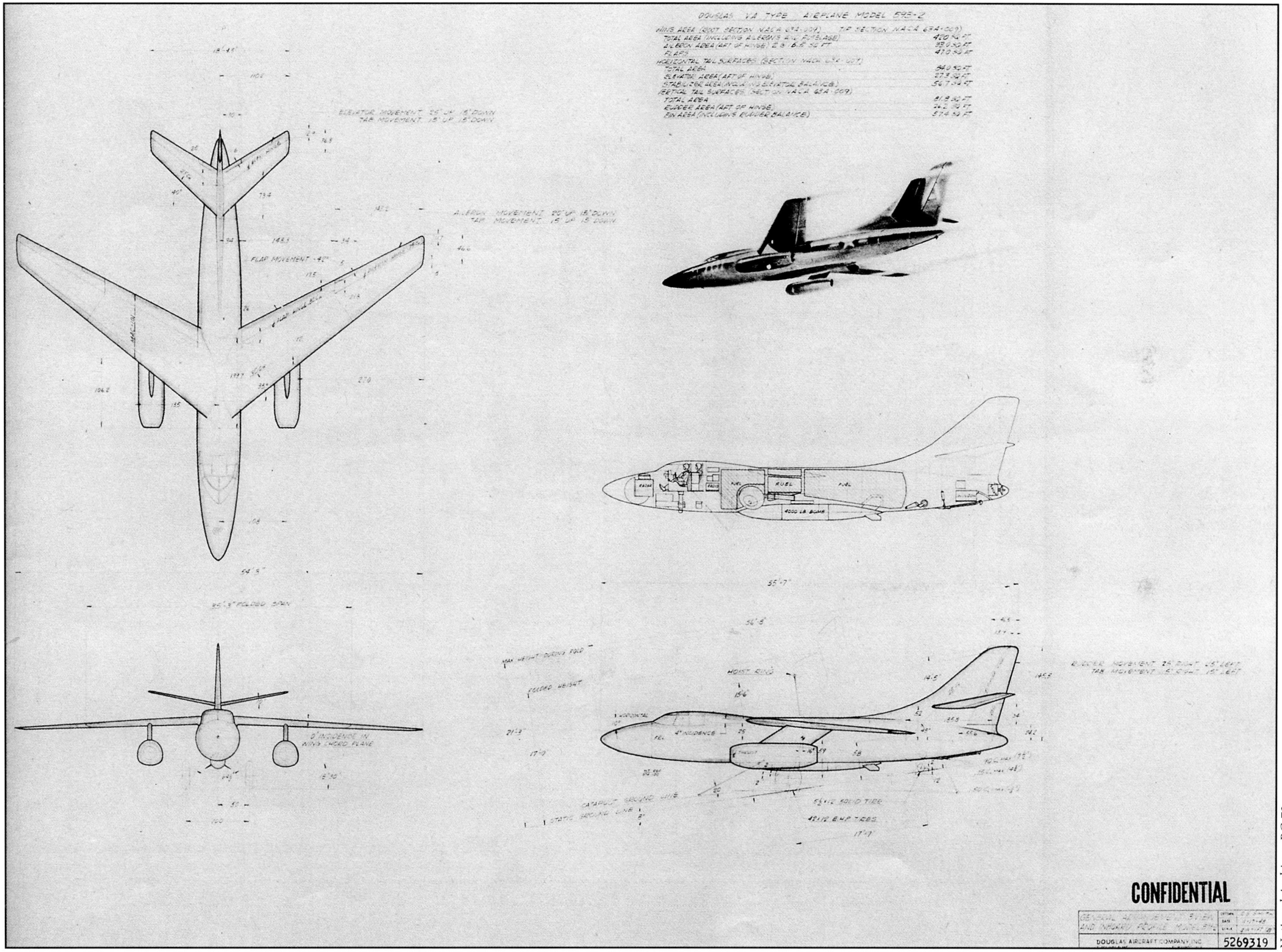

General arrangement drawing and inboard profile of the Model 593-2. This stripped down version of the basic Model 593 was capable of approximately the same performance as the larger airplane at half the cost, along with greatly improved overall utility.

National Archives, RG 72

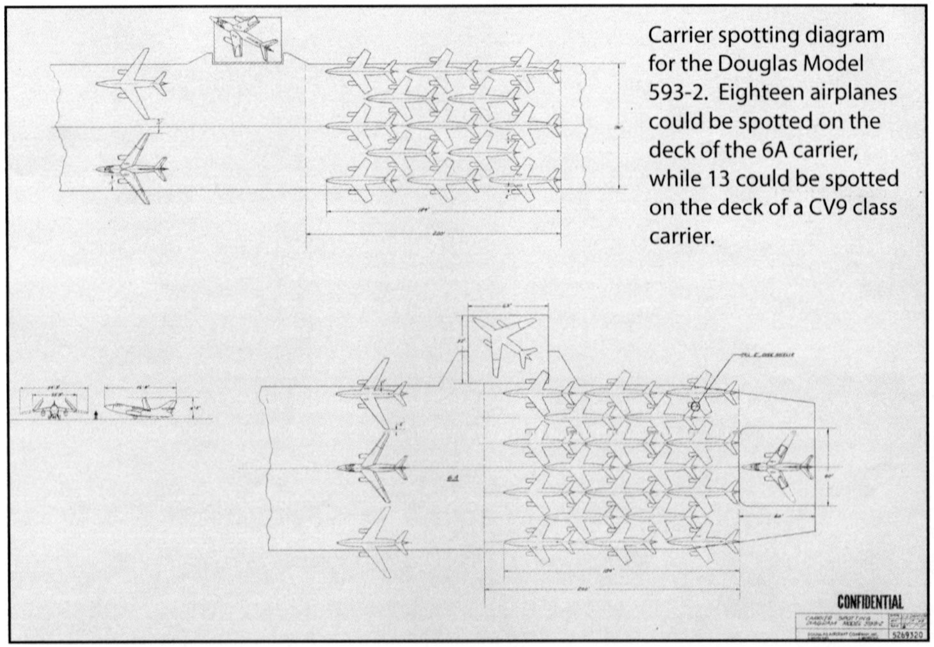

Carrier spotting diagram for the Douglas Model 593-2. Eighteen airplanes could be spotted on the deck of the 6A carrier, while 13 could be spotted on the deck of a CV9 class carrier.

National Archives, RG 72

MISSION AND DESCRIPTION

The primary mission of the Douglas Model 593-1 Airplane is the attack and destruction of enemy ground and surface targets. The airplane is designed to operate from land bases and from CVE and 6A carriers.

The airplane is a conventional swept wing structure with an all-metal two-spar wing and a semi-monocoque, circular section fuselage. The two turbo-jet engines are enclosed in under wing nacelles. Provisions are made for a three man crew, a pilot, a co-pilot navigator, and a bombardier-radar operator. The landing gear, wing fold, wing flaps, arresting hook and power boost mechanisms for rudder, elevator and ailerons are operated by hydraulic power. The adjustable stabilizer is electrically controlled.

Armament provisions consist of one 10,000# bomb completely enclosed in a bomb bay with hydraulically operated doors.

WEIGHTS

AIRPLANE
NORM. GROSS WT. ...... 87,500#
WEIGHT EMPTY ....

POWER PLANT

NO. & MODEL ....(2) XJ40-WE-12
MFR. .... WESTINGHOUSE
TURBO-JET WITHOUT AFTERBURNER

RATINGS

XJ40-WE-12 S.L.S. Thrust (lb)
MILITARY 8100
NORMAL 7300

XJ40 (FUTURE) S.L.S. Thrust (lb)
MILITARY 9125
NORMAL 8070

FUEL AND OIL

Gal. - No. Tanks - Location
4850 ...... 3 .... Fuselage
1714 ...... 2 .... Wing

OIL

2 gal. SEALED IN EACH ENGINE

ORDNANCE

1 - 10,000# Bomb

DIMENSIONS

SPAN .... 80'-4"
LENGTH (3 point) .... 77'-9"
LENGTH (level) .... 76'-3"
HEIGHT .... 26'-6"
TREAD .... 9'-6"
WING AREA .... 920□'
TURN RADIUS .... 52'

ELECTRONICS

RADAR ALTIMETER AN/APN-1
VHF COMM AN/ARC-1
RADAR BMB DIR MK5 .. AN/APB-2
MHF XMTR AN/ART-13
MHF REC. AN/ARR-15
NAV REC AN/ARR-12A
IFF .... AN/APX-C
ICS (3 place) AN/AIC-4
RANGE REC AN/ARC-5
LORAN AN/APN-4
TAIL WARNING RADAR
WINDOW DISPENSER

National Archives, RG 72

MISSION AND DESCRIPTION

The primary mission of the Douglas Model 593 Airplane is the attack and destruction of enemy ground and surface targets. The airplane is designed to operate from land bases and from CVB and 6A carriers.

The airplane is a conventional swept wing structure with an all-metal two-spar wing and a semi-monocoque, circular section fuselage. The two turbo-jet engines are enclosed in under wing nacelles. Provisions are made for a three man crew; a pilot, a co-pilot navigator, and a bombardier-radar operator. The landing gear, wing fold, wing flaps, arresting hook and power boost mechanisms for rudder, elevator and ailerons are operated by hydraulic power. The adjustable stabilizer is electrically controlled.

Armament provisions consist of one 10,000# bomb completely enclosed in a bomb bay with hydraulically operated doors and two 20 mm. guns in a radar controlled tail turret.

WEIGHTS

AIRPLANE
NORM. GROSS WT. ...... 87 500#
WEIGHT EMPTY .... 37 759#

POWER PLANT

NO. & MODEL .... (2) XJ40-WE-12
MFR. .... WESTINGHOUSE
TURBO-JET WITHOUT AFTERBURNER

RATINGS

XJ40-WE-12 S.L.S. Thrust (lb)
MILITARY 8100
NORMAL 7300

XJ40 (FUTURE) S.L.S. Thrust (lb)
MILITARY 9125
NORMAL 8070

FUEL AND OIL

Gal. - No. Tanks - Location
4850 ...... 3 .... Fuselage
1450 ...... 2 .... Wing

OIL

2 gal. SEALED IN EACH ENGINE

ORDNANCE

1 - 10,000# Bomb
1 - AERO XIIE Tail Turret containing 2 - 20 mm. guns with 500 rds ammo. per gun

DIMENSIONS

SPAN .... 80'-4"
LENGTH (3 point) .... 77'-9"
LENGTH (level) .... 76'-3"
HEIGHT .... 26'-6"
TREAD .... 9'-6"
WING AREA .... 920□'
TURN RADIUS .... 52'

ELECTRONICS

RADAR ALTIMETER AN/APN-1
VHF COMM AN/ARC-1
RADAR BMB DIR MK5 .. AN/APB-2
MHF XMTR AN/ART-13
MHF REC. AN/ARR-15
NAV REC AN/ARR-12A
IFF .... AN/APX-C
ICS (3 place) AN/AIC-4
RANGE REC AN/ARC-5
LORAN AN/APN-4

National Archives, RG 72

Above and Right: Selected Standard Aircraft Characteristics charts for the Douglas Models 593, 593-1, and 593-2 Class VA aircraft summarizing their key features.

MISSION AND DESCRIPTION

The primary mission of the Douglas Model 593-1 Airplane is the attack and destruction of enemy ground and surface targets. The airplane is designed to operate from land bases and from CVE and 6A carriers.

The airplane is a conventional swept wing structure with an all-metal two-spar wing and a semi-monocoque, circular section fuselage. The two turbo-jet engines are enclosed in under wing nacelles. Provisions are made for a three man crew, a pilot, a co-pilot navigator, and a bombardier-radar operator. The landing gear, wing fold, wing flaps, arresting hook and power boost mechanisms for rudder, elevator and ailerons are operated by hydraulic power. The adjustable stabilizer is electrically controlled.

Armament provisions consist of one 10,000# bomb completely enclosed in a bomb bay with hydraulically operated doors.

WEIGHTS

AIRPLANE
NORM. GROSS WT. ...... 87,500#
WEIGHT EMPTY ....

POWER PLANT

NO. & MODEL ....(2) XJ40-WE-12
MFR. .... WESTINGHOUSE
TURBO-JET WITHOUT AFTERBURNER

RATINGS

XJ40-WE-12 S.L.S. Thrust (lb)
MILITARY 8100
NORMAL 7300

XJ40 (FUTURE) S.L.S. Thrust (lb)
MILITARY 9125
NORMAL 8070

FUEL AND OIL

Gal. - No. Tanks - Location
4850 ...... 3 .... Fuselage
1714 ...... 2 .... Wing

OIL

2 gal. SEALED IN EACH ENGINE

ORDNANCE

1 - 10,000# Bomb

DIMENSIONS

SPAN .... 80'-4"
LENGTH (3 point) .... 77'-9"
LENGTH (level) .... 76'-3"
HEIGHT .... 26'-6"
TREAD .... 9'-6"
WING AREA .... 920□'
TURN RADIUS .... 52'

ELECTRONICS

RADAR ALTIMETER AN/APN-1
VHF COMM AN/ARC-1
RADAR BMB DIR MK5 .. AN/APB-2
MHF XMTR AN/ART-13
MHF REC. AN/ARR-15
NAV REC AN/ARR-12A
IFF .... AN/APX-C
ICS (3 place) AN/AIC-4
RANGE REC AN/ARC-5
LORAN AN/APN-4
TAIL WARNING RADAR
WINDOW DISPENSER

National Archives, RG 72

National Archives, RG 72

Artist's impression of the Douglas Santa Monica Model 1181 heavy attack aircraft. Like the Convair Class VA proposal, it was a trijet powered by three Westinghouse XJ40-WE-10 turbojets, though the engine arrangement was substantially different; note the secondary air intakes for the center engine located awkwardly underneath the engines mounted on the fuselage at the wing roots. The design almost has a Soviet look to it, accentuated by the natural metal finish the aircraft sports in this artwork.

CHAPTER 6 — *Douglas Santa Monica Model 1181*

Douglas Santa Monica performed design studies of several families of airplanes comparing different types, sizes, numbers of power plants, and various wing geometries with simultaneous changes in gross weight. In addition, studies were made of families of airplanes with turboprop and turbojet engines. Results of these studies indicated that to meet the high speed and altitude requirements of OS-111, the weight of the power plant for the turboprop more than offset its lower fuel consumption. Consequently, it was concluded that the turboprop engine would be inferior to the turbojet engine for this particular design. The studies also indicated that the use of the smallest number of the largest jet engines would result in the most effective and efficient airplane. With the fixed equipment and bomb loads called for in OS-111, it appeared essential to have an airplane of 100,000 lb takeoff weight if the desired combat radius was to be achieved, and other performance requirements dictated the necessity of approximately 20,000 lbs of takeoff thrust (dry). As this was more than the thrust available from two Westinghouse XJ40-WE-10 engines, it was found necessary to eliminate two-engine configurations from consideration in spite of their obvious arrangement advantages, and proceed with arrangements using three XJ-40 engines. Accordingly, the Model 1181 and its alternates -1, -2 and -3 were proposed to be powered by three Westinghouse XJ-40s. The Model 1181-4 was powered by two Wright TJ-6 turbojet engines, about which preliminary information had only recently become available. Detail studies were undertaken of practically all possible arrangements of jet powered airplanes to meet the requirements. Such items as engine arrangement, tail surface arrangement, wing thickness, sweep back, and aspect ratio were all studied exhaustively and evaluated by design personnel in order to obtain the most satisfactory combination of characteristics from the standpoint of usability and manufacturability in a tactical airplane of maximum performance and tactical utility.

The basic Model 1181 had the following arrangement:

a. The wing configuration was based on a sweep back of 35° and a reasonably low aspect ratio of 7, the combination of which was known to have excellent high speed, stability and structural characteristics when combined with a 10.1% thickness ratio.

b. The tail configuration was a conventional vertical and horizontal arrangement with horizontal tail located sufficiently high to preclude the possibility of any wake interference from the wing.

c. The engine arrangement was selected after considerable study as having the best general characteristics from the standpoints of accessibility, maintenance, minimal drag, an uninterrupted flap, and overall simplicity.

d. The bomb bay and landing gear configuration was chosen as providing the most reasonable combination of center of gravity travel with bomb loading, nose wheel liftoff speeds at takeoff, and landing gear geometry that would afford adequate stability without the necessity of outrigger gear, while permitting stowage of the retracted gear in the fuselage.

e. The crew arrangement was selected to provide the most efficient conditions

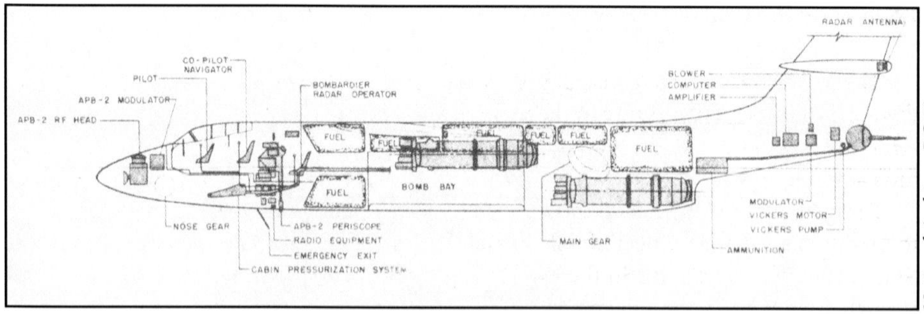

National Archives, RG 72

Simplified inboard profile of the Douglas Model 1181 Class VA Heavy Attack proposal.

in combat and retain full compliance with the general intent of the outline specification. Care was taken to assure the rapid escape of the crew in case of emergency, by means of ejection seats, a jettisonable canopy and an escape hatch through the lower section of the airplane. Normal crew entrance was through this same lower hatch.

The Model 1181 had ample reserve performance to ensure against obsolescence of the type. It was designed aerodynamically to cruise at Mach .85 and was designed structurally to operate at a high speed of Mach .92 and at a maximum speed of 60 knots above that in the basic configuration.

Aerodynamics

The basic aerodynamic problem was one of selecting a wing, tail and engine configuration that was optimum for the particular performance desired and that also permitted satisfactory stability and control characteristics over a particularly wide speed range up to Mach 1.024. Douglas Santa Monica took particular care in the selection of the wing planform, airfoil section and dihedral that would result in the best combination of lift, drag, and proper high and low speed stability and control characteristics. Special care was also necessary in the selection of the most desirable tail locations and geometry for proper control forces and effectiveness throughout the wide speed range.

After full consideration of these problems, the basic Model 1181 was chosen to have a quarter chord-line sweep back of 35°, a taper ratio of 0.4, a dihedral angle of -2.5° measured in the zero lift plane, a constant thickness ratio of 8.6% in the stream direction, washout and twist of 3°. Leading edge slats were provided in the outer 72% of the span, and ailerons were located over the outer 45% of the span.

Douglas double slotted flaps of 31% chord were located between the wing root nacelles and ailerons. A maximum deflection of 50° in the stream direction was used for carrier takeoff and landing.

Douglas contended that the configuration selected as the result of these aerodynamic considerations resulted in a maneuverable, compact airplane, with reasonable takeoff and landing characteristics, that cruised at a speed of Mach .85 for the combat radius set forth in OS-111.

Weight and Balance

The use of heavy plate construction and high strength alloys, combined with a high degree of structural continuity in the major structural arrangements, enabled an efficient structure which, with a low level of equipment weight, resulted in a high fuel weight-to-gross weight ratio.

Douglas carefully arranged the airplane to minimize the center of gravity travel and to maintain good nose wheel lift off characteristics at high gross weights. The main portion of the fuel was carried in the fuselage, grouped about the wing aerodynamic chord in such a way that fuel management required a minimum of attention to maintain balance with only nominal use of fuel control devices.

		Design Gross Wt (lbs)	Overload Gross Wt (lbs)
Model 1181	Weight Empty	48,700	48,700
	Useful Load	51,300	63,800
	Gross Weight	100,000	112,500
Model 1181-1	Weight Empty	49,900	49,900
	Useful Load	60,100	73,850
	Gross Weight	110,000	123,750
Model 1181-2	Weight Empty	49,741	49,741
	Useful Load	50,259	62,759
	Gross Weight	100,000	112,500
Model 1181-3	Weight Empty	52,191	52,191
	Useful Load	68,809	83,809
	Gross Weight	121,000	136,000
Model 1181-4	Weight Empty	44,325	
	Useful Load	55,675	
	Gross Weight	100,000	

Structures

Wing and Control Surfaces The wing design used thick tapered skin and thick extruded hat sections together with two spars and conventional ribs. The center wing contained 1,400 gallons of fuel in lightweight cells. Particular care had been taken in the proposed wing design to provide large and suitably located access doors to permit installation and removal of fuel cells as well as to allow rapid and thorough inspection of the system controls that were routed in the wing. The outer wing panels started at the flap and aileron junction, and were folded upward and inward by hydraulic power.

The fixed empennage surfaces were similar in construction to the wing consisting of thick tapered plates and extruded hats, spars and ribs. All movable control surfaces were metal covered.

The Douglas double slotted flaps located inboard of the aileron were metal covered and were extended by means of links supported from the wing structure. The outboard 72% of the wing span was fitted with slats. The slats were bussed from one side of the airplane to the other and were operated by the wing flap buss system. Space provisions for thermal anti-icing were maintained in the leading edge of the wing and tail surfaces.

Fuselage The fuselage primary structure was of all metal semi-monocoque construction incorporating aluminum alloy transverse frames and longitudinal stiffeners with smooth aluminum alloy sheet covering. Steel was used in the region of the engines where high temperatures were encountered.

The nose and tail sections were removable from the fuselage center section by means of bolted butt joints. The fuselage nose section, including the crew compartment but exclusive of the nose wheel and radome compartments, was designed for pressurization.

Construction of the canopy aft of the windshield consisted of metal framework with transparent plastic panels. The canopy was normally operated hydraulically for opening during takeoff and landing, and was arranged for emergency jettisoning.

Power Plant The power plant of the Model 1181 consisted of three Westinghouse XJ40-WE-10 turbojet engines, one installed on each side of the fuselage at the intersection of the wing and fuselage, and one located on the center line of the airplane in the lower aft portion of the fuselage. The duct system was as short as was compatible with high efficiency. The air duct arrangement consisted of a single inlet for each side mounted engine and a pair of inlets for the center engine. Each of these inlets had a boundary layer bleed duct ahead of it to assure high ram recovery. The air from these bleeds was utilized to cool the engine sections. Ground cooling and efficient disposal of the cooling air in flight was assured by the use of an ejector around the exhaust nozzle of each engine to which all the cooling air was ducted.

No oil system external of the engines was required since the oil tank, cooler and associated parts were all integrated into the engines. The fuel system was extremely simple, being divided into three sets of tanks of approximately equal capacities so that in normal operation all of the fuel in the airplane could be used in the proper sequence without manipulation on the part of the pilot. In addition to the normal filler neck for each tank, one connection for each set of tanks was provided through which it was possible to fill or empty the tanks in the proper sequence, at the rate of 150 gals per minute. When supplied with fuel under pressure at this rate, it would have been possible to fuel the airplane in less than 15 minutes.

Each engine was completely isolated from the airplane structure by a fume-tight enclosure. Each enclosure was subdivided by a transverse firewall separating the forward section of the engine, where the fuel handling pumps and lines were located, from the aft section which included the burners and turbine. The aft portion of each engine, where high temperature components were located, was isolated from the airplane by stainless steel. In addition, all inflammable fluids could be sealed off by means of shutoff valves. Valves were also installed outside the engine section in the cooling air ducts and connected so that in case of fire, both fuel and air supplies could be stopped by moving a single lever.

TABLE I

COMPARATIVE PERFORMANCE

SPECIFICATION ENGINE RATINGS

	TAKE-OFF GROSS WEIGHT (LBS.)	CRUISING SPEED (MACH. NO.)	MAXIMUM SPEED (MACH. NO.)	COMBAT ALTITUDE (FEET)
DESIRED CHARACTERISTICS	100,000	.85	.90	40,000
MODEL 1181	100,000	.85	.917	42,700
OVERLOAD	111,500	.85	.910	41,300
MODEL 1181-1	110,000	.85	.910	41,410
OVERLOAD	123,750	.85	.896	39,950
MODEL 1181-2	100,000	.90	.970	41,700
OVERLOAD	112,500	.90	.965	40,150
MODEL 1181-3	121,000	.90	.960	38,800
OVERLOAD	136,000	.90	.945	36,900
MODEL 1181-4	100,000	.85	.920	43,900
OVERLOAD	112,500	.85	.920	42,400

	RATE OF CLIMB TAKE-OFF CONFIG. S.L. HOT DAY (FT / MIN)	STALLING SPEED (KNOTS)	COMBAT RADIUS FULL ARMAMENT (NAUTICAL MILES)	COMBAT RADIUS NO ARMAMENT (NAUTICAL MILES)
DESIRED CHARACTERISTICS	500	115	1700	
MODEL 1181	970	110	1510	1610
OVERLOAD	620	113	1810	1910
MODEL 1181-1	680	114	1700	1790
OVERLOAD	594	117	2000	2080
MODEL 1181-2	865	111	1340	1420
OVERLOAD	515	115	1640	1710
MODEL 1181-3	530	118	1700	1780
OVERLOAD	220	122	1890	1960
MODEL 1181-4	625	107	1670	1780
OVERLOAD	520	111	1960	2065

National Archives, RG 72

TABLE IA

COMPARATIVE PERFORMANCE

ADVANCED ENGINE RATINGS

	TAKE-OFF GROSS WEIGHT (LBS)	CRUISING SPEED (MACH NO.)	MAXIMUM SPEED (MACH NO.)	COMBAT ALTITUDE (FT.)
DESIRED CHARACTERISTICS	100,000	.85	.90	40,000
MODEL 1181	100,000	.85	.92	44,720
OVERLOAD	112,500	.85	.92	43,380
MODEL 1181-1	110,000	.85	.92	43,500
OVERLOAD	123,750	.85	.92	42,200
MODEL 1181-2	100,000	.90	.97	44,200
OVERLOAD	112,500	.90	.97	42,600
MODEL 1181-3	121,000	.90	.97	41,300
OVERLOAD	136,000	.90	.97	39,350

	RATE OF CLIMB TAKE-OFF CONFIG. S.L. HOT DAY	STALLING SPEED (KNOTS)	COMBAT RADIUS FULL ARMAMENT (NAUTICAL MILES)	COMBAT RADIUS NO ARMAMENT (NAUTICAL MILES)
DESIRED CHARACTERISTICS	500	115	1700	
MODEL 1181	1228	110	1450	1540
OVERLOAD	870	113	1740	1830
MODEL 1181-1	930	114	1630	1720
OVERLOAD	595	117	1940	2020
MODEL 1181-2	1119	111	1290	1370
OVERLOAD	755	115	1560	1630
MODEL 1181-3	540	118	1690	1770
OVERLOAD	455	122	1880	1950

National Archives, RG 72

Estimated comparative performance figures for the Douglas Model 1181 studies using specification (top) and advanced (bottom) engine ratings.

In the interest of reducing drag during one engine out operation, valves were provided in each main engine air duct to shut off the air flow through the engine if it was shut down. For normal operation, it was expected that all engines would be in use at all times, but these provisions were to maximize mission completion in case of engine failure.

Hydraulics/Landing Gear Boost System

Hydraulics The hydraulic system was similar to that of the Douglas XA2D-1 and operated at a pressure of 3,000 PSI, provided by two engine-driven variable displacement pumps mounted on the wing root engines. The hydraulic system was depressurized when landing gear and flaps were up, canopy closed, and bomb door master switch was off, being actuated to open center by a solenoid-operated bypass valve energized by an electric timer to bypass the system 30 seconds after all handles were in the stated position. Upon operation of any of the aforementioned items, the electrical circuit was broken, closing the solenoid and make the system a normal closed-center type. Failure of the electrical system allowed the bypass to close and the system to become closed center. The following equipment was operated by the hydraulic system: landing gear, wing flaps, wing folding, bomb doors, arresting hook, canopy, and brakes. The landing gear control operated the main gear, nose gear, tail bumper, and air scoop doors, the latter being open only when the gear was down.

The bomb doors were of the snap action type, actuated by a solenoid operated four-way valve. The bomb door system was not pressurized until the bomb door master switch was placed in the "on" position. Actuating the bomb release opened the doors, dropped the bombs, and closed the doors in sequence. The bomb doors were actuated by a separate manual control valve when snap action was not desired.

An emergency hydraulic system provided for operation of main landing gear down, flaps down, and bomb doors. Pressure was provided to this system by an electrically driven hydraulic pump. If either main gear or wing flaps did not extend with the normal system, placing the control in "emergency down" position started the electric pumps and provided pressure to the actuating cylinders through shuttle valves which blocked off the normal system. The electric pump was shut off at the completion of the operation.

Control Boost System The control surface boost system was separate from the main hydraulic system and was also similar in operation to that on the XA2D-1. An engine driven pump was provided for normal operation, and an electrically driven standby pump was provided in case of failure of the main pump or engine. The booster system was of the open center type and provided boost assist for aileron, elevator, and rudder control.

Main Landing Gear The main landing gear attached to the fuselage at three points and retracted aft and inward into the fuselage aft of the bomb bay. A hydraulic cylinder between the fuselage structure and lower end of the oleo strut powered the retraction mechanism. The first part of the retracting cylinder stroke allowed the drag brace to fold. An uplatch fixed to the fuselage structure locked the gear in the retracted position. The uplatch was released by mechanical (cable) means as the landing gear control was placed in the "down" position. The main landing gear doors were actuated by a direct mechanical linkage to the bell crank connecting the gear and doors. The doors were closed when the gear was down.

Nose Gear The nose gear was similar to that of the Douglas R-5D airplanes in mounting retraction. Full 360° swiveling was accomplished by mounting the shimmy damper at the top of the oleo strut. A centering spring and cam centered the wheels forward. The drag brace consisted of two links fixed to the upper end of the oleo. These locking links were held on center by a spring bungee which also assisted in the raising part of the gear extension. To retract the gear, hydraulic pressure was applied to both the retracting cylinder and to the bungee. In the up position, the lock links were forced on center by pressure in the bungee and the gear was retained in the up position by a roller latch which held the locking links on center. Motion of the gear control to the down position raised the up latch roller, the bungee moved the lock link off center and the gear fell. Air and gravity forces were sufficient to lower the gear. Down locking of the gear was assured by the bungee.

The nose gear doors were actuated by a saddle and linkage arrangement similar to that used on the R-5D. Rotation motion of the connecting links between the saddle and each door caused the jaws of the saddle to engage the oleo piston so that the falling gear forced the doors open.

Controls

The general cockpit arrangement of the Model 1181 was planned in accordance with contemporary Navy specifications. Flight and engine accessory controls were provided for the pilot only in accordance with OS-111. A control wheel was used to improve control forces and add comfort for the pilot. To provide clearance for seat ejection, this wheel could be folded against the control column. Conventional rudder pedals with toe brakes were provided. Simultaneous pedal adjustments were made from a convenient hand crank. Special care was taken by Douglas to provide the best control system from the standpoint of rigidity and friction. Special attention was paid to reducing system friction by means of long straight cable runs, large diameter pulleys, and the use of the smallest approved cable diameter. By careful attention to cable travel and design linkage and brackets, control system rigidity was achieved.

The flap and slat operating system used anti-friction bearings for economy of space and to facilitate blow back. When flaps and slats were extended, their linkages were parallel to the air stream. The flaps and slats were operated simultaneously by a common cable system which extended across the airplane.

Cabin Pressurization, Heating and Ventilation

The cabin pressurization system pressure was bled from the three-engine air manifold and interconnected to a single duct which carried the air forward to the cabin. The entering air temperature to the crew space was modulated by a mixing valve controlled by a temperature sensitive element. A refrigerator unit located beneath the floor furnished cooled air from the pressurized area. The refrigeration unit consisted of an after-cooler, expansion turbine, and a coolant air exhaust fan. Coolant air for the after-cooler was derived from a flush scoop on the lower left hand side of the fuselage adjacent to the nose wheel door. The desired normal cabin differential of 4.0 PSI (including pilot selection from normal to combat pressure of 2.68 PSI) was maintained by a cabin pressure regulator. Pressure relief and vacuum relief valves were provided to control cabin pressures. A dump valve action on the vacuum relief valve permitted rapid depressurization in case of emergency.

Twenty pounds-per-minute total air flow to the crew space was required for cabin cooling, and a total of approximately 40 pounds-per-minute at sea level and 10 pounds-per-minute at 40,000 ft was required for cabin heating. The flow at 40,000 ft was limited by a flow control venture in the hot air duct.

The pilot's windshield was defogged by hot air taken from the compressed air duct upstream of the after-cooler. In accordance with OS-111, the pressure breathing oxygen system consisted of three 514 cubic inch capacity oxygen cylinders and three Model 2862-A1 regulators installed in the nose wheel well. One portable oxygen unit was also provided.

Electrical, Electronic, and Radio

The basic electrical system for the Model 1181 had three unparalleled three-phase alternators rated at 30 KVA each. Each engine drove one alternator and switching was so arranged that all loads could be supplied by any two alternators. Three sets of transformers and rectifiers supplied a 28-volt DC system for all loads requiring this type of power. Any two of these units were capable of supplying the total DC load. A 34-ampere hour battery was also installed in the system. For all loads requiring 400 cycle AC power, two 1,500 volt ampere inverters, one operating and one standby, were provided. The APB-2 radar bomb sight had additional inverters rated at 2,500 volt amperes.

Complete flight instruments were installed for the pilot only, as well as control panels for the command and liaison communication sets. The copilot/navigator had the autopilot format stick, radar altimeter indicator, and basic flight instruments as well as cockpit pressure controls. In addition, he had the tail radar indicator and control box, the Loran APM-4, and the navigation receiver and range receiver controls as well as the AC and DC electrical power control panel.

The bombardier/radar/radio operator had the APB-2 radar periscope bombsight computer, control box, camera, tracking lever and basic units as well as necessary instruments for his function. The communication equipment located in the bombardier's compartment comprised the following units: Command ARC-1, VHF Transmitter-Receiver, Liaison ART-13 Transmitter and ARR-15 Receiver, Navigation Receivers ARC-5 and ARR-12A.

The tail radar APG-25 units were located in the aft portion of the fuselage with the radar antenna located at the aft end of the intersection of the vertical and horizontal stabilizers.

The antennas for the VHF Command and IFF units were located in the tip of the vertical stabilizer. The Liaison and Loran antennas were located in the trailing edge of the ailerons. Flush slot type radio-altimeter antennas were located in the fuselage.

Furnishings

The crew of the Model 1181 was located in a single inhabited area of the fuselage permitting direct communication between them. The pilot occupied the most forward seat in the section and the copilot/navigator was directly aft. These two crew members had standard ejection type seats. The bombardier was seated aft of the copilot/navigator and had emergency egress by means of a pneumatically operated door below his station and to the right. Each crew station was equipped with its required instruments and adequate lighting and ventilation outlets. Insulating and soundproofing fiberglass blankets were used in occupied portions as required by considerations of sound level vibration and temperature requirements. No special installations were made for life rafts in the Model 1181 since the seat type parachute used was equipped with the parakit.

Armament

The armament of the Model 1181 consisted of one Aero X11E tail turret equipped with two 20 mm M34 cannons. Ammunition boxes were located in the aft portion of the main fuselage. Ammunition was fed to the turrets by means of chutes running aft to the turret. Armament was in accordance with OS-111 was incorporated.

The bomb bay of the Model 1181 was also in accordance with OS-111 and had a capacity for one 10,000 lb special purpose bomb or any combination of standard type bombs which could be contained within the envelope of 16 ft in length, 60 inches wide, and 66 inches high. Bomb doors were of the snap action type and incorporated a separate control system for opening for purposes of maintenance and loading. The bomb bay was accessible through a 24 inch diameter crawl tube from the inhabited portion of the airplane during unpressurized flight.

Ditching Characteristics

The general configuration of the Model 1181 was such that its ditching characteristics were expected to be satisfactory. The hydraulic shape of the fuselage was comparable to those of other Navy jet aircraft such as the Grumman XF9F-2 and the McDonnell XF2H-1. A volume adequate to float the airplane was contained in the inhabited portion of the fuselage, which was designed for pressurization, plus the fuselage and wing fuel tanks, which were likely to be empty in the event of a power loss sufficient to require ditching. The pilot's canopy was above the static water line, and being of the quick release type, provided a rapid emergency exit for the entire crew.

Producibility

The simplicity of the configuration and general arrangement lent itself to efficient production techniques. This type of design followed the pattern with which the contractor had a long production experience, so that a straightforward approach and an early solution to production problems was assured.

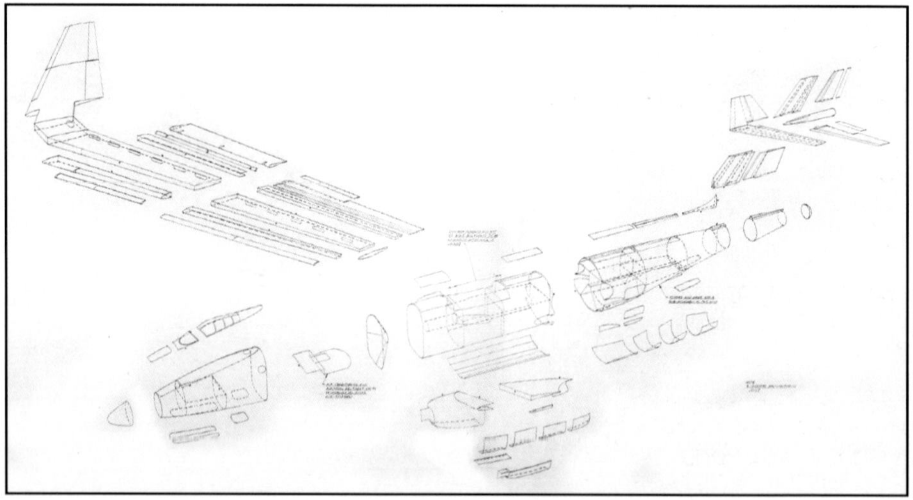

National Archives, RG 72

Structural breakdown of the Model 1181 showing the major subassemblies.

Production Breakdown The structural breakdown of reasonable structural assemblies and subassemblies was well integrated to the requirements for complete installation of equipment.

Structure The detail design practices were similar in principle to those employed on the R-5D, DC-4, and DC-6 airplanes employing predominantly skin stringer panels adaptable to machine riveting for both production economy and quality, as well as adaptable to a greatly expanded rate of production.

Douglas's experience with the 75S aluminum alloy and stainless steel which predominated in the structure of the Model 1181 indicated that their use would not have introduced any manufacturing disturbances, inasmuch as proven techniques, equipment and personnel were available at the Douglas plant.

All structural members included the wing plating were within the limitations of stretcher leveling equipment and the milled plate required for the wing employed only simple taper, scarfs and reliefs.

Equipment The equipment installations fell within the structural breaks except for the wing root power plants. Douglas's experience in master tooling techniques ensured interchangeability with this otherwise difficult production problem.

Alternate Configurations

Douglas also produced several alternate configurations for the basic Model 1181 in order to evaluate the relative importance of variations in design takeoff weight and design cruising speed on the combat radius and other characteristics of the resulting configurations. One alternate was also presented using two Wright TJ-6 jet engines, about which information had just become available even though this engine was not on the approved list in OS-111. General arrangement drawings and descriptions of the Douglas Model 1181 and it derivatives appear on the next five pages, followed by detail drawings of the type's major components.

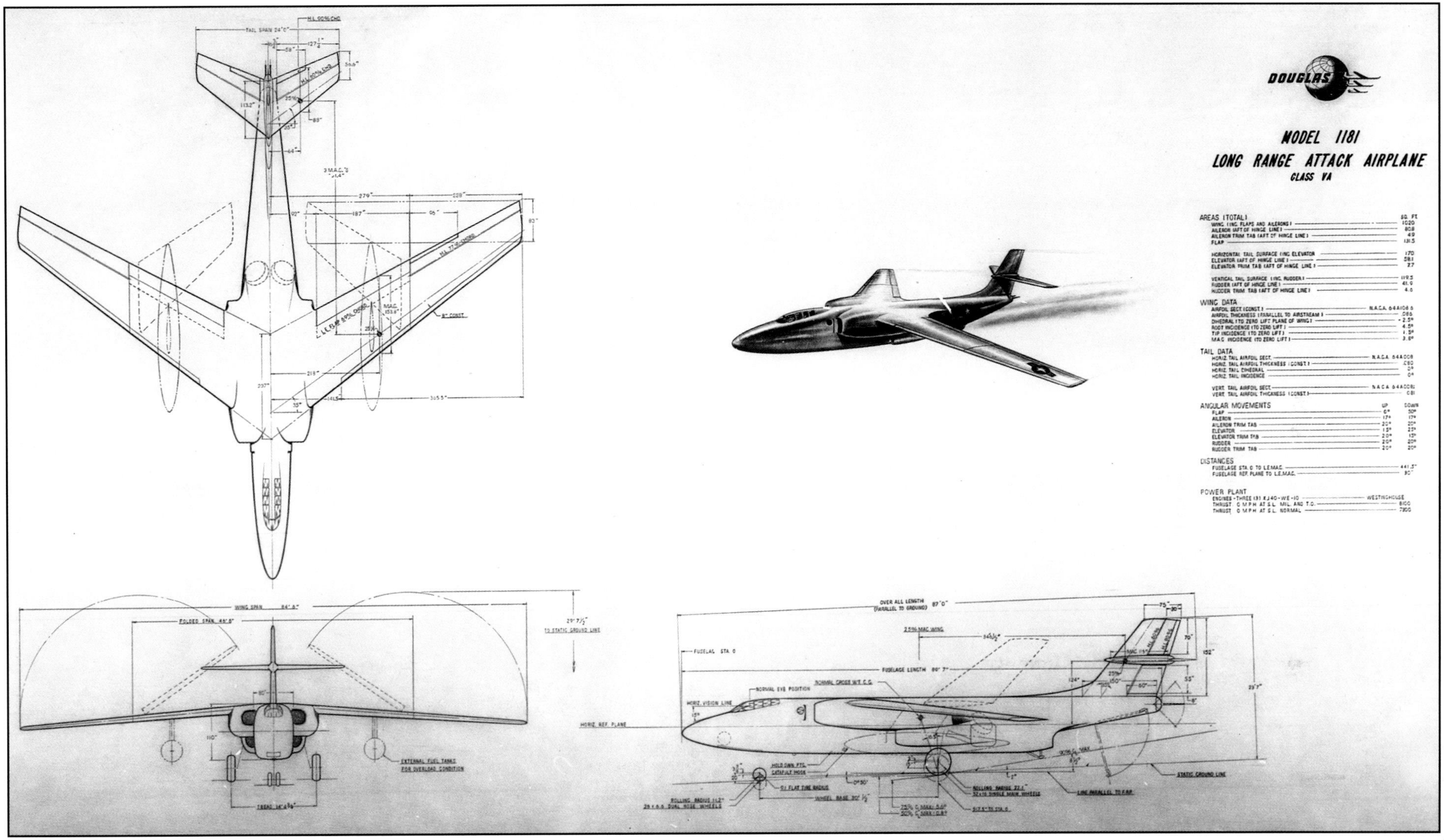

General arrangement drawing of the Douglas Model 1181 Class VA heavy attack aircraft. Key characteristics of the design included a 35° swept wing configuration with an aspect ratio of 7, a conventional tail arrangement with the horizontal surface located sufficiently high to reduce wake interference from the wing; a trijet power plant configuration (necessitated by the meager power of the Westinghouse XJ40-WE-10 turbojet engine) with a rather awkward installation of the secondary air intakes; tricycle landing gear that retracted into the fuselage; and an in line crew arrangement housed under a long, heavily braced canopy. While not the most attractive VA design submitted to BuAer, it was a generally competent design that closely followed the OS-111 requirements.

National Archives, RG 72

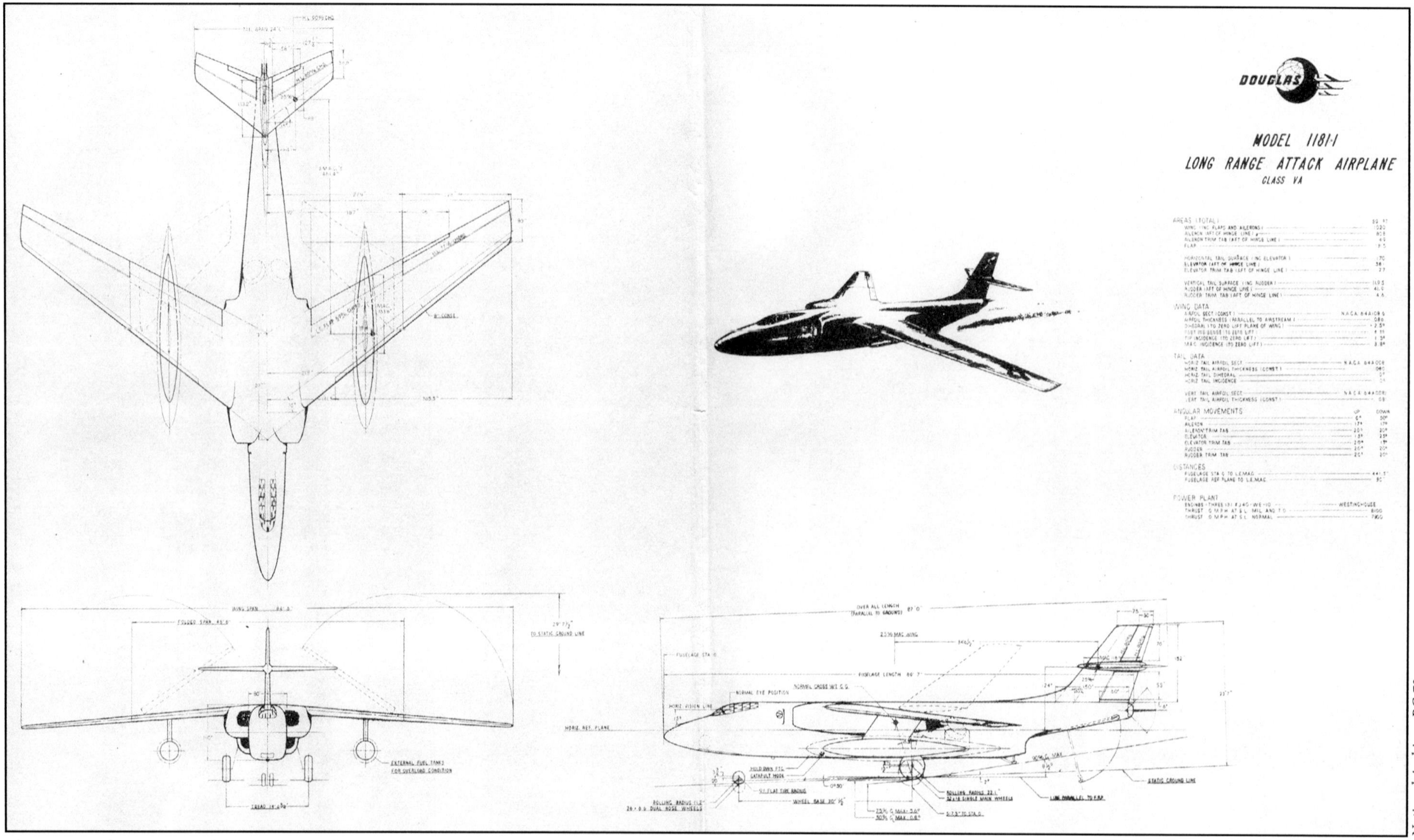

Alternate configuration Model 1181-1 was identical to its predecessor except that the design takeoff weight was increased to 110,000 lbs to permit accomplishment of the 1,700 nm desired combat radius requirement with full armament.

National Archives, RG 72

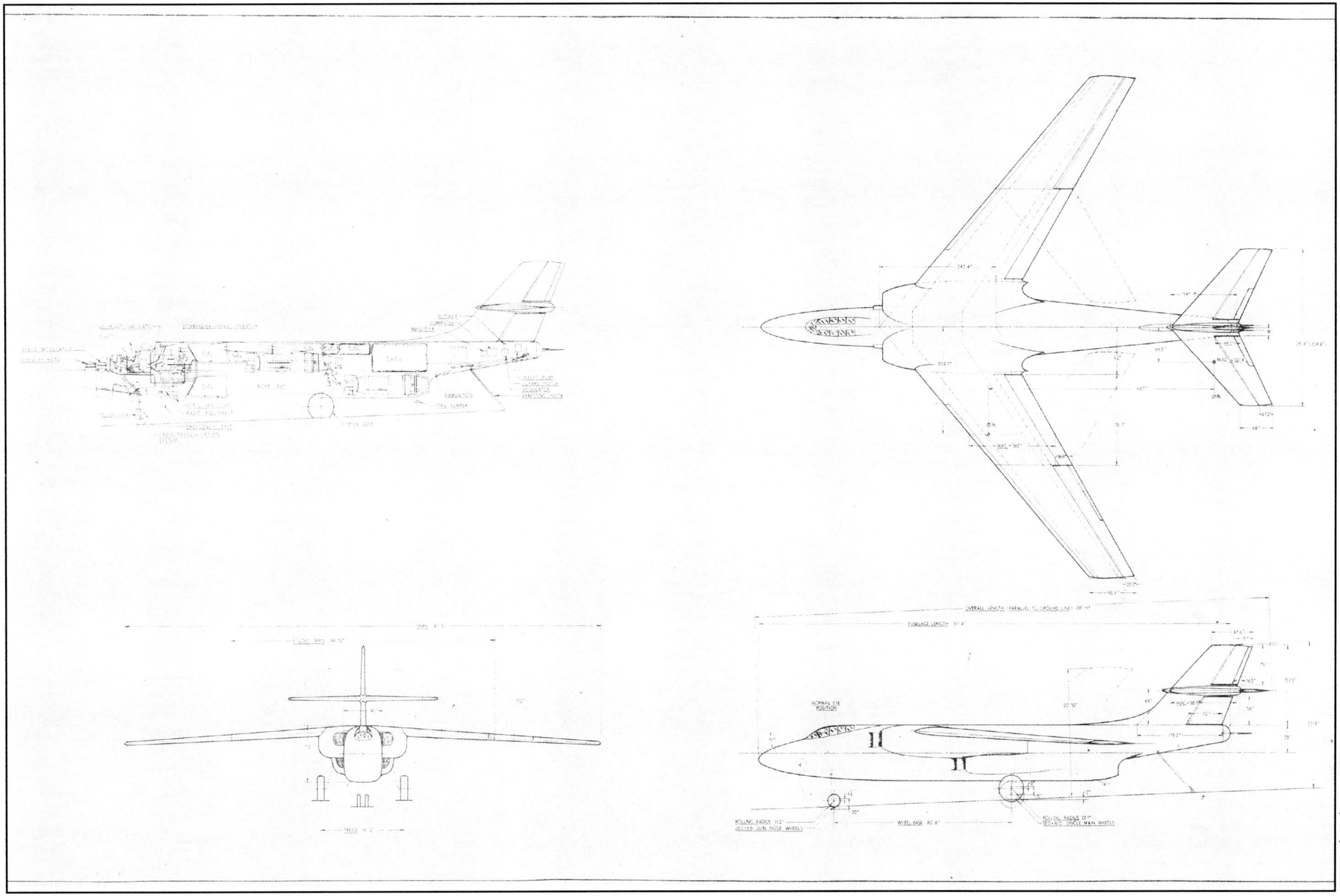

National Archives, RG 72

With the Douglas Model 1181-2, the basic Model 1181 configuration was revised as necessary to permit the cruising speed to be increased from Mach .85 to Mach .90. The wing and tail surfaces were given greater sweep and the inlets were subtly refined for higher speeds.

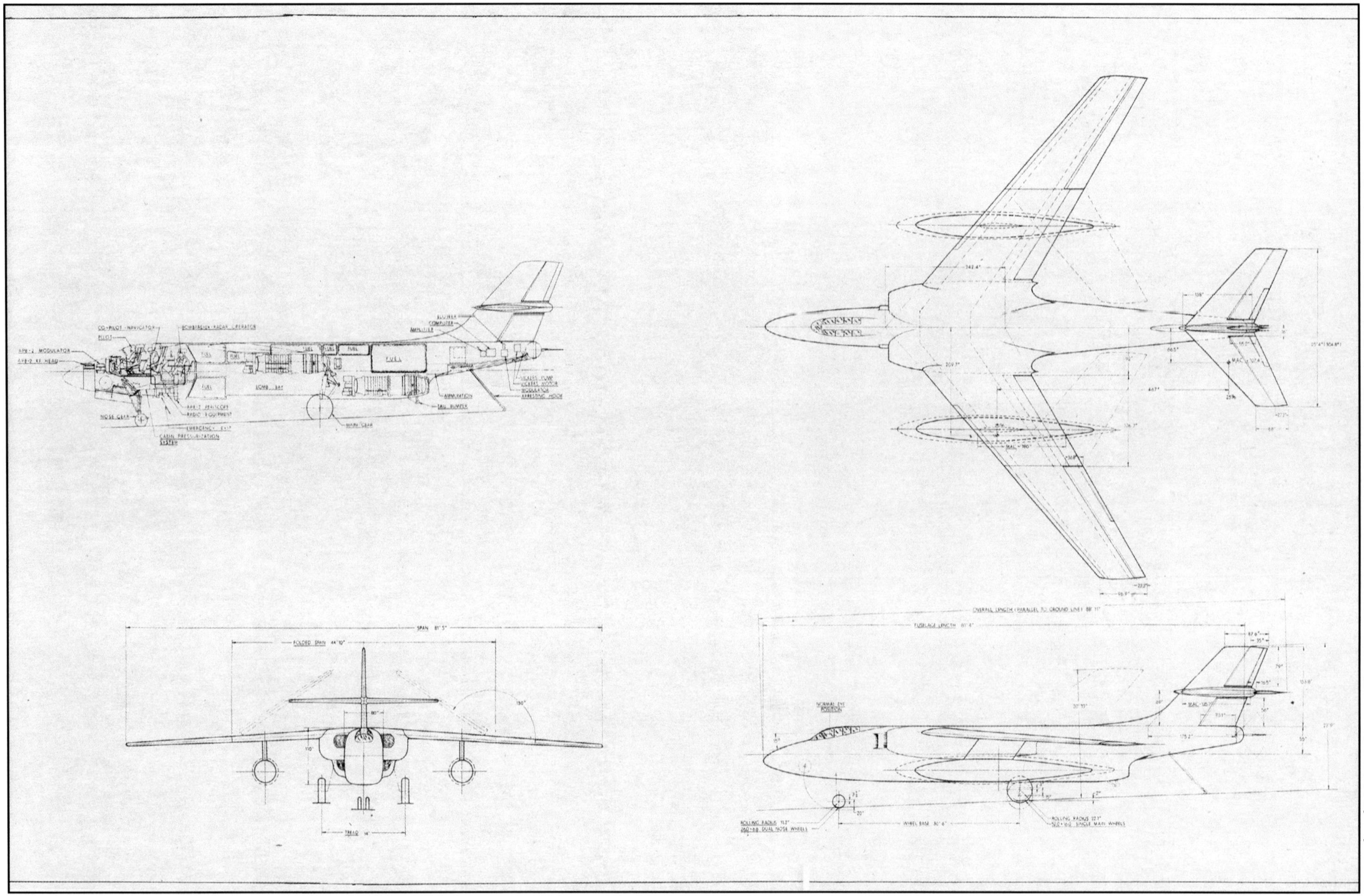

National Archives, RG 72

Alternate configuration Model 1181-3 was identical to Model 1181-2 except that the design takeoff weight was increased to 121,000 lbs to permit accomplishment of the 1,700 nm desired combat radius problem with full armament at a cruising speed of Mach .90.

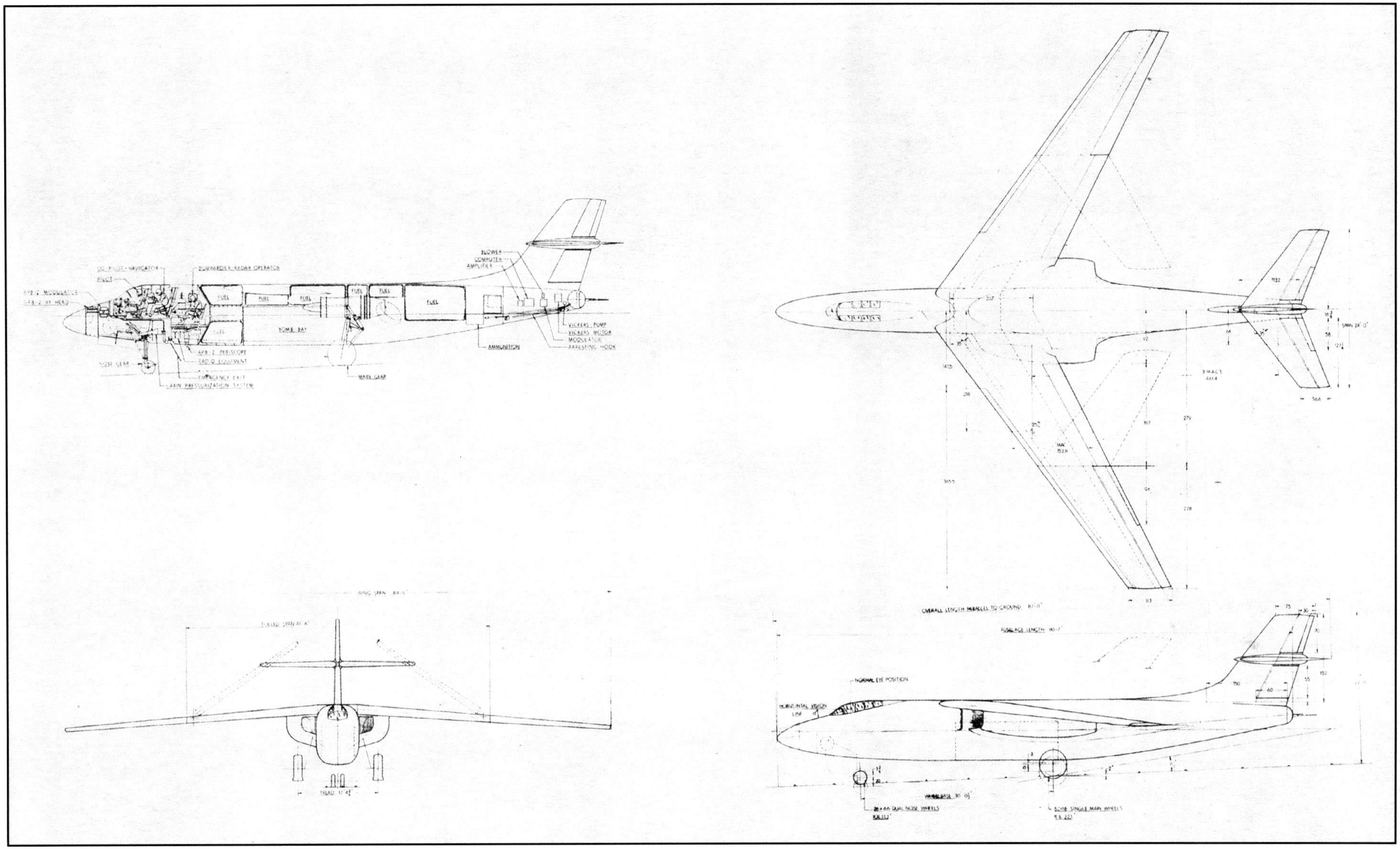

National Archives, RG 72

Alternate configuration Model 1181-4 was identical to the Model 1181 except for the modifications necessary to replace the three Westinghouse XJ40-WE-10 jet engines with two Wright TJ-6 turbojets. While the twin engine configuration was superior to the trijet in multiple respects, it depended upon the successful development of an engine that was still in its infancy and would ultimately be cancelled.

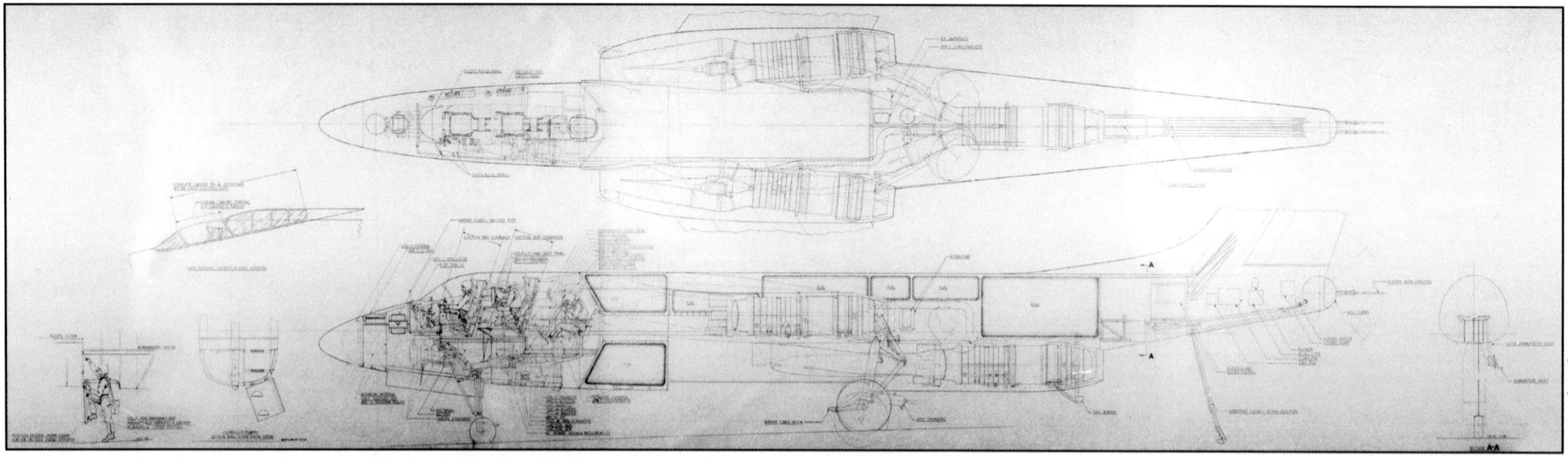

National Archives, RG 72

Detailed inboard profile of the basic Model 1181 showing the major internal details of this very large attack aircraft.

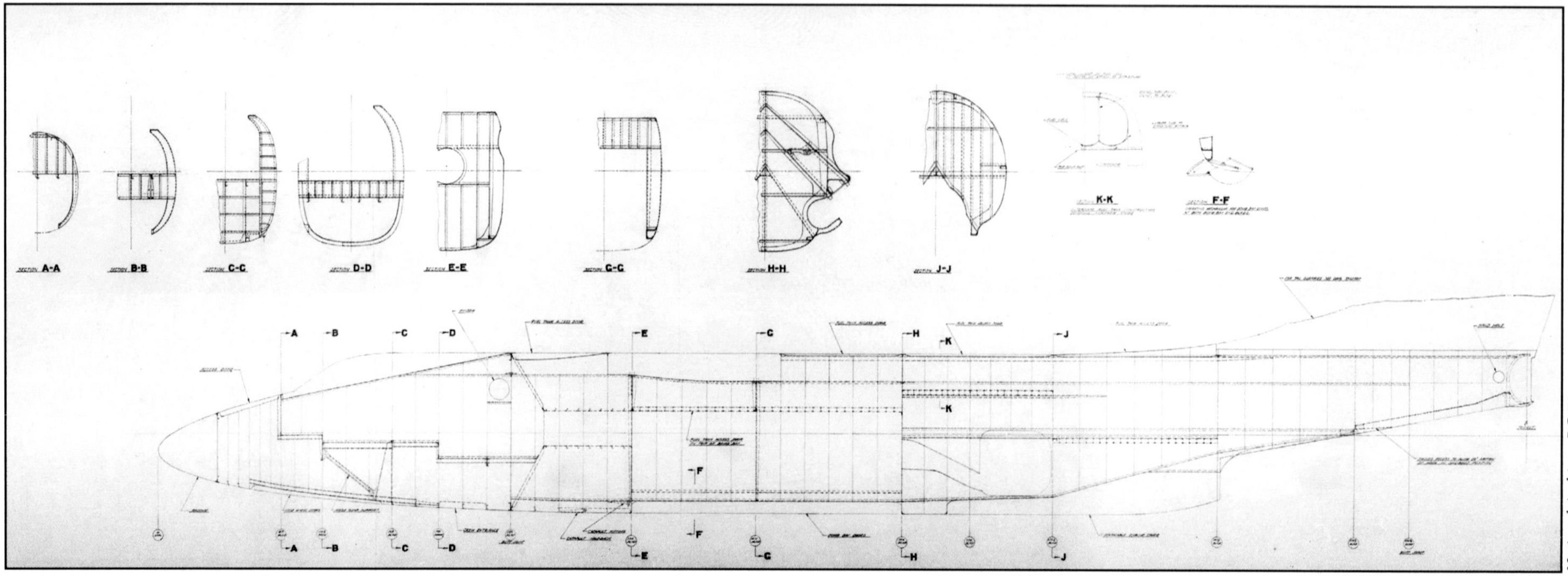

National Archives, RG 72

The basic fuselage structure of the Model 1181 was of all metal semi-monocoque construction incorporating aluminum alloy transverse frames and longitudinal stiffeners with smooth aluminum alloy sheet covering.

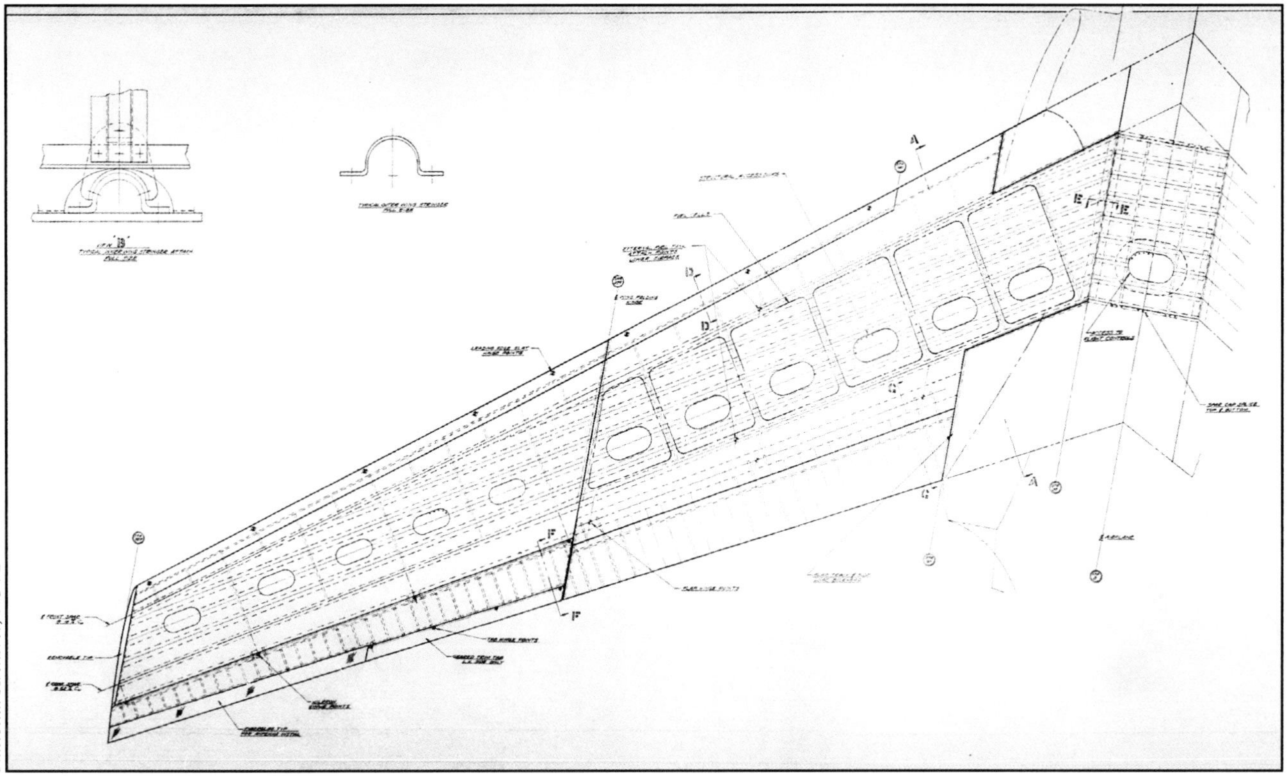

National Archives, RG 72

Left: Blueprint of the Model 1181 wing structure, which Consisted of a thick tapered skin and thick extruded hat sections together with two spars and conventional ribs. The center wing contained 1,400 gallons of fuel in lightweight cells.

Below: The structure of the Model 1181's empennage was similar in to that of the the wing, being constructed of thick tapered plates and extruded hats, spars and ribs. All movable control surfaces were metal covered.

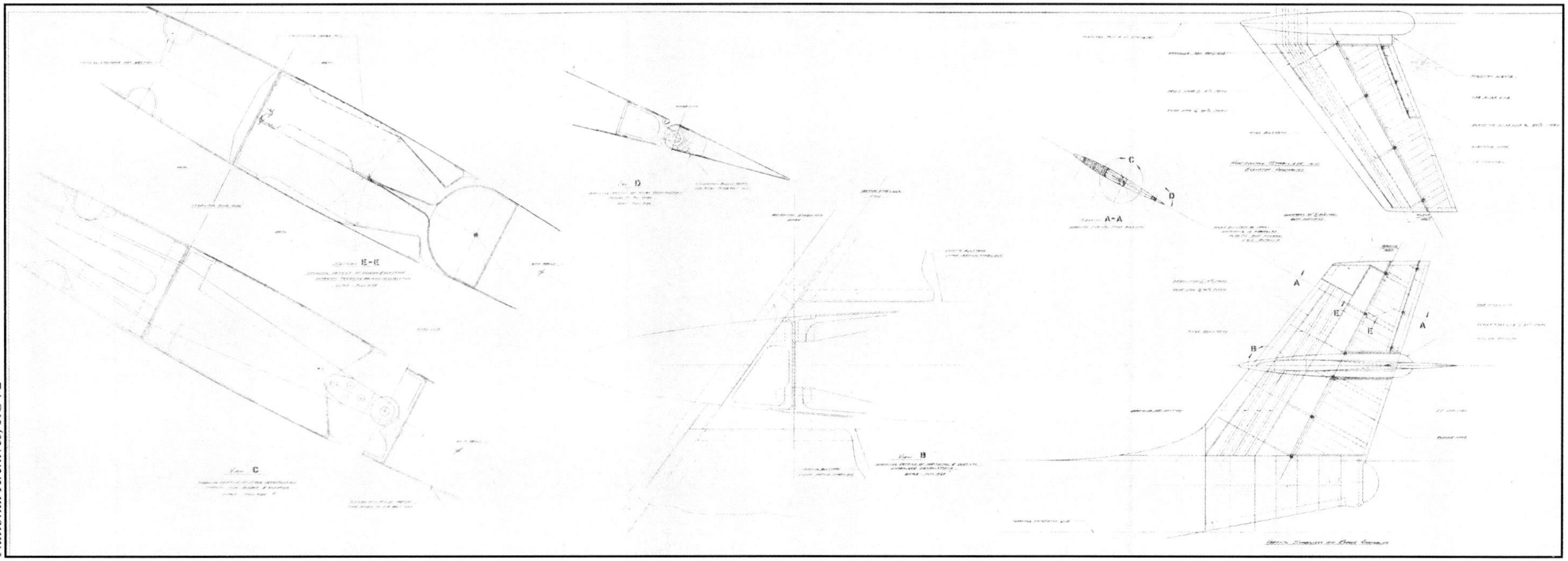

National Archives, RG 72

Right: Blueprint of the wing flight controls. The flaps and slats of the Model 1181 were operated simultaneously by a common cable system which extended across the airplane.

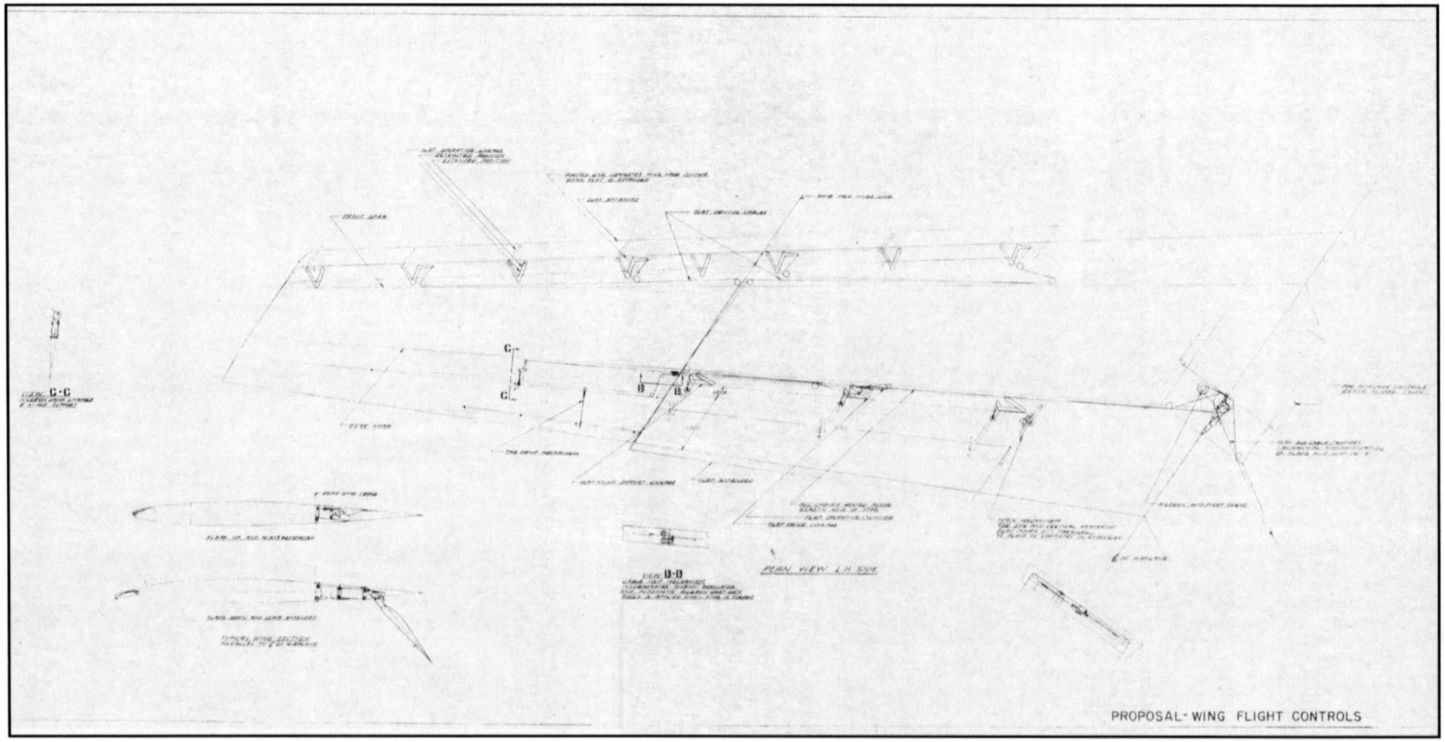

National Archives, RG 72

Below: Diagram of the fuselage accessory and flight controls, which featured long straight cable runs, large diameter pulleys, and small diameter cable to reduce friction.

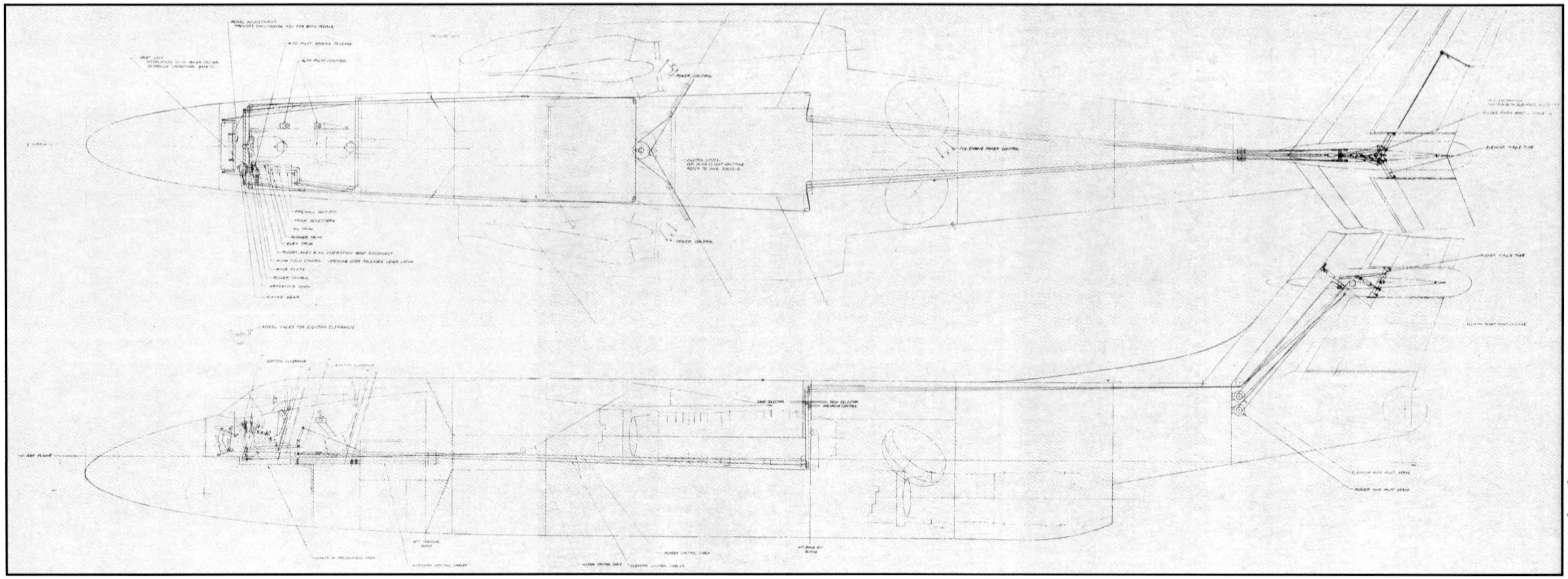

National Archives, RG 72

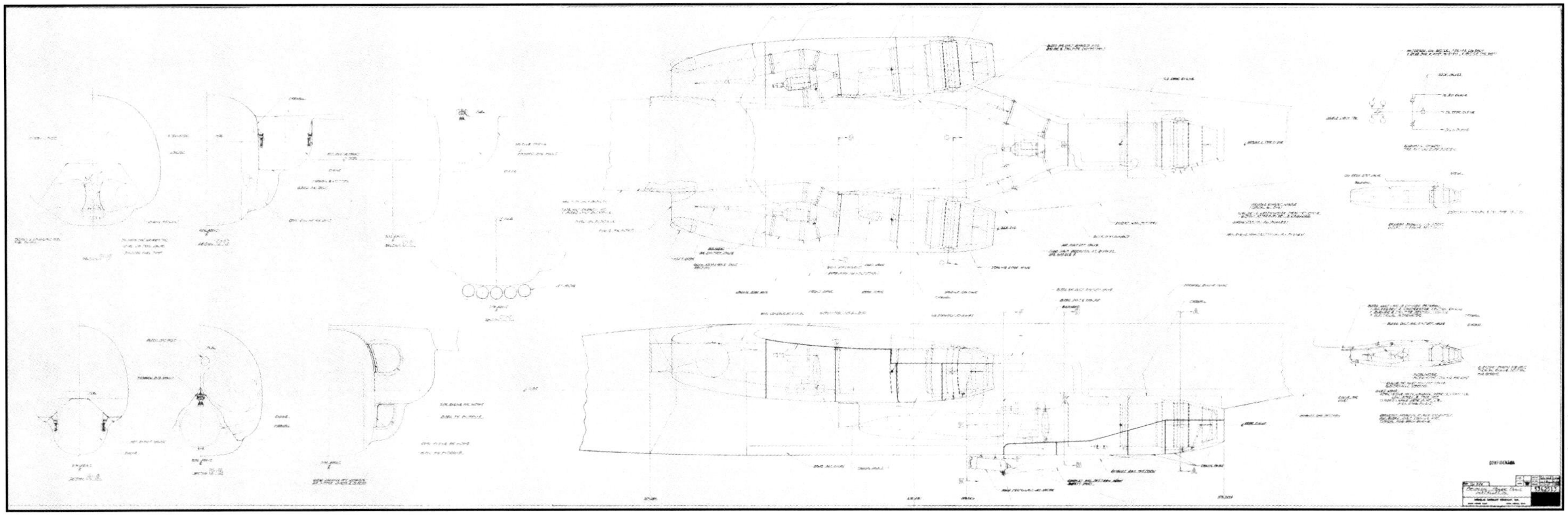

National Archives, RG 72

Above: The power plant installation of the Model 1181 consisted of three Westinghouse XJ40-WE-10 turbojets, one installed on each side of the fuselage at the intersection of the wing and fuselage, and one located on the center line of the airplane in the lower aft portion of the fuselage.

Below: Landing gear installation. The main gear attached to the fuselage at three points and retracted aft and inward into the fuselage aft of the bomb bay, while the nose gear swiveled a full 360° and retracted forwards into the fuselage.

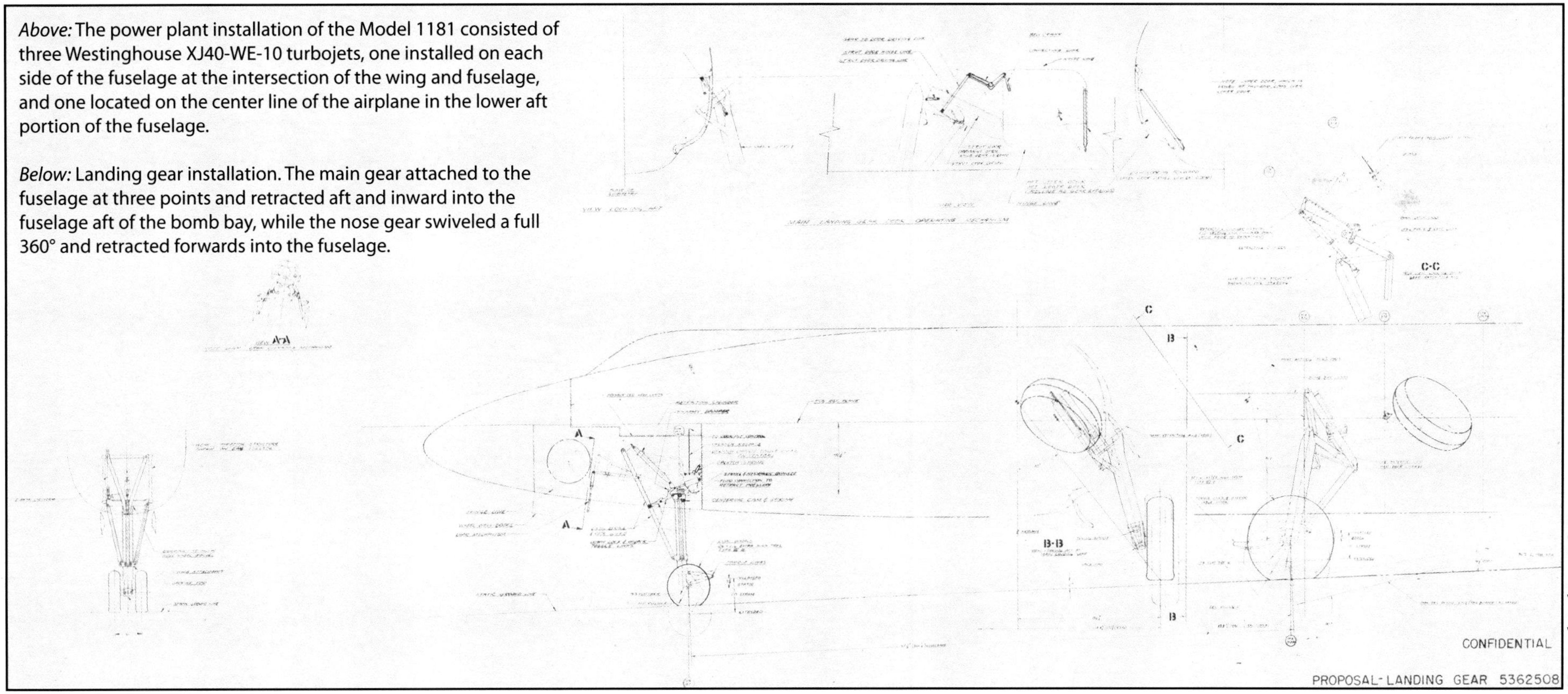

National Archives, RG 72

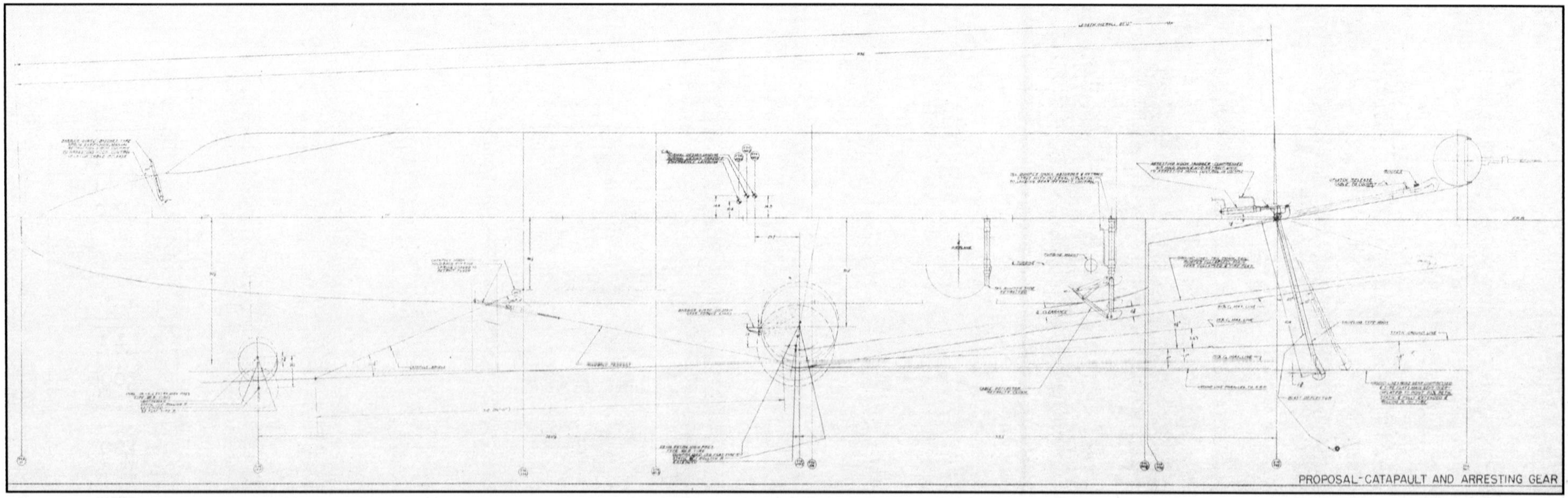

National Archives, RG 72

Above: The Model 1181 catapult and arresting gear arrangement. Note the retractable tail bumper, which was necessitated by the aft location of the arresting hook and fuselage configuration.

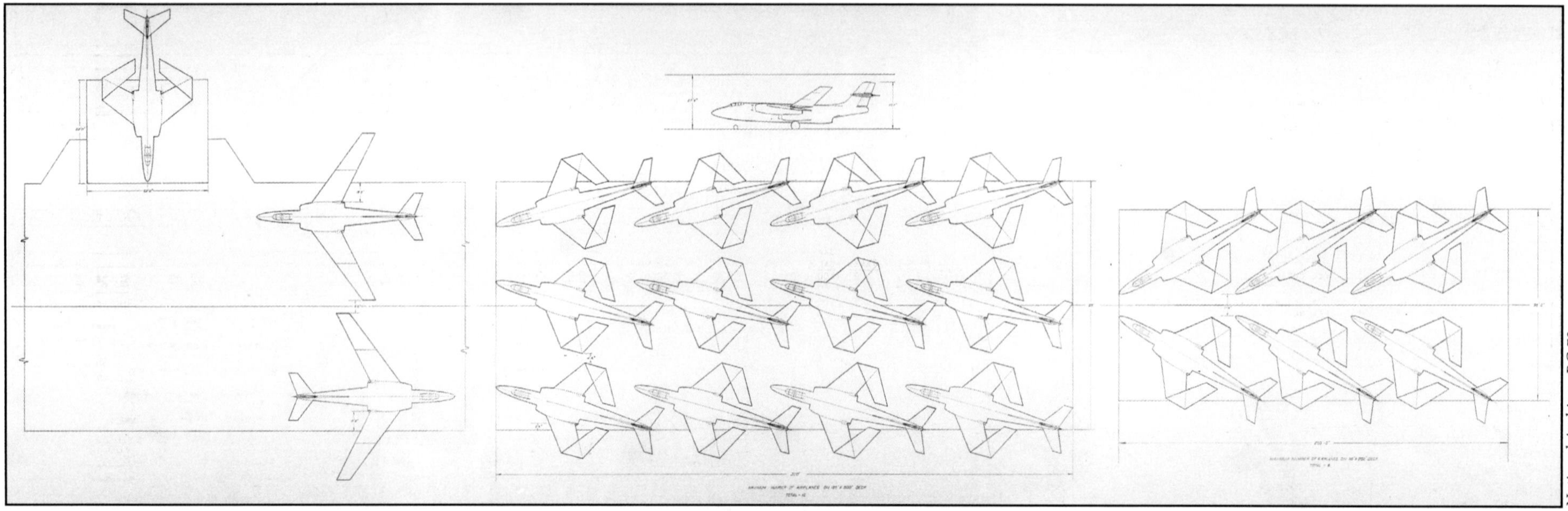

National Archives, RG 72

Above: Douglas Model 1181 carrier spotting diagram. Unlike the El Segundo branch, Douglas Santa Monica only considered the operation of the Model 1181 from the giant Project 6A supercarrier and not the smaller carriers in the Navy's inventory. This would prove to be a critical oversight and undoubtedly contributed to the type being passed over by BuAer.

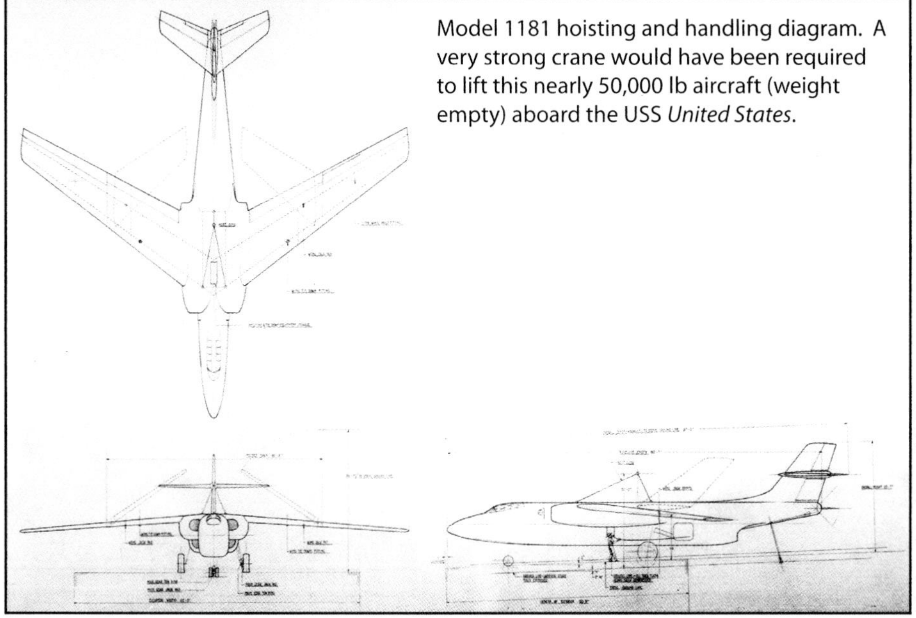

Model 1181 hoisting and handling diagram. A very strong crane would have been required to lift this nearly 50,000 lb aircraft (weight empty) aboard the USS *United States*.

National Archives, RG 72

POWER PLANT

MODEL..(3) XJ40-WE-10 (WITHOUT AFTERBURNER)

MANUFACTURER – WESTINGHOUSE ELECTRIC CORPORATION

SPECIFICATION – WAGT-XJ40E8-2 15 MARCH 1948

ENGINE RATINGS

	THRUST POUNDS	RPM
MILITARY	8100	7260
NORMAL	7300	7260
IDLE	495	3000

Mission and Description

THE MODEL 1181-1 IS A HIGH SPEED, HIGH ALTITUDE, LONG RANGE HEAVY ATTACK AIRPLANE. PROVIDED WITH AIR CONDITIONING AND PRESSURIZING EQUIPMENT, A CABIN OPERATING PRESSURE DIFFERENTIAL OF 4 PSI CAN BE MAINTAINED.

SPACE PROVISIONS ONLY SHALL BE MADE FOR THERMAL ANTI-ICING FOR THE WING AND TAIL SURFACES AND ENGINE AIR ENTRANCE SCOOPS. THE PILOT'S WIND-SHIELD SHALL BE ELECTRICALLY ANTI-ICED.

DROPPABLE EXTERNAL FUEL TANKS OF 1310 GALLONS AND 3430 GALLONS ARE PROVIDED FOR THE 110,000 LB. GROSS WEIGHT AND 123,750 LB. GROSS WEIGHT CONFIGURATIONS RESPECTIVELY.

THE ENGINE OIL TANKS ARE INCORPORATED WITHIN THE ENGINE UNITS.

WEIGHTS

LOADING	GROSS	LIMIT L. F.
WT. EMPTY	49,900(E)	
BASIC	50,565(E)	
DESIGN	110,000	2.25
COMBAT	76,900	
MAX. T.O.*	123,750	2.00
MAX. LDG.**	88,070	3.73

(E) ESTIMATED
* LIMITED BY STRUCTURE
** LIMITED BY SINKING SPEED OF 13.5 FPS AND 3.73 LIMIT LOAD FACTOR

FUEL

LOCATION	TANKS	CAP GAL
WING TANKS	2	1400
FUSE.-FWD.SEC.*	1	1460
FUSE.-CTR.SEC.*	1	400
FUSE.-1ST AFT SEC.*	1	810
FUSE.-2ND AFT SEC.*	1	600
FUSE.-REAR SEC.*	1	1300
EXTERNAL(DROPPABLE)	2	3430
TOTAL		9900

*SELF SEALING

OIL CAP........6 GAL.
GRADE .....SPEC. OIL

DIMENSIONS

SPAN	84.50 FT
LENGTH	86.58 FT
HEIGHT	23.58 FT
TREAD	14.17 FT
WING AREA	1020 SQ FT
SWEEPBACK	35° (25% CHORD LINE)
THICKNESS RATIO	10.1% (STRUCTURAL) 8.6% (STREAM DIRECTION)

BOMBS

NO.	SIZE	TYPE
1	10,000#	SPECIAL PURPOSE

OR

VARIABLE – DEPENDENT ON TYPE OF BOMB WHICH CAN BE CARRIED IN SPACE ENVELOPE DESIGNATED IN SPECIFICATION O.S.-111

GUNS

1 AGL TAIL TURRET AERO X11E CONTAINING 2 GUNS, 20 MM TYPE (M34)

500 ROUNDS AMMUNITION PER GUN.

ELECTRONICS

1	AN/APN-1	RADAR ALTIMETER
1	AN/ARC-1	VHF TRANS-REC.
1	AN/AFB-2	RADAR BOMB DIRECTOR (MKV)
1	AN/ART-13	MHF TRANSMITTER
1	AN/ARR-15	MHF RECEIVER
1	AN/ARR-12A	NAVIGATION REC.
1	AN/ARX-6	IFF EQUIPMENT
1	AN/AIC-4	(3 PLACE) INTERCOMMUNICATION EQUIP.
1	AN/ARC-5	(R-23 REC.) RANGE RECEIVER
1	AN/APN-4	LORAN (PROVISIONS ONLY)

National Archives, RG 72

Above and Right: Standard Aircraft Characteristics charts summarizing the key features of the Douglas Model 1181 proposal.

Basic Mission

RADIUS
Nautical Miles
2010
at 488 knots avg.
in 8.42 hours.

RANGE
Nautical Miles
3785
at 488 knots avg.
in 7.84 hours.

SPEED
Combat ---- Knots
530
at 35,000 ft alt., max pow.
Maximum -- Knots
581
at 12,300 ft alt., max pow.

CLIMB
T.O. Wt. ---Ft/Min
2150
Normal Power at S.L.
Combat Wt.-Ft/Min
6400
Maximum Power at S.L.

TAKE-OFF
Ground run ----Ft
10,700 No Assist
8000 With Assist
Over 50' height--Ft
12,650 No Assist
9200 With Assist

WEIGHT
Combat------- Lb
76,900
Take-Off------ Lb
123,750
Limited by: Structure

LOAD
BOMBS: 10,000 LB.
AMMUNITION: 1,000 RDS. 20 MM
FUEL: 9900 GAL.
PROTECTED: 51.3%
EXTERNAL DROPPABLE: 34.7%
JATO UNITS:
THRUST 14,600 LB.
TIME 12 SEC
WEIGHT 3,000 LB.

CEILING
Service -------- Ft
37,000
100 ft/min., T.O. weight maximum power
Combat--------Ft
44,900
500 ft/min., Combat wt. maximum power

S T A T U T E
0 1 2 3 4 5 6 7 8 9 0 1
0 1 2 3 4 5 6 7 8 9 0
N A U T I C A L

National Archives, RG 72

Combat Radius and Range

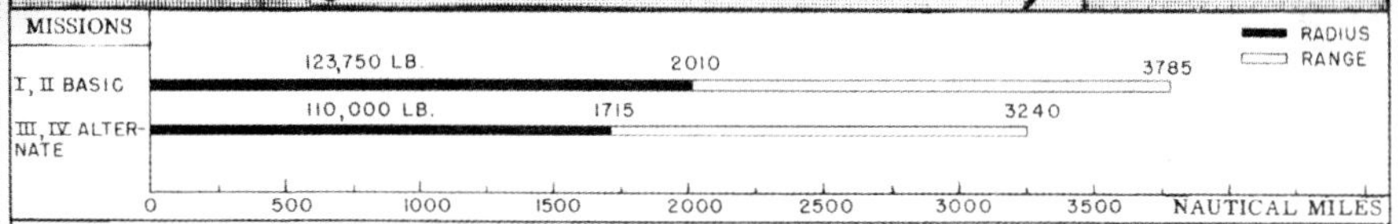

NOTES V FERRY RANGE: 4380 NAUTICAL MILES (5050 STATUTE MILES)

RATE OF CLIMB

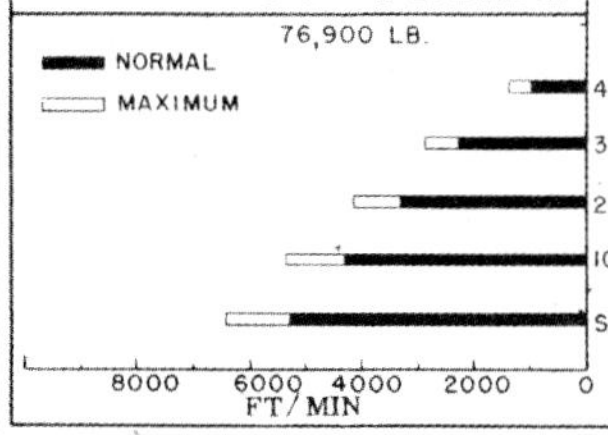

CEILING

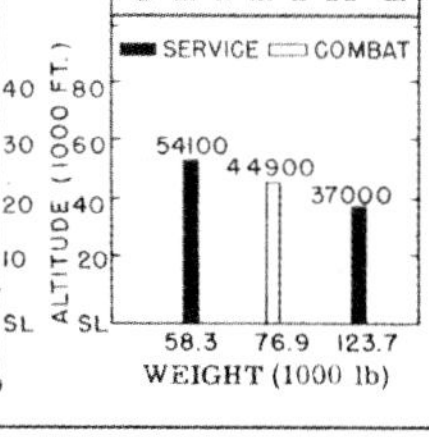

HIGH SPEED

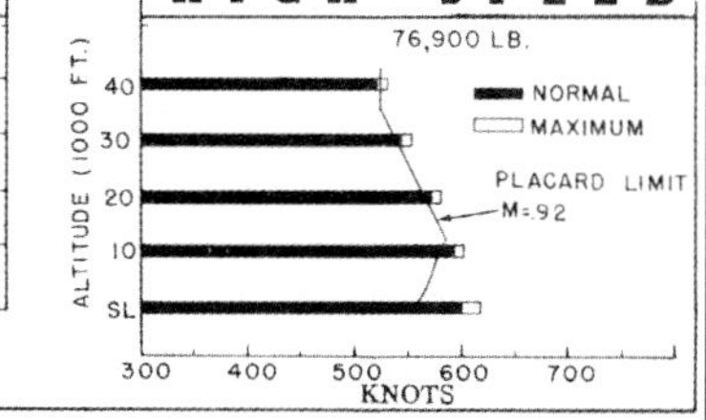

BASE REQUIREMENTS

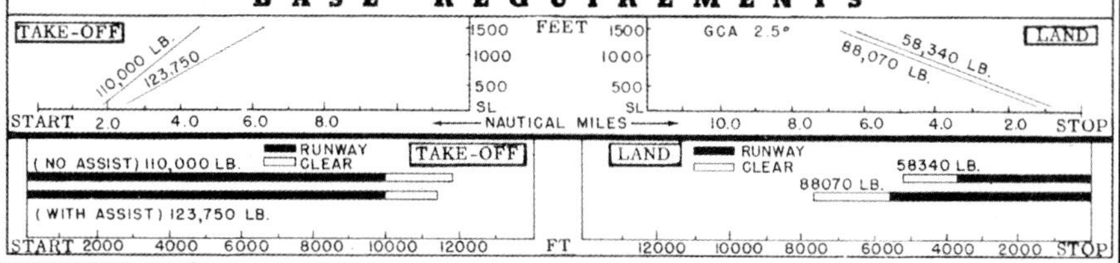

National Archives, RG 72

National Archives, RG 341

Artist's impression of the Fairchild M-121 taking off via a jet-assisted catapult. This unorthodox Air Force bomber project would serve as the basis for the M-128, Fairchild's submission to the Navy's requirement for a carrier-based long range heavy attack aircraft.

CHAPTER 7 — *Fairchild M-121 and M-128*

Fairchild submitted what was by far the most unconventional proposal in the Class VA competition - the Model M-128. It was based on the earlier Fairchild M-121, a bomber study designed to Air Force requirements. Both were largely the brainchild of Armand Thieblot, the talented chief engineer for Fairchild, who had designed such famous aircraft as the PT-19A trainer. The first part of this chapter covers the Air Force project, while the second focuses on the navalized derivative.

The Fairchild M-121 High Speed Long Range Bomber

Sometime between 1946 and 1948, Fairchild submitted to the Air Force a proposal for a highly unconventional bomber designated the M-121. The proposal was prepared in response to a series of Air Force-sponsored Generalized Bomber (GEBO) studies and symposiums. Fairchild recognized the requirement for a high speed, long range airplane capable of delivering a 10,000 lb bomb at 5,000 miles radius of action at speeds higher than 500 mph was particularly difficult to meet with conventional type airplanes.

Fairchild asserted that the main difficulty was the fact that airplane size increased rapidly with speed and range due to the fuel required. Any increase in size required additional power, which in turn meant still more fuel, etc. The practical limit was quickly reached. With other factors being equal, the gross weight of an airplane increased asymptotically with speed and range and the limits thus determined were far below the values required by military necessity.

Fairchild believed that its M-121 proposal constituted a solution not only to the principal problem outlined above, but also to those inherent to the bomb delivery, particularly at high speed regardless of altitude. The objectives that lead to the proposed design were those of the following military requirements:

1. Deliver one 10,000 lb bomb at 5,000 (statute) miles and return (corresponding to a range of 10,000 miles).
2. The target run was assumed to be a minimum of 500 miles each way, to be covered at a speed of 550 mph.
3. Cruising to and from the boundary of the target area was to be done at a minimum cruising speed of 450 mph at the most economical altitude.

To meet the above requirements, it was first necessary to investigate the ways and means of increasing the range independent of the airplane size.

Engine Selection and Power Plant Arrangement At the time, it was generally held that only propeller-driven aircraft could be designed for ranges of the order of 10,000 miles, because of the fuel economy attributed to propeller-engine combination. However, with increased speed and power, the propeller installation became a major problem and anticipated efficiencies at high Mach numbers were progressively getting lower than turbojet efficiencies. Turbojets were therefore selected because of equal or higher efficiency, lower weight and immediate availability. The power plant arrangement of the proposed airplane consisted of 10 Westinghouse 24C units arranged in a circle at the stern of the fuselage, around the bomb ejector tube. A multiplicity of comparatively small engines was selected to permit cruising at full power on a partial number of engines and therefore realizing the greatest economy.

National Archives, RG 341

Artist's impression of the Fairchild M-121 jettisoning its auxiliary wing, which also functioned as a large fuel tank. The wing would have been jettisoned some 2,500 miles from base, at which point the aircraft would have continued on in its mission to the target.

Fuel Storage, Airplane Size The most optimistic estimate on fuel economy, coupled with the lowest possible drag of an airplane of sufficient size to meet the range required, resulted in an impossible aircraft. In other words, for a range in excess of approximately 6,000 miles, the volume available in the airplane for fuel storage did not increase as fast as the volume of fuel required to go further. The trouble was found in the fact, that for the greatest part of the range, an unnecessarily large airplane burning a large quantity of fuel was being flown simply because of conditions at the beginning of the trip. The most efficient way of covering the range required necessitated a variable airplane, adjusted for initial conditions at each point of the trip. This point of view led to a pick-a-back design and the various schemes of refueling in the air through gliders or tankers, previously considered by aircraft designers.

The Fairchild proposal, as a solution to the problem, consisted of carrying an auxiliary, expandable gas tank in the form of a wing. The use of this auxiliary tank brought the actual starting point of the basic aircraft (when the wing had been jettisoned) some 2,500 miles from base and presented the following advantages:

1. Improved takeoff, by increasing the wing area in such a way that the wing loading was lower at high gross weight.
2. Permitted higher speed operation than was possible through the use of gliders

National Archives, RG 341

The bomb bay of the M-121 consisted of a tunnel similar to a torpedo tube from which the bomb would be ejected rearward at various speeds with respect to the airplane. In this artist's rendering, a pair of M-121s is shown in mid-bomb ejection over an urban target.

or tankers.

3. Greater overall fuel economy because of the low drag associated with the auxiliary fuel system.

The basic airplane configuration was such that its significant dynamic characteristics would not be adversely affected by the presence of the wing.

Basic Airplane Efficiency and Design This predominant factor in the general design of the basic airplane had been one of drag reduction to its lowest possible value. The wing planform had a 30° leading edge sweep back and the wing section used had a thickness ratio of 10%, no protuberances of any nature were allowed on the wing surface and nacelles and wing tip tanks were eliminated. The fuselage was made of sufficient size to house practically all the fuel required for the basic airplane, the power plants, and the equipment items required for the mission.

The canard configuration was chosen because of the low drag associated with the disposition of the lifting surfaces and also because the best usable fuselage volume to lateral area ratio could be obtained with this arrangement. In addition, it permitted an advantageous disposition of the power plant and bomb ejection system and reduced to a minimum the probability of collision and interference when jettisoning the auxiliary fuel tank.

In addition to increasing the critical Mach number, the swept back wing planform permitted a considerable reduction in stabilizing surface area and allowed a CG position and travel resulting in 100% utilization of fuselage volume. The wing thickness ratio was 10% for the main wing and varied from 18% at the root to 9% at the tip for the auxiliary wing. The reason for the increased thickness of the auxiliary wing was of course to provide the volume for the fuel capacity required.

The condition of minimum airplane drag for maximum usable volume led to the consideration of a rather large fuselage and comparatively thin wings. The particular disposition of the engines reduced the overall drag through the streamlining effect of the jets, the acceleration of the boundary layer of the fuselage directly ahead of the engines, and the following possibilities:

1. Pumping the fuselage boundary layer through the low pressure area at the center of the annular exhaust jet.
2. Combined boundary layer intake and rammed intake for maximum efficiency dependent upon condition of operation (cruising to target and target run).
3. Use of bomb ejection tube as thrust augmentation unit.

Gross Weights, Wing and Thrust Loading of the Proposed Airplane:

Condition	Gross Weight lbs.	Wing Loading W/S-lbs./sq.ft.	Thrust Loading W/T-10 Units-Statis Sea Level-Zero Duct Loss Normal Rating	Mil. Rating
Maximum with (3800 sq.ft.)	251,800	66.26	8.39	6.3
Normal with (1900 sq.ft.)	154,600	81.37	5.15	3.87
Des. Landing Gross Wt.	70,000	36.84	2.33	1.75

National Archives, RG 341

Auxiliary Systems Auxiliary systems were also a definite influence on the size and the general configuration of the airplane. All equipment items were kept to a minimum consistent with the mission of the airplane. The two most important auxiliary systems were the landing gear and the bomb release system.

If the landing gear were designed to take the full takeoff gross load, it would have been prohibitively heavy, and required additional wing area to carry the weight and additional power to propel the wing, etc. It was again a case of airplane weight empty rapidly increasing with the increasing weight of component parts.

The landing gear of the proposed airplane was designed for landing, only at a weight slightly in excess of the weight empty and corresponding to approximately weight empty/plus crew/plus 15% fuel (basic). The takeoff of the M-121 would have been jet-assisted on a catapult, with the airplane landing gear in the retracted position.

Bomb Bay Arrangement Numerous studies were made regarding bomb release at high speed. In the late 1940s, the principle obstacles were 1) the impact load on the bomb itself, causing failures of stabilizers; 2) the turbulence in the bomb bay, which was likely to cause bombing inaccuracies and structural damages to the airplane; and 3) with bomb release speed equal to that of the airplane, the airplane bomb separation could only be achieved from very high altitude, or through the use of parachutes.

The bomb bay of the proposed airplane consisted of a tube similar to a torpedo tube from which the bomb could be ejected rearward at various speeds with respect to the airplane. The turbulence was completely eliminated, the bomb hitting the air stream at an attitude of minimum drag with its longitudinal axis in the direction of motion. The bomb's velocity with respect to the ground could be controlled though the agent considered for the ejection, i.e., compressed air, catapult, slow burning powder, etc. Armand Thieblot and Roger W. Davis obtained US Patent no. 2,714,999 for this concept.

Fabrication and Maintenance In view of the fact that great stress had been laid on the fabrication and maintenance of combat aircraft, the airplane was designed with this ideal in mind. The airplane was fabricated in three basic parts: the central structure section, the forward bolted crew and equipment section and the rear power plant section.

The structural section was primarily built around a central core (bomb tunnel) enclosed between two vertical, longitudinal members, in the walls of which were housed all controls, wiring and plumbing, added access doors to the landing gear, engine accessories, and auxiliary wing and takeoff gear fittings, accessible for inspection or maintenance on the ground or during flight. The main spar frames formed a box section which efficiently transferred the gross overload condition of the auxiliary wing tanks directly to the auxiliary takeoff gear. The main wing, man and nose landing gear, engine mount forgings, and vertical surface members bolted directly to this section. The air intake cowling was bolted directly to the external skin. The individual engine was fastened to the engine mount members, allowing maintenance or replacement with the minimum amount of labor. The monocoque nose section housed the crew and equipment and was fully pressurized.

In the initial proposal, Fairchild indicated that provision could be made for jettisoning the entire section in case of emergency. Later, the company refined this idea, making the crew compartment completely jettisonable as an emergency escape system. The escape sequence was initiated by the shut-down of all engines, jettisoning the canard control surfaces, pyrotechnic separation of the nose section from the fuselage, extension of stabilizing fins, and the deployment of deceleration parachutes. The crew would have then abandoned the crew compartment using their individual parachutes.

Summary of Design The Fairchild M-121's purpose was to deliver a bomb load to a target sufficiently remote from the takeoff point to offer coverage of large areas of the earth's surface from any one base. Such range in a conventional bomber was obtained at a relatively low cruising speed. This airplane was intended to cruise at speeds sufficiently high to appreciably cut down the time to arrive at the target. In its target approach configuration, the M-121 had the performance of a fighter aircraft, which reduced its vulnerability to interception by enemy aircraft and anti-aircraft defenses.

In order to carry sufficient fuel for the long range offered, it was necessary to attach an auxiliary wing. Extra lift for sustained flight with auxiliary fuel was thereby afforded. Upon depletion of the fuel supply from the auxiliary wing, it was jettisoned. The airplane was then able to proceed to the target at a higher operating speed. Since the large fuel

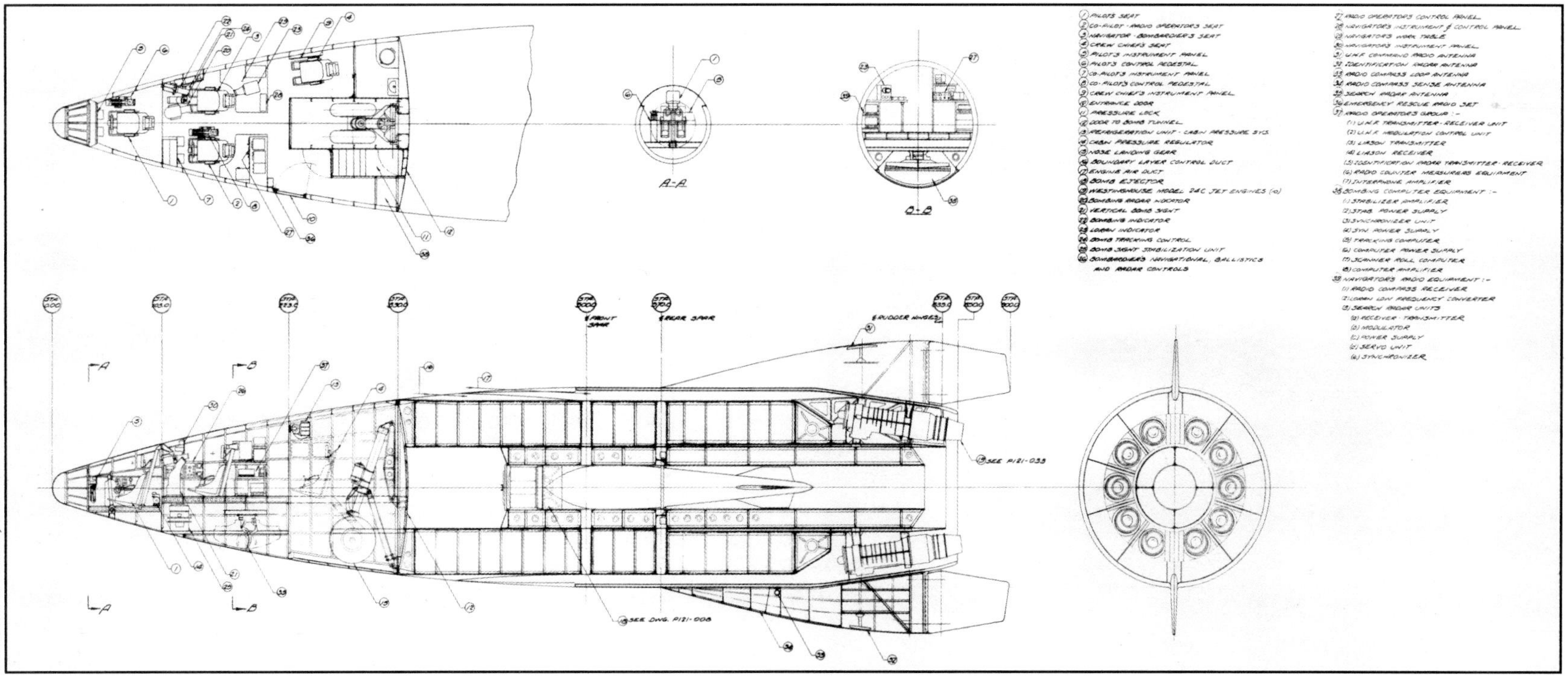

National Archives, RG 341

Inboard profile of the M-121. The circular arrangement of 10 Westinghouse 24C turbojets at the stern of the fuselage was but one of the radical features of this singular design.

National Archives, RG 341

Perspective cutaway illustration of the Fairchild M-121. This view emphasizes the bomber's large, streamlined greenhouse canopy which integrated into its projectile-like fuselage.

load would have been consumed by the time of landing after accomplishment of the mission, the wing loading would have been sufficiently low to allow a normal landing.

The design of the M-121 permitted a then-new bomb-dropping technique. Since it was propelled by turbojet engines mounted in a circular bank at the rear of the fuselage, a port was available at the center of the engine group. The bomb load could be ejected aft through this port without slowing down the airplane. The crew and airplane, therefore, were both better protected while in the target area. The period of time necessary for the bombardier to adjust his bomb launching control equipment was substantially reduced, as the airplane did not require retrimming when the bomb port was opened and before the bomb load was released. More accurate bomb drops were possible because of controlled conditions of the bomb ejection. These controlled conditions permitted duplication of bomb-load ejection on all missions.

With the M-121's sweptback wing and forward canard (called a "trimmer" by Fairchild), full utilization of the fuselage volume was possible. The crew compartment at the front gave optimum visibility. The cabin was pressurized. Boundary layer control was provided by an annular duct for removing the forward fuselage boundary layer. The basic structure was of conventional design using high strength alloys where possible to minimize weight.

This airplane was intended to effectively meet the requirements for a long range, high speed, bomb carrier suitable for tactical use by the United States Air Force.

Special Considerations It was possible to take off using the basic landing gear at a maximum takeoff gross weight of 81,600 lbs. This weight was based on maintaining a takeoff load factor of 3.0 as compared to the landing load factor of 3.5. With this loading, the airplane would have had the following takeoff and cruising performance with a crew of four:

Configuration		Clean	Aux. Wing On
Take-off Gross Wt.,	lbs.	81,600	81,600
Internal Fuel,	gal.	4,670	2,728
Take-off Distance over 50 Ft. Obst.	ft.	1,955	1,175
Max. Range with No Allowances,	mi.	3,120	1,310
Cruise Speed/Flt. Time	mph hr.	520/6.0	395/3.40
Range with Allowances for Warm-up, Take-off, Climb to Altitude,	mi.	2,430	722
Cruise Speed/Flt. Time	mph hr.	530/4.57	410/1.80

National Archives, RG 341

A special gear could be provided to allow operation without use of the dolly up to gross weights of 150,000 lbs for both takeoff and landing. Negligible additional built in structural weight penalties were involved; the only additional weight was in the gear itself. The gear would have been fully retractable in flight. With this gear installed, the airplane would have had the following takeoff and cruising performance with a crew of four:

Configuration		Clean	Aux. Wing On
Take-off Gross Wt.,	lbs.	150,000	150,000
Internal Fuel,	gal.	15,086	13,145
Take-off Distance over 50 ft. Obst.	ft.	5,945	3,215
Range with Allowances for Warm-up, Take-off Climb to Altitude	mi.	7,240	4,080
Cruise Speed/Flt. Time	mph hr.	495/14.58	420/10.22

National Archives, RG 341

The airplane could be landed with the auxiliary wing on if the fuel load in the auxiliary wing did not exceed 2,800 gallons (approximately 20% of auxiliary fuel capacity). Fairchild also considered wing tip fuel dumping as a rapid means of reducing the fuel load of the wing.

The auxiliary wing could also be jettisoned with fuel not exceeding 2,800 gallons (approximately 20% of auxiliary fuel capacity). Wing tip fuel dumping provisions were again considered for this case.

The clean airplane loaded to normal takeoff gross weight with bomb load was capable of a radius of action of 3,700 miles (15.63 hours flight time) with proper allowances for warm-up, takeoff, and climb. The bomb was dropped at mid-point.

For a long range mission loaded to the maximum takeoff gross weight of 251,800 lbs, the proper operational procedure was to utilize auxiliary fuel first and jettison the wing as quickly as possible. With this loading, the auxiliary fuel would have been exhausted after a distance of 2,400 miles from base. Since the total radius of action with the wing on at all times was 3,700 miles at the takeoff condition of 251,800 lbs, the airplane would still have had more than ample fuel to return to base.

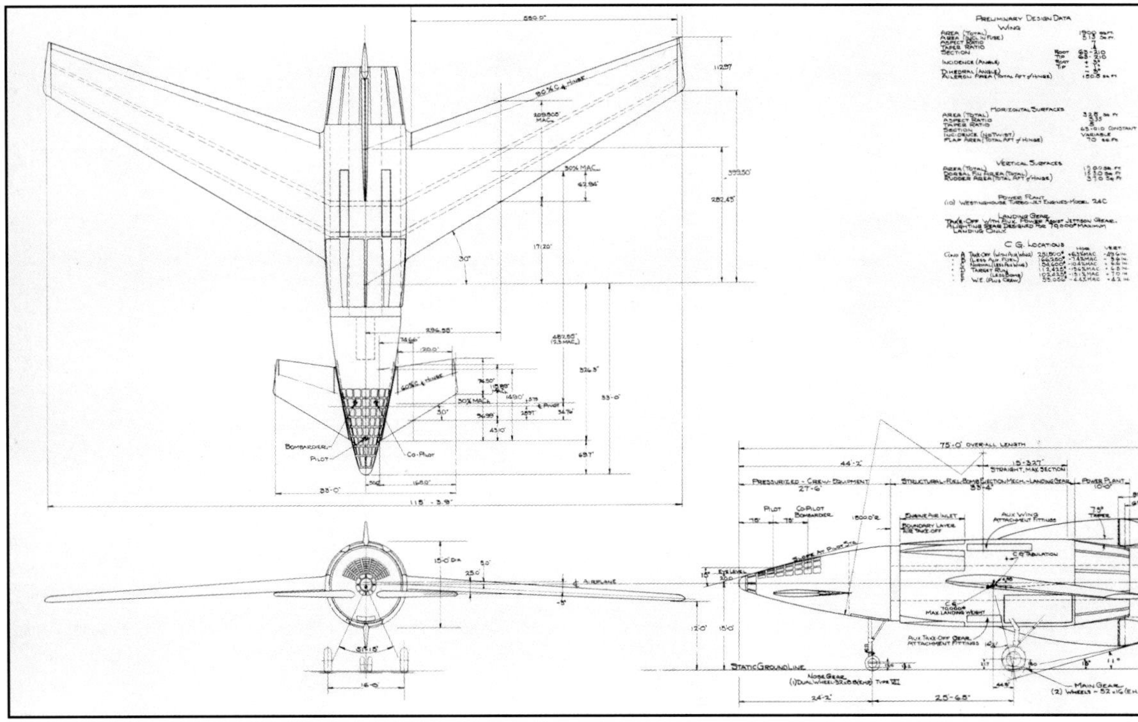

General arrangement drawing of the Fairchild M-121.

National Archives, RG 341

Further Developments Fairchild subsequently proposed the interchange of nose sections and the addition of associated equipment, converting the bomber to a reconnaissance aircraft or fighter escort. In the reconnaissance configuration, the nose section stations could accommodate K-22A and A-10 forward oblique cameras; K-17C, K-22A, K-37, K-38 vertical (stabilized mount) cameras; K-38, K-40 multi-camera; K-17C tri-metrogon; K-22A and K-38 right and left oblique cameras; K-37 and K-38 split vertical cameras; and a O-15 radar scope camera.

In the fighter escort configuration, the airplane's single bomb was replaced by a 16,000 lb thrust liquid oxygen JP-3 fuel "combat booster rocket engine" for high speed dashes. Its armament consisted of four 20 mm M-24 guns and 24 five-inch HVAR rockets or 24 Falcon air-to-air missiles.

Another M-121 variant was a refueling tanker. As a tanker, it would have been stationed at forward bases to refuel other M-121 bombers that had taken off from distant atomic bomb source bases. It could have also been used to refuel high speed fighter aircraft on special missions. Unfortunately, the author has been unable to locate drawings of these intriguing variants of the M-121.

The Air Force initially expressed interest in the Fairchild M-121, but dropped it due to the risks inherent in a design with so many unconventional features and the company's lack of experience in the construction of large bombers.

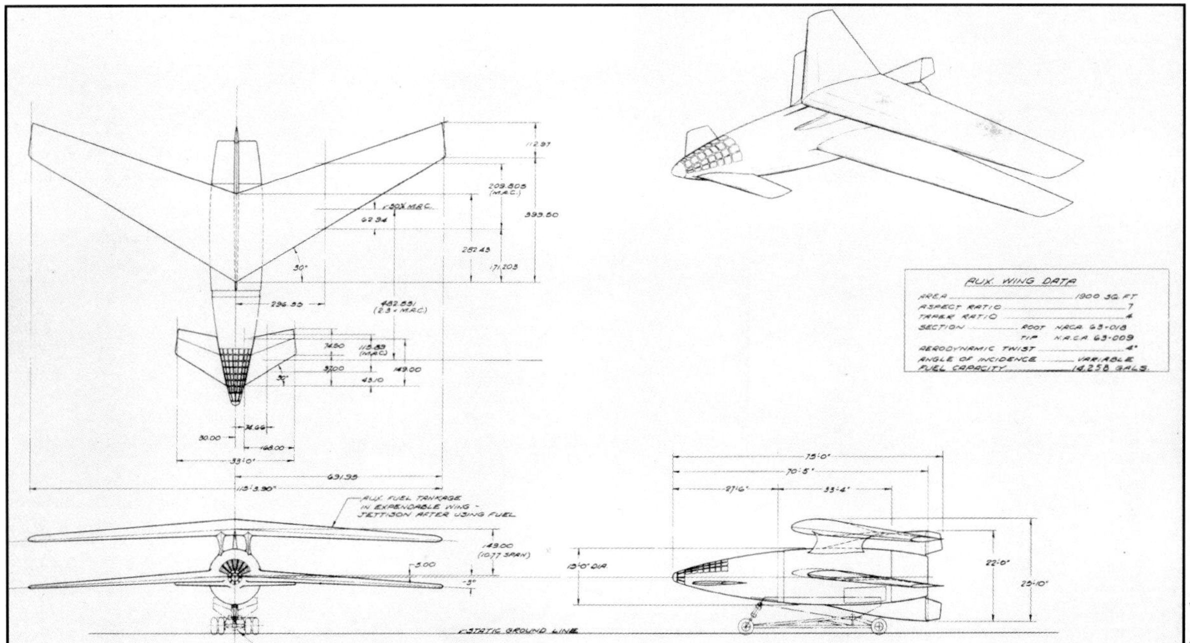

Three-view of the Fairchild M-121 with auxiliary wing and fuselage handling gear.

National Archives, RG 341

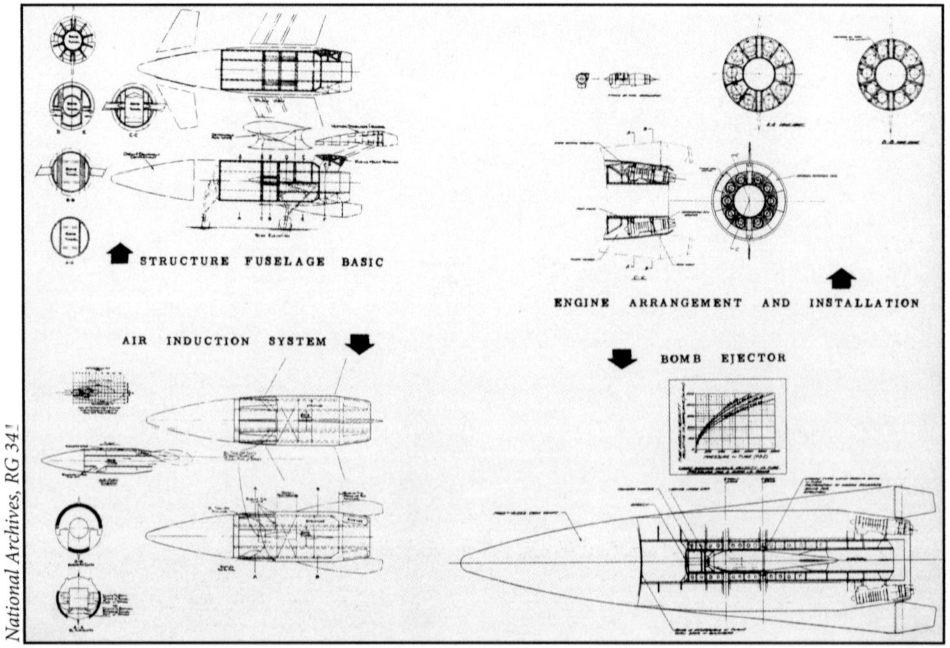

Above: Detail drawings of the M-121's basic fuselage structure, air induction system, engine installation, and bomb ejection system.

National Archives, RG 341

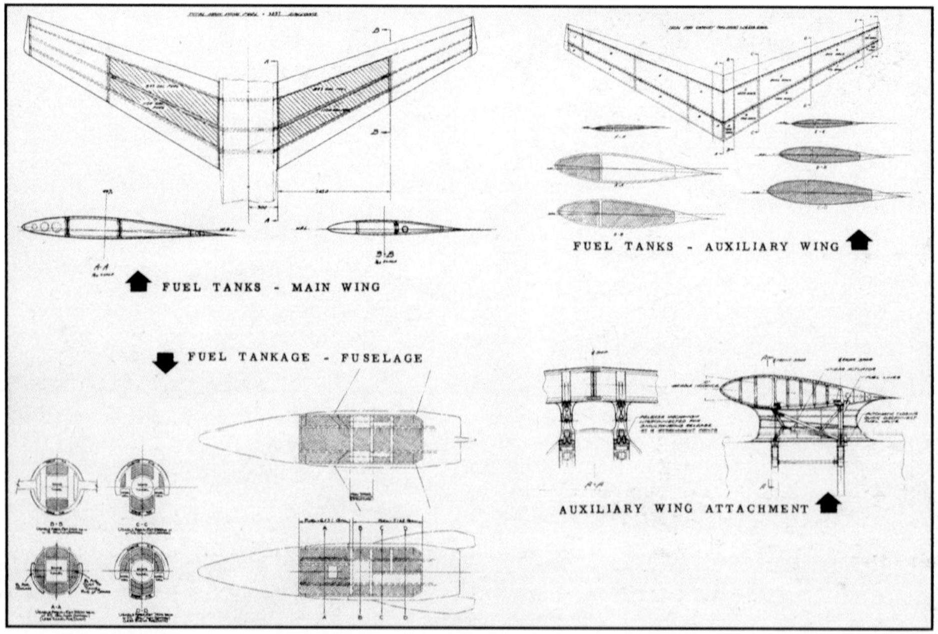

Above: These detail drawings of the M-121 show the bomber's fuel system and attachment of the auxiliary wing.

National Archives, RG 341

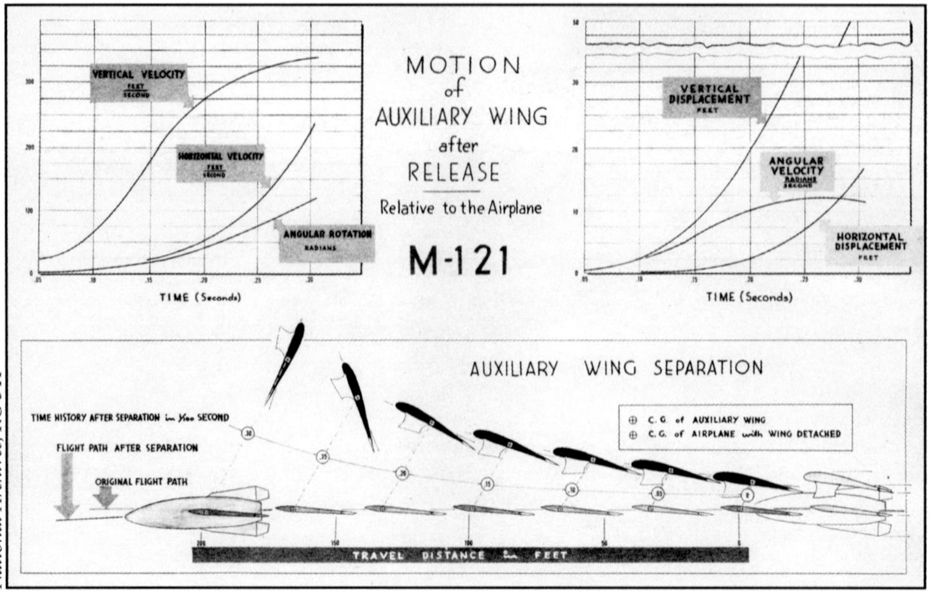

Above: Plots and a diagram showing in-flight separation of the auxiliary wing from the M-121.

National Archives, RG 341

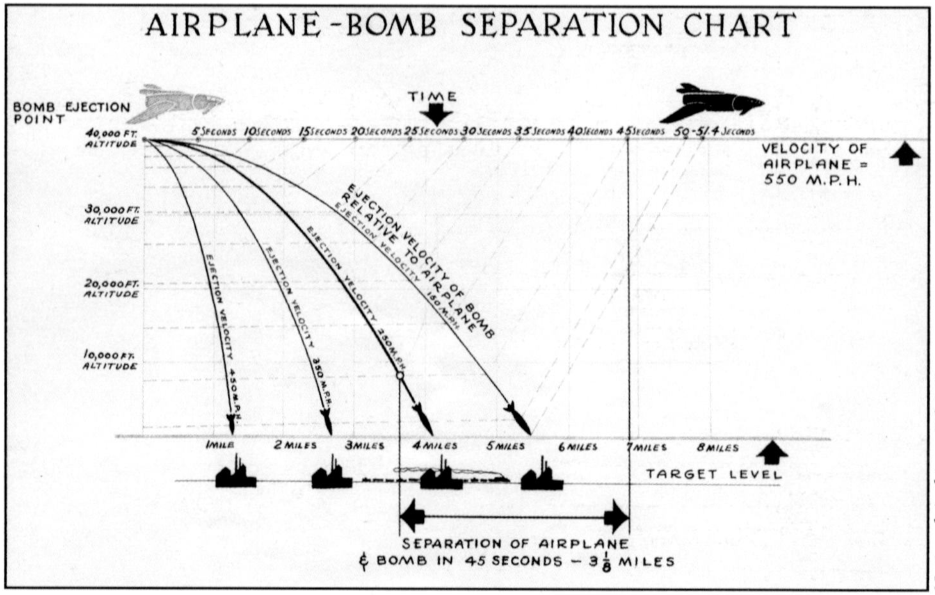

Above: This airplane-bomb separation chart shows that the M-121 was capable of ejecting a bomb rearward at various speeds with respect to the airplane. The bomb's velocity relative to the ground was to have been controlled through compressed air, catapult, slow burning powder, or other agents.

National Archives, RG 341

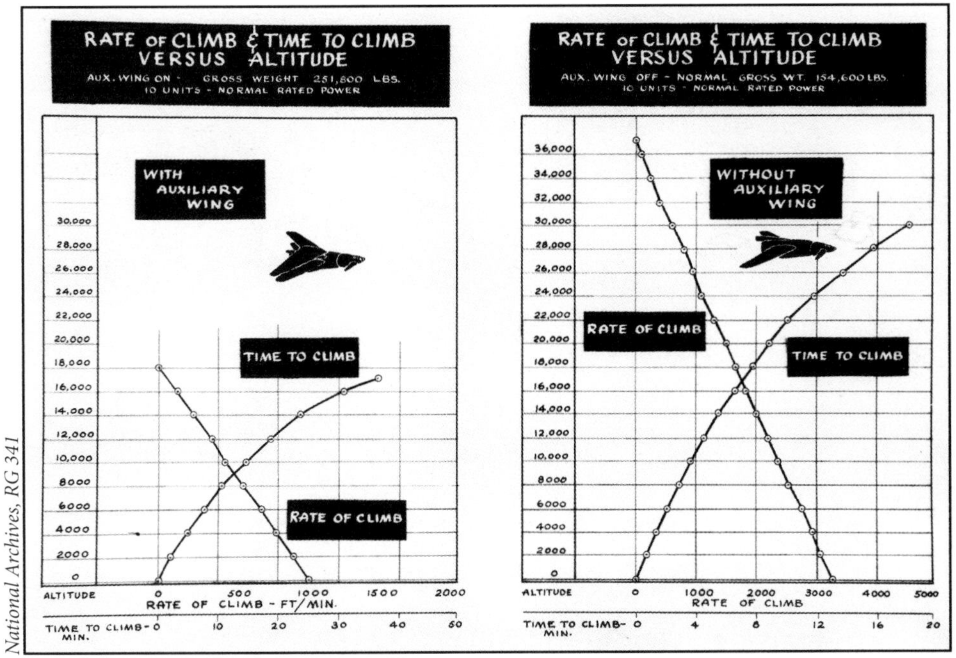

National Archives, RG 341

Above: Charts showing the rate of climb and time to climb versus altitude with and without the auxiliary wing; performance was markedly superior in the latter configuration.

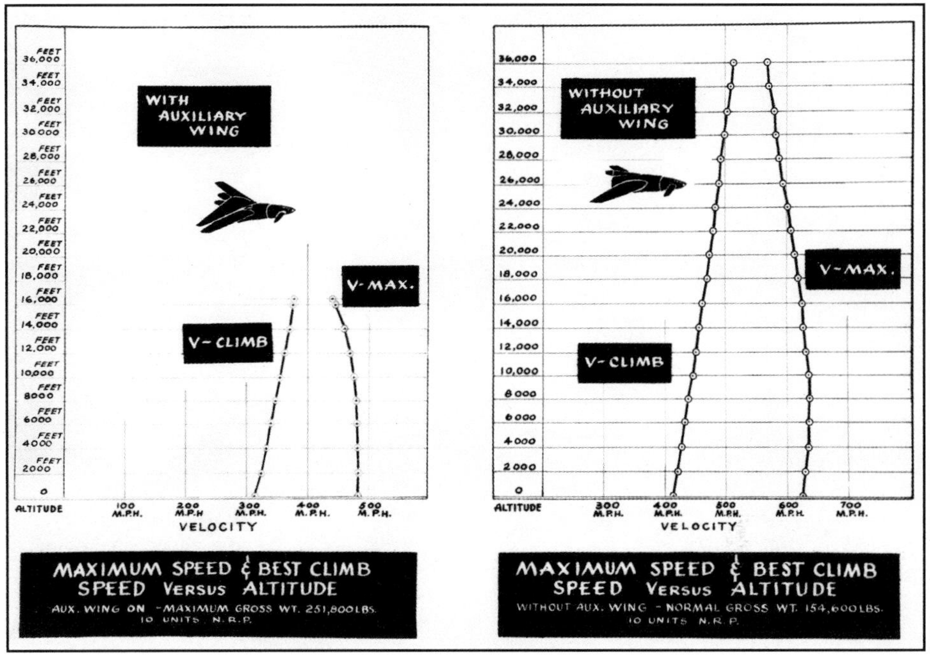

National Archives, RG 341

Above: These charts show the M-121's estimated maximum speed and best climb speed versus altitude with and without the auxiliary wing.

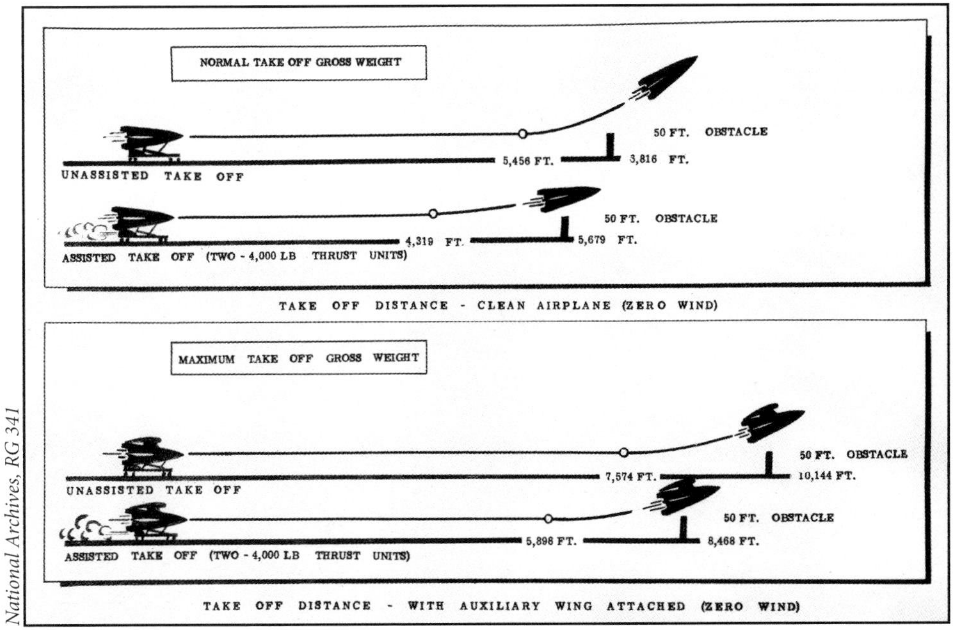

National Archives, RG 341

Above: Chart showing the takeoff distance of the M-121 at normal and maximum takeoff gross weight under various conditions.

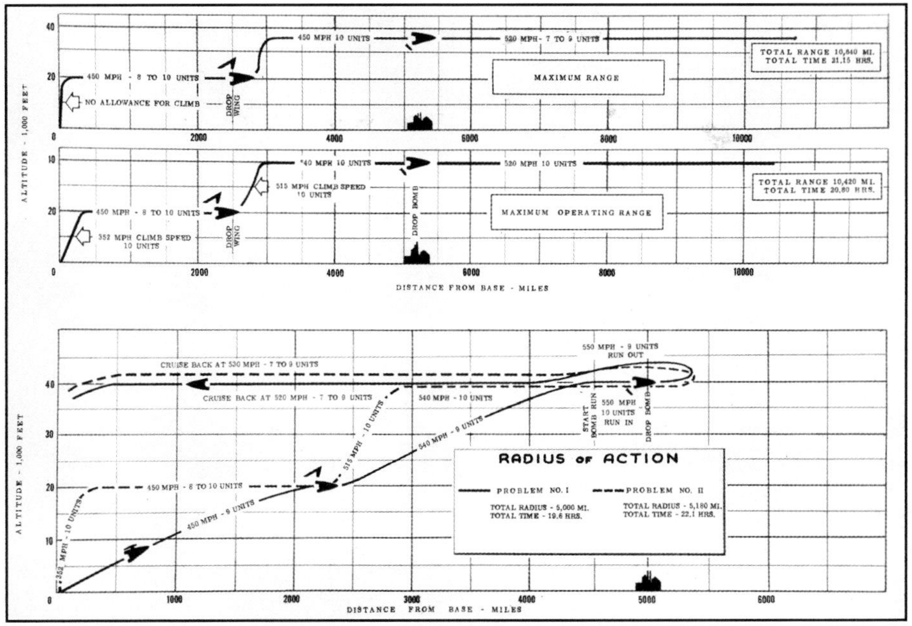

National Archives, RG 341

Above: Chart showing the radius of action of the M-121 under different mission scenarios.

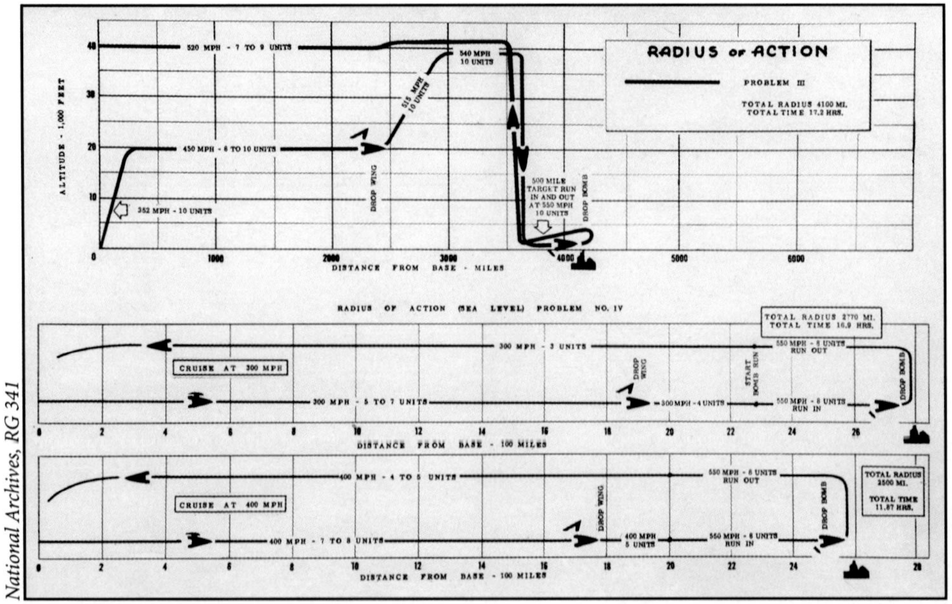

National Archives, RG 341

Above: Additional M-121 radius of action chart - note the dramatic 40,000 ft dive depicted in the upper scenario.

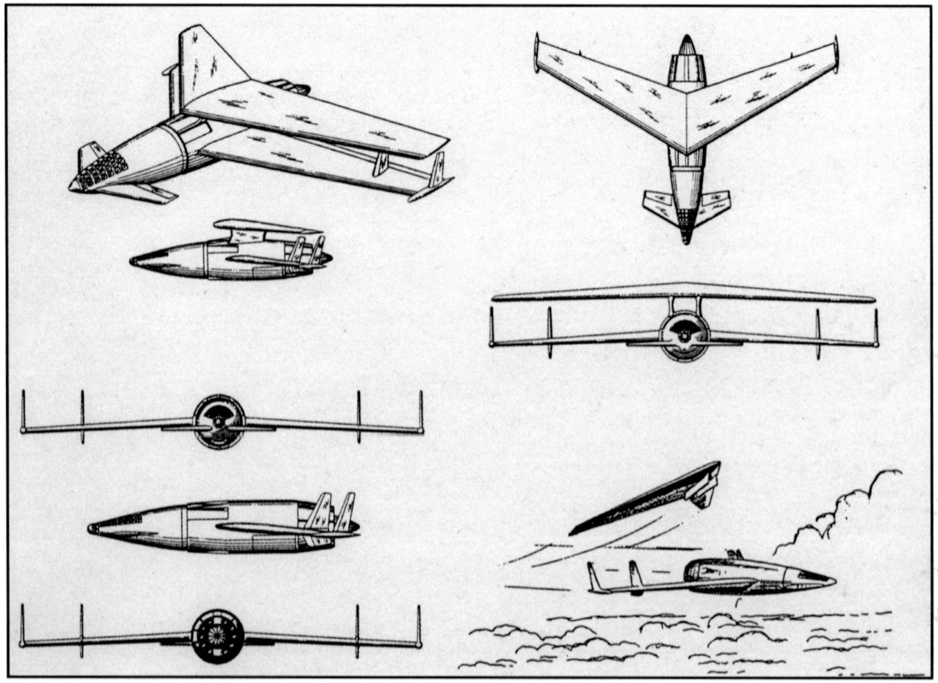

National Archives, RG 341

Above: Thieblot obtained US Patent nos. 173,771 and 173,772 for the basic M-121 design.

Below: Fairchild M-121 specification and performance data.

Loading Condition		Normal Take-Off Gross Weight	Maximum Take-Off Gross Weight
Airplane Characteristics			
Gross Weight	lbs.	154,600	251,800
Useful Load	lbs.	102,344	199,544
Weight Empty	lbs.	52,256	52,256 *
Internal Fuel Capacity	gal.	15,170	15,170
External Fuel Capacity	gal.		14,258
Total Fuel Capacity	gal.	15,170	29,428
Length Overall	ft.	75	
Wheel Base	ft.	25.5	
Wheel Tread	ft.	14	
Wing Area	sq. ft.	1,900	3,800
Aspect Ratio		7.01	4.24 (effective)
Wing Loading (W/S)	lbs./sq. ft.	81.37	66.26
Thrust Loading (W/T) - S.L., static			
Normal Rating	lb/lb.	5.15	8.39
Military Rating	lb./lb.	3.87	6.3
Engine Characteristics			
Model		Westinghouse 24-XX	Westinghouse 24-XX
Number of Units		10	10
Static Ratings (S.L. - zero duct losses)			
Normal	lbs. thrust/unit	3,000	3,000
Military	lbs. thrust/unit	4,000	4,000

* Auxiliary wing and supporting struts weight empty of 11,650 lbs. is included in useful load since they are considered expendable items.

National Archives, RG 341

PERFORMANCE SUMMARY

Loading Condition		Normal Take-Off Gross Weight	Max. Take-Off Gross Weight
Performance			
V Max. at Sea Level	mph	626	486
V Max. at 10,000 ft.	mph	635	478
V Max. at 20,000 ft.	mph	614	
V Max. at 30,000 ft.	mph	587	
Maximum Speed	mph	636	487
Altitude for Max. Speed	ft.	8,000	2,000
Rate of Climb at S.L.	ft./min.	3,240	1,000
Rate of Climb at 10,000 ft.	ft./min.	2,350	445
Rate of Climb at 20,000 ft.	ft./min.	1,460	
Rate of Climb at 30,000 ft.	ft./min.	580	
Time to Climb to 10,000 ft.	min.	3.6	13.8
Time to Climb to 20,000 ft.	min.	8.9	
Time to Climb to 30,000 ft.	min.	18.2	
Service Ceiling	ft.	35,800	16,300
Absolute Ceiling	ft.	37,100	18,100
Stall Speed - Power-Off - S.L.			
Full Load	mph	162.8	147.0
Full Load Less 1/2 Fuel	mph	136.8	118.3
Full Load Less Fuel	mph	104.4	80.3

Loading Condition		Normal Take-Off Gross Weight	Max. Take-Off Gross Weight
Take-Off Distance - T.O. Power - Zero Wind			
Unassisted			
Ground Run	ft.	5,456	7,574
Over 50 ft. Obstacle	ft.	6,816	10,144
With Jato (2-4000 lb. Units)			
Ground Run	ft.	4,319	5,898
Over 50 ft. Obstacle	ft.	5,679	8,468
Landing Distance - Zero Wind at Design			
Landing Gross of 70,000 lbs.			
Ground Run	ft.	1,910	
Over 50 ft. Obstacle	ft.	3,480	
Range and Radius of Action (1)			
Maximum Range	mi.		10,690
Maximum Operating Range	mi.		10,420
Radius of Action			
Problem I	mi.		5,000
Problem II	mi.		5,180
Problem III	mi.		4,100
Problem IV at 300 mph	mi.		2,770
at 400 mph			2,500

Note: (1) The actual problems are graphed in figures immediately following.

National Archives, RG 341

National Archives, RG 72

Artist's impression of the Fairchild M-128 taking off from a flush deck carrier. While conceptually similar to the M-121, it featured numerous modifications to meet BuAer requirements.

The Fairchild M-128 Class VA Long Range Heavy Attack Aircraft

Fairchild believed that the requirement for a long range carrier-based heavy attack airplane capable of delivering a 10,000 lb bomb load at 1,700 nm radius of action at speeds higher than 500 mph required an unconventional solution. Leveraging what it had learned in the design of the M-121, it proposed an aircraft of similar layout with numerous modifications to meet the requirements of OS-111. The dimensions of the airplane were specifically limited by carrier operation.

Engine Selection and Power Plant Arrangement The power plant arrangement of the proposed airplane consisted of 6 Westinghouse XJ-46 units arranged in a circle at the stern of the fuselage, around the bomb ejector tube. A multiplicity of comparatively small engines was selected to permit cruising at full power on a partial number of engines and realizing therefore the greatest fuel economy.

Fuel Stowage, Airplane Size The most optimistic estimate on fuel economy, coupled with the lowest possible drag of an airplane of sufficient size to meet the conditions established, led to an impractical arrangement considering BuAer requirements. The trouble was found in the fact that, for the greatest part of the range, an unnecessarily large airplane burning a large quantity of fuel was being flown simply because of conditions at the beginning of the mission. The most efficient way of covering the conditions required necessitated a "variable" airplane, which could be adjusted for initial conditions at each point of the trip.

The Fairchild M-128 was a solution to this problem, with its auxiliary, expendable fuel tank in the form of a wing. The use of this auxiliary tank brought the actual starting point of the basic aircraft (when the wing had been jettisoned) a considerable distance from takeoff, and presented the following advantages:

1. Permitted takeoff from a carrier, by increasing the wing area in such a way that the wing loading was lower at high gross weight.
2. Permitted higher speed operation than was possible through the use of a glider or tanks.
3. Greater overall economy because of the low drag associated with the auxiliary fuel system.

The basic airplane configuration was such that its significant dynamic characteristics would not be adversely affected by the presence of the wing.

Basic Airplane Efficiency and Design The predominant factor in the general design of the basic airplane was one of drag reduction to its lowest possible value. The wing planform had a 30° leading edge sweep back and the wing section used had a thickness ratio of 10%, no protuberances of any sort were allowed on the wing surface, and nacelles were eliminated. The fuselage was designed to be of sufficient size to house practically all the fuel required for the basic airplane, the power plants, and the equipment items required for the mission. The circular fuselage was developed from the lines of the best artillery shell.

The canard type was chosen because of the low drag associated with this arrangement of the lifting surfaces and also because it produced the best usable fuselage volume to lateral area ratio. The canard/trimmer was free floating. In addition, it permitted an advantageous disposition of the power plant bomb ejection system, reducing to a

National Archives, RG 72

Like the earlier M-121, the M-128 featured a jettisonable auxiliary wing, which permitted takeoff from a carrier by decreasing wing loading, enabled higher speed operation than other methods of external fuel carriage, and provided greater overall fuel economy.

minimum the probability of collision and interference when jettisoning the auxiliary fuel tank.

The sweptback wing planform not only increased the critical Mach number, but also permitted a considerable reduction in stabilizing surface area and allowed a CG position and travel resulting in 100% utilization of fuselage volume. The wings were arranged for folding so that overall span and length did not exceed 58 ft by 58 ft to fit carrier elevators. The wing thickness ratio was 10% for the main wing and varied from 18% at the root to 9% at the tip for the auxiliary wing. The reason for the increased thickness of the auxiliary wing was of course to provide the volume for the fuel capacity required.

The condition of minimum airplane drag for maximum usable volume led to the consideration of a rather large fuselage and comparatively thin wings. The particular disposition of the engines chosen by Fairchild was an attempt to reduce the overall drag by streamlining the effect of the jets, the acceleration of the boundary layer of the fuselage directly ahead of the engines, and offered the following possibilities which were to have been wind tunnel tested:

1. Pumping the fuselage boundary layer through the low pressure area at the center of the annular exhaust jet.
2. Combined boundary layer intake and rammed intake for maximum efficiency dependent upon condition of operation (cruising to target and target run).
3. Use of bomb ejection tube as a thrust augmentation unit.

Gross Weights, Wing and Thrust Loading of the Proposed Airplane:

Condition	Gross Weight lbs.	Wing Loading W/S-lbs./sq.ft.	Thrust Loading W/R-6 Units-Static Sea Level-Duct Losses Included Normal Rating	Mil. Rating
Maximum with (2400 sq. ft.)	113,000	47.2	5.15	4.28
Normal with (1200 sq. ft.)	72,988	60.8	3.32	2.76
Des. Landing Gross Wt. (1200 sq. ft.)	62,988	52.4	2.86	2.38

National Archives, RG 72

Auxiliary Systems All equipment items were kept to a minimum consistent with the mission of the airplane since they also had a definite influence on the size and general configuration of the airplane. The various items were taken into account in accordance with the BuAer Outline Specification OS-111 for the airplane.

Bomb Bay Arrangement Numerous studies had been made during and after WW II regarding bomb release at high speed. The principle obstacles were: the impact load on the bomb itself, causing failures of stabilizers, and the turbulence in the bomb bay which was likely to cause bombing inaccuracies and structural damage to the airplane. In addition, with bomb release speed equal to that of the airplane, the airplane bomb separation could only be achieved from very high altitude, or through the use of parachutes.

Structure Basically the airplane was fabricated in three parts, the central structural section, the forward bolted crew and equipment section, and the rear power plant section. The pressurized monocoque nose section housed the crew and equipment. Provision could have been made for jettisoning the entire section in case of emergency.

The structural section was primarily built around a central core (the bomb bay) enclosed between two vertical, longitudinal members, in the walls of which were housed the controls, wiring and plumbing, and access doors to engine accessories, auxiliary wing fittings, landing gear, etc. for inspection or maintenance. The air intake cowling was bolted directly to the external skin. The individual engine cowling was fastened to the engine mount members, allowing maintenance or replacement with the minimum amount of labor.

The bomb bay of the proposed airplane accorded with the OS-111 specification. A tube, not unlike a torpedo tube, was included through which the bomb could be ejected rearward at various speeds with respect to the airplane. The actual diameter of the ejector tube was taken as that given for a standard 10,000 lb bomb. The turbulence was completely eliminated. As with the M-121, the bomb hit the air stream at an attitude of minimum drag with its longitudinal axis in the direction of motion; the velocity with respect to the ground could be controlled through the agent considered for the ejection, i.e., compressed air, catapult, slow burning powder, etc.

Gun Turrets The general arrangement of the proposed airplane made use of the specified single tail turret impractical. Accordingly, Fairchild proposed placing a turret at each tip of the main wing, thereby greatly increasing the firepower of this armament.

Fabrication and Maintenance In view of the fact that BuAer laid great stress on the fabrication and maintenance of combat aircraft, the airplane was designed with this ideal in mind.

The Fairchild M-128 was undoubtedly the most unorthodox of the proposals known to have been submitted to fulfill OS-111. The innovative features of the type offered both the potential for high performance as well as considerable risk. Given the existence of the earlier Air Force proposal, the M-128 appears to be an example of a company tailoring a pet concept to a specification, rather than developing a clean sheet of paper design to fulfill the specification more closely. Furthermore, Fairchild had little experience in fabricating such a large and complex aircraft or working with the Navy, which had unique requirements. These are probably just a few of the reasons Fairchild's bold and radical design never left the drawing board.

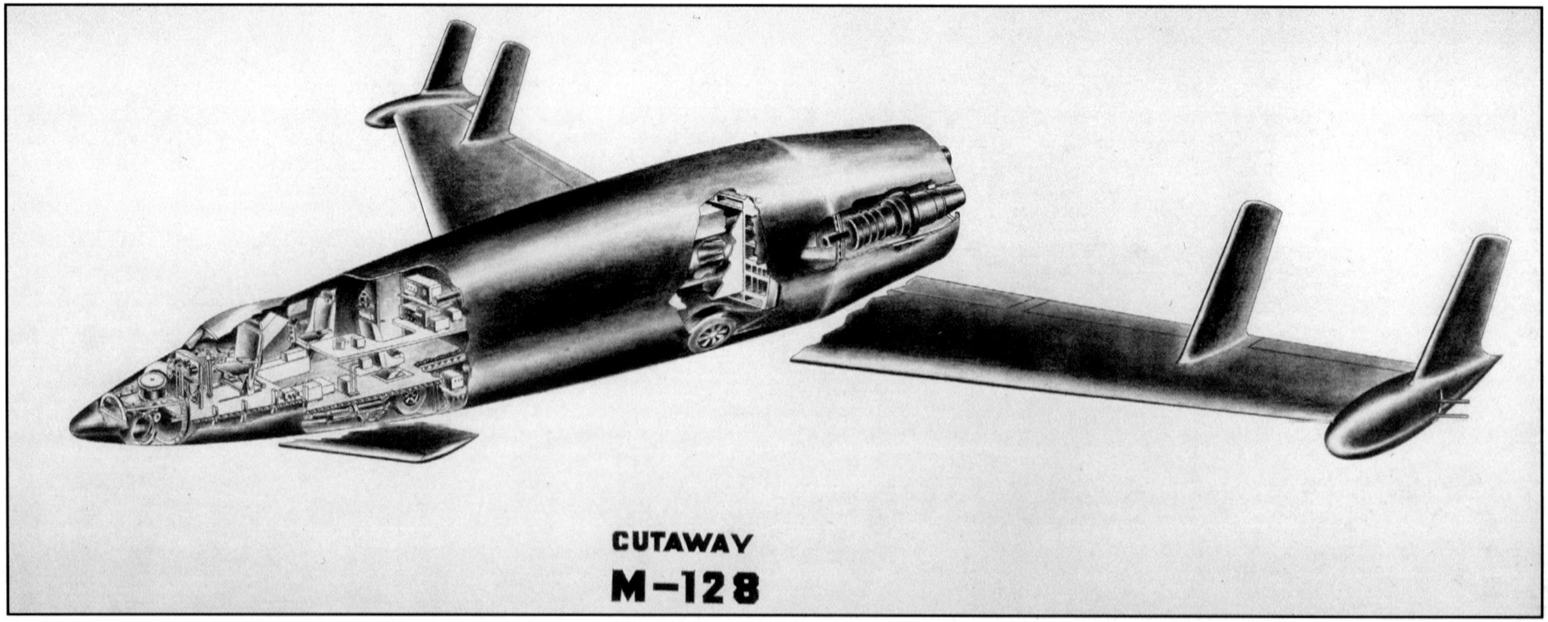

Right: Perspective cutaway view of the Fairchild M-128 Class VA Heavy Attack aircraft. Unlike the earlier M-121, the M-128 featured a bubble canopy and a different crew arrangement.

National Archives, RG 72

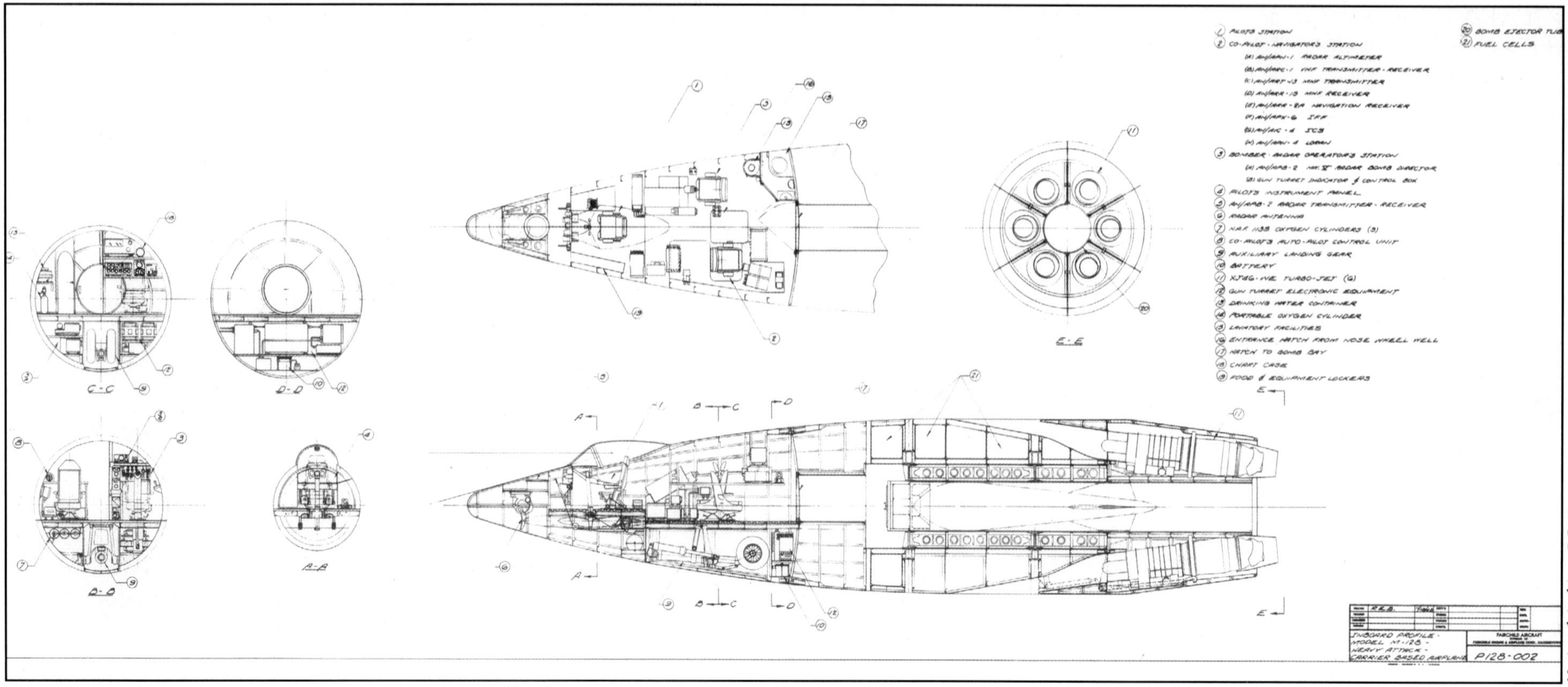

Below: This inboard profile of the Fairchild M-128 shows that it was powered by 6 turbojets, 4 fewer than the M-121. The 6 Westinghouse XJ-46 units were arranged in a circle at the stern of the fuselage, around the bomb ejector tube.

National Archives, RG 72

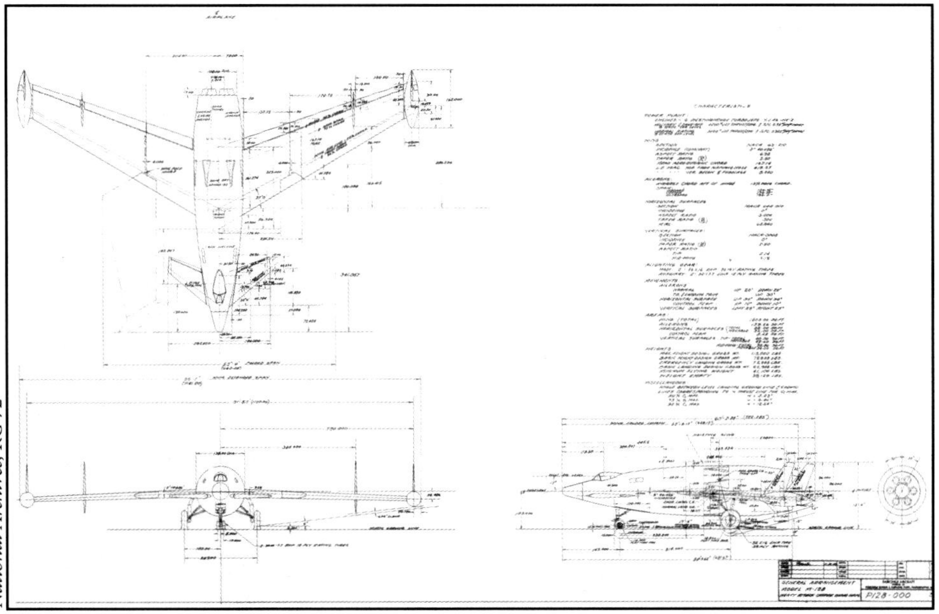

National Archives, RG 72

Above: Three-view drawing of the basic Fairchild M-128. Unlike the M-121, the naval version of Thieblot's unusual bomber design featured two unit-type vertical tails on each wing, wing folding, and wing tip turrets for defense.

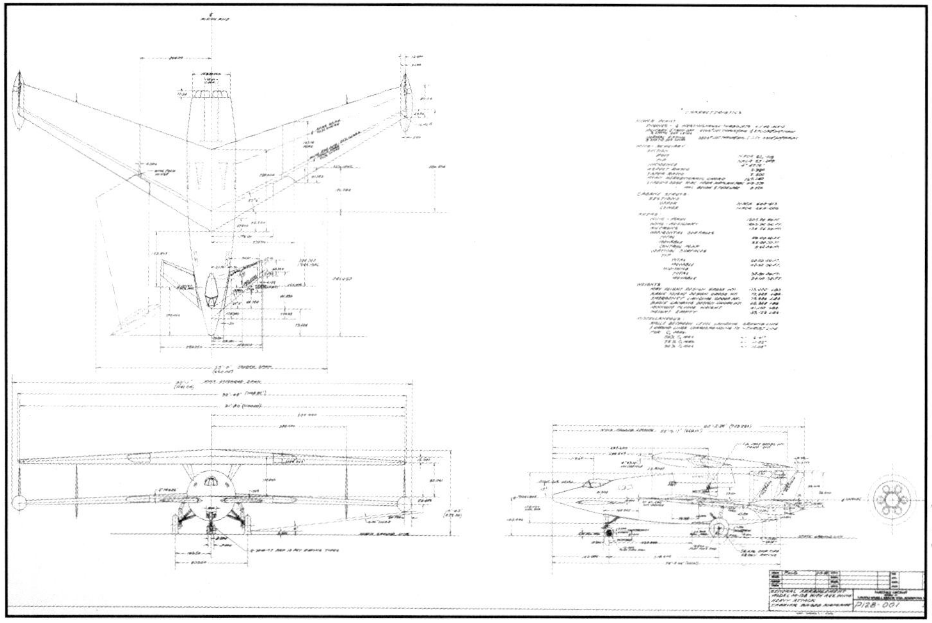

National Archives, RG 72

Above: Three-view drawing of the Fairchild M-128 with the auxiliary wing. Unlike the M-121, the landing gear of the M-128 was stressed for takeoff at full gross weight with the auxiliary wing attached, as utilization of a launching cart was impractical for carrier operations.

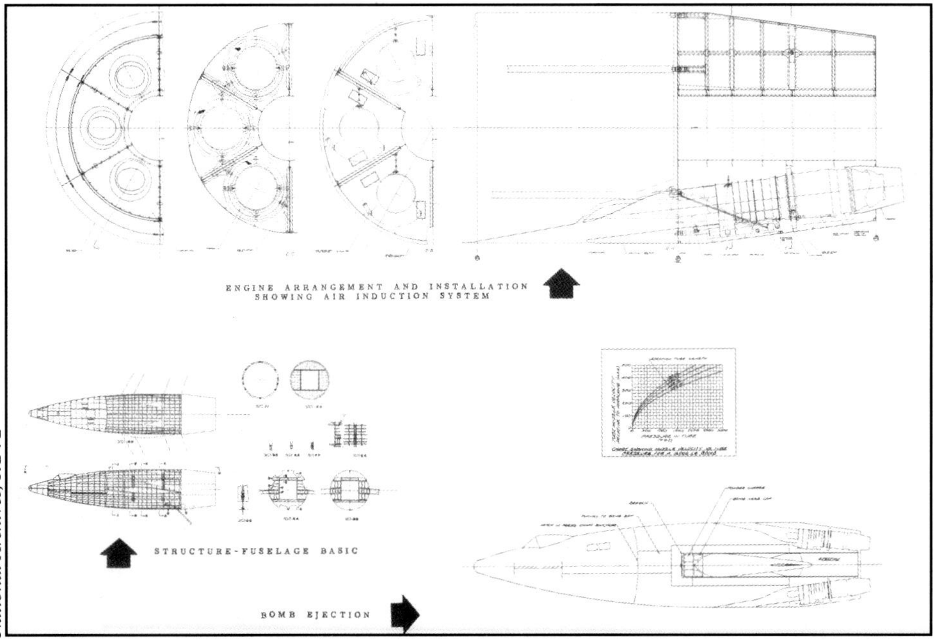

National Archives, RG 72

Above: Detail drawings of the engine installation, the fuselage structure, and the bomb ejection system. *Right:* Detail drawings of the M-128's fuel system and auxiliary wing attachment.

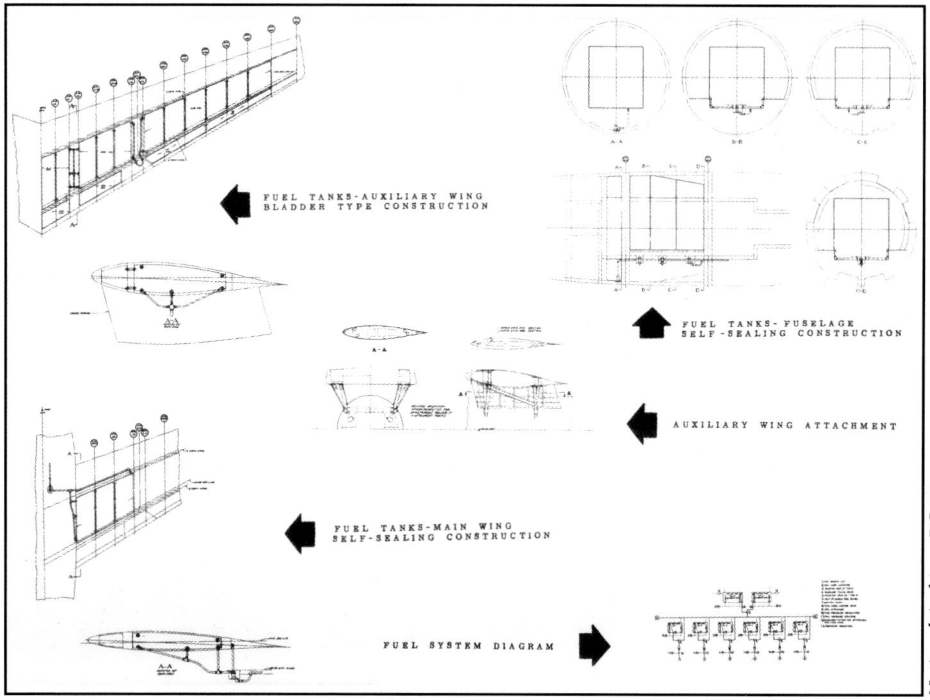

National Archives, RG 72

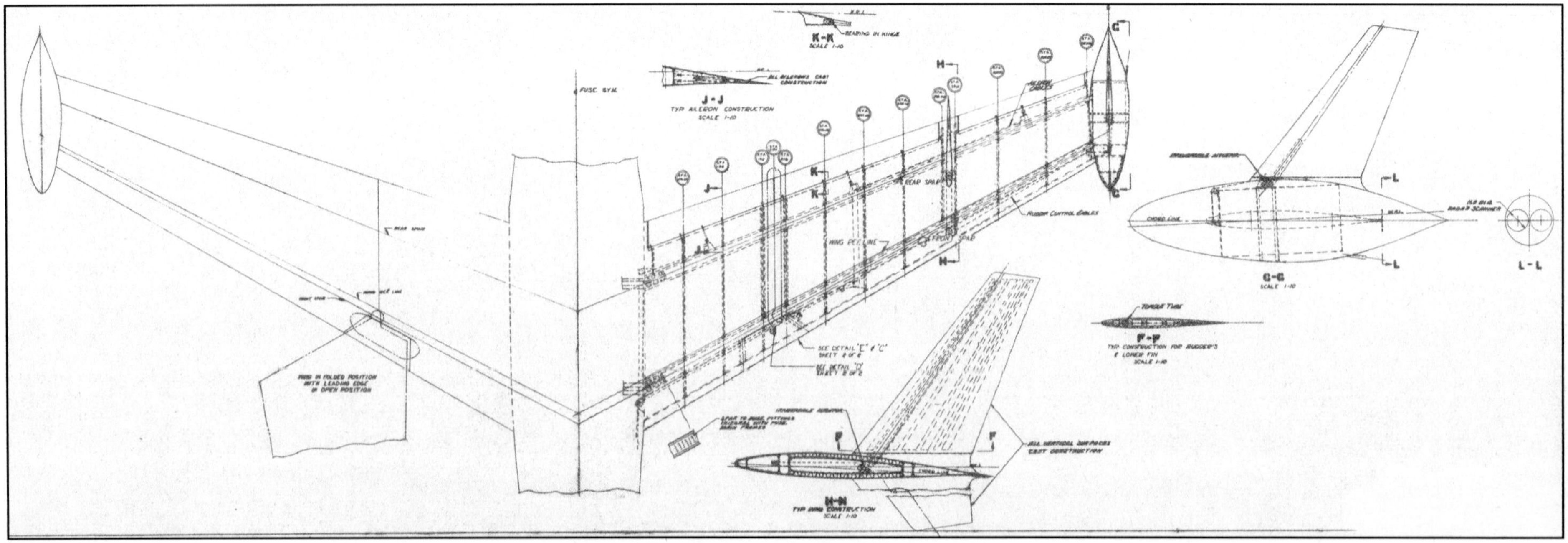

Above: Blueprint of the M-128 main wing and vertical tail structures. The wing featured a 30° leading edge sweepback and a wing section with a thickness ratio of 10%.

National Archives, RG 72

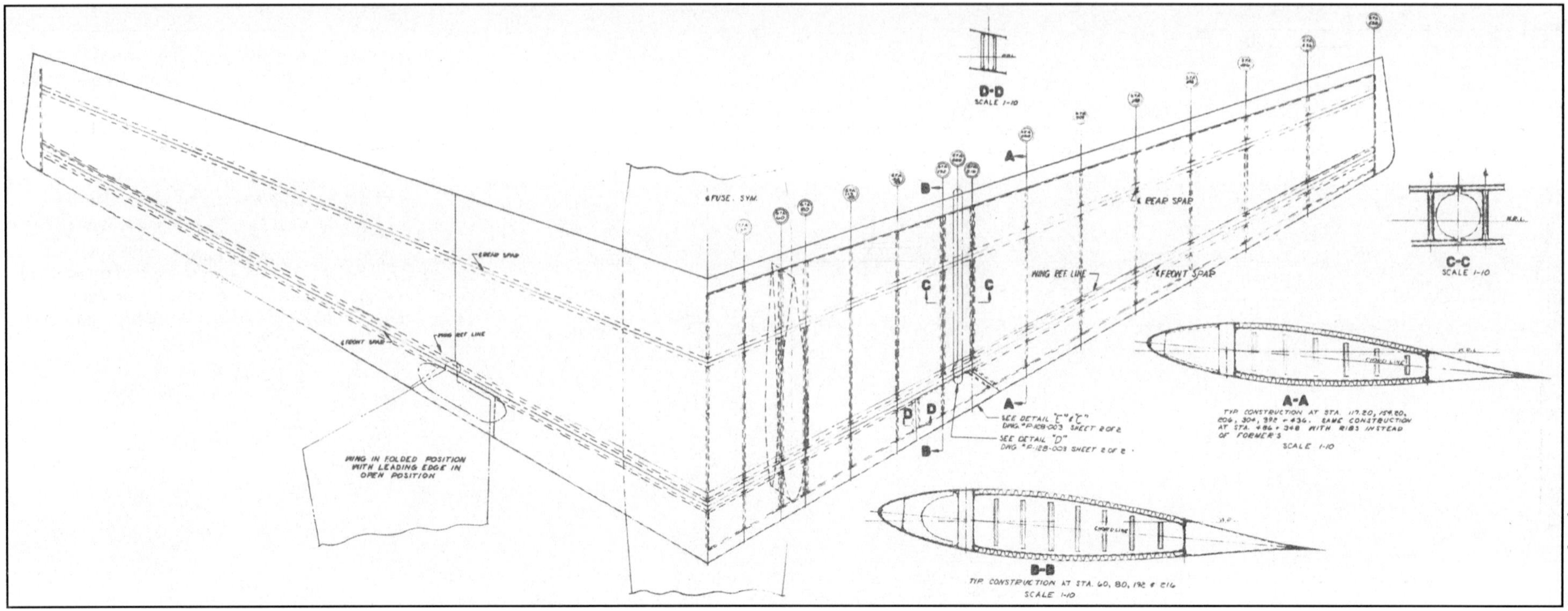

Above: Structure of the M-128's auxiliary wing, which functioned both as an additional lifting surface and enormous fuel tank.

National Archives, RG 72

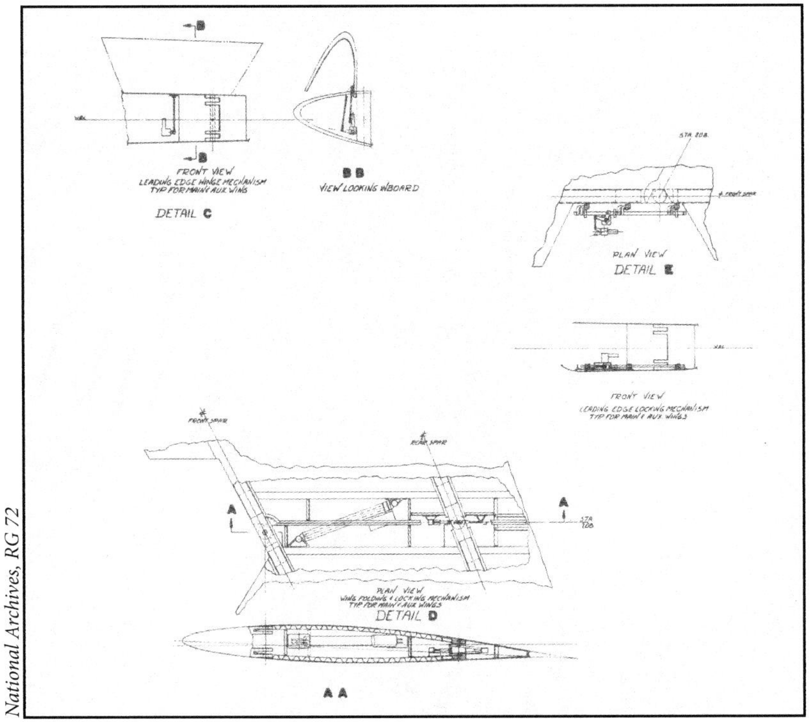

National Archives, RG 72

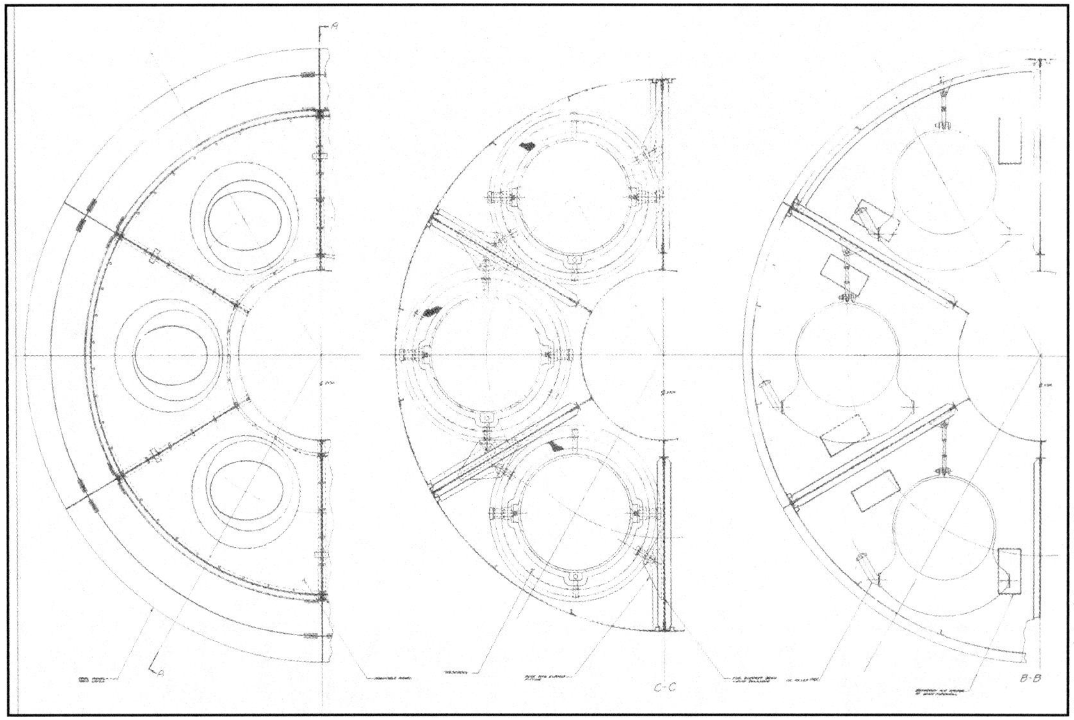

National Archives, RG 72

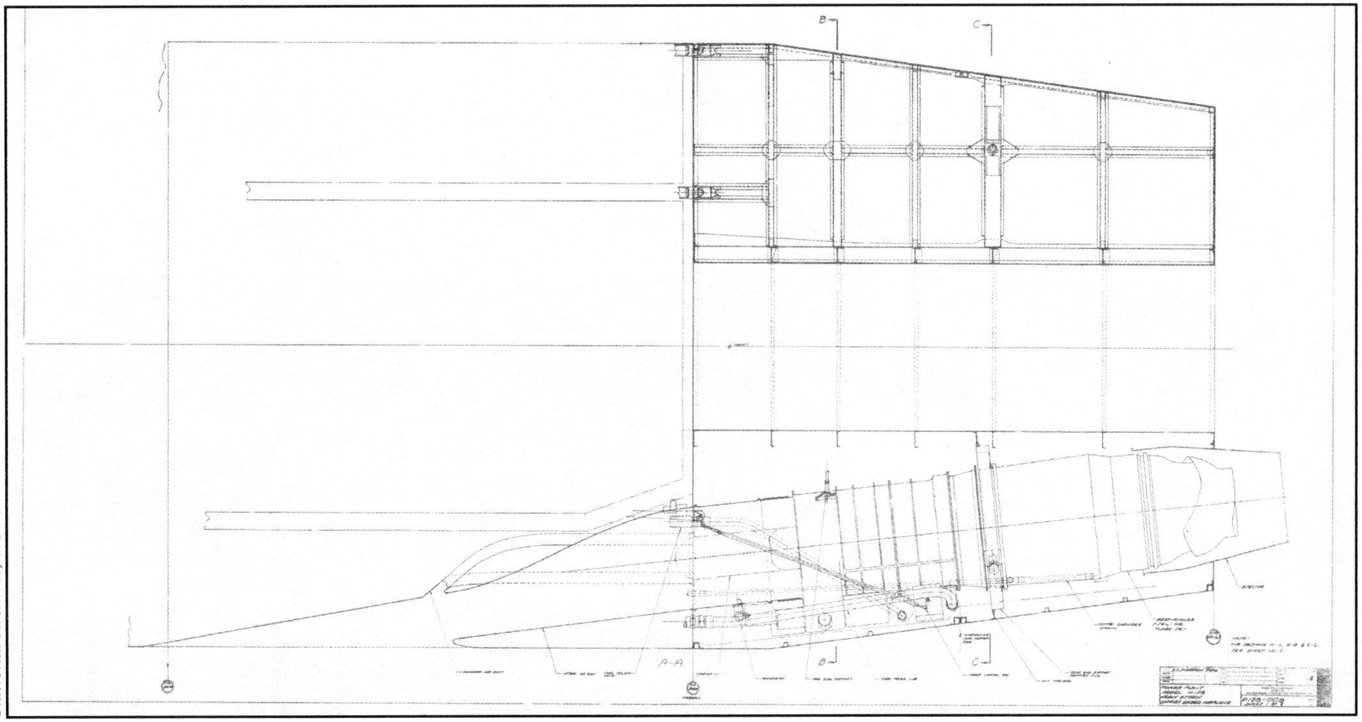

National Archives, RG 72

Above Left: Additional section drawings of the auxiliary wing shown on the previous page.

Above Right: Cross sections of the M-128 fuselage showing the powerplant installation.

Left: Blueprint of the Westinghouse XJ46-WE power plant installation. Fairchild was one of the few manufacturers to select this engine for its Class VA proposal, employing 6 of these small turbojets to permit cruising at full power on a partial number of engines, resulting in improved fuel economy.

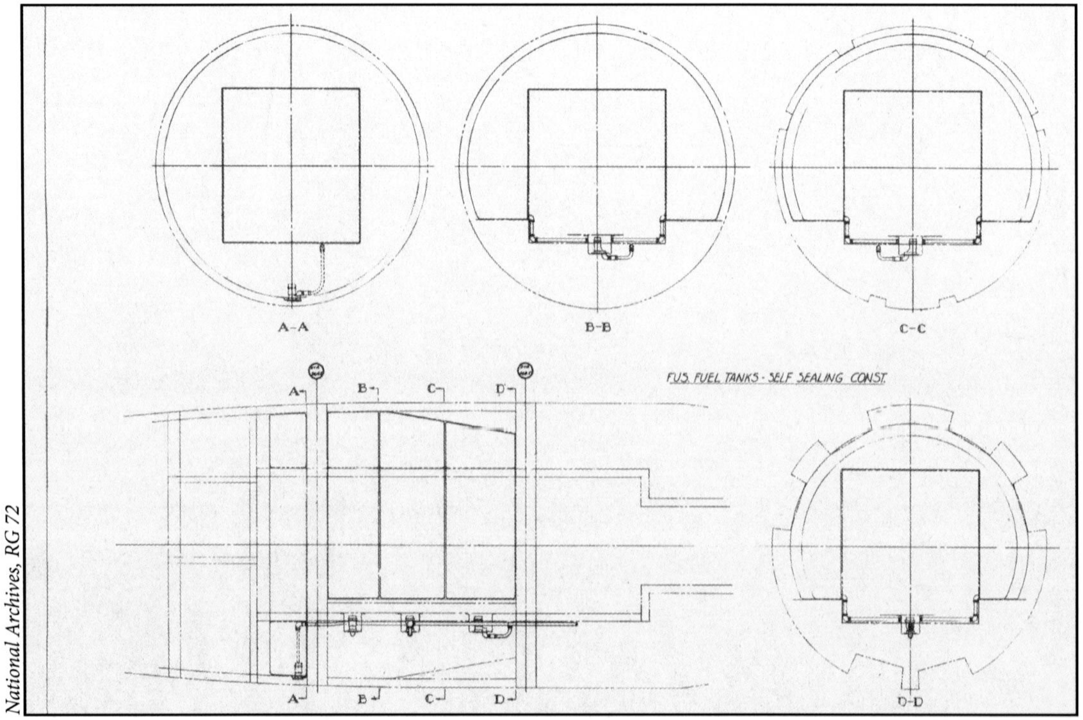

National Archives, RG 72

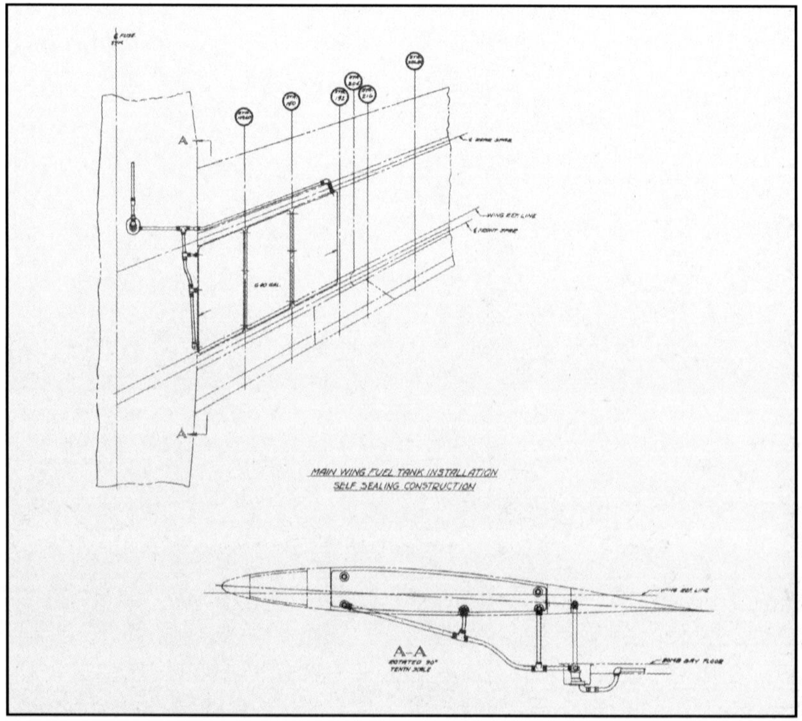

National Archives, RG 72

Above Left: Blueprint of the fuel tank installation in the M-128 fuselage.

Above Right: Installation of the main wing fuel tanks.

Right: The structure of the M-128's fuselage was fabricated in three parts: a central structural section, a forward bolted crew and equipment section, and a rear power plant section.

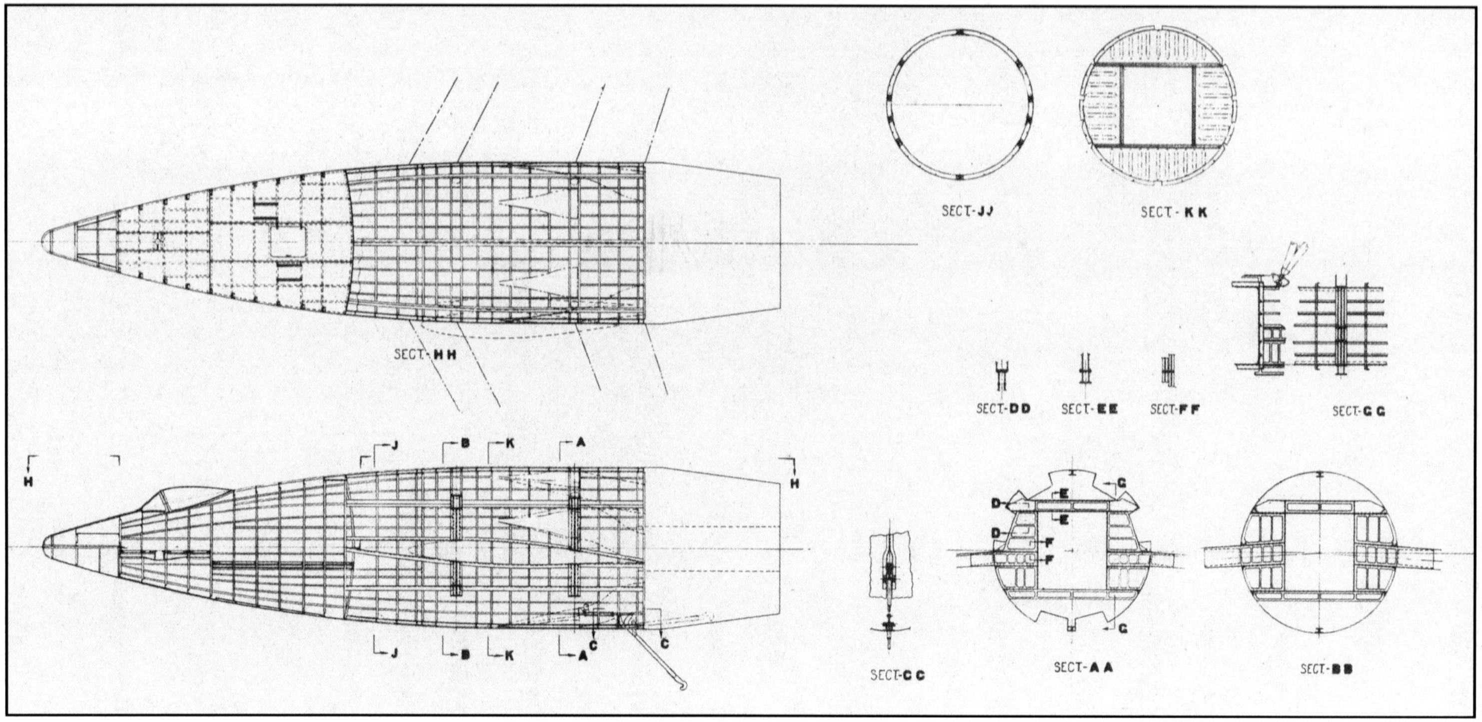

National Archives, RG 72

Blueprint of the landing gear installation.

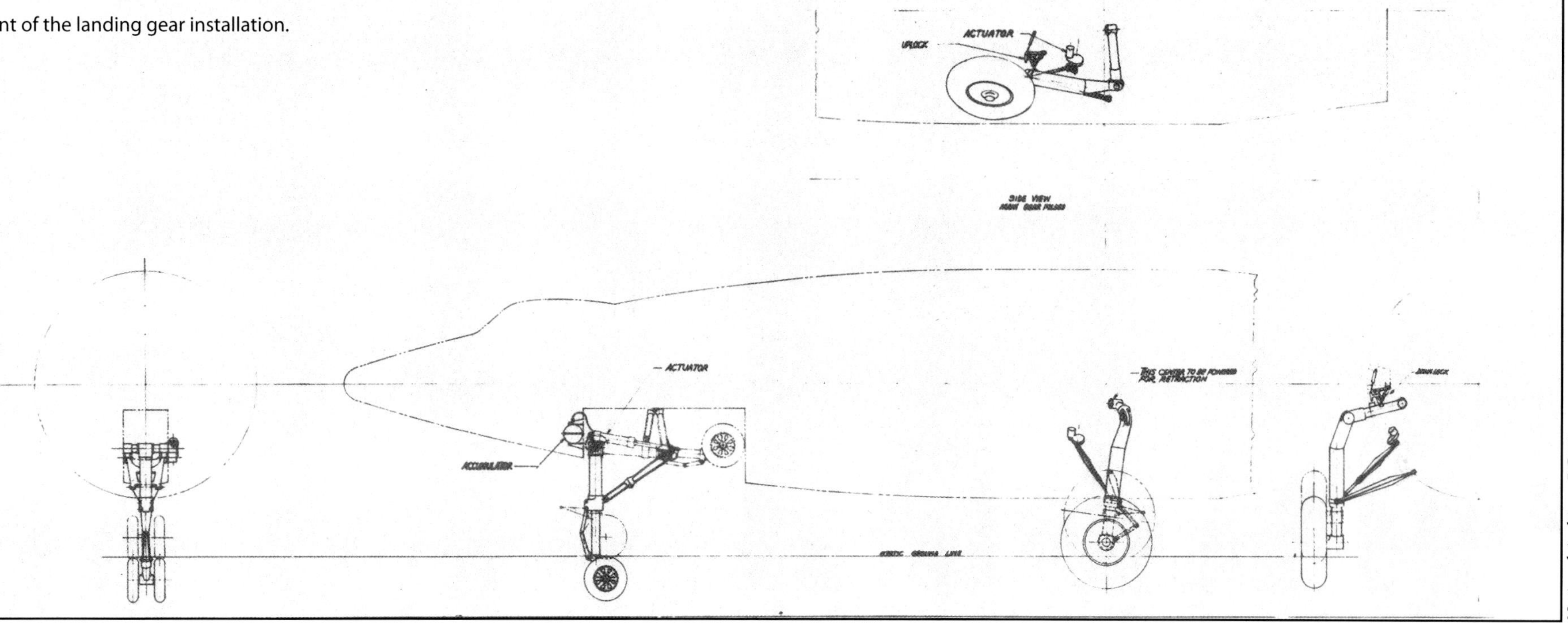

National Archives, RG 72

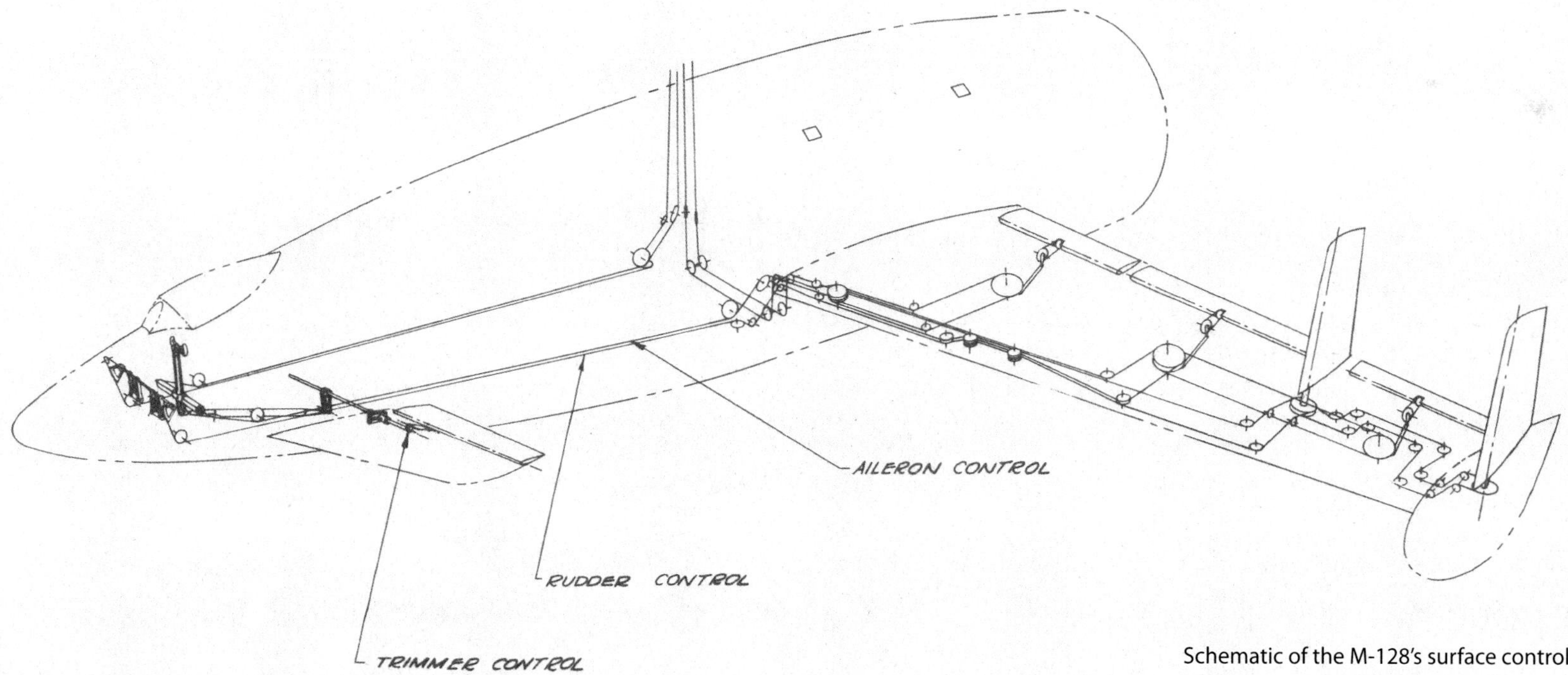

Schematic of the M-128's surface control system.

National Archives, RG 72

Right: Field of fire diagrams for the M-128's dual wing tip-mounted X11E turrets. The unique layout of Fairchild's bomber made the use of a single tail turret (as specified in OS-111) impractical.

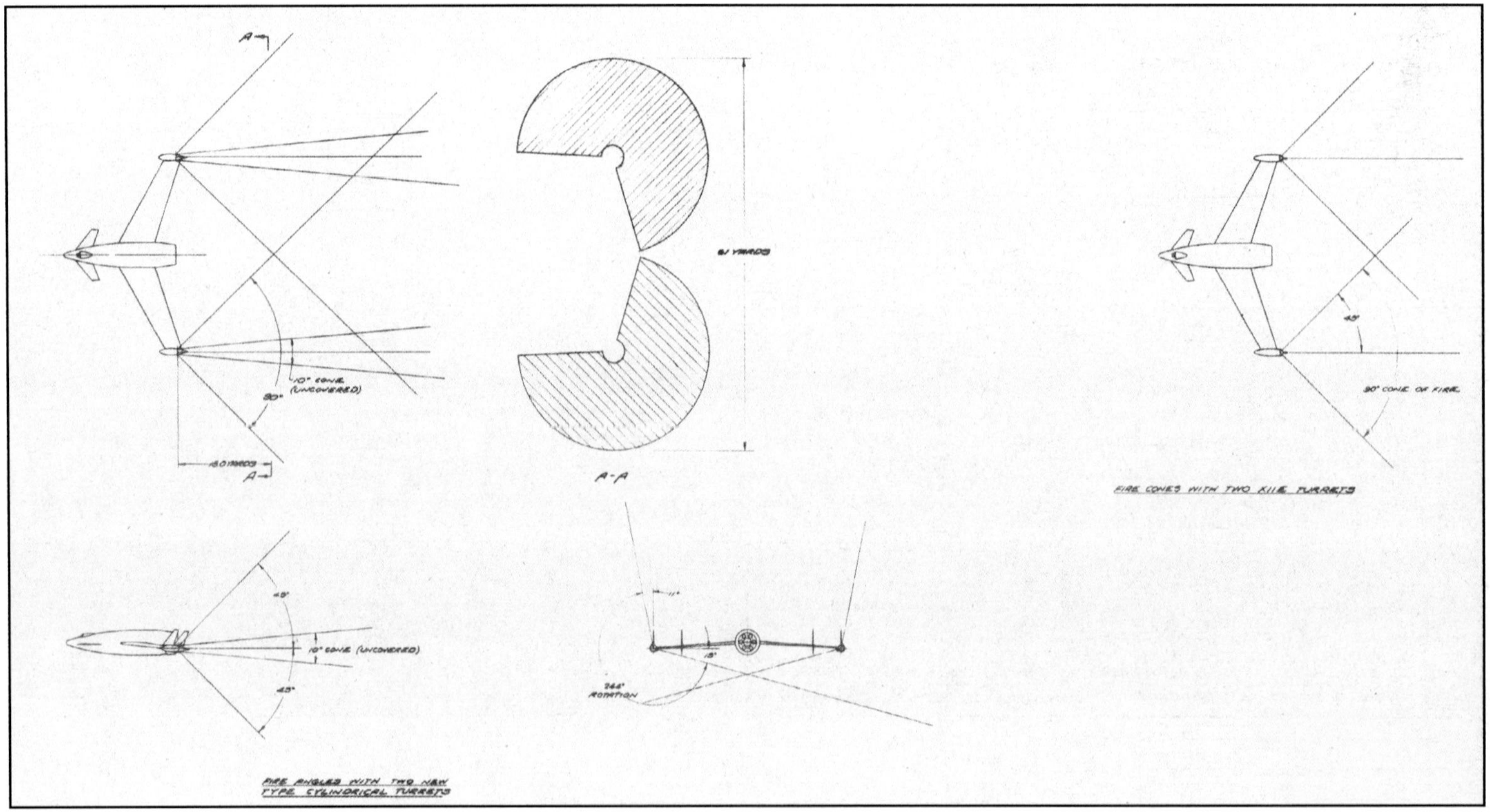

National Archives, RG 72

Below: Catapult and arresting diagram of the M-128.

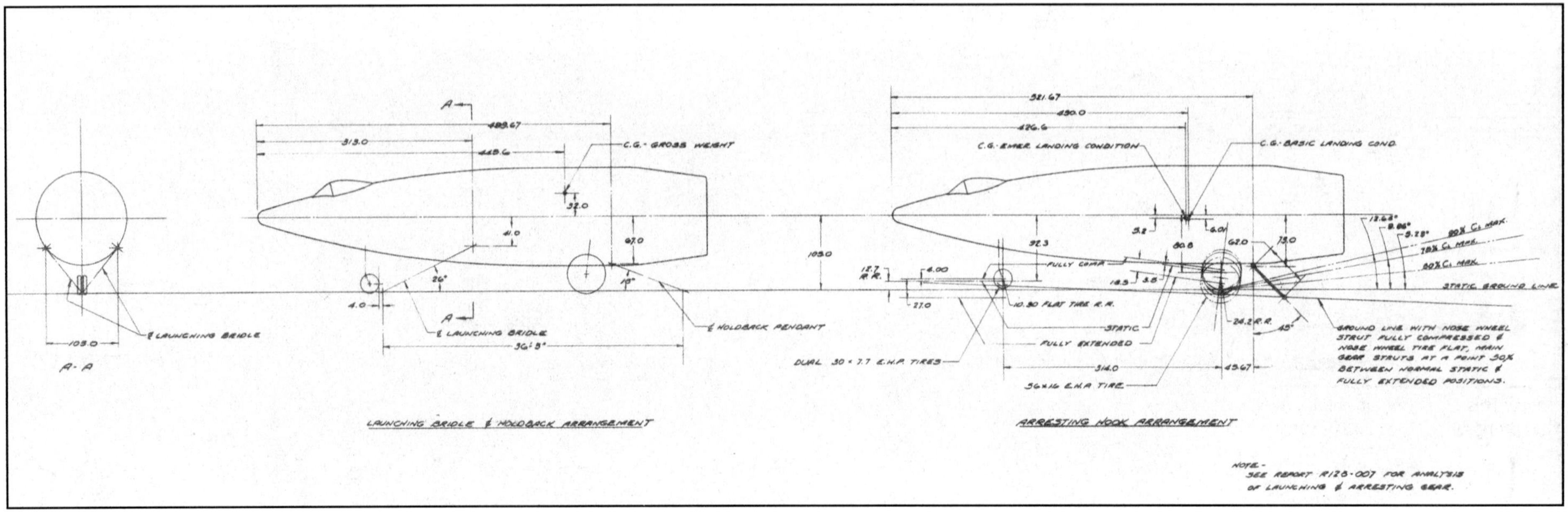

National Archives, RG 72

Carrier spotting and clearance diagram. When stowed, the Fairchild M-128 certainly had an unusual silhouette with its forward folding wings!

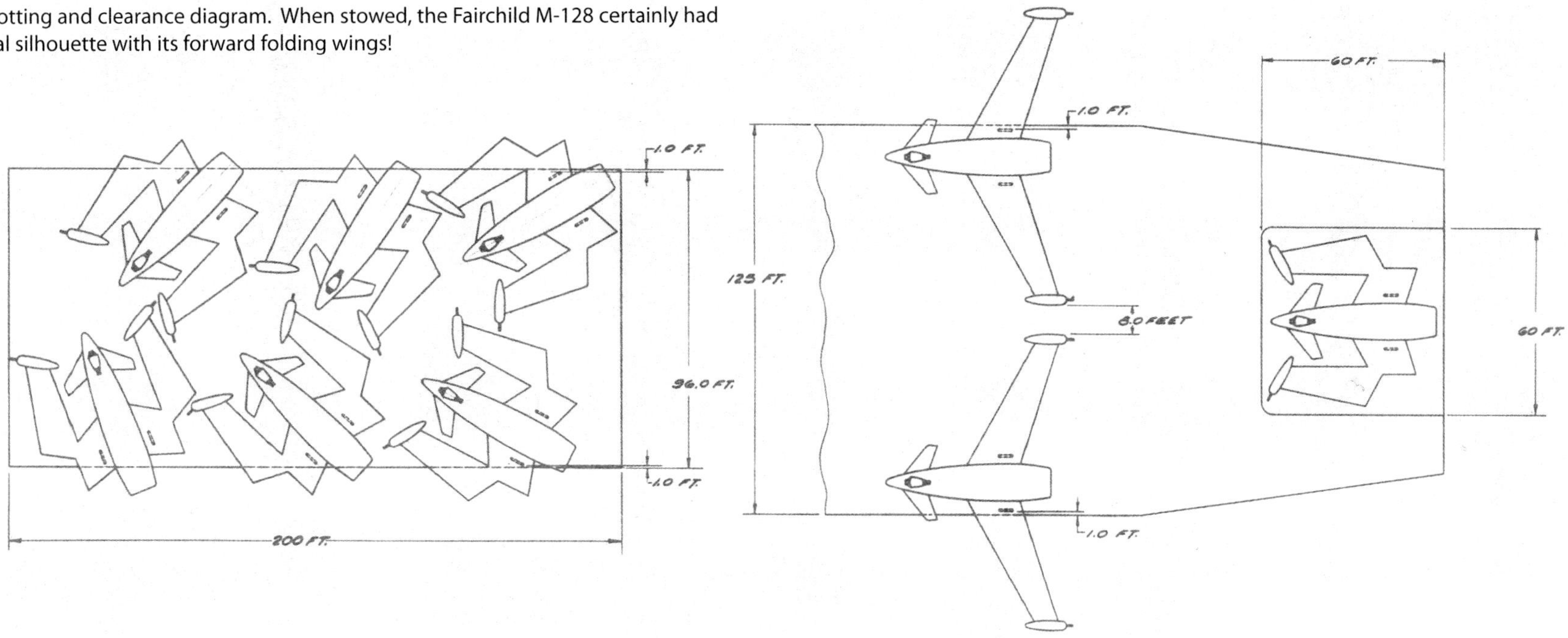

National Archives, RG 72

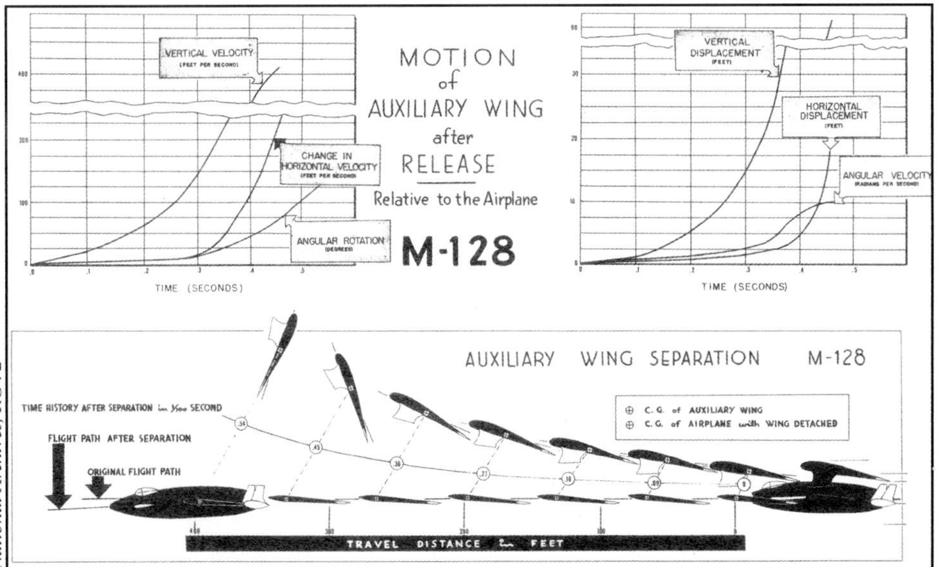

National Archives, RG 72

Above: This chart prepared for the M-128 showing auxiliary wing separation is quite similar to that prepared for the M-121.

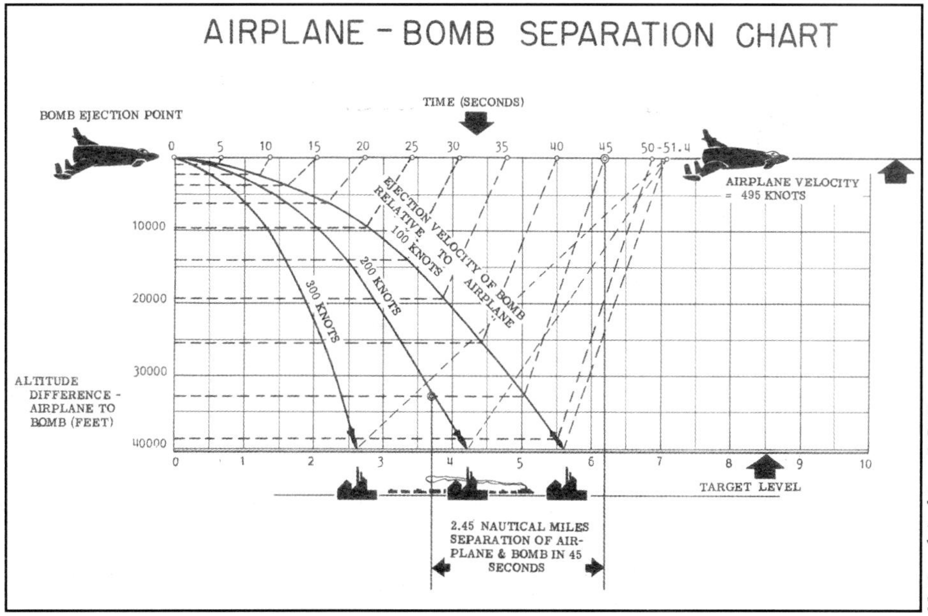

National Archives, RG 72

Above: As with the M-121, the M-128 was capable of ejecting a bomb rearward at various speeds by means of an agent such as compressed air, catapult, slow burning powder, etc.

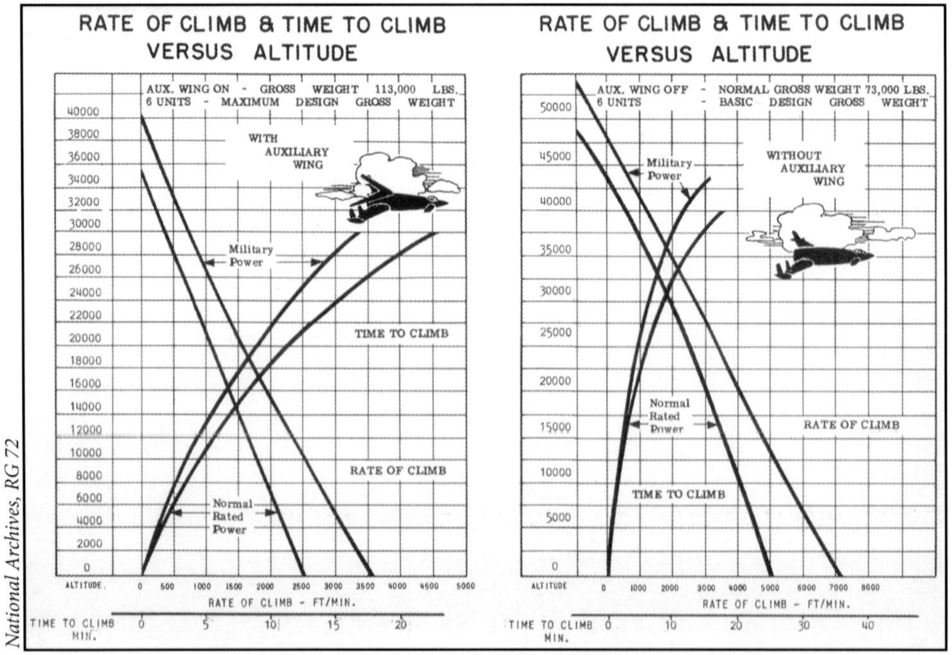

National Archives, RG 72

Above: Plots of rate of climb and time to climb versus altitude, with and without the auxiliary wing.

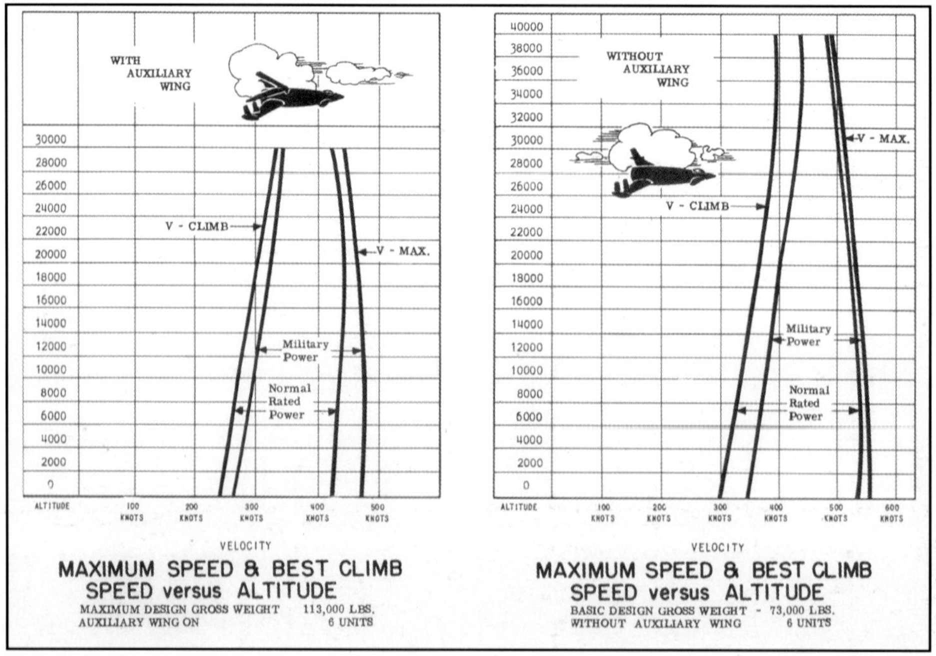

National Archives, RG 72

Above: Plots of maximum speed and best climb speed versus altitude with and without auxiliary wing for the M-128.

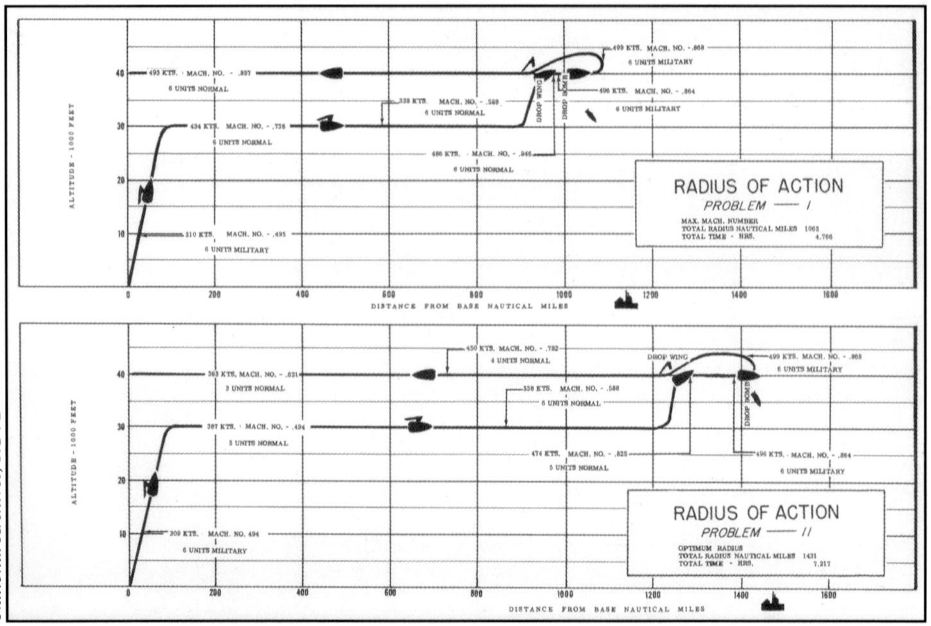

National Archives, RG 72

Above: Charts showing the radius of action of the M-128 at 1,062 nm and 1,431 nm.

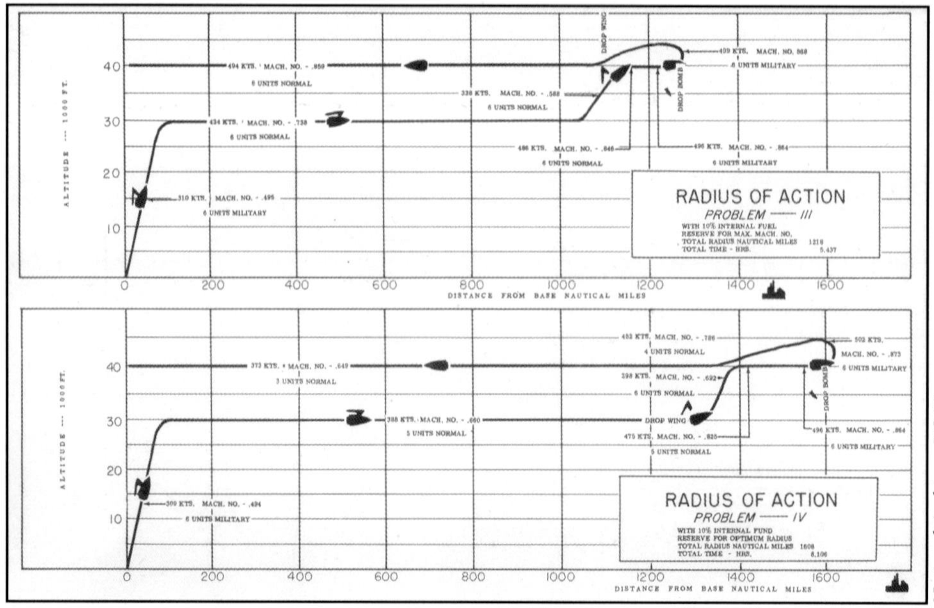

National Archives, RG 72

Above: Charts showing the radius of action of the M-128 at 1,218 nm and 1,608 nm.

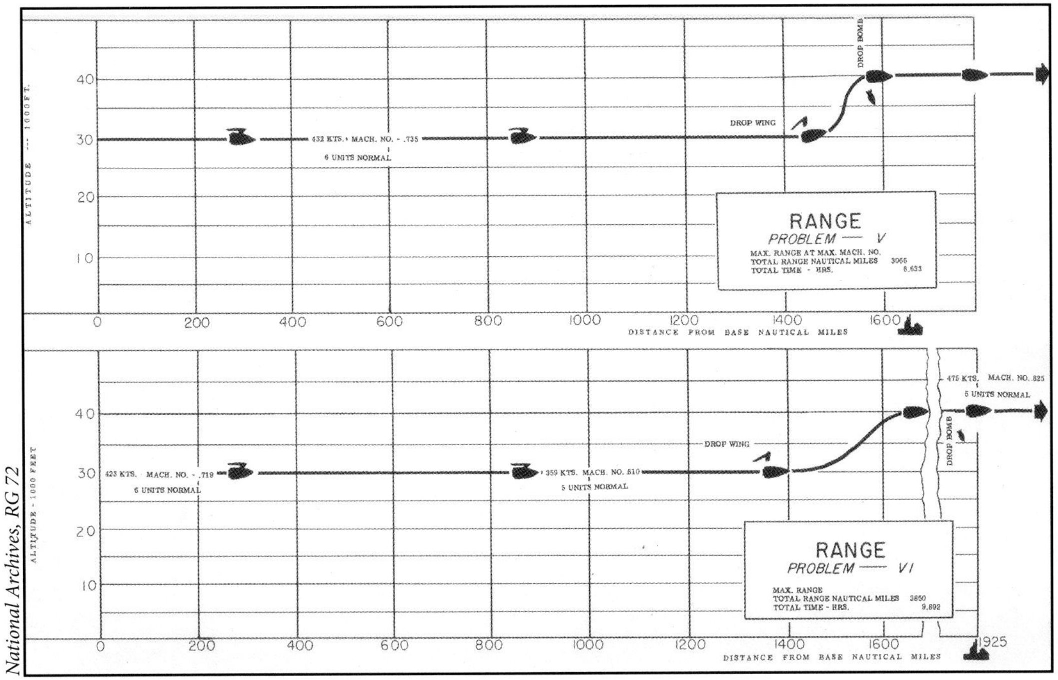

National Archives, RG 72

Above: Chart showing range (3,066 nm) at maximum Mach no. /maximum range (3,850 nm) generally.

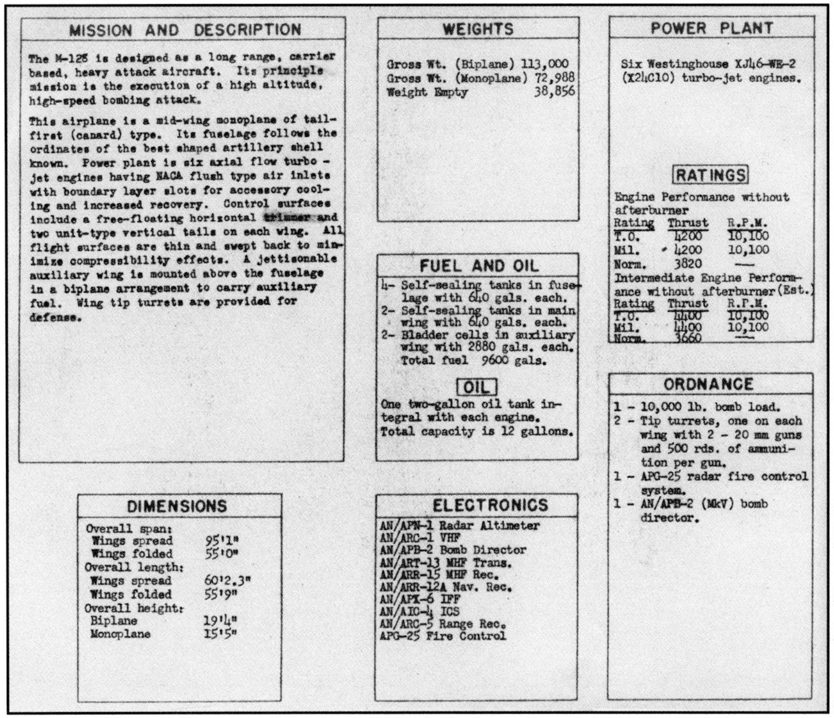

MISSION AND DESCRIPTION

The M-128 is designed as a long range, carrier based, heavy attack aircraft. Its principle mission is the execution of a high altitude, high-speed bombing attack.

This airplane is a mid-wing monoplane of tail-first (canard) type. Its fuselage follows the ordinates of the best shaped artillery shell known. Power plant is six axial flow turbo - jet engines having NACA flush type air inlets with boundary layer slots for accessory cooling and increased recovery. Control surfaces include a free-floating horizontal trimmer and two unit-type vertical tails on each wing. All flight surfaces are thin and swept back to minimize compressibility effects. A jettisonable auxiliary wing is mounted above the fuselage in a biplane arrangement to carry auxiliary fuel. Wing tip turrets are provided for defense.

WEIGHTS

Gross Wt. (Biplane) 113,000
Gross Wt. (Monoplane) 72,988
Weight Empty 38,856

POWER PLANT

Six Westinghouse XJ46-WE-2 (X24C10) turbo-jet engines.

RATINGS

Engine Performance without afterburner

Rating	Thrust	R.P.M.
T.O.	4200	10,100
Mil.	4200	10,100
Norm.	3820	—

Intermediate Engine Performance without afterburner (Est.)

Rating	Thrust	R.P.M.
T.O.	4400	10,100
Mil.	4400	10,100
Norm.	3660	—

FUEL AND OIL

4- Self-sealing tanks in fuselage with 640 gals. each.
2- Self-sealing tanks in main wing with 640 gals. each.
2- Bladder cells in auxiliary wing with 2880 gals. each.
Total fuel 9600 gals.

OIL

One two-gallon oil tank integral with each engine. Total capacity is 12 gallons.

ORDNANCE

1 - 10,000 lb. bomb load.
2 - Tip turrets, one on each wing with 2 - 20 mm guns and 500 rds. of ammunition per gun.
1 - APG-25 radar fire control system.
1 - AN/APB-2 (MkV) bomb director.

DIMENSIONS

Overall span:	
Wings spread	95'1"
Wings folded	55'0"
Overall length:	
Wings spread	60'2.3"
Wings folded	55'9"
Overall height:	
Biplane	19'4"
Monoplane	15'5"

ELECTRONICS

AN/APN-1 Radar Altimeter
AN/ARC-1 VHF
AN/APB-2 Bomb Director
AN/ART-13 MHF Trans.
AN/ARR-15 MHF Rec.
AN/ARR-12A Nav. Rec.
AN/APX-6 IFF
AN/AIC-4 ICS
AN/ARC-5 Range Rec.
APG-25 Fire Control

National Archives, RG 72

Above Right: Standard Aircraft Characteristics chart summarizing the main features of the Fairchild M-128 design.

Left: Physical and performance characteristics taken from the M-128 proposal brochure.

Loading Condition		Basic Design Gross Wt.	Maximum Design Gross Weight	
Configuration		MONOPLANE	BIPLANE	
Airplane Characteristics				
Gross Weight	lbs.	72988	113000	
Internal Fuel Capacity	gal.	3840		
External Fuel Capacity	gal.		5760	
Total Fuel Capacity	gal.	3840	9600	
Wing Area	sq.ft.	1203	2406	
Aspect Ratio		6.98	4.24	(effective)
Wing Loading (W/S)	lbs/sq.ft.	60.68	46.97	
Thrust Loading (W/T) S.L., Static with Duct Losses				
Normal Rating	lb/lb.	3.32	5.15	
Military Rating	lb/lb.	2.76	4.28	
Engine Characteristics				
Model		Westinghouse XJ46-WE		
		Intermediate Ratings		
Number of Units		6		
Static Ratings (S.L. with duct losses)				
Normal	lbs/ Thrust/unit	3660		
Military	lbs/ Thrust/unit	4400		

National Archives, RG 72

		Basic Design Gross Wt. MONOPLANE		Maximum Design Gross Weight BIPLANE	
		Normal	Military	Normal	Military
Vmax at Sea Level	Knots	535	560	420	470
Vmax at 10,000 ft.	Knots	537	551	434	475
Vmax at 20,000 ft.	Knots	524	531	441	463
Vmax at 30,000 ft.	Knots	505	511	420	441
Vmax at 40,000 ft.	Knots	485	494		
Maximum Speed	Knots	539	560	441	475
Altitude for Max. Speed	ft.	6,000	S.L.	20,000	10,000
Maximum Mach Number			.875		.755
Altitude for Max. Mach Number	ft.		35,000		22,000
Rate of Climb at S.L.	ft/min.	5,160	7,200	2,500	3,520
Rate of Climb at 10,000 ft.	ft/min.	4,180	5,610	1,790	2,510
Rate of Climb at 20,000 ft.	ft/min.	3,150	4,090	1,040	1,540
Rate of Climb at 30,000 ft.	ft/min.	2,040	2,750	310	710
Rate of Climb at 40,000 ft.	ft/min.	900	1,520		
Rate of Climb at S.L. - Navy Hot Day,					
Gear Down - 95% CLMAX	ft/min.		2,270		650
Time to Climb to 10,000 ft.	min.	2.2	1.5	4.7	3.3
Time to Climb to 20,000 ft.	min.	4.8	3.6	11.6	8.2
Time to Climb to 30,000 ft.	min.	8.7	6.5	26.0	16.9
Time to Climb to 40,000 ft.	min.	18.0	11.1		

National Archives, RG 72

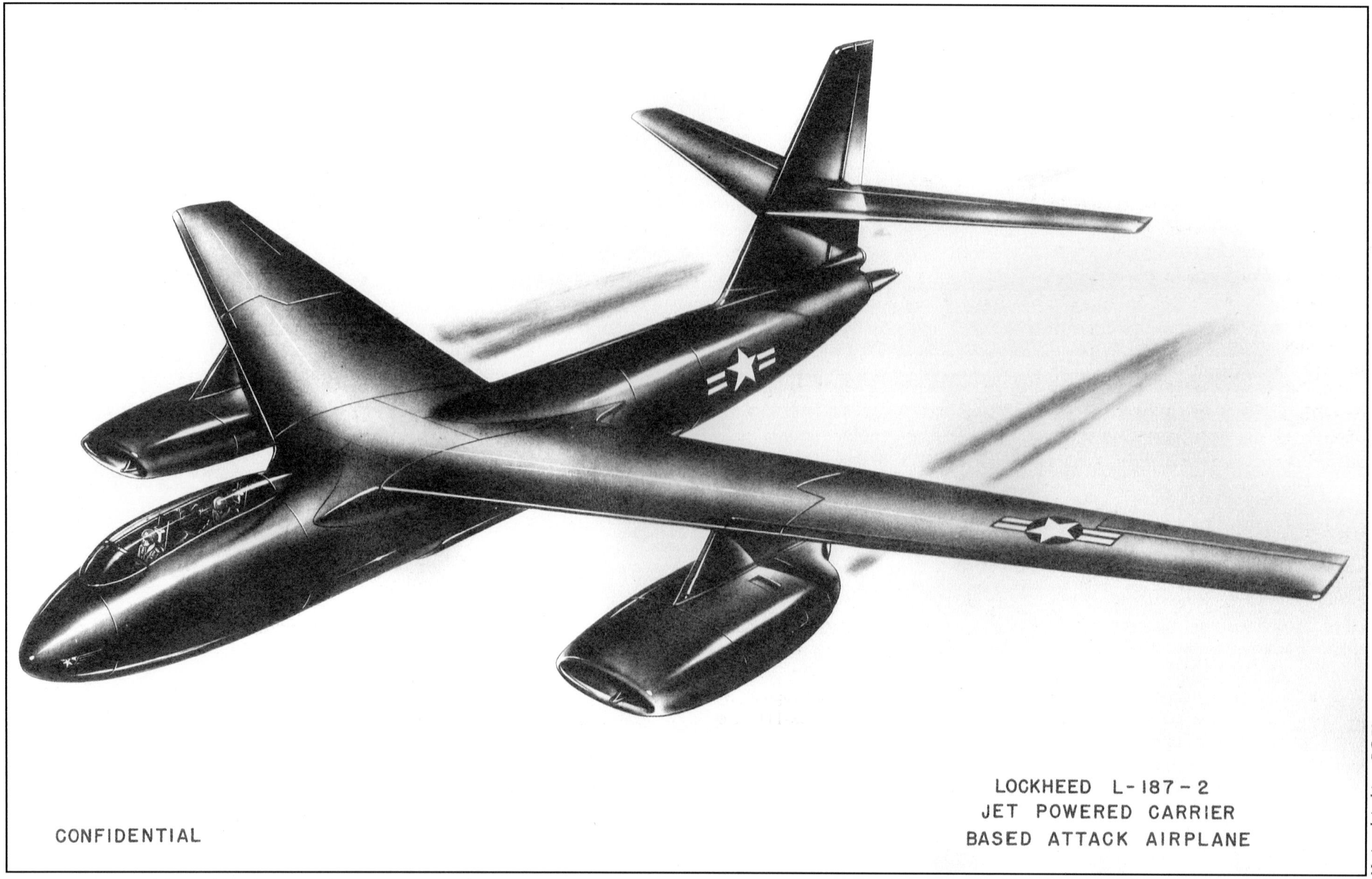

National Archives, RG 72

Artist's impression of the Lockheed L-187-2 Class VA proposal, a four engine jet airplane powered by the Westinghouse XJ-40. The engine nacelles were similar to those of the Convair XB-46, though they were mounted on pylons like the Boeing B-47. Lockheed claimed that this airplane met substantially all of the requirements of OS-111 except combat radius and exceeded the requirements for top speed.

CHAPTER 8 — *Lockheed L-187*

In the competition to design a Class VA aircraft capable of fulfilling OS-111, Lockheed was the only company known to have devoted a substantial portion of its proposal to a turboprop-powered aircraft. Lockheed had been considering the problem of long and medium range bombardment for some time, with the conviction that the most successful way for delivering bomb loads was at extremely high speeds either at sea level or very extreme altitudes. A further conviction was that to do this kind of operation, it was necessary to have a heavily loaded small airplane that would have probably required a considerable amount of takeoff assist in order to be practical. Finally, it was felt that an extreme simplification of crew function, armament protection, and general airplane design had to be made before the desired speeds and small size could possibly be achieved.

A number of airplanes were studied ranging from conventional types to extremely unconventional configurations in attempting to achieve the requirements of the specification and to determine the most desirable of all of the designs studied. The lack of time caused by the required finish date of November 22, 1948 had not allowed full completion of this study and, as a result, Lockheed presented two airplanes for the Navy's consideration. Both of these airplanes fell short of full compliance with OS-111.

Lockheed's investigations of OS-111 led to the conclusion that no practical airplane design could be developed with contemporary technology to comply fully with all of the requirements of the specification. As a result, two design proposals were submitted, each of which fulfilled the majority of the requirements but were deficient in others.

The first design, Model L-187-2, was a four engine jet airplane using four Westinghouse XJ-40 power plants without tail pipe burners. This airplane filled substantially all of the requirements except combat radius and exceeded the requirements for top speed. The second design, Model L-187-7, was a turboprop powered airplane of almost identical configuration except for the power plants. This design utilized two Allison 503 engines (XT-44-A) equipped with long extension shafts and twelve bladed high activity factor Curtiss propellers. The L-187-7 met most of the requirements of OS-111 except that both the combat radius and top speed were deficient. The radius, however, was greater for the same maximum allowable gross weight of 100,000 lbs than with the jet powered version.

Performance studies were made with both airplanes and further study had been made with both airplanes and a further study was made to determine the effect of improvements in power plant performance if a Wright TJ-6 jet engine were substituted for the two XJ-40 engines in each nacelle of the L-187-2. The future range capabilities of the TJ-6 airplane were considerably greater than that of an XJ-40 airplane since basically the airplane drag was lower and the weight was considerably reduced.

A further study was made of the two specification airplanes in an attempt to achieve the maximum range with the guaranteed engine performance as approved by BuAer. In this investigation, the airplanes which complied fully with the specification requirements were methodically stripped in an effort to reduce weight and increase fuel capacity until an airplane with the maximum possible range was achieved. A 1,690 mile radius could

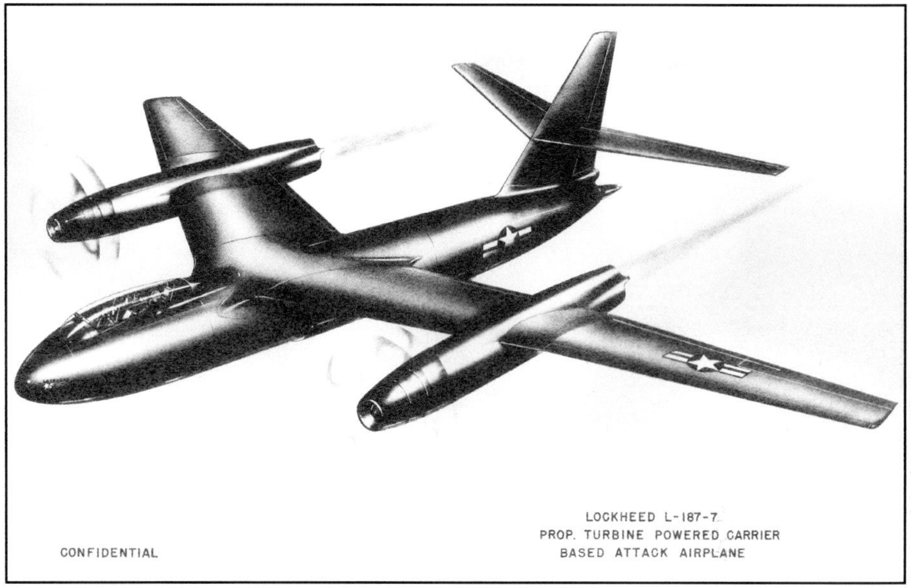

National Archives, RG 72

Artist's impression of the Lockheed L-187-7, a turboprop powered airplane of almost identical configuration to the L-187-2 except for the power plants. Powered by two Allison 503 engines (XT-44-A) equipped with long extension shafts and twelve bladed Curtiss propellers, the L-187-7 met most of the requirements of OS-111 except for combat radius and top speed.

be obtained with the jet airplane and a radius of 1,950 miles could be achieved with the propeller airplane if the following reductions in additional requirements were made:

A. Jet Airplane
   1. Removal of tail gun turret.
   2. Removal of crew access to bomb bay.
   3. Removal of bullet sealing on all fuel.
   4. Addition of skids in place of all landing wheels and utilization of takeoff cart.
   5. Reduction in bomb size and reduction in bomb weight to 6,000 lbs.
   6. Reduction from 3 to 2 in crew size.
   7. Removal of wing flaps.

B. Propeller Airplane
   1. Removal of tail gun turret.
   2. Removal of crew access to bomb bay.
   3. Removal of bullet sealing on all fuel.
   4. Reduction in bomb size and reduction in bomb weight to 6,000 lbs.
   5. Reduction from 3 to 2 in crew size.

Lockheed also studied the range performance gained by overloading up to the maximum capability of a practical amount of JATO (4,000 lbs thrust). It was determined that the L-187-2 had a radius of 1,240 miles and the L-187-7 had a radius of 1,620 miles. The overload gross under these conditions was only 110,780 lbs.

From these studies, Lockheed recommended that a jet version of the airplane be constructed essentially as outlined in its proposal and that serious consideration be given

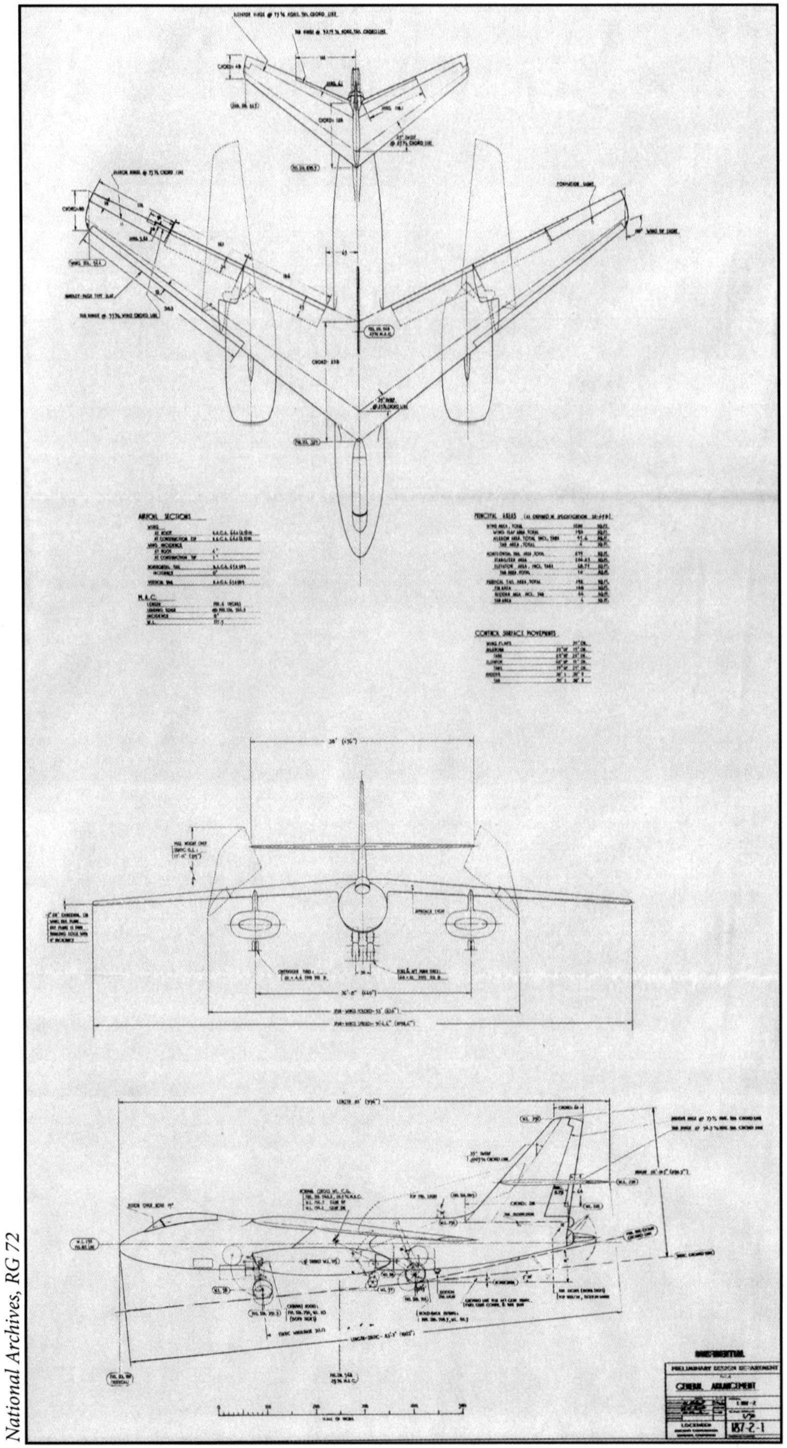

National Archives, RG 72

during the design to a quickly interchangeable power plant so that the Wright TJ-6 or similar engine could be easily installed to improve the range.

If maximum range was required before power plant improvements became available, a stripped airplane could have been constructed to achieve the radius of 1,590 miles, and if overloaded for takeoff a radius of over 1,880 miles could have been obtained with the XJ-40 engines.

It was the conclusion of Lockheed's study that the propeller driven airplane was impractical since:

1. Gear boxes, extension shafts, counter-rotating high activity factor propellers of twelve blades and large spinners with built-in fans and hub fairings had to be developed.
2. The airplane did not meet the high speed requirements which were number 2 on the priority list below cruising speed.
3. Future improvements in the power plant were not expected to change the airplane speed, whereas future improvements in the simpler, more predictable and developed jet engines could be expected to remove the deficiencies in range.
4. The stability in pitch of the propeller airplane was marginal in spite of extensive changes in configuration to obtain adequate stability.

General Arrangement

The configurations of both the propeller and jet-powered airplanes were very nearly identical except for the power plant installations. The general arrangement was basically conventional with the engines enclosed in nacelles on a 35° swept high wing. Wing sections were 10% thick measured parallel to the fuselage center line. The empennage was conventional with the exception that the horizontal tail had been raised on the vertical to avoid disturbance from the wing and power plants. All sections on the empennage were 9% thick and the sweep angle was identical to the wing (35° and on the ¼ chord line). The landing gear on the two airplanes was of the bicycle type with the main gears equally distant from the normal center of gravity of the airplane.

The wing arrangement on the two airplanes was different since the clearance problems of the propellers on the deck did not permit as much negative dihedral as was desired for stability reasons. Thus, to obtain stability characteristics adequate for flight, it was necessary to put anhedral in the outer wing panels only. The clearance of the nacelle and the deck on the two airplanes required, of course, two different outrigger gears. A further change required by the differences in the nacelles was the arrangement of the wing flaps. In the propeller airplane, these flaps had to be broken to clear the aft end of the nacelle, thus reducing the flap area and adding to the complication of the flap system.

Fuselage and Interior Arrangement

The nose of the fuselage was reserved for the installation of the Mk. 5 bomb director antenna and this area was followed immediately by the portion of the fuselage reserved for the crew. The pilot and copilot were arranged in tandem for minimum drag and to increase the space available around both crew members for the installation of the additional equipment required for operating the airplane to permit the copilot enough space so that he could act as a competent navigator. The copilot was raised somewhat above the pilot in order to provide good vision down over the nose and to raise his eyes above the side sills of the canopy to provide good vision over the side of the airplane. The only controls provided for the copilot

Left: Three-view drawing of the Lockheed L-187-2 Class VA proposal.

were the autopilot flight control and engine shutoff controls. All of the navigation equipment was arranged around the copilot's station within easy reach.

In the pilot's station full flight controls were available, including all power controls, landing gear controls, and the basic flight instruments. The bomb tender's station was located aft and below the copilot to provide easy access to the passage through the forward fuselage to the bomb bay and to provide adequate width for the radar equipment associated with the tail gun firing and the control panel for bomb monitoring. The passage from the crew quarters aft to the bomb bay was on the right side of the airplane and consisted only of a floor and opening in the major bulkheads. The only pressurized door in the system was the door at the aft pressure bulkhead of the crew compartment which was used as the normal means of entrance to the cabin through the wheel well.

Emergency exit procedure for this crew arrangement was quite simple. Both the pilot and copilot were equipped with explosive ejection seats and the canopy was provided with a similar type of emergency jettisoning device. This type of system had been developed at the Lockheed Company for use on its jet trainer version of the standard F-80 fighter. Emergency exit for the bomb tender was provided by an opening in the lower portion of the fuselage directly under his seat. The opening had a pressurized cover which was attached to the seat which in turn was mounted on guide rails so that the seat could be ejected in a downward direction through the belly of the crew quarters. The ejection would have either been of the spring or light explosion type depending upon the amount of energy required to actually push the seat out of the opening while guided by the seat mount rails. Emergency exit for the bomb tender during ditching was provided by a large opening aft of the copilot's position which was uncovered when the canopy was jettisoned. Separate controls were, of course, provided for the canopy and explosive seats so that the canopy could be removed during a ditching operation without activating the seat charges.

Aft of the crew quarters was the fuselage area devoted to the forward gas tanks and the forward main gear. Retraction of the main gear was in a forward direction so that extension was simple under emergencies when the main actuating system was inactive. Fuel tanks in this area contained 1,959 gallons, which was considerably less than was possible if the passage to the bomb bay had not been required.

The bomb bay was located aft of the forward tank area so that the bomb CG corresponded with the normal airplane CG. This area had not been designed in any great detail since information on the bomb load had not been divulged - secrecy regarding the atomic bomb was exceptionally tight during this period. Bomb bay doors were of the roll-up type and were completely external to the airplane so that during opening, the doors themselves had no loads greater than in the closed position and caused no additional drag or pitch changes to the airplane other than that caused by the bomb opening itself.

Aft of the bomb bay was an additional tank bay and landing gear bay containing the aft gear and the aft tank system. The aft gear retracted in an aft direction in order to provide adequate structure on the gear so that it could be used as the hold-back point for the catapult. The geometry of the gear and the fact that it was too short to have extreme air loads made it possible to extend the gear under gravity alone in an emergency in spite of the aft retraction motion. The

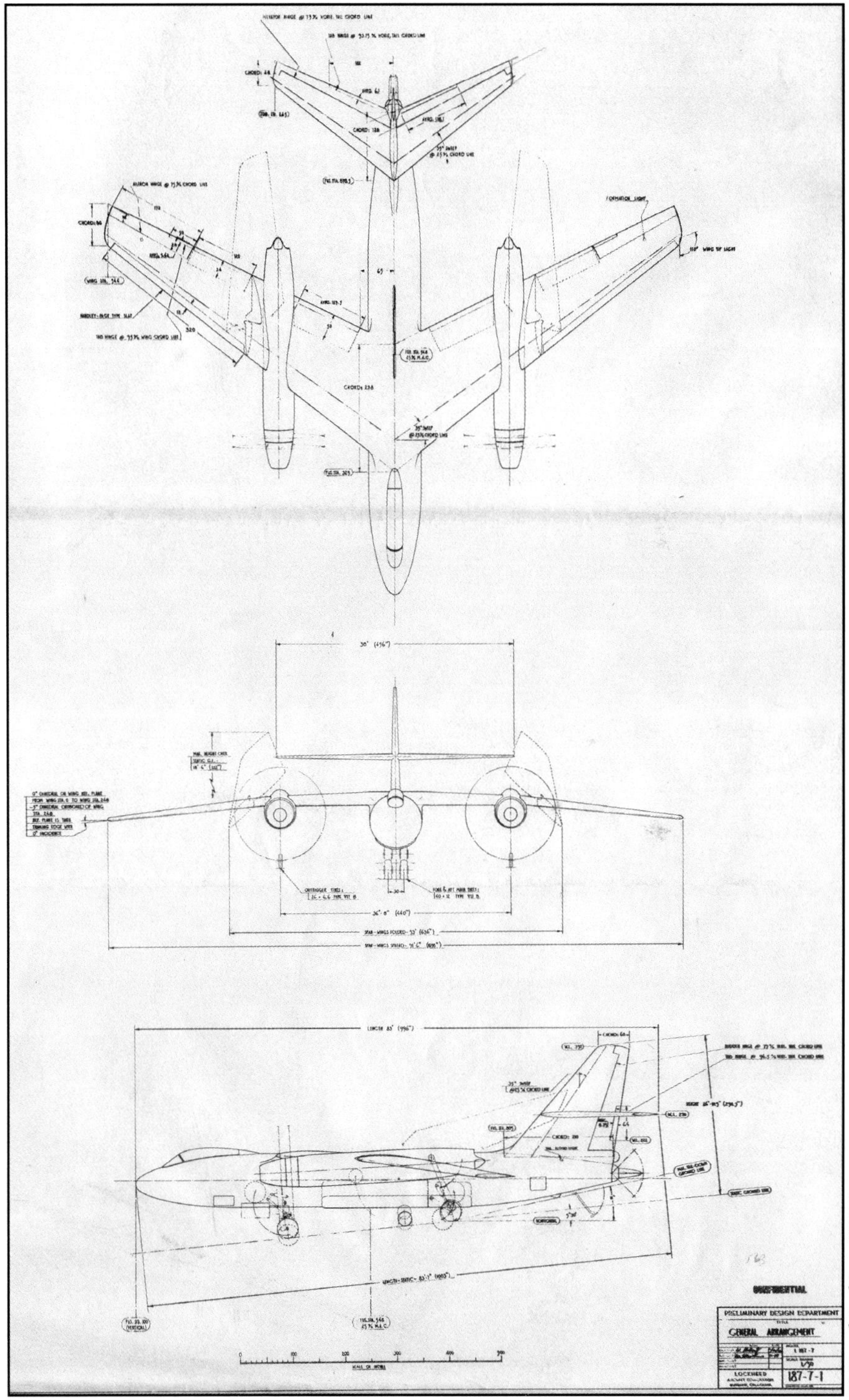

National Archives, RG 72

Right: Three-view drawing of the Lockheed L-187-7 Class VA proposal; note the anhedral added to the outer wings to ensure sufficient flight stability.

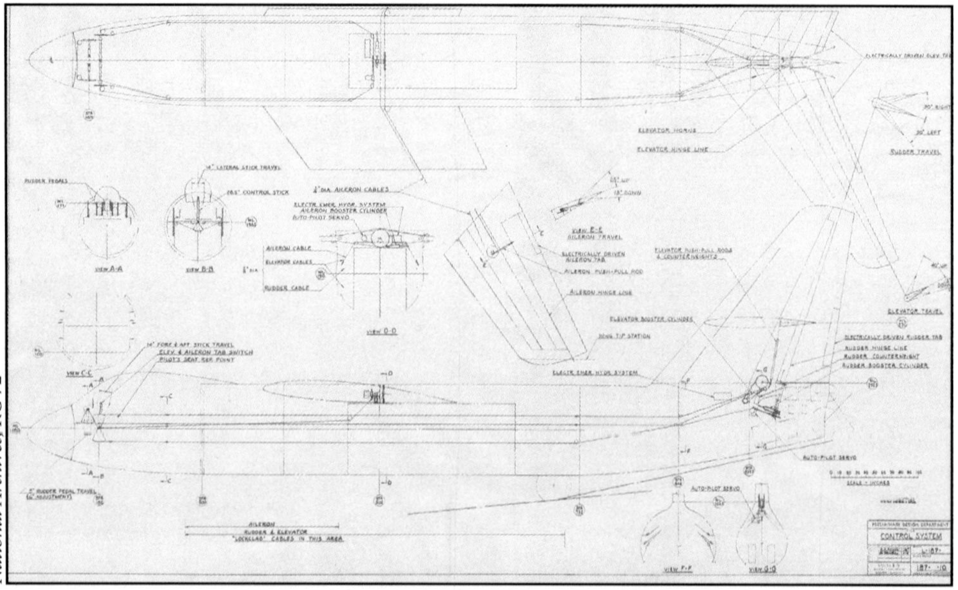

National Archives, RG 72

Above: Diagram of the control system, which was common to both L-187 airplanes.

aft tank bay contained 1,450 gallons of fuel.

In the empennage area the XAR-6 tail turret was installed along with the radar scanner for its control. Ammunition was stowed in low ammunition boxes on the lower surface of the fuselage to avoid interference with the tail controls. Since the guns of this tail turret were close together, it was decided to add a fairing to the tail turret so that cruise drag was improved. Lockheed believed that the additional hinge moment caused by this fairing would not be substantial enough to cause difficulty in the operation of the guns.

Arresting and Catapult Provisions

Considerable study was expended on this arrangement since the airplane incorporated a bicycle gear and the catapult loads appeared to be very nearly the most critical on this airplane. Forward catapult hooks were installed on the main lower fuselage longerons in the region of the forward gear fulcrum attachment. This was a strong point on the fuselage and the loads from the catapult could be taken directly into the main load carrying members of the fuselage. Two hooks were provided, one on each side of the fuselage, to be used with a long bridle on the carrier. Fenders were provided on the nose gear and the aft gear to prevent the bridle when disengaged from entangling either set of wheels.

Since the airplane could not be airborne under full load at the end of the catapult, it was necessary for both wheels of the main gear to roll over the bridle unless the carrier design was such that the bridle was swallowed by some device on the carrier deck. Experiments

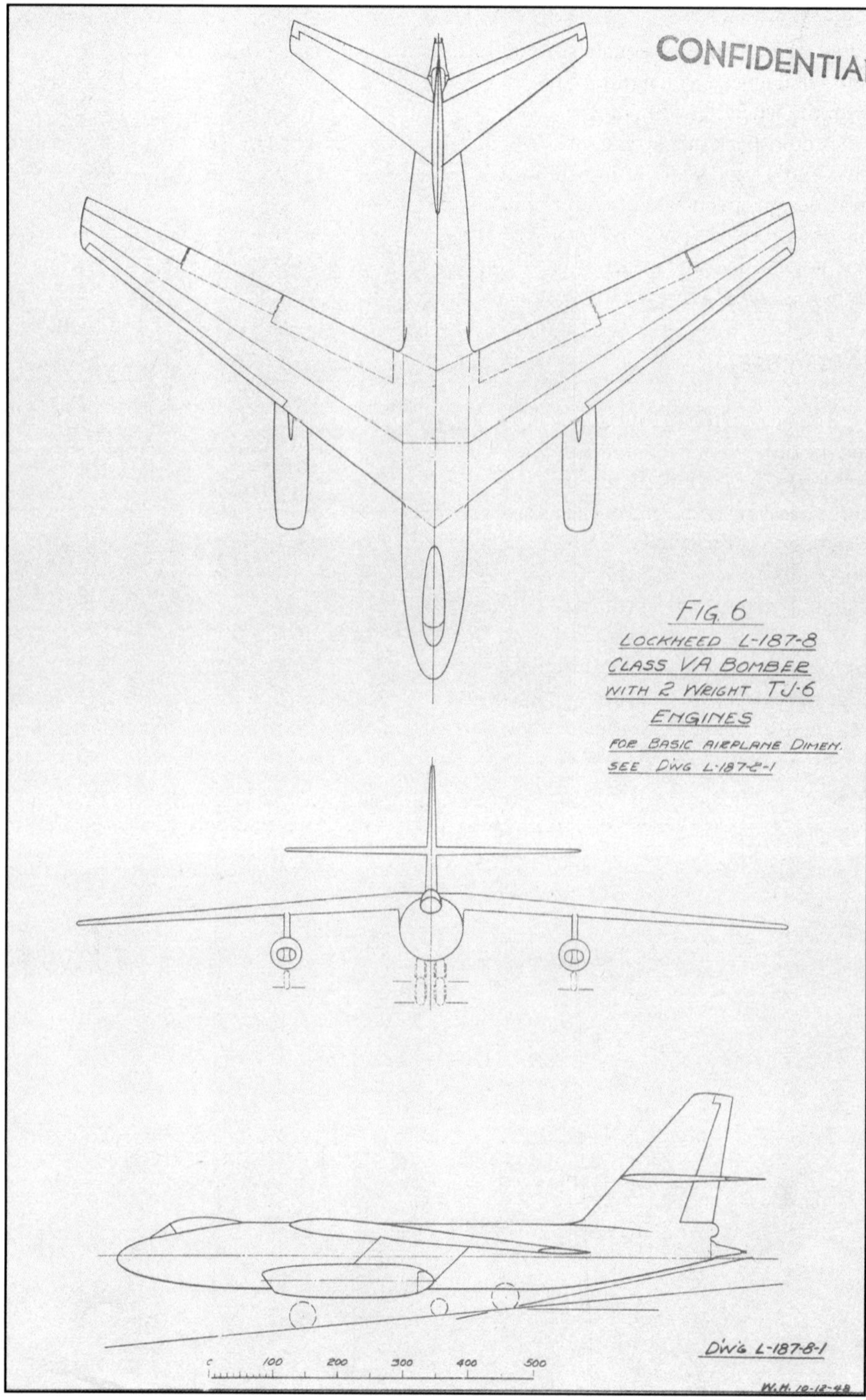

National Archives, RG 72

Right: Three-view drawing of the L-187-8, a modification of the L-187-2 powered by a pair of Wright TJ-6 engines. The estimated range of this variant was superior to that of the L-187-2 airplane due to the reduction in both airplane drag and weight.

with other high speed airplanes at Lockheed indicated that the wheels could roll over a cable which was of adequate size to be the bridle, and since this cable was of large size and relatively short length, it was not expected that any difficulty would be experienced with the wheels picking up the cable while rolling over it.

A hold-back fitting was attached at the axle between the two rear wheels of the main gear and a very short fitting connected this to the deck hold-back. The main landing gear design specifically accommodated this fitting in that the drag link of the gear had been attached to the aft end of the two main longerons in the fuselage in a direct line with the hold-back of the deck. Thus, no eccentricities existed and no additional loads were imposed on the aft gear by this hold-back function.

Wing Design

The basic wing design differed little between the airplanes, the major distinction being the difference in dihedral angles and in the cut-out for the flap in the propeller engine version. The basic structure of the wing was of the three spar type which permitted cutting down the length of the contour formers and reducing their weight. The former weight was of substantial importance on a wing designed for high speeds since the major portion of the load carried by the surface of the wing was pressure loaded, the bending being carried by concentrated caps on the spars with high material allowables.

The leading edge of the wing incorporated space provisions only for heat anti-icing aft to the 15% chord point. It was this provision which prevented the use of the leading edge as space for fuel. Leading edge slots were provided outboard of the nacelles to control the tip stall characteristics associated with the high degree of sweep and taper ratio necessitated on this airplane. These slots were of the automatic type and were not interconnected. They were controlled, however, by the landing flaps through a brake installed on the slot system so that its automatic features were operable only when the main wing flaps had been extended. Heat was provided to the leading edge slots by means of flexible or slide tubes in the event that heat anti-icing was provided on the airplane.

The flaps were of the Fowler type and were interconnected across the airplane. These flaps were not full-span because of the difficulty of obtaining an adequate spoiler type of aileron control system on a 10% thick wing and because the full-span flap gained very little CL maximum because of the high pitching moment encountered without compensating downwash on the horizontal tail which required not only a down-tail load to trim but required a large change in stabilizer incidence that was not required with partial span flaps. Thus, the full-span flaps carried substantial weight penalties because of the complication of the flap system, the aileron system, and an adjustable empennage system.

Normal ailerons with sealed hinges were provided which were boost operated. The wing folding mechanism consisted of an oblique hinge with hinge points on the 40% chord cap strips. This type of wing folding was selected since it permitted the main bending members to be continuous through the joint without a slide bolt fastening and since the wing during folding did not exceed the height in the hangar deck. With a straight folding mechanism in which the outer panel tip was folded up and over toward the fuselage, the height exceeded hangar deck ceiling limitations which would have prevented the wing tip folding mechanism from being checked out in the hangar deck.

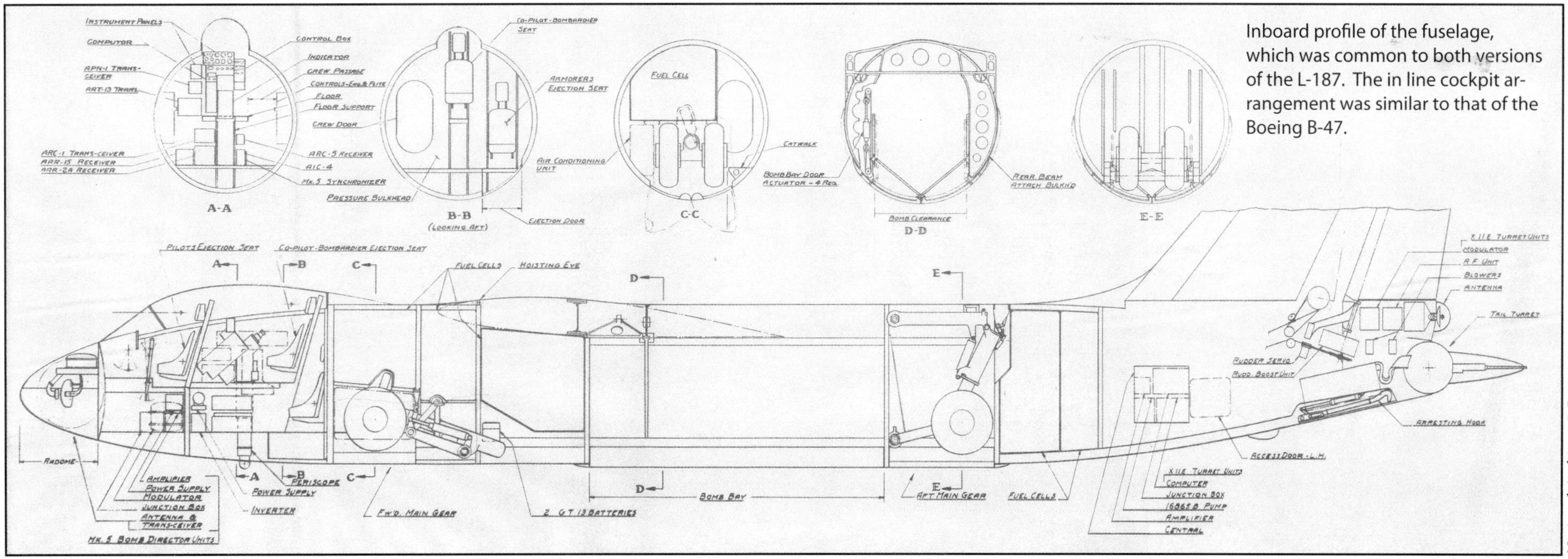

Inboard profile of the fuselage, which was common to both versions of the L-187. The in line cockpit arrangement was similar to that of the Boeing B-47.

National Archives, RG 72

Power Plant Installation

The jet engine installation was of the pedestal mount type in which the two engines were located below and forward of the wing, and were mounted side by side with a streamline strut between the engines, providing a connection to the basic wing structure. The location of the nacelle, while not superior in drag to other types of nacelles, was at least equal to other installations and so its practical value dictated its use. With the engines located close to the deck and surrounded by only that structure necessary to cowl and mount the engine, power plant accessibility was ideal. Furthermore, having concentrated connections to the wing as provided by the strut, it became entirely feasible to make a quick change power plant in order to keep the airplane operational in spite of minor power plant faults by replacing a faulty power plant and leaving it behind for more leisurely maintenance and troubleshooting. (Right and left hand power plants were interchangeable on the jet airplane only). A further advantage of this type of power plant was the fact that all of the fire sources associated with power plant operation were divorced by considerable distance from the wing structure and its tanks. Therefore, fire control and danger from uncontrolled fire was reduced to a minimum. This was a decided advantage for any tactical airplane and Lockheed felt that it would have went far in

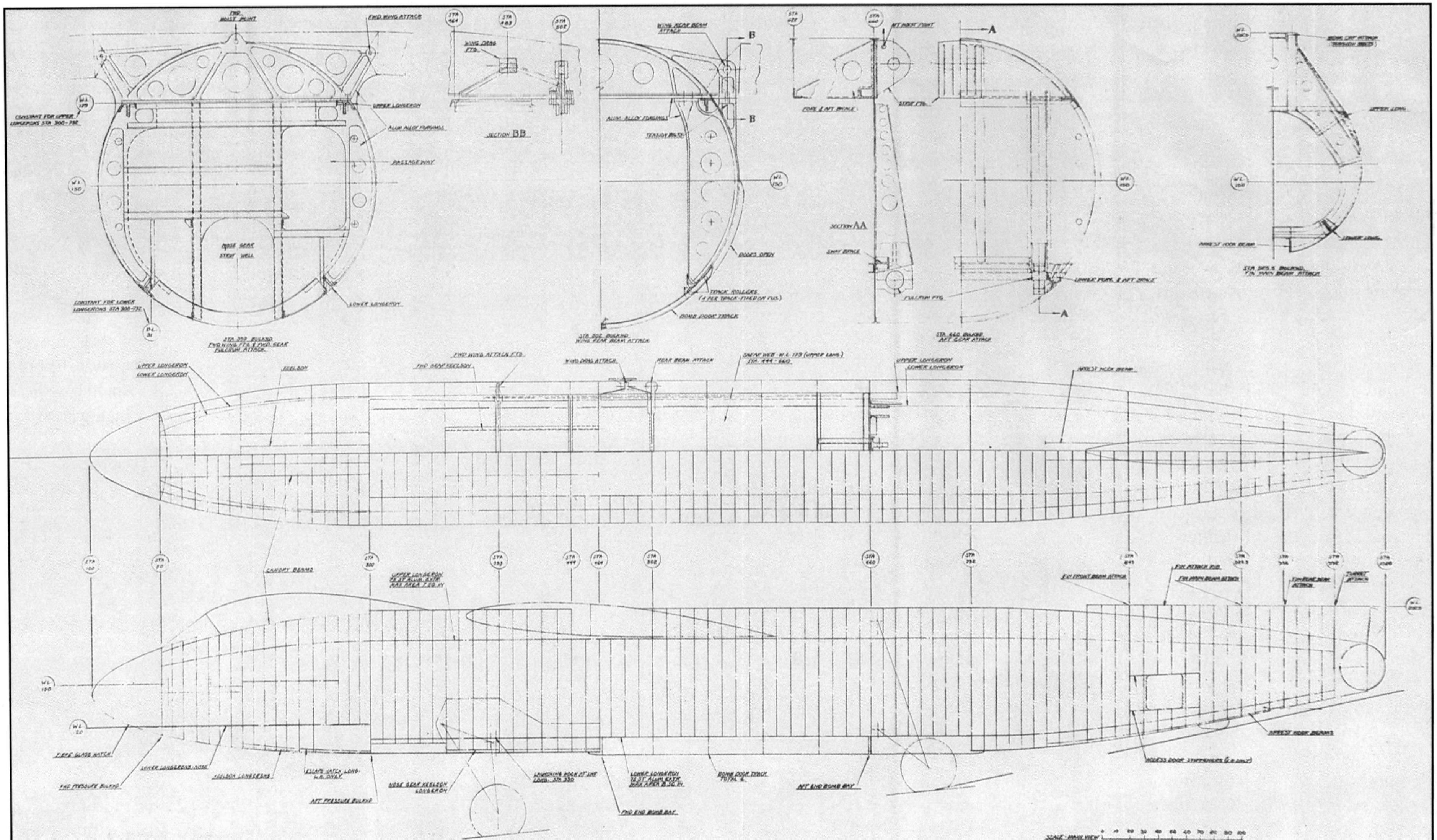

Blueprint of the L-187 fuselage structure, which was of the conventional longeron-ring type.

National Archives, RG 72

improving crew morale and reducing the percentage losses during missions.

The turbine propeller power plant was considerably more complicated than the jet engine. Stability studies showed the necessity of anhedral and a nose down thrust line with the highest possible position of the thrust line with respect to the vertical airplane CG. All of these requirements necessitated a high nacelle position, higher than could be obtained with the engines under the wing. Thus, the engines were located aft of the rear spar and extension shafts were utilized to place the propellers far enough forward of the wing to properly clear the leading edge and to balance the power plant CG for flutter prevention on the wing. Thus, long extension shafts (one extending through the wing structure), long ducts, and a long outrigger gear were dictated by the effects of the propeller on flight characteristics. The penalties added to the necessity of putting the required anhedral in the outer panel only, adding substantially to the weight of the propeller installation.

Structural Design

The structural design of both aircraft was relatively conventional with the exception of the very heavy surface gauges required by the high speed pressure loads and the necessity of maintaining minimum surface structure depth in order to utilize all possible interior space. It was proposed that the surface structure of the upper and lower surfaces of the wing and leading edge be of rolled or machined skin in production versions of the airplane since this type of structure represented the lightest and thinnest which was possible to achieve within the necessary wing weight for the airplane. Lockheed had been experimenting with this type of structure and it was being used to a limited extent in production airplanes. A major research project had been the design and construction of an outer wing panel for the Constellation transport. This study showed that the machine surfaces could be utilized without large increases in cost at a considerably lighter weight. Furthermore, a smoother structure was achieved as compared to the more conventional sheet-stringer-riveted or spotwelded construction.

Lockheed also proposed investigation of a new method of structure on the flaps, ailerons and movable control surfaces in which the surfaces were constructed with relatively light gauges and the entire interior space was filled with a foamed plastic which was cast into the structure and cured. This type of surface had been developed at Lockheed and successful efforts to date had led to its inclusion as a production structure for tabs on high performance fighter airplanes.

Empennage structure would have been conventional, unless it had been possible to obtain rolled sheet with integral stiffeners for use as a surface material. The fuselage structure was of the longeron-ring type. The major portion of the bending loads were carried by four main longerons, the lower ones bordering the wheel wells and bomb bay, the upper ones passing below the main wing center section structure. Closely spaced rings supported the surface structure between the longerons. Bulkheads were located within the fuselage structure at highly concentrated load points and were suitably reinforced for these loads. Main bulkheads were located at the aft pressure bulkhead in the cockpit, at the nose gear fulcrum, fore and aft of the bomb bay, at the main wing attachment, at the aft gear supporting points, and at the main empennage attachment points. A keel was located on the bottom center line of the rear fuselage to carry the landing hook loads and distribute them into the longerons through shear in the lower surface skin structure.

Landing Gear

The landing gear consisted of main and outrigger landing gear units. As previously noted, the main gears were identical for either the propeller or the turbojet airplane, whereas the outriggers were different due to the different nacelle configurations. The main gears utilized 40" x 12" type VII B tires mounted in dual units and incorporating brakes on both the fore and aft wheels. The nose gear was steerable from a wheel in the cockpit at the pilot's station. By means of quick disconnect, it was possible to swivel the nose gear through a full 360° for ease in maneuvering the airplane on deck. No disconnect was required for plus or minus 90° deck towing angles.

It was proposed that large hooks be installed on the rear main gear for the purpose of guiding a barrier cable onto the rear gear where structure was available to withstand the barrier loads. This would have required a device similar to that proposed by the designers of carrier equipment in which the barrier cables laid flush with the deck and were raised by a nylon line which was engaged by the nose gear when the airplane passed over the barrier area. Hooking the barrier to the aft gear would have undoubtedly involved damage to the propellers and the outrigger wheels in the case of the propeller airplane and would have probably caused damage to the outrigger of the jet airplane unless a drag load could be arrived at under which the retracting mechanism of the outboard gear would have allowed the gear to trail as the barrier cable hit it. In spite of this, the rear gear was used to withstand the barrier crash condition because its structure was the most easily capable of handling these extreme loads. In addition, the airplane would have been stable in the forward direction as the rear gear caught the cable, not swinging sideways when the barrier halted its forward speed.

A 26" x 6.6" type VII B single tire was used on each outrigger of the propeller airplane whereas 20" x 4.4" type VII B dual tires were used for the outrigger of the jet airplane. This difference in tire size was dictated by the necessity of making the outrigger fully swiveling through 360° on the jet airplane and the nacelle was too low to the deck to allow a larger size tire to swivel beneath it. The single tire was used on the propeller driven airplane since the gear had to be narrow to retract between the two lower extension shafts of the Allison 503 engine.

Effect of Equipment and Power Plants on Performance

As part of Lockheed's investigation, an effort was made to determine what penalty in equipment carried or other sacrifices were required to make the airplanes capable of the full desired radius and what additional improvements could be made to the power plant for the same purpose.

Advanced Power Plants The estimated performance of Lockheed's turboprop airplane was based on a BuAer study of the Allison 503 turboprop engine. BuAer estimates showed that no increase in range could be obtained with the engine by means of a reduction in fuel consumption unless unreasonably high component efficiencies were assumed. Since this study showed no improvement on the XJ-40 jet engine either, it was decided to make a brief study with different jet power plants of a more advanced nature in order to compare the airplane with the propeller version using the Allison 503.

Lockheed prepared general arrangement and power plant installation drawings for the L-187-8 airplane using the proposed Wright Aeronautical Corporation TJ-6 engine. The potential power of this engine meant that only two were required to meet the specifications for rate of climb and to meet the high speed requirements. Thus, a substantial weight saving was possible along with a substantial drag reduction. The improvement achieved by the use of the more advanced jet power plant was obvious and the configuration of the airplane was such that this improvement was a relatively simple change that could have been made when the engine became available. Lockheed noted that even more advanced engines were being proposed by some manufacturers and with the configuration of the airplane selected, the installation of practically any engine or even number of engines was relatively simple.

Equipment Reduction (Stripping) Since neither the propeller airplane nor the jet airplane as proposed by Lockheed fully complied with the radius requirements, a serious effort was made to reduce the size and weight of the airplane by eliminating numerous detail specification requirements in order to improve weight and range characteristics. The items studied include:

1. Reduction in bomb size and weight below specification values but within values known to be reasonable for certain types of bomb loads.
2. Reduction in fuel protection in order to gain space and weight relying only on speed to provide protection.
3. Reduction in landing gear facilities and/or landing gear entirely for the purpose of specialized missions.
4. A reduction in crew size.
5. Removal of all gun fire protection.
6. An investigation of the use of external fuel stores and/or bomb storage.
7. Removal of access to the bomb bay on the basis that automatic monitoring of the bomb had to be developed and the passage space could be used for fuel.
8. Removal of flaps on the basis that they were not required in landing; other aids could be used for takeoff.

All of these items had, of course, an influence on the range capabilities of the airplane and it only remained for the users of this type of airplane to determine which, if any, of these reductions in basic requirements were justified for additional performance.

Lockheed studied three fuselages designed around the space limitations imposed by the various requirements. "A" was the standard fuselage shown in the inboard profile. "B" showed the size reduction possible by reducing the crew by one, by the reduced bomb size, a reduction in wheel size assuming only carrier operation, and by a reduction in the requirement of providing passage from the cockpit to the bomb. Fuselage "C" was the ultimate in the reduction of airplane size in which the landing gear was removed entirely and the remaining crew located inside the fuselage instead of under an all-round vision canopy.

In this maximum stripped proposal a takeoff cart was incorporated which weighed

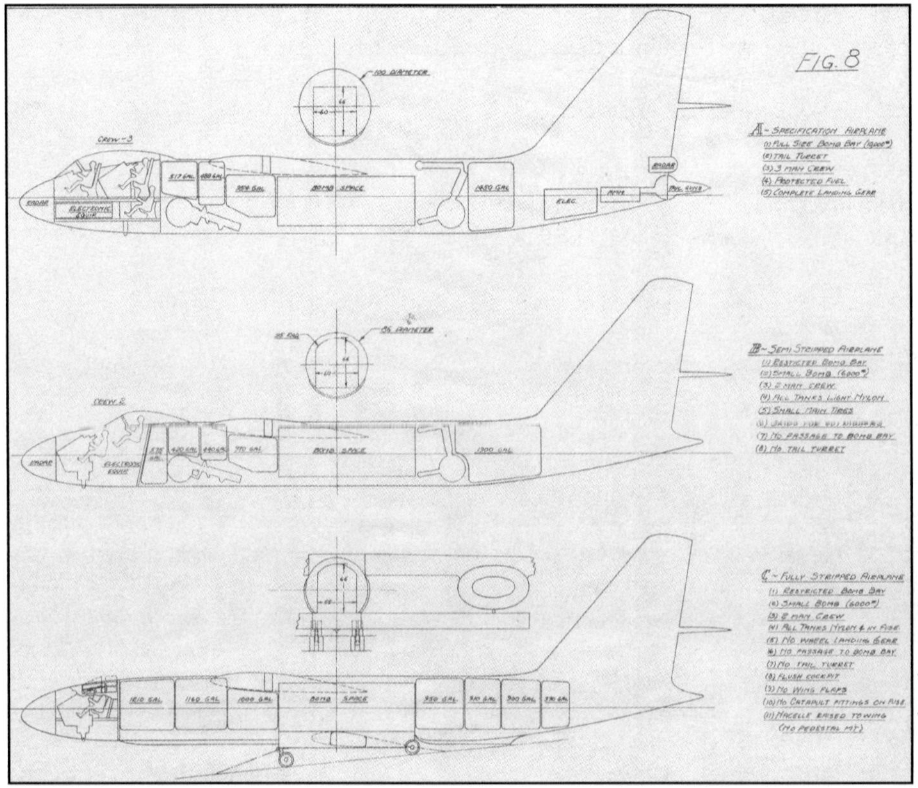

National Archives, RG 72

Lockheed studied several ways of reducing the size and weight of the L-187 to meet OS-111 radius requirements. From top to bottom: fuselage "A" was the baseline design; "B" had only two crew, a smaller bomb and wheels, and no passage to the bomb bay; and "C" had the two crew inside the fuselage in an all-round vision canopy with the landing gear removed entirely. A takeoff cart was provided for this last variant.

approximately 3,000 lbs. This cart contained industrial type wheels with solid tires and incorporated the catapult and hold back fittings. It was made to fit securely on the lower bomb bay longerons with the bomb bay doors open. Wings of 500 square feet area were added to increase the airplane lift so that flaps were not required. This cart was dropped after takeoff and the bomb bay doors closed.

A comparison of the designs indicated that the ultimate reduction in requirement compliance increased the fuel capacity and the radius of the jet airplane by approximately 645 nm. Similar reductions could have been made to the propeller driven airplane and these also gave a sizable increase in radius of approximately 600 nm, enough to exceed substantially the 1,700 nm requirement.

Some of the more radical reductions in weight performed on the jet airplane were impractical on the propeller airplane because of the propellers themselves. The landing gear represented the most important of these. The gear could not be removed and replaced by skids because the propeller clearance was inadequate to protect this expensive device in a skid landing. On the jet airplane skids on the nacelles sufficed and the fuselage belly could have been made replaceable if damage was done. Bomb bay doors were opened during skid landings, thereby reducing the possibility of their suffering damage.

Aerodynamic Design Considerations

The design objectives of this high speed, carrier based bomber airplane dictated the aerodynamic requirements of the configuration if a conventional type of design was chosen. Thus, for Lockheed's proposal, the following requirements were important:

1. Average cruising speed of Mach .85 demanded a critical Mach number of .85 or greater.
2. A high speed of at least Mach .90 at a minimum of 40,000 ft altitude stipulated that the compressibility drag rise had to be minimized. To satisfy these two requirements either an extremely thin straight wing of extremely low aspect ratio was required, or a moderately thin wing with sweep. The latter was chosen as a 10% thick wing with 35° sweep, which gave a negligible compressibility drag increase at cruising speed and which, with the normal difference between normal and military engine ratings, allowed the attainment of the desired high speed. Although additional sweep and reduced thickness was obviously beneficial to performance, investigations proved that the weight and stability penalties involved were excessive compared to the benefits gained.
3. A combat altitude of at least 40,000 ft was not restrictive because of the range performance gained by high altitude flight and because of the power requirements for the takeoff specification.
4. A desired radius of action of 1,700 miles emphasized the aerodynamic benefits of high aspect ratio and moderate power. However, wing weight was of equal importance with fuel weight. A careful evaluation of net range for an airplane with an initial gross weight of 100,000 lbs, with various aspect ratios resulted in the optimum value AR= 7.0. Furthermore, the optimum number of engines for range considerations alone was three of the XJ-40 type.
5. The takeoff problem was unique in its limitations. The catapult on the carrier deck provided a speed of 129 kts in a 150 ft run for all weights up to 100,000 lbs. For higher weights, JATO assist could have been used to maintain the catapult end speed of 129 kts but the catapult acceleration was high and considerable JATO was required because net thrust per JATO unit was low.

   On the hot day required in the takeoff problem, the catapult end speed of 129 kts true air speed may not have been sufficient for flight unless sufficient wing area and/or high lift devices were incorporated. However, 33 ft of deck run remained to allow the airplane to accelerate to a speed at which it could have flown; that is, where the lift equaled the weight with an adequate margin from the wing stall. The time on the catapult was on the order of 1.5 seconds, and from the catapult end to deck end, approximately 1.5 seconds. Thus, it was assumed that the attitude of the airplane could not have been altered during the deck run and, therefore, that the attitude developed sufficient lift to equal airplane weight at deck end speed, on a hot day. A takeoff of this type

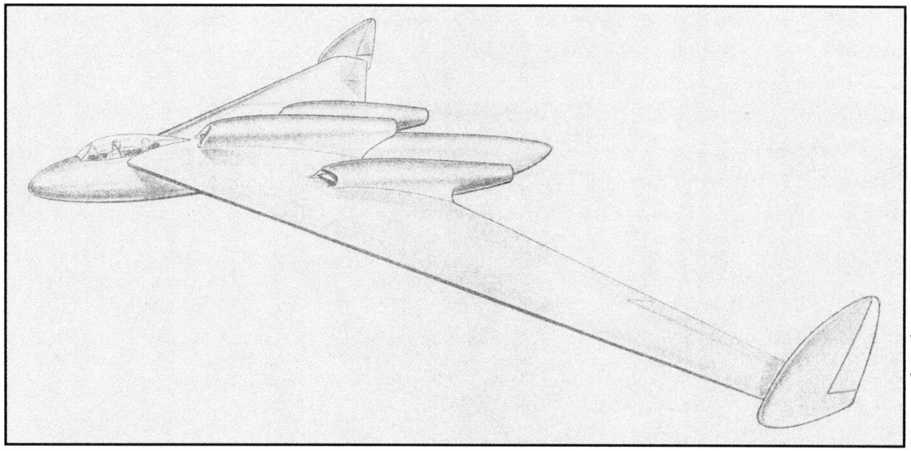

National Archives, RG 72

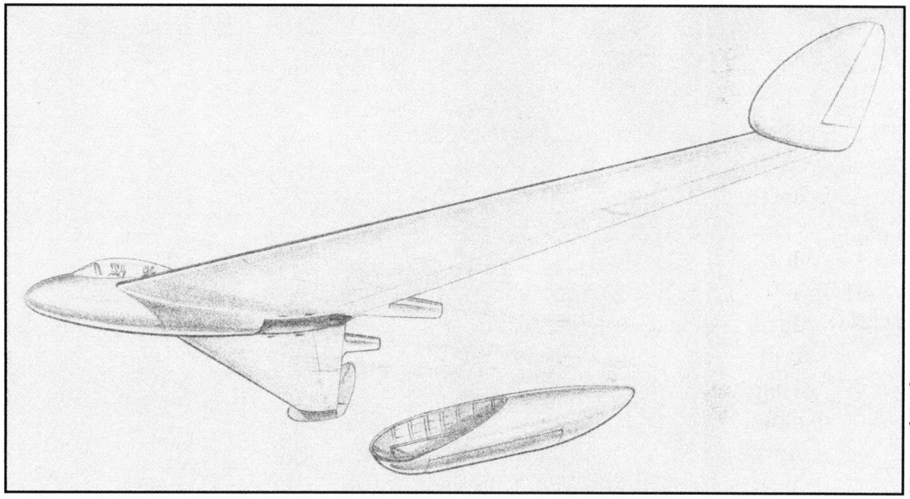

National Archives, RG 72

The L-187-3 was a study for a flying wing with a droppable fuselage containing the bomb and major portion of the fuel tanks. Lockheed's research determined that it was not weight efficient for high design speeds, and the configuration was abandoned early on.

was similar to takeoff from a runway in that the airplane had to have reserve lift coefficient at takeoff. The assumption was made that the takeoff lift coefficient was 90% of the maximum available.

The takeoff problem continued to the point where a 500 ft per minute rate of climb was available with the thrust of the engines alone at which point the JATO could be dropped. Because of the aspect ratio, wing sweep and thickness were dictated by the cruise, high speed, and range considerations, the variation of drag and speed could have been large.

Analysis of this takeoff problem showed little advantage to reducing the wing area to the point where JATO was required for takeoff. A 1,200 sq ft wing area allowed takeoff on a hot day with engine power plus catapult. An indication of the critical nature of this takeoff requirement was shown by the fact that it took 14,000 lbs of JATO for takeoff on a hot day at an overload gross weight of 110,780 lbs (780 lbs being the JATO weight).

6. The stalling speed at design landing weight was not to exceed 115 kts. This requirement did not dictate because with a conventional design takeoff and landing flap positions were identical, and the takeoff problem was most severe.

Unconventional Designs

Expendable Components Studies of expendable lift components, such as added wing area or high lift devices, proved practical only if the landing gear was eliminated. Expendable area at the wing tips was not advantageous because aspect ratio was desirable for flight as well as takeoff. The weight cost of retractable high lift devices was relatively small compared to that of added area where this area was retained throughout the flight.

Studies of expendable fuselage components showed that the most costly part of the flight in terms of fuel was going out to the target. The added fuel cost of increased fuselage drag caused by the by design with droppable fuselage components (bomb bay, fuel tanks, etc.) due to poorer aerodynamic shape and local interferences, practically cancelled the fuel saving on the return flight with the clean configuration.

The Flying Wing The degree of wing sweep back required and the thought of droppable fuselage components suggested a configuration of a flying wing. The takeoff problem, however, dictated 80% more wing area. This, coupled with the large fuselage on the outgoing flight and the increased wing drag due to control surfaces and trim control setting, resulted in similar fuel requirements and excessive empty weight values.

The Canard The tail first design was attractive from the importance of the takeoff problem. Such a configuration was possible but Lockheed's experience, based on numerous wind tunnel tests and analyses in the past, demonstrated that the allowable center of gravity range, limited on one end by stability and on the other by trim requirements, was very restrictive. All configura-

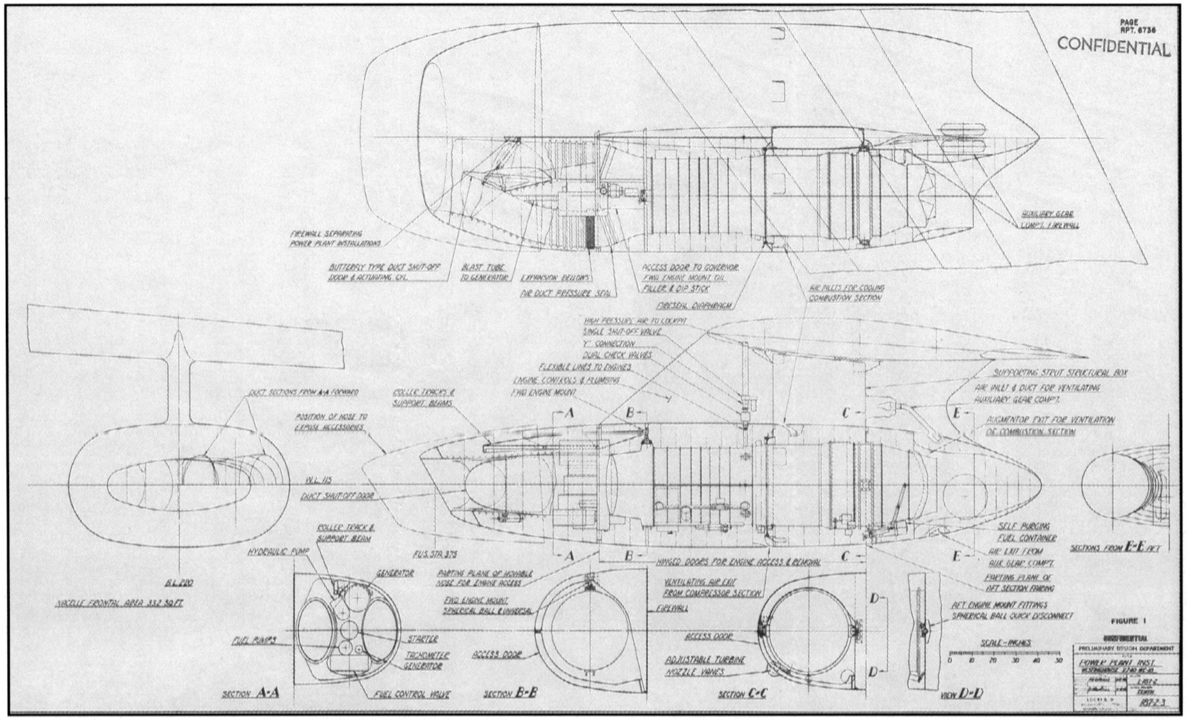

National Archives, RG 72

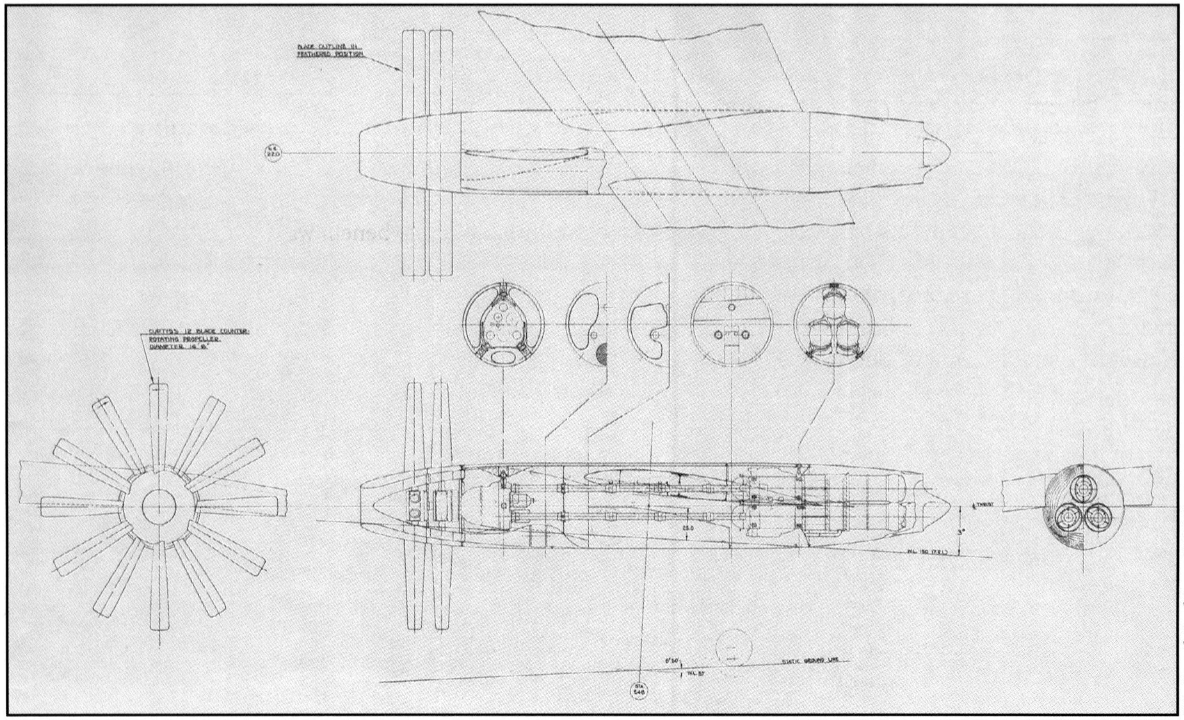

National Archives, RG 72

Right: Blueprints of the power plant installations. The L-187-2 nacelle featured 2 Westinghouse XJ40-WE-10 turbojets (top), while the L-187-7 nacelle housed an Allison 503 (XT-44-A) turboprop (bottom). Note the long extension shafts and ducting of the latter, which were dictated by the aftward placement of the engines to balance the power plant center of gravity.

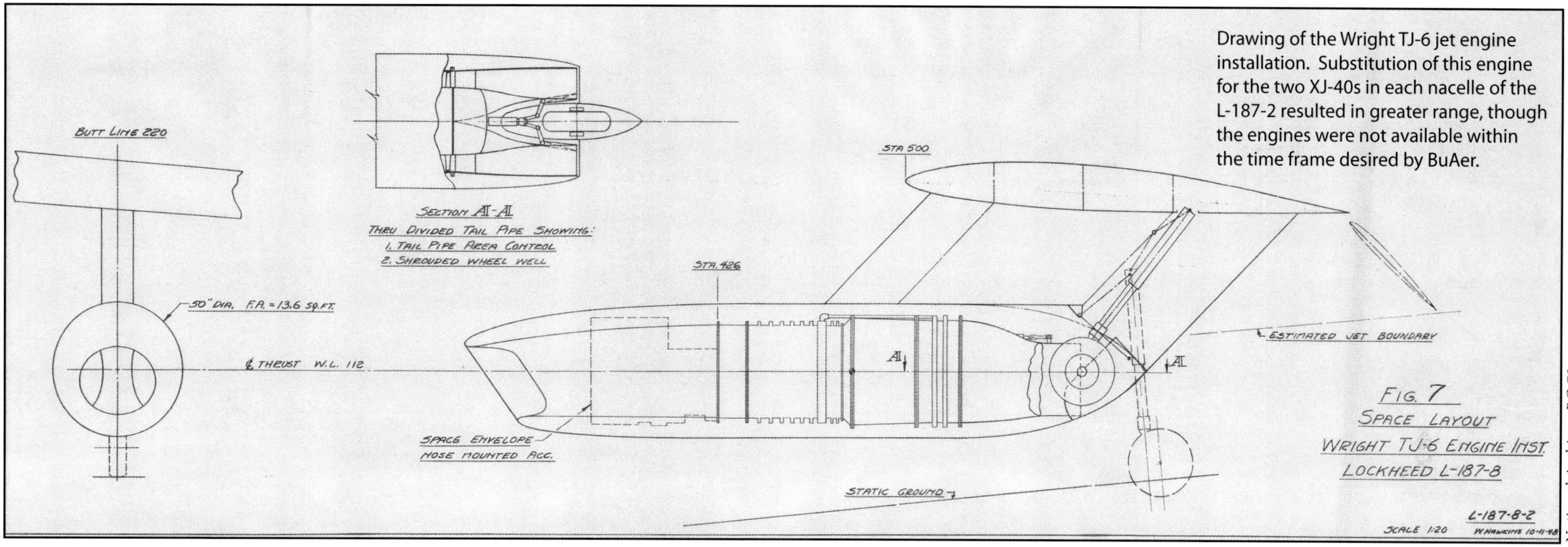

Drawing of the Wright TJ-6 jet engine installation. Substitution of this engine for the two XJ-40s in each nacelle of the L-187-2 resulted in greater range, though the engines were not available within the time frame desired by BuAer.

National Archives, RG 72

tions tried on this proposal required a normal range of center of gravity travel. Therefore, barring the use of "synthetic" stabilizing devices as impractical, the canard type was not satisfactory.

Variable Sweep A design with variable sweep was attractive from the standpoint of high lift and low drag for takeoff, and high critical Mach number for high speed flight. The movement of the MAC had to be limited, however, and the degree of this movement was directly a function of aspect ratio. To attain benefits for takeoff commensurate with the weight penalty involved, a relatively low aspect ratio was required. To attain optimum cruise conditions, high aspect ratio was required. The trigonometry of wing sweep was opposite from this relationship. Therefore, on careful analysis, no benefit was derived.

Boundary Layer Control In the foregoing, it had been assumed that the aerodynamic refinements were limited to optimum airfoil shapes and component fairings. However, the utilization of boundary layer control for increased lift and reduced drag was highly beneficial to all the airplane configurations studied and would have strongly influenced the choice of the optimum. Lockheed recommended that practical application of the theoretical and experimental knowledge then available should be attempted, so that the benefits to be derived in an airplane such as the L-187 could be obtained. The use of the turbine engine as the airplane power source, with excess power for cruise operation, made the adoption of boundary layer control more readily adaptable. However, although the development was suitable for a tactical airplane, Lockheed felt that it could not be presented on a proposal as specific in detail design requirements as this one. The practical application of boundary layer control itself could dictate an airplane configuration in which the maximum benefits would be realized. Lockheed welcomed an opportunity to pioneer in this field, but it was of the opinion that such a development was outside the realm of this particular bid proposal.

Power Plant

Two types of airplanes were proposed, one powered by the turbojet engine and one by the turboprop engine. The optimum jet engine of those listed in OS-111 was the Westinghouse XJ40-WE-10 rated at 8,100 lbs static sea level thrust. The Westinghouse engines appeared superior to others in terms of thrust per unit frontal area and in specific fuel consumption. The XJ-40 engine was chosen rather than the XJ-46 because of the reduced number of units and simplified installation problems. The consideration of the inclusion of afterburning (then referred to as "tail pipe burning") depended upon the best balance between takeoff and cruise performance and installation conditions.

Lockheed's research yielded the following conclusions:

1. Although the XJ-40 engine was effectively equivalent to two XJ-46 engines, a net advantage in range and speed was obtained if XJ-40 engines were used.
2. If only two XJ-40 engines were used, tail pipe burning had to be included to accomplish the takeoff and high speed requirements.
3. If three or more XJ-40s were used, the thrust was sufficiently great to attain the required takeoff and high speed requirements. The installation of tail pipe burners would have caused an increase in empty weight and in fuel requirements, with only a small advantage in high speed which was not warranted.
4. The higher operating altitude available with three XJ-40 engines instead of 2, plus the elimination of the tail pipe burner, saved sufficient fuel to result in a

greater net range.

5. The addition of a fourth engine increased slightly the fuel required for a given range and the empty weight of the airplane. High speed and altitude were obviously improved. Installation factors, not apparent aerodynamically, governed the final choice of four XJ-40 engines.

The three engines required two nacelles plus one fuselage installation. This interfered with armament provisions, made the landing gear design difficult and in fact appeared impractical from many other standpoints.

The optimum propeller engine proved to be the Allison XT-44A. The dual XT-40-A type had insufficient power at altitude to attain the altitude and thus the range requirements. The Pratt and Whitney XT-48-P resulted in a slightly underpowered airplane and showed no net performance or weight advantage. Two XT-44A engines satisfied the altitude and cruise speed requirements, and came close to the high speed requirements.

The high speed deficiency of the XT-44-A airplane could have been eliminated by several methods. The wing sweep could have been increased or wing thickness reduced to increase the critical Mach number. Structural and dynamic load penalties of reduced thickness discouraged this method. Structural, stability, carrier takeoff, and control penalties due to increased sweep eliminated this approach. An additional jet engine could have been included in the airplane for high speed purposes only, but the weight complications involved eliminated any range advantages which could have been gained by a propeller engine. Therefore, the composite configurations were eliminated.

As a result, the two airplane types presented were basically similar in all respects except power plant. Thus, an excellent comparison of advantages of propeller versus jet power was obtained.

Nacelles

The propeller engine nacelles were by necessity conventional. The configuration of the jet engine nacelles was a result of considerable investigation. Four types of jet engine installations were considered. Engines in the fuselage were attractive if only two engines were considered and if the tail gun installation was eliminated. The requirement for more engines discouraged this possibility. The net loss due to a nacelle installation was relatively small, however, due to the fact that the engine ram pressure loss with nacelle engines was only one-half that with a fuselage installation.

The types of nacelles compared were: four separate nacelles on struts, two double nacelles on struts, and two double nacelles on the wing. Wind tunnel tests were made to evaluate these three types from the aerodynamic standpoint. The four separate nacelles had no advantage and were immediately eliminated. The advantages of the other two were as follows:

1. The nacelle drag of the wing installation was 12% less than that of the strut design. However, the nacelle-swept wing interference of a wing nacelle installation reduced the amount of flap available. Thus, the strut installation had the highest CL maximum. Assuming equal lift required, the drag of the added wing area required when the double nacelle was faired into the wing tended to balance the extra nacelle drag when a pylon mount for the nacelle was used.
2. The power effect of the strut installation was a reduction of 8% in stability. However, the horizontal tail size was dependent on trim as well as stability and therefore the difference in tail size was small.
3. Reference reports indicated that the critical Mach number of both installations was above that of the wing itself.
4. The ram available in either installation was good.

Since the net aerodynamic qualities were approximately equal, the strut installation was chosen for the sake of power plant installation simplicity.

Maximum Lift

Experience in the design study and testing of the XF-90 airplane showed that slats were required for a 35° swept wing with aspect ratio greater than 3.0. If 70% span slats were used, the stalling characteristics of aspect ratios from 3 to at least 10 could have been made satisfactory. Thus, the criterion did not enter into the aspect ratio choice.

The question of the extent of span of the wing flap was decided from consideration of the takeoff problem. Full-span flaps had the advantage of lower drag at high lift and higher center of lift maximum for a given type flap. However, partial span flaps had the advantage of markedly lower pitching moments on a swept wing. Full-span flaps dictated the use of an adjustable stabilizer to meet trim requirements. Furthermore, partial span flaps retained the use of ailerons for lateral control which was considered doubly important for a carrier-based aircraft in the ability to raise the low wing. The advantage in lift of full-span flaps was only on the order of 5% which was not considered sufficient benefit to warrant the added complications.

Guaranteed and Estimated Performance

OS-111 stated that guaranteed performance was based on guaranteed engine ratings and estimated performance would be predicated on advanced engine ratings. Lockheed's basic calculations were made based on engine manufacturer's guarantees in the performance report. Performance summary data, curves, and characteristic chart information were all presented to the Navy on the "guaranteed" basis.

Estimated engine ratings were checked following the system prescribed by BuAer. The result of these calculations, using the turbine and jet efficiencies specified, indicated very similar results when compared to the engine manufacturer's specifications. Unless these component efficiencies were arbitrarily increased, no advantage could be found. Therefore, in the performance data Lockheed presented to BuAer, estimated performance was derived in the identical manner as guaranteed performance.

Based on the OS-111 suggestion of estimated performance, the use of an engine not listed in the Outline Specification Appendix II was also studied. This engine was the WAC TJ-6. The specific fuel consumption was slightly less optimistic than that of the XJ-40 but with the high design pressure ratio, the thrust per unit frontal area was optimum for this design. Two TJ-6 engines were equivalent to four XJ-40 types. The fuel requirements to attain the desired range were slightly reduced due to lower nacelle drag. The empty weight was considerably reduced, increasing the fuel allotment.

Propeller Efficiencies

The propeller efficiencies used in Lockheed's performance analysis were derived directly from the specified BuAer Report DR-1065. Following the system prescribed, a 14.5 ft twelve bladed dual rotating propeller was chosen to give maximum efficiency for cruise and high speed and sufficient thrust for takeoff. Although the engine manufacturer's specified propeller gear ratio was 18 to 1, it was necessary to assume that a change could be obtained to make this gearing 25 to 1 to obtain optimum results. Furthermore, to obtain maximum propulsive thrust, a 33% propeller spinner was used, following the system of DR-1065. The result was an efficiency value on the order of 70% for cruise speed and 60% for high speed.

The Curtiss Propeller Corporation presented their propeller analyses which, if revised to fit the airplane, could have offered even higher cruise and high speed efficiencies. Lockheed felt that it was not judicious to use more optimistic values than DR-1065 until these at least had been substantiated by experimental research. Therefore, no improvement in efficiencies over those prescribed was even estimated.

Propeller efficiency assumptions were one of the most critical basic parameters in the design analysis. With the assumptions stipulated in BuAer Report DR-1065, the range of the propeller airplane was considerably superior to that of the jet airplane, flying at a Mach number of .85. To emphasize the importance of propeller efficiency, Lockheed studied the miles per pound of fuel for the jet and propeller types. The calculations were simplified for this comparison by using the same weight, wing area, and drag coefficient for both airplanes and neglecting the increment of compressibility drag at high speed. Furthermore, the XT-44 and XJ-40 specific fuel consumptions were assumed constant at an average value.

Relative to the basic problem of obtaining maximum range at a cruise Mach number of .85, Lockheed's analysis showed the propeller airplane 37% superior to the jet airplane, using the assumptions of DR-1065, half of which was due to the use of a 33% spinner. Based on the best test results available, the propeller airplane was 27% worse. The test results were based on peak efficiencies and idealized conditions. Further, they were propeller efficiencies, not propulsive efficiencies. Wind tunnel tests with practical blades, with dual rotation, and at equivalent power coefficients were badly needed to get the answer to this important parameter.

Stability and Control

The horizontal tail area was derived from a careful study of the jet airplane requirements. The decision to use the strut nacelle design set the horizontal tail area at 275 sq ft to attain the desired stability. The cost in stability of this versus a wing installation was on the order of 8% but with the high nacelle, trim ability was critical and the saving in tail area was small. Longitudinal control and trim were satisfactory with the use of the standard Lockheed-developed power boost system.

For the propeller airplane, the stability problem was more severe. Although the instability increment of the nacelle was less, the destabilizing effect of power calculated considerably higher at low speeds. Past experience indicated that increased tail area to account for propeller slip stream effects was extremely inefficient. The horizontal tail size determined theoretically would have been excessive. Therefore, the area had been chosen identical to that of the jet air-

National Archives, RG 72

National Archives, RG 72

Lockheed performed preliminary wind tunnel tests to determine the ideal nacelle configuration for the L-187. This particular configuration consisted of four single jet nacelles supported on struts; additional test photos can be found on pages 119-120.

plane, pending further research. This further research would have entailed wind tunnel tests on a powered scale model to determine the actual effects of slip stream on a swept wing and power effects on stability for high disc loading contra-rotating propellers. No experimental information was currently available on these factors.

Preliminary calculations showed the propeller airplane to be stable based on P2V airplane data. However, the effects of power on a swept wing and high disc loading on a dual rotating propeller were unknown. The thrust line was purposely put high to increase stability. Extensive wind tunnel tests were required to solve these problems.

The vertical tail area was relatively large (16% of wing area) due to the dictates of yaw control with inoperative engines and due to dynamic lateral stability considerations. For yaw control the BuAer control requirement of control with one jet engine inoperative was met with the jet airplane. However, for the propeller airplane, the definition of what comprised one engine was confused. Each nacelle housed three turbine engines geared to one propeller unit. If it was assumed that a gear, shaft or propeller failure occurred, the propeller airplane as presented was unsatisfactory. If it was assumed that one turbine engine alone became inoperative and that the other engines continued to operate, the control problem was relatively simple because of the increased propeller efficiency at low power.

Dynamic lateral stability was critical on swept wing type airplanes. Preliminary analysis indicated that the configuration of this airplane was critical for both low and high speed regimes. NavAer Report SR-119B presented a chart which illustrated a dividing line between "satisfactory" and "unsatisfactory" airplane Dutch roll characteristics in terms of time to damp and period. To attain "satisfactory" characteristics for low speed low altitude and cruise speed high altitude flight, without artificial means, considerable anhedral was required. However, a second criterion was the aerodynamic dihedral effect required for "satisfactory" control. These two criteria worked in opposite directions such that positive dihedral was desired for high speed flight control and negative dihedral was desired for low speed flight stability. A compromise was reached in this design between the two. If this proved to be unsatisfactory for stability, Lockheed suggested the use of an artificial means, such as a gyro driving the ailerons or rudder

In summary, the propeller airplane was not as satisfactory in terms of stability and control as the jet airplanes. The theoretical and wind tunnel research required for the propeller airplane was considerably greater due to the unknowns than for the jet airplane.

Internal Airflow

According to Lockheed, engine intake pressure recovery was excellent on both airplanes. Calculation for the propeller airplane was complex due to the air intake through the faired hubs of twelve propeller blades and the unknown character of the complicated diffuser. Theoretical calculations indicated small power loss due to pumping action. However, practical limitations of design and manufacture could have reduced the pumping efficiency and thus increase the pumping power markedly. This would have been an item of considerable design investigation.

Pressurization and air conditioning of the cockpit was straightforward on the jet airplane designs because high pressure ratios were available. Deicing requirements for the jet airplane had been studied and a mixed air type with jet pumps appeared to be optimum for the inboard wing and tail and unmixed engine air for the slats and nacelles. For the propeller airplane, a change would have been required in the compressor air tap position. The pressure ratio from the existing tap was insufficient but it appeared possible to move this tap to a higher pressure point.

Additional Investigations

When it was realized that a relatively conventional airplane would not fulfill the requirements of OS-111, Lockheed entered into other fields of investigation. None of these efforts was successful, but Lockheed presented a summary to the Navy for purposes of comparison with the two airplanes finally proposed.

Increased Gross Weight Before the importance of the catapult limitations was realized, the most promising field of endeavor was an increase in design gross weight until the operating radius of specification requirements was fulfilled. This approach led to the use of a four engine jet powered configuration similar to the L-187-2 with the exception that the normal takeoff gross weight of 100,000 lbs was exceeded as required.

Two versions of the airplane were proposed:

1. Airplane with constant wing area and increased wing loading, also increasing catapult end speeds.
2. Airplane with constant wing loading (constant catapult end speed) and increased wing area.

Each of these airplanes fulfilled all of the OS-111 requirements except for gross weight. The resulting design characteristics are shown in the following table:

COMPARISON OF HIGH GROSS WEIGHT AIRPLANES

	Constant Wing Area 1200 sq. ft.	Constant Wing Loading = 83.4 lbs./ft.^{2}
Area sq. ft.	1,200	1,925
T.O. Gross Weight (Lbs.)	146,000 lbs.	160,400
Fuel Load (Lbs.)	54,000 lbs.	62,100
Radius	1,700	1,700
T.O. Speed (C_L T.O. = 1.6) Kn.	150	124

Calculations of JATO required for each of these airplanes showed impractical values and the conclusion of the study was that different catapult characteristics were required to make either of these models practical. Lockheed emphasized that this conclusion pointed to the only method of achieving all of the desired requirements for equipment, bomb load, speed and range. This method was the redesign of the catapult to achieve higher weights at the same speed, or higher speeds and weights. The higher takeoff speeds, of course, implied higher load factors or longer catapults. The latter was recommended since the existing catapult load factor was very nearly prohibitive for the pilot and many of the structural units.

Other Configurations Lockheed investigated three additional designs to meet OS-

111, each of which had peculiar advantages.

The L-187-1 was a twin engine airplane which incorporated XJ-40 engines with tail pipe burners. This airplane, though clean aerodynamically, did not have sufficient thrust to attain a satisfactory cruising altitude for low fuel consumption. Furthermore, it was impractical to install a tail turret between tail pipes with afterburners.

The L-187-6 was a three engine airplane utilizing XJ-40 engines. This airplane had the best range of all the jet configurations studied. However, the center power plant installation was impractical from a maintenance and structural standpoint and the ram recovery for all power plants was questionable. Furthermore, a tail turret could not be installed.

The L-187-3 was an attempt to utilize a flying wing with the hope that a fuselage containing the bomb and major portion of the fuel tanks could have been dropped, thus leaving a very clean wing for the return trip. The calculated weight of the wing, however, was large and the required gross weight reached a total of 135,000 lbs without provisions for tail guns or access to the bomb bay. One of the reasons for the failure of a flying wing to be weight efficient for high design speeds was the fact that the high local pressures designed the wing structure rather than the bending loads and thus the expected weight saving due to low wing loading and relatively large depth did not materialize.

It was the conclusion of these investigations that a more conventional and simple airplane more realistically fulfilled the requirements of OS-111 and so the configurations represented by L-187-2 and L-187-7 were chosen.

Conclusions

Lockheed believed that the two designs it submitted to BuAer represented a practical solution for the carrier-based attack problem. Its conclusions were as follows:

1. No design could fully comply with OS-111 within the limits of the approved power plants and the equipment requirements.
2. A stripped jet airplane could have been made which fulfilled and exceeded all performance requirements, but this airplane could not have complied with the armament specification, with the carrying of a full bomb load, nor would all of the equipment and crew requirements have been fulfilled.
3. A completely spec jet airplane could have been built which was capable of carrying the required bomb load on a bombing mission of 1,240 miles radius utilizing a reasonable overload gross weight (110%) and a reasonable JATO (14,000 lbs for 5 seconds). This airplane exceeded the high speed requirements of Mach = .90 by achieving Mach .93 at the combat altitude.
4. A completely spec propeller turbine airplane could have been built which was capable of a bombing mission with a full bomb load of 1,620 miles radius using the same overload and JATO. Unlike the jet airplane, the propeller version did not comply with the required high speed of Mach = .90 since the maximum Mach number was .88.

Lockheed submitted both designs for consideration on a study basis but recommended the selection of the jet airplane because:

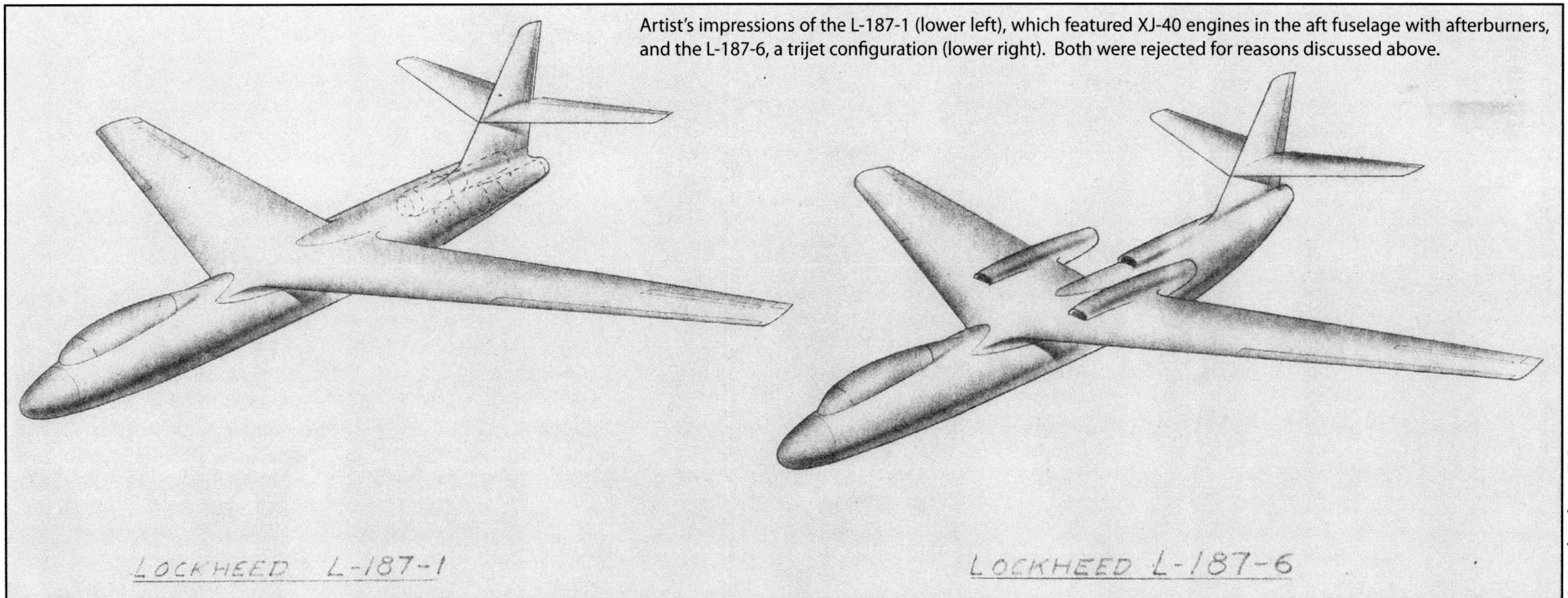

Artist's impressions of the L-187-1 (lower left), which featured XJ-40 engines in the aft fuselage with afterburners, and the L-187-6, a trijet configuration (lower right). Both were rejected for reasons discussed above.

National Archives, RG 72

1. The development of the jet airplane and its engine was considerably simpler and the resulting airplane because of its speed and simplicity would have been a more practical tactical weapon.
2. The progress in jet engine development would have eventually provided a power plant which would have permitted the achievement of the desired range.
3. Propeller development, control development, gear box and clutch development all appeared to be extremely difficult programs that could have continued so long that future jet developments would have made the propeller airplane obsolete before completion.
4. Control and stability problems on the propeller airplane could have made the research programs on the airframe as extensive as on the power plant whereas the jet airplane appeared to have required considerably fewer programs.
5. It was doubtful whether the propeller efficiencies assumed could have ever been achieved in practice and it was nearly certain that the high speed requirements were not achievable with a propeller. Thus, even if practical problems could have been surmounted, the advantage of longer range with the propeller would have been negated.

Overall, Lockheed's was among the longest and most detailed of the proposals submitted to BuAer. One wonders, however, if the company would have had more success in eliminating the turboprop variant entirely and further developing the jet-powered airplane instead.

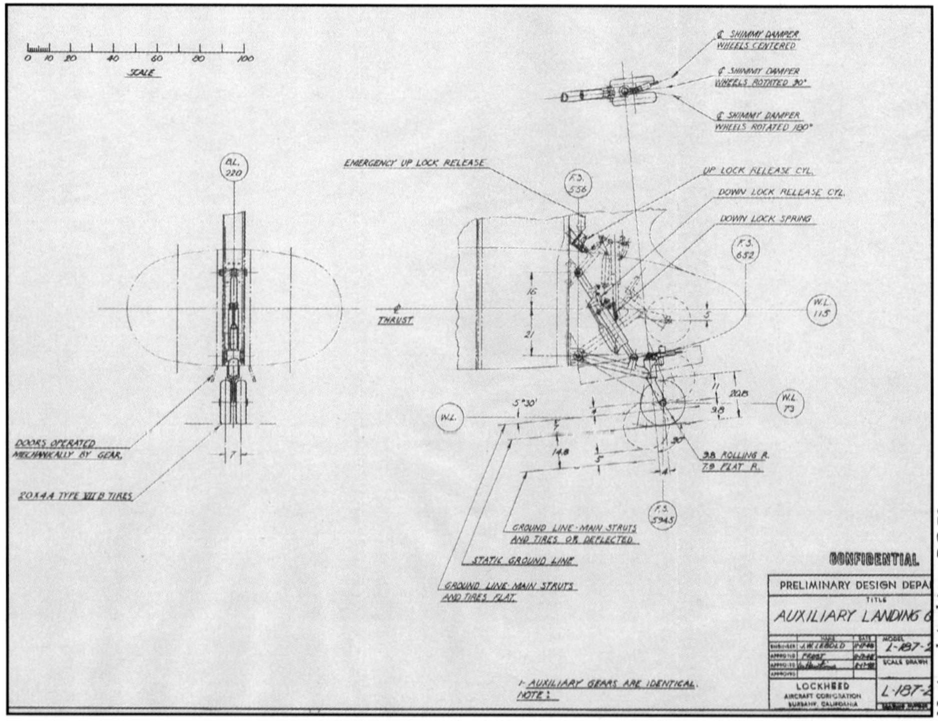

National Archives, RG 72

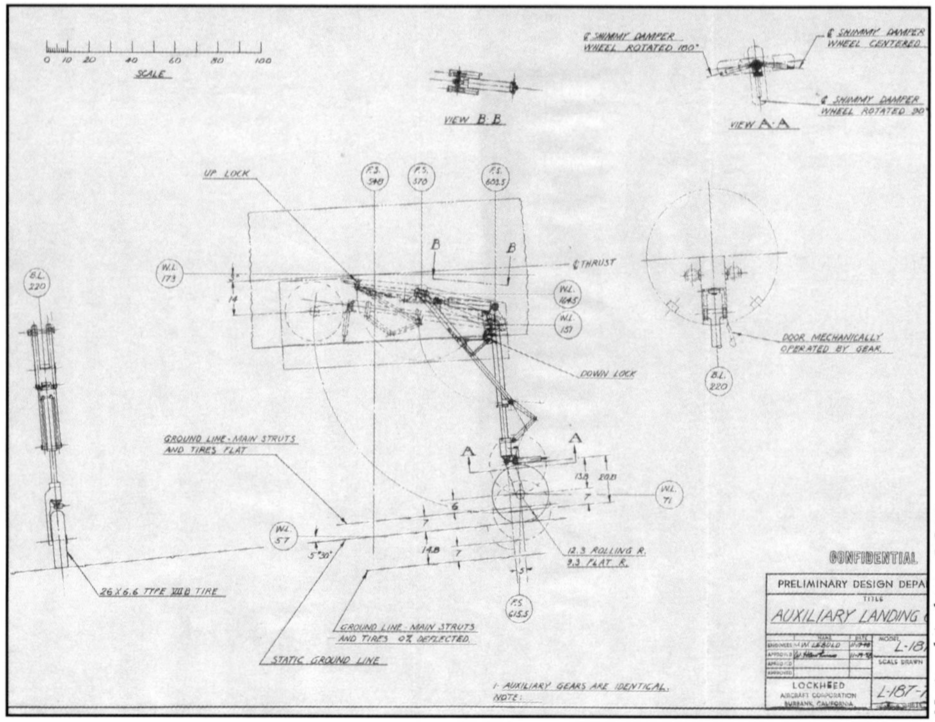

National Archives, RG 72

Right: Blueprints of the auxiliary landing gear installations for the L-187-2 (top) and the L-187-7 (bottom). The high nacelle position resulted in very tall outrigger gear for the latter.

Left: The forward main landing gear, which retracted forward to simplify extension during emergencies when the main actuating system was inactive.

Below: The aft main landing gear, which retracted aftwards in order to provide adequate structural strength for it to be used as the hold-back point for the catapult.

Next Page

Top Left: Blueprint of the L-187-2 wing structure.

Top Right: Blueprint of the empennage structure, common to both aircraft.

Bottom Left: Blueprint of the L-187-7 wing structure.

Bottom Right: Drawing showing nacelle configurations wind tunnel tested by Lockheed for the L-187 proposal.

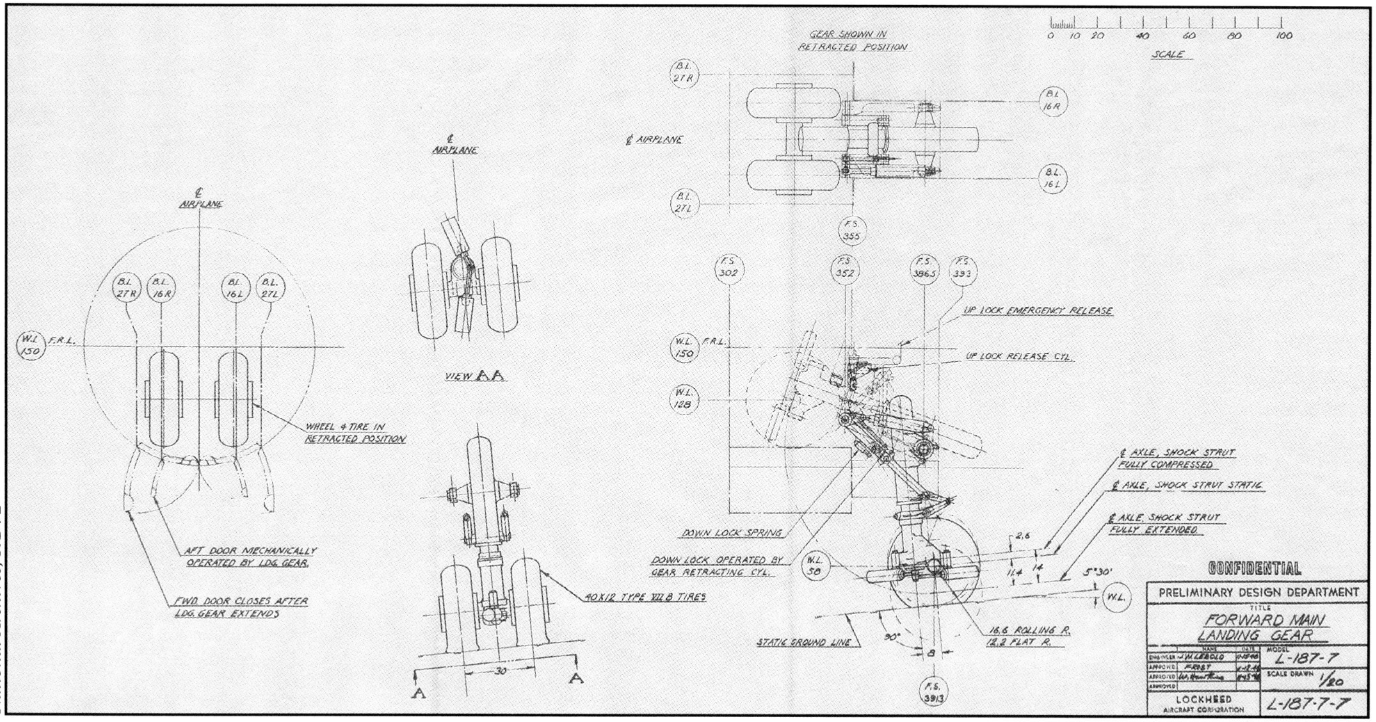

National Archives, RG 72

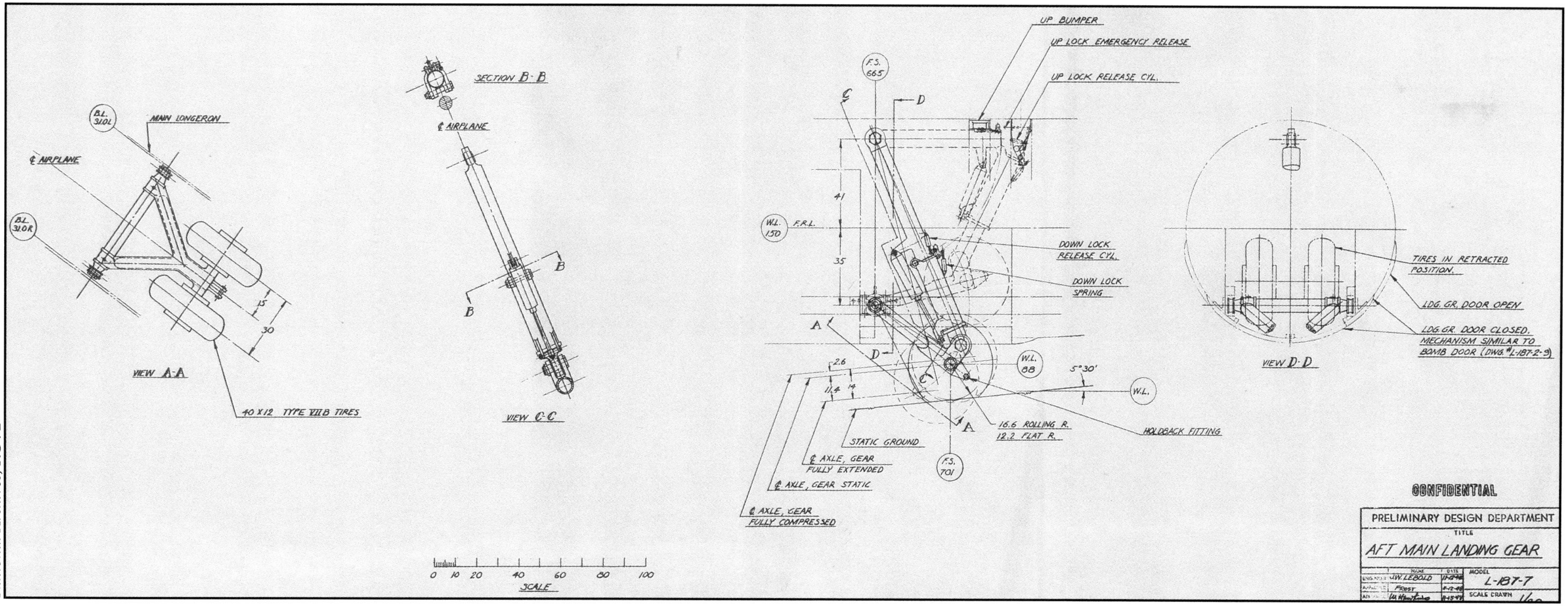

National Archives, RG 72

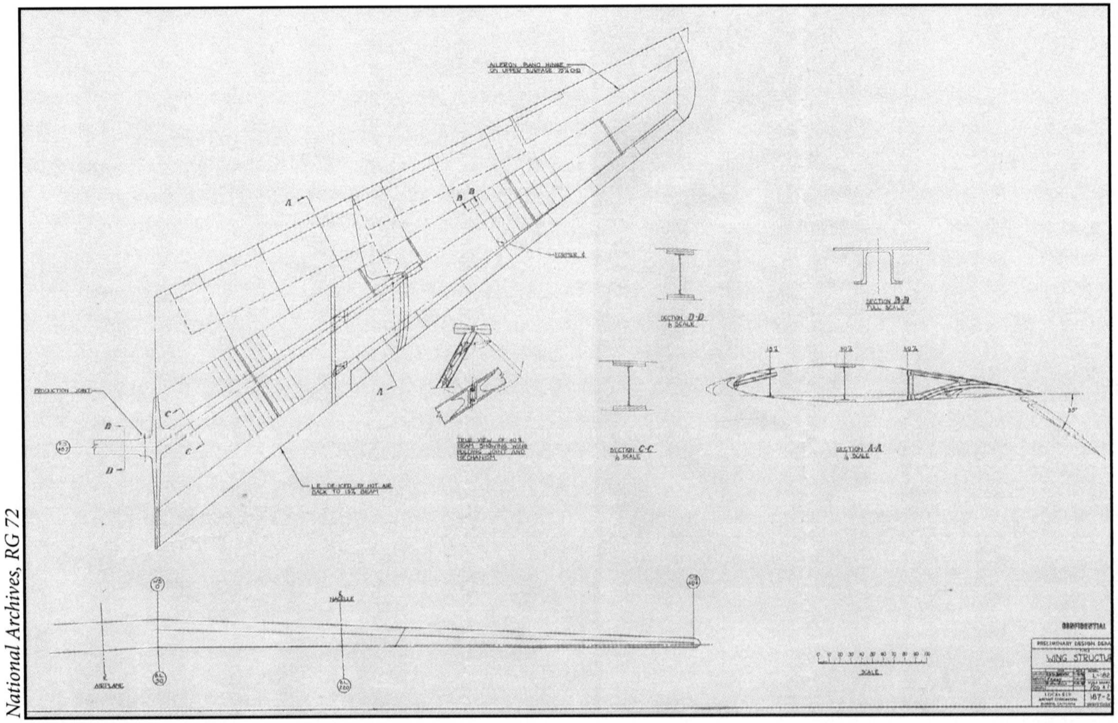

National Archives, RG 72

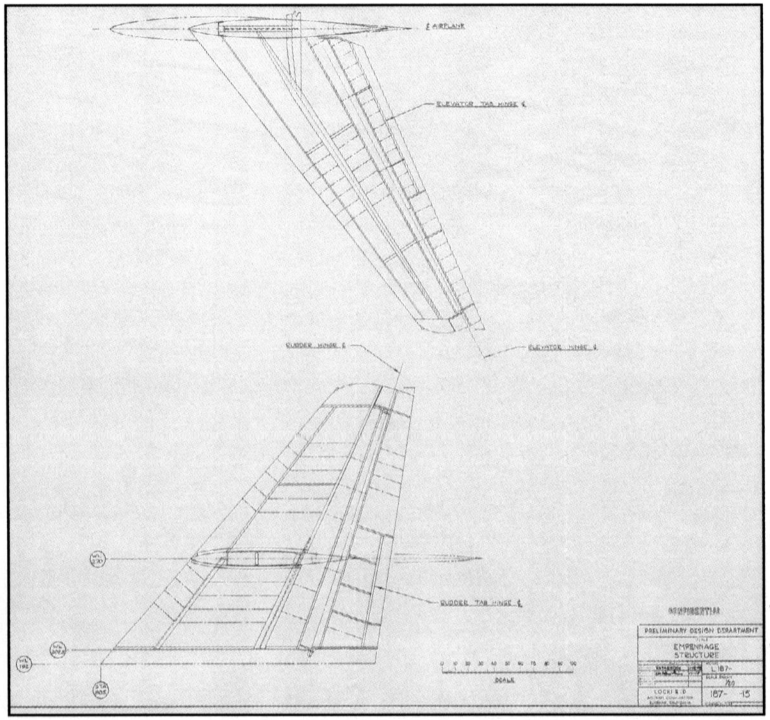

National Archives, RG 72

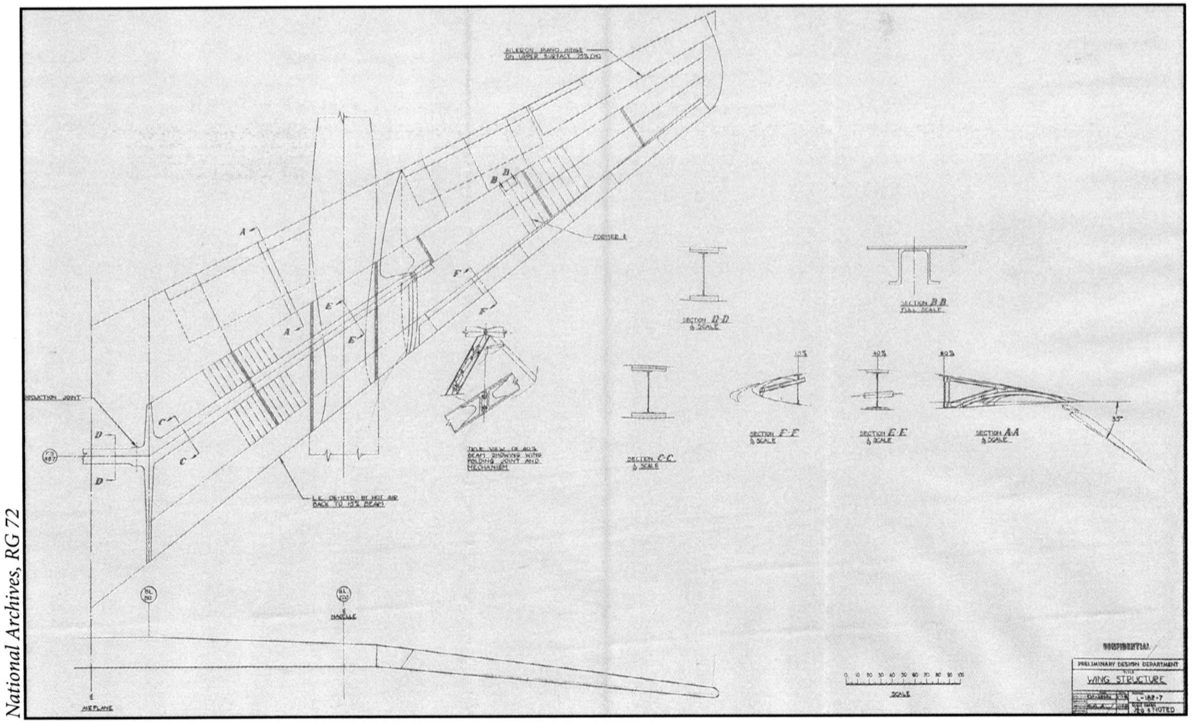

National Archives, RG 72

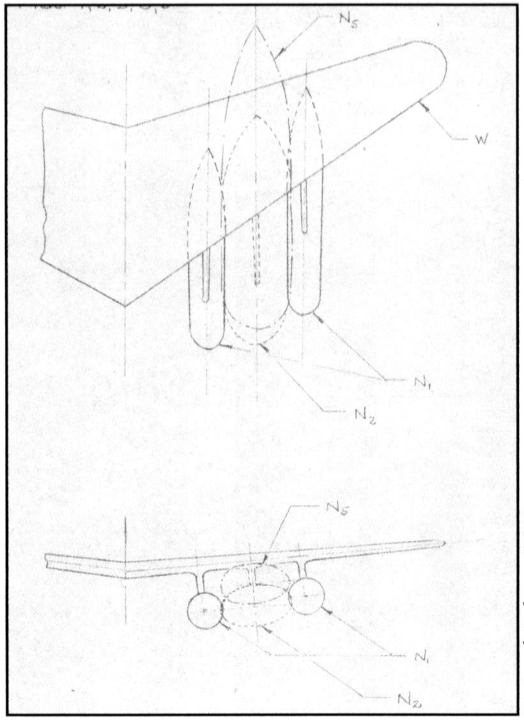

National Archives, RG 72

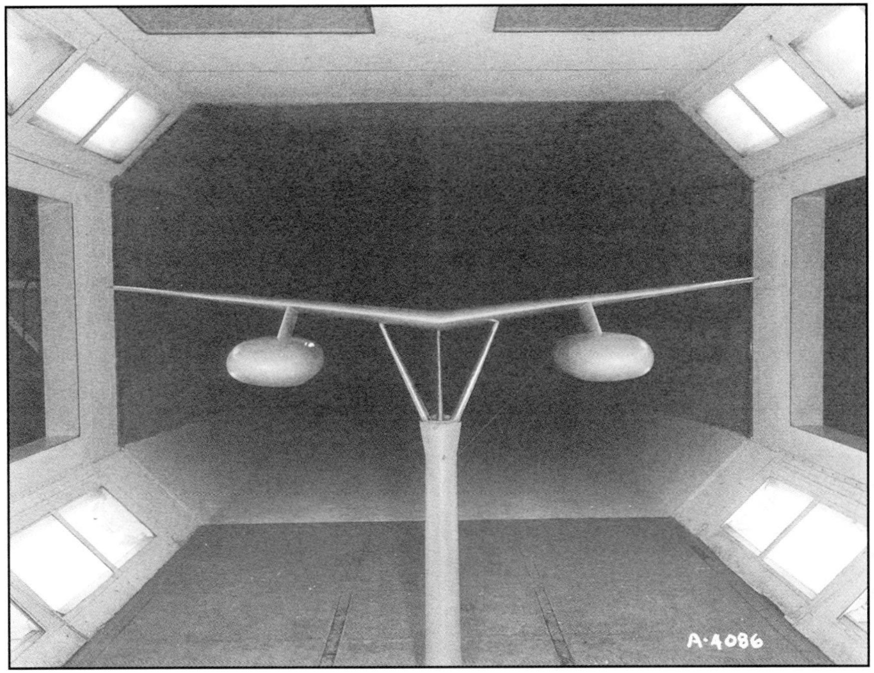

National Archives, RG 72

National Archives, RG 72

National Archives, RG 72

Above: In the wind tunnel, Lockheed tested a configuration with two double jet nacelles on short struts, similar to what was actually adopted on the L-187-2. The test wing was a stock item that differed considerably from what was eventually chosen, however.

National Archives, RG 72

Above: This arrangement consisted of two double jet nacelles mounted directly on the wing, similar to the North American B-45 Tornado.

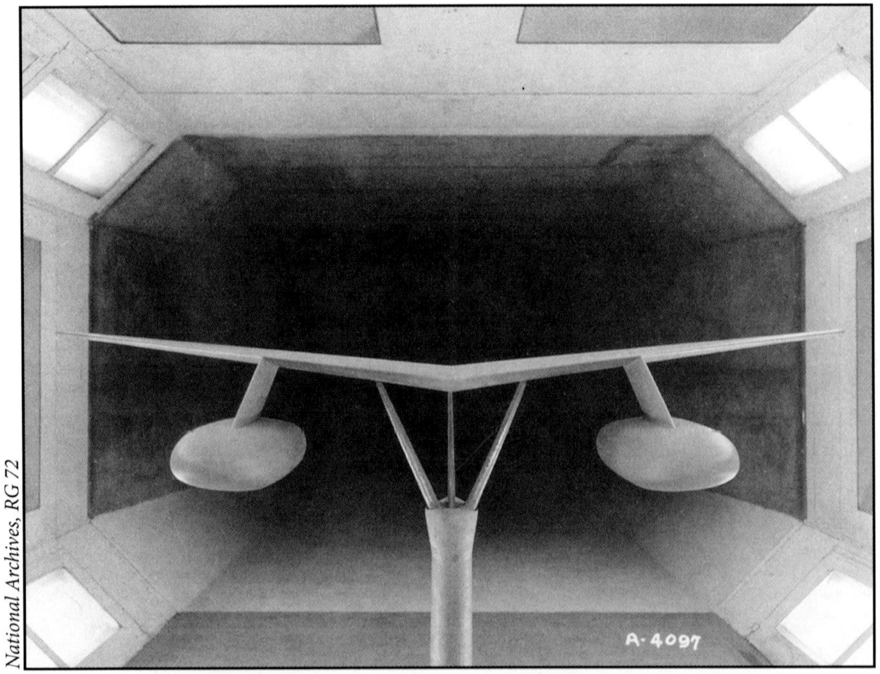

National Archives, RG 72

National Archives, RG 72

Above: Lockheed also tested an arrangement with two double jet nacelles on long struts. This probably would have presented carrier deck clearance problems and necessitated taller landing gear, increasing overall weight.

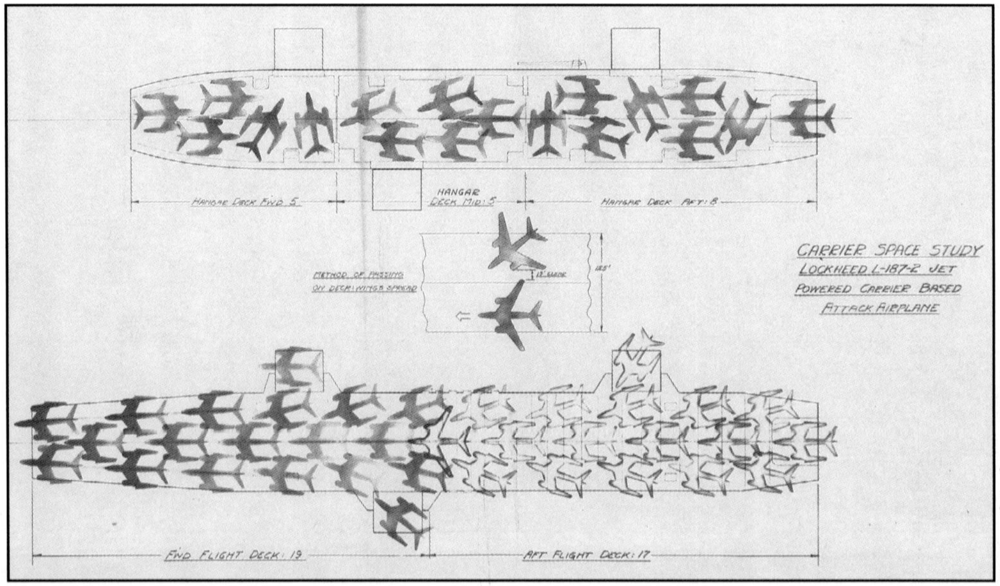

National Archives, RG 72

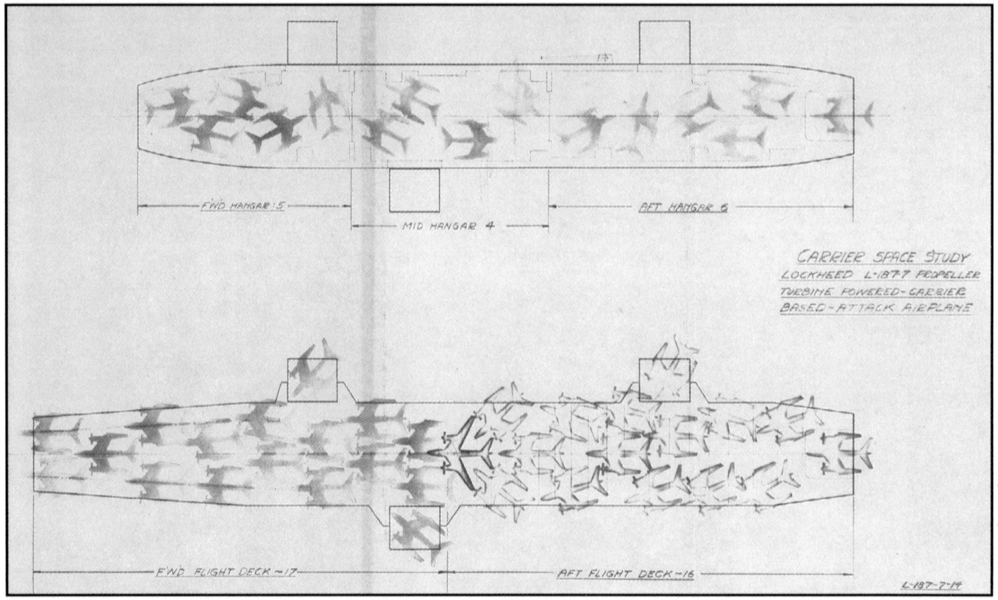

National Archives, RG 72

Above: Carrier spotting diagrams for the L-187-2 (top) and L-187-7 (bottom). Approximately 36 L-187-2s could be accommodated on the flight deck and 18 on the hangar deck. The larger nacelles of the L-187-7 reduced these numbers to 33 on the flight deck and 15 on the hangar deck, a distinct disadvantage.

Next Page

Left Column: Charts showing the effects of power plant selection on combat radius.

Right Column: Standard Aircraft Characteristics charts for the L-187-2 (top) and L-187-7 (bottom).

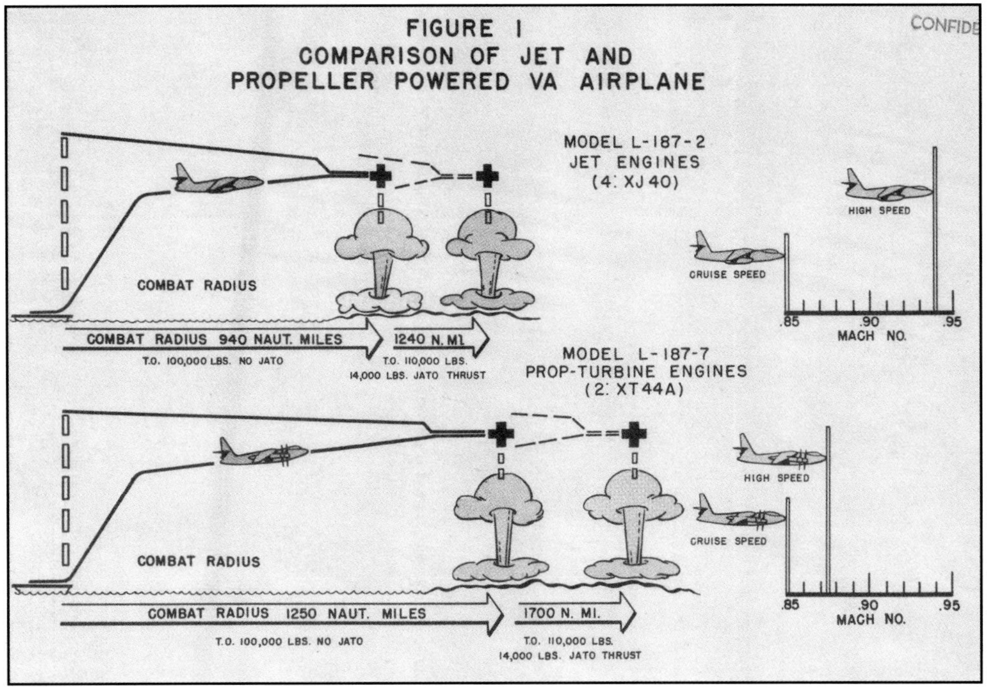

FIGURE 1
COMPARISON OF JET AND PROPELLER POWERED VA AIRPLANE

National Archives, RG 72

MISSION AND DESCRIPTION

Execution of high altitude horizontal bombing attack mission with large bombs and special weapons of 10,000 lbs. weight. Designed with the specific mission of high transonic speed long-range "hit and run" attack and to be operated off and on the new class CVB flush deck carriers.

Configuration features sweptback wing with dual-jet engines mounted side by side in two underslung strut-suspended nacelles, crew of three in pressurized cabin with access to bomb bay in flight, and fully retractable dual tire bicycle landing gear with outriggers mounted on and retracting into the nacelles.

WEIGHTS

Loading	Gross Lbs.	L.F.
Empty	61,013	
Basic	63,000	
Design	88,000	2.84
Combat	74,580	
Max.T.O.	100,000	2.25
Max. Landing	74,000	

POWER PLANT

No. & Model . . . Four XJ40-WE-10

Mfr. . . . . Westinghouse

RATINGS

Rating	Thrust	RPM
Military	8100	7260
Normal	7300	7260

FUEL AND OIL

Location	Gal.
Fuselage*	2230*
Wing and Fuse.	2270
Total	4500
Fuel Grade	
Fuel Spec.	AN-F-58

OIL

Nacelles	8
Oil Grade	1010
Oil Spec.	AN-0-9

*Self Sealing

ORDNANCE

Basic Mission --

10,000 Lb. Missile

Requiring
5 ft. x 5½ ft. x 16 ft. space envelope
Combination optical and Radar aids in the APB-2 Radar Bomb Director.

Tail Turret --
Automatic gun-laying, uninhabited, Aero XII E type with APG-25 radar. Two M-24 20 mm guns with 500 rounds ammunition per gun.

DIMENSIONS

Wing Area	1200 sq. ft.
Span	91'6.6"
Aspect Ratio	7.0
Sweep	35°
Length	83'7"
Height	24'10.5"
Tread	36'8.2"

ELECTRONICS

Radar Bomb Director (MKV)	APB-2
Comm. VHF	ARC-1
Trans.& Rec. MHF	ART-13
	ARR-15
Nav. Homing	ARR-2A
Range Receiver	ARC-5
IFF	APX-6
Radar Alt.	APN-1
Interphone	AIC-4
Loran (Prov.)	APN-4

National Archives, RG 72

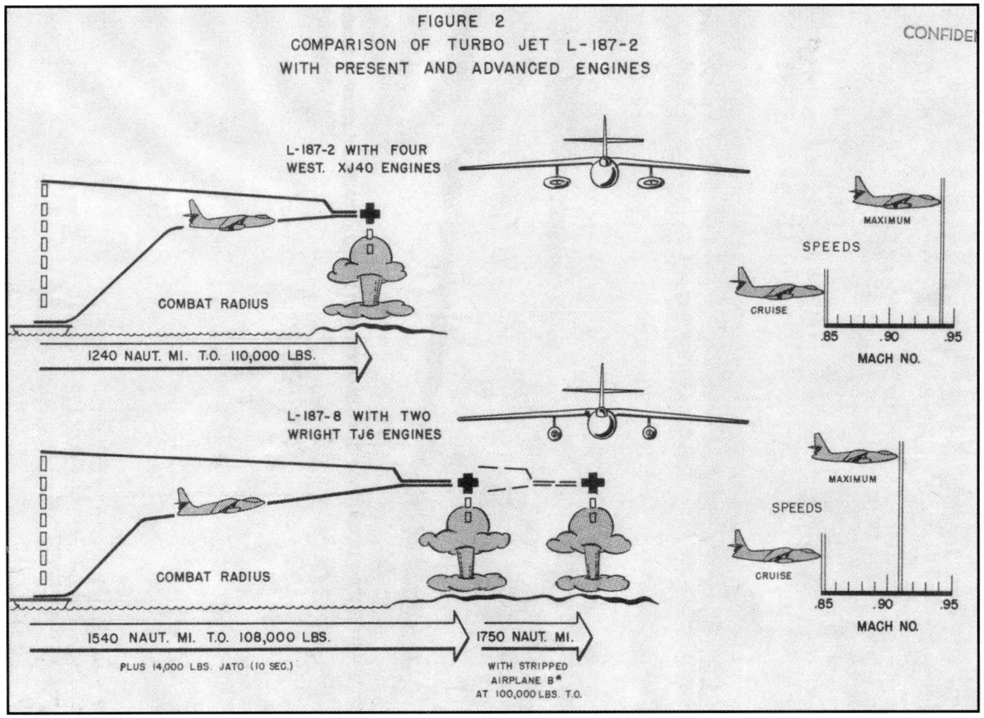

FIGURE 2
COMPARISON OF TURBO JET L-187-2 WITH PRESENT AND ADVANCED ENGINES

National Archives, RG 72

MISSION AND DESCRIPTION

Execution of high altitude horizontal bombing attack mission with large bombs and special weapons of 10,000 lbs. weight. Designed with the specific mission of high transonic speed long-range "hit and run" attack and to be operated off and on the new class CVB flush deck carriers.

Configuration features sweptback wing with two triple-turbo-prop engines geared into 12 blade dual rotating propellers, crew of three in pressurized cabin with access to bomb bay in flight, and fully retractable dual-tire bicycle landing gear with outriggers mounted on and retracting into the nacelles.

WEIGHTS

Loading	Gross Lb.	LF
Empty	63,263	
Basic	65,790	
Design	89,100	2.80
Combat	75,800	
Max.T.O.	100,000	2.25
Max. Landing	75,475	

POWER PLANT

No. and Model Two XT-44-A

Mfr. . . . . . . Allison

RATINGS

Rating	Static ESHP* at Sea Level	RPM
Take-off	11,250	13,620
Military	11,250	13,620
Normal	9,400	13,620

$$\text{*Static ESHP} = \text{SHP} + \frac{\text{Static Thrust}}{2.5}$$

FUEL AND OIL

Location	Gal.
Fuselage*	2605*
Wing and Fuse.	1430
Total	4035
Fuel Grade	100/130
Fuel Spec.	AN-F-48

OIL

Nacelle	50
Oil Grade	1010
Oil Spec.	AN-0-9

*Self Sealing

ORDNANCE

Basic Mission - -
10,000 Lb. Missile

Requiring
5 ft. x 5½ ft. x 16 ft. space envelope
Combination optical and radar aids in the APB-2 Radar Bomb Director

Tail Turret - -
Automatic gun-laying, uninhabited, Aero XII E type with APG-25 radar. Two M-24 20 mm guns with 500 rounds ammunition per gun.

DIMENSIONS

Wing Area	1200 sq.ft.
Span	91'6.6"
Aspect Ratio	7.0
Sweep	35°
Length	83'7"
Height	24'10.5"
Tread	36'8.2"

ELECTRONICS

Radar Bomb Director(MKV)	APB-2
Comm. VHF	ARC-1
Trans.&Rec.MHF	ART-13
	ARR-15
Nav. Homing	ARR-2A
Range Receiver	ARC-5
IFF	APX-6
Radar Alt.	APN-1
Interphone	AIC-4
Loran (Prov.)	APN-4

National Archives, RG 72

CHAPTER 9 — *North American RD-4554*

North American's Class VA proposal is notable for its brevity and lack of detail, indicating that the company had little real interest in the project or was so busy with other work that it did not have the resources to produce a fully developed design with a serious chance of winning. In the documents it submitted to BuAer on November 19, 1948, the company claimed that it had analyzed a variety of airplane configurations, all of which incorporated swept back wings in order to attain the high drag divergence Mach number necessitated by the cruising speed requirements of OS-111. In all cases, the wing loadings were determined by OS-111 low speed operation requirements. A wing aspect ratio of 6.0 was established after investigations showed that the type of operation desired plus carrier space requirements would not have justified a larger aspect ratio.

Evidence of the severity of the Combat Radius requirement was noted early in the generalized design studies. As the studies progressed, it was noted that very unrealistic parameters had to be assumed to create a design which could have met all the performance requirements, including Combat Radius. Therefore, in accordance with OS-111 instructions, the design studies presented to the Navy were made for a reduced Combat Radius requirement consistent with realistic values for all airplane parameters.

Generalized performance studies made for the purpose of power plant selection showed that the Combat Radius available with a turbo-propeller airplane could have been made equivalent to a turbojet airplane only if propulsive efficiencies in excess of 0.75 could have been achieved on the highly loaded propellers at the specified cruising

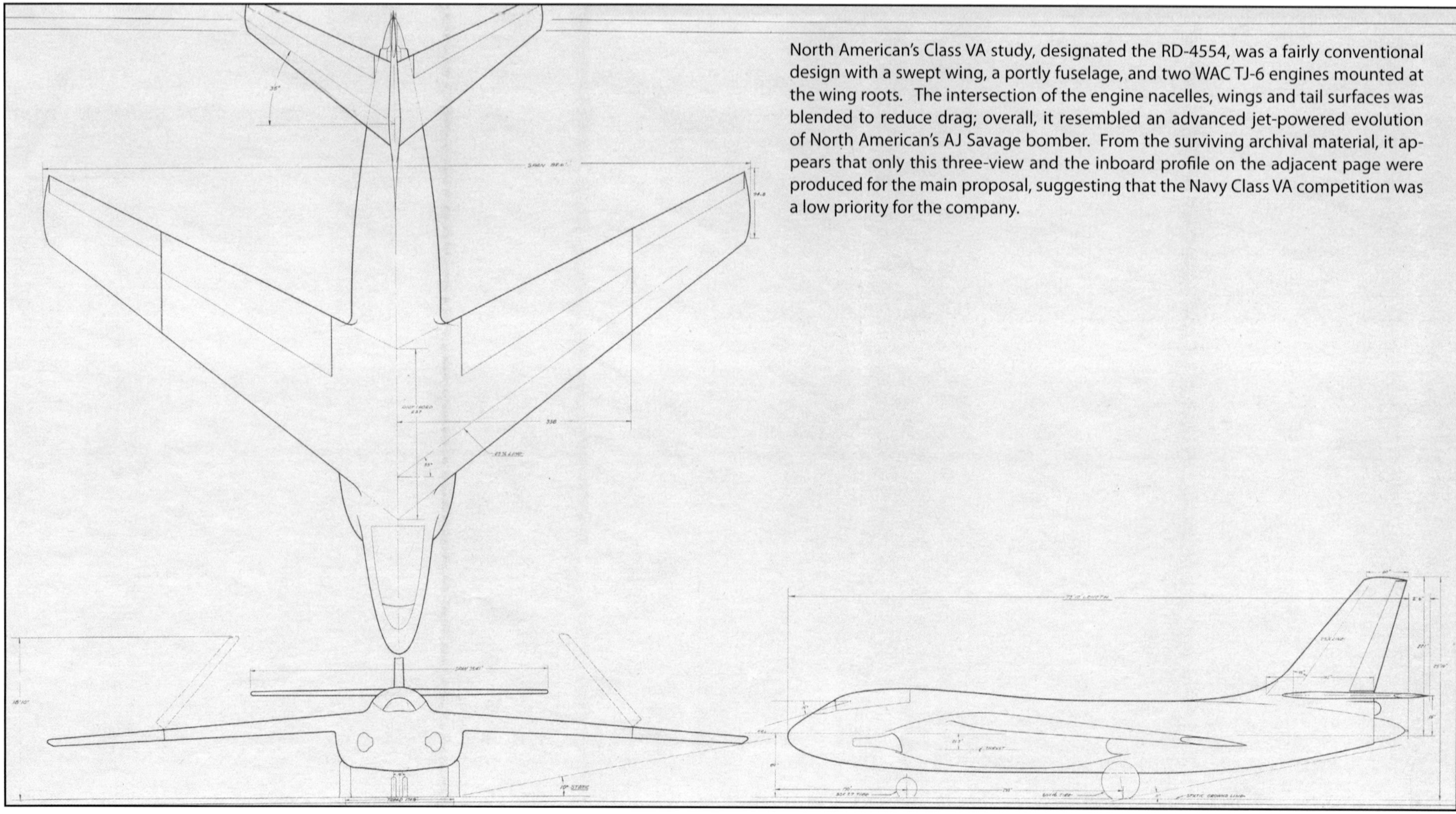

North American's Class VA study, designated the RD-4554, was a fairly conventional design with a swept wing, a portly fuselage, and two WAC TJ-6 engines mounted at the wing roots. The intersection of the engine nacelles, wings and tail surfaces was blended to reduce drag; overall, it resembled an advanced jet-powered evolution of North American's AJ Savage bomber. From the surviving archival material, it appears that only this three-view and the inboard profile on the adjacent page were produced for the main proposal, suggesting that the Navy Class VA competition was a low priority for the company.

National Archives, RG 72

Mach number of .85. Since there appeared to be little possibility of exceeding efficiencies of this order by an appreciable amount, and in view of the mechanical complexity and undesirable aerodynamic interferences, no further consideration was given to a propeller driven airplane.

Further generalized studies to determine the best turbojet airplane and engine combination showed that the maximum Combat Radius configuration could have been obtained with the Wright TJ-6 turbojet. The chief advantages of this engine for this airplane were in its high thrust (11,000 lbs, sea level static, without augmentation) and its low weight (3,000 lbs). It made possible a two engine airplane, whereas the use of engines from the OS-111 list necessitated a three engine airplane. The installation advantages of two versus three turbojets were obvious. Therefore, North American based its proposals upon two Wright TJ-6 turbojets.

In view of the apparent superiority of the TJ-6 engine for the OS-111 airplane requirement, North American suggested that BuAer give this engine serious consideration before awarding a final phase airplane contract. Following the generalized studies, one specific design received final consideration in this study.

It was evident from the above tabulation that this airplane would have satisfied all requirements of OS-111 with the exception of Combat Radius. The estimated radius performance was substantially below the desired value. The specific design represented a configuration which was established to give maximum possible airplane radius within the operational limits set in OS-111. Aerodynamic and structural parameters consistent with the best engineering practices were used in the design analysis. North American noted, however, that improvements in radius performance were possible with additional study of the aerodynamic and structural aspects of the design. Furthermore, a more detailed study of strength requirements, with design limitations imposed in keeping with the tactical objective of OS-111, could have lead to reduction in structural weight. For example, the elimination of critical gust design requirements by a reduction in limit speed at sea level would have resulted in a structural weight saving.

Additional study of similar structural as well as aerodynamic aspects of the problem would have resulted in a closer accomplishment of the stringent specification requirements. Such study, however, was beyond the scope of a design proposal and more logically belonged in a phase one contract stage.

Aerodynamics

General Performance Considerations The general performance investigations conducted during the initial stages of the design study included all possible airplane designs considered feasible for OS-111.

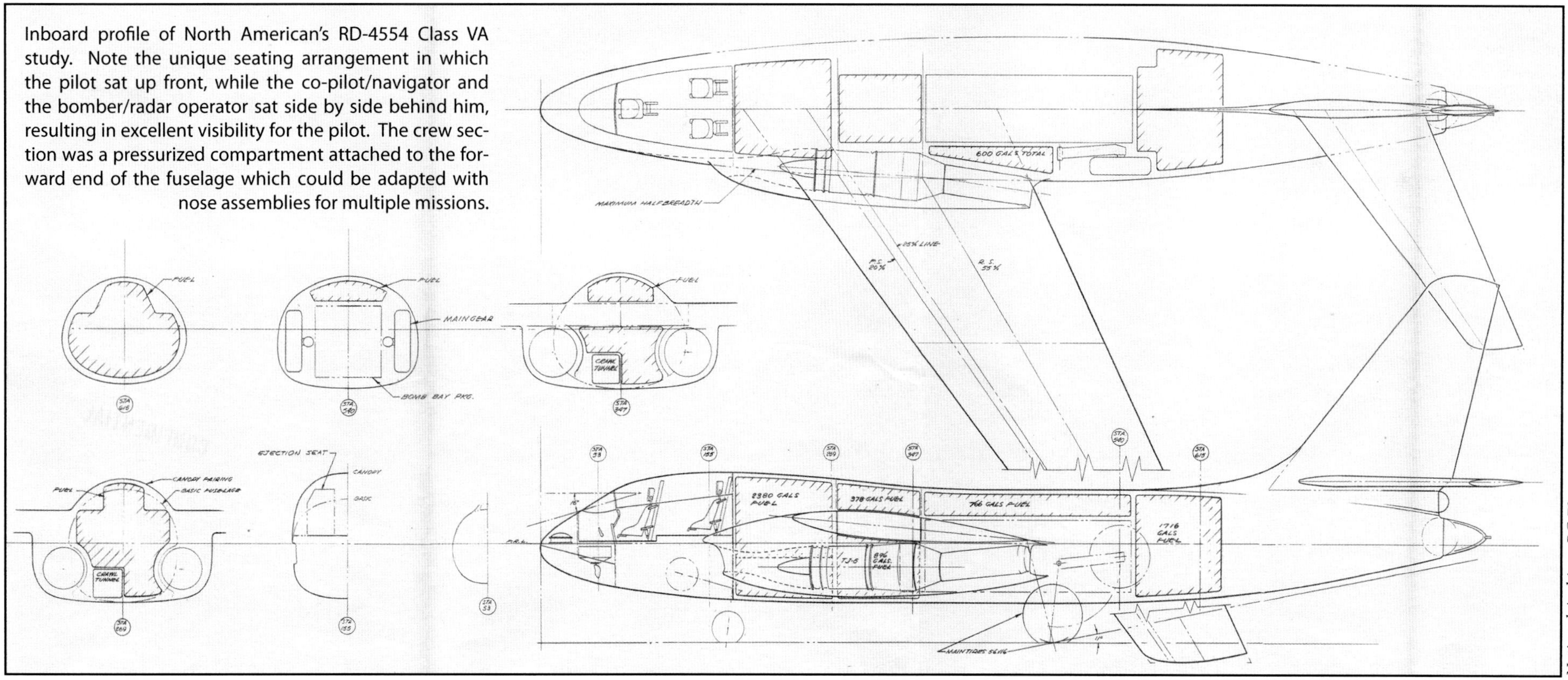

Inboard profile of North American's RD-4554 Class VA study. Note the unique seating arrangement in which the pilot sat up front, while the co-pilot/navigator and the bomber/radar operator sat side by side behind him, resulting in excellent visibility for the pilot. The crew section was a pressurized compartment attached to the forward end of the fuselage which could be adapted with nose assemblies for multiple missions.

National Archives, RG 72

Certain general design characteristics were decided very early in the investigations. First, a swept-back wing was considered to be the best method for attaining high drag divergence Mach numbers, on the basis of weight studies which included preliminary analyses of wing flutter characteristics. Second, the wing area was determined by the low speed operation requirements in connection with the maximum attainable lift coefficient. Third, an aspect ratio of 6.0 was considered a maximum practical value in view of low speed stability carrier handling requirements, and the small gains experienced with larger values.

The total thrust requirements for these generalized designs were compared to the fuel load requirements for a given range and plotted as curves. These relationships were possible for airplane designs which cruised at constant speed above 35,000 ft altitude and at constant throttle setting. Curves of this type could be considered independent of airplane size to a first approximation, and airplane configuration affected only the selection of drag coefficient.

North American then compared fuel availability to the characteristics of particular designs. Fuel availability was based on the known fixed weight items and estimated structural weight, and was drawn for a given takeoff gross weight with a wing loading established by low speed requirements. An optimum selection of total engine thrust was then shown by identifying the point at which the fuel available line which gave the maximum radius.

After determining the total thrust requirement for a given design in the aforementioned manner, different power plant installations were studied which approached this value. A desirable power plant was one which had a low weight/thrust ratio, convenient dimensions, and a thrust rating which permitted use of a small, even number of engines. The Wright TJ-6 engine, which was not on the OS-111 list, fulfilled these requirements better than any other engine studied. Other turbojet engines were studied as well as turboprop engines during the investigation.

North American also checked the takeoff operation (including rate of climb at the end of the deck) before finally approving the total thrust requirements. In some designs, the total thrust determined by the cruising condition did not permit the airplane to satisfy the rate of climb requirement. When considering turbojet engines in this manner, it was necessary to determine the thrust from the propeller in terms of the shaft horsepower and thereby select the engines

Propeller Considerations Propellers were carefully investigated in the early stages of the design study since it had been the usual experience that greater range was attained by propeller driven airplanes than by comparable turbojet-driven airplanes.

Certain initial handicaps were encountered in the propeller investigation of this design due to lack of test data on a desired type propeller at Mach numbers of .85 to .90, and also, an uncertainty of the effects of a propeller on a swept-back wing.

North American determined the propeller efficiencies at Mach .85 to be extremely low. So low, in fact, that further considerations of propellers on this basis were unnecessary. If the spinner diameter were increased until reasonable propeller efficiencies were obtained, then the resulting diameter was too large for a reasonable airplane design.

Advanced propeller designs which were more applicable to this type of airplane were investigated. It was considered possible to attain propeller efficiencies of approximately .77 at Mach numbers between .85 and .90.

Since the performance investigations determined that a propeller efficiency of approximately .75 was necessary in order for the propeller driven airplane to be equivalent to the turbojet driven airplane, it appeared that, at best, very little gain was to be expected from a propeller installation.

In light of the above facts, further considerations of propeller installations were dropped since the additional mechanical complexity of the airplane, and the very uncertain effects on the aerodynamic charac-

North American RD-4554 Class VA Study - Specifications and Performance Characteristics

Wing:

Area	1136 sq ft
Aspect Ratio	6
Span	82.6 ft
Airfoil Section	64A-010
Sweepback	35 degrees

Power Plant:

Mfg.	Wright
Model	TJ-6
Number	2

Tail:

Total Area	363.5 sq ft

Fuselage:

Length	73.9 ft
Width	14.9 ft

Total Airplane Wetted Area = 4567 sq ft

Performance characteristics of this design in comparison to requirements of OS-111 are as follows:

Airplane		OS-111 Requirements	N.A.A. Design
Take-Off Gross Weight	(lb)	100,000	100,000
Total Fuel Load	(gal)		6736
Bomb Load	(lb)	10,000	10,000
Combat Radius	(naut mi)	1700	1220
Cruising Speed	(Mach no)	0.85	0.85
	(knots)		490
Stalling Speed Without Power	(knots)		132

Airplane		OS-111	NAA Design
Rate Of Climb At Sea Level At End Of Deck (Navy Standard Hot Day)	(fpm)	500	666
Basic Flight Design Gross Weight (See Note 1)	(lb)		81,812
Maximum Speed	(Mach no)	0.90	0.90
Combat Altitude	(ft)	40,000	41,000
Design Landing Weight (See Note 2)	(lb)		65,750
Stalling Speed Without Power	(knots)	115	107

NOTES:

(1) Basic flight design gross weight is take-off weight less 45% of total fuel.

(2) Basic landing gross weight is take-off weight less bombs and 60% of total fuel.

National Archives, RG 72

teristics of the airplane high Mach numbers were not justified.

Drag Considerations Drag data for these design studies was based on North American's flight test and wind tunnel experiences together with all available data from other agencies. The drag figures represented minimum attainable figures with contemporary fabrication methods and good design practices, excluding unusual engine and equipment requirements which modified the exterior of the airplane and/or interior airflow.

The airplane drag divergence Mach number had been set at a value which would not have compromised the drag at the cruising condition. The effect of compressibility at a Mach number of .85 was considered to increase the low speed airplane drag coefficient by .0030. The wing area of the proposed bomber was 1,136 sq ft and total airplane surface area was 4,570 sq ft; North American calculated the equivalent skin friction coefficient as .0035. This low speed drag coefficient was based on the wing area and did not include any of the drag increase due to compressibility effects. No Reynolds number extrapolation was applied to the study.

Stability The specific design configuration selected by North American was required to meet NavAer SR-119B specification dated June 1, 1948, "Specification for Flying Qualities of Piloted Airplanes." As a preliminary investigation, only the critical requirements of the above specification were considered. Wind tunnel test results of the F-86 and similar type configurations were used as a basis for the evaluation.

Low speed flying qualities and stalling characteristics were foremost in the critical design considerations for carrier-based aircraft. The single slotted trailing edge flap used on the F-86 airplane was incorporated into the RD-4554. The inherently poor longitudinal stability at the stall and poor stalling characteristics of swept wings were overcome by the use of the full automatic leading edge slats used successfully on the F-86 airplanes.

Maximum lift coefficient for takeoff and landing were estimated from wind tunnel and flight tests of the aerodynamically similar F-86 wing configuration. With the full-span leading edge slat and the .50 b/2 single slotted trailing edge flap in its optimum position, it was estimated that a maximum lift coefficient of 1.5 was obtainable.

The center of gravity range was chosen so that a five percent static margin was maintained at low speeds. Based on F-86 wind tunnel and flight data, the increased margin at high Mach numbers did not produce undesirable shifts. An adjustable stabilizer and elevator provided sufficient longitudinal control in landing and takeoff.

Based on F-86 wind tunnel and flight correlation, the airplane was provided with sufficient vertical tail to provide satisfactory static directional stability; North American predicted that it would also exhibit satisfactory dynamic lateral and directional stability characteristics. With the engine arrangement proposed, single engine direction control would not have been critical. Considering both the F-86 tunnel and flight results and the reduced requirements for this type of airplane, the ailerons would have probably produced sufficient lateral control.

Stick and pedal forces were to have been set within specification requirements by adjusting the control boost ratio. Stick-free stability was to have been maintained by an irreversible boost system with built-in pilot feel.

Weight Study

In order to evaluate the feasibility of the class VA airplane outline in OS-111, North American conducted a weight study of the RD-4554. In consideration of the design and performance requirements, it was not apparent that a 100,000 lb airplane would meet the required combat radius. The weight study conducted laid particular emphasis on the two principle design parameters, namely, the ratio of the fuel weight to takeoff weight and the ratio of the fuel weight to takeoff weight and the ratio of structural weight to the basic flight design gross weight where the latter was the same as defined in OS-111. Consideration was given to the structural design criteria including such factors as the magnitude of flight and landing gross weight, design speeds, maneuver load factors, gust criteria and miscellaneous other criteria affecting the structural weight.

The weight data used in North American's studies were taken from a collection of statistical data adapted in empirical form suitable for use with various structural parameters. The statistical data included weight information from a large number of existing bombardment and attack type airplanes as well as a brief investigation of the possible weights that might be required in the wing of high speed attack type airplanes.

The first case studied was that of a 100,000 lb takeoff gross weight airplane that strictly adhered to the strength criteria as given in OS-111. The structural weight estimate was predicated on a preliminary structural design gross weight as defined. To this structural weight was added the remainder of the weight empty and all items of useful load with the exception of fuel. The amount of fuel permissible without exceeding the takeoff weight of 100,000 lbs was, therefore, insufficient to achieve the combat radius of 1,700 nm. North American's study presented its estimate of the structural weight required to make the 100,000 lb airplane possible disregarding the combat radius. It became evident that the percent of the structural design gross weight comprising the structural weight was 32.7%.

In view of the fact that the gust requirements at sea level were greater than the minimum maneuvering load factors and since OS-111 permitted a reduction in limit speeds at sea level in order to meet the structural design requirements without undue weight penalty, North American executed a second weight study. The second weight study was on the same basis with the exception that the gust strength requirements did not exceed those required for maneuvering. Hence, based on the strength requirements for maneuvering purposes only, the second study resulted in slightly lower structural weights, specifically 31.8% of the structural design gross weight. This slight gain was insufficient to allow higher fuel weights to meet the combat radius requirement.

Having thus investigated the required structural weight, North American then proceeded with a third weight study. The third study was likewise predicated on a takeoff gross weight of 100,000 lbs but included as one of the basic parameters the fuel required to meet the combat radius of 1,700 nm. To the basic fuel weight was added the remainder of the weight empty and useful load items necessary to meet all design requirements except those compatible with strength criteria. The weight remaining thus constituted the available structural weight for a 100,000 lb airplane capable of satisfying the performance requirements. Structural weight was 18.7% of the basic design flight gross weight in this study.

North American believed that a 100,000 lb airplane did not appear adequate to meet the combat radius requirements for a VA type airplane as outlined in OS-111. In submitting these preliminary weight studies to BuAer, the company did not believe that their estimates were unduly conservative; rather, it was pointed out that these weight estimates reflected North American's consideration of the problems anticipated in this type of airplane. The problems included relatively high speeds and Mach numbers for an airplane of this type, basic structural arrangements including pressurization, elevated structural temperatures, high shipboard landing requirements, transient load effects, etc. In the course of this preliminary study, North American was not able to reconcile the difference between the structural weight required for a 100,000 lb airplane designed to meet the requirements of OS-111, with the exception of the combat radius, and the permissible structural weight if all performance requirements were met. This difference was manifested in the 32.7% structural weight required to satisfy the strength criteria and the 18.7% structural weight permissible to meet the performance criteria for the configuration described.

In view of these preliminary weight studies, the feasibility of the 100,000 lb attack airplane outlined in OS-111 was not apparent. North American believed that it was necessary to conduct a study proportionate to a Phase I contract in order to narrow the above difference to a point where the feasibility of the 100,000 lb airplane became more apparent.

Design Features

This airplane was designed specifically for ease of operation and maintenance on the CVA (flush-deck) class carrier. Swept wing and tail surfaces were used to meet the high speed requirements. Engines were housed in the fuselage to reduce total wetted area, preserve a clean wing and simplify the power plant systems. The tricycle landing gear was also in the fuselage. The fuel was disposed in seven fuselage tanks. The radar and crew section was located in a pressurized compartment attached to the forward end of the fuselage and was adaptable to replacement with nose assemblies for other combat

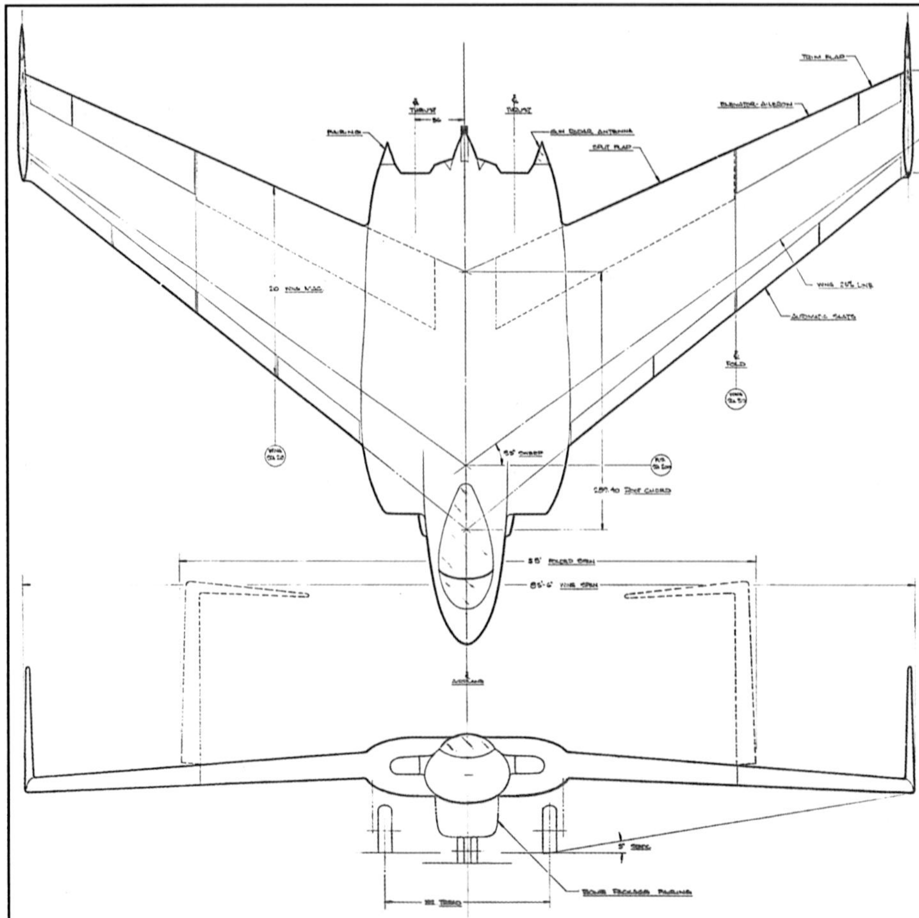

RD 4554 Navy VA Tailless Study - Specifications

Wing	**Area**	1,428 sq ft
	Aspect Ratio	5
	Span / Span Folded	55ft / 85ft 6in
	Taper Ratio	.4
	Sweep back	35°
Tail	**Area**	171.36 sq ft
	Aspect Ratio	1.5
	Taper Ratio	.4
	Sweepback	42.5 degrees
Fuselage	**Length Overall**	51ft 4in
Height	**Wings Folded**	23ft 4in
Weight	**Take Off Gross**	100,000 lbs

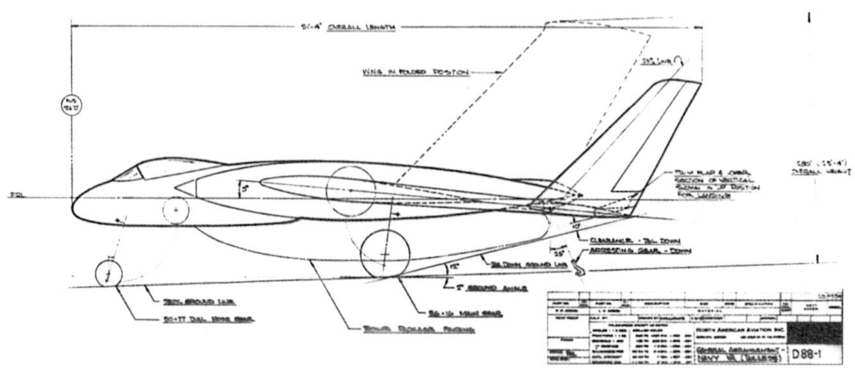

Three view drawing of the RD 4554 Navy VA Tailless study.

National Archives, RG 72

uses. Visibility was extremely good in this arrangement.

The RD-4554 Navy VA Tailless Study

North American also drew up a design called the "Navy VA Tailless" under the RD-4554 designation. Only the drawings for this aircraft have been found in BuAer files; it does not appear to have been part of North American's main proposal; perhaps it was sent to BuAer to demonstrate the pros and cons of a more unconventional design. The following information has been gleaned from the surviving blueprints.

Like the Lockheed L-187-3 study discussed in Chapter 8, the tailless RD-4554 was equipped with a large droppable bomb package. In a maximum range operation, the package functioned as follows:

1. The 1,000 gals of non self sealed fuel in the droppable package was used going to target.
2. The bomb control intervalometer ejected the door and dropped the bomb.
3. The package was dropped to effect weight and drag reduction for the return leg of the flight.

Doors were provided to close off the bomb bay after the package was jettisoned. North American also envisioned a smaller non droppable auxiliary bomb package for long range bombing when general purpose type bombs or depth charges were required.

Like the conventional RD-4554, the tailless study was powered by a pair of Wright TJ-6 turbojets. The air intakes were mounted on the fuselage sides and featured boundary bumps to improve airflow. The total fuel capacity was 6,696 gals, the majority of which was contained in self sealing tanks in the fuselage and wing.

The large wing was swept at 35° and featured trailing surfaces made up of a split flap, elevator/aileron, and trim flap. The leading edge of the wing had automatic slats and vertical surfaces were mounted at the wing tips. The wings were foldable for carrier stowage.

The pilot and copilot sat side by side in the front of the cockpit under a wide canopy, while the radar/bomb operator sat aft, offset to the right. Each crew member was provided with an ejection seat, though the ejection path for the radar/bomb operator did not meet the BuAer vertical clearance requirement. The cockpit entrance was on the bottom of the nose through the nose gear well. A narrow crawl tunnel was provided to access the bomb bay during flight.

The extreme aft part of the fuselage featured three cone-shaped fairings. The central fairing housed an Aero XIIE tail turret with a 90° cone of coverage, while the left fairing housed the gun radar antenna and associated computer equipment. The antenna had a 110° cone of coverage.

The tailless RD 4554 had a tricycle landing gear. The dual wheel nose gear retracted backwards, while the main gear retracted forwards into the wing.

North American's Class VA proposal was eliminated/disqualified early on by BuAer; the company wasn't even listed as an official participant in subsequent Navy correspondence concerning the competition. Nonetheless, the designs it submitted are of historical curiosity, providing an interesting comparison to those prepared by other manufacturers.

Below: Inboard profile of the tailless RD 4554 showing the large droppable bomb package.

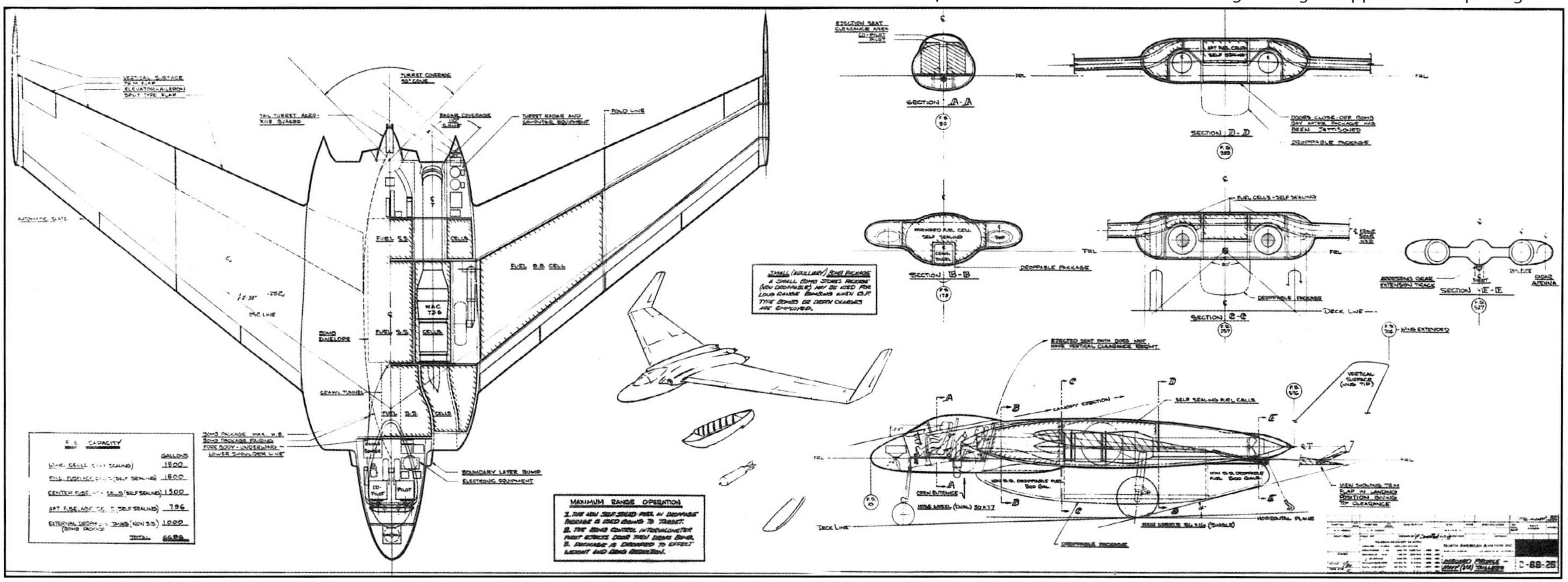

National Archives, RG 72

CHAPTER 10 — *Republic NP-50*

Republic's submission to OS-111, designated the NP-50, was an elegant design influenced by the company's work on the Air Force XF-91 Thunderceptor, which was under development at the time of the Navy Class VA competition. The influence was especially apparent in the design of the aircraft's prominent V-tail and variable incidence wing. The NP-50 was a three place, carrier based, heavy attack aircraft designed for the execution of high altitude attacks with large bombs and special weapons within a radius of action of not less than 1,700 nm. The design bomb load was 10,000 lbs.

General Description

Fuselage The fuselage was of semi-monocoque, stressed skin construction and was composed basically of Alclad and aluminum alloy transverse bulkheads and continuous stringers.

The three man crew was housed in a pressurized compartment forward of the bomb bay with the pilot's station situated to allow 15° vision over the nose. The copilot/bombardier was seated directly behind the pilot and all navigating and bombing apparatus was conveniently located with respect to his position. The armorer was seated behind the copilot/bombardier in a position next to the door into the bomb bay passage. The three crew member stations were covered by a single cockpit enclosure which provided

Artist's impression of Republic's handsome Class VA proposal, the design of which relied heavily on their experience with the XF-91 Thunderceptor.

National Archives, RG 72

maximum vision and was jettisonable to provide safe emergency egress from the aircraft by means of ejection seats. Access to each of the three crew stations and the bomb bay was provided by a passageway on the right side of the fuselage. The main crew door was located on the right hand side of the crew compartment and was jettisonable in flight to provide an alternate exit for all of the crew members.

The bomb bay, located behind the crew compartment, was designed for carrying a bomb load with maximum envelope dimensions of 16 ft long, 5 ft wide, and 5 ½ ft high. A bomb stabilizing flap and flush opening bomb bay doors were provided to permit bomb release at all flight speeds up to the maximum speed without damage to the aircraft or reduced bombing accuracy. The stabilized radar antenna for the AN/APB-2 bomb director was housed in a radome in the fuselage nose.

The tail portion of the fuselage housed a power-operated, uninhabited, automatic gun laying turret containing two 20 mm M-24 guns. The associated radar antenna was in the extreme tail position directly under the turret. The AGL electronic apparatus and ammunition boxes for 1,000 rounds of ammunition were arranged in the tail section immediately forward of the turret.

Wing The wing had a span of 85 ft, a mean aerodynamic chord of 14.7 ft, a sweep back angle of 41.5° at the leading edge, a dihedral of -3°, an area of 1,200 sq ft, and a thickness ratio of 11%. Its incidence angle was variable from -1° to +5° by means of two ball bearing screw jacks driven by a hydraulic motor.

Four spar stressed tapered skin construction was used in the wing center section and three spar stressed tapered skin construction was used in the outer panels. The wing was fabricated mainly from 24-ST and 75-ST aluminum alloy sheet, extrusions, and forgings, and in addition aluminum alloy castings, magnesium castings and forgings, and steel fittings were used.

The outer wing panels folded in a vertical plane by hydraulic actuation and were readily removable by removing the hinge pins and disconnecting the controls and actuating mechanism. The maximum span with wings folded was 49 ft.

Empennage The aircraft was equipped with a swept back V-type tail with a total area of 380 sq ft and a horizontal span of 42 ½ ft. Each portion of the tail had a chord of

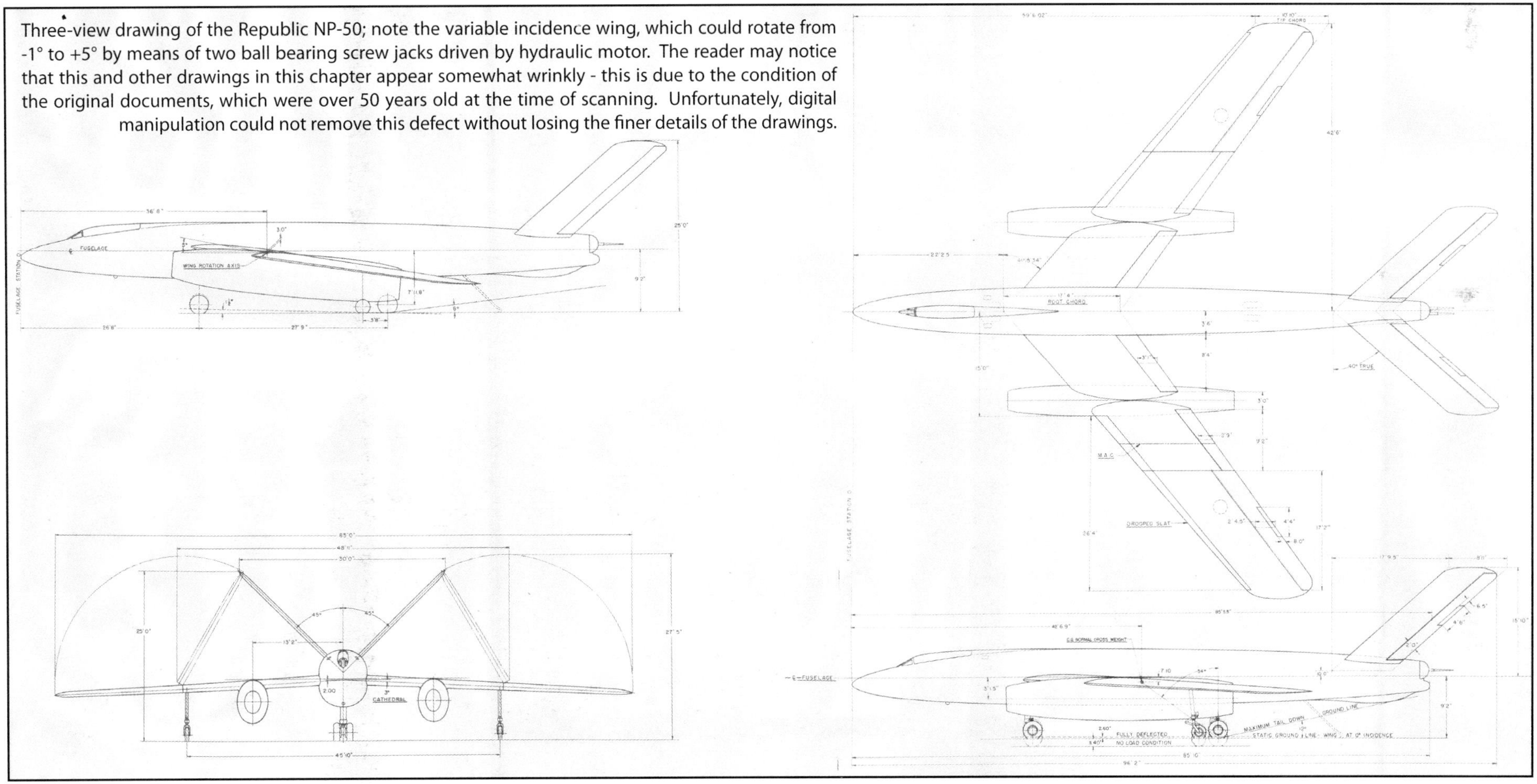

Three-view drawing of the Republic NP-50; note the variable incidence wing, which could rotate from -1° to +5° by means of two ball bearing screw jacks driven by hydraulic motor. The reader may notice that this and other drawings in this chapter appear somewhat wrinkly - this is due to the condition of the original documents, which were over 50 years old at the time of scanning. Unfortunately, digital manipulation could not remove this defect without losing the finer details of the drawings.

National Archives, RG 72

8.8 ft, an 11% thickness ratio, an incidence angle of zero, a 40° sweep back angle, a 4.75 aspect ratio, and a 45° dihedral angle. The height over the highest part of the tail was 25 ft.

The fixed tail surfaces had tapered skins machined from 75-ST Alclad sheet. The spars and ribs were formed from 75-ST aluminum alloy sheet. The "elerudders" were constructed of the same material as the fixed surfaces.

Power Plant The NP-50 was powered by four Westinghouse turbojet engines, two each of model XJ40-WE-12 and model XJ46-WE-2. The turbojets were housed in two wing nacelles, each nacelle containing one XJ-40 and one XJ-46 engine.

Armament A 10,000 lb bomb installation, an AN/APB-2 Mark V bomb director, and a two-gun Aero XIIE automatic gun laying tail turret installation compromised the aircraft's useful armament load.

Flight Controls The aileron and elerudder main flight controls were operated in the conventional manner by a control stick located at the pilot's station. A combination of cables and push-pull rods carried the control stick movements to the ailerons and to a lever assembly in the tail. The "elevator" and "rudder" motions were changed by the lever assembly to move the two elerudders differentially or in the same direction as required. A push-pull rod connected the elerudder change-over mechanism to the elerudders. Three hydraulic boosters were included in the aileron, "elevator," and "rudder" control systems to reduce control surface loads and permit high rates of control surface movement. Each booster unit incorporated a variable "feel back" device, operated by an electric motor, which allowed the pilot to adjust the control stick force to correspond with control surface loads and thus eliminate the tendency to over-control during cruising flight. In the event of failure of the hydraulic boosters the pilot could control the ailerons and elerudders directly by disengaging the hydraulic boost cylinders. Conventional motor operated trim tabs were used on the control surfaces.

The flaps and the combination drag brake and bomb stabilizing flap were operated by hydraulic cylinders controlled through selector valves. The leading edge wing slats were operated through a linkage connected to the flap actuating cylinders.

Manual control of the aircraft was accomplished only by the pilot as no flight controls were provided for the copilot. Automatic flight control was governed either by the pilot or the copilot as each was provided with the necessary controller and flight instruments for the P-3 autopilot.

Design Features

The NP-50 was an aircraft specifically designed for the performance of its particular mission but throughout the design emphasis had also been placed on convenience of ground handling and servicing.

Service Accessibility All components of the aircraft were readily accessible for inspection and maintenance through conveniently located access openings. Where equipment was so located that it could not be conveniently reached through the wheel wells, bomb bay doors, crew compartment openings, or removable access panels, special accessibility provisions were made. The hinged nose section for servicing the equipment in

This Page and Next: Inboard Profile of the NP-50. Like several other manufacturers, Republic chose a bicycle landing gear to save weight.

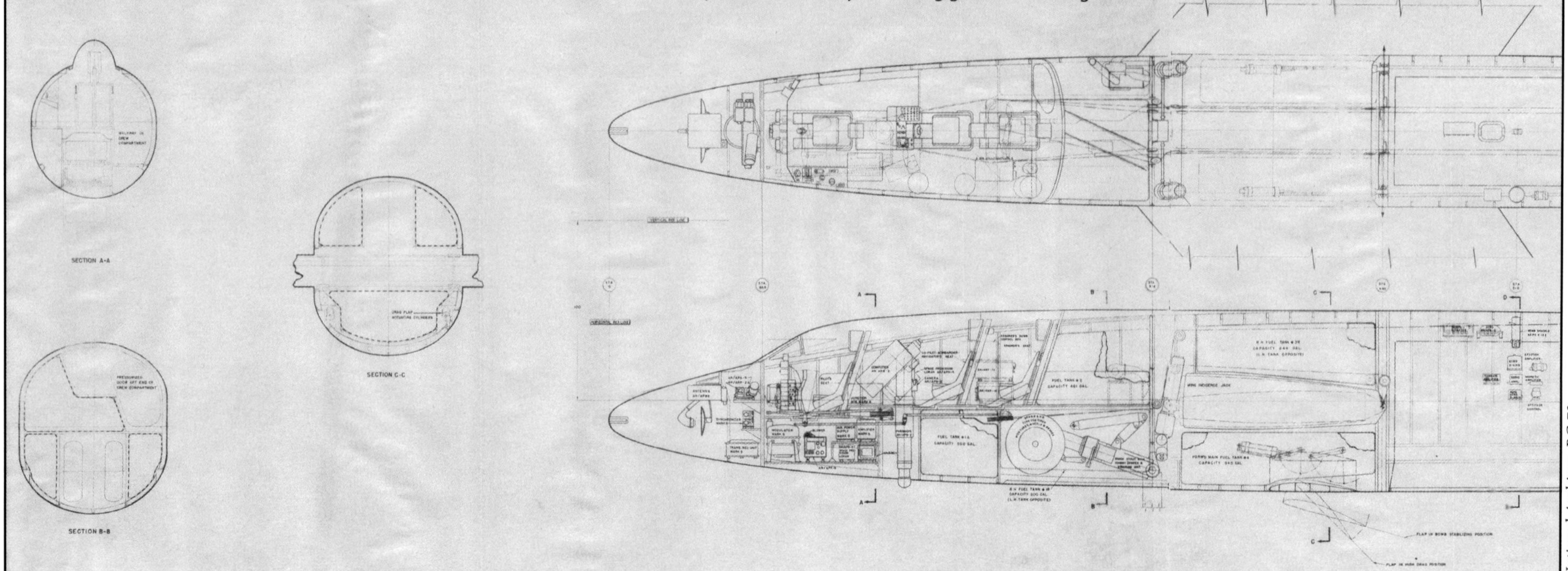

National Archives, RG 72

the forward portion of the fuselage, and the installation of the battery and portions of the electronic systems on elevators to permit lowering for maintenance from the deck were exemplary of the design consideration given to maintenance requirements.

Power Plant Arrangement The arrangement of the XJ-40 and XJ-46 engines in the two wing nacelles was such that each nacelle presented the least possible frontal area and a desirable fineness ratio. The engines were readily accessible for maintenance by opening the forward hinged section of the nacelle and opening the lower hinged portions of the nacelle skin. Any engine could be independently removed or replaced by a wheeled deck handling engine lift or torpedo hoist with adapter which was attached through the lower nacelle openings.

Engine Starting As the initial starting of the engines was accomplished on the ground by pneumatic starters supplied with compressed air from an external source, provisions were incorporated for engine starting in flight without carrying an auxiliary compressor unit. Either engine in each nacelle group could be started during flight by operating the compressed air starter of the stopped engine from compressed air bled from the running engine. This provided a positive means of restarting in case a temporary engine shutdown was required during the mission.

Landing Gear The use of a tandem main landing gear on the underside of the fuselage resulted in considerable overall weight saving by reducing the required length of the struts. The full swiveling provision of the main and auxiliary landing gear wheels facilitated deck handling and maneuvering.

Variable Incidence Wing The incorporation of a variable incidence wing in the NP-50 aircraft enabled the tail to be lowered at takeoff and the aircraft's angle of attack to be increased to the optimum value in spite of the location of the rear tandem wheel aft of the CG. It also provided a means of maintaining the pilot's over-the-nose vision during the high wing angles of attack required for takeoff and landing.

Varying the wing incidence provided a means of rapidly accomplishing trim changes required for flight at transonic speeds and allowed alignment of the aircraft fuselage with the line of flight to reduce drag.

V-tail The V-tail had been incorporated in the design as test data indicated that it provided better stability and control characteristics and less drag at transonic speeds than was obtainable with conventional vertical and horizontal tail surfaces.

Jettisonable Cockpit Enclosure The single jettisonable cockpit enclosure provided a quick open escape hatch for the emergency exit of the crew members in flight or after a ditching or crash landing. The cockpit enclosure was removable to permit access to the crew compartment for overhaul or equipment modifications.

Ejection Seats The ejection type seats provided for the crew members permitted safe emergency egress from the aircraft under conditions of high speed and possibly uncontrolled flight. This means of emergency exit had been selected as recent successful bailouts at speeds of approximately 550 mph had demonstrated the safety of ejection of crew members into the air stream at these speeds. The ejection seat was particularly suited for vertical exit in V-tailed aircraft.

Hydraulic Control Surface Boost The three hydraulic boosters included in the flight control system reduced control stick forces and permitted high rates of control sur-

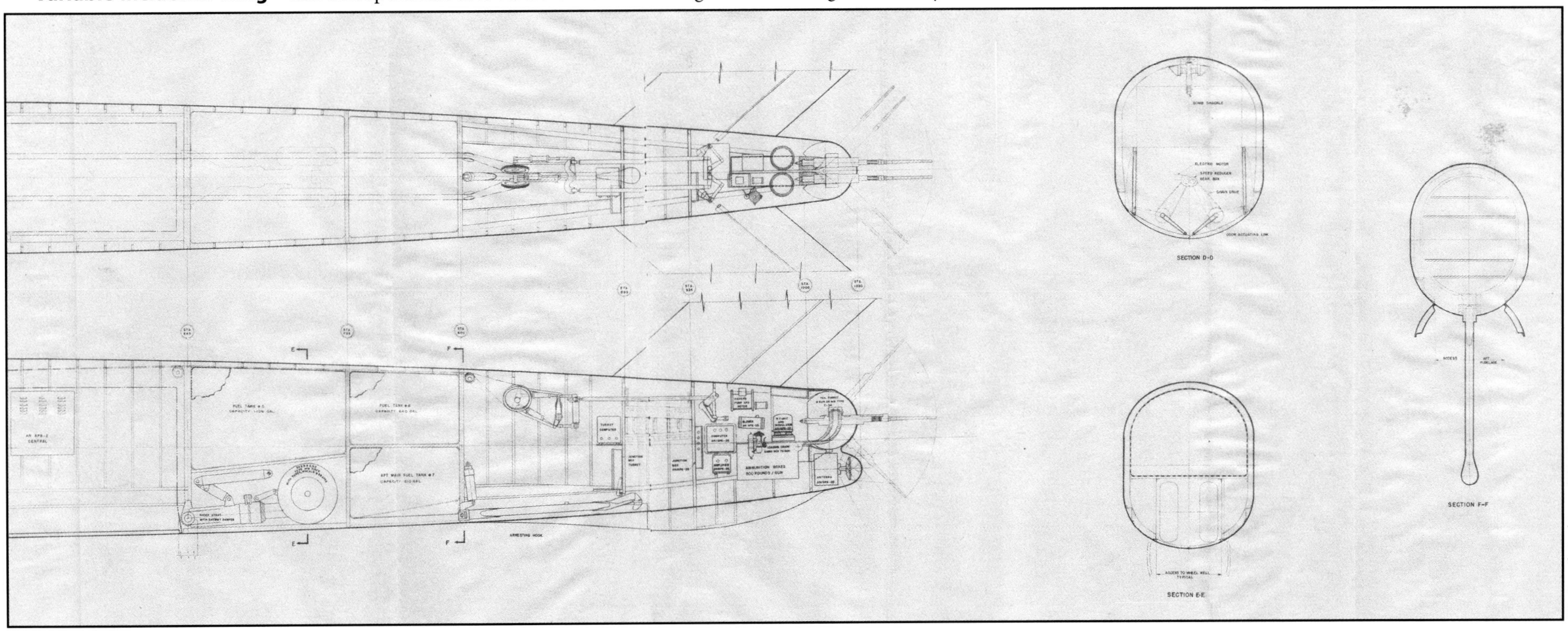

National Archives, RG 72

face movement. The hydraulic cylinders could have been disengaged for direct manual control of the aircraft. Each booster unit incorporated a variable "feel back" device, operated by an electric motor, which allowed adjustment of control stick force in the desired proportion to control surface loads to eliminate over-controlling during cruising flight.

Engineering Background

Republic Aviation Corporation had engaged in extensive research and development in the field of high performance aircraft with performance ranges and sizes which included the requirements of the Class VA Attack Airplane. Ability to develop and manufacture large aircraft of advanced design was exemplified by the Republic XR-12 reconnaissance airplane. Tactical evaluation tests had demonstrated that the XR-12 was one of the most outstanding high altitude long range reciprocating engine aircraft in the world.

NP-50 Crew Compartment Mockup

A partial mockup of the NP-50 crew compartment was built and revised as necessary during the initial fuselage layout studies. The location of navigation, communication, bombing and flight control apparatus, the accessibility of the three crew stations for interchange of crew members in flight, the relative location of crew stations to each other and to the fuselage and bomb bay entrance doors, and the suitability of the seating arrangement for emergency exit through the jettisonable canopy were investigated in preliminary studies until a suitable and convenient crew compartment arrangement was obtained.

National Archives, RG 72

Photograph of Republic's crude mockup of the NP-50 crew compartment.

Aerodynamic Testing of V-tail

Wind tunnel and free flight testing of V-tailed models had been accomplished through NACA and other facilities in connection with the development of the Republic XF-91 airplane. These tests showed that the V-tail resulted in 12% less drag at transonic speeds than obtained when conventional vertical and horizontal tail surfaces were employed. A comparison of tests conducted on V-tailed models and tests conducted on similar models with conventional tails showed that changes in normal acceleration with Mach number were considerably less for the V-tail, indicating improvement in stability and control characteristics at transonic and supersonic speeds when the V-tail was used.

National Archives, RG 72

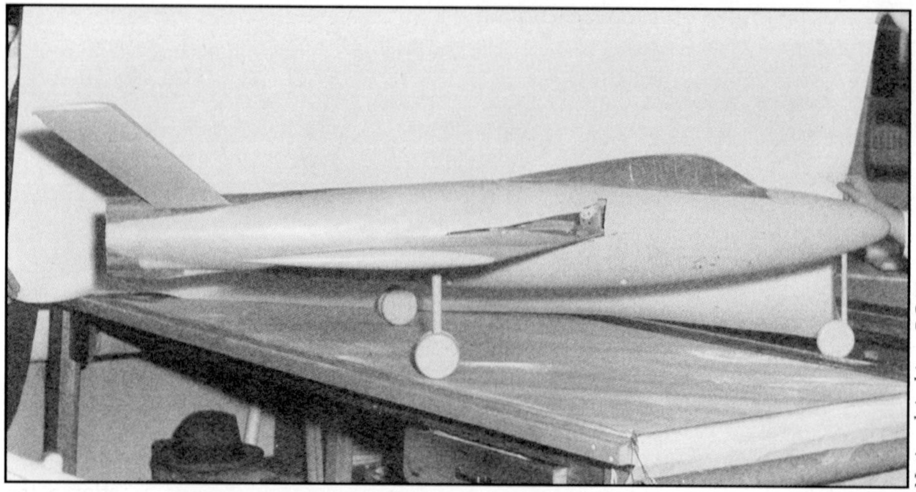

National Archives, RG 72

Photographs of a Republic XF-91 model used in wind tunnel tests to determine the viability of the V-tail configuration. Results were encouraging enough to also employ the unusual tail arrangement on the Republic NP-50 design.

Spin recovery characteristics of an airplane were considerably better with the V-tail than with the conventional tail. This advantage had been demonstrated by comparison of Republic models in spin tunnel tests and resulted from the fact that with the "V" configuration, no part of the tail surface that was effective in spin recovery was blanketed, whereas a large section of the vertical portion of the conventional tail configuration was hidden by the horizontal tail surface at the large angles of attack.

Development of the Variable Incidence Wing Mechanism

The low increase in lift with angle of attack of swept back wings offered serious takeoff and landing problems which could be minimized by the use of a variable incidence wing to reduce the required ground angle and increase the pilot's vision. The variable incidence wing was desirable for aligning the aircraft fuselage with the line of flight to reduce airplane drag and improve the pilot's vision at high altitude, and also provided a means of rapidly accomplishing trim changes required for flight in the transonic speed range.

Republic had completed the design and development testing of a variable incidence wing installation and operating mechanism. The wing was hinged at the rear of the fuselage opening and attached at the forward end of the opening to the two jacks which supplied power for varying the incidence angle. Republic constructed a test rig at their research laboratory for proof testing the system as installed on a fighter aircraft.

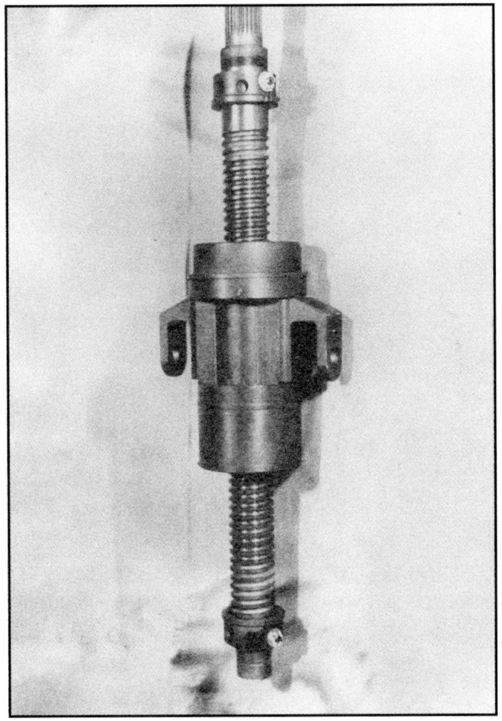

National Archives, RG 72

Ball bearing type screwjack used in the variable incidence wing of the XF-91; a similar mechanism would have been employed in the NP-50.

The adjustable angle of incidence feature of the wing presented the problem of sealing the opening in the fuselage through which the wing operated. A sliding closure plate for sealing the opening had been developed and tests had been conducted in the Republic research laboratory to study the performance of the sliding closure and the action of the surrounding structure under simulated flight conditions. The test specimen was subjected to estimated critical flight loads and the sliding closure operated satisfactorily at all increments up to the limit load. The force required to adjust the position of the closure at limit load was less than 2% of that available for wing incidence adjustment.

Control Surface Booster Mechanism Research

Republic engineers had performed extensive research and experimental testing for the design of a control surface booster mechanism with desirable control characteristics. An improved, simple, and highly satisfactory aileron control system was developed, tested and installed on all Republic production F-84 airplanes and contributed immensely to the elimination of "control stick fatigue." This system, which had merited pilot approval, was characterized by the following:

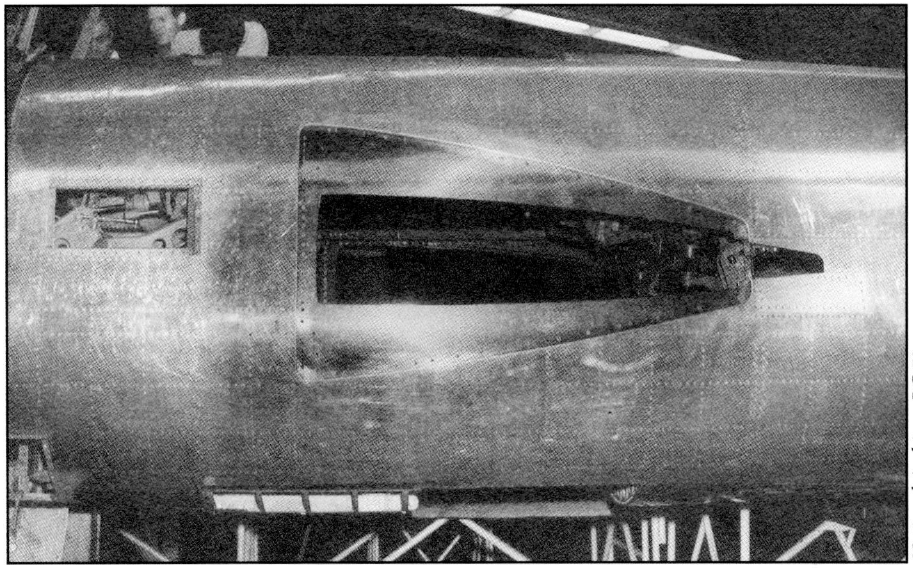

National Archives, RG 72

Photo of the variable incidence wing installation in the Republic XF-91 fuselage.

1. Light pilot stick forces with feel back in direct proportion to aileron load.
2. Smoothness of operation.
3. Speed and accurate response of the boost control
4. Elimination of vibration.
5. Non-hunting, self-centering system.
6. Ease of manual boost-off operation.
7. Provisions for changing the boost feel-back ratio in flight.
8. Provision for turning the hydraulic boost on or off in flight.
9. Provision for emergency disconnection of the hydraulic boost from the mechanical system in combat.

Booster mechanism studies were conducted in the Republic research laboratory for use in the development of control system adaptable to high performance interceptor aircraft.

Miscellaneous Testing / Development of Servicing and Training Equipment

A considerable amount of miscellaneous testing had been accomplished at Republic with results which were directly applicable to the proposed NP-50 attack aircraft design. This work included research on cabin pressurization, cabin heating and cooling for pilot comfort, diffuser and duct testing, and windshield and canopy defrosting.

Republic had been active in the development of special tools, handling equipment, and training aids for use in facilitating aircraft servicing and in developing proficiency of maintenance crews. The engine handling dolly developed for the F-84 airplane was a typical example of the attention given to the development of specialized equipment for minimizing the time requirement for engine change operation.

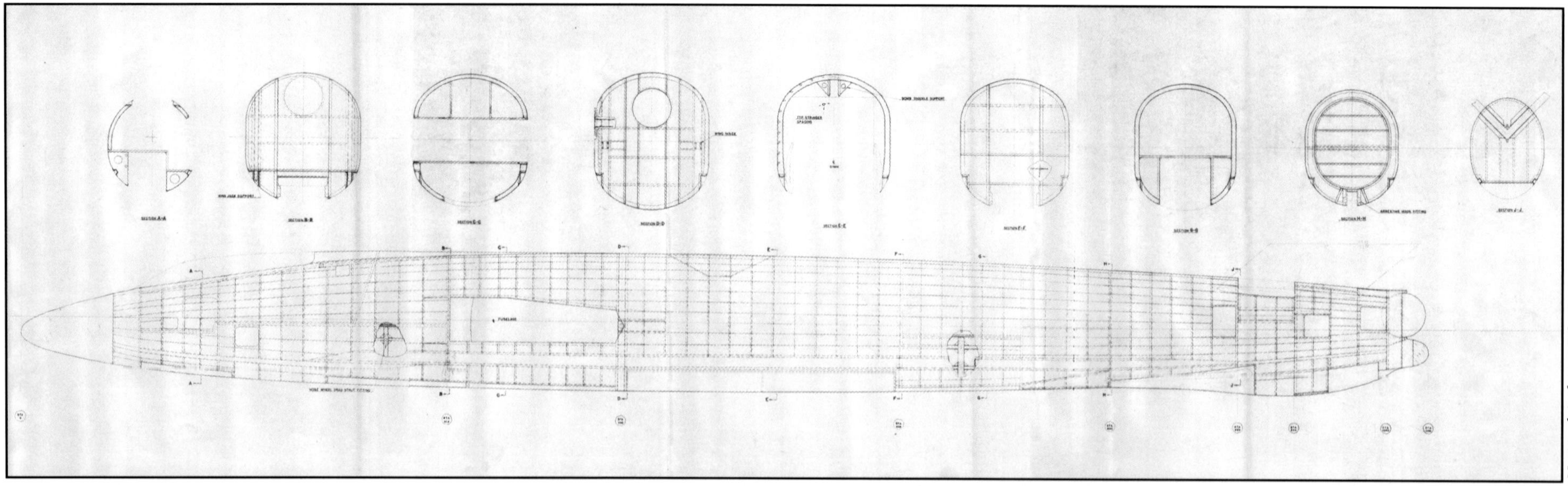

National Archives, RG 72

Above: NP-50 fuselage structure, which was of semi-monocoque, stressed skin construction and was composed basically of Alclad and aluminum transverse bulkheads and continuous stringers.

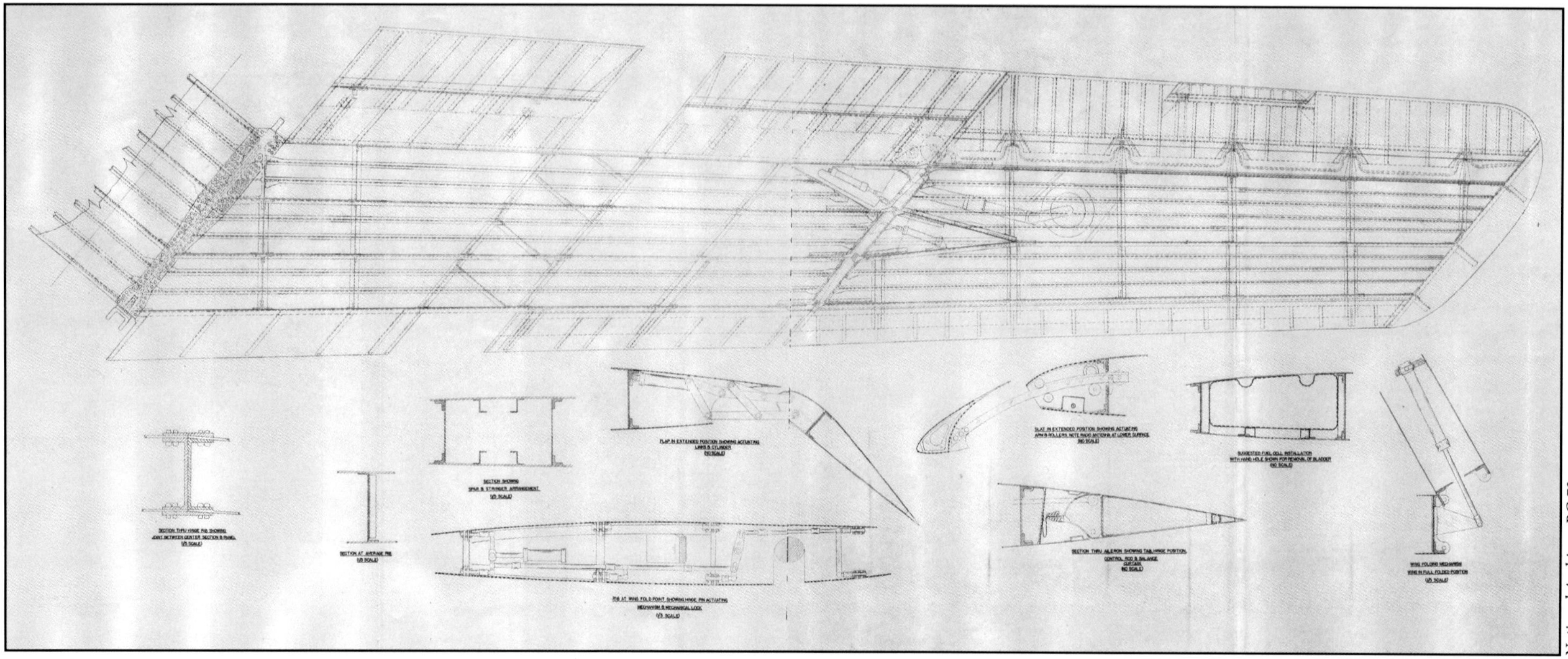

National Archives, RG 72

Above: The wing structure, which was of four spar stressed tapered skin construction in the wing center section and three spar stressed tapered skin construction in the outer panels.

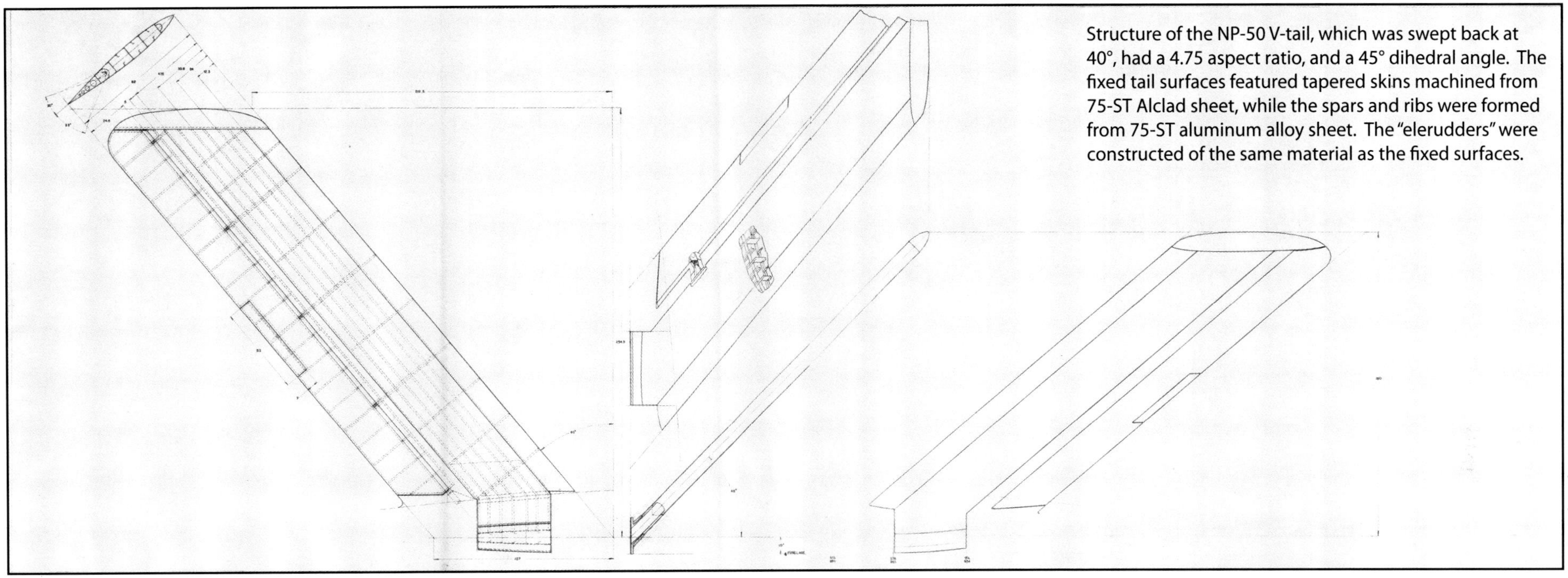

Structure of the NP-50 V-tail, which was swept back at 40°, had a 4.75 aspect ratio, and a 45° dihedral angle. The fixed tail surfaces featured tapered skins machined from 75-ST Alclad sheet, while the spars and ribs were formed from 75-ST aluminum alloy sheet. The "elerudders" were constructed of the same material as the fixed surfaces.

National Archives, RG 72

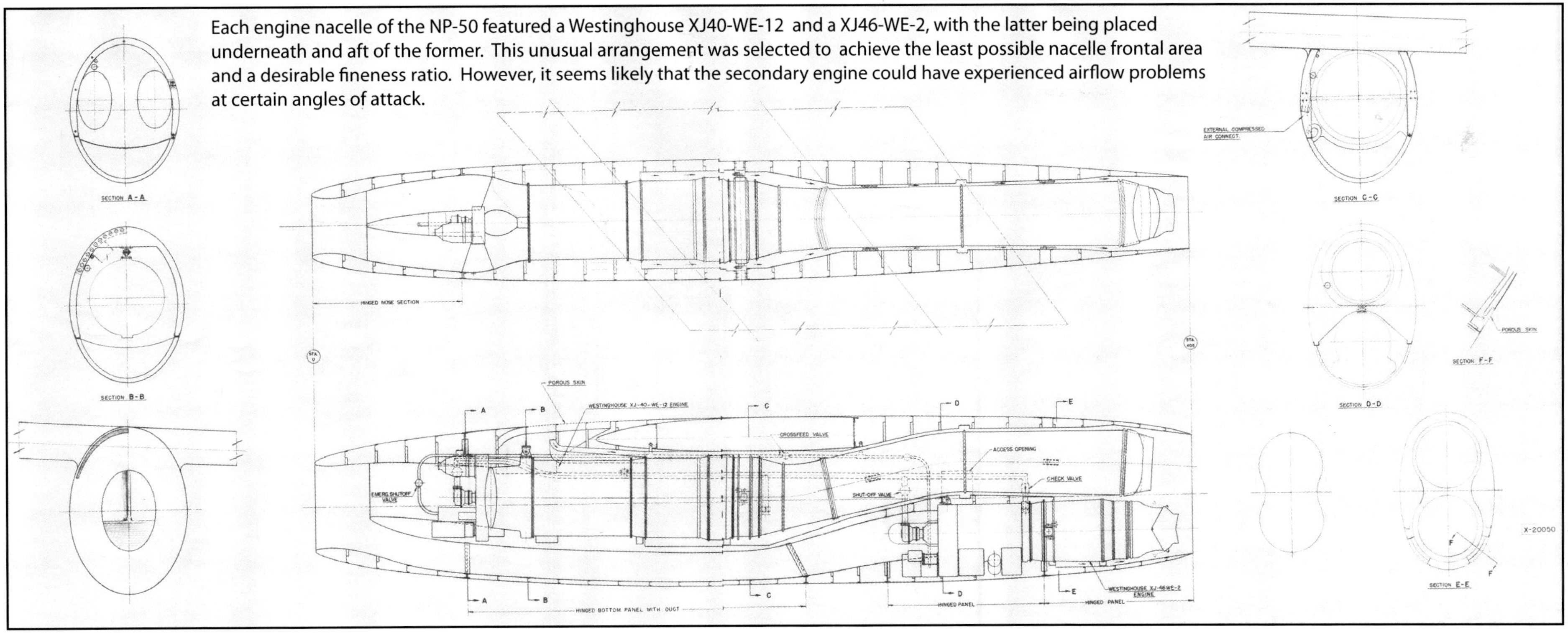

Each engine nacelle of the NP-50 featured a Westinghouse XJ40-WE-12 and a XJ46-WE-2, with the latter being placed underneath and aft of the former. This unusual arrangement was selected to achieve the least possible nacelle frontal area and a desirable fineness ratio. However, it seems likely that the secondary engine could have experienced airflow problems at certain angles of attack.

National Archives, RG 72

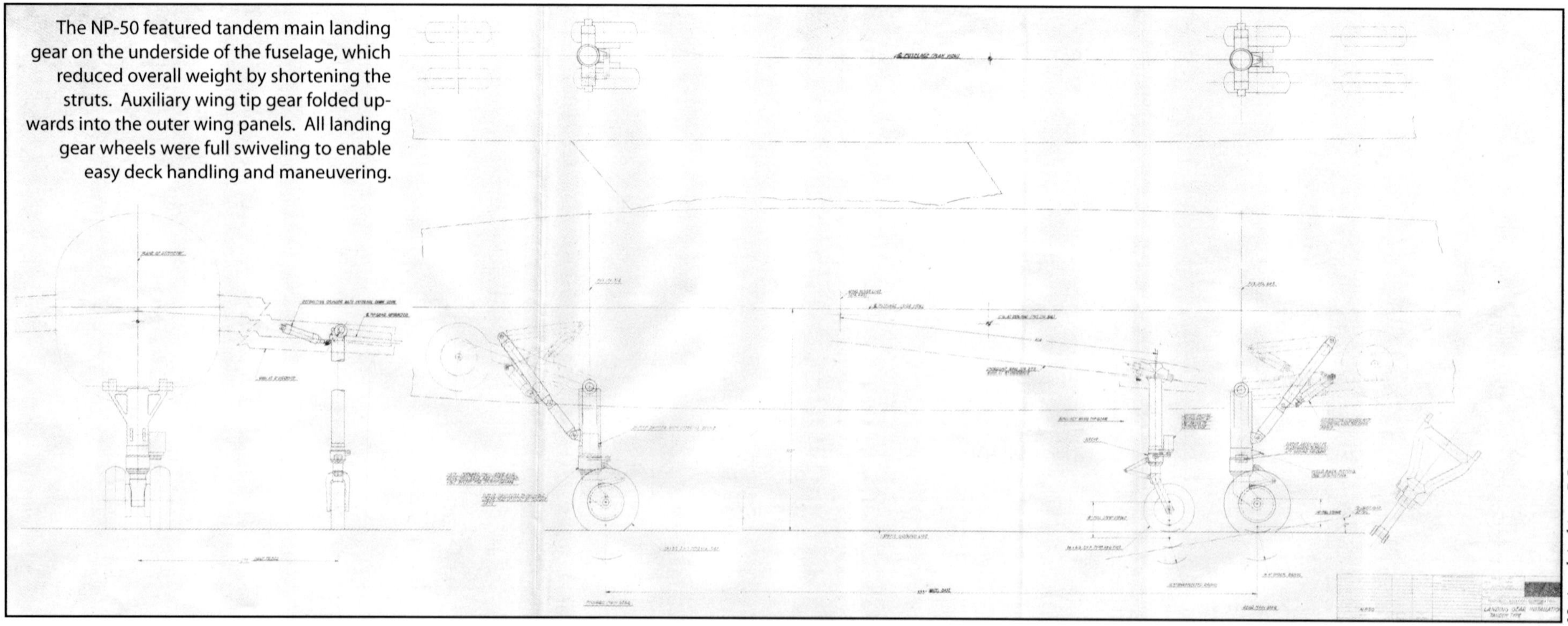

The NP-50 featured tandem main landing gear on the underside of the fuselage, which reduced overall weight by shortening the struts. Auxiliary wing tip gear folded upwards into the outer wing panels. All landing gear wheels were full swiveling to enable easy deck handling and maneuvering.

National Archives, RG 72

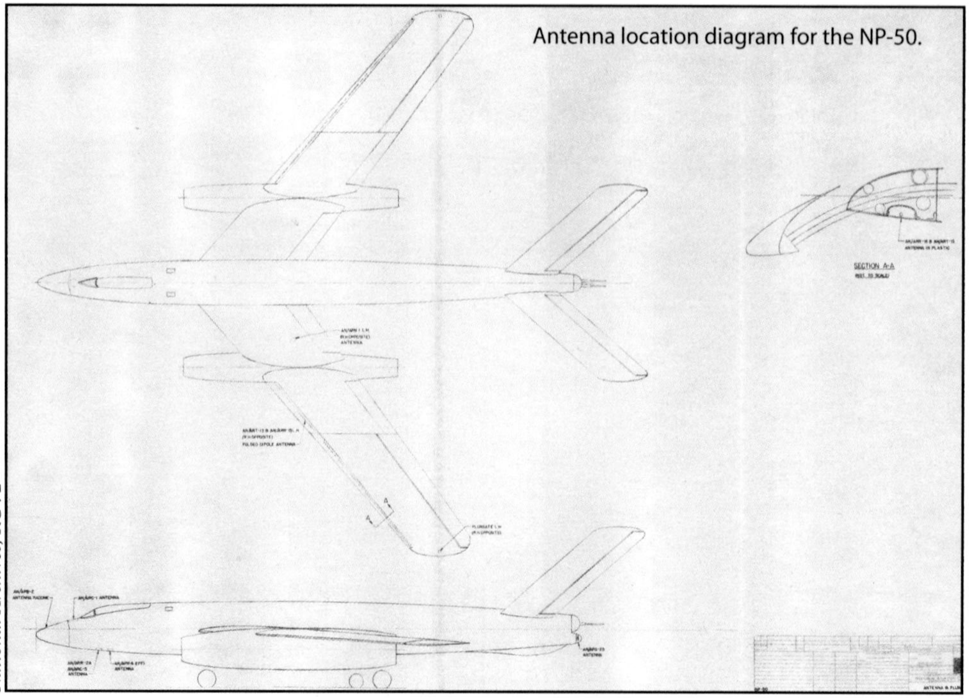

Antenna location diagram for the NP-50.

National Archives, RG 72

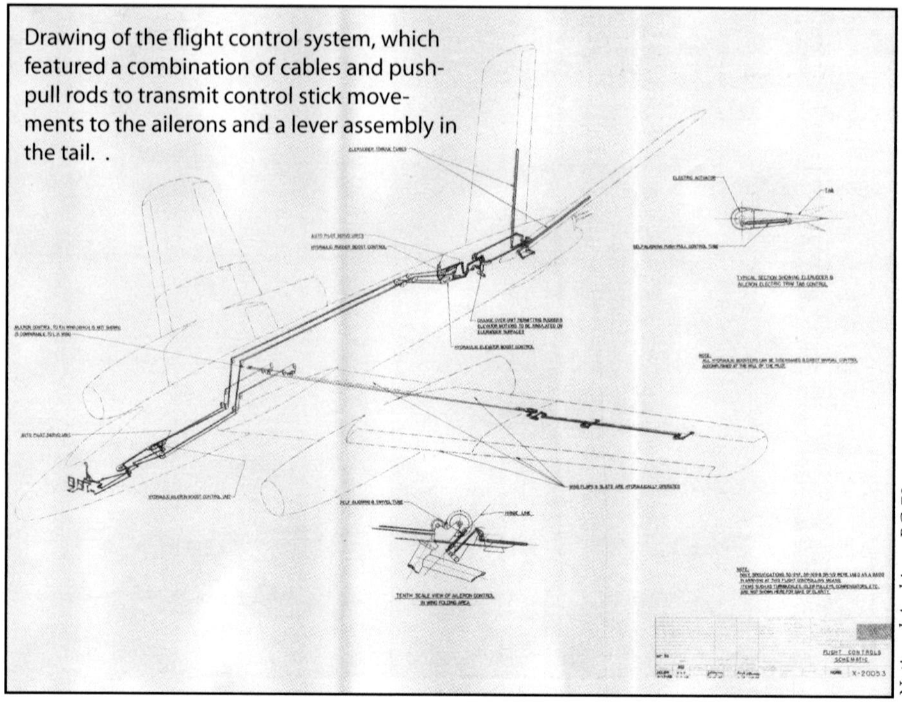

Drawing of the flight control system, which featured a combination of cables and push-pull rods to transmit control stick movements to the ailerons and a lever assembly in the tail. .

National Archives, RG 72

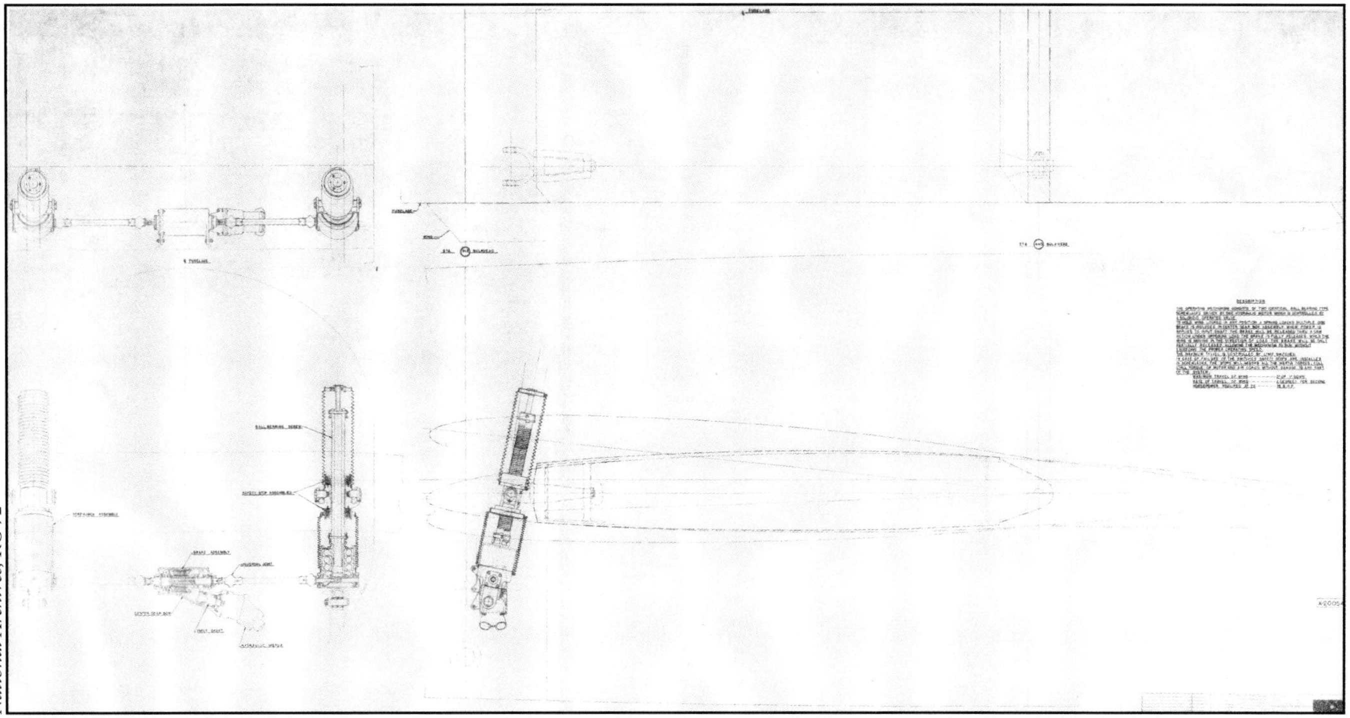

National Archives, RG 72

Left: Blueprint of the NP-50 wing incidence control. The wing was hinged at the rear of the fuselage opening and was attached at the forward end of the opening to two jacks which supplied power for varying the incidence angle. A sliding closure plate sealed the opening in the fuselage through which the wing operated.

Below: Installation of the two-gun Aero XIIE automatic gun laying tail turret.

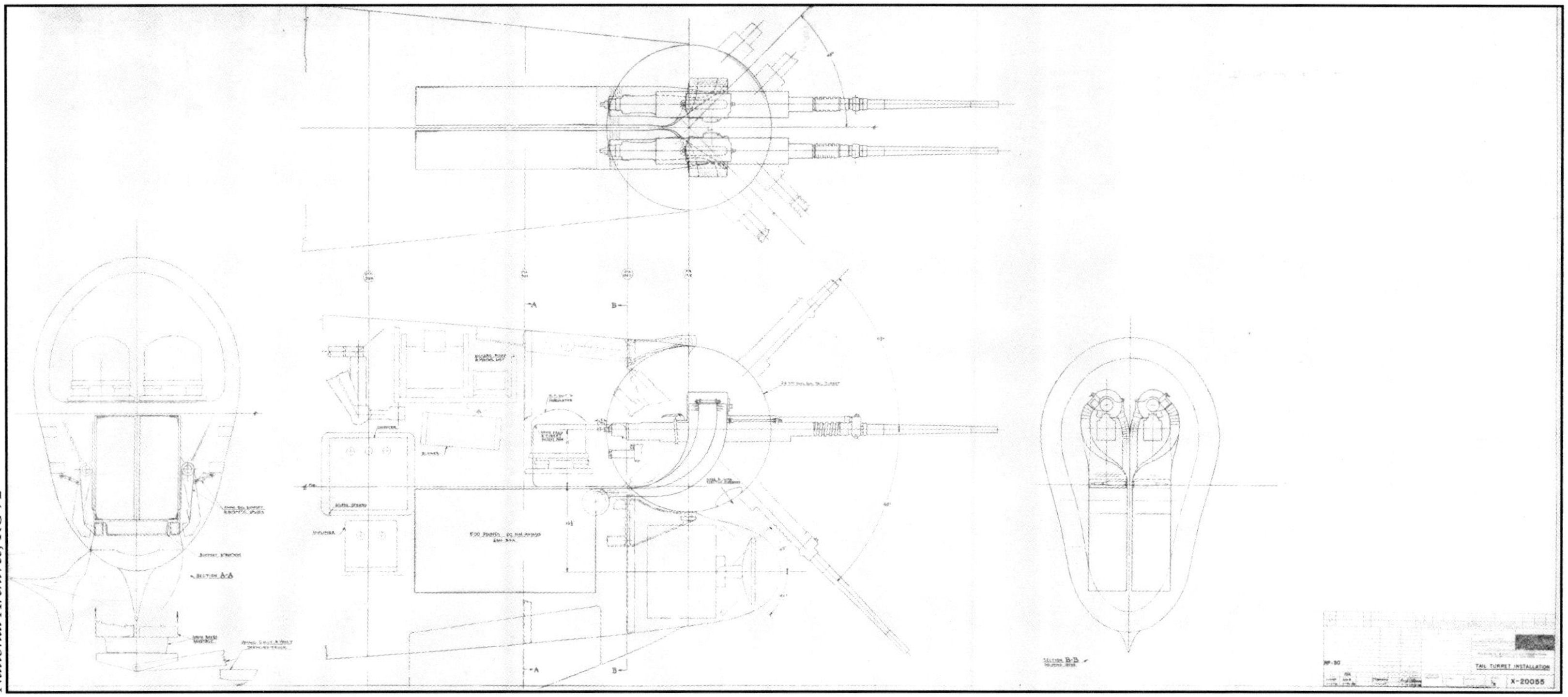

National Archives, RG 72

Right: Diagram showing location of NP-50 fuel tanks and their removal provisions.

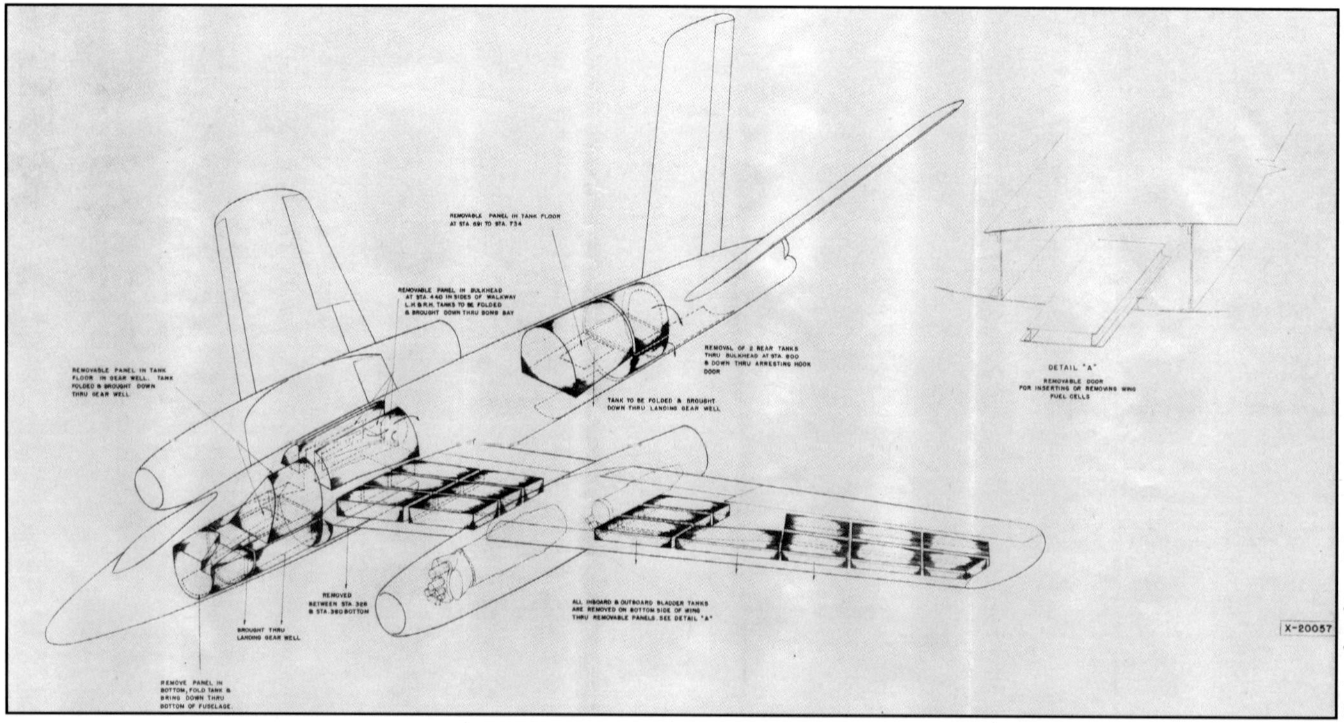

National Archives, RG 72

Below: Schematic of the NP-50 fuel system.

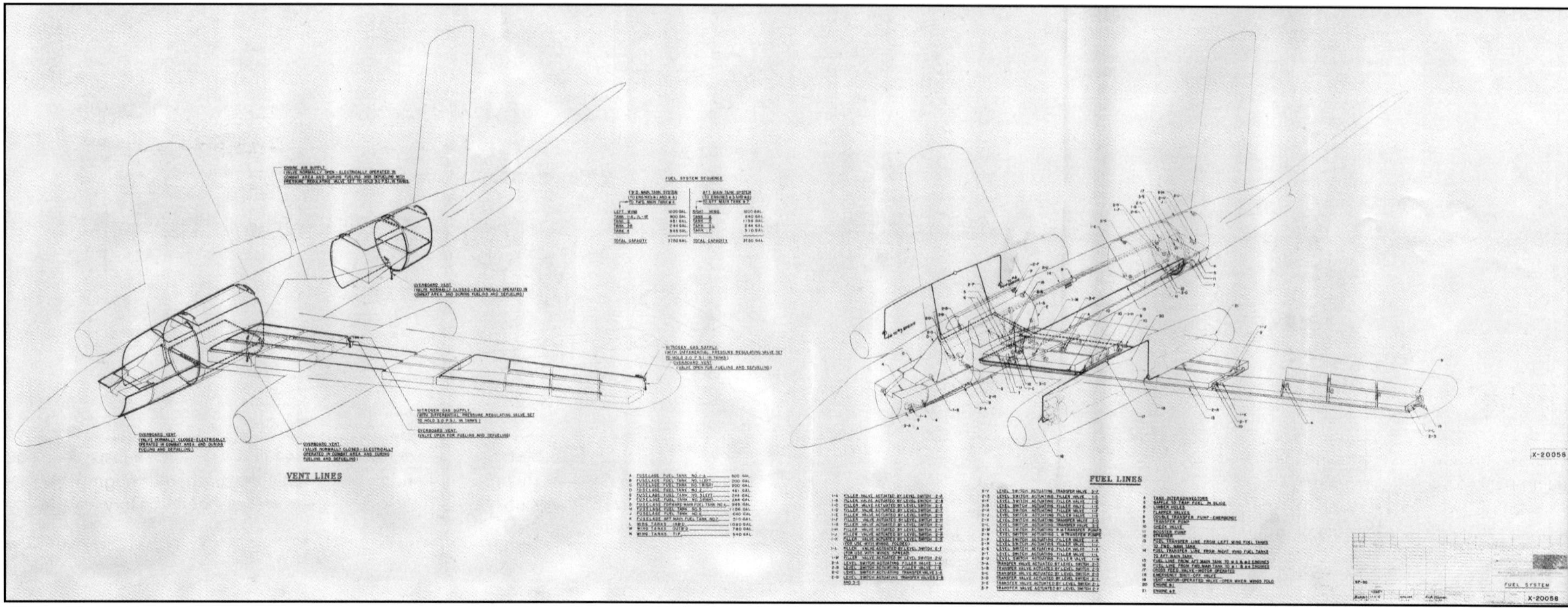

National Archives, RG 72

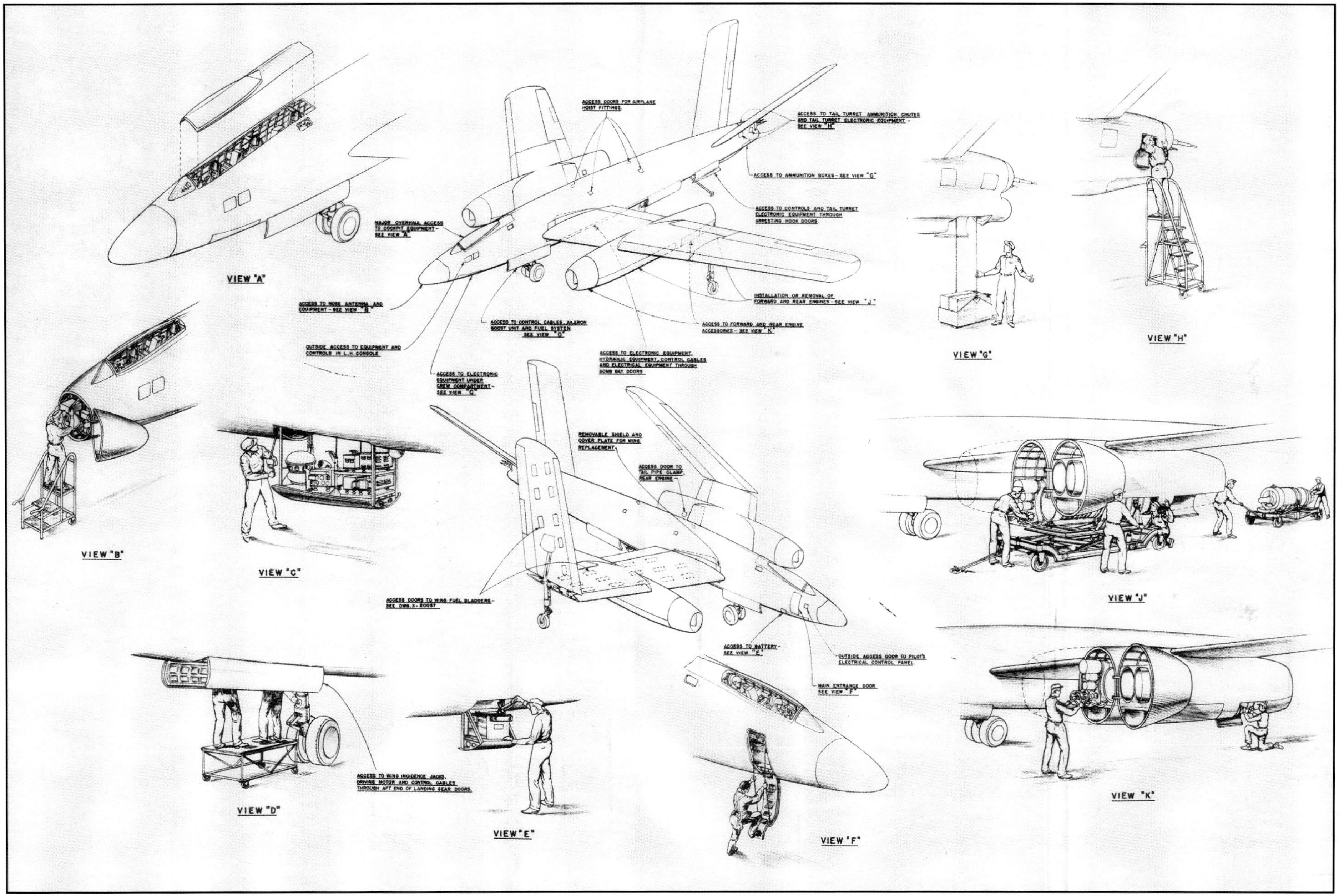

National Archives, RG 72

These exquisitely drawn pen and ink illustrations depict service access locations for the NP-50. Republic endeavored to make all components of the aircraft readily accessible for inspection and maintenance through conveniently located access openings. The manufacturer made special accessibility provisions where equipment could not be conveniently reached through the wheel wells, bomb bay doors, crew compartment openings, or removable access panels. Notable servicing features included a hinged nose section for servicing the equipment in the forward portion of the fuselage and the installation of the battery and portions of the electronic systems on elevators to permit lowering for maintenance from the deck.

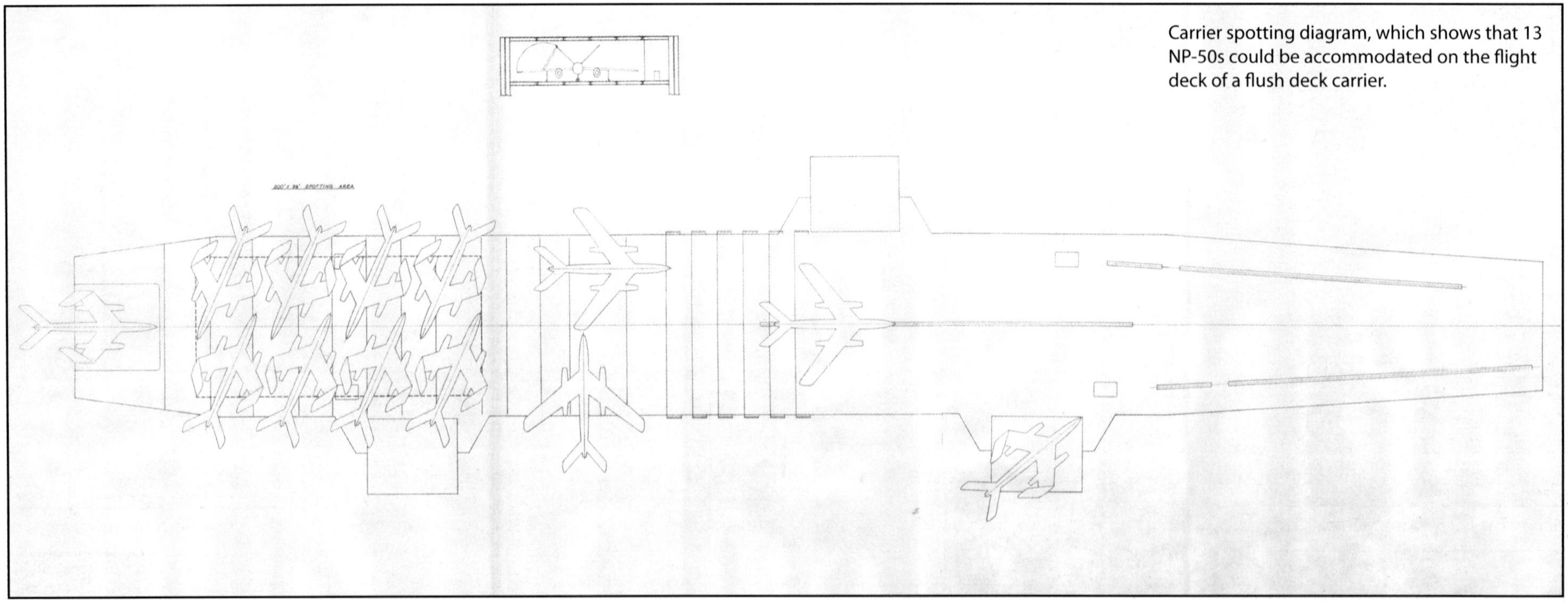

Carrier spotting diagram, which shows that 13 NP-50s could be accommodated on the flight deck of a flush deck carrier.

National Archives, RG 72

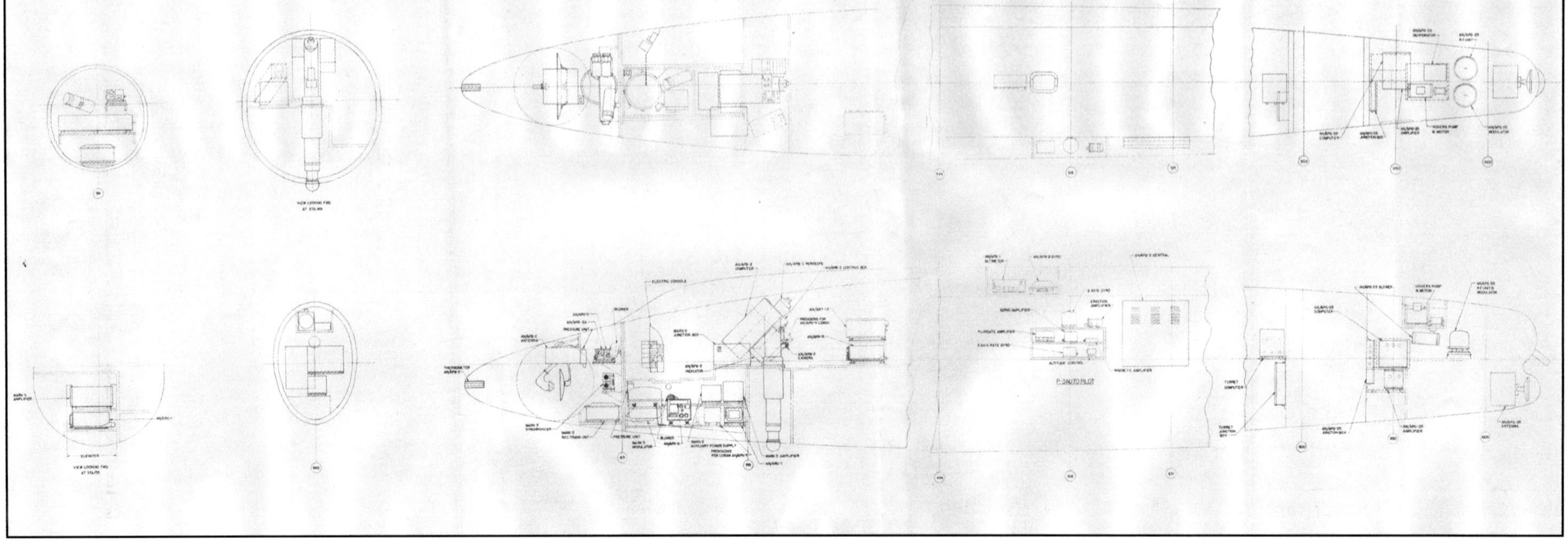

Blueprint showing the electronics arrangement for Republic's heavy attack aircraft.

National Archives, RG 72

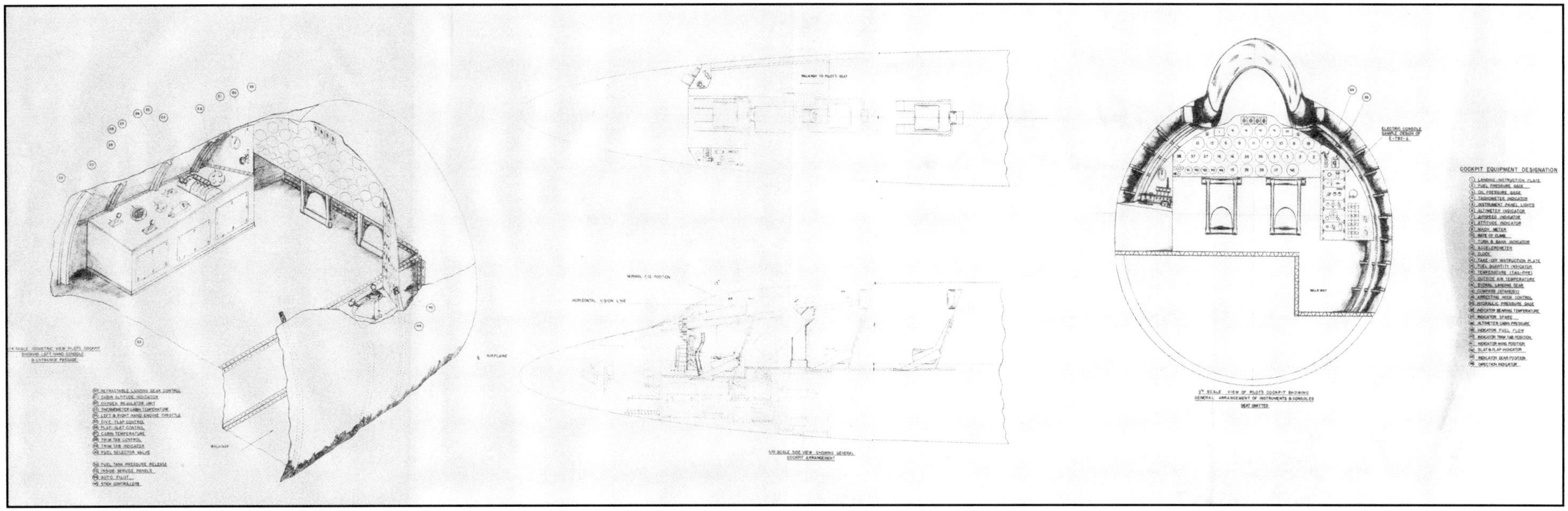

National Archives, RG 72

Above: The NP-50 cockpit installation consisted of a pressurized compartment housing three crew forward of the bomb bay, to which a tunnel was provided on the right side of the fuselage.

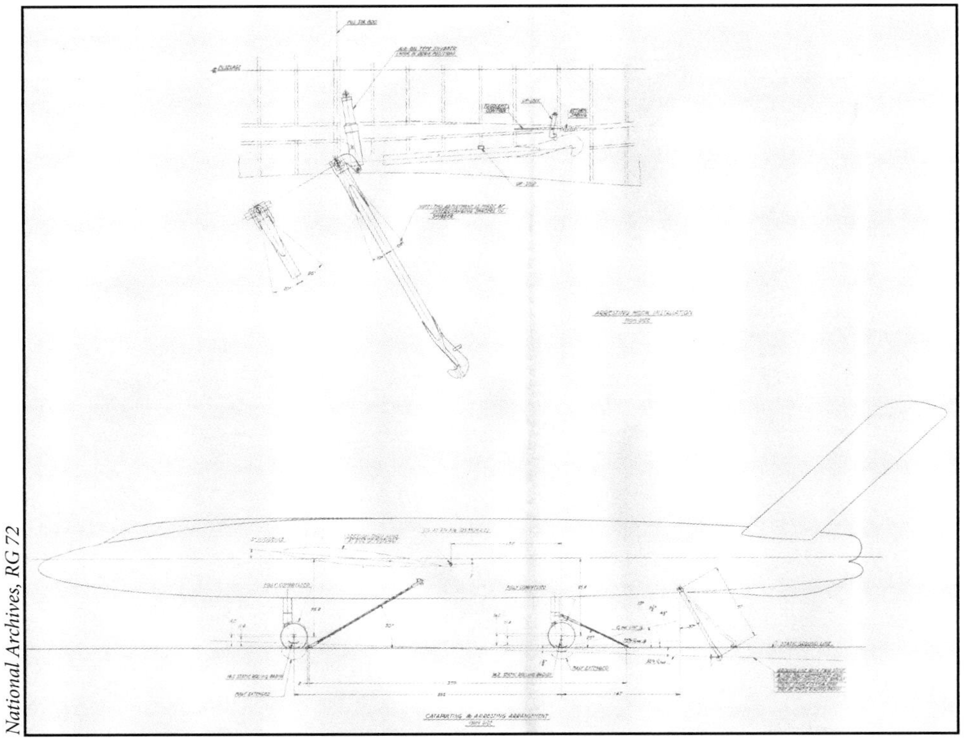

National Archives, RG 72

Above: Catapulting and arresting arrangement for the NP-50 Class VA proposal.

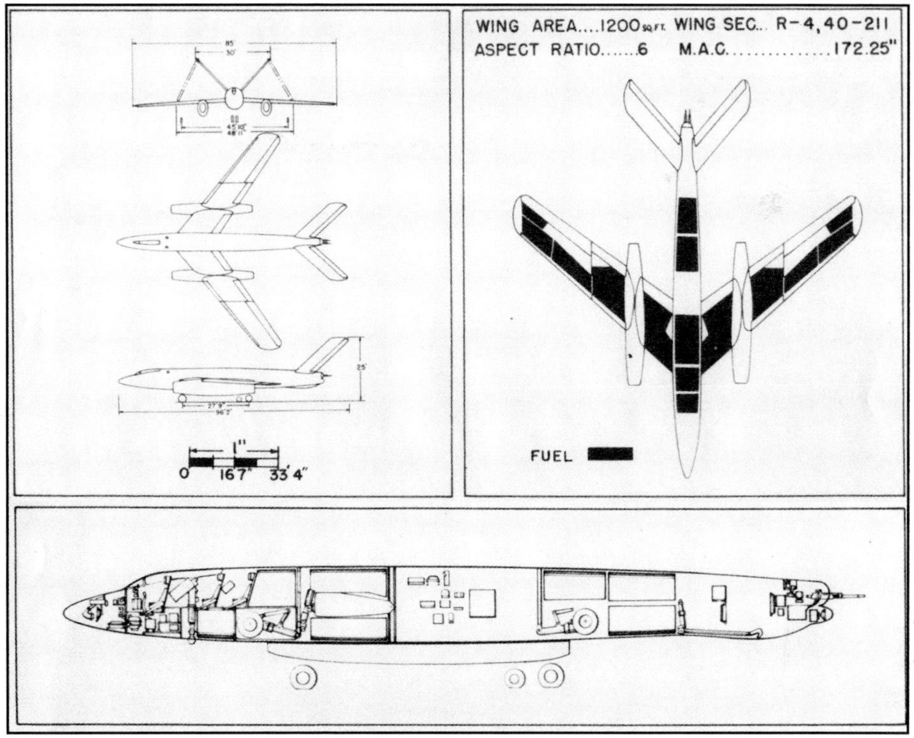

National Archives, RG 72

Above: Simplified NP-50 drawings from the type's Standard Aircraft Characteristics charts.

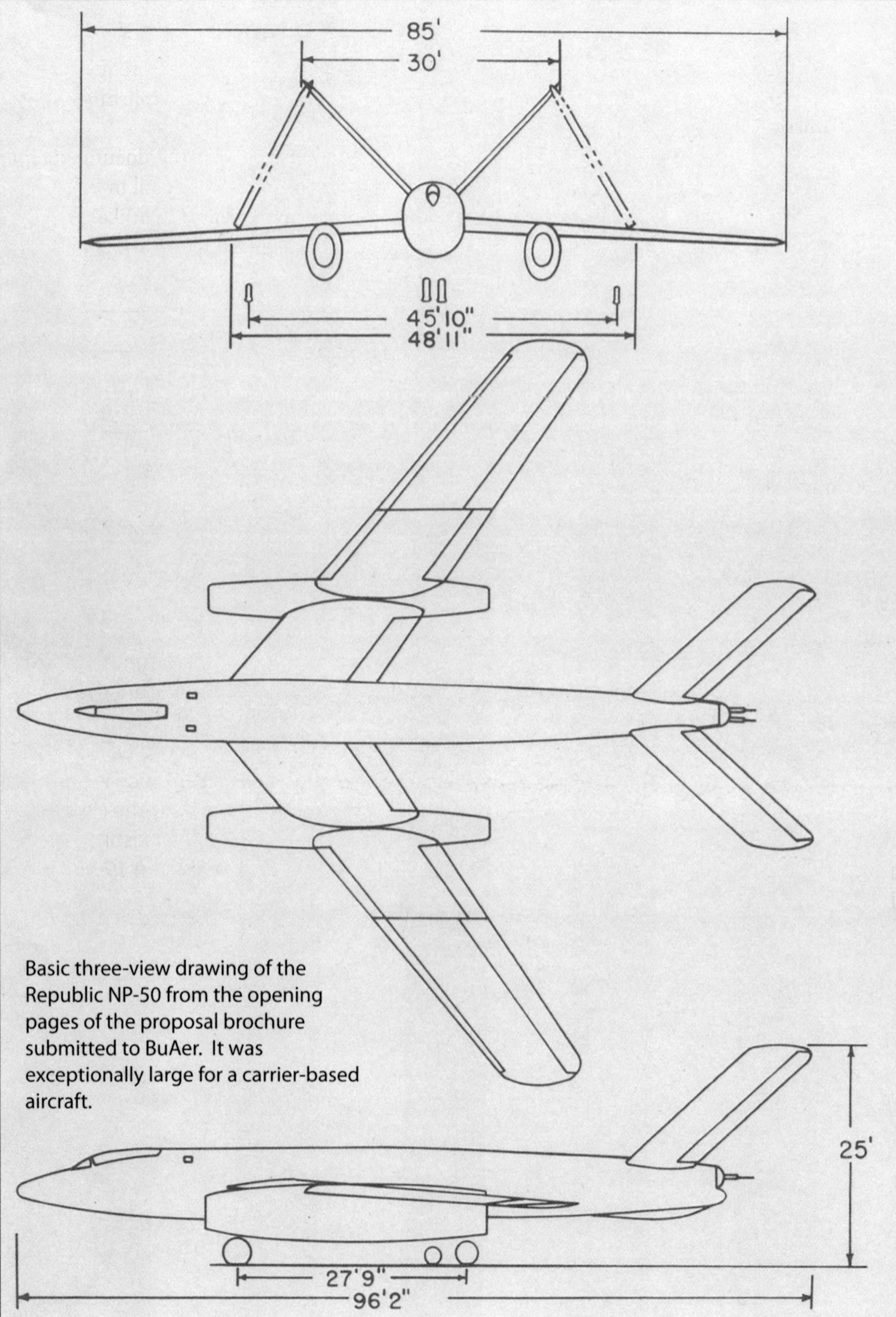

Basic three-view drawing of the Republic NP-50 from the opening pages of the proposal brochure submitted to BuAer. It was exceptionally large for a carrier-based aircraft.

National Archives, RG 72

MISSION AND DESCRIPTION

The primary mission of this airplane is the execution of a high altitude horizontal bombing attack with large bombs and special weapons at a point not less than 1700 nautical miles from the point of take-off.

The Republic NP-50 aircraft is a four engined jet-powered aircraft employing a swept-back variable incidence wing, vee tail, and a dual wheel tandem type gear. The engines are housed in two nacelles supported under the wing structure. The bomb bay is designed to carry a special bomb load of 10,000 pounds.

WEIGHTS

Weight Empty	50,273Lbs
Useful Load	56,827Lbs

POWER PLANT

Two (2) Westinghouse XJ40-WE-12
Two (2) Westinghouse XJ46-WE-2

RATINGS

	Guaranteed	Advanced
XJ40	8100 Lbs	9000Lbs
XJ46	4200 Lbs	4870Lbs

FUEL AND OIL

7500 Gals Aviation Gasoline

OIL

Self Contained in Engine

ORDNANCE

A power operated, uninhabitated AGL turret system containing 2 - 20 mm M-24 guns is installed on the aircraft. 500 rounds of ammunition are provided per gun and fire is controlled by APG-25 radar.

Provisions are made to carry a 10,000 pound bomb load in a bomb bay of the size specified.

DIMENSIONS

Over-all Length	96'-2"
Span	85'
Folded Span	48'-11"
Height	25'
Tread(Auxiliary Gear)	45'-10"

ELECTRONICS

AN/APN-1	Radar Altimeter
AN/ARC-1	VHF Trans Rec
AN/APB-2	Radar Bomb Director(MkV)
AN/ART-13	MHF Trans
AN/ARR-15	MHF Rec
AN/ARR-12A	Navigation Rec
AN/APX-6	IFF
AN/AIC-4	(3 Place)ICS
AN/ARC-5	(R-23Rec) Range Rec
AN/APN-4	Loran (Provisions only)

National Archives, RG 72

Data Based on Guaranteed Engine Ratings

PERFORMANCE SUMMARY

LOADING CONDITION		Basic Mission			
TAKE-OFF WEIGHT		107,100			
Fuel	lbs	44,988			
Bombs	lbs	10,000			
Ammunition	lbs	630			
Wing/Power Loading (A) lbs/sq.ft. lbs/lb		89.2/4.7			
Stall Speed--Power off	kn	112			
Stall Speed--Power off - No Fuel,Bombs	kn	72			
Stall Speed--Power on	kn	108			
Maximum Speed/Alt (B)	kn/ft	544/40,000			
Take-off Distance, deck -- calm	ft	Catapult			
Take-off Distance, deck 25kn.	ft	Catapult			
Take-off Distance, Airport	ft	8,300			
Rate of climb -- sea level (B)	ft/min	3,650			
Service Ceiling (B)	ft	41,500			
Time-to-climb 35,000 ft. (B)	min	16.9			
Time-to-climb 41,500 ft. (B)	min	34.			
Combat Range/V av 40,000 ft.	n.mi/kn	3210/491			
Combat Radius/V av 40,000 ft.	n.mi/kn	1685/491			
LOADING CONDITION					
GROSS WEIGHT	lbs	86,855			
Engine power		Military			
Fuel	lbs	24,743			
Bombs/Tanks		10000Lb/None			
Ammunition	lbs	630			
Max. speed at sea level	kn	613			
Max. speed 35000ft.	kn	556			
Combat speed/Alt.	kn/ft	550/40,000			
Rate of climb SL	ft/min	5,600			
Ceiling for 500 fpm R/C	ft	44,200			
Time-to-climb/Alt.	min/ft	19/44200			

NOTES

(A) Wing Loading = T.O.G.W./1200
Power Loading= T.O.G.W./S.L. Static T.O. Thrust

(B) Normal Thrust

National Archives, RG 72

Above: Standard Aircraft Characteristics charts summarizing the NP-50 proposal.

CHAPTER 11 — *Outline Specification 115*

Concurrent with Outline Specification 111, BuAer drafted Outline Specification 115 for a Class VA, Long Range Special Attack airplane, which was released on August 24, 1948. The requirements of OS-115 were far more challenging than those of OS-111, resulting in proposals that were among the most radical and unconventional aircraft ever considered for carrier-based operations.

The Navy required an attack airplane capable of delivering a large bomb load at extreme ranges. The nature of possible targets and probable future developments in enemy defensive weapons dictated that such an airplane, in order to survive, had to be capable of traveling at higher altitudes and continuous cruise speeds than was then considered practical for conventional aircraft. While the guided missile attained the speeds and altitudes desired, great difficulties still posed themselves in the problem of combining these qualities with adequate range and accuracy of guidance. Therefore, the Navy elected to modify the requirements then imposed on both piloted aircraft and guided missiles to produce a vehicle embodying an approach to the speed and altitude performance of the missile while retaining the range and accuracy of guidance of the conventional airplane.

The vehicle was conceived as a single mission, composite aircraft which was capable of discarding or jettisoning, during the course of its flight, such parts of the vehicle that were not required for completion of its mission. It had to, however, be capable of a) being launched by any feasible means including JATO and/or conventional or special launching devices from a CVA class carrier and b) being able to return the crew to the point at which the flight originated. Concerning the latter requirement, it was desired but not mandatory that the component returning the crew be capable of landing aboard a carrier of the Essex (CV-9) class. It was highly desirable that the airplane be adaptable to use for training operations from land bases.

The Navy desired that the maximum gross weight at takeoff in the configuration to attain the prescribed radius did not exceed 100,000 lbs. The performance and tactical requirements are summarized in the following section. BuAer emphasized that high altitude performance and minimum weight were of greater importance than increasing the combat radius above the minimum specified.

General

The arrangement of the airplane would provide for a crew of two, namely a pilot who would also serve as radio operator and a bomber who would also serve as radar operator and navigator. Both of the crewmen would be provided with ejection seats. Personnel access to the bomb bay in flight was not required.

The design would be predicated on power plants that could reasonably be expected to be available by the time required for installation. Self-sealing fuel tanks would not be required.

Electronic equipment could be limited to VHF, with certain exceptions. A Mk 5 bomb director or equivalent would be installed. The installed weight was approximately 1,070 lbs, which included a radar scanner with a required hemispherical clearance of 40 inch diameter. This equipment was a radar optical bomb sight containing provisions for ground position indication and radar search. Armor plate was not required. Furnishings and equipment were required only as necessary for the accomplishment of the mission.

The time frame for OS-115 has not been indicated in the surviving documents thus far discovered; given the very challenging requirements and lack of detail in the specification, it appears to have been more of a long term research project. Unlike OS-111, a small number of manufacturers are known to have submitted proposals to OS-115; these highly unorthodox designs are covered in the following 5 chapters.

Bomb Load	10,000 lbs
Maximum Gross Weight	100,000 lbs
Operating Altitude	not less than 40,000 ft
Combat Altitude at Basic Flight Design Gross Weight	40,000 ft or higher
V cruise out at Operating Altitude	not less than Mach 1.20
V cruise back at Operating Altitude	not less than Mach 0.92
Combat Radius	1,700 nm

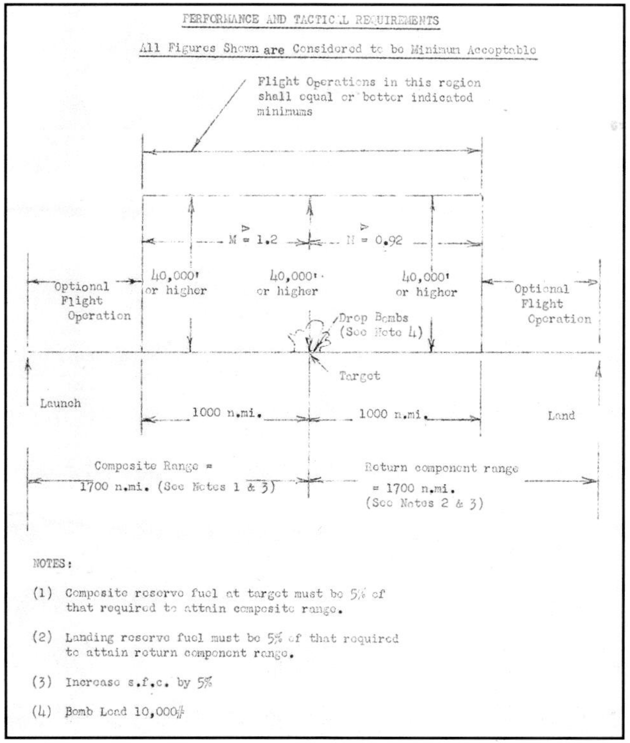

Left: Diagram of the performance and tactical requirements of a standard OS-115 mission, which was well beyond the capability of any existing naval aircraft in 1948.

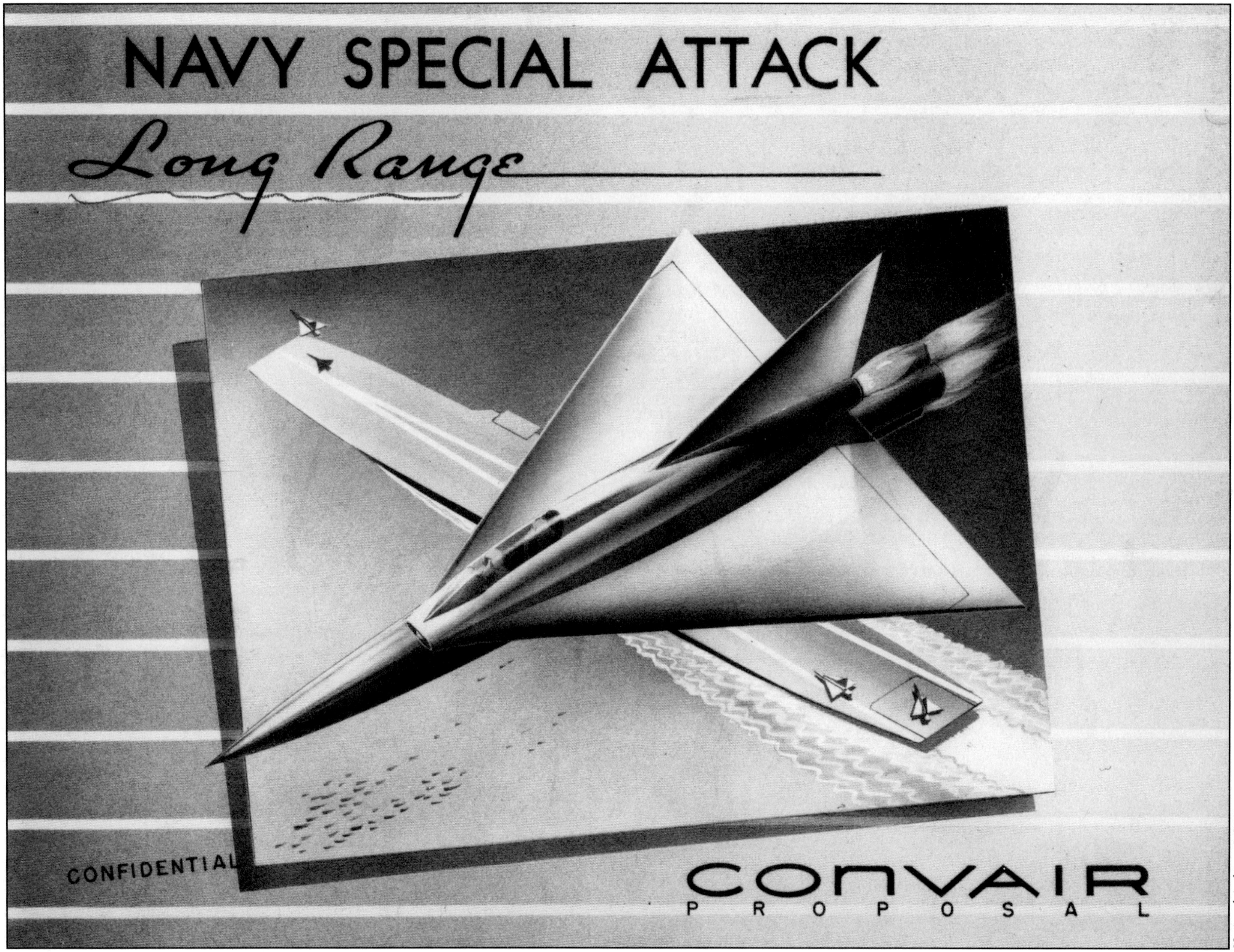

National Archives, RG 72

CHAPTER 12 — *Convair Class VA Long Range Special Attack Airplane*

Convair's proposal was for a carrier based long range special attack airplane designed to fulfill the requirements outlined in OS-115. Convair claimed that the proposed design equaled or exceeded all of the requirements set forth therein:

SPECIFIED ITEMS	REQUIRED	ATTAINED
SPECIAL DESIGN CONSIDERATIONS	THE AIRPLANE MAY BE A SINGLE MISSION COMPOSITE AIRCRAFT WHICH IS CAPABLE OF DISCARDING OR JETTISONING, DURING THE COURSE OF THE FLIGHT, SUCH PARTS AS ARE NOT REQUIRED FOR THE COMPLETION OF ITS MISSION.	FUSELAGE "POD" JETTISONED, BASIC AIRPLANE (I.E. RETURN COMPONENT) RETURNED TO CARRIER.
MAXIMUM TAKE-OFF GROSS WEIGHT (IN THE CONFIGURATION TO ATTAIN THE PRESCRIBED RADIUS)	LB. 100,000	LB. 96,260
MISSION COMBAT RADIUS BOMB LOAD OPERATING ALTITUDE - NOT LESS THAN CRUISE-OUT SPEED (AT OPERATING ALT.) - NOT LESS THAN- CRUISE-BACK SPEED(AT OPERATING ALT.) - NOT LESS THAN-	 NAUT.MI. 1,700 LB. 10,000 FT. 40,000 MACH NO. 1.2 MACH NO. .92	 NAUT.MI. 1,700 LB. 10,000 FT. 40,000 MACH NO. 1.34 TO 1.37 MACH NO. 1.01 TO .92
TAKE-OFF	OPERATION FROM A CVB CLASS CARRIER, BY ANY FEASIBLE MEANS INCLUDING JATO AND/OR CONVENTIONAL OR SPECIAL LAUNCHING DEVICES.	TAKE-OFF FROM CVB CARRIER DECK WITH JATO ASSIST (TAKE-OFF GEAR JETTISONED).
LANDING	A CONFIGURATION UTILIZING A RETURN COMPONENT CAPABLE OF LANDING ABOARD A CV-9 CLASS CARRIER IS DESIRED, BUT NOT REQUIRED.	BASIC AIRPLANE (I.E. RETURN COMPONENT) LANDS ON CV-9 CARRIER.
ADAPTABILITY TO TRAINING	OPERATIONS FROM LAND BASES ARE HIGHLY DESIRABLE BUT NOT REQUIRED.	TRAINING GEAR PROVIDED FOR OPERATION FROM LAND BASES.
CREW OF TWO (BOTH PROVIDED WITH EJECTION SEATS)	1. PILOT (WHO WILL ALSO SERVE AS RADIO OPERATOR.) 2. BOMBER (WHO WILL ALSO SERVE AS RADAR OPERATOR AND NAVIGATOR.)	AS REQUIRED

National Archives, RG 72

Possible Configurations

In the design of an airplane to meet the performance requirements, three possible configurations were evident:

1. An airplane which returned from the mission as a complete article.
2. An airplane which expended only secondary structure, such as bomb bay, fuel tankage, etc. over the target area.
3. An airplane which expended primary and secondary structure and equipment over the target area and returned as the smallest possible flying component capable of returning the crew only.

Selection of Configuration

In analyzing the speed and range requirements of the problem, Convair determined that, with the power plants and ratings to be considered, an airplane with no expendable components, i.e. configuration "A" above, was impossible within the allowable gross weight of 100,000 lbs. Further study showed that the requirements were attainable with the expenditure of only secondary structure containing the bomb bay, fuel tankage and the additional power plants necessary to attain supersonic cruising speed with the outbound configuration.

A study of the return component, configuration "C" above, showed that the wing necessary to accomplish this approached in size that required for the outbound portion of the problem.

Selection of Wing

In the choice of the type of wing best suited for the problem, analyses were made of various delta and highly swept back wing designs. A 60° delta wing was selected as it resulted in the smallest airplane where launching was considered. Based on the flight problem only, a highly swept back wing (55°) gave a 10% smaller design, though a 60 kt higher launching speed was required.

In addition, available aerodynamic data on the two types of wing showed that many unsolved problems of stability, control and undesirable flow separation at cruising lift coefficients existed for the highly swept back wing. In contrast, satisfactory aerodynamic characteristics had been obtained during extensive wind tunnel tests at subsonic, transonic and supersonic speeds of the 60° delta wing in the development of Convair's Model 7002 (XF-92A) airplane.

Since September 1948, several successful flights had been made with the Model 7002 at altitudes up to 12,000 ft. Although early flights were devoted mainly to pilot familiarization and to adjustment of the power operated control system, maneuverability and

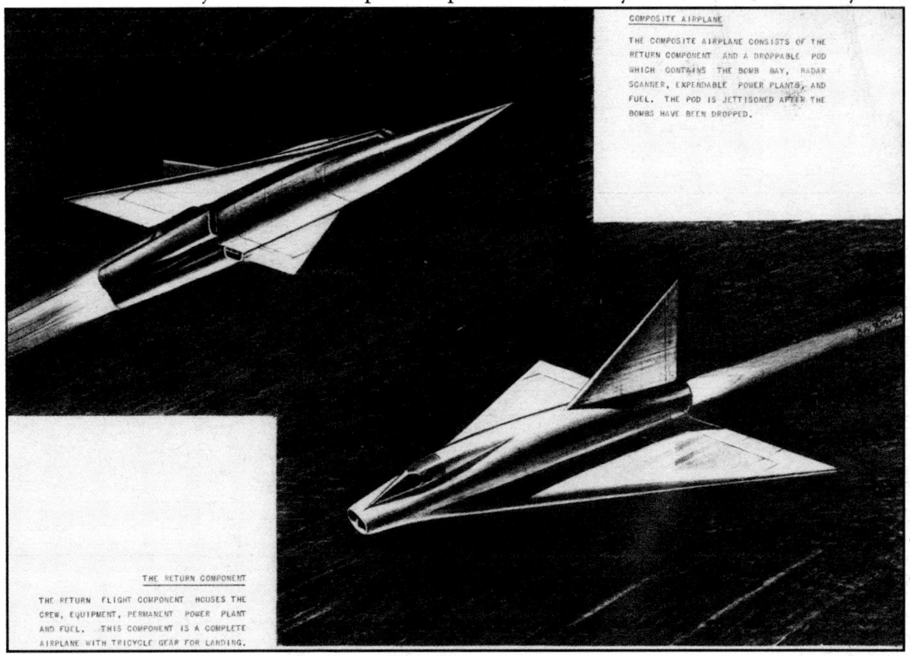

National Archives, RG 72

Artist's impression of the Convair LRSA before and after release of its enormous drop pod.

Facing Page: Cover to the brochure for the Convair Long Range Special Attack (LRSA) proposal, a remarkable composite aircraft made up of a piloted component with a delta wing and a large expendable drop pod/missile.

stability were indicated to be satisfactory. Structural analysis and tests of the Model 7002 showed the advantages of inherent light weight and rigidity.

General Description

The complete composite airplane in its takeoff configuration consisted of the following main components:

1. A droppable takeoff gear and JATO which were jettisoned after takeoff.
2. A droppable pod which contained the bomb bay, radar scanner, expendable power plants and fuel. The pod was jettisoned after the bombs were dropped.
3. A return component which housed the crew, equipment, permanent power plant, and fuel. This component was a complete airplane with tricycle gear for landing.

The airplane had a 60° delta wing with a NACA 63 series symmetrical 5% thick section (measured parallel to the plane of symmetry). Longitudinal and lateral control was effected by means of elevons located at the wing trailing edge and actuated by means of a power operated system. A manually operated rudder was provided for low speed landing operation at the carrier.

The power plants were four Westinghouse XJ40-WE-10 turbojets (per Westinghouse

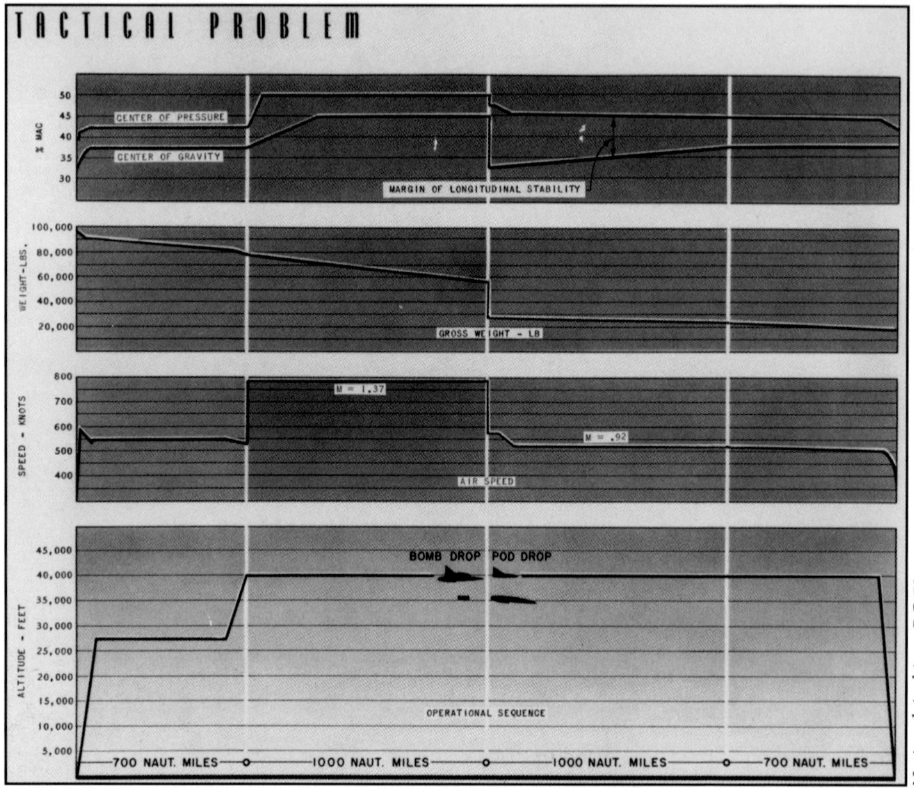

National Archives, RG 72

Above: The challenging mission requirements of OS-115 necessitated a radical approach.

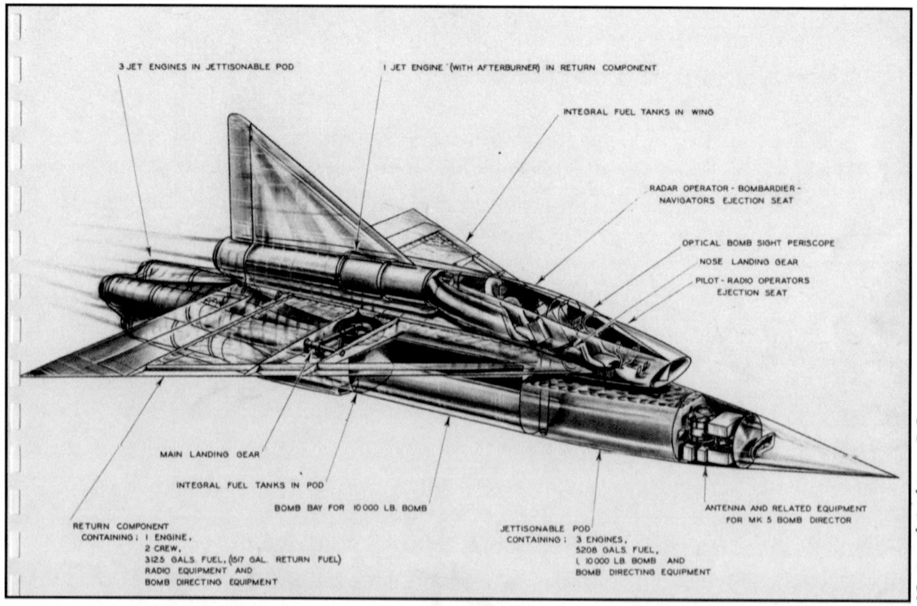

National Archives, RG 72

Above: Cutaway illustration depicting the major components of the Convair LRSA.

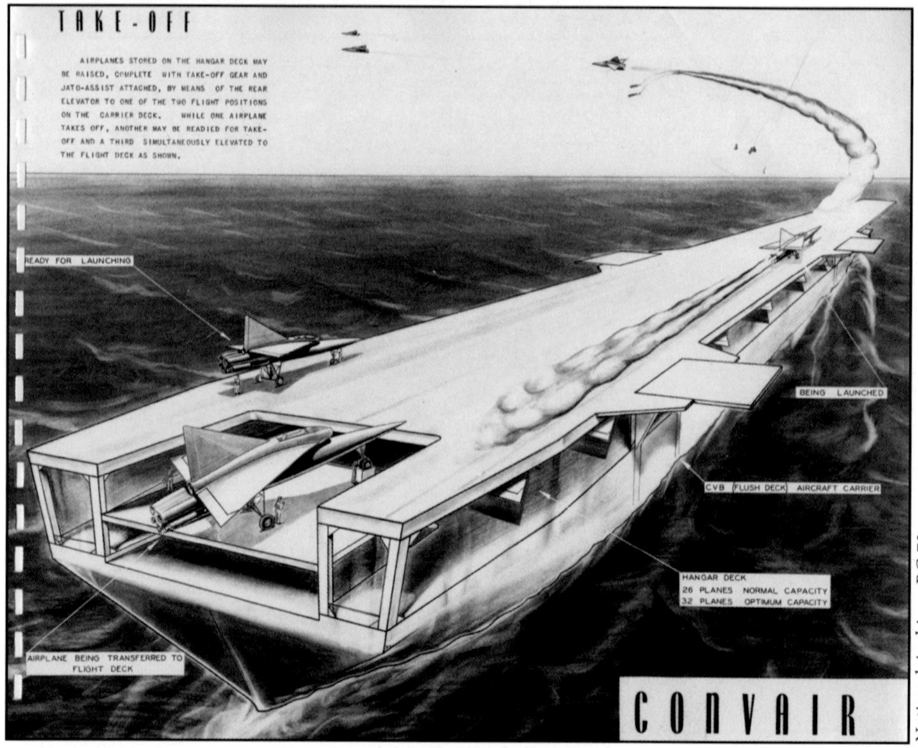

National Archives, RG 72

Above: To keep the Convair LRSA as light as possible, JATO assist and a droppable take off gear was employed to launch the composite aircraft from a CVB class aircraft carrier.

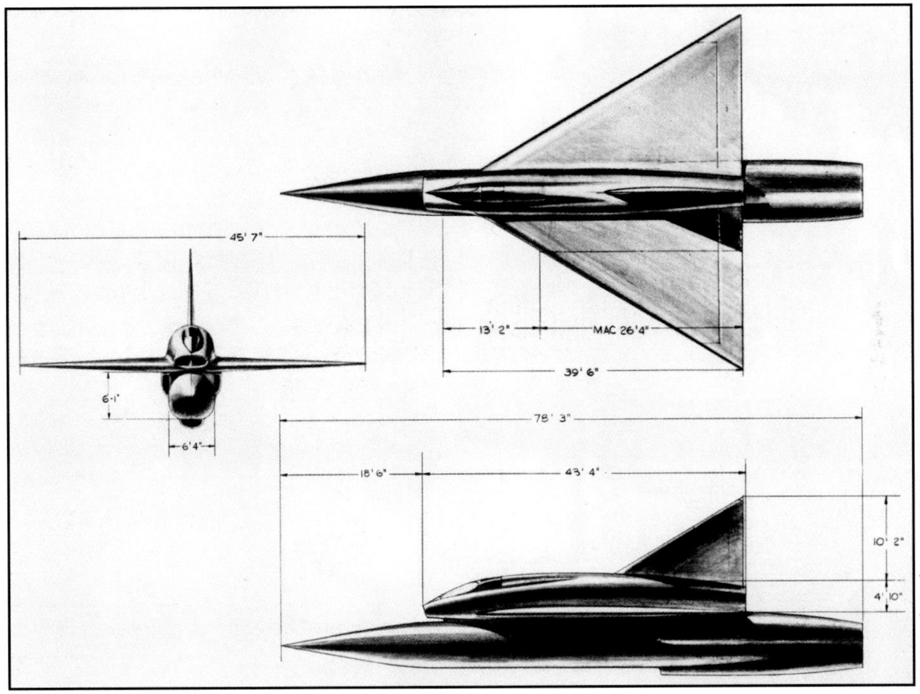

National Archives, RG 72

Above: Shaded three-view drawing of the unconventional Convair LRSA proposal, a relatively compact design given the demanding requirements of OS-115.

Specification WAGT-X40E8-2 dated March 15, 1948). Three of the units were located in the expendable pod and one permanent unit was located in the return component. This permanent unit was provided with an afterburner to retain high performance on the return trip.

Performance and Aerodynamic Characteristics

In general, the favorable drag characteristics of the 60° delta wing configuration were shown in the adjacent plot of drag for various wing planforms. Further advantage with respect to drag was obtained with the delta wing by the use of low wing thickness without unacceptable compromises in wing weight and structural stiffness.

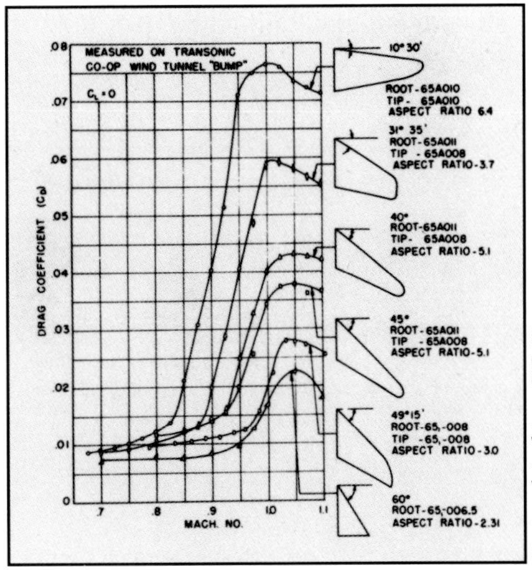

National Archives, RG 72

Satisfactory stability and control were obtained with the 60° delta wing at subsonic, transonic and supersonic speeds in a tailless configuration. Hence, the problem of tail buffet was eliminated. High lift conditions at landing were free of tip stall and did not require the use of auxiliary devices such as leading edge slats to produce satisfactory flight characteristics.

Longitudinal and lateral control was obtained by elevons at the wing trailing edge. Flight tests of the 60° delta, XF-92A airplane had indicated that the rudder could be eliminated and the airplane made basically two-control. However, a rudder had been provided on the proposed design for use in landing aboard carrier where three-control was desirable. Further work in this respect would have shown if a rudder was needed.

The XJ-40 engine with advanced ratings was used in order to obtain a realistic design. Development of new engines in the future would have undoubtedly improved both power and fuel consumption to a major degree. However, as long as the problem could be met with realistic engine characteristics, any future developments would have served to improve the tactical advantage of this type of design.

PERFORMANCE DATA

TAKE-OFF WEIGHT	LB	96,260
TARGET WEIGHT	LB	57,300
RETURN WEIGHT	LB	28,550
LANDING WEIGHT	LB	19,880
HIGH SPEED WITH MILITARY RATING* @ 40,000 FT		
COMPOSITE AIRPLANE @ TARGET WEIGHT	KNOTS	920(M 1.6)
RETURN COMPONENT @ RETURN WEIGHT	KNOTS	585(M 1.02)
COMBAT RADIUS	N.MI.	1,700
AVERAGE CRUISING AIR SPEED		
DURING 1,000 N.MI. APPROACH TO TARGET @ 40,000 FT	KNOTS	785(M 1.37)
DURING 1,000 N.MI. RETURN FROM TARGET @ 40,000 FT	KNOTS	530(M .92)
DECK SPEED @ TAKE-OFF	KNOTS	191
RATE OF CLIMB @ TAKE-OFF MILITARY RATING	FT/MIN	2,165
CEILING (100 FT/MIN RATE OF CLIMB) MILITARY RATING		
TARGET WEIGHT	FT	48,000
RETURN WEIGHT	FT	41,500
DECK SPEED @ LANDING WEIGHT	KNOTS	60

* AFTERBURNER ON RETURN COMPONENT ENGINE OPERATING

AIRCRAFT DIMENSIONAL DATA

WING		
AREA - TOTAL	SQ FT	900
- EXPOSED	SQ FT	695
SPAN	FT	45'7"
ROOT CHORD	FT	39'6"
MEAN AERODYNAMIC CHORD	FT	26'4"
AIRFOIL SECTION	NACA	63-005 MOD
WING INCIDENCE	DEGREES	0°
AERODYNAMIC WASHOUT	DEGREES	0°
DIHEDRAL	DEGREES	0°
SWEEPBACK OF LEADING EDGE	DEGREES	60°
ASPECT RATIO		2.31
VERTICAL TAIL		
AREA	SQ FT	90
ASPECT RATIO		1.15
ELEVONS		
TOTAL AREA	SQ FT	90
PERCENT SPAN	PERCENT	86
POD		
LENGTH	FT	78'3"

National Archives, RG 72

History of the Convair Model 7002/XF-92A

Appreciation that a delta wing might have desirable characteristics at airplane speeds in the range of Mach 1.0 to 2.0 induced a study and test program by Convair that began in 1945. The delta wing was compared with wings of more conventional planform in numerous analyses of aerodynamic, dynamic and stress conditions. Preliminary wind tunnel tests of models designed to explore effects of wing configuration changes substantiated the conclusions formulated in the original study program.

Incorporation of the tailless 60° delta wing configuration in a tactical airplane, the

Inboard profile of the Convair LRSA return component, the design of which was based heavily on the contemporary Convair Model 7002/XF-92A research aircraft built for the Air Force.

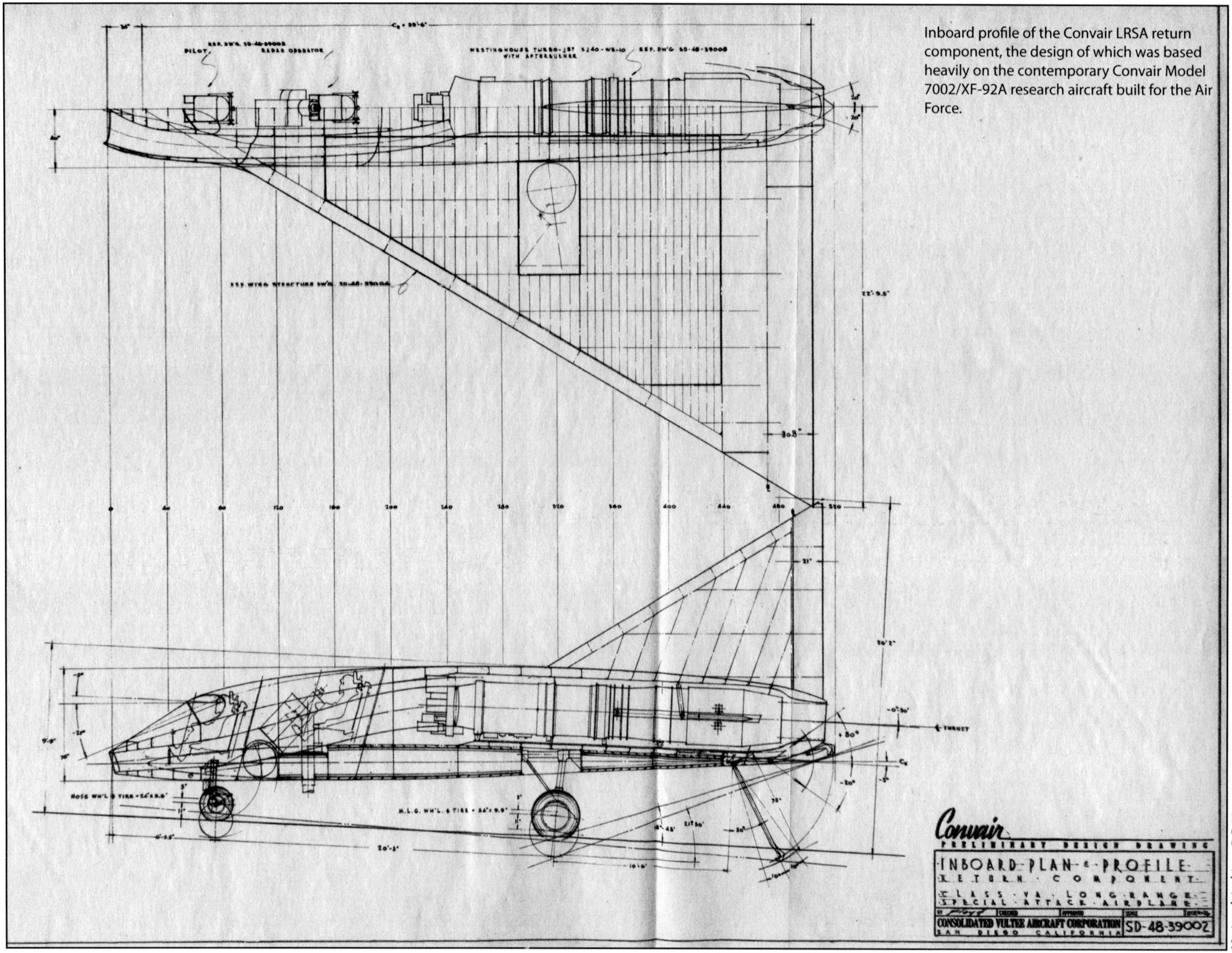

National Archives, RG 72

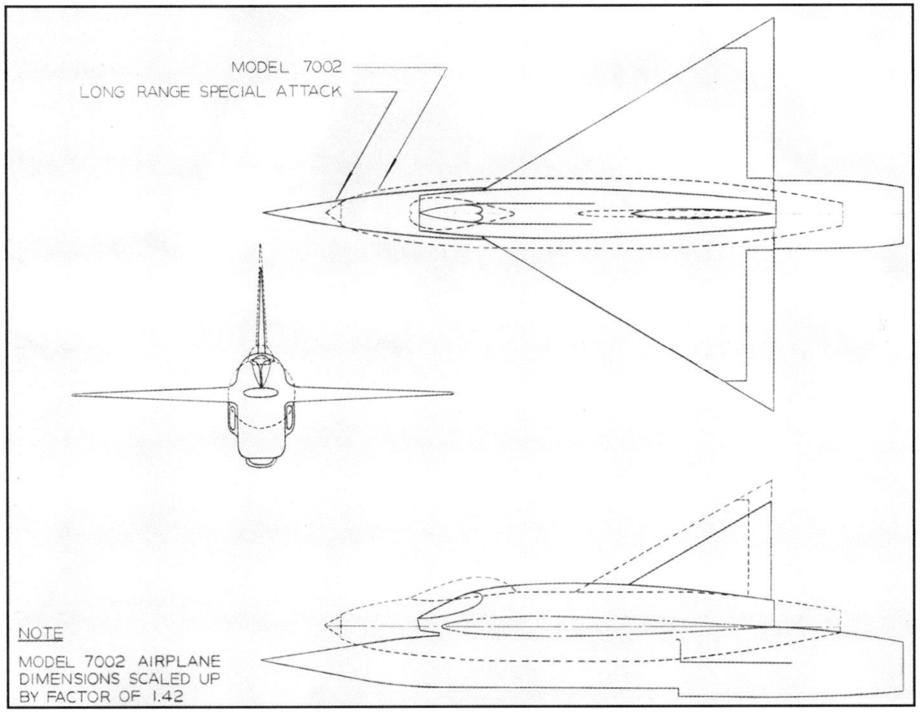

National Archives, RG 72

Drawings comparing the layout of the Convair LRSA study to the XF-92A, which had a more substantial fuselage relative to its delta wing and tail than the Navy aircraft.

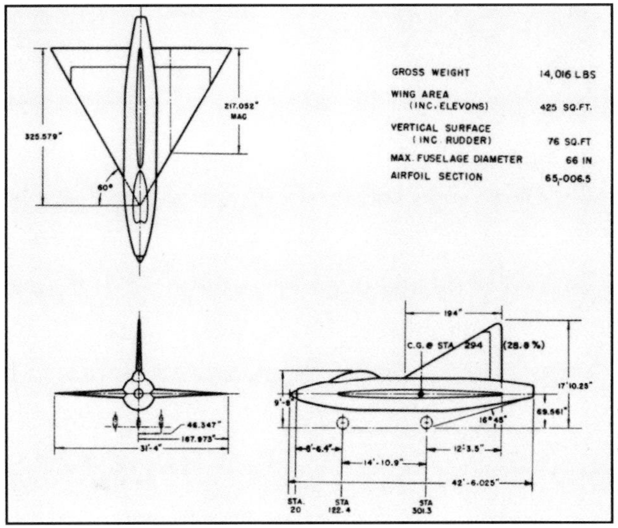

National Archives, RG 72

Three-view drawing of the Convair Model 7002/XF-92A.

XF-92A, of advanced power plant design was then undertaken. To accelerate the aerodynamic development of this airplane, work was started late in 1946 on a full-scale flight test version, Convair's Model 7002. The delta wing and tail configuration of the XF-92A and an existing proven turbojet engine were utilized for the Model 7002. Meanwhile, extensive wind tunnel tests were conducted at subsonic, transonic and supersonic speeds to evaluate experimentally the aerodynamic characteristics. These tests indicated a tailless 60° delta wing configuration to be definitely superior to conventional swept-back configurations from the standpoint of stability and control characteristics in the transonic and supersonic regions and for speeds greater than Mach 0.9.

Full-scale wind tunnel tests of the Model 7002 were conducted at the NACA Moffet field tunnel in late 1947. In April 1948, the Model 7002 was taken to Muroc Air Base for high speed taxi and flight tests. Since September 18, 1948, several successful flights had been made at altitudes up to 12,000 ft and in durations up to approximately 20 minutes.

National Archives, RG 72

National Archives, RG 72

Photographs of the Convair XF-92A, America's first delta wing aircraft and a heavy influence on the Convair LRSA proposal.

Weights

The similarity of the proposed configuration to the Convair Model 7002 airplane, which was then undergoing exhaustive flight tests, made it possible to take full advantage of the Model 7002 actual weight data, structural test results, design details, etc., and by comparison to validate the structural weights of the proposed design as obtained from preliminary stress analyses. It was believed that this had resulted in the attainment of realistic and accurate weight estimates that would not have been possible without this previous design and construction experience with the delta wing configuration.

Stress Analysis

The load calculations for determining the air loads and air load distribution for Convair's proposal were justified by data obtained from flight tests, full scale wind tunnel tests, and transonic and supersonic wind tunnel tests of the Model 7002 airplane. Design and estimated weight of the fuselage and wing were based on the stress analysis shown in an accompanying report, on design studies, structural tests and actual weights of the

Model 7002 airplane.

The 60° delta wing configuration gave a low structural weight due to:

1. Low aspect ratio (2.3), which gave low wing bending moments.
2. Long root chord, which gave negligible chord bending stress and good structural thickness for thin wings (5%).
3. Only one movable surface at the wing trailing edge (no leading edge slats were required).

As a consequence, the proposed wing comprised only 7% of takeoff gross weight or 9.5% of the basic flight gross weight. The major part of the wing area was used as integral fuel tank, therefore the wing was designed with open section stringers on upper and lower surfaces. Wing bending and shear structure were continuous through the fuselage, passing below the engine. The fuselage was supported for its entire length by wing structure which gave low fuselage weight. Fuselage and vertical tail weights were based on the Model 7002. Magnesium was utilized for pod skin and skin support structure where weight saving was attainable thereby. The landing gear was short and loads were taken directly into the major wing structure. The takeoff gear attached directly to the major pod wing attachment bulkheads.

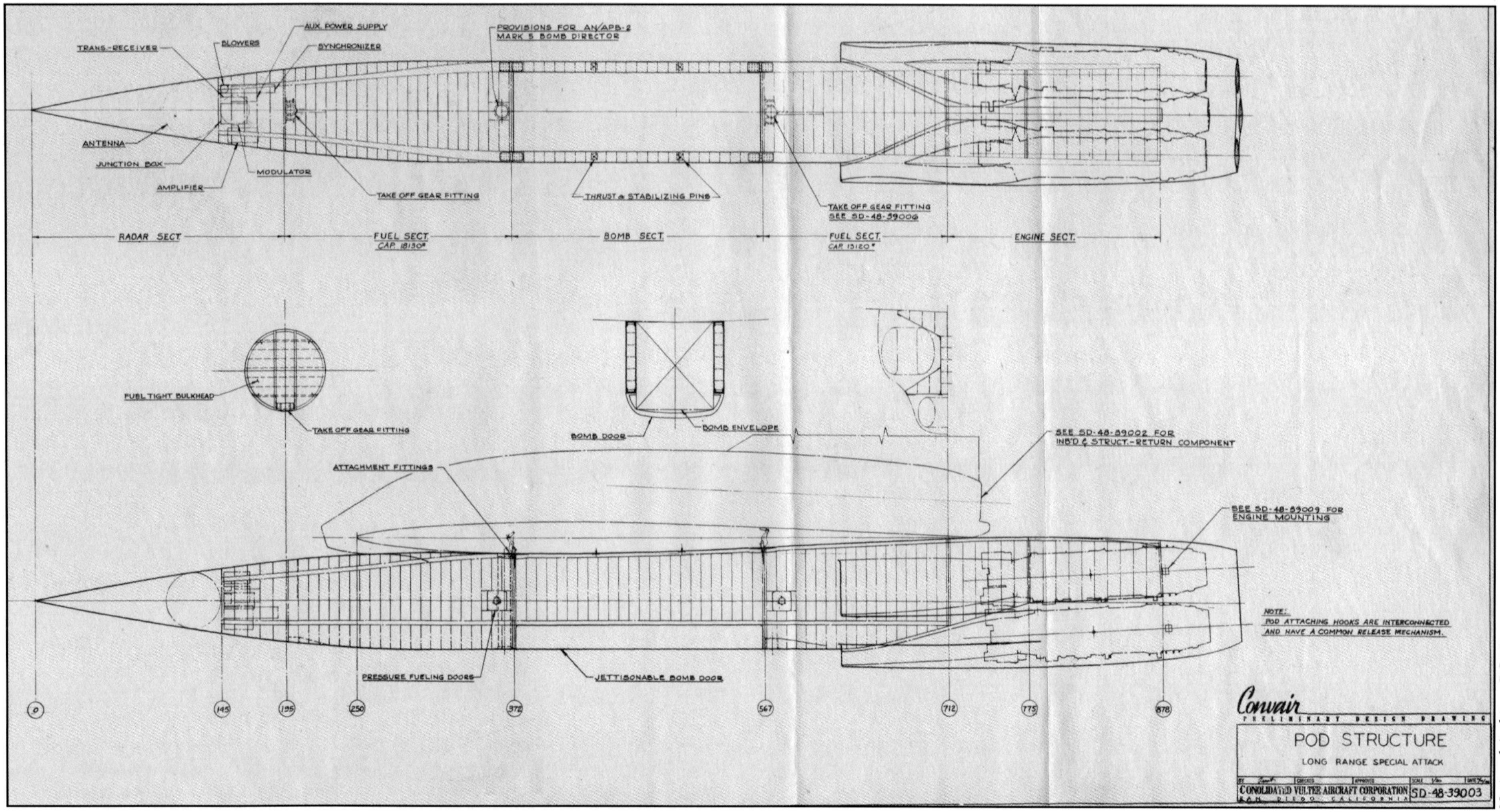

National Archives, RG 72

Blueprint of the Convair LRSA pod structure, which utilized magnesium for the pod skin and skin support structure to save weight.

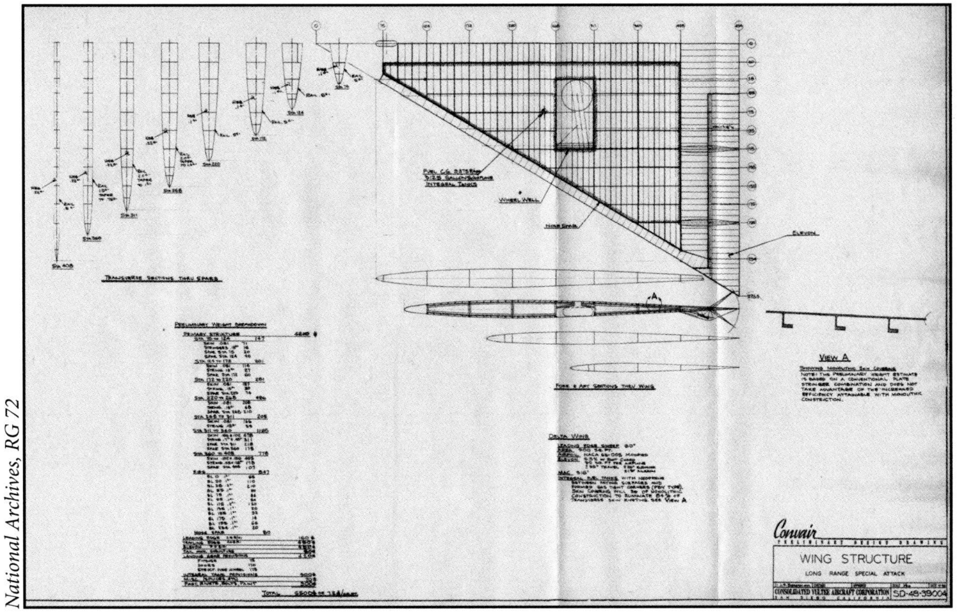

National Archives, RG 72

The wing structure featured an integral fuel tank and also provided support to the fuselage.

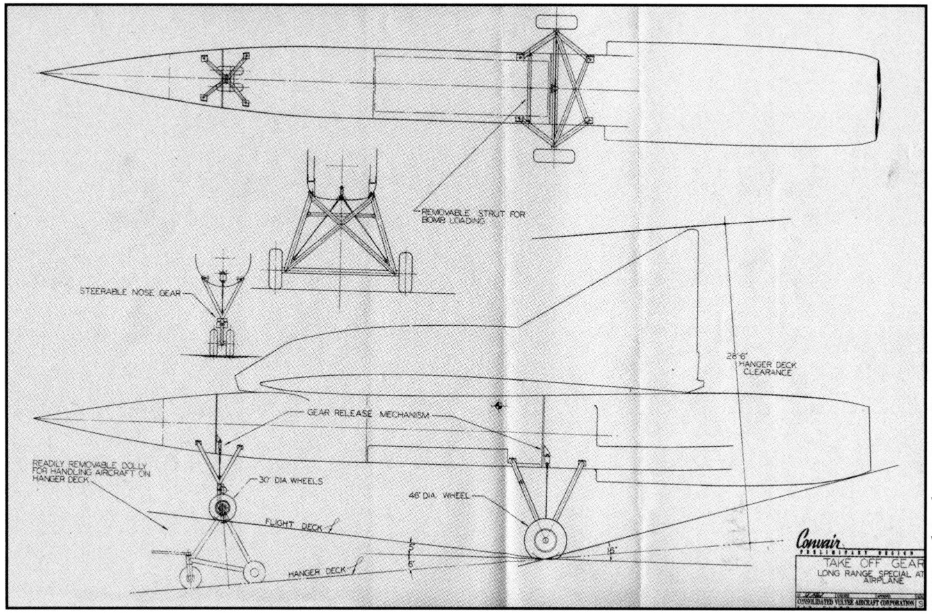

National Archives, RG 72

Blueprint of the Convair LRSA droppable takeoff gear; note the extreme nose down attitude.

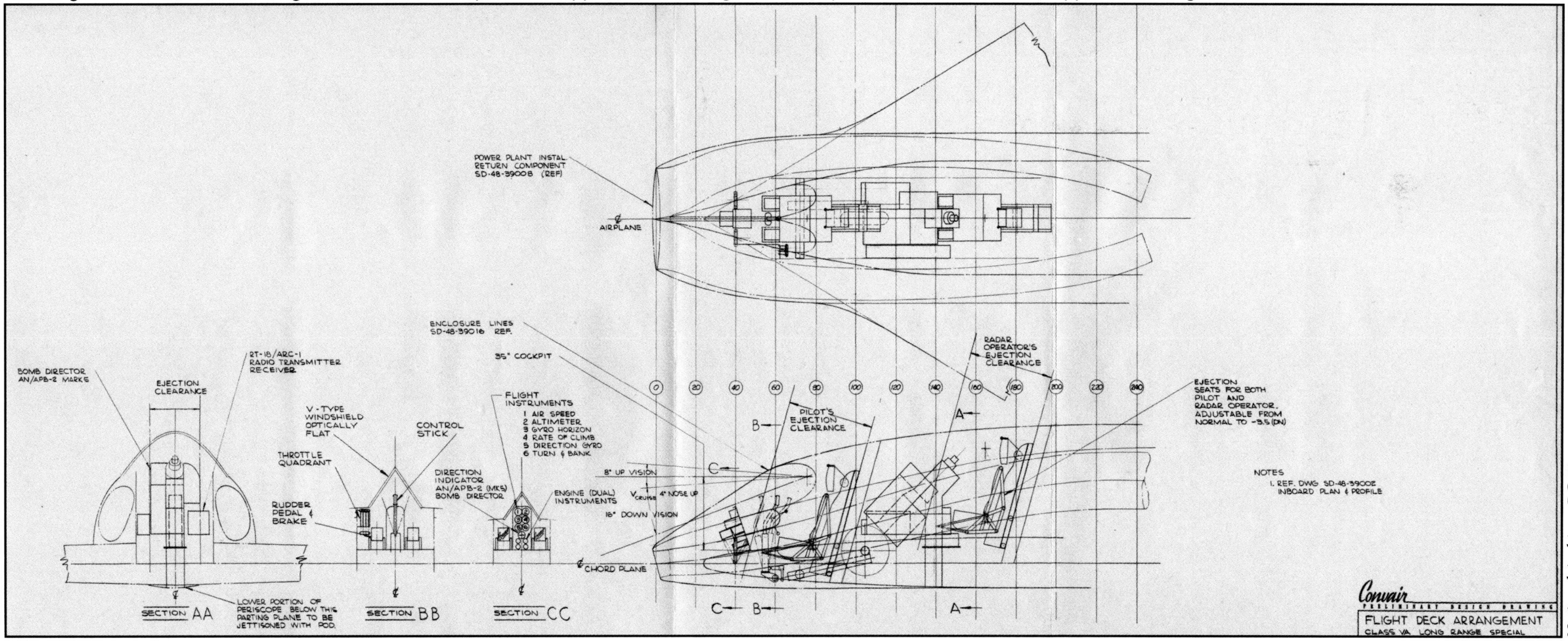

National Archives, RG 72

The flight deck of the Convair LRSA had the pilot and radar operator sitting in tandem, with curved intake tunnels on either side leading from the nose to the XJ40-WE-10 turbojet in the rear.

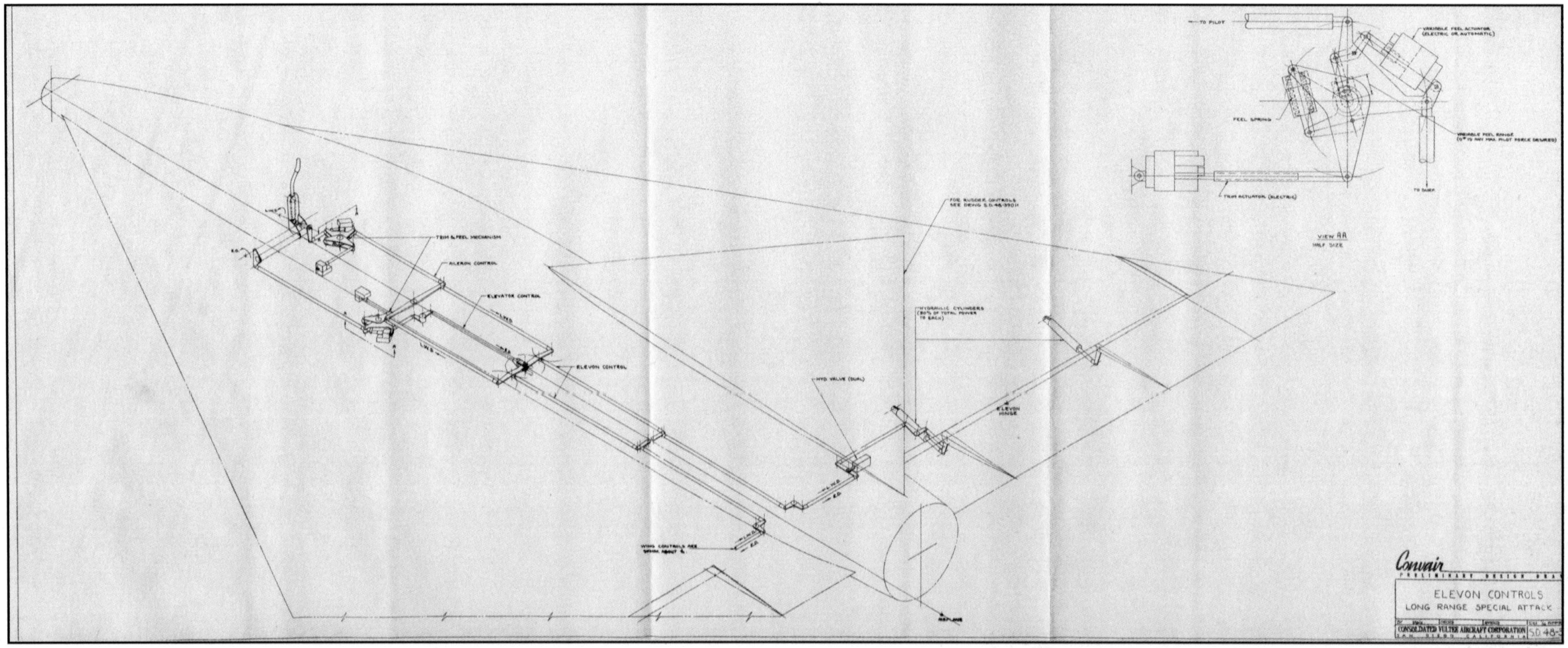

National Archives, RG 72

Above: Diagram of the return component's elevon control system.

Right: Diagram of the return component's rudder control system.

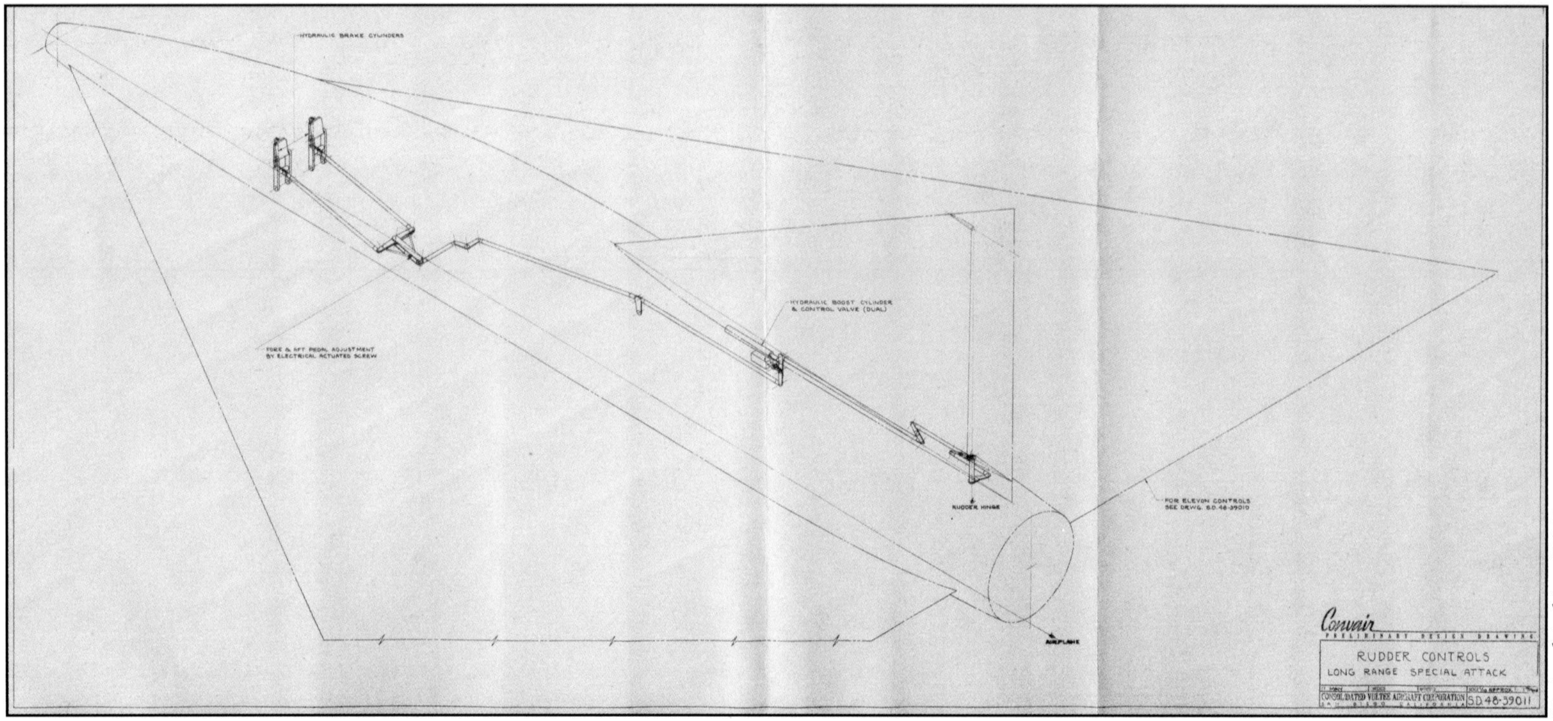

National Archives, RG 72

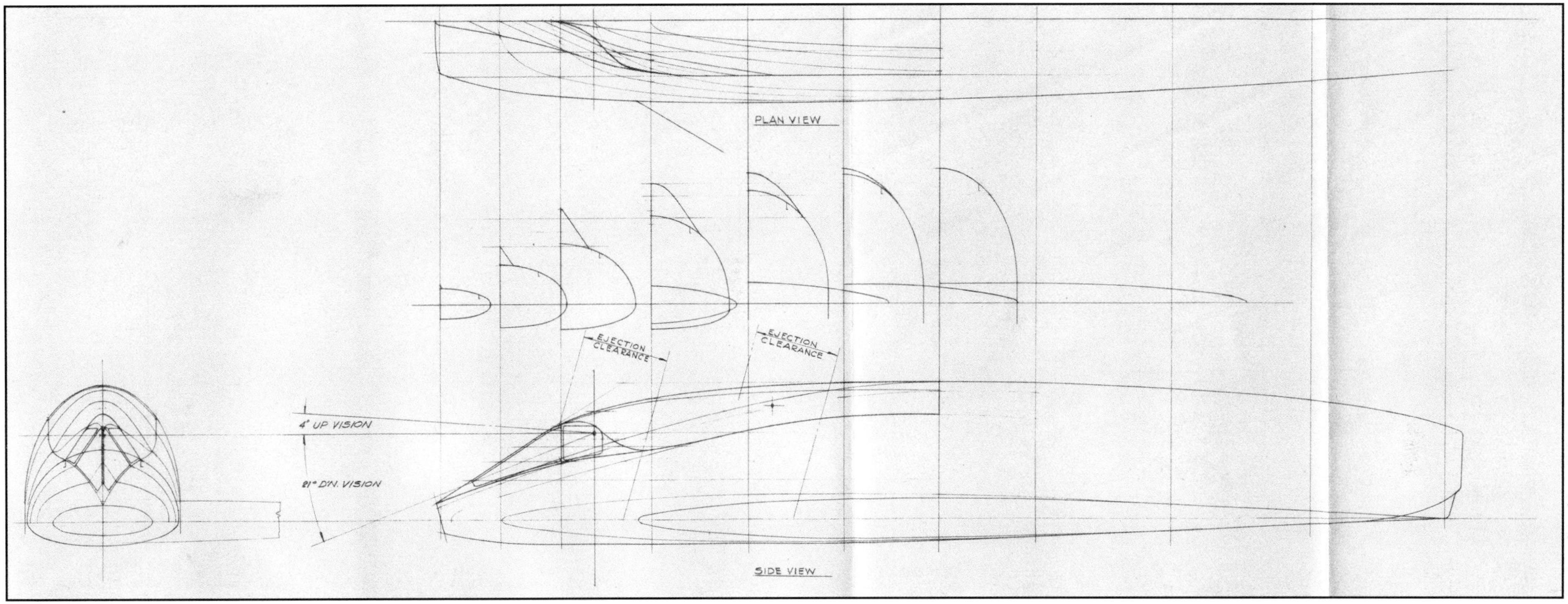

National Archives, RG 72

National Archives, RG 72

Above: Fuselage loft lines for the return component of the Convair LRSA proposal.

Left: This carrier spotting diagram shows that the hangar deck of a CVA class carrier could accommodate a maximum capacity of 32 Convair LRSAs, or aa normal capacity of 26.

Right: The power plant installation of the return component consisted of a single Westinghouse XJ40-WE-10 turbojet equipped with an afterburner.

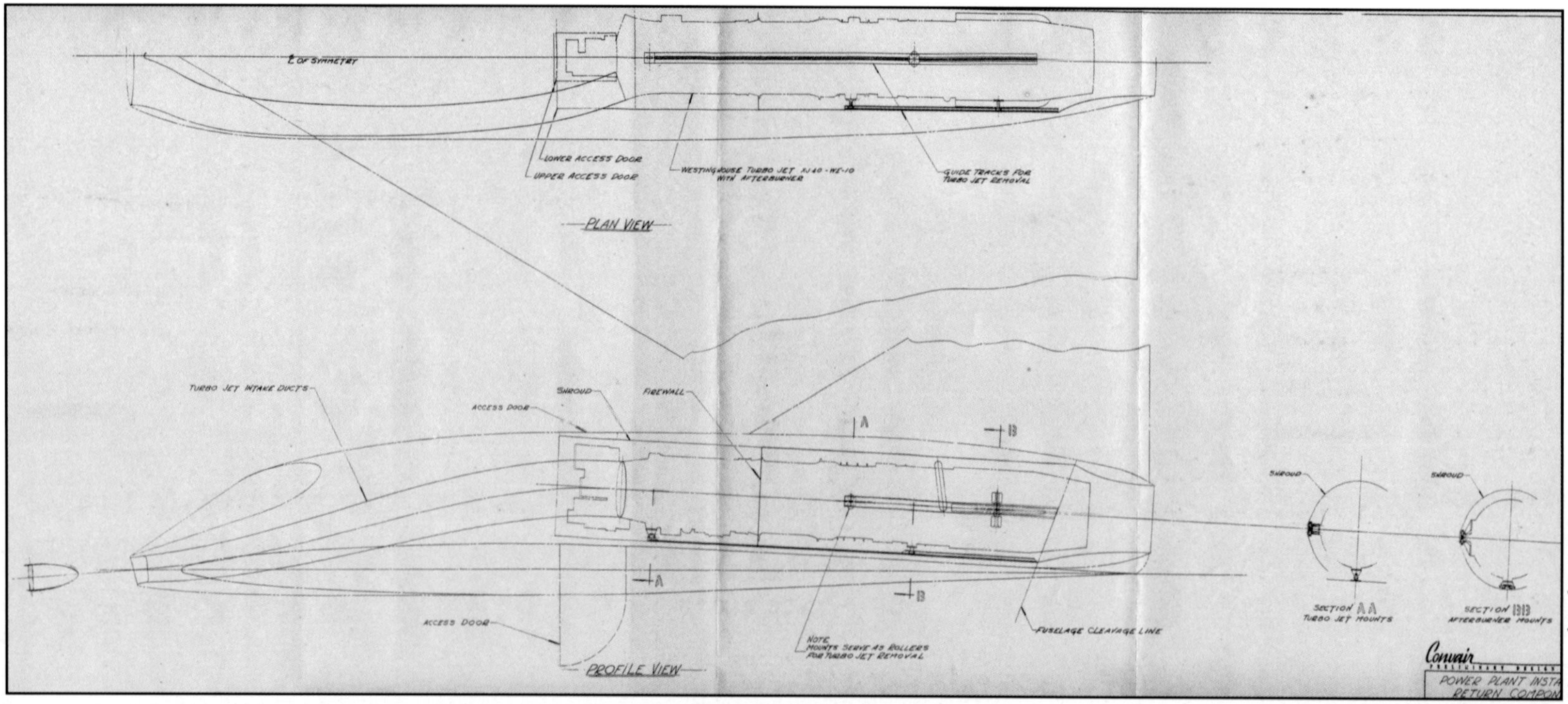

National Archives, RG 72

Below: The power plant installation of the drop pod featured three XJ40-WE-10 turbojets mounted at the aft end of the pod, each fed by a separate intake duct. JATO units would have been attached for takeoffs.

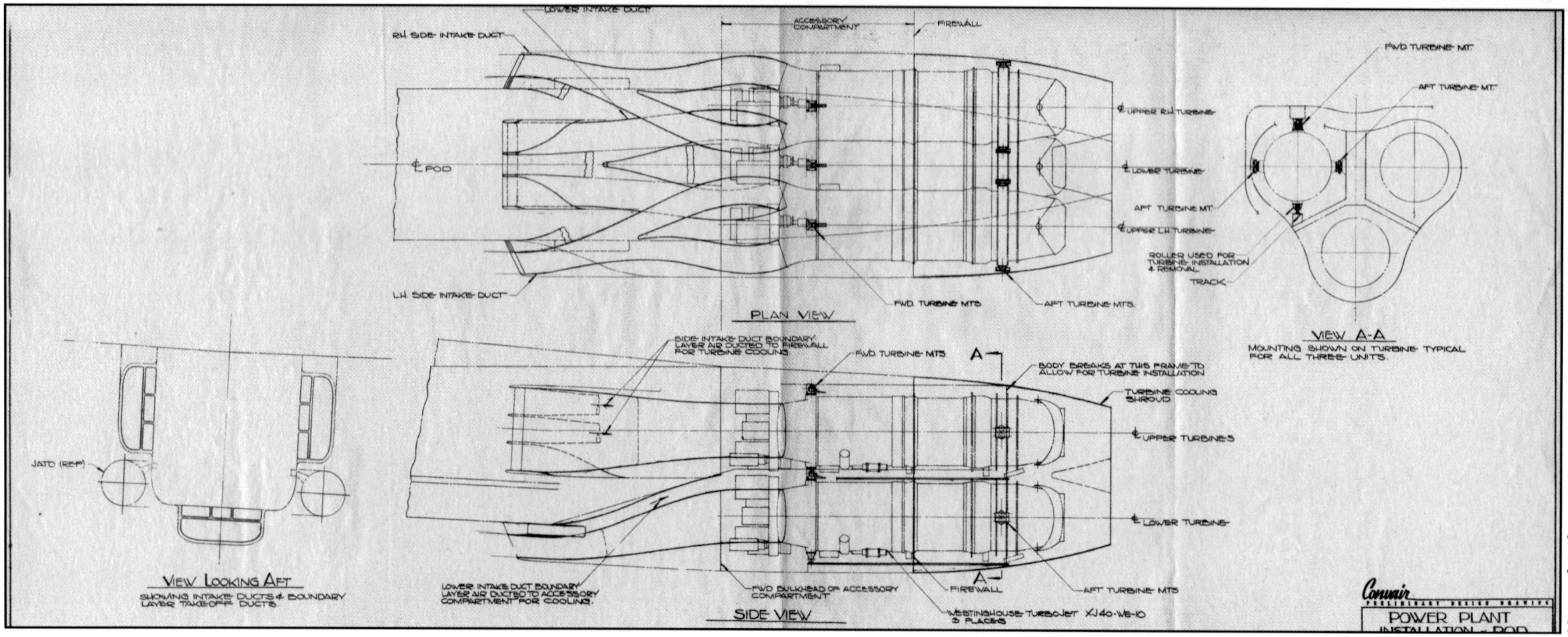

National Archives, RG 72

Photograph of Convair Class VA Long Range Special Attack desktop model. Of the four manufacturers known to have submitted proposals to OS-115, Convair was the only one to make this extra effort. Additional photos of this handsome model are found on the next page.

National Archives, RG 72

National Archives, RG 72

National Archives, RG 72

National Archives, RG 72

National Archives, RG 72

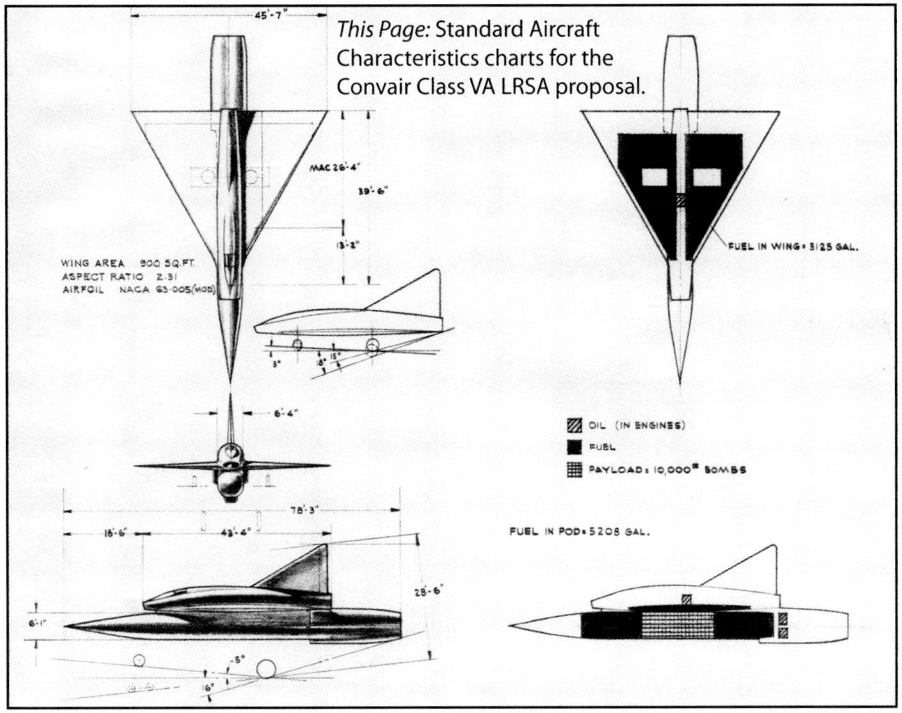

This Page: Standard Aircraft Characteristics charts for the Convair Class VA LRSA proposal.

National Archives, RG 72

MISSION AND DESCRIPTION

MISSION:– DELIVERY OF LARGE BOMB LOAD AT EXTREME RANGES AT HIGH ALTITUDE AND HIGH AIRSPEED. AIRPLANE IS CAPABLE OF TAKING OFF WITH ASSIST FROM CVB CLASS CARRIER AND RETURNING THE CREW TO CV-9 CLASS CARRIER.

DESCRIPTION:– THE AIRPLANE IS OF THE COMPOSITE TYPE CONSISTING OF A RETURN COMPONENT AND A DROPABLE POD.

THE RETURN COMPONENT INCLUDES 60 DEGREE DELTA WING AND VERTICAL TAIL, AND A FUSELAGE WITH PRESSURIZED CREW SPACE AND ONE TURBO-JET ENGINE AND AFTERBURNER. INTEGRAL FUEL TANKS ARE LOCATED IN THE WING.

THE POD CONTAINS RADAR GEAR, INTEGRAL FUEL TANKS, A BOMBBAY AND THREE TURBO-JET ENGINES. IT IS RELEASED FROM THE RETURN COMPONENT AFTER THE BOMB IS DROPPED.

TAKE OFF IS ACCOMPLISHED ON JETISONABLE GEAR WITH JATO ASSIST. THE RETURN COMPONENT IS EQUIPPED WITH RETRACTABLE LANDING GEAR AND ARRESTING HOOK.

THE TWO MAN CREW CONSISTS OF A PILOT-RADIO OPERATOR AND A BOMBER-RADAR OPERATOR-NAVIGATOR.

WEIGHTS

WEIGHTS
COMPOSITE AIRPLANE

EMPTY	– 35,510
DESIGN	– 63,520
TAKE OFF	– 96,260

RETURN COMPONENT

EMPTY	18,700
COMBAT	28,550
MAX. LANDING	26,675

FUEL AND OIL

LOCATION		TYPE	GALS.
WING:	FORWARD	INT.	1605
	AFT	INT.	1520
POD:	FORWARD	INT.	3022
	AFT	INT.	2187
(AVIATION GASOLINE)		TOTAL	8334

OIL

OIL SYSTEMS AND RESERVOIERS INTEGRAL WITH ENGINES. 10 GALS. PER ENGINE IS ALLOWED.

POWER PLANT

FOUR WESTINGHOUSE XJ40-WE-10 TURBO-JET ENGINES, ONE WITH AFTERBURNER.

TWO JATO UNITS

RATINGS

TURBO-JET ENGINE RATINGS CONFORM TO WEC BID SPEC. WAGT-X40E8-2, 3-15-48, AS MODIFIED BY NAVAER REPORT NO. 1045.

JATO UNITS
80,000 LBS. THRUST EACH FOR 8 SECONDS.

ORDNANCE

10,000 LB. BOMB LOAD
ENVELOPE 16 FT. IN LENGTH, 66 INCHES HIGH AND 60 INCHES WIDE INCLUDING FALL CLEARANCES.

DIMENSIONS

SPAN	45' 7"
LENGTH:	
COMPOSITE AIRPLANE	78' 3"
RETURN COMPONENT	43' 4"
HEIGHT:	
*COMPOSITE AIRPLANE	30' 10"
RETURN COMPONENT	20' 3"
TREAD (COMPONENT)	18' 4"
WING AREA	900 SQ.FT.

*OVERTAIL, ON TAKE-OFF GEAR

ELECTRONICS

AN/APX-2 IFF
AN/ARC-1 COMMAND VHF
INTERPHONE
MARK 5 BOMB DIRECTOR
(RADAR OPTICAL BOMBSIGHT INCLUDING GROUND POSITION INDICATION AND RADAR SEARCH)

National Archives, RG 72

PERFORMANCE SUMMARY

LOADING CONDITION		COMPOSITE AIRPLANE (TAKE OFF)	COMPOSITE AIRPLANE (TARGET)	RETURN COMPONENT (TARGET)	RETURN COMPONENT (LANDING)
GROSS WEIGHT		96,260	57300	28550	19880
Fuel	lbs	50,000	11040	9100	430
Bombs	lbs	10,000	10000	0	0
	lbs				
WING/THRUST LOADING (A) lbs/sq.ft.lbs/	LB	107.0/2.75	63.5/1.64	31.7/3.26	22.0/2.27
Stall Speed--Power off *	kn	209*			93*
Stall Speed--Power off - No Fuel	kn				
Stall Speed--Power on	kn				
Maximum Speed/Alt (B)	kn/ft	660/S.L	667/S.L.		
Take-off Distance, deck -- calm	ft				
Take-off Distance, deck 33kn (JATO ASSIST)	ft	950			
Take-off Distance, Airport	ft				
Rate of climb -- sea level (B)	ft/min	8100	15000	4000	6350
Service Ceiling (B)	ft		44000		
Time-to-climb ft. (B)	min				
Time-to-climb ft. (B)	min				
Combat Range/V av ft.	n.mi/kn		3400 N.MI./785	Kn & 530 Kn	
Combat Radius/V av ft.	n.mi/kn		1700N.MI./785	Kn & 530 Kn	
LOADING CONDITION					
GROSS WEIGHT	lbs				
Engine power					
Fuel	lbs				
Bombs/Tanks					
Max. speed at sea level	kn				
Max. speed ft.	kn				
Combat speed/Alt.	kn/ft				
Rate of climb SL	ft/min				
Ceiling for 500 fpm R/C	ft				
Time-to-climb/Alt.	min/ft				

* MINIMUM FLIGHT SPEED CORRESPONDING TO A WING ANGLE OF ATTACK OF 20° (SEE EXPLANATION SEC. 7 CVAC REPORT ZA-189- "STABILITY & CONTROL ANALYSIS OF THE CLASS VA LONG RANGE SPECIAL ATTACK AIRPLANE")

NOTES

(A) STATIC THRUST AT SEA LEVEL
(B) NORMAL THRUST

National Archives, RG 72

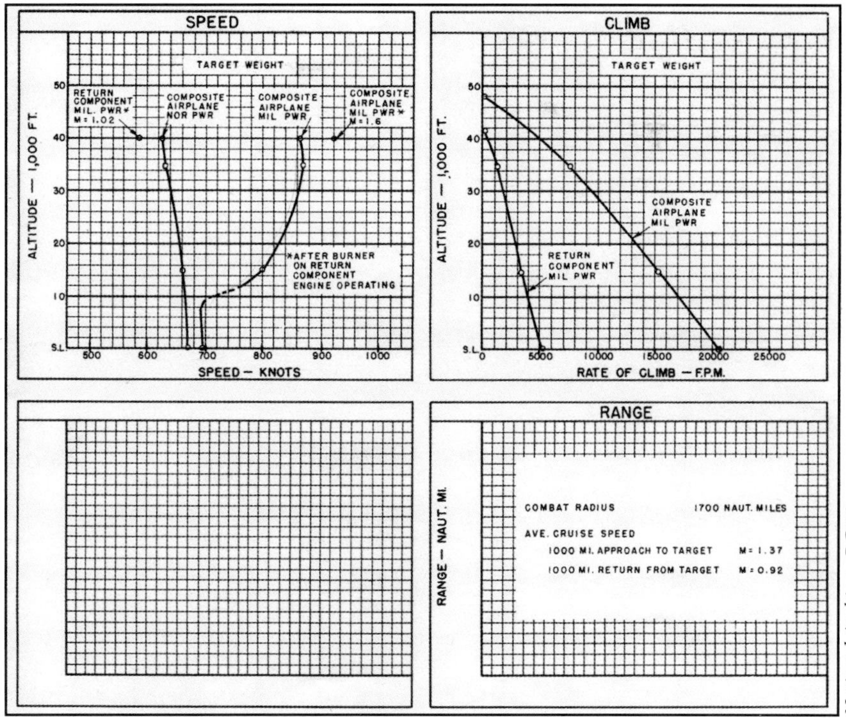

National Archives, RG 72

Trainer

Since the composite airplane involved no provisions for landing with the pod in place, special considerations were required for crew training. It was not economically desirable to have to drop a pod on each training flight of the composite airplane; therefore, a special "training pod" incorporating a landing gear was proposed for this purpose.

In addition, it was considered desirable that the training configuration be one capable of demonstrating the high speed characteristics of the airplane; therefore the proposed training gear was completely retractable within the space normally occupied by the bomb bay and radar equipment on the tactical pod.

The required high landing, takeoff attitude, and the length of the pod, together with the high CG and the restricted diameter of the "pod," presented a major problem in main gear retraction as indicated by the accompanying drawings.

The design shown required two folding sequences for retraction. One sequence folded the gear down to the center and the second sequence folded it forward into the bomb bay. Convair emphasized that further study would have resulted in considerable simplification. Weight was not necessarily restrictive in the design of the landing gear for the training pod. Ballast was also necessary, as discussed below. Cost was considered to be the primary factor and the design was visualized as consisting mainly of welded chrome molybdenum steel tubing. Standard braking provisions were to have been incorporated. The CG shift on extending the gear, in the landing gross weight condition, was approximately 3% of the MAC. The nose gear was of conventional design.

The size and shape of the training "pod" was to have been identical to that of the tactical pod, and the engine and ducting installations of the two would have been the same. The structure of the training pod would have been redesigned as required to accommodate the landing gear. Ballast tanks were to have been provided to attain the tactical gross weight. Approximately 40,000 lbs of jettisonable water ballast would have been carried in the space normally occupied by the fuel tanks and radar equipment of the tactical pod. In order to provide for the center of pressure shift at supersonic speeds, it would have probably been desirable to provide a means of shifting the ballast by pumping water

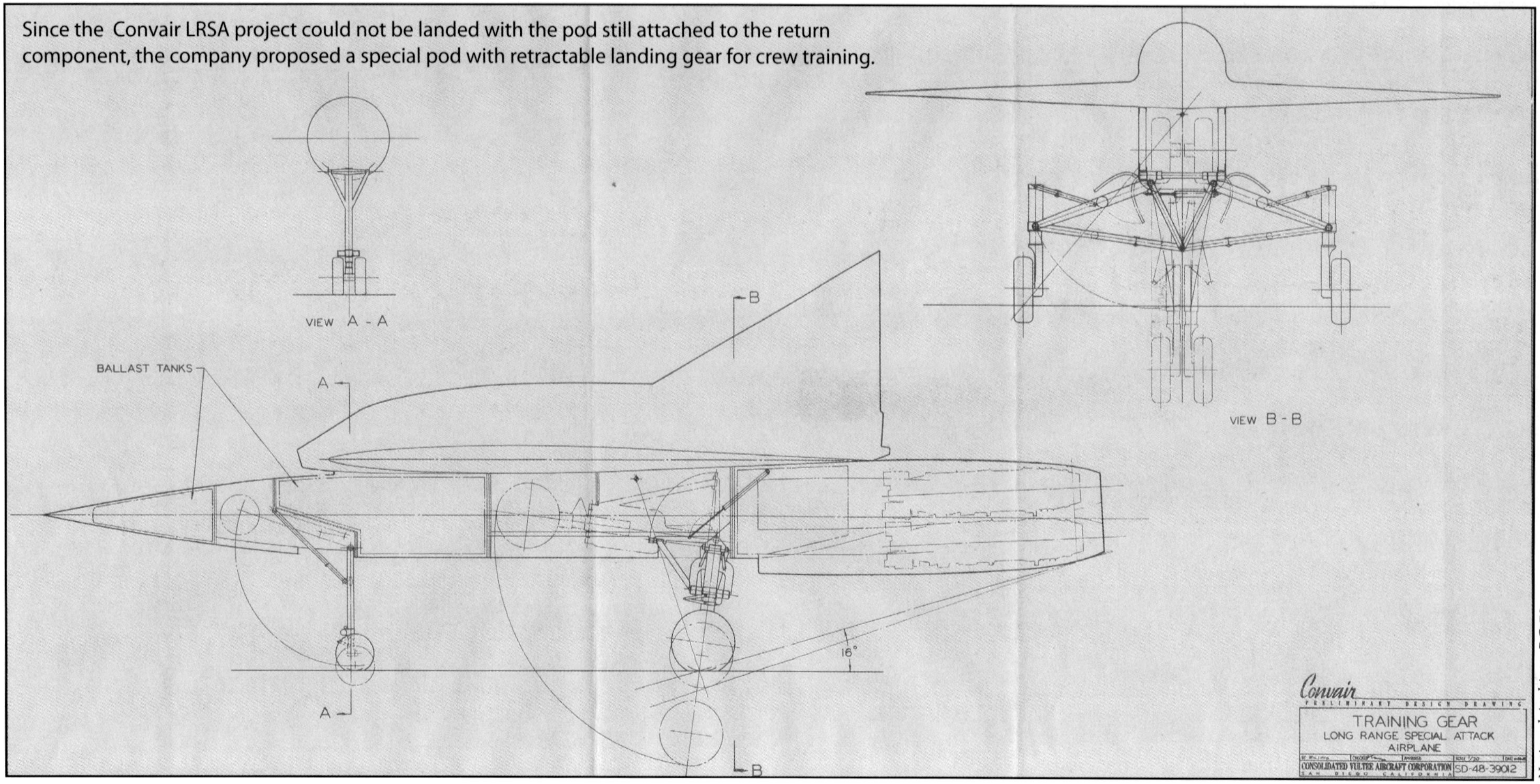

Since the Convair LRSA project could not be landed with the pod still attached to the return component, the company proposed a special pod with retractable landing gear for crew training.

National Archives, RG 72

between the fore and aft tanks.

In the landing condition (approximately 53,000 lbs gross weight, including reserve fuel but minus all disposable ballast) the stalling speed of the training airplane was approximately 153 kts (CG = 34% MAC). The training gear was designed for the standard impact velocity of 12 ft per second at the aforementioned landing design gross weight. The return component, being a complete airplane in itself, could have been used directly for crew training.

Fighter

The basic arrangement of the Special Attack Airplane design submitted to BuAer on November 2, 1948 consisted essentially of a flight component plus a jettisonable pod housing radar, fuel, bombs and expendable engines. This "bomber pod" could have been replaced by a smaller "fighter pod" to obtain an arrangement with performance exceeding the requirements of both BuAer Interceptor Specification OS-113 and BuAer Fighter Specification OS-116.

This fighter pod was non-jettisonable and required changes in the landing gear and arresting hook. The landing gear, used in the attack version, was designed only for landing of the flight component after the pod was jettisoned. This gear was removed and a lengthened gear with larger wheels was installed to accommodate the greater weight of the fighter version and to provide clearance for the non-jettisonable fighter pod. The arresting hook was lengthened in accordance with the change in landing gear.

National Archives, RG 72

Artist's impression of the fighter/interceptor variant of the Convair LRSA aircraft, which featured a smaller "fighter" pod in lieu of the larger jettisonable bomb pod.

The wing structure of the attack version was designed to a load factor of 2.25 at the full takeoff weight of 100,000 lbs. The takeoff weight with the fighter pod was on the order of 36,000 lbs, depending on the particular mission considered. At this reduced weight, the wing structure was good for a load factor of approximately 6.0. For combat, where 40% fuel was assumed expended, the allowable load factor was increased to approximately 7.0.

The power plant of the fighter version consisted of one XJ40-WE-10 with afterburner installed in the flight component (same as attack version) plus a second XJ40-WE-10 with afterburner installed in the pod. These two units gave a high speed of 912 kts at 35,000 ft (Mach 1.59) and 800 kts at 50,000 ft (Mach 1.39) based on the advanced ratings of BuAer reports DR1045 and 1046. Performance was based on a 20° nose cone which required some development with respect to radar operation. Contemporary radar required approximately a 40° nose cone.

PERFORMANCE SUMMARY

Power Plant - Two XJ40-WE-10 turbojets with afterburners (advanced ratings per BuAer Reports DR 1045 and 1046) (11,750 lb. static thrust/unit @ S.L. with afterburner).

INTERCEPTOR MISSION

Item		Estimated Performance	Requirements Interceptor Spec. OS-113
Take-off weight	lb.	34,565	
Fuel	lb.	8,960	
High speed with afterburner, combat weight*			
35000 ft.	knots	912(M=1.59)	
40000 ft.	knots	903(M=1.57)	
50000 ft.	knots	800(M=1.39)	546(M=.95)
Time to climb to 50,000 ft. with afterburner, take-off weight	min.	4.0	6.0
Rate of climb @ S.L. with afterburner, combat weight*	ft/min.	41,000	
Combat ceiling with afterburner combat weight* (500 ft/min.R.C.)	ft.	55,000	
Rate of climb at launching speed @ S.L. with afterburner, take-off weight, gear extended, 95°F day	ft/min.	4,400	500

* Combat weight = Take-off weight less 40% fuel.

PERFORMANCE SUMMARY

Power Plant - Two XJ40-WE-10 turbojets with afterburners (advanced ratings per BuAer Reports DR 1045 and 1046) (11,750 lb. static thrust/unit @ S.L. with afterburner)

FIGHTER MISSION

Item		Estimated Performance	Requirements Fighter Spec. OS-116
Take-off weight	lb.	37,305	
Fuel	lb.	11,700	
High speed with afterburner, combat weight*			
35000 ft.	knots	912(M=1.59)	546(M=.95)
40000 ft.	knots	903(M=1.57)	
50000 ft.	knots	800(M=1.39)	
Time to climb to 50000 ft. with afterburner, take-off weight	min.	4.5	
Rate of climb @ S.L. with afterburner, combat weight*	ft/min.	39,500	
Combat ceiling with afterburner, combat weight* (500 ft/min. R.C.)	ft.	54,000	
Rate of climb at launching speed @ S.L. with afterburner, take-off weight, gear extended, 95°F day	ft/min.	3,900	

* Combat weight = Take-off weight less 40% fuel.

PERFORMANCE SUMMARY

Power Plant - Two XJ40-WE-10 turbojets with afterburners (advanced ratings per BuAer Reports DR 1045 and 1046) (11,750 lb. static thrust/unit @ S.L. with afterburner)

FIGHTER MISSION (ALTERNATE)

Item		Estimated Performance	Requirements
Take-off weight	lb.	35,605	
Fuel	lb.	10,000	
High Speed with afterburner combat weight*			
35000 ft.	knots	912(M=1.59)	
40000 ft.	knots	903(M=1.57)	
50000 ft.	knots	800(M=1.39)	
Time to climb to 50,000 ft. with afterburner, take-off weight	min.	4.3	
Rate of climb @ S.L. with afterburner, combat weight*	ft./min.	40,500	
Combat ceiling with afterburner, combat weight* (500 ft/min. R.C.)	ft.	54,500	
Rate of climb at launching speed @ S.L. with afterburner, take-off weight, gear extended, 95°F day	ft./min.	4,200	

* Combat weight = Take-off weight less 40% fuel.

National Archives, RG 72

Performance summaries for the Convair LRSA interceptor, fighter, and alternate fighter missions.

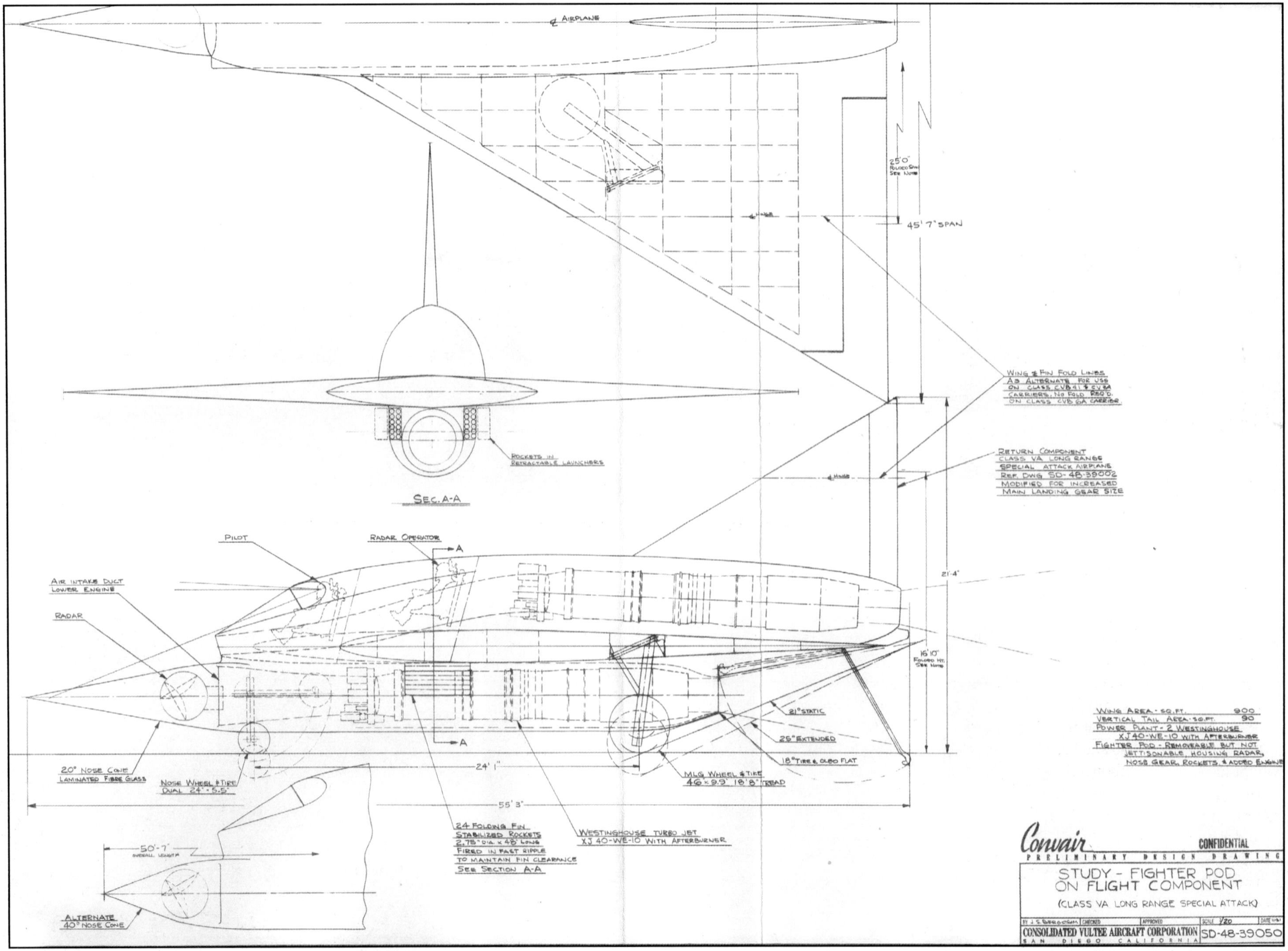

National Archives, RG 72

Plan and inboard profile of the fighter/interceptor variant of the Convair Class VA Long Range Special Attack proposal. The fighter pod was substantially smaller and lighter than the bomb pod, as it only had a single Westinghouse XJ40-WE-10 engine. Armament consisted of 24 folding fin stabilized rockets in retractable launchers, similar to the installation on the North American F-86D.

Miscellaneous Studies

As a preliminary to selecting an appropriate configuration to meet the requirements of OS-115, numerous ideas and available technical data were reviewed. A few of the ideas which appeared worthy of further investigation are listed below. All configurations were basically of the composite type where appropriate portions of the airplane and various installations were jettisoned in the course of flight. Early calculations indicated that takeoff to landing weight ratios on the order of 5 were required to meet the range and speed problem, and return of the entire airplane after completion of the mission appeared impossible.

1. Highly swept back tailless with droppable pod.
2. Delta wing tailless with droppable pod.
3. Delta wing tandem canard with return of tail component/Delta wing tandem (tail aft) with return of tail component.
4. Highly swept back dual airplane with return of small airplane.
5. Variable sweep wing with droppable pod.
6. Designs of the above type with boundary layer removal.
7. Power plants
   a. Turbojet
   b. Ducted fan
   c. Ram jet
   d. Expendable turbojet
   e. Wright Aero Corporation turbojet
8. Ditching considerations.

Each of the above ideas is discussed in detail below.

1. Highly swept back tailless (Robert T. Jones) with droppable pod Using the data of NACA report TN #1350, *Estimated Lift-Drag Ratios at Supersonic Speed*, authored by Robert T. Jones, as a basis, with allowances for detail differences in wing and fuselage design, it appeared that a modified Robert T. Jones configuration could accomplish the range problem of the Navy Special VA requirement. The airplane at takeoff had a gross weight of 85,000 lbs (including 39,000 lbs of fuel) and required three engines equivalent to that specified in Westinghouse Bid Specification WAGT X40E8-2, dated March 15, 1948, with future thrust ratings and fuel consumptions as shown in BuAer DR Report #1045, dated April 1948 and Supplement dated August 1948. Upon landing, the airplane would have weighed about 21,000 lbs and would have been equipped with one engine of the type specified above. With 700 sq ft of wing area (required for cruising at CL for the maximum lift/drag ratio) and a maximum lift coefficient of .5, the takeoff airspeed would have been about 265 kts and the landing air speed would have been about 130 kts. It was apparent from these figures that special procedures, or devices other than the normal catapult would have been required for takeoff. The landing problem could have been disregarded to a certain extent since the special VA requirement did not make the ability to land mandatory.

Brief studies were also made of a modified Robert T. Jones configuration having a gross weight of 95,000 lbs, four engines of the same type specified above for the smaller version, and 1,100 sq ft wing area which enabled takeoff and landing airspeeds of about 225 kts and 120 kts, respectively. At landing, this airplane would have weighed about 26,000 lbs and would have been equipped with one engine of the type specified above. Using the data of NACA report TN #1350 as a basis, it appeared that the airplane could have also accomplished the range problem and the Special VA requirement in spite of operation at lift coefficients below those required for a maximum lift/drag ratio. The primary penalties paid for attainment of more reasonable takeoff and landing speeds were the higher gross weight and the addition of one engine.

In addition to the problem of takeoff for the smaller airplane above, data included in a report titled *NACA Conference on Supersonic Aerodynamics* dated August 30-31, 1948, showed pronounced laminar separation on wings of these types in small scale supersonic tests. If any separation of this type was encountered at full scale, the data of NACA report TN #1350 would no longer have held for performance calculations and range, which in this study was marginal for the Special VA requirement, becoming sub-marginal in direct proportion to the decrease in the maximum lift/drag ratio. In addition to the effect on performance, flow separation could have also caused stability and control problems. It was believed that boundary layer control could have been used, if necessary, to alleviate problems caused by separation at full scale, but whether the alleviation would have been sufficient to enable attainment of the necessary stability and control and/or the performance shown by the NACA report, could have only been determined by extensive wind tunnel and flight tests.

In these preliminary studies, the problems of aileron reversal speeds were not considered thoroughly. It was therefore possible that the wing weights used for performance checks were optimistic. However, Convair believed that problems caused by this fact

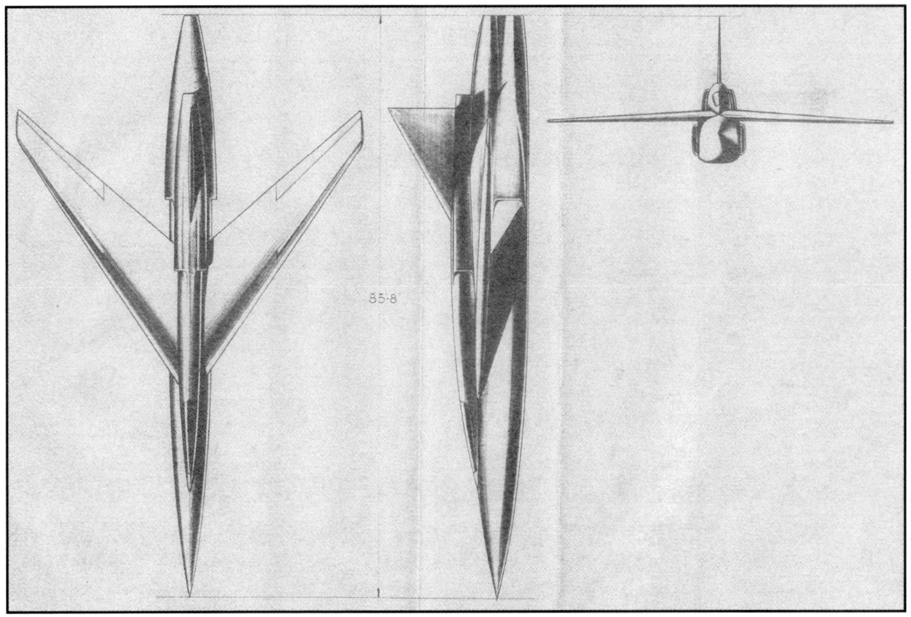

National Archives, RG 72

The first of the miscellaneous studies drafted to fulfill OS-115 was designated "Study A," which featured a "Robert T. Jones" wing, a highly swept back tailless configuration.

were solvable with sufficient study.

2. Delta wing tailless with droppable pod This configuration was selected as the most promising and was used as the basis for the design proposal.

3./4. Delta wing tandem canard with return of tail component / Delta wing tandem (tail aft) with return of tail component Two tandem delta wing type airplanes were studied. On both of these versions, the main wing had approximately 900 sq ft area and the tail unit (which formed the wing of the return component) had about 40% of the area of the main wing.

The curve of the lift/drag ratio vs. CL for either complete tandem airplane was very nearly the same as for the tailless delta wing version. The larger total wing area of the tandem types, however, resulted in operation at lift coefficients lower than optimum and therefore at lower attainable values of lift/drag than for the tailless delta wing type. This result, for the complete tandem type airplane, resulted in it being unable to attain the supersonic performance outlined by the special VA requirements, even with advanced engine ratings.

In addition, the minimum possible fuselage size required to enclose the returnable equipment was physically the same for the tandem types as for the tailless type, while the return wing area for the tandem was considerably smaller. This decreased the maximum attainable value of the maximum lift/drag ratio for the return component of the tandem type, as compared with the tailless type, to the point where flight of the return component was not possible at the prescribed conditions with the single engine included in the Convair study.

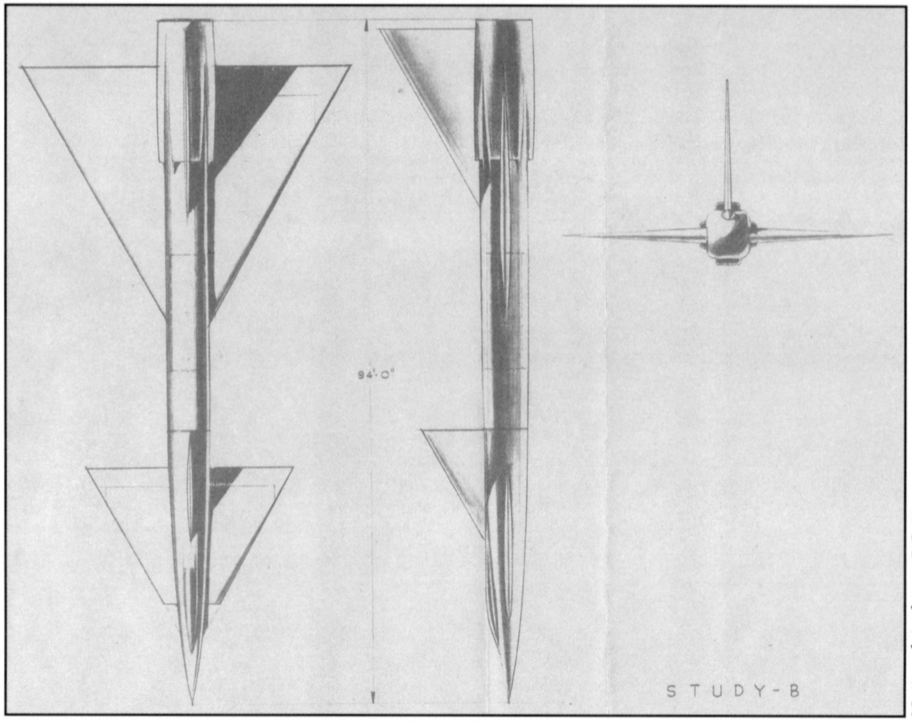

Convair examined the canard layout in Study B, in which the parasite aircraft attached to the front of the expendable component, much like a modern two stage rocket.

National Archives, RG 72

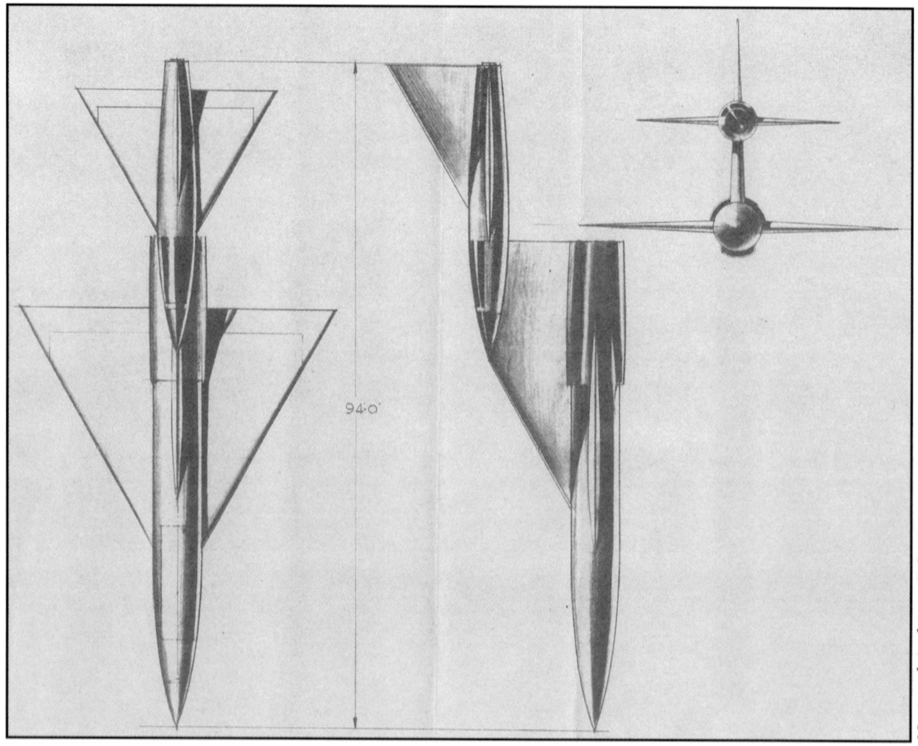

Study C was a tandem delta wing design which mounted the parasite aircraft on the vertical tail of the bomb component, making for a truly unorthodox configuration.

National Archives, RG 72

Other proportioning of the total wing area between the two components, or changes in total wing area, resulted in even lower overall performance. The tandem types, due to lower takeoff wing loading and higher landing wing loading, would have had lower takeoff speeds and higher landing speeds than the tailless delta wing type airplane.

The foregoing discussion dealt only with the performance aspects of the tandem delta wing types. In addition, due to possible interaction between the two wings of the tandem types, stability and control problems could have been encountered, and performance might not have been as good as indicated by these studies wherein interference effects were neglected.

Convair noted that the tandem delta types would have been more complex to fabricate and would therefore have been more expensive types than the tailless delta wing type airplane.

5. Highly swept back dual airplane with return of small airplane Using fundamental assumptions similar to those used for the highly swept back tailless design, it appeared that a dual airplane type could have also accomplished the range problem of OS-115. The airplane at takeoff would have had a gross weight of nearly 100,000 lbs and would have been equipped with four engines of the type specified for the tailless

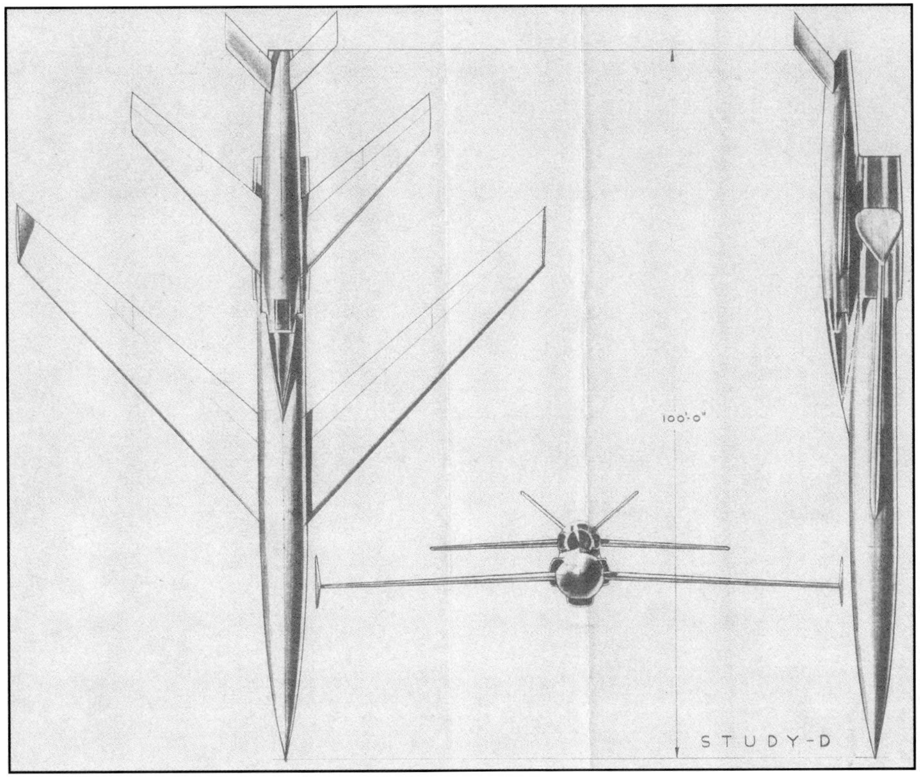

National Archives, RG 72

Both components of Study D featured highly swept back wings, with the parasite aircraft attaching directly to the aft fuselage of the missile.

airplane. The return component would have been the small airplane and it would have been powered by one of the four engine units.

This airplane would have been subject to the same questions regarding airflow separation and aileron reversal speed as those raised for the tailless configuration. In addition, it would have been necessary to have two sets of controls, one for the complete airplane and one for the return component. If any interference effects were encountered between the various lifting surfaces, performance, stability, and control might have all been adversely affected.

This type of airplane would have been considerably more complex to fabricate than the tailless type with pod. It would therefore have been more expensive than the latter types in terms of initial cost, and in addition would have expended a more expensive component on each operational flight.

6. Variable sweep wing with droppable pod These studies showed two methods of obtaining relatively high aspect ratio (and low wing sweep) for takeoff, climb, low speed cruise, and landing while retaining the ability to obtain greater sweep back and lower aspect ratio (favoring structure) for operation at Mach numbers near or greater than before. Although mechanical and structural details involved in varying the sweep had not been worked out for either of these possibilities, it was probable that appropriate

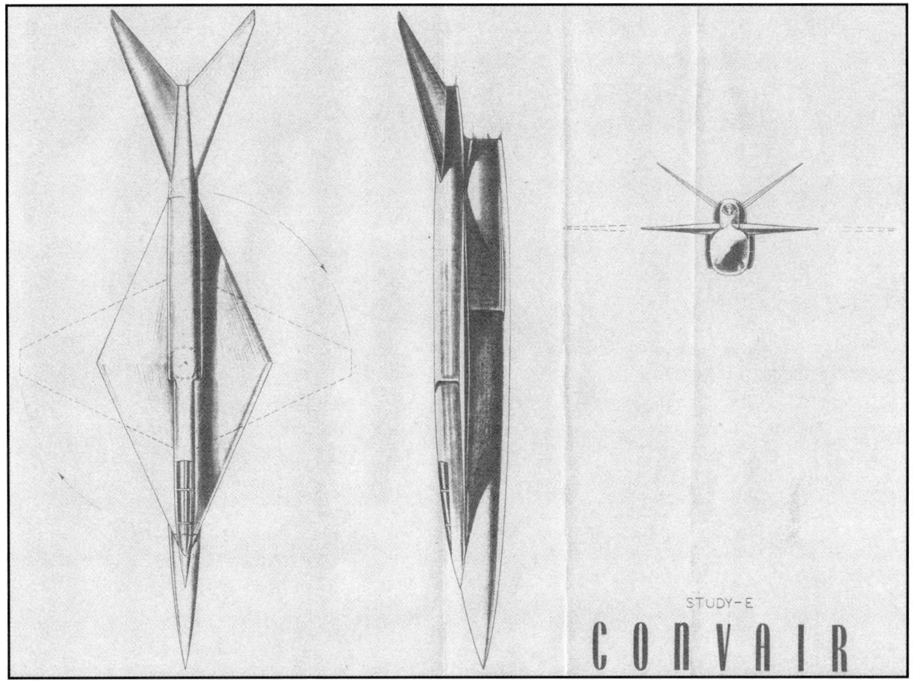

National Archives, RG 72

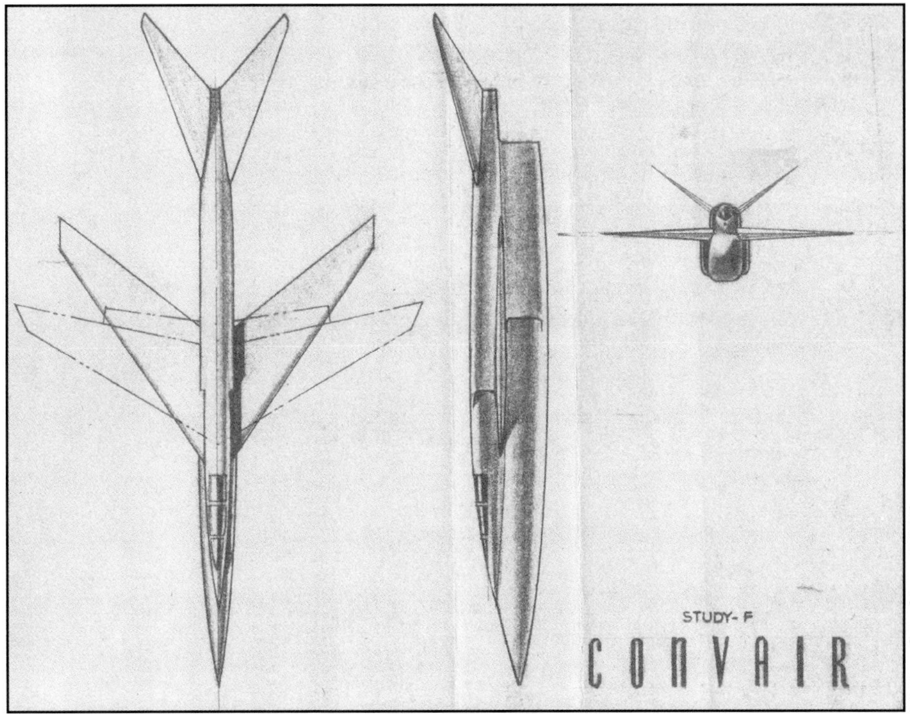

National Archives, RG 72

Above: Convair Studies E and F featured different types of variable geometry wings.

center of gravity control could have been obtained without any additional mechanical complications to produce wing translation. It appeared that the large proportion of fuel to gross weight for the VA design would have allowed center of gravity control through selective use of fuel.

7. Designs of the above type with boundary layer removal The accumulation of the low-energy air in the boundary layer next to the wing surface resulted in a number of adverse aerodynamic effects at both low and high speeds. The advantages of removing this boundary layer for improving the stall of straight wings and for decreasing the drag by permitting more extensive laminar flow were well known.

Of greater importance to the high speed aircraft was the possibility of improving the drag rise through the transonic speed range by removing the abnormally thickened boundary layer that occurred in the vicinity of the normal shock wave. This boundary layer air resulted in separated flow with the consequent large increase in wake drag, the "shock stall." Even without complete removal, the possibilities of changing the character of boundary layer flow offered means of reducing the drag in the transonic regime.

The large spanwise pressure gradients existing on swept wings induced a spanwise flow of the boundary layer air which accumulated, in the case of the swept back wing (such as the Robert T. Jones type wing), near the wing tips. This accumulation of low-energy air augmented separation of the airflow on the outboard portion of the wing with resulting longitudinal and lateral loss of stability and lateral control. (Convair noted that, due to the low aspect ratio of the delta wing planform, the above difficulties at the stall were not present). The usual method of controlling the stall was to use large, heavy leading edge slats on the outboard portion of the wing, sometimes in conjunction with wing fences. Other means, such as dropped leading edges, had also been used. A more satisfactory solution would have been to remove the boundary layer by the use of suitable slots or porous surfaces. The turbojet power plant provided an excellent means of pumping the air, particularly at speeds near the stall where the full thrust was not required for propulsion.

Convair recognized that, in spite of the notable progress that had been made in recent years, many problems still remained to be solved before boundary layer control could be considered satisfactory. Convair stated that it would continue toward the realization of practically boundary layer control in later phases of the Special VA project, in order to obtain the highest airplane performance possible.

8. Power Plants The following power plants were considered:

a. Turbojet Preliminary estimates of the fuel requirements for the Combat Radius Problem showed that, of the various types of engines under development, only the turbojet had performance characteristics which made a solution possible. In order to achieve as realistic a design as possible, only engines then in prototype development as listed by BuAer were considered.

The engine chosen for the designs was the XJ40-WE-10. Considerations of specific fuel consumption, takeoff and altitude thrust ratings, thrust-weight ratio, and number of units necessary dictated the decision.

It was believed, however, that future engines of higher thrust rating and lower fuel consumptions would have supplanted the XJ-40 as the logical choice in the development of the Special VA airplane, but the consideration of such engines at the time of the proposal would not have led to realistic airplane design.

b. Ducted fan Information on the J-49 project (Packard Motor Car Company Specification No. 203a Rev. 18 dated June 1948) showed that thrust to engine weight ratio, engine size, and fuel consumptions were inferior to the XJ-40 data. Also, satisfactory operation of the ducted fan type power plant at supersonic speeds appeared questionable.

c. Ram jet Early calculations indicated that approximately 50,000 lbs of ram jet fuel would have been required for the supersonic portion of the flight (i.e., 1,000 nm out of a total of 3,400 nm). Therefore, the possibility of using ram jets was not investigated further. Mach nos. up to 2.0 were considered in these calculations.

d. Expendable turbojet Information on the Turbodyne III (Turbodyne Corporation letter dated October 22, 1948, classified Secret) showed that the expendable type unit under development might eventually replace the three expendable XJ-40 turbojets specified for the pod. However, the estimated specific fuel consumptions for the Turbodyne III were too high to warrant its choice, but Convair recommended consideration of future developments of this engine with a variable area nozzle to reduce fuel consumption because of simplicity of installation and possible decrease in pod frontal area.

e. Wright Aero Corporation Turbojet Data on the two proposed developments (TJ-6 Specification No. AC-141 and TJ-7 Specification No. AC-142, both dated September 1, 1948) indicated that the TJ-6 engine, which was to have been available in 1951, had a higher thrust to weight ratio and equivalent specific fuel consumptions as compared to the XJ-40, while the TJ-7 scheduled for 1955 showed improved specific fuel consumptions. Engines of this size, 11,000 to 12,000 lbs static takeoff thrust, would have simplified power plant design, while the TJ-7 fuel consumptions would have reduced the fuel requirements and consequently the size of the airplane for the combat problem.

9. Ditching Considerations Consideration was given to ditching only the return component as the pod would have been jettisoned in the event of a forced landing in the water prior to the return flight. Without a hydrodynamic sustention device at the nose, it appeared that the airplane would have had unsatisfactory ditching characteristics. A hydrofoil or hydroski could have been designed in conjunction with the nose wheel gear, which would have kept the airplane from diving when water contact was made. It was estimated that a hydroski of less than one square foot would have sufficed.

Ditching tests with scale models could have shown unsatisfactory cartwheeling tendencies. Some simple device would have been necessary in this respect.

Convair OS-115 Miscellaneous Studies - Dimensions

Designation	*Overall Length (entire composite aircraft)*	*Notes*
Study A	85.67 ft	
Study B	94.00 ft	
Study C	94.00 ft	
Study D	100.00 ft	Excludes V-tail of parasite aircraft
Study E	105.22 ft	Estimated - assumes drawing is to same scale as Study D
Study F	105.63 ft	Estimated - assumes drawing is to same scale as Study D

Convair GEBO II Study for the USAF

Like the other proposals in the OS-115 competition, the Convair Long Range Special Attack airplane never left the drawing board; the reasons for this are speculated upon in Chapter 17. In January of 1950, Convair would recycle the basic design for the Air Force Generalized Bomber (GEBO) II Study, proposing that it be carried as a parasite bomber under a B-36 Peacemaker. While this aircraft also never made it beyond the study stage, GEBO would ultimately evolve into the famous B-58 Hustler, which first flew on November 11, 1956. More information concerning this project can be found in Chapter 3 of *Convair B-58 Hustler* by Jay Miller.

CONVAIR GEBO II PARASITE ON EXTENDED TRAPEZE

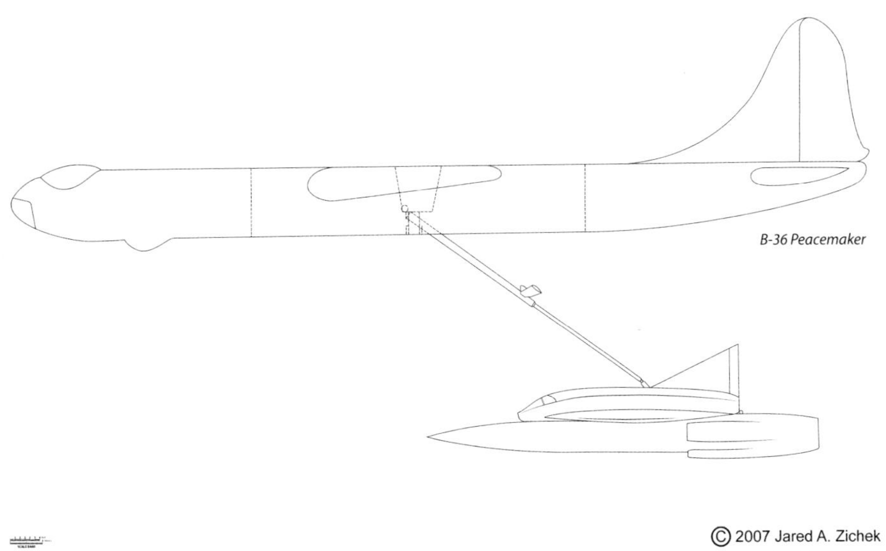

CONVAIR GEBO II PARASITE

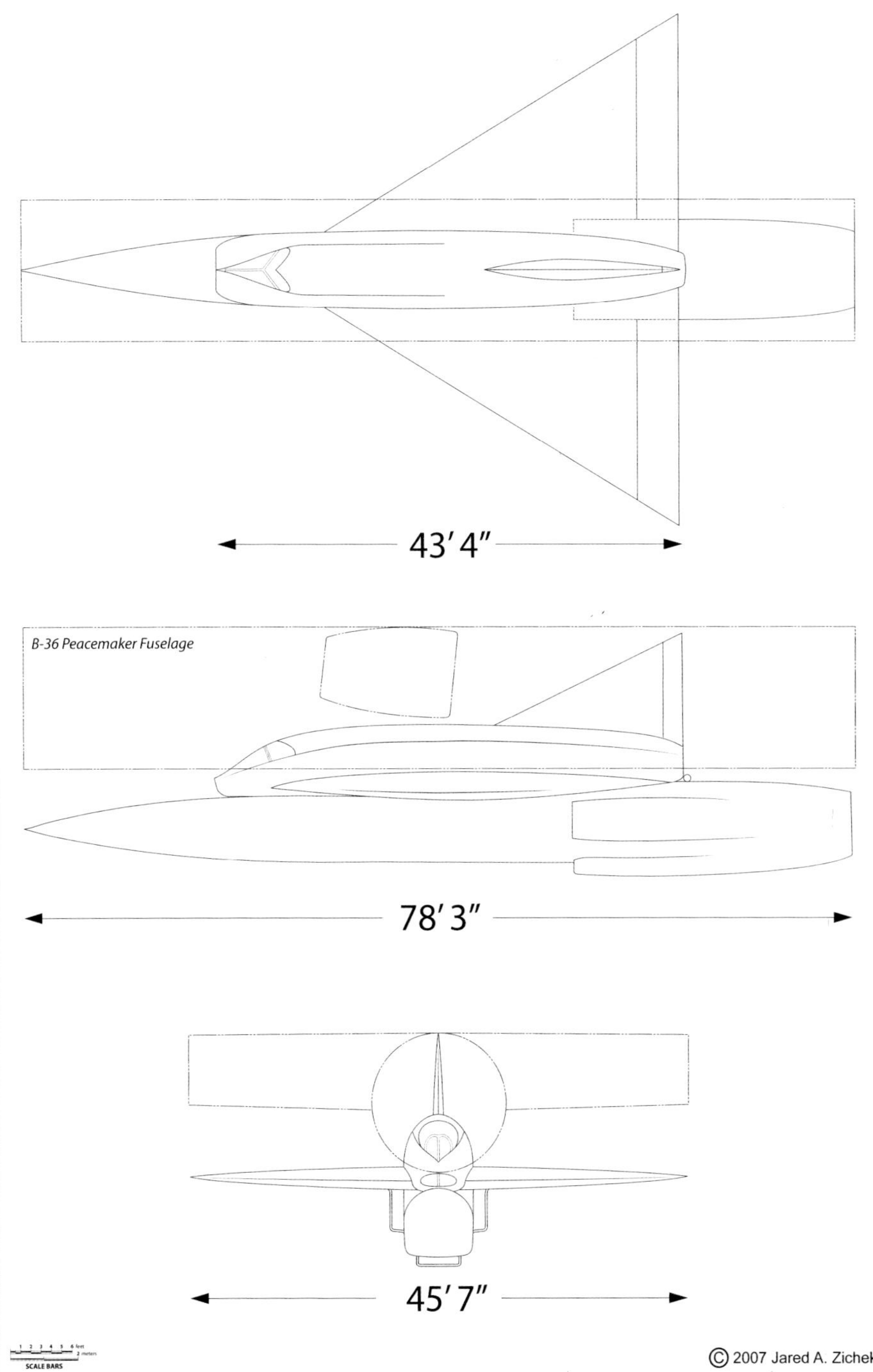

CHAPTER 13 — *Douglas El Segundo Model 594*

As with OS-111, Douglas divided its design efforts between its El Segundo and Santa Monica branches, submitting two different Special Attack proposals. Each branch produced four studies for a composite attack aircraft made up of a large missile and a piloted return component, each optimized for high speed flight. The brevity of the surviving proposal documents suggests that Douglas did not anticipate OS-115 producing a lucrative near term production contract; thus, none of the special attack studies was developed to the level of detail shown in the OS-111 proposals. The El Segundo studies fell under the Model 594 designation and showed noticeable influence from the company's work on the X-3 Stiletto and F4D Skyray. The Santa Monica studies were produced under the Model 1186 designation and were even more heavily influenced by the X-3; these remarkable designs are covered in the following chapter.

Douglas Model 594

The first of Douglas' special attack studies was designated the Model 594. This radical composite aircraft had the following characteristics:

Weight The takeoff weight of the complete Model 594 was 100,000 lbs, with the gross weight of escape vehicle being 18,595 lbs.

Escape Vehicle The escape vehicle was a two-place conventional airplane having accommodations for a pilot and radio operator/navigator/bomber. The wing featured an area of 300 sq ft, and aspect ratio of 5, and a thickness of 8% in the direction of flight.

External Store The external store contained the bomb, two turbojet power plants and fuel; it was provided with a wing and empennage. Aileron, elevator and rudder controls were provided and acted simultaneously with those of the escape vehicle.

Power Plant Power plants consisted of XJ-40 turbojets modified to provide 11,000

National Archives, RG 72

Above: Artist's Impression of the extraordinary Douglas Model 594 special attack aircraft; note the similarity to the X-3 in the design of the escape vehicle's fuselage.

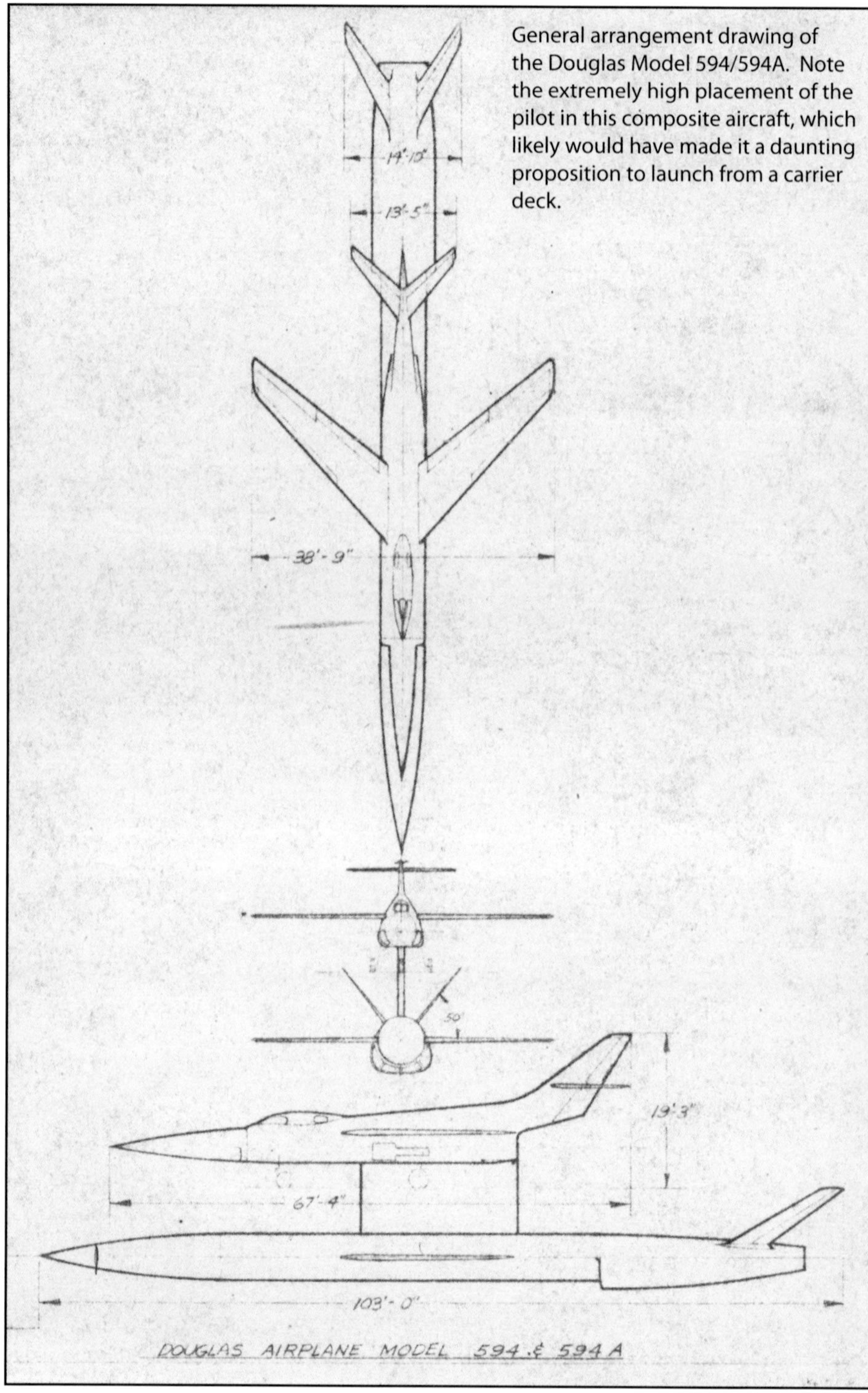

General arrangement drawing of the Douglas Model 594/594A. Note the extremely high placement of the pilot in this composite aircraft, which likely would have made it a daunting proposition to launch from a carrier deck.

National Archives, RG 72

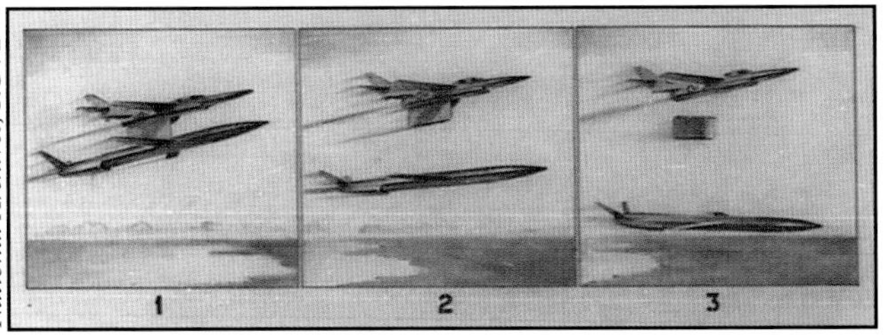

National Archives, RG 72

Illustration of the Model 594 external store separation sequence; BuAer likely would have required extensive wind tunnel testing to ensure the cleanest possible release of the missile component.

lbs static thrust without afterburner and 15,950 lbs static thrust with afterburner. The power plant weight was assumed to be the same as for the XJ40-10 turbojet. Specific weights of new turbojets proposed by Wright Aeronautical Company substantiated this weight. If the XJ-40 turbojet could not be modified as assumed, the Wright Aeronautical TJ-6, which had theoretically equivalent performance, would have been substituted.

One turbojet was located in the escape vehicle and two turbojets in the store. On the way to the target, the store turbojets were operated at military thrust plus afterburning. Since the turbojet in the escape vehicle was not expendable, it was operated only at normal thrust plus afterburning except for limited times during the climb and acceleration periods.

In order to operate at the maximum speed of Mach 1.75 for prolonged periods, it could have been necessary to insulate the fuel tanks in order to prevent fuel vaporization. Douglas did not consider the weight for this in its calculations, but the tanks were designed for a pressure of 9 lbs per square inch.

Fuel Capacity The fuel capacity in the escape vehicle for return flight was 4,370 lbs; in the store, it was 55,152 lbs. This fuel was supplied to all three engines on outgoing flight.

Armament The armament of the Model 594 was a 10,000 lb bomb 5 ft in diameter by 9 ft long. Douglas realized that the envelope described in OS-115 specified an overall length of 16 ft. It was assumed that the after part of the bomb was made up of an empennage and, therefore, could have been removed in this installation. If this assumption was invalid, the bomb envelope could have been increased without serious effect upon performance. Douglas did not include the weight of the bomb installation in its performance calculations, as it assumed that this would have been bal-

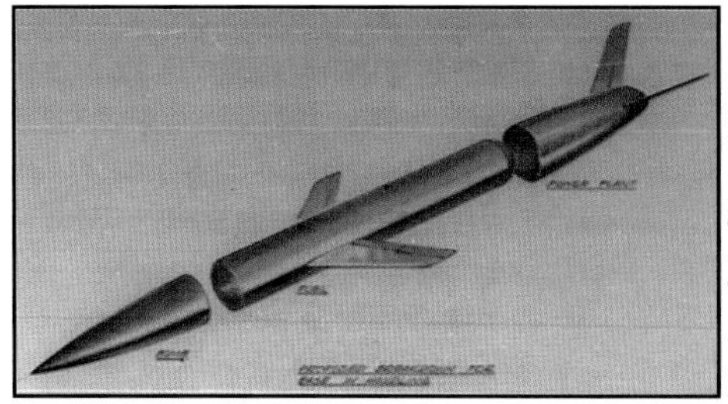

National Archives, RG 72

Above: Breakdown of the external store, which featured a 10,000 lb bomb in the nose, fuel in the central fuselage, and the power plant in the aft component.

National Archives, RG 72

Above: The Model 594 launching cart was to have been propelled either by a slotted tube catapult or JATO.

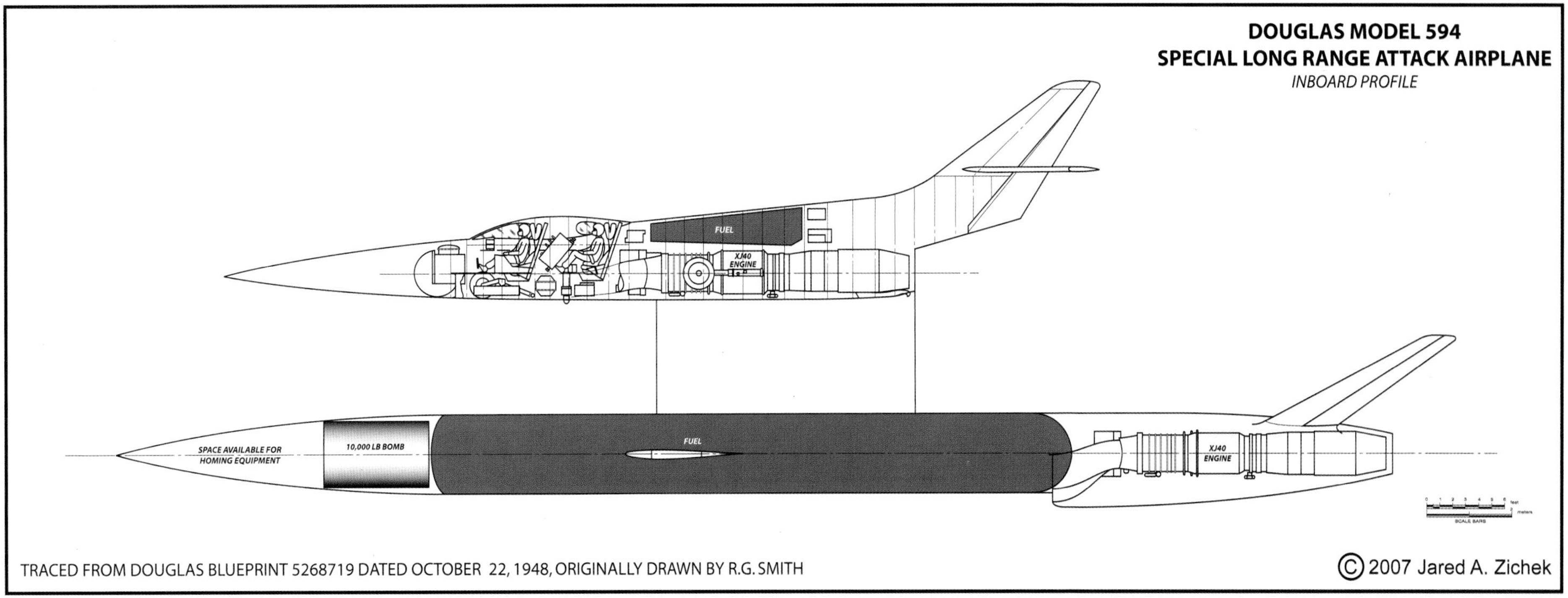

anced by the weight of the empennage removed.

It was assumed that the wings would have remained on the store when dropped. With this arrangement, a homing device or automatic pilot could have been used to direct the store to the target.

Takeoff and Landing Takeoff was accomplished with the aid of a launching dolly propelled either by a slotted tube catapult or JATO. The takeoff stalling speed was 191 kts. In a 600 ft run with a 25 kt wind, this speed could have been reached with an average acceleration of 2G. The escape vehicle was equipped with a tricycle landing gear and an arresting hook and could land aboard CV9 class carriers. The landing speed was 103 kts.

Training For training from land bases, the launching dolly could have been propelled by JATO along a railroad track. In order to salvage the store and engines, a parachute could have been used.

Strength The aircraft was designed for an indicated speed corresponding to Mach 1.09 at sea level. The applied load factors were 2.25 at takeoff gross weight and 2.67 at combat weight. Because of the high wing loading, the gust condition would not have been critical. When operating at the maximum speed of Mach 1.75 at altitude, there would have been a strength reduction of approximately 5% due to temperature effects.

Performance In the combat radius problem, proper allowance was made in the subsonic portion of the run out for fuel to accelerate to the supersonic speed.

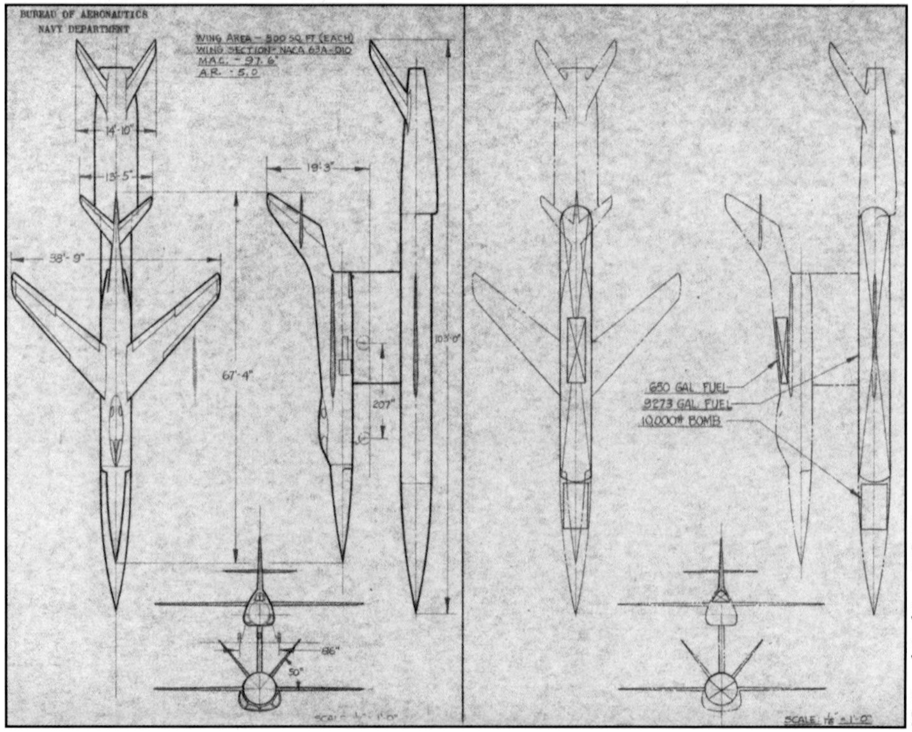

National Archives, RG 72

Above & Above Right: Extracts from the Standard Aircraft Characteristics charts for the Douglas Model 594.

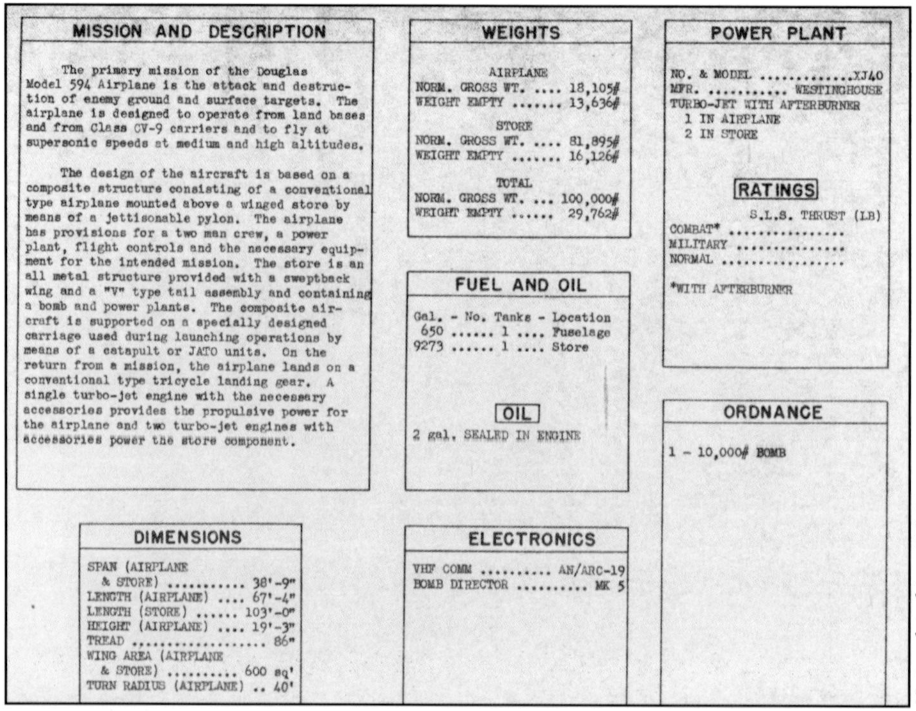

MISSION AND DESCRIPTION

The primary mission of the Douglas Model 594 Airplane is the attack and destruction of enemy ground and surface targets. The airplane is designed to operate from land bases and from Class CV-9 carriers and to fly at supersonic speeds at medium and high altitudes.

The design of the aircraft is based on a composite structure consisting of a conventional type airplane mounted above a winged store by means of a jettisonable pylon. The airplane has provisions for a two man crew, a power plant, flight controls and the necessary equipment for the intended mission. The store is an all metal structure provided with a sweptback wing and a "V" type tail assembly and containing a bomb and power plants. The composite aircraft is supported on a specially designed carriage used during launching operations by means of a catapult or JATO units. On the return from a mission, the airplane lands on a conventional type tricycle landing gear. A single turbo-jet engine with the necessary accessories provides the propulsive power for the airplane and two turbo-jet engines with accessories power the store component.

WEIGHTS

AIRPLANE
NORM. GROSS WT. .... 18,105#
WEIGHT EMPTY .... 13,636#

STORE
NORM. GROSS WT. .... 81,895#
WEIGHT EMPTY .... 16,126#

TOTAL
NORM. GROSS WT. ... 100,000#
WEIGHT EMPTY ...... 29,762#

POWER PLANT

NO. & MODEL XJ40
MFR. .... WESTINGHOUSE
TURBO-JET WITH AFTERBURNER
1 IN AIRPLANE
2 IN STORE

RATINGS

S.L.S. THRUST (LB)
COMBAT* ....
MILITARY ....
NORMAL ....

*WITH AFTERBURNER

FUEL AND OIL

Gal. - No. Tanks - Location
650 ...... 1 .... Fuselage
9273 ...... 1 .... Store

OIL

2 gal. SEALED IN ENGINE

ORDNANCE

1 - 10,000# BOMB

DIMENSIONS

SPAN (AIRPLANE & STORE) .... 38'-9"
LENGTH (AIRPLANE) .... 67'-4"
LENGTH (STORE) ...... 103'-0"
HEIGHT (AIRPLANE) .... 19'-3"
TREAD .... 86"
WING AREA (AIRPLANE & STORE) .... 600 sq'
TURN RADIUS (AIRPLANE) .. 40'

ELECTRONICS

VHF COMM AN/ARC-19
BOMB DIRECTOR .... MK 5

National Archives, RG 72

Douglas Model 594A

The Douglas Model 594A was physically identical to the Model 594 except that Wright Aeronautical Company Model TJ-7 turbojets were substituted for the modified XJ-40 turbojets, improving overall performance.

Douglas Model 594-1

The rationale behind the Model 594-1 was to reduce weight and improve overall performance and economy. While the resulting aircraft deviated from the requirements of OS-115, it had the advantage of being more practical and affordable for the Navy. The vehicle had the following characteristics:

Weight The takeoff gross weight was 60,000 lbs., with the weight of the escape vehicle being 16,385 lbs.

Escape Vehicle For this case, Douglas assumed that the mission could have been accomplished by one crew member. Therefore, the escape vehicle provided only for a pilot. In other respects, it was similar to that of the Model 594.

External Store The external store was similar to that of the Model 594 except that only one turbojet was used and the wing area was reduced.

Power Plant The Model 594-1 was powered by two Wright Aeronautical Company Model TJ-7 turbojets rated at 12,000 lbs static thrust without afterburner and 17,400 lbs static thrust without afterburner.

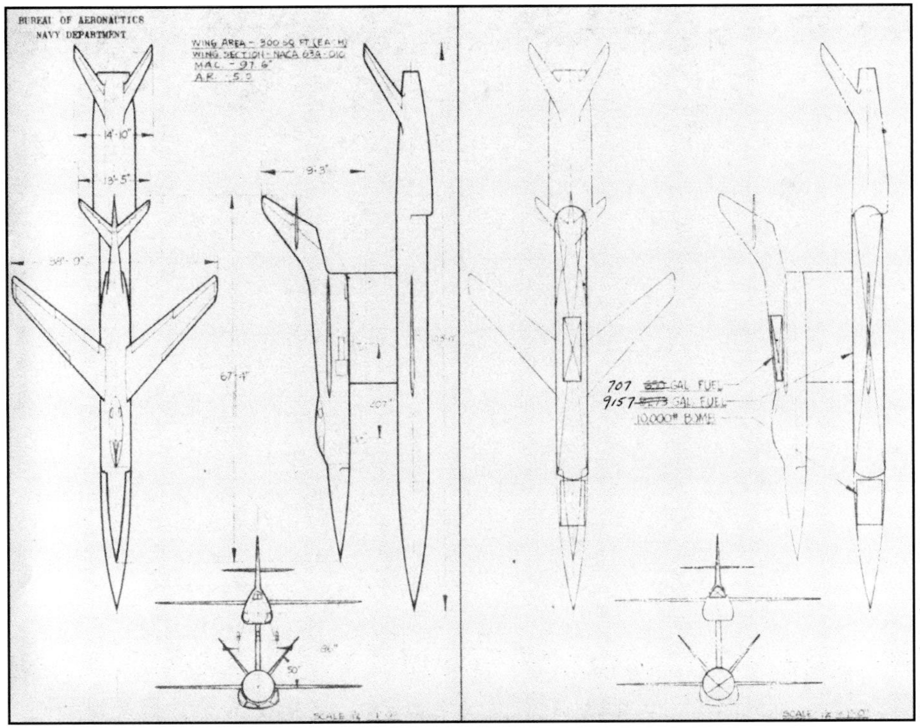

National Archives, RG 72

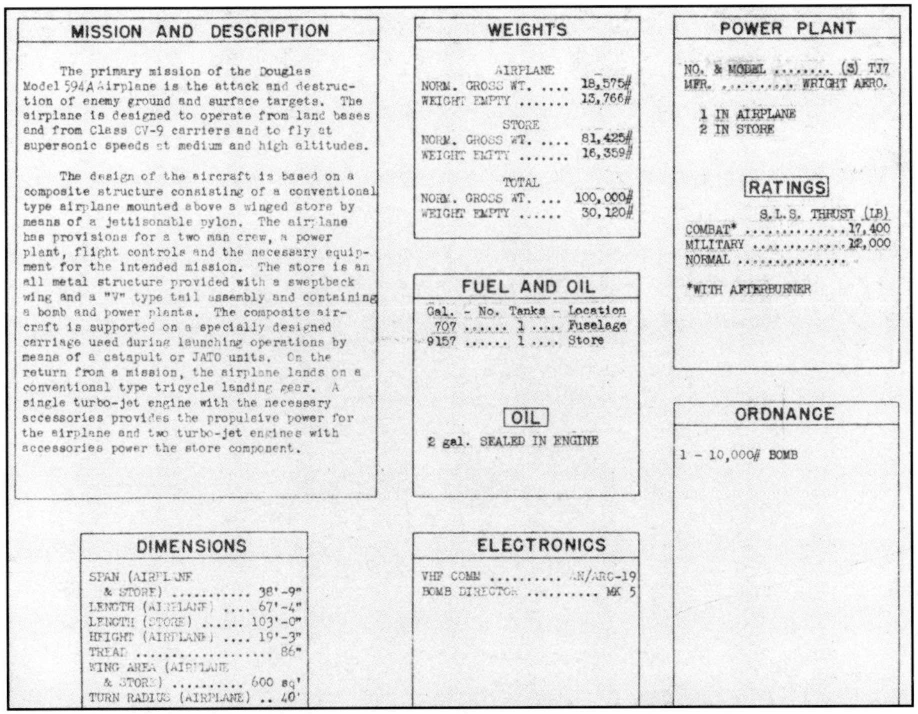

MISSION AND DESCRIPTION

The primary mission of the Douglas Model 594A Airplane is the attack and destruction of enemy ground and surface targets. The airplane is designed to operate from land bases and from Class CV-9 carriers and to fly at supersonic speeds at medium and high altitudes.

The design of the aircraft is based on a composite structure consisting of a conventional type airplane mounted above a winged store by means of a jettisonable pylon. The airplane has provisions for a two man crew, a power plant, flight controls and the necessary equipment for the intended mission. The store is an all metal structure provided with a sweptback wing and a "V" type tail assembly and containing a bomb and power plants. The composite aircraft is supported on a specially designed carriage used during launching operations by means of a catapult or JATO units. On the return from a mission, the airplane lands on a conventional type tricycle landing gear. A single turbo-jet engine with the necessary accessories provides the propulsive power for the airplane and two turbo-jet engines with accessories power the store component.

WEIGHTS

AIRPLANE
NORM. GROSS WT. .... 18,575#
WEIGHT EMPTY .... 13,766#

STORE
NORM. GROSS WT. .... 81,425#
WEIGHT EMPTY .... 16,359#

TOTAL
NORM. GROSS WT. ... 100,000#
WEIGHT EMPTY ...... 30,120#

POWER PLANT

NO. & MODEL .... (3) TJ7
MFR. .... WRIGHT AERO.

1 IN AIRPLANE
2 IN STORE

RATINGS

S.L.S. THRUST (LB)
COMBAT* 17,400
MILITARY 12,000
NORMAL ....

*WITH AFTERBURNER

FUEL AND OIL

Gal. - No. Tanks - Location
707 ...... 1 .... Fuselage
9157 ...... 1 .... Store

OIL

2 gal. SEALED IN ENGINE

ORDNANCE

1 - 10,000# BOMB

DIMENSIONS

SPAN (AIRPLANE & STORE) .... 38'-9"
LENGTH (AIRPLANE) .... 67'-4"
LENGTH (STORE) ...... 103'-0"
HEIGHT (AIRPLANE) .... 19'-3"
TREAD .... 86"
WING AREA (AIRPLANE & STORE) .... 600 sq'
TURN RADIUS (AIRPLANE) .. 40'

ELECTRONICS

VHF COMM AN/ARC-19
BOMB DIRECTOR .... MK 5

National Archives, RG 72

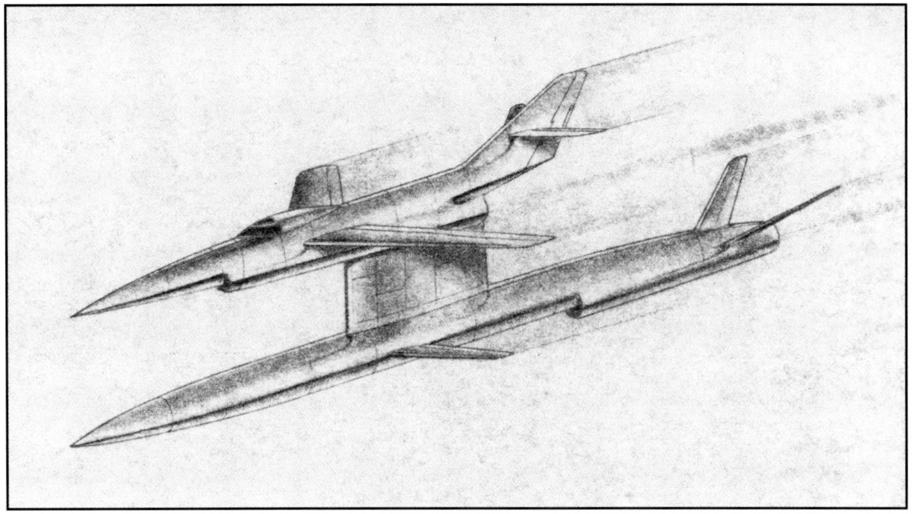

National Archives, RG 72

Above: Artist's impression of the Model 594-1, a lighter version of the Model 594A; note the smaller wing of the external store compared to the preceding study.

Fuel Capacity The fuel capacity in the escape vehicle for return flight was 3,910 lbs; in the store for outgoing flight, it was 30,874 lbs.

Armament With the Model 594-1, Douglas assumed that the armament could have been reduced to a 4,000 lb bomb of approximately 2 ft diameter by 6 ft in length. If this assumption proved overly optimistic, the 10,000 lb bomb could have been carried with some reduction in combat radius.

Training Since the store on this model had only one turbojet engine, the expense of training would have been less than for the Model 594 in the event that it was impracticable to recover the store after release.

National Archives, RG 72

Left: Another artist's impression of the Model 594-1, shown from the bottom. Artwork by the incomparable R.G. Smith.

Left: Extracts from the Standard Aircraft Characteristics charts for the Douglas Model 594A, which featured WAC TJ-7 turbojets and improved performance over the Model 594. Note the handwritten corrections to the fuel figures in the drawing on the upper left.

DOUGLAS MODEL 594-1
SPECIAL LONG RANGE ATTACK AIRPLANE

INBOARD PROFILE

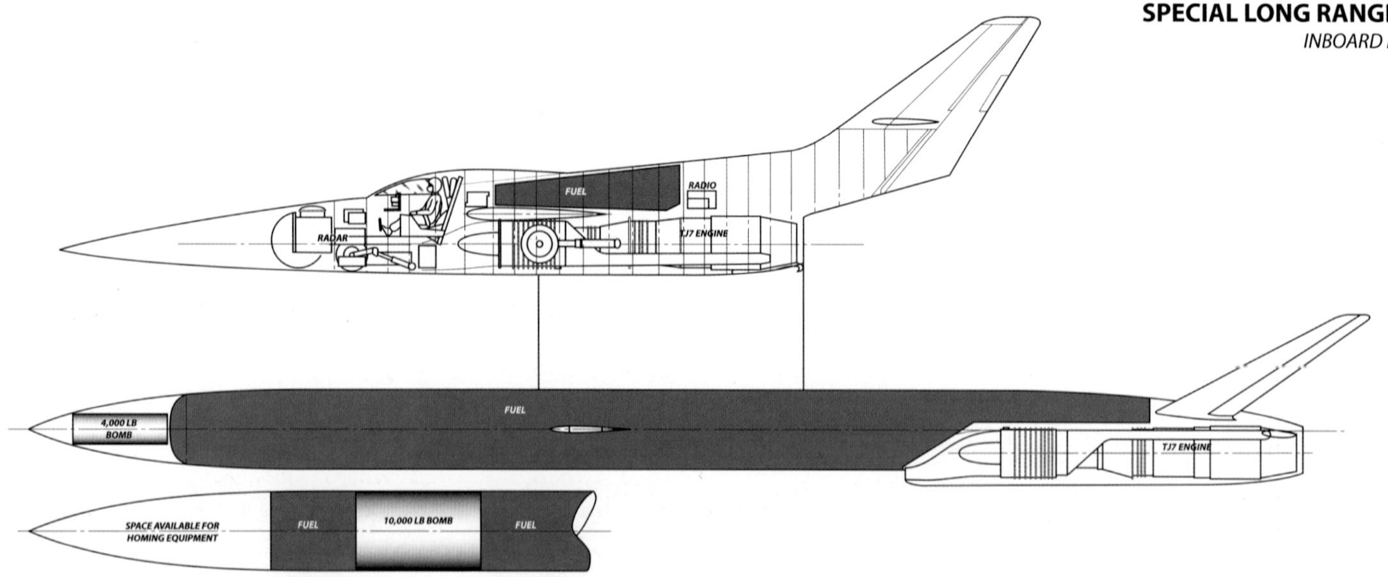

TRACED FROM DOUGLAS BLUEPRINT 5268720 DATED OCTOBER 26, 1948, ORIGINALLY DRAWN BY R.G. SMITH

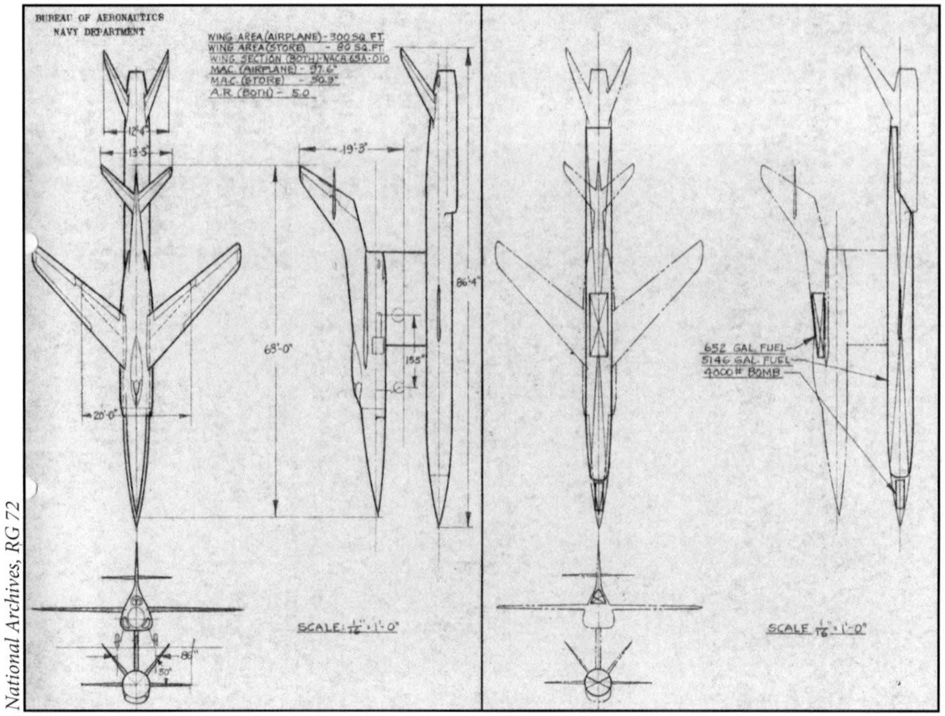

MISSION AND DESCRIPTION

The primary mission of the Douglas Model 594-1 Airplane is the attack and destruction of enemy ground and surface targets. The airplane is designed to operate from land bases and from Class CV-9 carriers and to fly at supersonic speeds at medium and high altitudes.

The design of the aircraft is based on a composite structure consisting of a conventional type airplane mounted above a winged store by means of a jettisonable pylon. The airplane has provisions for a one man crew, a power plant, flight controls and the necessary equipment for the intended mission. The store is an all metal structure provided with a sweptback wing and a "V" type tail assembly and containing a bomb and power plant. The composite aircraft is supported on a specially designed carriage used during launching operations by means of a catapult or JATO units. On the return from a mission, the airplane lands on a conventional type tricycle landing gear. A single turbo-jet engine with the necessary accessories provides the propulsive power for the airplane and two turbo-jet engines with accessories also power the store component.

WEIGHTS

AIRPLANE
NORM. GROSS WT. ..... 16,385#
WEIGHT EMPTY .... 12,168#

STORE
NORM. GROSS WT. ..... 43,615#
WEIGHT EMPTY .... 8,626#

TOTAL
NORM. GROSS WT. ..... 60,000#
WEIGHT EMPTY .... 20,794#

FUEL AND OIL

Gal. - No. Tanks - Location
652 ...... 1 .... Fuselage
5146 ...... 1 .... Store

OIL

2 gal. SEALED IN ENGINE

POWER PLANT

NO. & MODEL .... (2) TJ7
MFR. .... WRIGHT AERO.

1 IN AIRPLANE
1 IN STORE

RATINGS

S.L.S. THRUST (LB)
COMBAT* 17,400
MILITARY 12,000
NORMAL ....

*WITH AFTERBURNER

ORDNANCE

1 - 4,000# BOMB

DIMENSIONS

SPAN (AIRPLANE) .... 38'-9"
SPAN (STORE) .... 20'-0"
LENGTH (AIRPLANE) ..... 63'-0"
LENGTH (STORE) .... 86'-4"
HEIGHT (AIRPLANE) ..... 19'-3"
TREAD .... 86"
WING AREA (AIRPLANE) .. 300 sq'
WING AREA (STORE) ..... 80 sq'
TURN RADIUS (AIRPLANE) ... 38'

ELECTRONICS

SUITABLE BOMB DIRECTOR

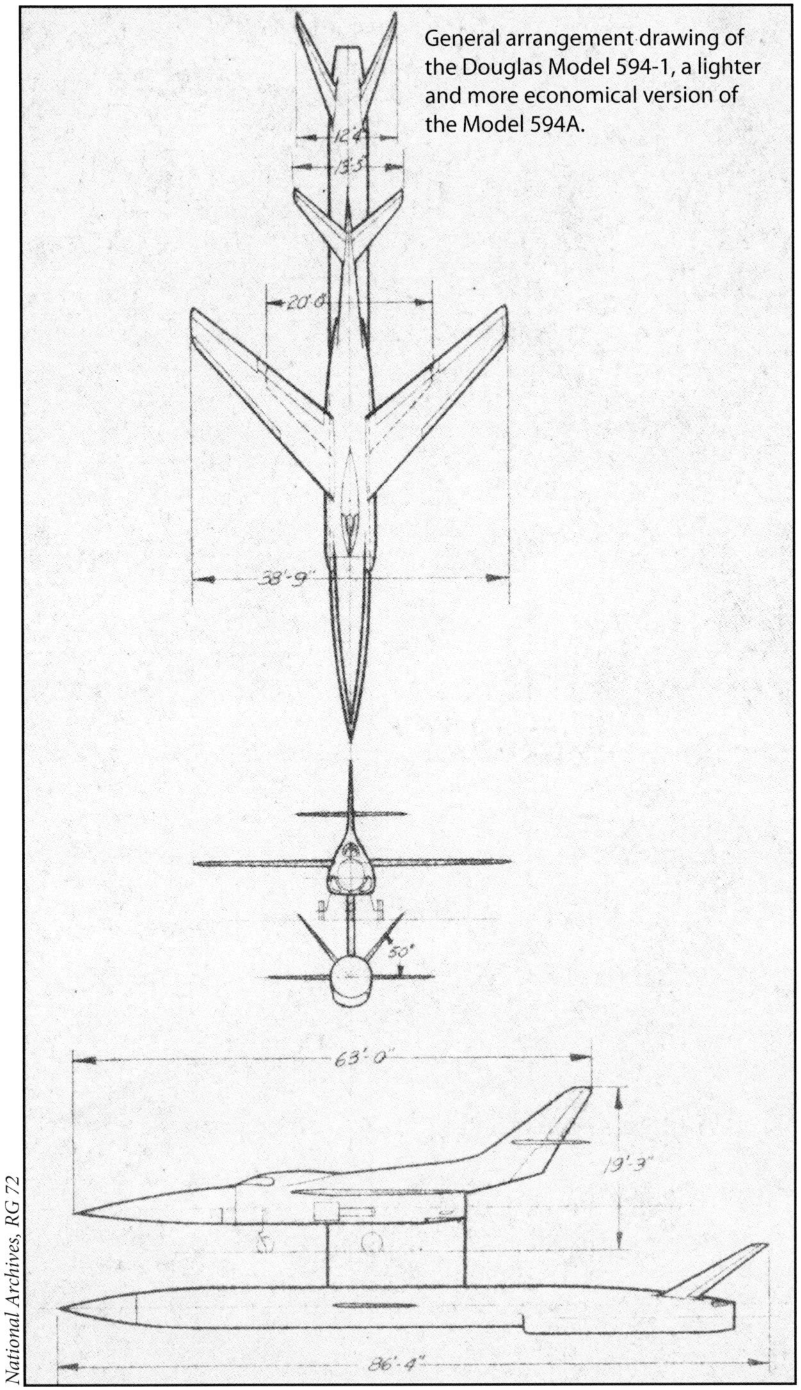

General arrangement drawing of the Douglas Model 594-1, a lighter and more economical version of the Model 594A.

National Archives, RG 72

Facing Page: Douglas Model 594-1 inboard profile and selected Standard Aircraft Characteristics charts.

Douglas Model 594-2

The final study in the Model 594 series, the Model 594-2 featured a new escape vehicle heavily influenced by the company's work on its F4D Skyray fighter. The characteristics of the study were as follows:

Weight The takeoff weight of the Model 594-2 was 64,000 lbs; the escape vehicle weighed 25,214 lbs.

Escape Vehicle The escape vehicle was a single place tailless aircraft having a delta planform and powered by two turbojet engines. It was heavily influenced by research undertaken in the development of the Douglas F4D Skyray fighter, which was then under development at the company.

Wing The wing had an area of 609 sq ft, an aspect ratio of 2, a span of 35 ft, and a thickness ratio of 7% at the root and 4.5% at the tip.

External Store The external store contained only fuel and the bomb. No wing was provided and no movable controls were contemplated.

Power Plant Two Wright Aeronautical Company TJ-7 turbojets rated at 12,000 lbs static thrust without afterburner and 17,400 lbs static thrust with afterburner. Bother power plants were located in the escape vehicle and, therefore, were not considered expendable. One power plant, however, would have been operated at military thrust plus afterburner during all of the high speed run to the target.

Fuel Capacity The fuel capacity in the escape vehicle for the return flight was 7,230 lbs; in the store for outgoing flight, it was 31,672 lbs.

Armament The armament was the same as for the Model 594-1. The 10,000 lb bomb could have been carried, if necessary, with some reduction in combat radius. In this case the store had no wing and, therefore, a gravity drop was required.

Training Since there were no power plants in the store and no movable controls were contemplated, the store could have been considered expendable for training purposes. Therefore, the Model 594-2 was the most promising from this point of view.

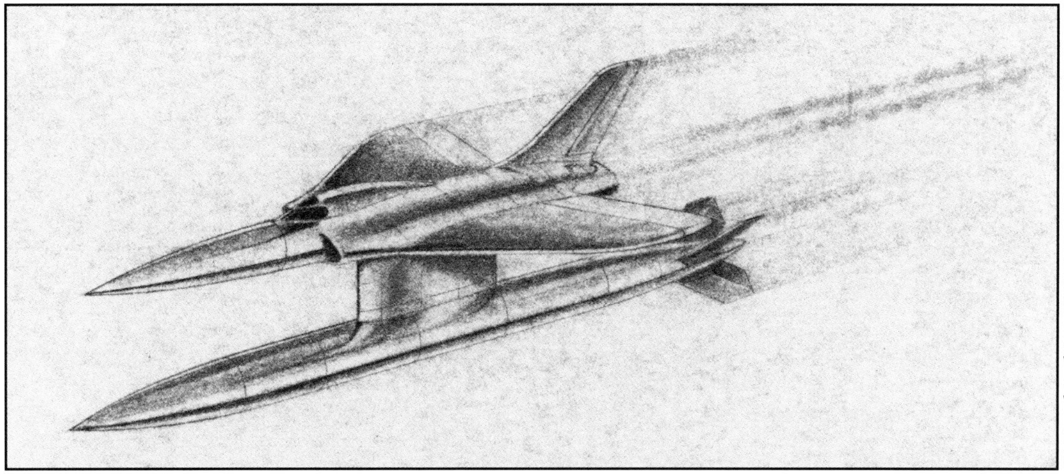

National Archives, RG 72

Above: Artist's impression of the Douglas Model 594-2, which resembled a high speed twin engine F4D Skyray with a gigantic central store. The large wing area and high power of the escape vehicle permitted the deletion of the wings and power plant from the expendable component.

DOUGLAS MODEL 594-2
SPECIAL LONG RANGE ATTACK AIRPLANE
INBOARD PROFILE

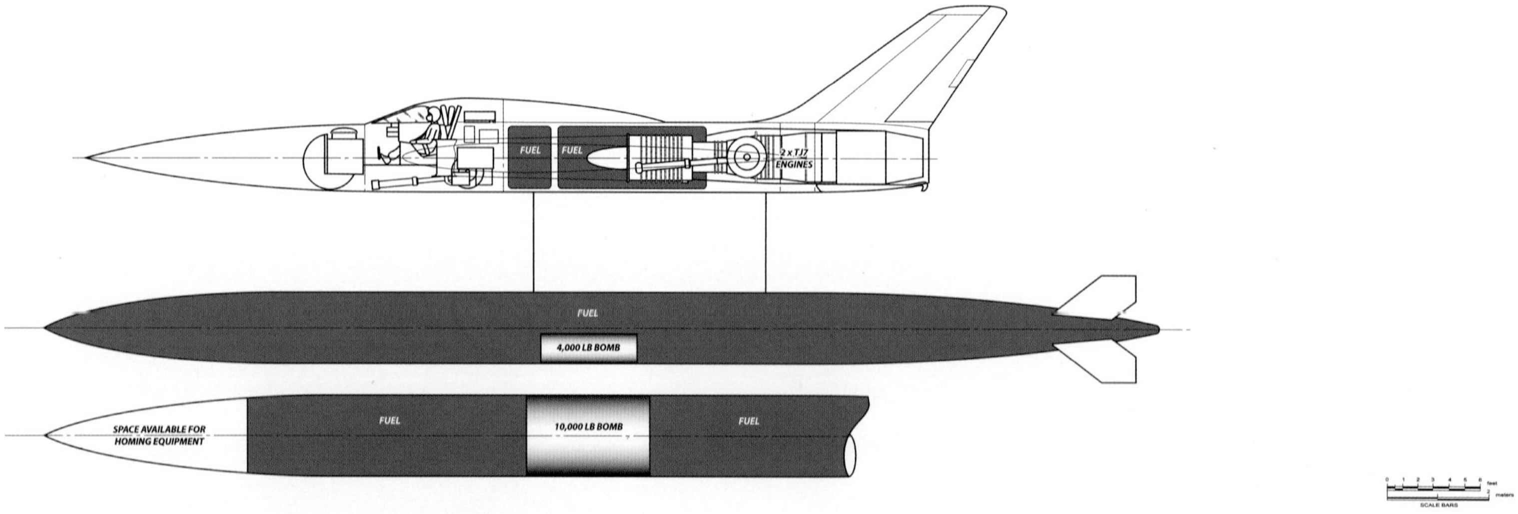

TRACED FROM DOUGLAS BLUEPRINT 5268721 DATED OCTOBER 26, 1948, ORIGINALLY DRAWN BY R.G. SMITH

DOUGLAS MODEL 594-2
SPECIAL LONG RANGE ATTACK AIRPLANE
PROPOSED FUTURE DEVELOPMENTS TO IMPROVE LOGISTICS, TRAINING AND ECONOMY

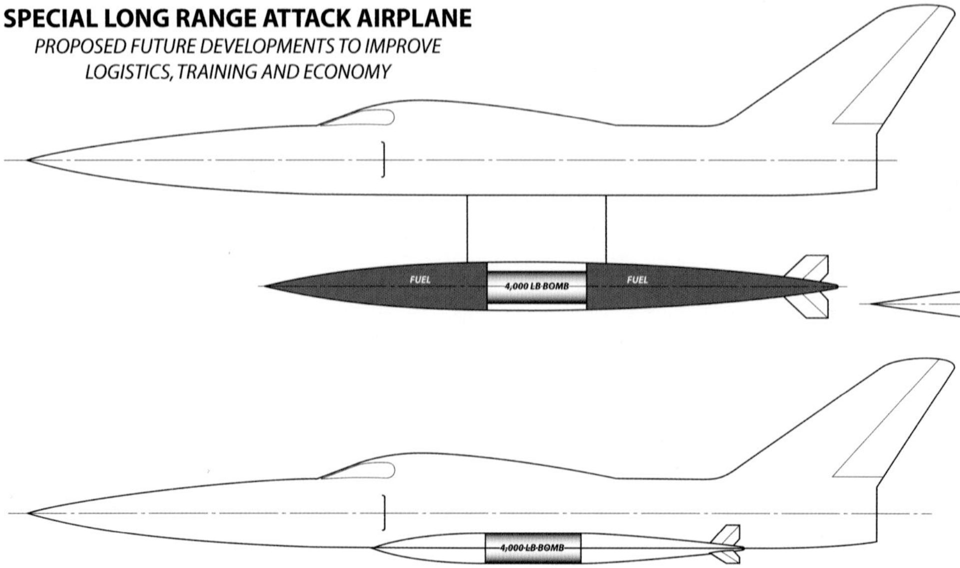

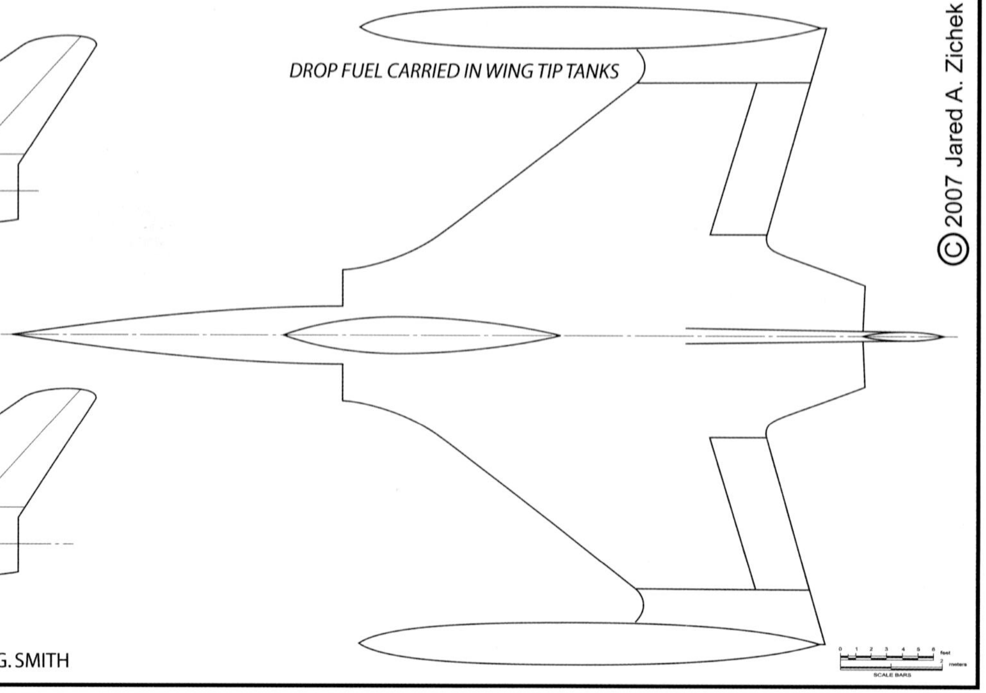

TRACED FROM DOUGLAS BLUEPRINT 5268721 DATED OCTOBER 26, 1948, ORIGINALLY DRAWN BY R.G. SMITH

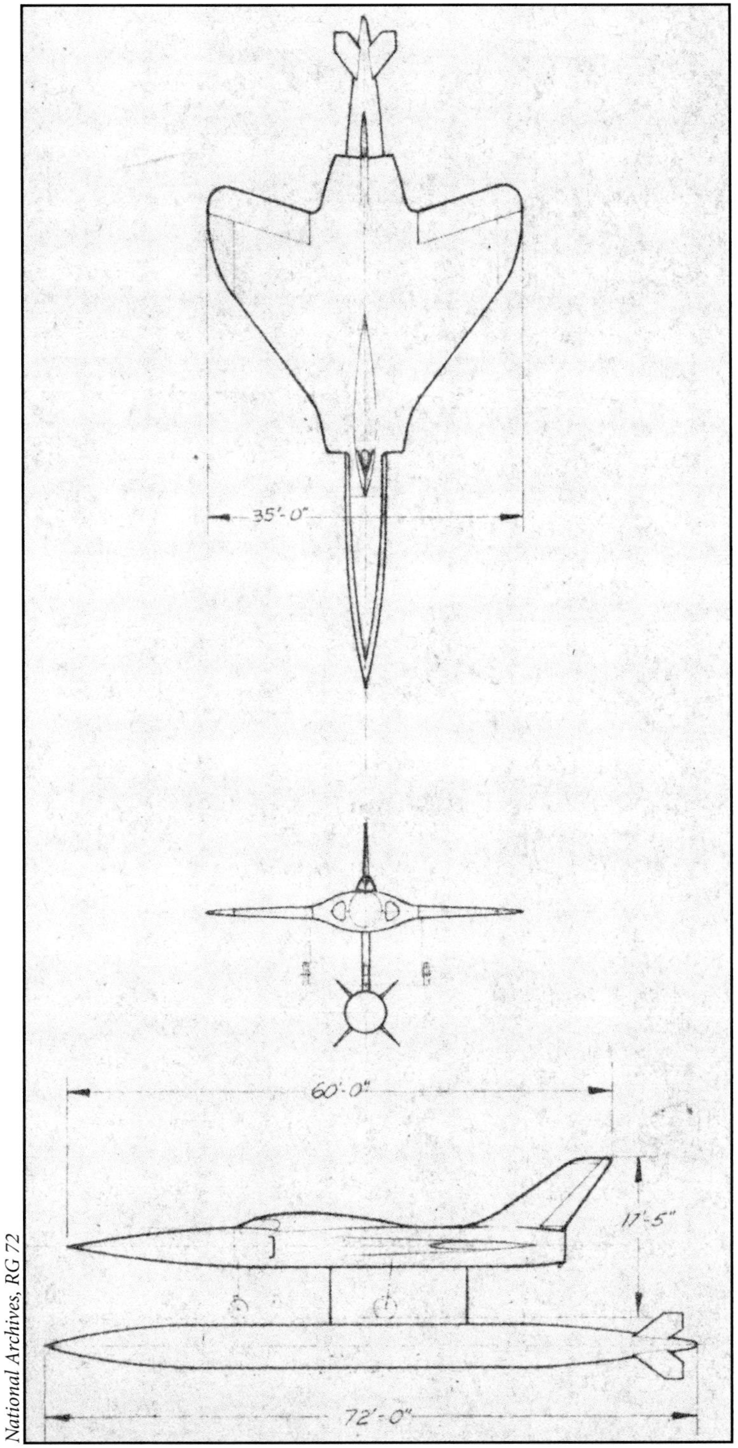

National Archives, RG 72

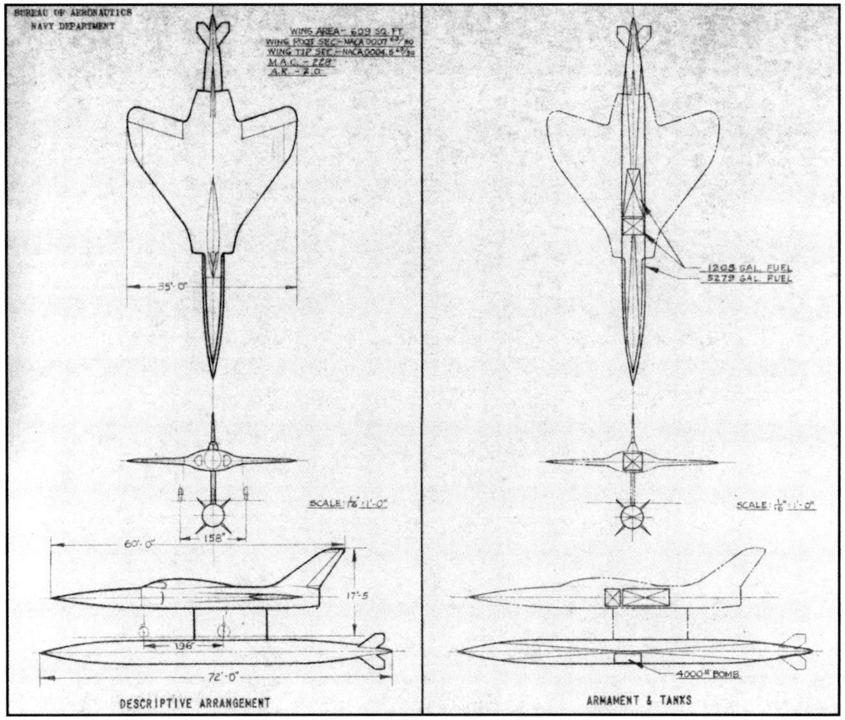

National Archives, RG 72

Left & Below: General arrangement drawing and selected Standard Aircraft Characteristics charts for the Douglas Model 594-2 special attack aircraft.

MISSION AND DESCRIPTION

The primary mission of the Douglas Model 594-2 Airplane is the attack and destruction of enemy ground and surface targets. The airplane is designed to operate from land bases and from Class CV-9 carriers and to fly at supersonic speeds at medium and high altitudes.

The design of the aircraft is based on a composite structure consisting of a Delta wing type airplane mounted above a store by means of a jettisonable pylon. The airplane has provisions for a one man crew, a power plant, flight controls and the necessary equipment for the intended mission. The store design is based on the Douglas external store shape with an increased slenderness ratio. It contains a bomb and fuel. The composite aircraft is supported on a specially designed carriage used during launching operations by means of a catapult or JATO units. On the return from a mission, the airplane lands on a conventional type tricycle landing gear. Two turbo-jet engines with the necessary accessories provide the propulsive power for the airplane.

DIMENSIONS

SPAN .... 35'-0"
LENGTH (AIRPLANE) .... 60'-0"
LENGTH (STORE) .... 72'-0"
HEIGHT (AIRPLANE) .... 17'-5"
TREAD .... 158"
WING AREA .... 609 sq'
TURN RADIUS (AIRPLANE) .. 37'

WEIGHTS

AIRPLANE
NORM. GROSS WT. .... 25,214#
WEIGHT EMPTY 17,652

STORE
NORM. GROSS WT. .... 38,786#
WEIGHT EMPTY .... 3,054#

TOTAL
NORM. GROSS WT. .... 64,000#
WEIGHT EMPTY .... 20,706#

FUEL AND OIL

Gal.	No. Tanks	Location
1205	1	Fuselage
5279	1	Store

OIL

2 gal. SEALED IN ENGINE

ELECTRONICS

SUITABLE BOMB DIRECTOR

POWER PLANT

NO. & MODEL .... (2) TJ7
MFR. .... WRIGHT AERO.

2 IN AIRPLANE

RATINGS

	S.L.S. THRUST (LB)
COMBAT*	17,400
MILITARY	12,000
NORMAL	

*WITH AFTERBURNER

ORDNANCE

1 - 4,000# BOMB

National Archives, RG 72

TABULATED PERFORMANCE SUMMARY

Model			594	594-A	594-1	594-2
Engine in Return Component			One J40θ	One TJ7	One TJ7	Two TJ7
Engine in External Store			Two J40θ	Two TJ7	One TJ7	None
Wing Planform			45° Sweep	45° Sweep	45° Sweep	Low Aspect Ratio Swept Wing
Composite Airplane	Take-off Weight	(lb.)	100,000	100,000	60,000	64,000
	Target Weight*	(lb.)	47,606	47,806	30,670	33,912
	Fuel, Total	(lb.)	59,522	59,181	34,784	38,902
	Bomb Load	(lb.)	10,000	10,000	4,000	4,000
	Wing Area	(sq.ft.)	600	600	380	609
	Span	(ft.)	38.75	38.75	38.75	35
	High Speed at 40,000 ft.** (Target Weight)	(knots/Mach No.)	1015 (1.76)	1000 (1.74)	952 (1.66)	868 (1.51)
	High Speed at 50,000 ft.** (Target Weight)	(knots/Mach No.)	944 (1.64)	978 (1.70)	915 (1.59)	645 (1.12)
	Rate of Climb at Sea Level** (Take-off Weight)	(fpm)	31,800	18,200	19,220	20,160
	Stalling Speed (Take-off Weight)	(knots)	191	191	191	191
	Combat RadiusØ/Target Approach Distance at M=1.2	(n.mi.)	1700/570	1700/1000	1700/550	1700/430
	Combat RadiusØ/Target Approach Distance at M = 1.2	(n.mi.)	1400/700	1700/1000	1413/713	1306/606
	Combat RadiusØ/Target Approach Distance at High SpeedØØ	(n.mi.)	1700/420	1700/650	1700/450	1700/350
	Combat RadiusØ/Target Approach Distance at High SpeedØØ	(n.mi.)	1300/600	1486/786	1354/654	1224/524
	High SpeedØØ for Target Approach	(Mach No.)	1.58	1.63	1.47	1.39
Return Component	Initial Weight	(lb)	18,595	18,575	16,385	25,214
	Fuel	(lb)	4370	4240	3910	7230
	Wing Area	(sq.ft.)	300	300	300	609
	Span	(ft.)	38.75	38.75	38.75	35
	Aspect Ratio		5.0	5.0	5.0	2.0
	High Speed at Sea Level	(knots/Mach No.)	809 (1.22)	673 (1.02)	673 (1.02)	711 (1.08)
	High Speed at 40,000 ft.	(knots/Mach No.)	869 (1.51)	856 (1.49)	862 (1.50)	976 (1.70)
	High Speed at 50,000 ft.	(knots/Mach No.)	765 (1.33)	829 (1.44)	834 (1.45)	967 (1.68)
	Rate of Climb at 40,000 ft.	(fpm)	12,840	14,860	17,150	41,390
	Rate of Climb at 50,000 ft.	(fpm)	6370	8170	9700	24,410
	Stalling Speed at Landing Weightψ	(knots)	103	103	96	102

θ Estimated future J40 having sea level military static thrust of 11,000 lb. (Ref. 1)
* Take-off weight less fuel to target (reserve fuel at target included in target weight).
** Military plus afterburning thrust for all engines.
Ø Combat radius problem defined on page .
ØØ High speed with normal plus afterburning thrust for one engine, military plus afterburning thrust for all other engines.
ψ Less all fuel except reserve fuel.

National Archives, RG 72

Above: Table summarizing the key physical and performance characteristics for the Douglas Model 594 series of studies.

Right: Artist's impression of the Douglas Model 594-2 in flight by R.G. Smith. This view emphasizes the cleanliness of the design relative to the other Model 594 studies.

National Archives, RG 72

CHAPTER 14 — *Douglas Santa Monica Model 1186*

Douglas Santa Monica's approach to the Special Attack competition was similar to that of its El Segundo counterpart, employing a small piloted parasite aircraft atop a large expendable missile for each of its Model 1186 studies. However, these studies definitely showed more influence from the work conducted on the Douglas Model 499C, better known as the X-3 Stiletto. Both the piloted and expendable components generally had high fineness ratios, low-aspect ratio wings, and air intakes very similar to those of the X-3. Overall, Douglas Santa Monica's Model 1186 studies were among the most radical and futuristic studies known to have been submitted to BuAer for the Special Attack competition.

Submitted on October 27, 1948, the Douglas Santa Monica proposal followed the general concepts of the OS-115 mission requirements, but no attempt was made to meet the detailed requirements listed in the specification. Designated Model 1186, the study was made with a view toward increasing speed and allowing other aspects of performance to be reduced accordingly. The experience and knowledge gained in the intensive studies conducted for the design of the X-3 supersonic research aircraft (then known as the Douglas Model 499C/Project MX-656) heavily influenced the design of their proposal. Since it was desired to provide a cruising speed that would be competitive with missiles and the fastest fighter aircraft that would likely be operating at the time the Model 1186 became available, and since the knowledge derived from the X-3 project was based primarily on a Mach number of 2.0, this speed was chosen as the cruise Mach number of the airplane. Various arrangements were studied and the combat radius as defined in OS-115 was determined as a function of the percentage of the radius flown at Mach 2.0.

From the study performed by Douglas Santa Monica, it was concluded that a large expendable aircraft carrying the bomb load and a small escape airplane (i.e., a parasite airplane) was best suited for the requirements. The combat radius with a takeoff weight of 100,000 lbs was about 500 nm with 20% of the distance flown at a Mach 2.0. Altitude over the target was approximately 54,000 ft. By overloading the airplane to 150,000 lbs., the radius was increased to 1,010 miles, with 20% of the radius at Mach 2.0. However, more carrier deck run had to be provided than was then available after the catapult run in this overloaded condition.

Four arrangements were considered for the Model 1186. These designs were all heavily influenced by past research by Douglas for the development of the X-3. In each case, the vehicle was assumed to be made up of an expendable component and a crew escape

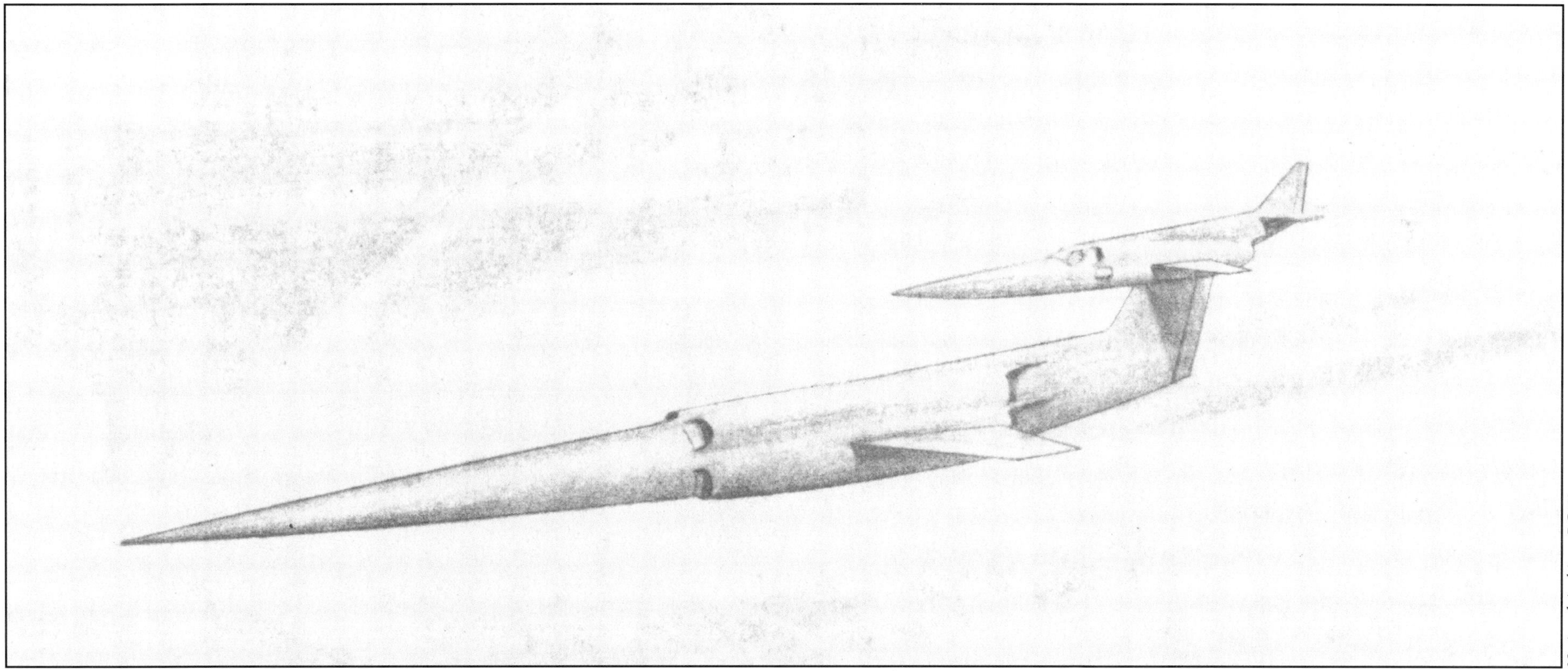

National Archives, RG 72

Above: Artist's impression of the Douglas Santa Monica Model 1186-A, which featured an escape vehicle not unlike the X-3 Stiletto mounted on the vertical fin of an expendable component, using the wings of the escape airplane as the horizontal tail of the combination. This artwork was part of the Standard Aircraft Characteristics charts submitted with the proposal to BuAer.

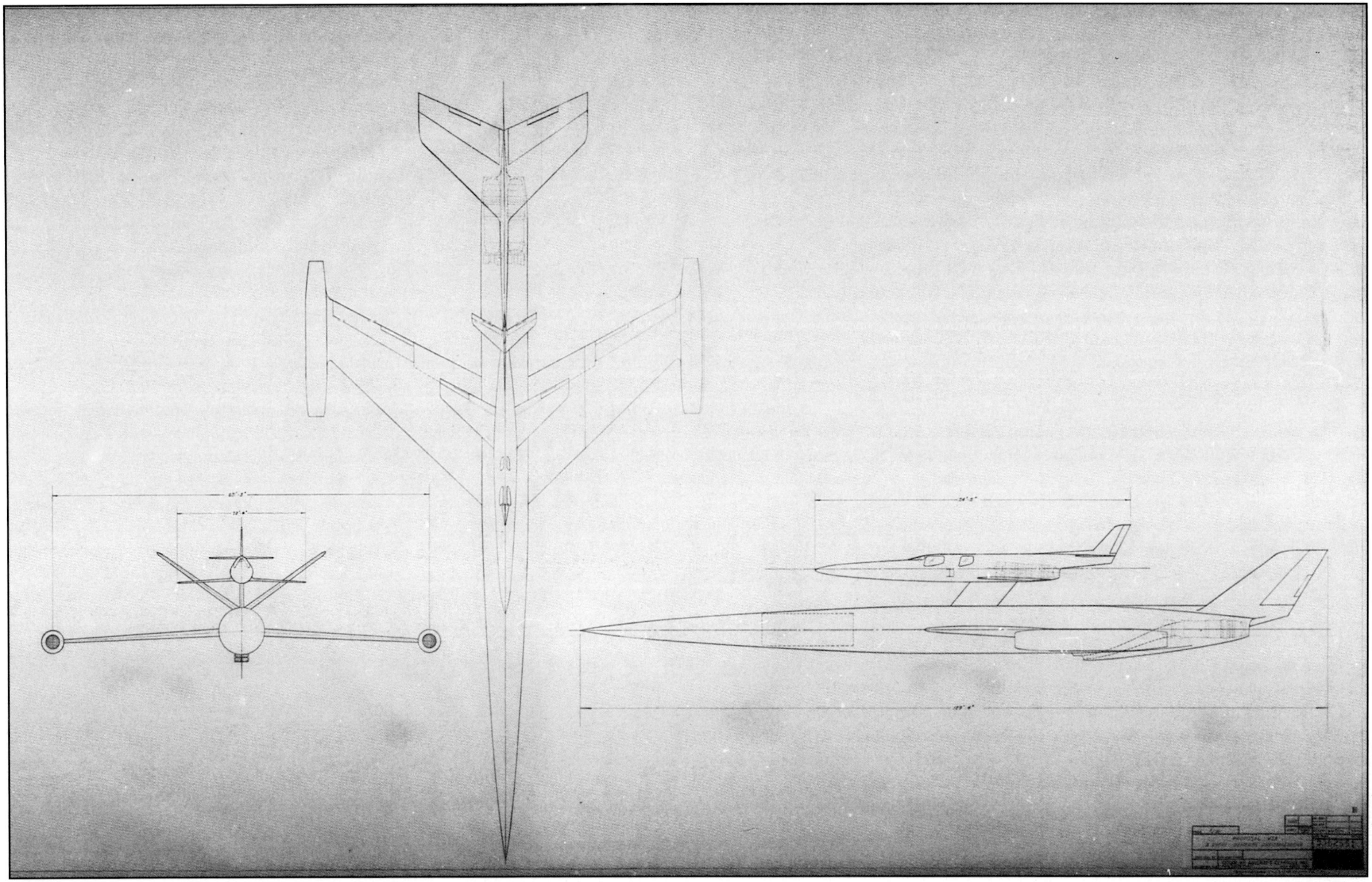

National Archives, RG 72

Above: The earliest known Douglas Special Attack configuration study, designated simply as the Model 1186. With its prominently swept wing, the escape vehicle bears only a minor resemblance to the X-3. The expendable component appears to be powered by four Westinghouse XJ40-WE-10 engines.

component.

The escape component was essentially the same for each design. It was powered by a single Westinghouse X24C-10 engine, incorporated tricycle landing gear, and an arresting hook for carrier landings. Escape provisions for the two-man crew were provided with downward seat ejection. The pilot maneuvered the expendable component by means of a remotely controlled automatic pilot system. The bombardier operated the radar sighting equipment located in the expendable component by remote control. Only the minimum amount of equipment was located in the crew escape vehicle.

The four arrangements considered were to be launched from a catapult, utilizing a cradle or dolly instead of normal landing gear, and would have required assisted thrust

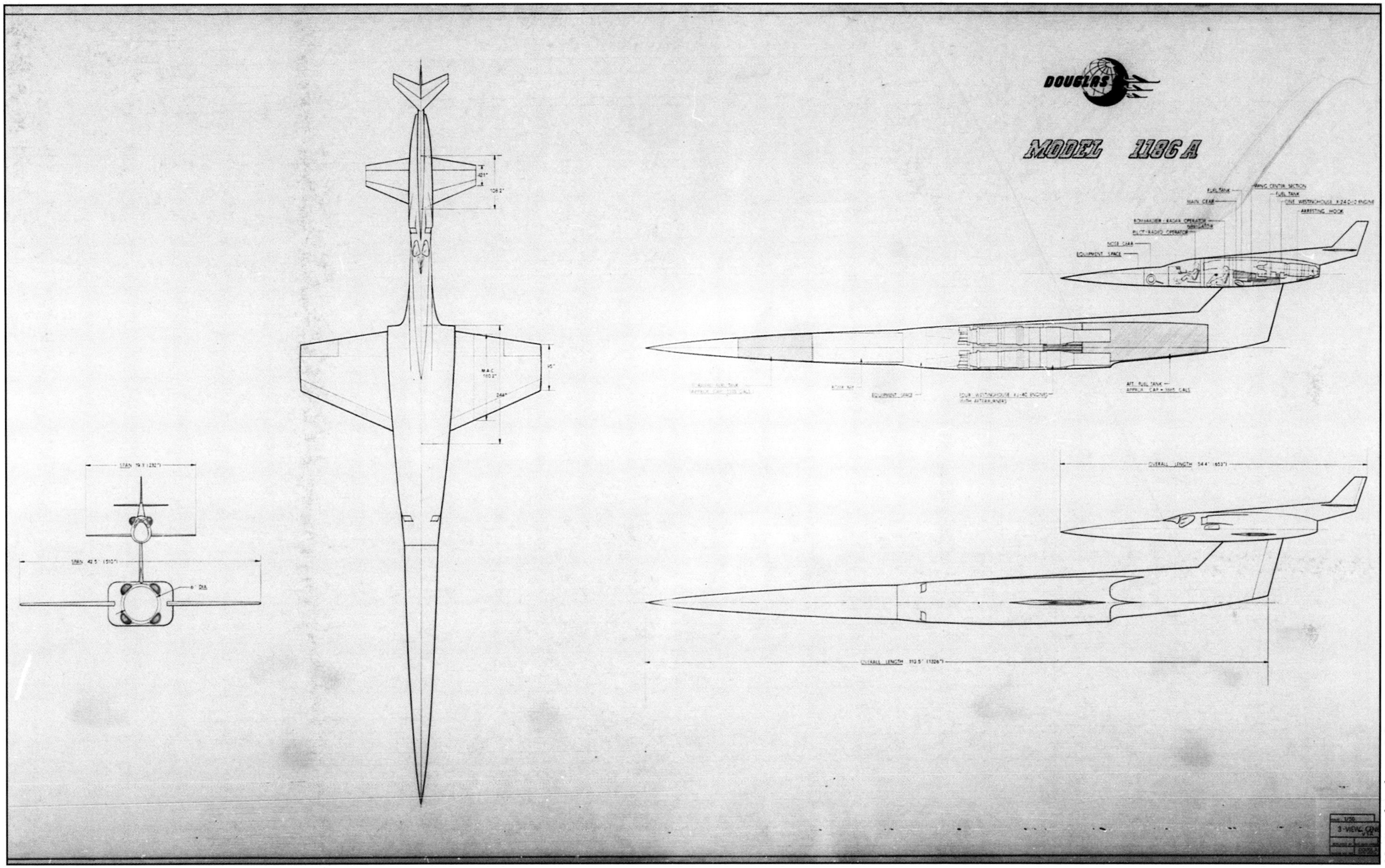

National Archives, RG 72

Above: The Model 1186-A appears to have been Douglas's preferred design among the four Model 1186 configurations officially submitted to BuAer. Structural weight was saved by using the wings of the escape airplane as the horizontal tail of the composite aircraft.

for takeoff when launched from a CVA class carrier. A basic description of each arrangement follows.

Model 1186-A

This study featured the escape vehicle mounted on the vertical fin of the expendable component, using the wings of the escape airplane as the horizontal tail of the combination. The bomb compartment was located far forward in the nose section, and fuel was

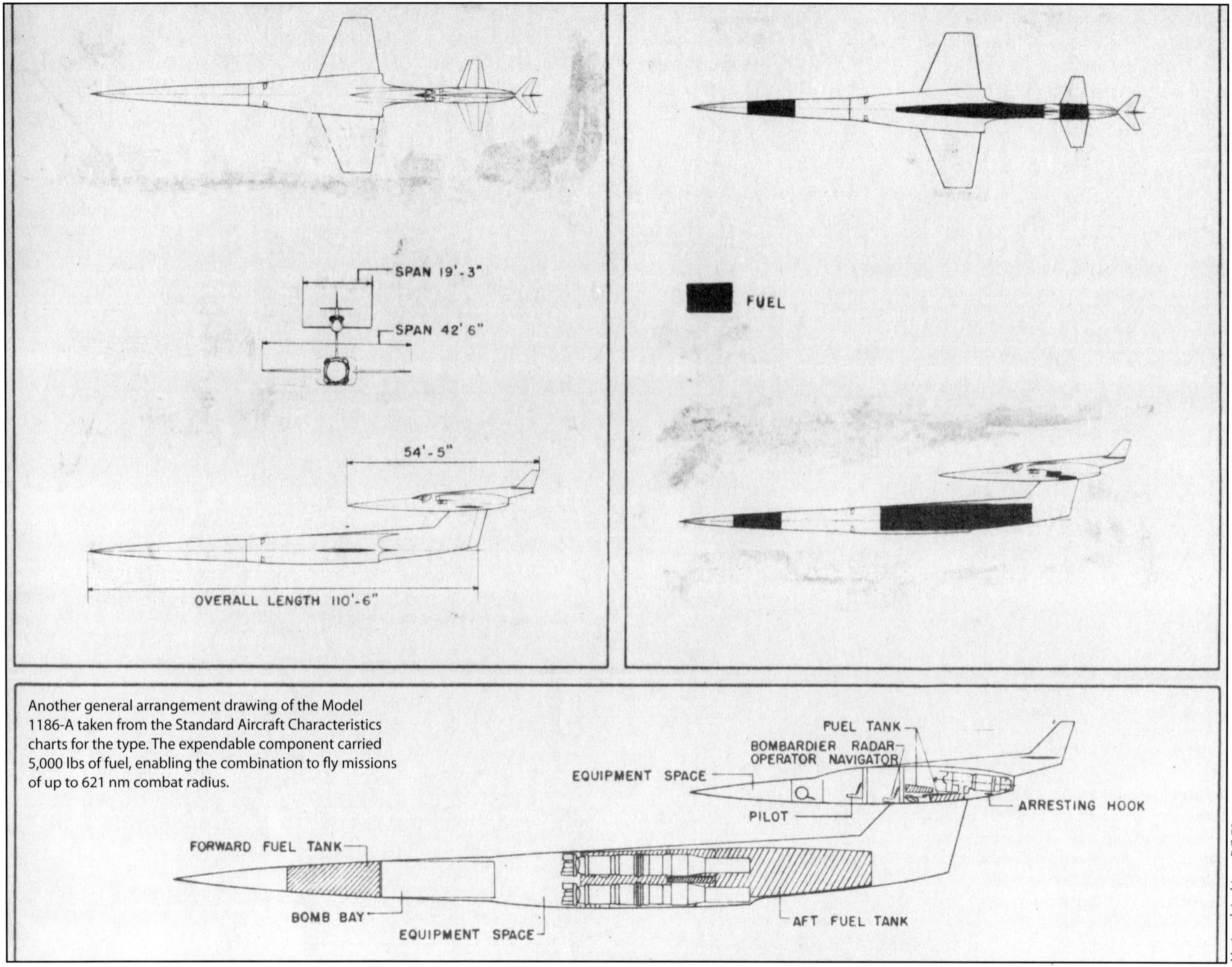

Another general arrangement drawing of the Model 1186-A taken from the Standard Aircraft Characteristics charts for the type. The expendable component carried 5,000 lbs of fuel, enabling the combination to fly missions of up to 621 nm combat radius.

National Archives, RG 72

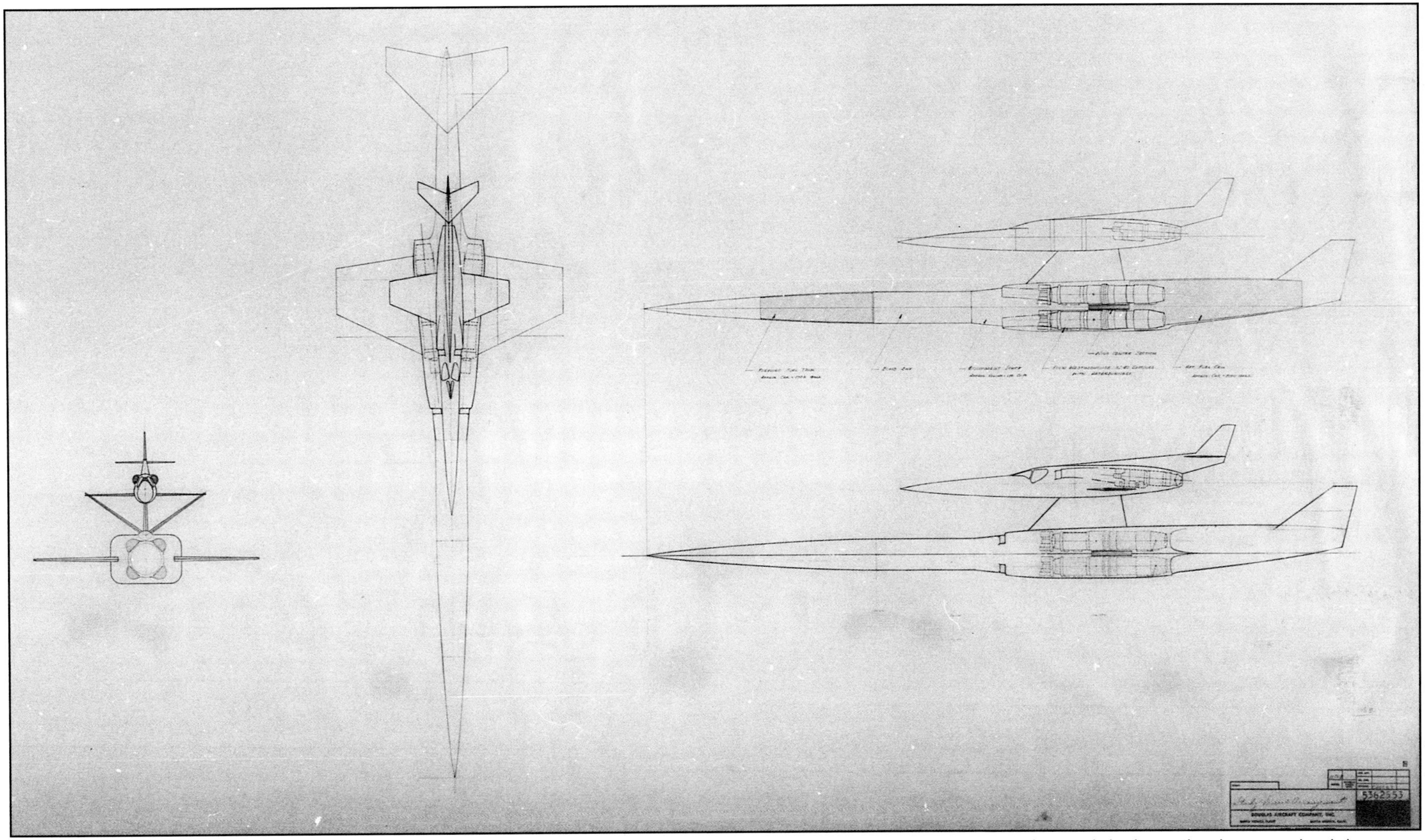

National Archives, RG 72

Above: An early drawing of the Model 1186-B, which featured the escape airplane mounted atop the expendable component on a pylon. The missile had a V-tail and a tremendously long nose that housed the bomb bay and part of the fuel load.

disposed fore and aft to maintain proper CG location. The four Westinghouse XJ40-WE-10 engines with afterburners were located in the fuselage. The inclined ramp at the air intakes served to produce oblique shock waves to reduce the stress Mach number ahead of the normal shockwave at the intake. These provisions were made so that when the airflow was reduced to subsonic velocity at the intake, it was achieved with as weak a normal shockwave as possible to minimize ram losses.

The Model 1186-A appears to have been the study Douglas saw the most potential in, as the company went to the trouble of performing detailed performance calculations for it in the Standard Aircraft Characteristics charts submitted to the Navy as part of the proposal.

Model 1186-B

The Model 1186-B was similar to the Model 1186-A except that the escape airplane was mounted on a pylon above the wing of the expendable component. Stability and control was maintained by the use of a V-type tail, which also allowed continuous opera-

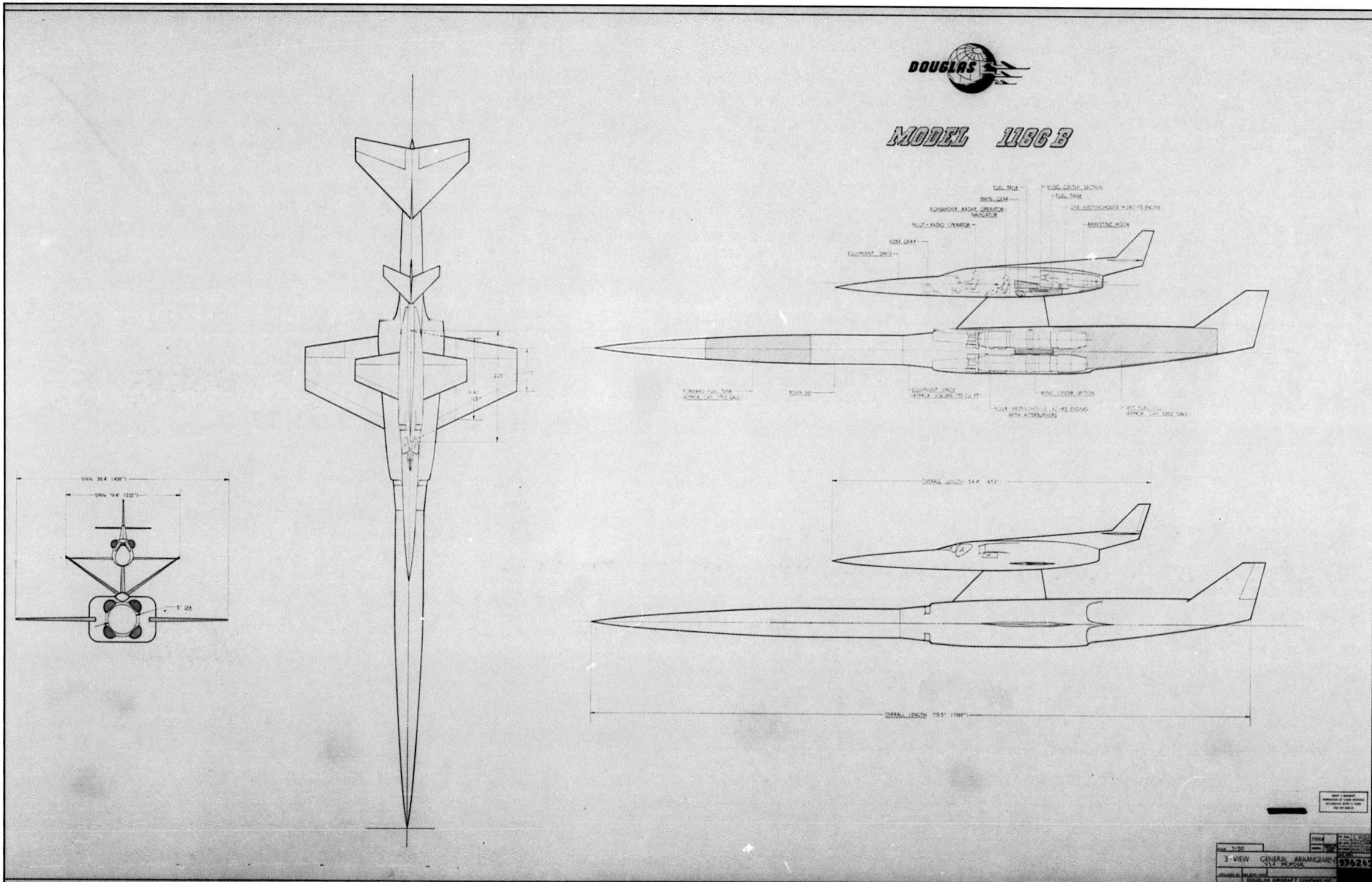

National Archives, RG 72

Above: Finalized general arrangement drawing of the Model 1186-B submitted to the Navy. While quite similar to the preliminary sketch, this blueprint features more detail in the inboard profile of the escape vehicle, as well as small windows below the intake for the second crewman. Crew accommodations would have likely been very cramped.

tion of the engine in the escape component. In this arrangement, both the wings of the escape and expendable components contributed to the lift, allowing a small reduction in the wing area of the expendable unit.

Model 1186-C

The "C" version utilized the pylon to house two of the XJ-40 engines. The other two engines were mounted in tip nacelles. The double wedge in the leading edge of the pylon

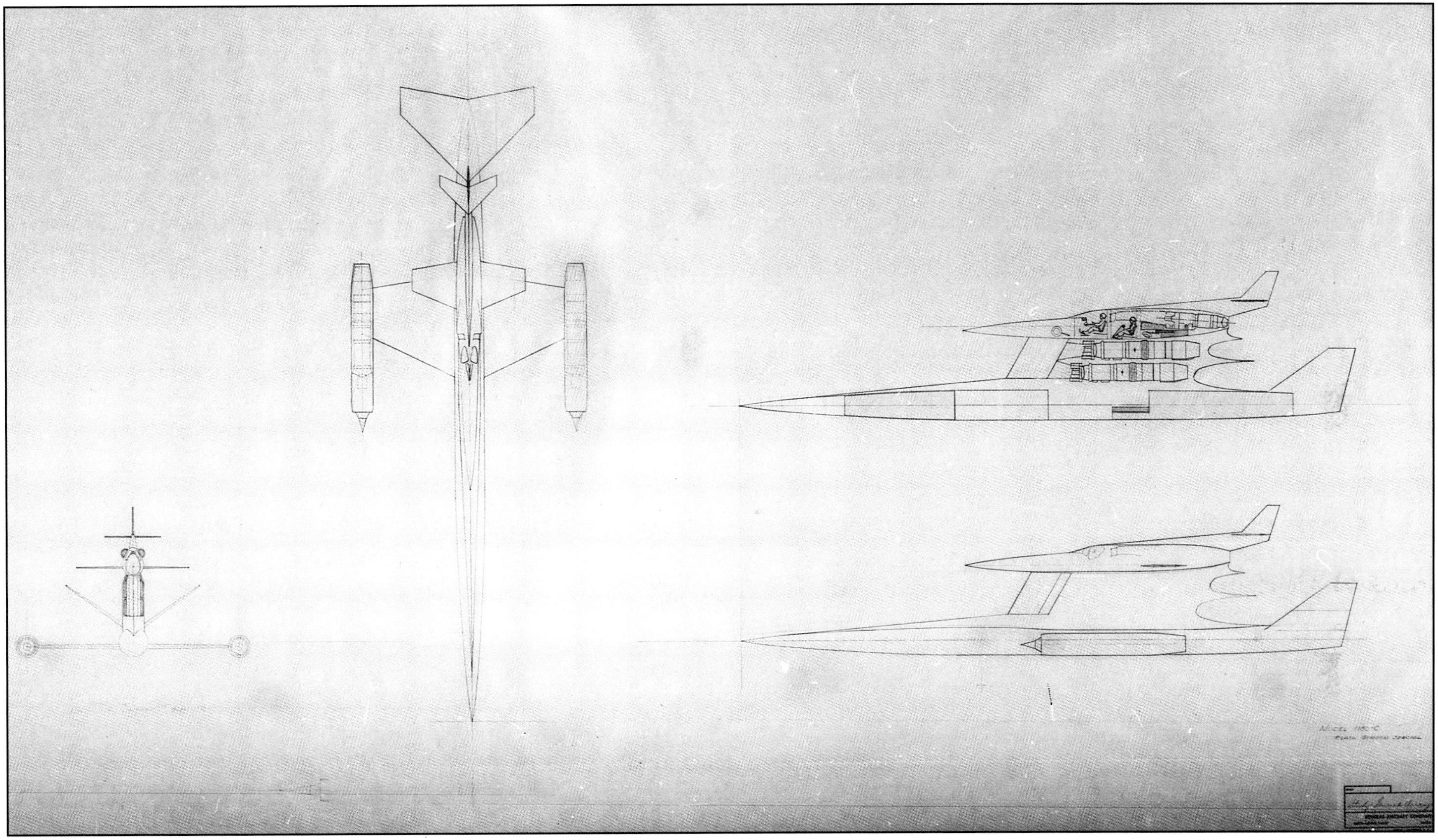

National Archives, RG 72

Above: The most unusual looking study in the VSA series was the Model 1186-C, shown here in this preliminary drawing of the type. The expendable component of the Model 1186-C was powered by two XJ-40 turbojets stacked inside a large dorsal pylon with a double wedge air intake and by two additional XJ-40s on the wing tips. The drawing is labeled amusingly as "The Flash Gordon Special" in the lower right hand corner. This baroquely futuristic aircraft would have certainly been at home in Alex Raymond's classic sci-fi comic strip!

replaced the ramp intakes used with the buried installations. The conical shapes served the same purpose on the tip-mounted units. The fuel, bomb, and equipment were disposed in the fuselage of the expendable component in a manner similar to Models 1186-A and –B. Some reduction in fuselage length was permitted by the engine relocation.

Model 1186-D

The final study presented an arrangement wherein the escape component was partially submerged into the expendable unit. The high wing and straight leading edge on the expendable component was fitted against the trailing edge of the escape airplane. In this version, positive mechanical ejection of the escape unit was incorporated, and its engine could not be used during flight to target. Two of the engines of the expendable compo-

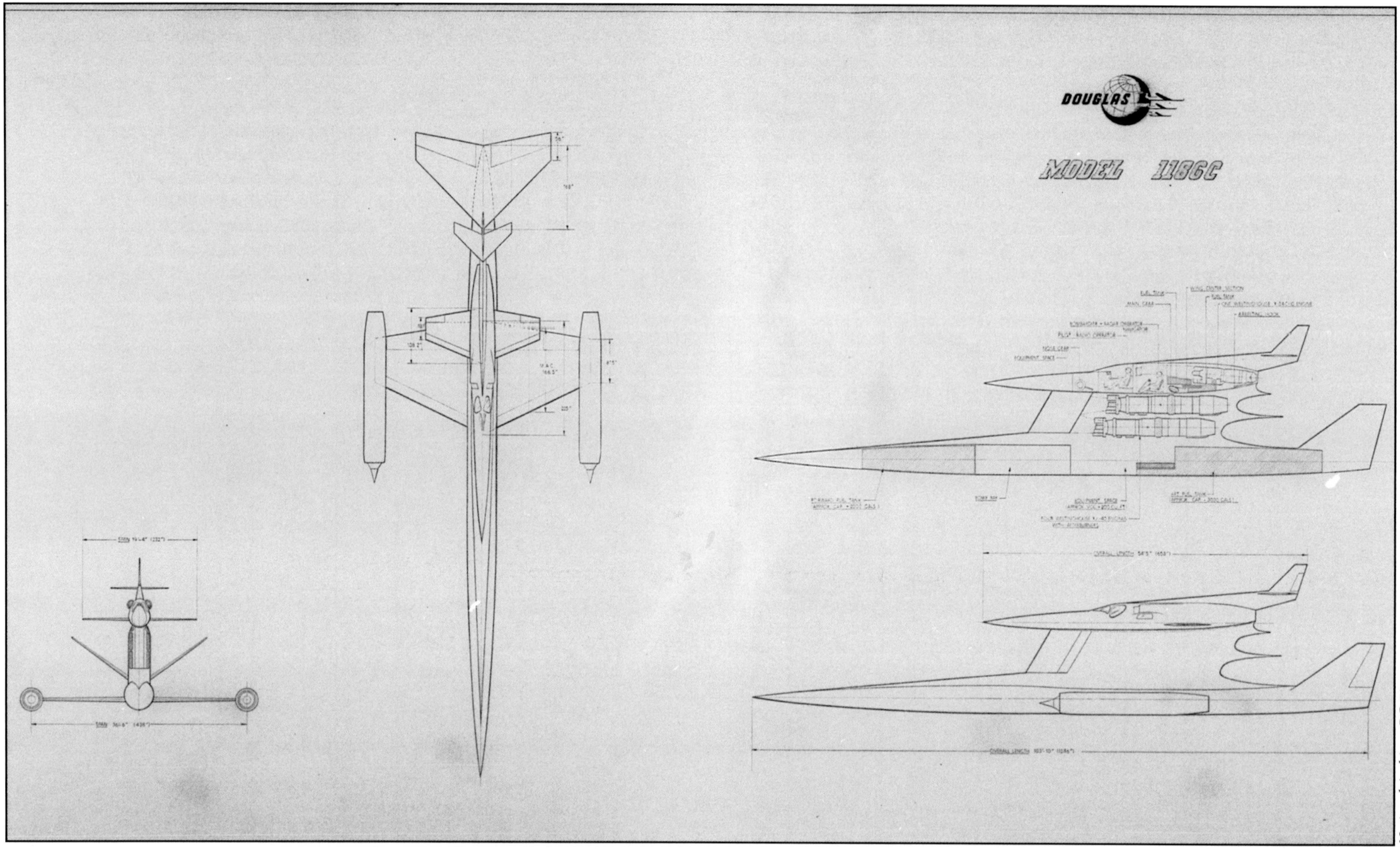

National Archives, RG 72

Above: The finalized drawing of the Model 1186-C as officially submitted to BuAer. The aft edge of the central pylon retained the pronounced scalloped effect present in the original drawing, which was presumably incorporated to improve the aerodynamics of this bizarre composite aircraft.

nents were in tip nacelles, and two were mounted aft in the fuselage. The fuel, equipment and bomb were disposed in the fuselage for proper CG location.

Conclusion

It was not expected that a normal bomb run would be made at the speeds considered in the proposal. The arrangements presented did not incorporate bomb bay doors or other normal bombing equipment. It was conceived that the expendable unit could become an aimed missile or that the entire component could be broken up after the escape vehicle had disengaged so that the rate of descent of the bomb could be reduced and additional escape time for the crew provided. Douglas noted that tactical use of such a weapon as the Model 1186 would have been governed by the development of bomb directing and control equipment.

In the designs presented, the visual sighting component had been eliminated, based

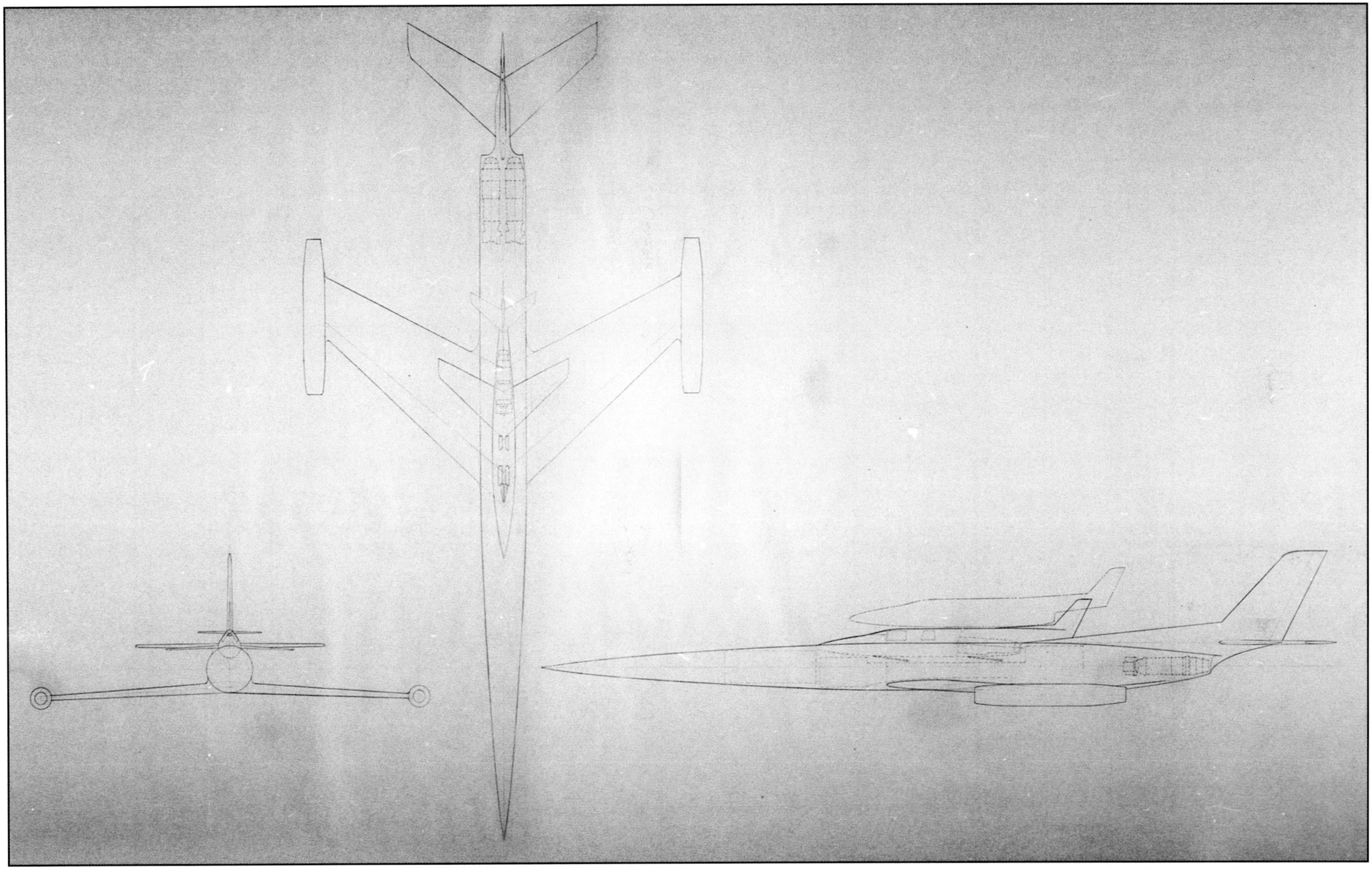

National Archives, RG 72

Above: The Model 1186-D rounded out the configuration studies submitted to the Navy in the Special Attack competition; this blueprint depicts the initial configuration. The vehicle had the escape airplane partially submerged into the upper fuselage of the expendable component, reducing the drag of the overall combination. The escape airplane is quite different from the others in the series, most of which appeared virtually identical to the X-3 Stiletto.

on assumed improvements in the radar equipment. Location of search antenna in the area of the air intake ramp limited the forward range of the radar. At the time of the proposal, studies were underway to determine the effect on the drag and high speed for a modified nose section to provide a more suitable location for the antenna.

Douglas Santa Monica's VSA studies were truly radical, sacrificing all other attributes in the name of speed. While probably impractical from an operational standpoint, they were nonetheless beautiful expressions of high performance aircraft design.

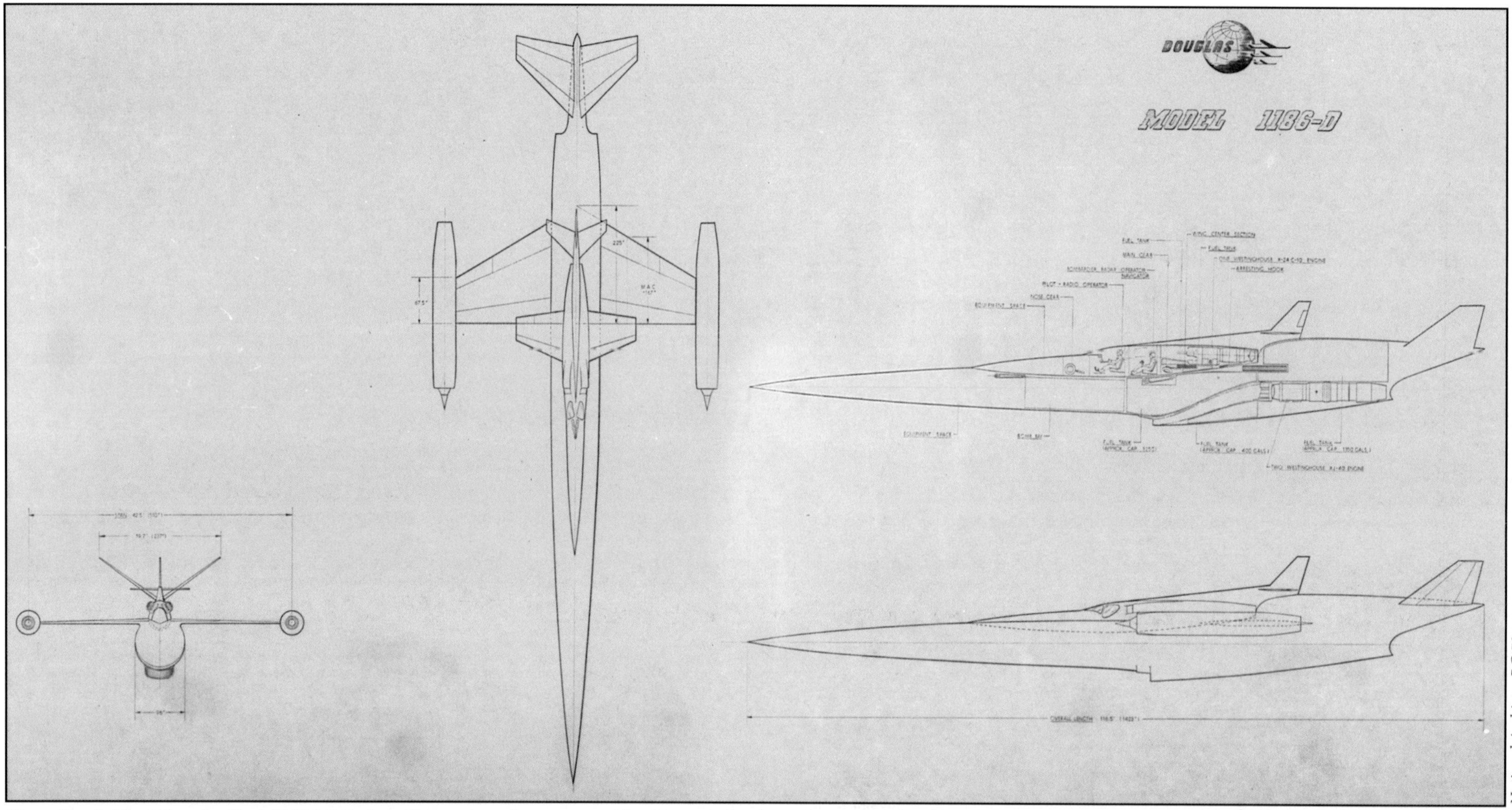

National Archives, RG 72

Above: The finished Douglas Model 1186-D design. This study underwent considerable evolution from the original sketch on the previous page, the main similarity being the submerged position of the piloted component into the upper fuselage of the expendable. This arrangement prevented the engine of the escape airplane from being used until the missile was released.

Douglas Santa Monica Model 1186 VSA Studies - Basic Dimensions

	Escape Airplane		*Expendable Component*		
Model No.	**Span (ft)**	**Length (ft)**	**Span (ft)**	**Length (ft)**	**Comments**
1186	22.33	54.42	65.25	129.33	Span of expendable measured from centers of turbojet nacelles mounted on wing tips
1186-A (Final)	19.33	54.40	42.50	110.50	
1186-B (Preliminary & Final)	19.33	54.40	36.33	113.50	
1186-C (Preliminary & Final)	19.33	54.42	36.50	103.83	Span of expendable measured from centers of turbojet nacelles mounted on wing tips
1186-D (Preliminary)	22.17*	47.65*	64.97*	138.00*	Span of expendable measured from centers of turbojet nacelles mounted on wing tips
1186-D (Final)	19.33*	54.40*	42.50	118.50	Span of expendable measured from centers of turbojet nacelles mounted on wing tips

*Estimated

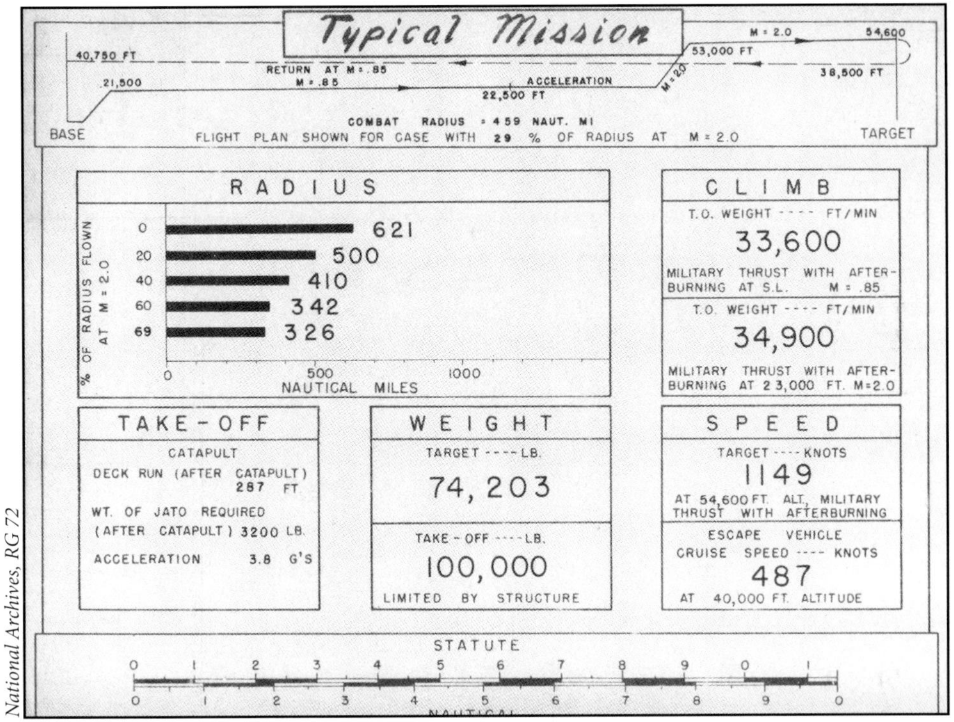

National Archives, RG 72

POWER PLANT

Expendable Component
Mfgr. . . Westinghouse
Model(4). XJ40-10 with after-burners

Escape Component
Mfgr. . . Westinghouse
Model(1). X24C-10

Mission and Description

The Model 1186 is a high speed, special attack type airplane designed as a single mission composite weapon. It is made up of an expendable component housing the bomb load, and the majority of the engines, fuel, and equipment. There is an attached escape component for the crew of two. The composite airplane is launched from a cradle or dolly from the deck of a CVB class carrier. Landing gear and arresting hook are provided only in the escape vehicle. In this version, the wing of the escape component serves as the horizontal tail of the composite aircraft.

The modified diamond shape airfoil has been used in the thin wings of both components consistent with the supersonic speed range of the airplane.

WEIGHTS

Loading	Weight (Lbs.)	Limit L.F.
Expendable Component:		
Wt. Empty	53,253	
Basic	62,853	
Design	100,000	2.25
Max. T.O.	100,000 plus launching gear & jato.	
Escape Component:		
Wt. Empty	7,652	
Basic	8,340	
Design	9,500	2.67
Max. T.O.	9,500	

ENGINE RATINGS

	Jet Thrust (Pounds)
XJ40	
Military	10,000
Normal	9,000
X24C-10	
Military	5,200
Normal	4,700

FUEL

Location	Capacity (Gals.)
Expendable Component:	
Fwd. Fuse.	1,115
Aft. Fuse.	3,885

DIMENSIONS

	Expend.	Escape
Span	42'6"	19'4"
Length	110'6"	54'4"
Wing Area (Sq.Ft.)	600	125
Sweepback	0° at 75% Chord	
Thickness Ratio	4.5%	4.5%

BOMBS

No.	Size	Type
1	10,000#	Special Purpose

National Archives, RG 72

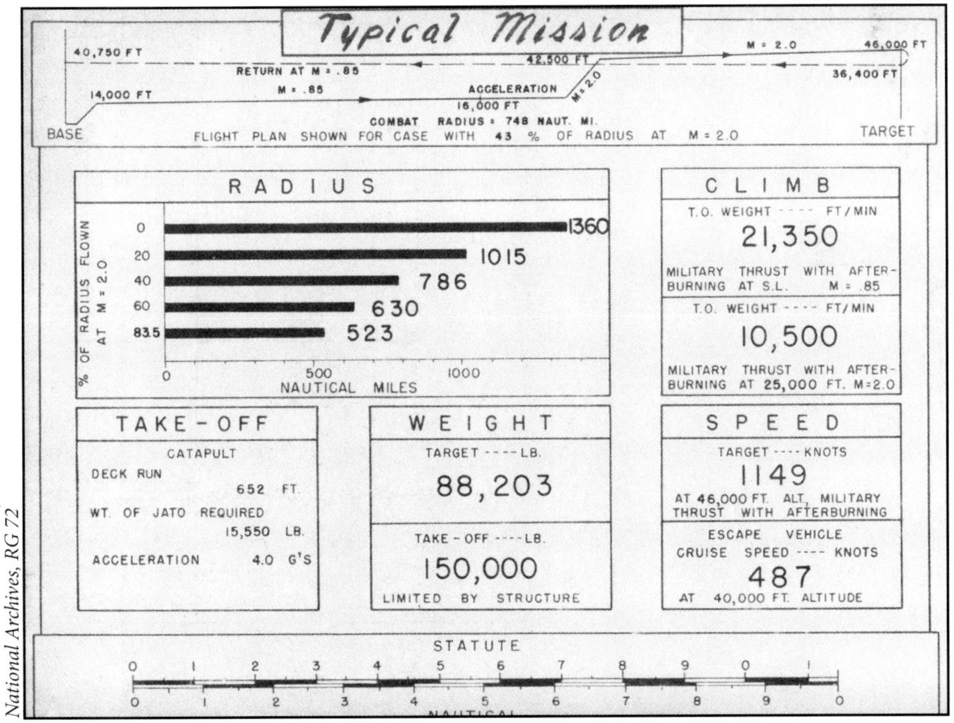

National Archives, RG 72

NOTES

1. Radius Formula

All radius values include fuel and distance allowances as follows:

Accelerate from take-off speed to Mach No. = 0.85.

Climb to optimum subsonic cruising altitude at a Mach No. = 0.85.

Cruise at Mach No. = 0.85 at optimum subsonic cruise altitude.

Accelerate from Mach No. = 0.85 to Mach No. = 2.0

Climb to the optimum supersonic cruising altitude at a Mach No. = 2.0

Cruise at Mach No. = 2.0 to target at optimum supersonic cruise altitude. The expendable vehicle is dived into the target at Mach No. = 2.0, and the escape component returns to home base at a Mach No. of 0.85 at its optimum cruising altitude.

For all radius values the reserve fuel is 5% of the total fuel carried. In addition, the specific fuel consumption is increased 5%.

The radius shown with 0% of the radius flown at M = 2.0 includes the acceleration to a Mach No. of 2.0. At that instant the airplane is over the target.

The radius case showing the highest percent of the radius flown at M = 2.0 is a case in which all range is flown at M = 2.0 except for the acceleration distance to M = 0.85, climb to the subsonic cruise altitude, and the acceleration at that altitude to M = 2.0.

2. Take-off

(a) 100,000 lb. take-off weight airplane.

The take-off data assume the use of the X9HD catapult and jato assist from a CVB carrier for the 100,000 lb. weight case. The jato thrust is the thrust required to accelerate from the catapult speed to a speed of V_{stall} + 10 knots on a 90°F hot day at sea level with a 25 knot headwind and an available deck length of 287 ft. (ref: BuAer Sk. No. S.1. 1142 dtd July 21, 1948)

(b) 150,000 lb. take-off weight airplane.

The take-off data assume a jato assisted take-off without use of catapult. The deck length quoted is the deck length required for the airplane assuming the entire take-off is jato assisted and the major portion of the deck length is available for take-off. A maximum acceleration of 4 g's is assumed.

National Archives, RG 72

This Page: Standard Aircraft Characteristics charts for the Model 1186-A. A notional 150,000 lb. version with a superior mission radius is mentioned; this large and heavy aircraft would have been quite a challenge to operate from a carrier, even one as large as the USS *United States*.

CHAPTER 15 — *Fairchild Model M-130*

The Fairchild Model M-130 Special Attack proposal was quite similar to its previous M-128 Heavy Attack design. The chief differences consisted of a revised power plant installation with 8 Westinghouse XJ46-WE-2 engines; an integral greenhouse canopy similar to that of the original M-121 designed for the Air Force; removal of the inner pair of vertical tail surfaces; and deletion of the auxiliary wing. Judging by the surviving documents, substantially less effort went into the Fairchild Model M-130 proposal than into the M-128, as only a pair of blueprints and few basic reports were submitted to the Navy describing it.

In the Model M-130 Detail Specification submitted to BuAer on November 4, 1948,

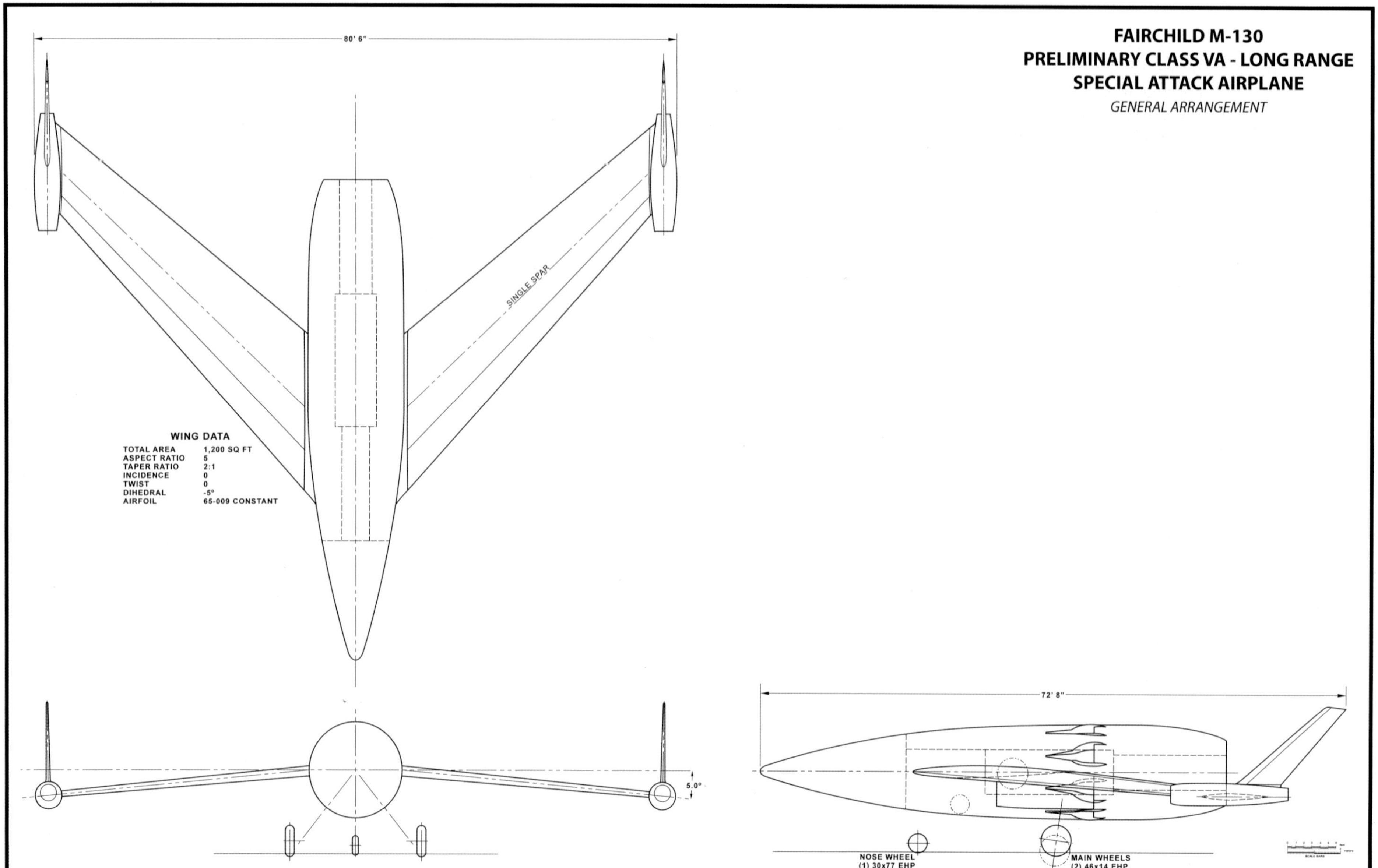

TRACED FROM FAIRCHILD BLUEPRINT P130-000 DATED NOVEMBER 4, 1948

Fairchild put forward an airplane design which it claimed to be capable of delivering a large bomb load at long range while traveling at higher altitudes and higher continuous cruise speeds than had, up till that point, been considered practicable for conventional types of aircraft. The speed and altitude attained by this airplane were comparable to that of a guided missile, and the presence of a crew with navigational instruments and bomb director equipment permitted much greater accuracy while approaching the target than was possible with pilotless aircraft. Inasmuch as no part of this proposed aircraft was discarded during its mission (a feature that was of importance to those in BuAer concerned about cost), the airplane could have landed and been prepared for additional flights with the extent of maintenance being no greater than other turbojet airplanes of this size. The crew compartment of the M-130 was pressurized, and ejectable seats were provided for emergency exit of the two man crew from the airplane. The M-130 would have been capable of being launched with JATO from a CVA class carrier. It would have also been possible to adapt the airplane for use in training and land-based operations.

The gross weight of the M-130 was 100,000 lbs; the useful load was 52,055 lbs; and the weight empty for this airplane was 47,945 lbs. Total wing area, including elevons and horizontal control surfaces, was 1,200 sq ft. Total vertical control surface area was 100 sq ft.

General Dimensions

Wing span	77.5 ft
Wing taper ratio	2:1
Wing sweep back	45° at 25% chord

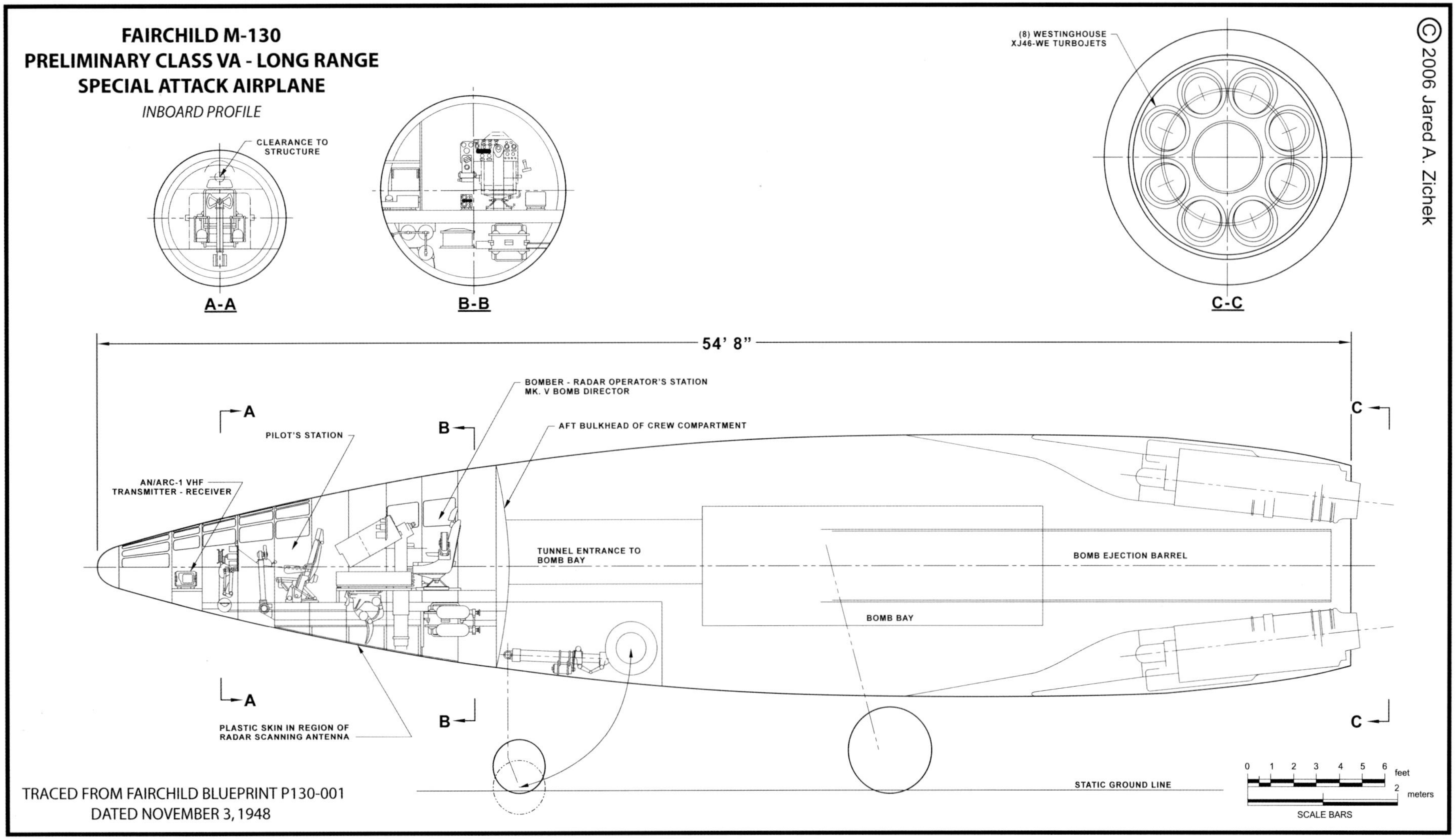

Wing section	NACA 65009
Fuselage length	58 ft
Height over vertical control surfaces	21 ft
Main wheel diameter	46 in
Nose wheel size	30 x 7.7 EHP

Wing Group

The wing arrangement was a mid-wing with a 45° sweep back along the 25% chord line. The wing was comprised of two inner panels and two outer panels. The inner panels each mounted a horizontal control surface on the trailing edge and contained fuel cell provisions. Each outer panel mounted an elevon along the trailing edge.

Tail Group

No tail group was provided; however, elevator control was obtained by use of the horizontal control surfaces and directional control was obtained by vertical control surfaces located at the tip of each wing surface.

Body Group

The fuselage was of a projectile shape and constructed of aluminum alloy. Suitable provisions were made within the fuselage for a pressurized crew compartment, retractable tricycle landing gear, engine compartment, fuel compartment, bomb bay and necessary equipment.

Surface Control System

The surface control system featured the use of power boost.

Propulsion

The power plant consisted of ten XJ46-WE-2 turbojet engines, eight arranged peripherally within the aft end of the fuselage and on each wing tip. The XJ46-WE-2, Westinghouse Model X24C10, engines were in accordance with Westinghouse Specification WAGT X24C10-2B dated April 7, 1948. The rating of each engine was revised on the basis of BuAer Report DR-1045 with Amendment No. 1 dated August 1948, was estimated to be as follows:

Takeoff	5,166 lbs static thrust at 10,100 RPM at sea level
Military	5,166 lbs static thrust at 10,100 RPM at sea level
Normal	4,699 lbs static thrust at ? RPM at sea level

Fuel System

The arrangement of the fuel system provided for approximately 3,500 gallons of fuel in the fuselage just forward of the engine compartment, and for 3,400 gallons of fuel in the wing. All fuel was contained in bladder-type interconnected cells.

Other Features

A hydraulic system was provided for power operation of the main wheel brakes. A suitable electrical system was to have been provided for the ignition, lighting, electronic, and instrument system; and for operation of the landing gear, arresting gear, power boost, and other miscellaneous installations requiring actuators. Suitable VHF equipment was to have been installed. Suitable ejections seats were provided for each crew member.

Provision was to have been made for attaching JATO units as required to assist in taking off from the deck of a carrier. Fairchild did not include the weight of this installation in the normal weight empty. Catapulting provision was not required.

The crew consisted of a pilot/radio operator and a bomber/radar operator/navigator weighing a total of 400 lbs. The M-130 was to have carried 6,900 gals of fuel and 20 gals of oil. Armament consisted of a single 10,000 lb bomb load installation.

FAIRCHILD M-130

T.O. Gross Wt.	Lbs.	100,000
Bomb Load	Lbs.	10,000
Fuel	Gals.	6,900
Stall Speed	Kts.	157
Operating Altitude	Ft.	40,000
Vcruise out @ Op. Alt.		650 N. Mi. @ M =1.1
Vcruise back @ Op. Alt.		650 N. Mi. @ M =.92
Combat Radius	N. Mi.	1350
Crew		2
Power Plant		10XJ46-WE-2
Wing Span/Area	Ft./Sq.Ft.	80'6"/1200
Overall Length/Sweepback	Ft.In./°	72'8"/45°
Special Features	8 engines grouped peripherally within the aft end of the fuselage and 1 on each wing tip. Bomb is ejected aft through tube in center of fuselage. Airplane has no horizontal tail. Twin vertical tails at wing tips. There is no expendable component.	

National Archives, RG 72

CHAPTER 16 — *Martin Model 245*

Martin Aircraft Company took a completely different approach to the Special Attack competition, proposing a large delta wing aircraft that could operate from the water as a flying boat, from a carrier, or from a land base. Extracts from its lavish promotional brochure are reproduced in this chapter. Martin described its Model 245 as a new concept of airborne weapon which, in cooperation with other Naval units, would carry the attack to the heart of any aggressor. While definitely a unique and exciting concept, the questionable practicality and economy of the Model 245 likely played a big part in its failure.

Tactical Mission

Martin claimed that the Model 245 combined the speed and altitude of a guided missile with the range and accuracy of a piloted aircraft, having the ability to perform the mission outlined in OS-115. The particular virtue of the basic concept of this airplane, however, was found in its ability to perform not only this, but other types of missions in a variety of highly effective ways.

Such versatility was sought and designed into the Model 245 upon analysis of the practical methods available for the accomplishment of the primary bombing mission. In view of the great investment in time and resources necessary to perfect any aircraft for this mission, and considering the logistics involved in the manufacture and operation of such an airplane, Martin argued that it was desirable for the airplane to be versatile enough to initiate its attack in whatever manner was dictated by the governing tactical situation, and in addition, could effectively perform normal bombing or reconnaissance missions in a conventional manner.

The Model 245 fulfilled these requirements. For maximum range missions, it could have been used as an expendable airplane operating either from water or from an aircraft carrier. For shorter range missions, however, it would not have been expended; after initiating its attack from water or an aircraft carrier, it would have alighted back aboard the carrier or on land. This airplane also lent itself very simply to any type of testing or training operation.

Basically an efficient high speed long range airplane, the Model 245 was arranged to accommodate the installation of various types of launching and alighting components. The basic combinations of flight and launching components possible with the Model 245 design were assigned dash numbers for convenient identification. The combinations were as follows:

National Archives, RG 72

Above: Artist's impression of the Martin Model 245 basic flight component to which a droppable hull and floats or a droppable wheeled gear could be attached for maximum operational flexibility. The resemblance of the proposal to the British Avro Vulcan is noteworthy.

a. Model 245: Basic flight component containing provisions for attachment of a droppable hull and floats or a droppable wheeled gear.
b. Model 245-1: Composite airplane with droppable hull and auxiliary floats.
c. Model 245-2: Composite airplane with droppable wheeled takeoff gear.
d. Model 245-3: Testing and training configuration.
e. Model 245A: Model 245 modified for the installation of carrier landing and arresting gear.

Model 245-1 – Composite with Droppable Hull

The droppable hull used for staging flights or training. The hull was dropped after takeoff on combat missions with the flight component continuing at high speed.

Weights (lbs)	
Flight Component	100,000
Hull and Floats	11,635
JATO	10,080
Total Takeoff Weight	121,715

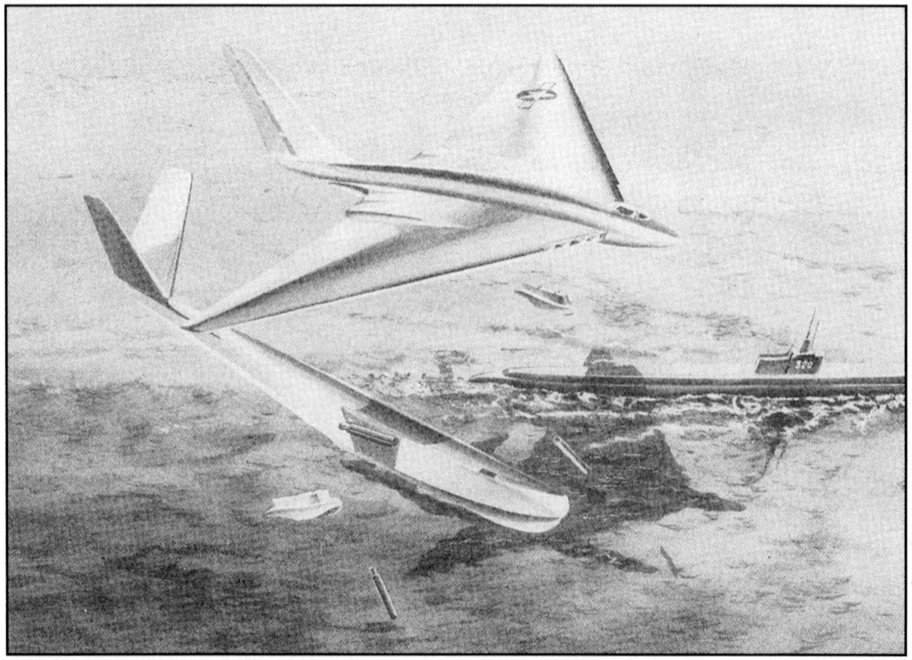

National Archives, RG 72

The Model 245-1 featured a droppable hull, enabling it to cooperate with submarines in a combination staging and combat mission. This eliminated the necessity of risking large aircraft carriers, and also made possible surprise attacks that could have been difficult to detect or intercept.

Model 245-2 – Composite with Droppable Gear

The droppable gear was used for takeoff from the carrier on combat missions. The gear was dropped immediately after takeoff.

Weights (lbs)	
Flight Component	100,000
Droppable Gear	3,890
JATO	5,040
Total Takeoff Weight	108,930

Model 245-3 – Testing and Training Configuration

This configuration featured a retractable tricycle gear used for any normal testing and training flights. This could have been combined with the Model 245-1.

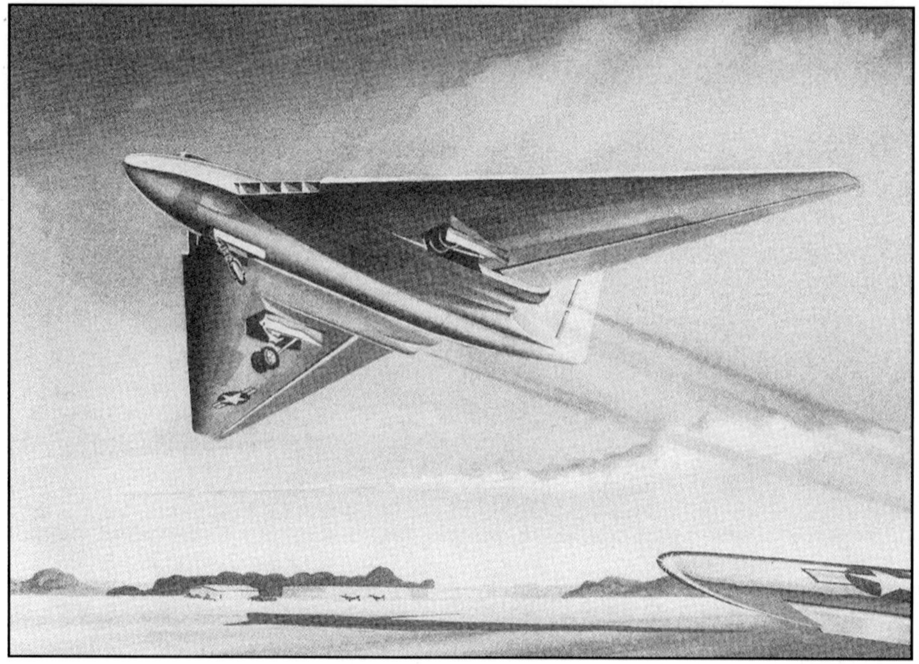

National Archives, RG 72

The Model 245-3 had a fully retractable tricycle landing gear for initial flight testing, production check flying, and training operations.

Model 245A – Carrier Landing Configuration

This variant was equipped with an arresting hook and was capable of operating conventionally from a Project 6A carrier. It could have been combined with Model 245-1.

Weights (lbs)	
Maximum Flight Weight	100,000
JATO	5,040
Total Takeoff Weight	105,040

The Model 245 Studies In Depth

Basic Flight Component

Description The basic flight component of the Model 245 featured a sweptback, low aspect ratio, highly tapered wing, low wing loading, elimination of the horizontal tail, and propulsion by four XJ40-WE-6 turbojet engines installed in nacelles which were almost completely submerged within the wing contour. Provisions for a crew of two, a pilot/radio operator, and bomber/navigator/radar operator, sealed in tandem were contained in a pressurized compartment in the nose of the airplane, with the pilot located in front where he commanded excellent forward vision over the nose, and with the bomber/navigator/radar operator located just in back of the pilot in a roomy compartment which permitted a convenient arrangement of his bombing and navigating equipment. Ejection seats were provided for both crew members.

For this airplane, a novel rotary bomb bay was selected, in the interest of minimizing the aerodynamic disturbances created by opening the bomb bay at high speed, improving the ease of loading bombs either from the bottom or the top of the airplane, and in order to locate the heavy bomb bay structure in the bottom of the airplane to improve strength for ditching or belly landings.

Electronic equipment installed in the Model 245 included the Mk 5 Bomb Director, VHF Command radio, and radio compass. The radar antenna for the Mk 5 Bomb Director system was located in the nose of the airplane to improve strength for ditching or belly landings.

Provisions were made for the alternate installation of a retractable or a droppable nose gear beneath the floor of the crew compartment. Provisions for the alternate retractable or droppable main gear units were contained in the wing just outboard of the engine nacelles. Provisions were also made in the fuselage for attachment of the droppable hull, and in the wing for attachment of the droppable auxiliary floats.

In order to obtain an extremely smooth wing surface, multi-spar construction was used with covers of Honeycomb blankets.

Selection of Configuration The aerodynamic configuration of the Model 245 was arrived at through the analysis of systematic variations of wing area, aspect ratio, and wing sweep back from the standpoint of range, cruising speed, landing and takeoff performance, and potential transonic and supersonic stability and control characteristics. This theoretical evaluation was backed up by low speed wind tunnel tests of two different configurations and many minor variations thereon. Throughout this wing planform evaluation, only planforms that produced stable stalling characteristics were considered, in the interest of providing the best possible flying characteristics, even with a sweptback wing. The planform study showed that a relatively low aspect ratio wing of large area produced the best range, speed, and performance. The large usable wing volume provided space for efficient spanwise distribution of engines, fuel, and alighting gear, which resulted in a reduction in size of the fuselage and reduction of wing structural weight. The arrangement also resulted in minimum parasite drag, since fuselage and nacelles were largely hidden by the wing. The low wing loading permitted elimination of flaps and horizontal tail, thereby reducing drag and weight. Combination ailerons and elevators, called elevons, were provided along the trailing edge of the wing for pitch and roll control.

Performance Efficiency of the aerodynamic and structural configuration, together with the elimination of the alighting gear dead weight and minimization of equipment, resulted in an airplane with rather remarkable performance capabilities, combined with the versatility to perform a number of necessary and effective tactical missions. The illustration on page 190 shows the area of Russia covered by the tactical operating radius of the Model 245 from water areas around the perimeter of the Asiatic continent.

Model 245-1 Composite with Droppable Hull

Description Model 245-1 was the composite airplane consisting of the basic Model 245 flight component combined with a droppable hull and auxiliary floats. The long after-body hull was attached to the airplane by means of electric bomb shackles mounted in the hull and picking up recessed lugs on the fuselage at the center end rear spar bulkheads. Combination compression and shear pads completed the structural attachment. A V-tail was carried on the hull to produce additional longitudinal pitch control for realization of reduced takeoff and landing speeds for water operations, and to provide adequate stability for the composite airplane. The auxiliary floats were mounted in a manner similar to the hull, with electric bomb shackles in the pylons picking up lugs recessed in the lower surface of the wing. When dropping these launching components, it was necessary to break only the electrical connections to the bomb shackles and the electrically operated V-tail trimming surfaces. Provisions were made on the sides of the hull for the installation of JATO units which, together with the JATO units that could be mounted beneath the wing, produced a very short takeoff distance desired for rough water takeoffs.

Employment It was anticipated that the Model 245-1 would have been employed in a combination staging and combat mission in cooperation with submarines, thereby eliminating the necessity of risking large aircraft carriers, and also making possible surprise attacks that would have been difficult to detect or intercept. In this type of mission, the composite airplane would have flown directly from the continental United States to a rendezvous with a submarine within striking distance of the target. After refueling from the submarine, the airplane would have taken off, dropped its hull and floats, and continued on its attack mission. Returning to the submarine after the attack, the crew would then have either bailed out or ditched the airplane and been picked up by the submarine for return to base. The illustration on page 194 depicts the staging routes that could have been followed in arriving at several points where the attack mission could have been initiated.

Model 245-2 Composite with Droppable Gear

Description The Model 245-2 was a composite airplane consisting of a combination of the basic Model 245 flight component with droppable wheeled tricycle gear components. These droppable components were of welded steel tube construction, and mounted oversize low pressure tires which were used in lieu of conventional shock struts for takeoff from an aircraft carrier of the CVA type or larger. The structural attachments points for the droppable gear were the same as for the retractable gear units of the Models 245-3 and 245A. Release of the droppable units was accomplished with standard bomb shackles.

Employment After takeoff from the carrier deck, this airplane jettisoned the droppable gear components, and proceeded on its normal bombing mission at high speed and high altitude. Upon completion of the mission, the airplane returned to the carrier, or to a submarine, destroyer, or flying boat, and the crew either ditched or bailed out, to be picked up and returned to base.

Performance & Weights Summary

The following performance figures represent the take-off characteristics of the composite airplane with the droppable gear attached. Performance after release of the gear is the same as for Model 245.

Performance		Weights	
1. Take-off Distance, Deck, 25 Knot Wind with JATO, Std. Day - Feet	385	Flight Component Gross Weight	(100,000)
		Droppable Gear	3,890
		JATO (Two 12HC24000)	5,040
2. Take-off Distance, Airport, No Wind, with JATO, Std. Day - Feet	647	Take-off Gross Weight	108,930
3. Take-off Distance, Airport, No Wind, without JATO, Std. Day - Feet	2,410	Take-off Gross Weight less JATO	103,890

National Archives, RG 72

Model 245-3 Testing and Training Configuration

A fully retractable tricycle landing gear was provided for initial flight testing, production check flying, and training operations with the Model 245-3. This gear could have been installed together with the droppable hull and float components for test dropping of the hull, or for tactical missions in which it was desired to stage an over-water mission in a manner similar to that described for the Model 245-1, and alight on land at the completion of the mission.

Martin assumed that the testing and training airplane would have been restricted in gross weight so that landing loads would not have penalized the structural weight of the basic flight component. For proposal purposes, therefore, the gross weight of the Model 245-3 was restricted to 80,000 lbs. Subsequent study could have altered this gross weight restriction.

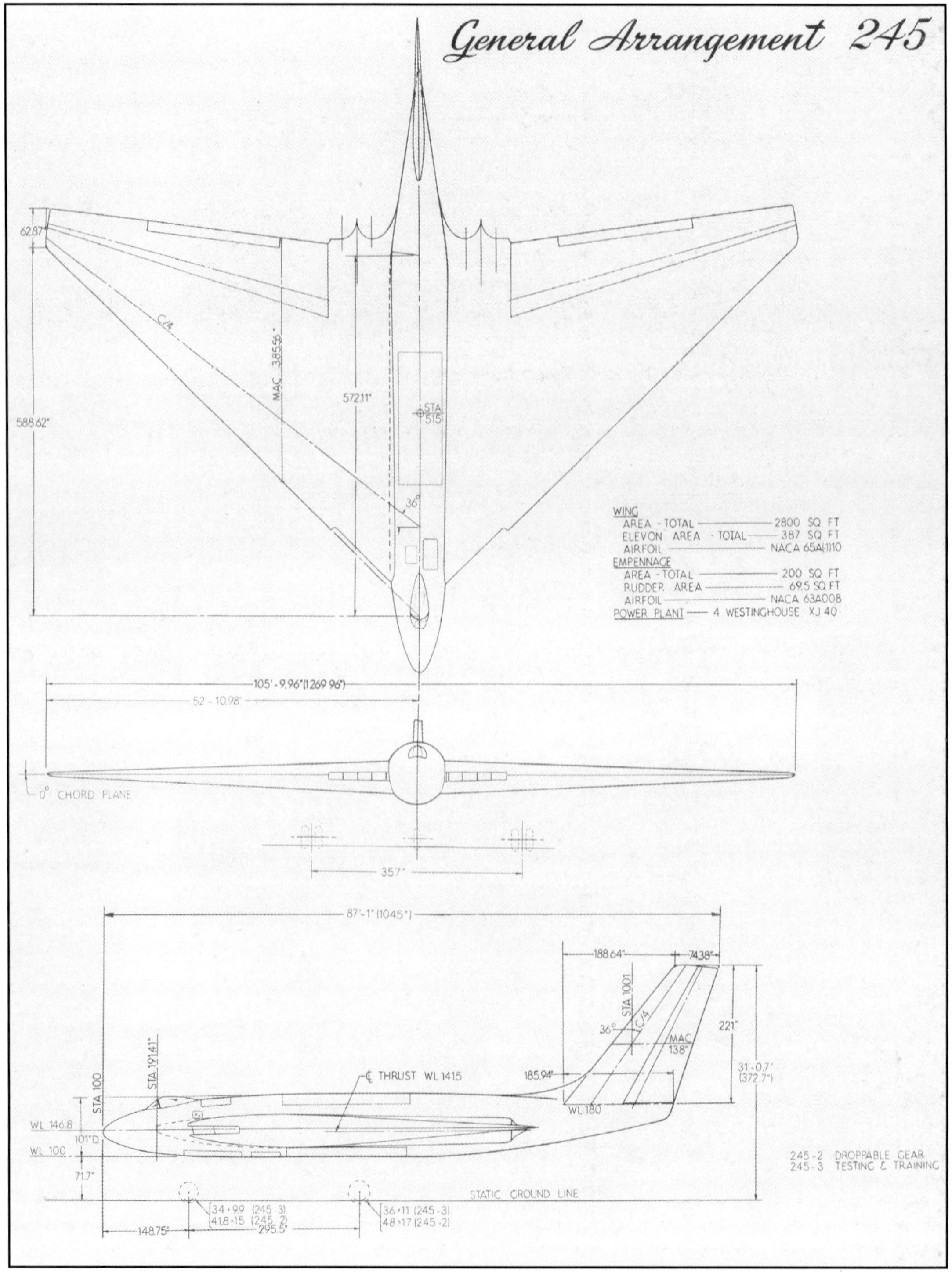

National Archives, RG 72

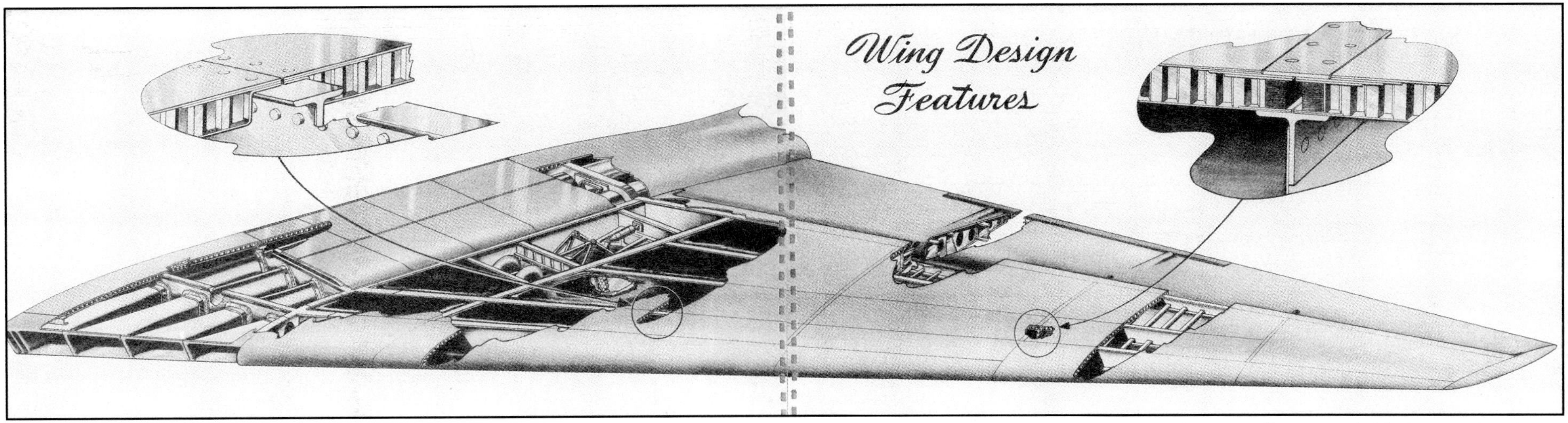

Above: The Model 245 flight component was a tailless design with a sweptback, low aspect ratio, highly tapered wing. Multi-spar construction with covers of honeycomb blankets was used to obtain an extremely smooth wing surface.

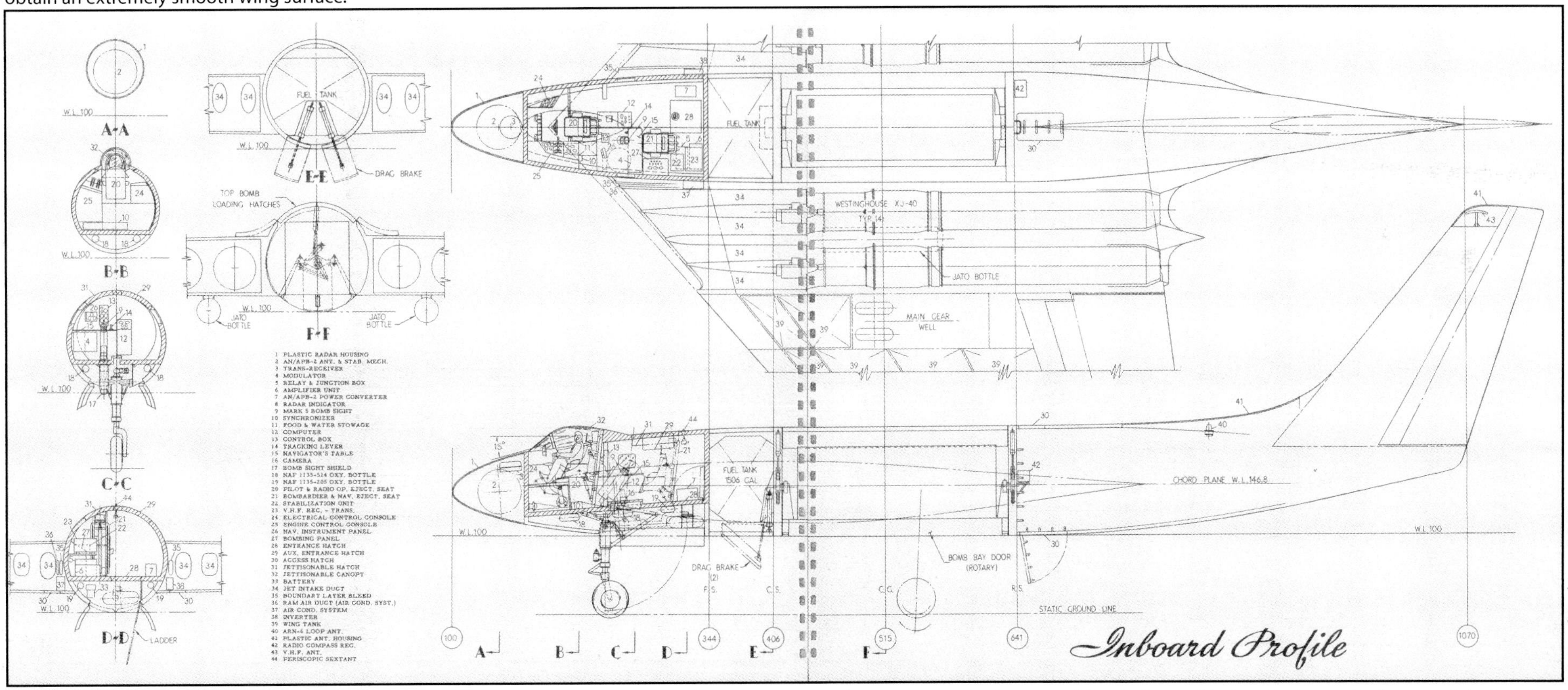

Above: Inboard profile of the Model 245 flight component. The crew of two sat in tandem in a pressurized compartment in the nose of the airplane, with the pilot located in front, and the bomber/navigator/radar operator behind him. Ejection seats were provided for both crew members.

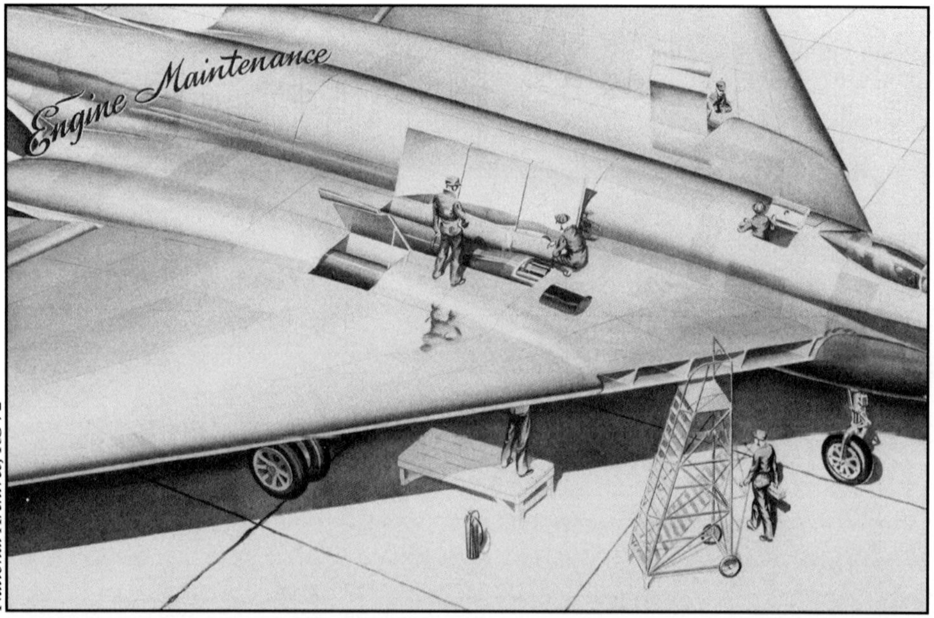

National Archives, RG 72

Above: The Model 245 was powered by four XJ-40-WE-6 turbojet engines installed in nacelles which were almost completely submerged within the wing contour.

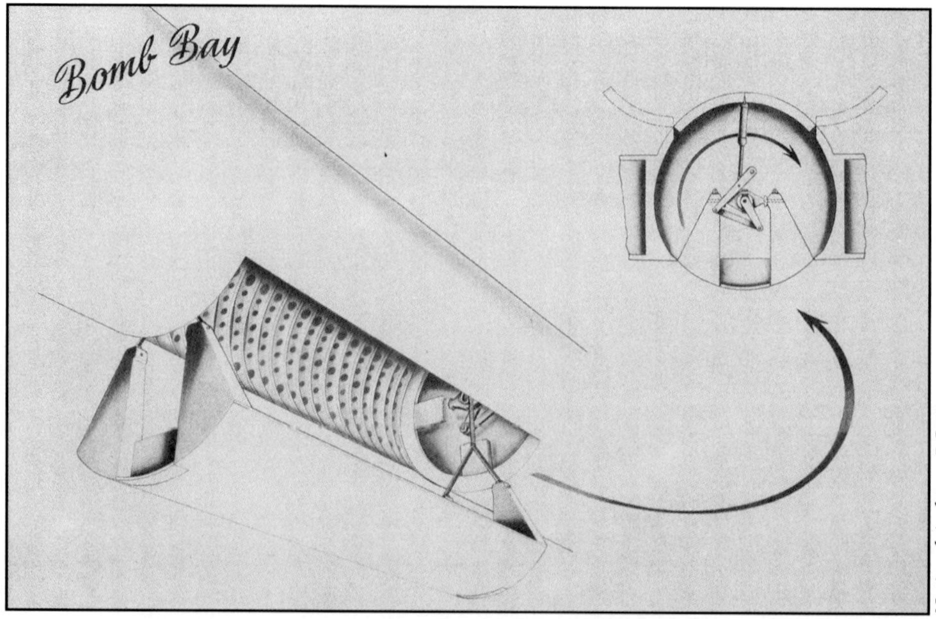

National Archives, RG 72

Above: The aircraft's rotary bomb bay minimized the aerodynamic disturbances created by opening the bomb bay at high speed and improved the ease of loading bombs.

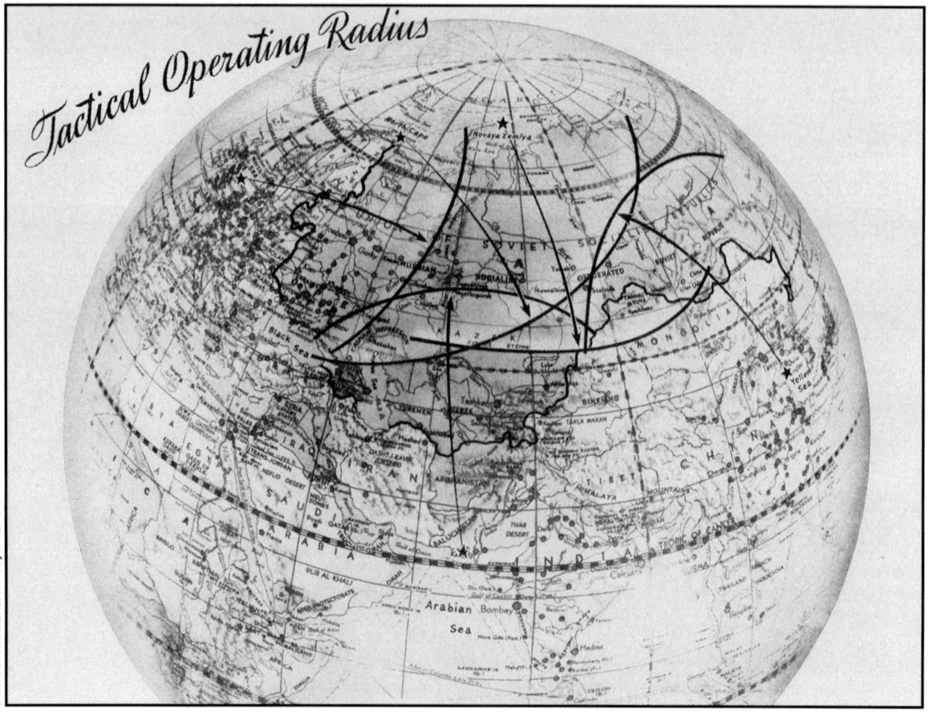

National Archives, RG 72

Above: The Model 245's maximum tactical operating radius of 1,916 nm permitted it to strike deep into the heart of the Soviet Union from a variety of locations.

Performance

1.	Tactical Operating Radius with 10,000 lb. Bomb Load - Naut. Mi.	1,700
2.	Average Cruising Speed in Combat Zone on above mission - Knots/Mach No.	536/.93
3.	Bombing Altitude on above mission - Feet	46,500
4.	Max. Tactical Operating Radius (300 ft./min. Combat Ceiling) with 10,000 lb. Bomb Load - Naut. Mi.	1,916
5.	Average Cruising Speed in Combat Zone on above mission - Knots/Mach No.	522/.91
6.	Bombing Altitude on above mission - Feet	50,100
7.	Maximum Mach No., Level Flight, Target Weight, Military Power	.95
8.	Altitude for Max. Mach No. - Feet	35,332
9.	Rate of Climb at Sea Level, Normal Power, Flight Component Gross Weight - Ft./Min.	4,550
10.	Stalling Speed, Flight Component Gross Weight - Knots	110
11.	Stalling Speed, Flight Component Gross Weight less Bomb Load and 90% Fuel - Knots	75

Weights

Item	Weight
WEIGHT EMPTY	(40,012)
Wing Group	13,310
Tail Group	942
Body Group	5,031
Engine Section	1,290
Power Plant Group	14,445
Fixed Equipment Group	4,994
USEFUL LOAD	(59,988)
Crew	588
Fuel - Usable	48,913
Fuel - Trapped	240
Oil	60
Bomb Installation	10,000
Equipment	187

Item	Weight
Flight Component Gross Weight	100,000
Basic Design Gross Weight (Average weight during run-in to target)	76,000
Target Weight (Actual)	68,017
Flight Component Gross Weight Less 10,000 Lbs. Bomb Load And 90% Fuel	45,975

National Archives, RG 72

Above: Performance and weight data for the basic Martin Model 245.

National Archives, RG 72

Model 245A Carrier Landing Configuration

Description The Model 245A was an alternate version of the basic Model 245 airplane, obtained through the installation of a retractable tricycle landing gear and modification of the aft fuselage for the installation of an arresting hook. Provisions for the droppable components of the 245-1 and 245-2 were retained in this configuration,

National Archives, RG 72

Above: For the surprise attack mission, the Model 245-1 would have flown directly from the continental United States to a rendezvous with a submarine within striking distance of the target. After refueling from the submarine, the airplane would have taken off, dropped its hull and floats, and continued on its attack mission.

Previous Page: The Model 245-1 flying boat would have made an impressive sight during takeoff, as this handsome artist's impression conveys. A V-tail was carried on the detachable hull to produce additional longitudinal pitch control to reduce water takeoff and landing speeds, and to provide adequate stability for the composite aircraft.

National Archives, RG 72

Above: As a flying boat, the Model 245-1 required bomb loading through the top of the fuselage. Given the complications of water-based operations, this Model 245 variant would have likely been the most expensive to service and maintain of those proposed by Martin.

thereby providing the same versatility as was found in the configurations described in the preceding sections of this chapter.

The landing gear proposed for the Model 245A was identical to that used in the testing and training version, the Model 245-3. The arresting hook was fully retractable, being enclosed within flush doors when not in use. The retraction system utilized the hydraulic snubbing cylinder normally provided to hold the hook down in position for arrested landings. A roller type hook was employed to minimize damage to the carrier arresting cables.

This Page: General arrangement drawing, staging route diagram, and performance and weight data for the Martin Model 245-1 composite flying boat.

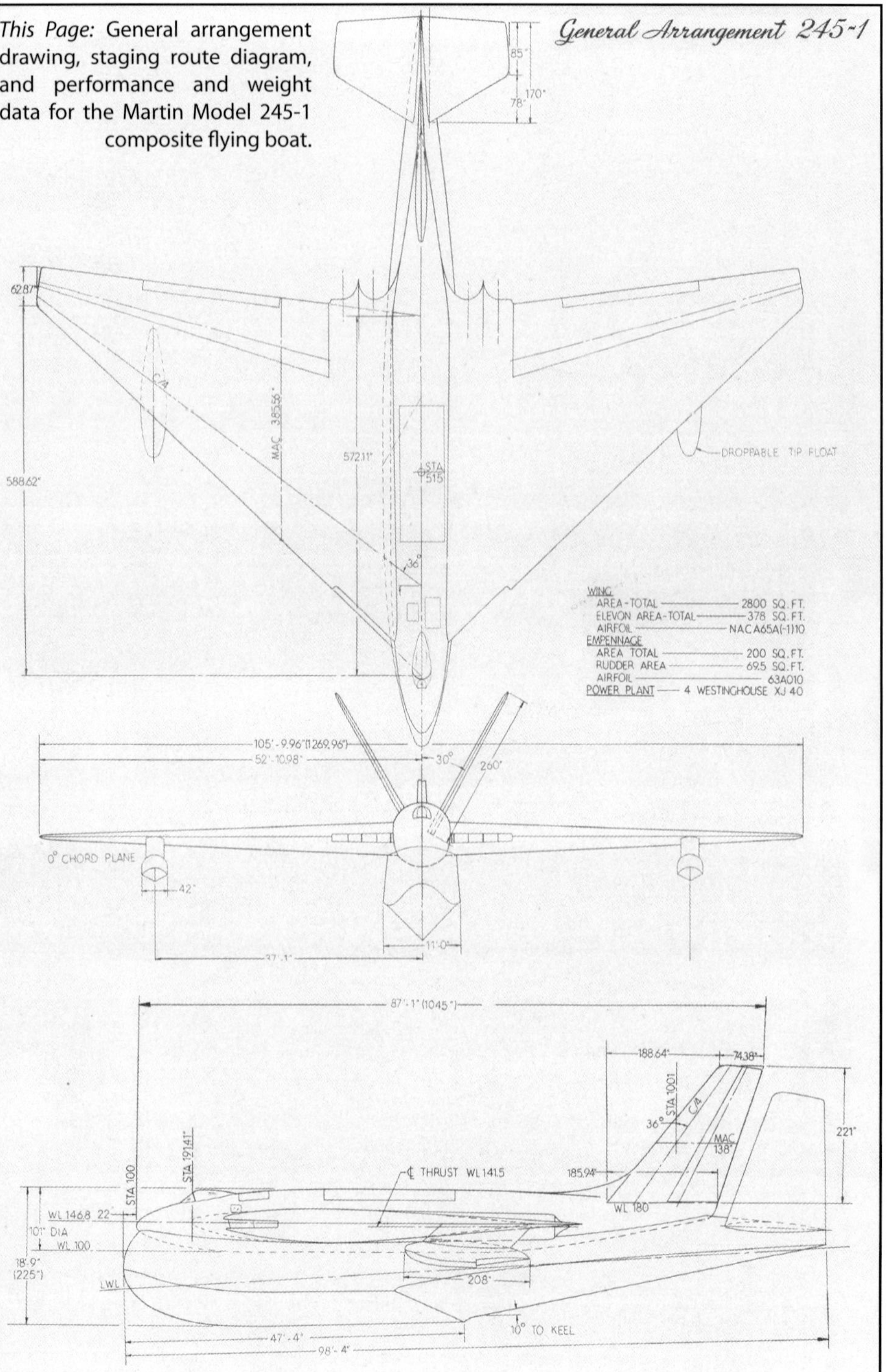

National Archives, RG 72

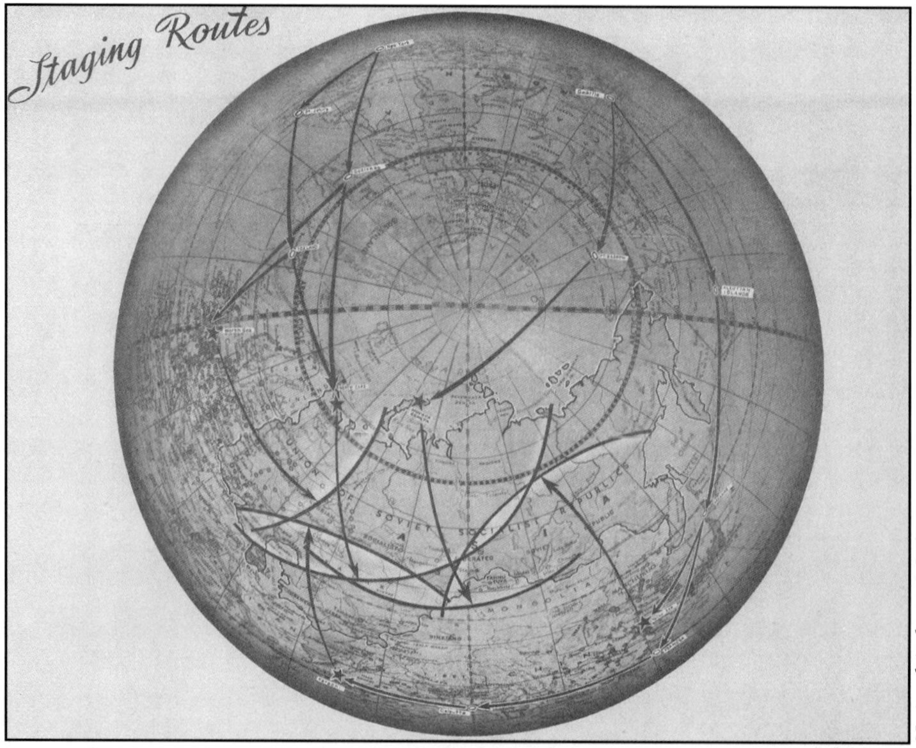

National Archives, RG 72

Performance

The following performance figures correspond to the composite airplane with hull attached. Performance after release of the hull is the same as for Model 245.

1. Take-off Distance with JATO - Feet 590
2. Take-off Time with JATO - Seconds 6.1
3. Take-off Speed with JATO - Knots 95
4. Stalling Speed with Hull and 10,000 lb. Bomb Load but less JATO and 90% Fuel - Knots 86
5. Range with 10,000 lb. Bomb Load carried entire distance, at 300 ft./min. ceiling - Naut. Mi. 1,810
6. Average Cruising Speed on above mission - Knots 402
7. Maximum Speed at Take-off Gross Weight less JATO - Knots 449
8. Altitude for Maximum Speed - Feet 23,000
9. Rate of Climb at Normal Power, Take-off Gross Weight less JATO - Ft./Min. 2,960

Weights

Flight Component Gross Weight 100,000

Droppable Hull 10,985
Droppable Floats 650
JATO (Four 12HC24000) 10,080

Take-off Gross Weight 121,715

Landing Gross Weight 67,613
(With hull and 10,000 lb. bomb load but less JATO and 90% Fuel)

Take-off Gross Weight less JATO 111,635

National Archives, RG 72

National Archives, RG 72

Preceding Page: The Model 245-2 dropping its detachable gear and JATO bottles as it takes off from a carrier. Upon return, the crew would have had to ditch or bail out, sacrificing the aircraft component entirely.

The overall size and configuration of the Model 245A permitted normal handling and spotting of nine airplanes on the flight deck of the Project 6A carrier.

Performance In this configuration, the performance of the basic Model 245 type airplane was unimpaired, except that range was reduced somewhat because of the increased structural weight and addition of the non-droppable landing gear. With two droppable JATO units, this airplane had the takeoff performance necessary for operation from the deck of a Project 6A carrier. Landing speeds and weights were also well within the capacity of the arresting gear projected for this carrier.

Performance & Weights Summary

(All performance shown at Gross Weight of 80,000 Lbs.)

1. Take-off Distance, Airport, No Wind, Std. Day - Feet	1,340
2. Take-off Distance, Deck, 25 Knot Wind, Std. Day - Feet	660
3. Stalling Speed - Knots	98
4. Maximum Mach No., Military Power	.95
5. Altitude for Maximum Mach No. - Feet	35,332
6. Rate of Climb at Sea Level, Normal Power - Ft./Min.	5,850
7. Service Ceiling, Normal Power, (100 ft./min.) - Feet	48,600
8. Ferry Range, no Bomb Load - Naut. Mi.	2,893
9. Average Speed for above range - Knots	522
Fuel Load	24,118
Bomb Load	10,000
Take-off Gross Weight	80,000

National Archives, RG 72

Basic Aerodynamics of the Model 245 Series

Prior to the final establishment of the Model 245 configuration, several systematic aerodynamic studies and tests were made. In a report dated October 25, 1948, Martin presented a cruising performance comparative planform study, stability analyses of several configurations, and complete low speed wind tunnel tests of two configurations were made to serve as a basis for the design of the Model 245. Photographs from these tests cover pages 2061 to 2083.

The planform study indicated that the maximum range was obtained with the following wing configuration:

Wing Area, sq ft	2,500
Aspect Ratio	4.5
Sweep back Angle	32°
Taper Ratio	6.66

However, the planform selection was tempered by considerations of controllability and stability at high transonic Mach numbers. It was believed that 36° of sweep back was the minimum tolerable quarter chord sweep back. The wing area had to be compromised in deference to considerations of landing stall and sinking speeds, and fuel volume capacity required for the desired percent fuel load. Consequently, the best compromise planform was found to have the following characteristics:

Wing Area, sq ft	2,800
Aspect Ratio	4.0
Sweep back Angle	36°
Taper Ratio	9.1:1

A plot of the stability and control characteristics for the Model 245 showed that the airplane would have exhibited very desirable flying qualities both at low speeds and high speeds.

This airplane featured an inverted camber airfoil which was expected to yield a higher critical Mach number at high speed lift coefficients and a positive pitching moment at zero lift which would have otherwise required the employment of elevon deflection.

Conclusion

Overall, Martin submitted a comprehensive and imaginative proposal to fulfill the challenging requirements of OS-115. However, evidence suggests that it tried to adapt a pet concept it had been developing internally to a specification that called for a different type of aircraft. BuAer was specifically looking for an aircraft/missile composite to fly from (and justify the existence of) its newest giant supercarrier, not an aircraft that could be adapted as a flying boat or land-based attacker. Martin ignored this obvious fact, much to its detriment.

National Archives, RG 72

Above: Bomb loading of the Model 245-2/-3 was accomplished through the bottom of the fuselage, as shown in this artist's impression. Interestingly, the artist has depicted a prominent island on the carrier, indicating perhaps that Martin intended that its Special Attack aircraft be operated from smaller, non-CVA class carriers.

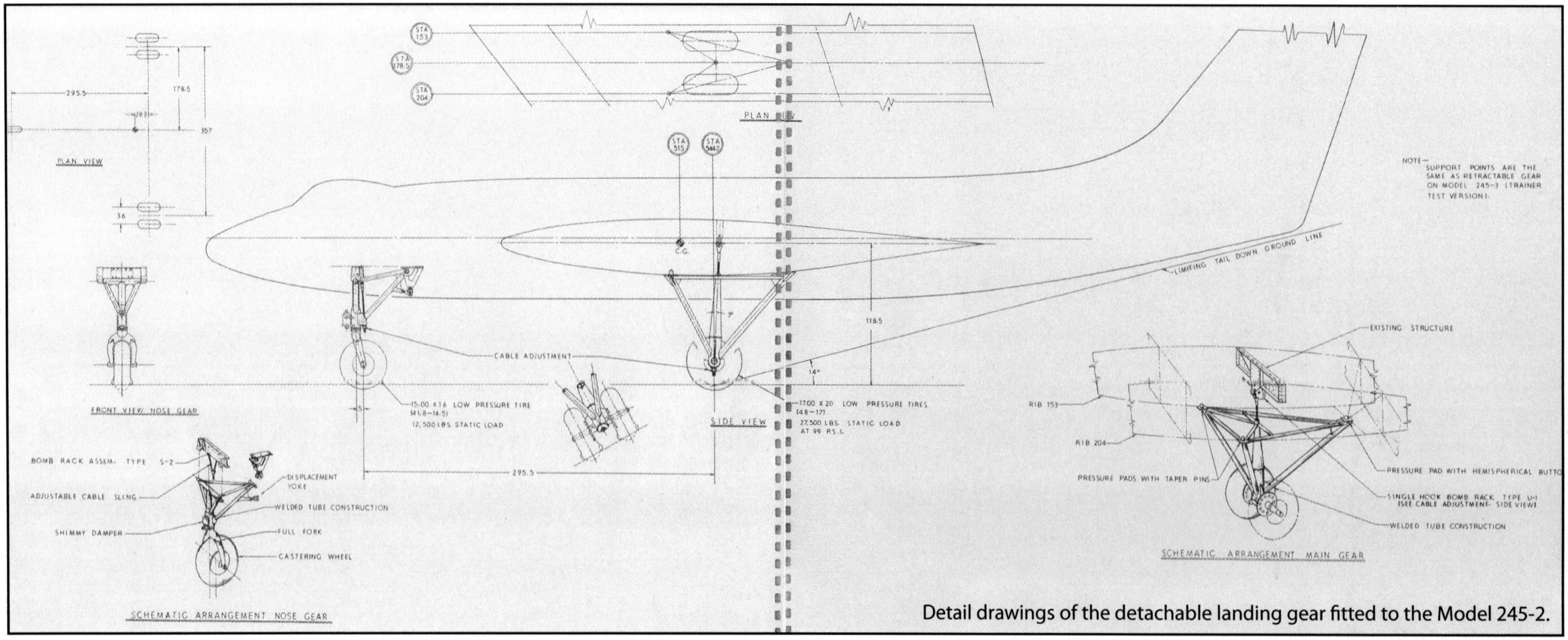

Detail drawings of the detachable landing gear fitted to the Model 245-2.

National Archives, RG 72

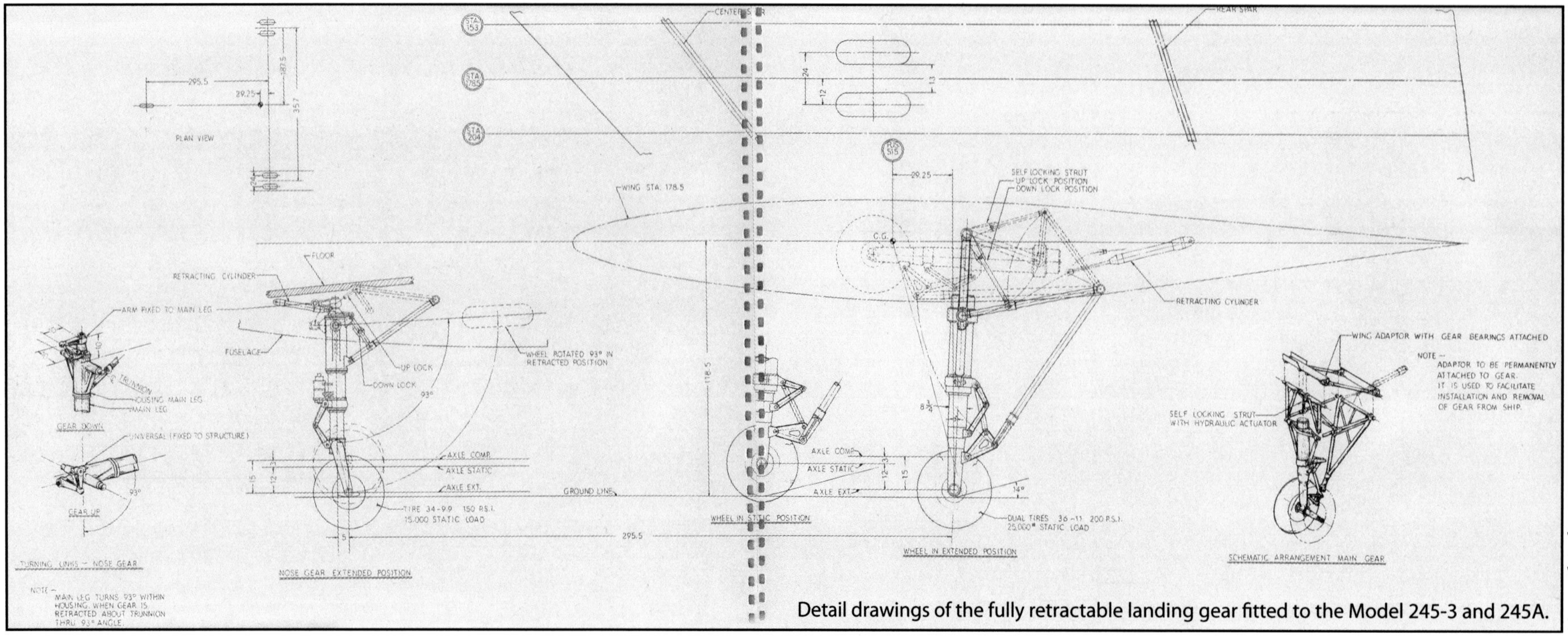

Detail drawings of the fully retractable landing gear fitted to the Model 245-3 and 245A.

National Archives, RG 72

National Archives, RG 72

Above: Artist's impression of the Model 245A landing on an aircraft carrier with its retractable landing gear and arresting hook extended.

Performance & Weights Summary

Performance

1.	Tactical Operating Radius at 300 ft./min. Combat Ceiling with 10,000 lb. Bomb Load - Naut. Mi.	1,617
2.	Average Cruising Speed in Combat Zone on above mission - Knots/ Mach No.	522/.91
3.	Bombing Altitude on above mission - Feet	49,000
4.	Maximum Mach No. at Target Weight, Military Power	.95
5.	Altitude for Max. Mach No. - Feet	35,332
6.	Rate of Climb at Sea Level, Normal Power, Take-off Weight less JATO - Ft./Min.	4,550
7.	Take-off Distance, Deck, 25 Knot Wind, with JATO - Feet	340
8.	Take-off Distance, Airport, No Wind, without JATO - Feet	2,210
9.	Stalling Speed, Take-off Weight less JATO - Knots	110
10.	Stalling Speed, Take-off Weight less JATO, Bomb Load, and 60% Fuel - Knots	88

Weights

WEIGHT EMPTY	(45,257)
Wing Group	13,310
Tail Group	942
Body Group	5,031
Landing Gear	4,995
Carrier Arresting Hook Installation	250
Engine Section	1,290
Power Plant Group	14,445
Fixed Equipment Group	4,994
USEFUL LOAD	(54,743)
Crew	588
Fuel - Usable	43,668
Fuel - Trapped	240
Oil	60
Bomb Installation	10,000
Equipment	187

Maximum Flight Weight (or Take-off Gross Weight less JATO)	100,000
JATO (Two 12HC24000)	5,040
Take-off Gross Weight	105,040
Basic Design Gross Weight (Average Weight during run-in to target)	80,200
Target Gross Weight (Actual)	71,797
Landing Gross Weight (Take-off Weight less JATO, Bomb Load and 60% Fuel)	63,799

National Archives, RG 72

Above: Martin Model 245A performance and weight data.

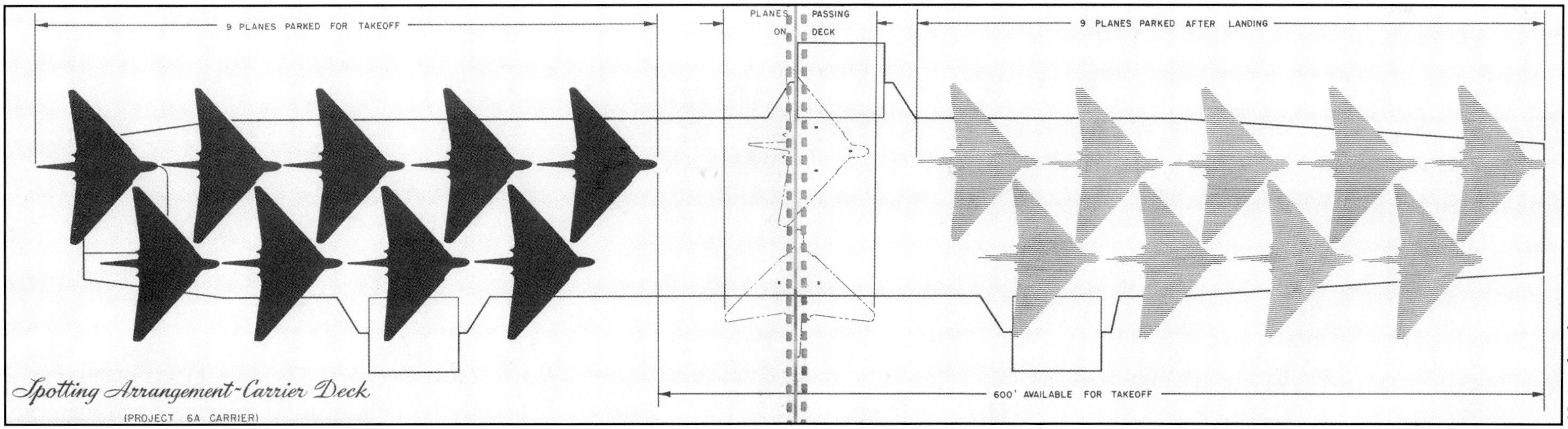

National Archives, RG 72

Above: Nine Model 245A aircraft could be accommodated on the flight deck of the Project 6A carrier; more could have likely been carried if wing folding had been incorporated into the design.

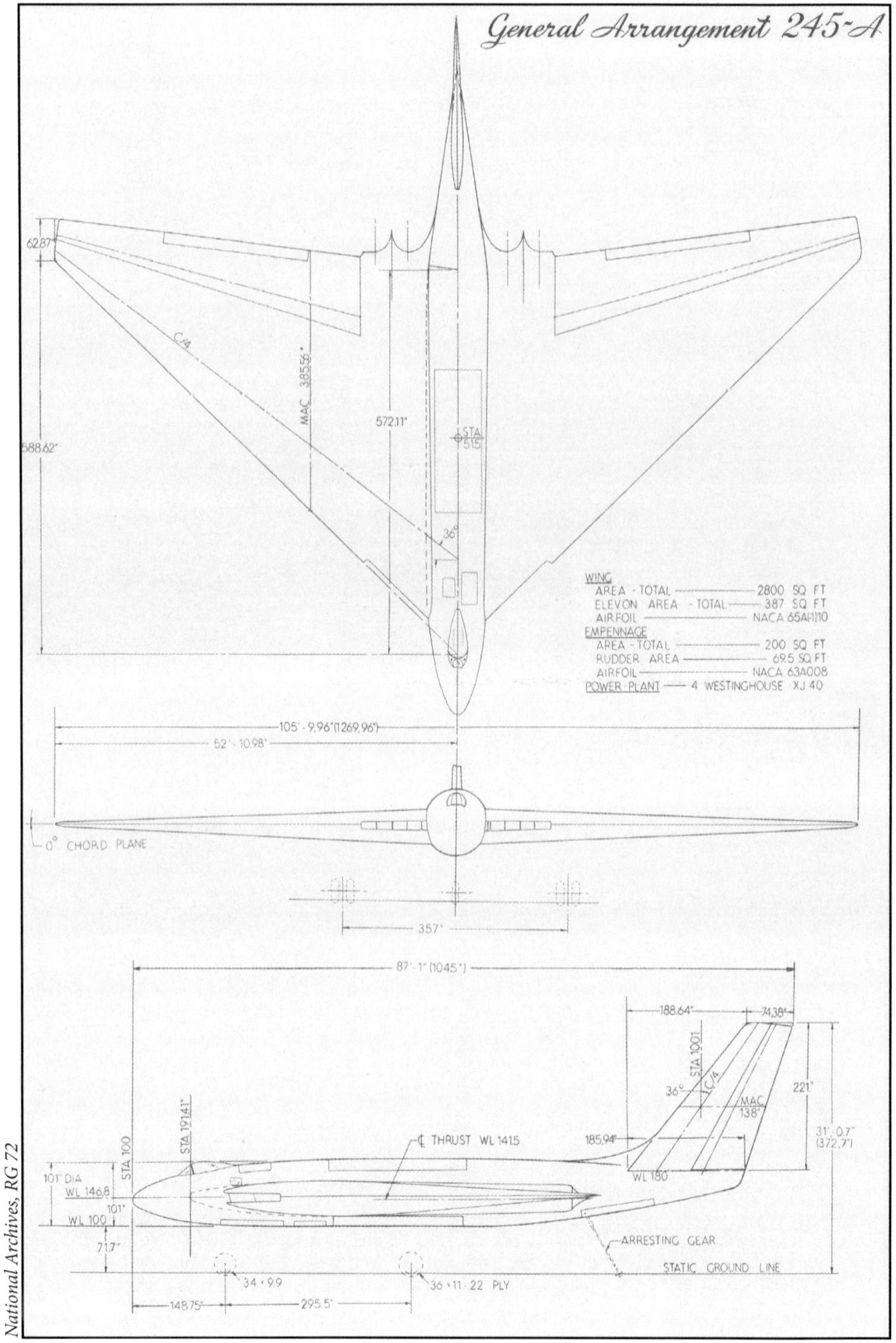

National Archives, RG 72

MISSION AND DESCRIPTION

The mission of this airplane is the delivery of bombing attacks against any ground or water target in the world from water bases.

Martin Model 245 is conceived as an extremely high speed composite aircraft which, with the addition of suitable launching and landing components, can operate from the surface of the water, from an aircraft carrier, or from land, and return its crew to the point of origin of the mission. With a droppable hull, (Model 245-1) it can operate as a flying boat, refueling at sea from a submarine. With a droppable wheel type gear (Model 245-2) it can take off from an aircraft carrier. With a retractable gear, it can serve as a testing and training airplane, and with a retractable gear and an arresting hook (Model 245A) it can operate conventionally as a carrier based aircraft.

This airplane features a low aspect ratio, highly tapered sweptback wing, and the elimination of a horizontal tail. It is manned by a crew of two, a pilot-radio operator, and a bomber-navigator-radar operator.

WEIGHTS

Loadings	Gross,Lbs.	L.F.
Empty	40,012	
Basic Flt. Des.	76,000	3.3
Alt. Flight Des.	111,635	2.25
Max. T. O.		
245 (a)	100,000	--
245-1	121,715 (b)	3.42
245-2	108,930 (c)	2.0
245-3	80,000	2.0
245A	105,040	2.0
Landing		
245	45,975 (d)	--
245-1	67,613 (e)	3.30
245-2	(See 245)	--
245-3	80,000	2.62
245A	63,799 (f)	3.3

Notes:
(a) Flight component weight.
(b) With hull and JATO.
(c) With droppable gear and JATO.
(d) T. O. weight less any droppable component, JATO, bomb, and 90% fuel.
(e) With hull and bomb, but less 90% fuel.
(f) T. O. weight less bomb, and 60% fuel.

ELECTRONICS

(1)	ARC-1	VHF Command
(1)	AIC-5A	Interphone
(1)	ARN-6	Radio Compass
(1)	MK-5	Bomb Director

FUEL AND OIL

Gals.	No. Tanks	Location
6680	14	Wing
1472	1	Fuselage
Fuel Grade		Fuel Spec.
100/130		AN-F-48

OIL

Cap. 8.1 Gals. (Total)
Spec. AN-0-9

(Oil System and Tanks contained in Engines)

DIMENSIONS

Wing Area	2800 Sq.Ft.
Wing Span	105'-9.96"
Wing M.A.C.	385.56"
Max. Airplane Length	87'-1"
Max. Airplane Height	31'-0.7"
Gear Tread	357"

ORDNANCE

Design bomb load 10,000 Lbs.

POWER PLANT

No. & Model	4 XJ-40-WE-6
Mfr.	Westinghouse
Type	Turbo-jet

RATINGS

Static Sea Level

T.O.	7500 Lbs.	7260 RPM
Military	7500 Lbs.	7260 RPM
Normal	6800 Lbs.	7260 RPM

525 Knots - 45000 Ft.

Military	1890 Lbs.	7260 RPM
Normal	1700 Lbs.	7260 RPM

National Archives, RG 72

MODEL 245
WEIGHT SUMMARY FOR VARIOUS LOADING CONDITIONS

CONDITIONS	MODEL	TAKE-OFF	FLIGHT	BOMB LOAD	INTERNAL FUEL	EXTERNAL FUEL	TOTAL FUEL	EXTERNAL TANKS	DROP HULL	DROP GEAR	DROP FLOAT	JATO	FUEL TRANSFER
Basic - Water Take-off	245-1	121,715	100,000	10,000	48,913	—	48,913	—	10,985	—	650	10,080	—
Basic - Carrier T.O.-Drop Gear	245-2	108,930	100,000	10,000	48,913	—	48,913	—	—	3,890	—	5,040	—
Basic - Test and Training	245-3	80,000	80,000	10,000	24,118	—	24,118	—	—	—	—	—	—
Basic - Carrier Land. Gear	245-A	105,040	100,000	10,000	43,668	—	43,668	—	—	—	—	5,040	—
WATER TAKE-OFF													
Carrier Land. Gear-No Refuel Equipment	245-1A	121,715	100,000	10,000	43,668	—	43,668	—	10,985	—	650	10,080	—
Carrier Land. Gear-Equipped for Refuel	245-1A	121,715	100,000	10,000	40,300	—	40,300	2,268	10,985	—	650	10,080	—
Flight Refueling - Carrier Land. Gear	245-A	—	135,250	10,000	53,053	22,497	75,550	2,268	—	—	—	—	41,850
CARRIER TAKE-OFF													
Take-off with Refuel Equipment Installed - Carrier Land. Gear	245-A	105,040	100,000	10,000	40,700	—	40,700	1,880	—	—	—	5,040	—
Flight Refueling - Carrier Land. Gear	245-A	—	130,900	10,000	53,053	18,547	71,600	1,880	—	—	—	—	37,500
TANKERS													
Water Take-off and Landing - No Land. Gear-Refuel Equipment Installed.	245-1	121,715	111,635	—	56,913	—	56,913	—	—	—	—	10,080	—
Carrier T.O. and Land -Refuel Equipment Installed	245-A	105,040	100,000	—	51,668	—	51,668	—	—	—	—	5,040	—

National Archives, RG 72

Above: Standard Aircraft Characteristics chart and a weight summary table for the Martin Model 245 series of studies.

Left: Three-view of the Martin Model 245A Long Range Special Attack aircraft.

National Archives, RG 72

Above: Photo of one of the wind tunnel model configurations tested by Martin to determine the ideal planform for the Model 245. Multiple combinations of various wing leading edge, nose, and fuselage shapes were tested in a low speed wind tunnel, as shown in the photos on the next two pages.

National Archives, RG 72

National Archives, RG 72

National Archives, RG 72

National Archives, RG 72

National Archives, RG 72

National Archives, RG 72

National Archives, RG 72

National Archives, RG 72

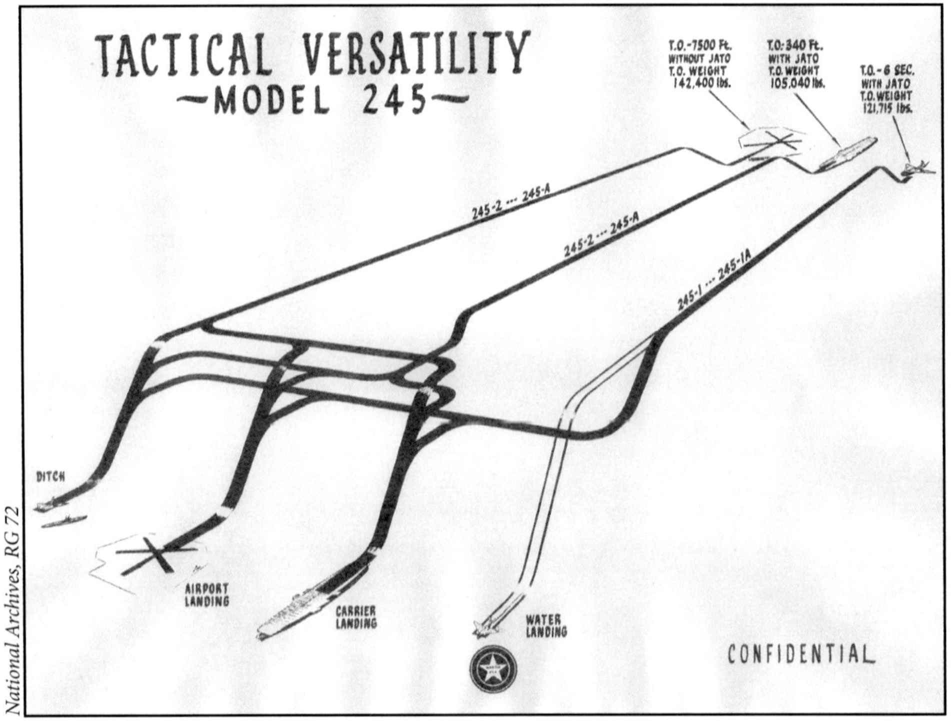

National Archives, RG 72

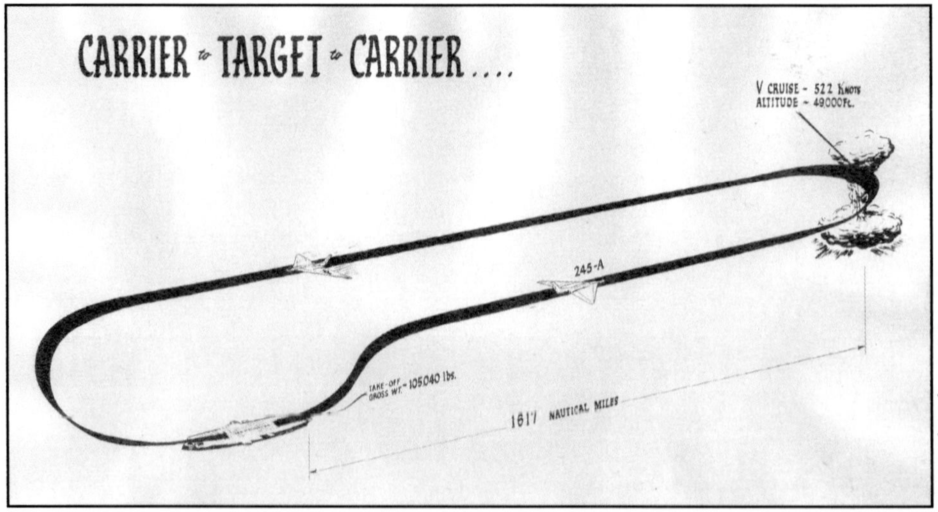

National Archives, RG 72

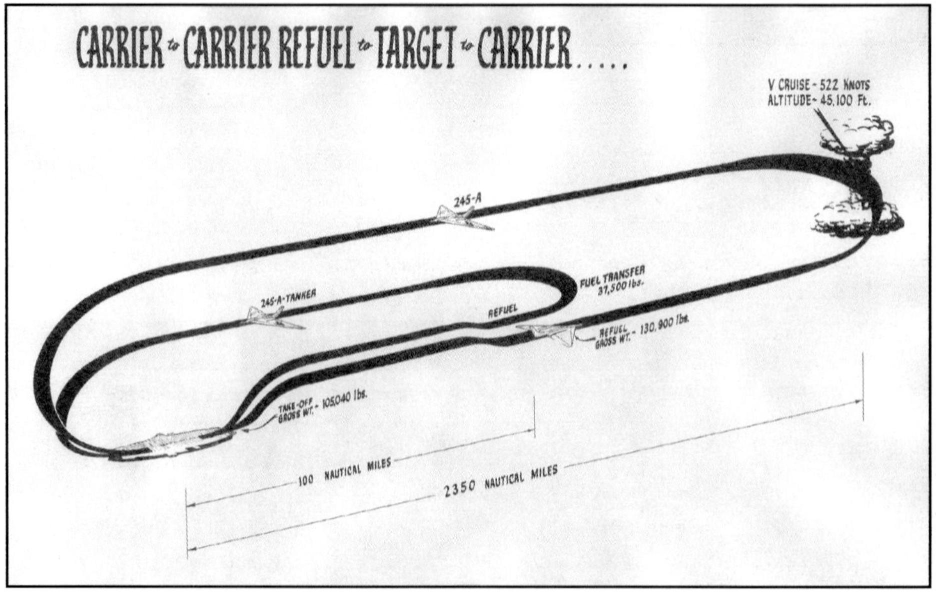

National Archives, RG 72

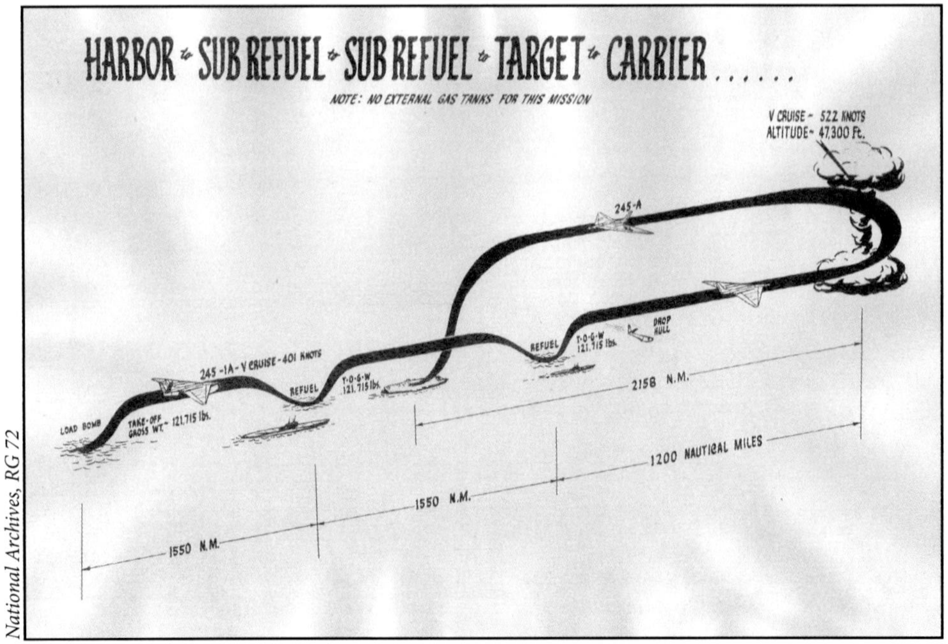

National Archives, RG 72

This Page: In a report dated January 3, 1949, Martin presented a few of the many different types of tactical operations they believed to be possible with the Model 245 Airplane. The range data presented in the report was calculated using fuel loads corresponding to weights presented in the table on Page 200. Adequate allowances were made for external droppable fuel tank installations, local structural modifications, and equipment changes where necessary, to present realistic weight and drag estimates. Illustrations from this report cover this and the next 1½ pages.

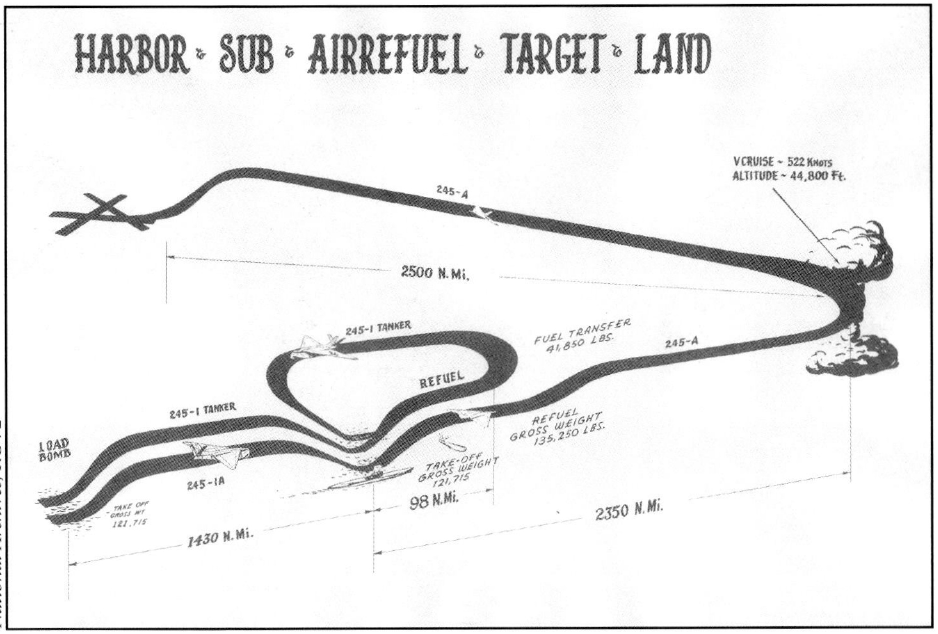

National Archives, RG 72

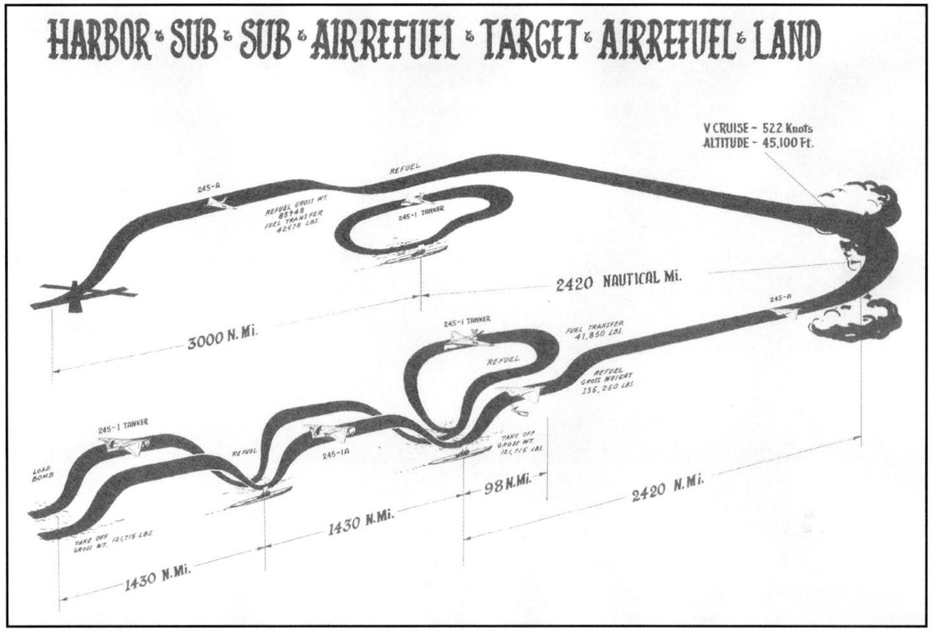

National Archives, RG 72

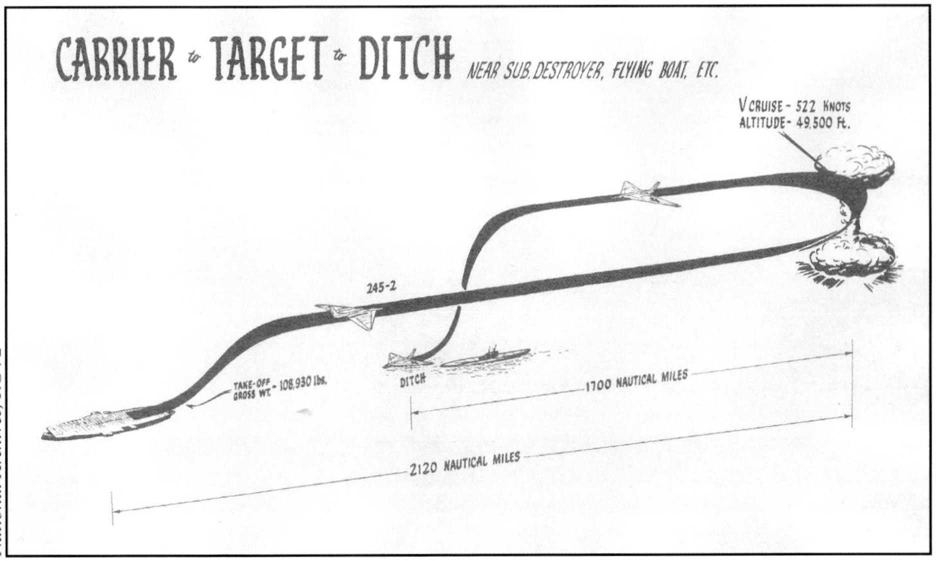

National Archives, RG 72

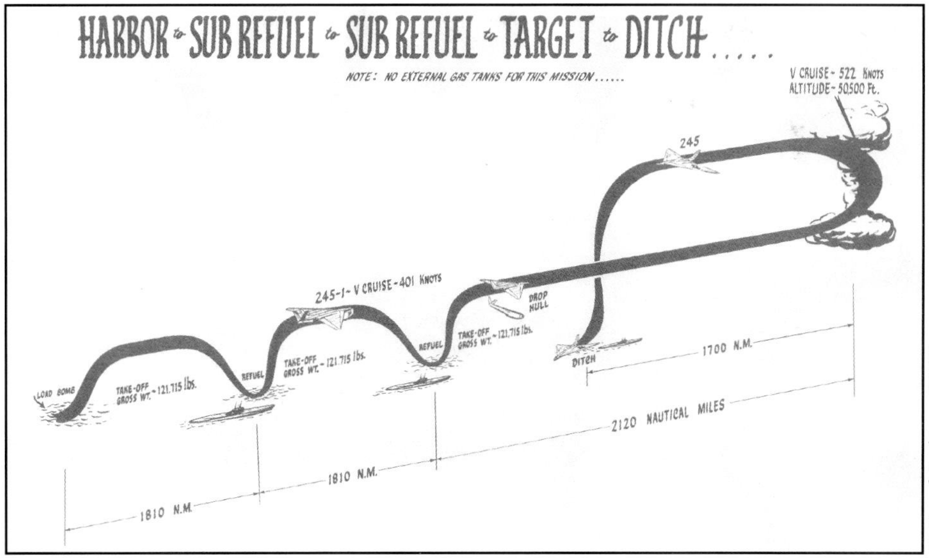

National Archives, RG 72

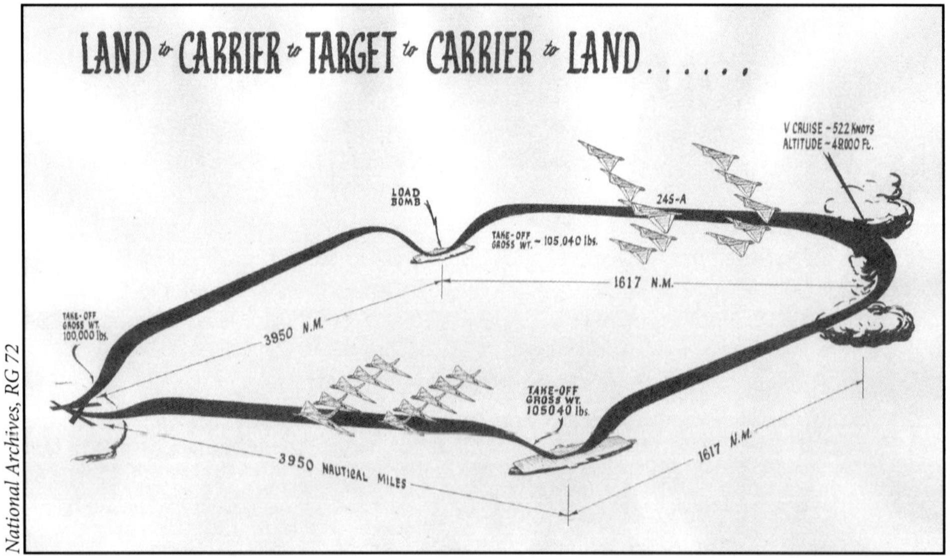

National Archives, RG 72

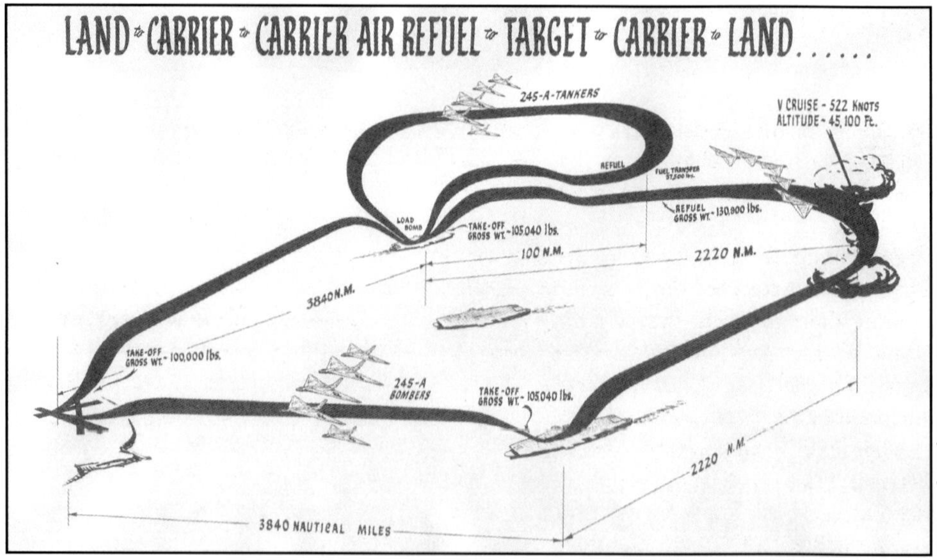

National Archives, RG 72

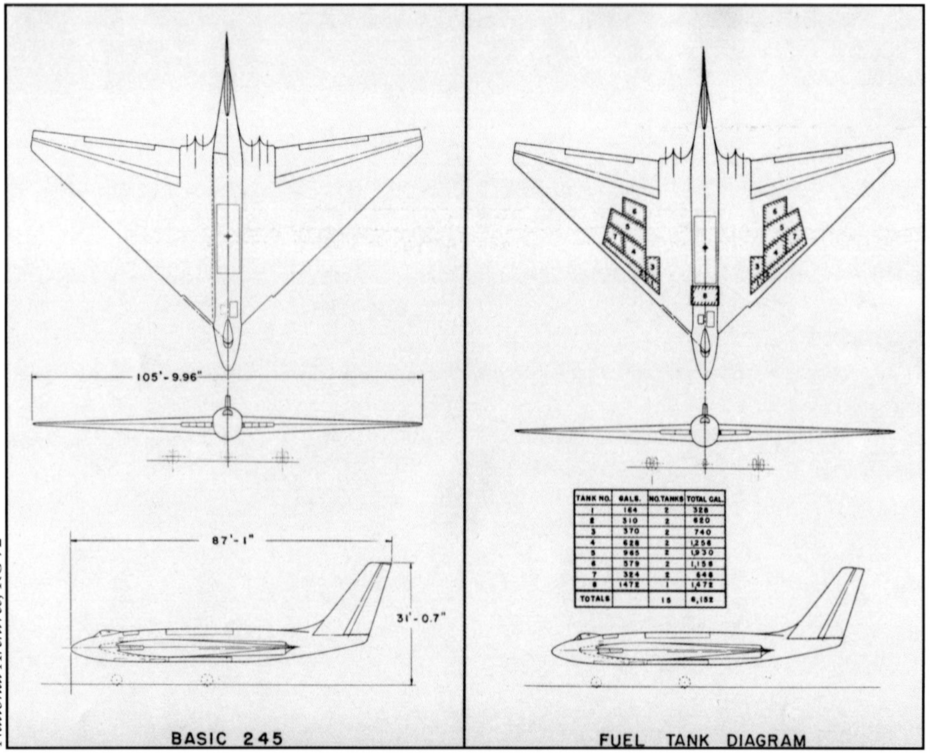

National Archives, RG 72

Above: General arrangement drawing and fuel tank diagram of the Martin Model 245 taken from the Standard Aircraft Characteristics charts prepared for the type.

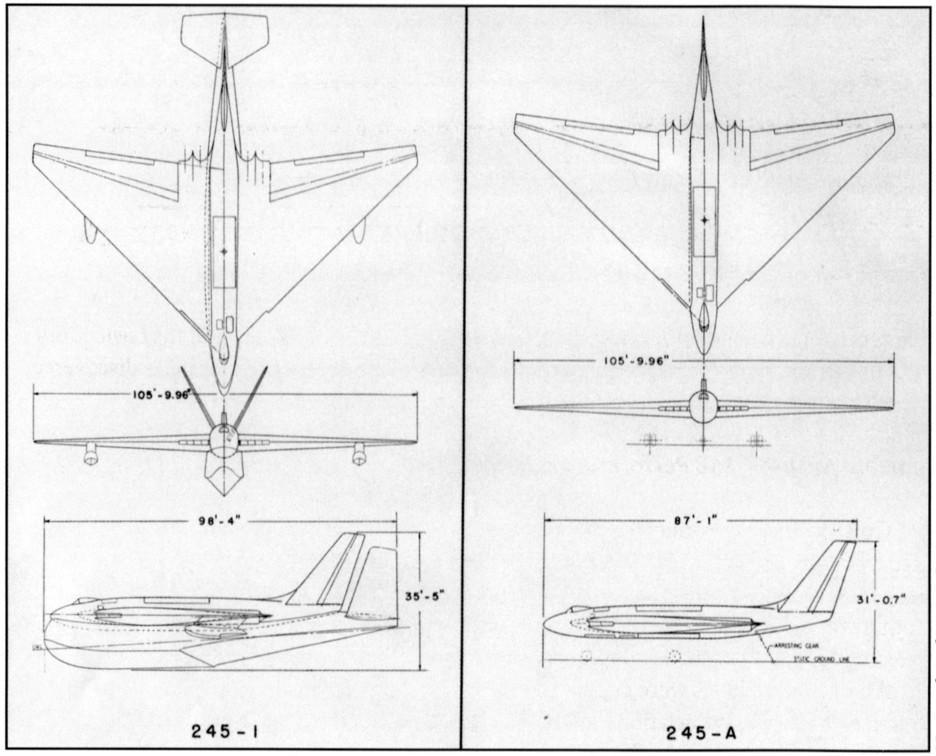

National Archives, RG 72

Above: General arrangement drawings of the Model 245-1 and -A excerpted from the same document.

CHAPTER 17 — *Winners and Losers*

William Z. Frisbie, Director of the Evaluation Division at BuAer, forwarded the proposal charts submitted by the contractors in the Class VA, Heavy Attack competition to various Assistant Chiefs and Directors within BuAer on November 24, 1948. Martin requested that their Model 245A and alternates, which had been submitted in the Long Range Special Attack competition, also be considered as their proposal for the Long Range Heavy Attack competition. A total of 21 designs, including alternates, was submitted by eight contractors in this competition. North American's submission, which was comparatively superficial in scope and neither met the requirements of OS-111 nor its associated specifications, was quickly eliminated and not included in this tally.

Competitive bids were submitted on December 3, 1948 by Convair, Curtiss, Douglas, Fairchild, Martin and Republic. While BuAer reviewed the proposals, Douglas El Segundo used company funds to further refine the Model 593, resulting in the informal submission to the Navy of four revised designs: the Model 593-3, -4, -5 and -6. Convair, Fairchild, Martin and Republic were ultimately eliminated; unfortunately, the author has been unable to locate documents detailing BuAer's evaluation and ultimate rejection of these designs. On March 1, 1949 Curtiss and Douglas were requested to submit cost proposals for Phase 1 studies. Both companies furnished the requested information by late March, Curtiss-Wright submitting a report describing various performance modified versions of the P-558 (discussed below), and Douglas submitting the Model 593-7, a further iteration of its proposal. On March 31, Curtiss and Douglas received Phase 1 contracts for $808,340 and $810,586, respectively for further development of their designs.

Douglas Models 593-3 to 593-7

No reports have been found describing these follow-on developments of the basic Model 593 in detail; only blueprints of Models 593-3, -6 and -7 have thus far been discovered, which are presented on this and the following pages.

Curtiss-Wright P-558 Performance Modified Versions

Curtiss-Wright produced a study of the performance characteristics of several modified versions of the P-558 long range heavy attack aircraft on March 25, 1949. These revisions included those specifically requested by BuAer in addition to several other configurations which were considered essential for a complete evaluation of the airplane selected for the Phase 1 development program.

All of the airplanes were generally similar in external appearance. The principal differences were due to variations in range, bomb load or armament and the effect of these variations on the airplane size and weight. Several corollary investigations were made in order to determine specifically the possible benefit which could be obtained by either

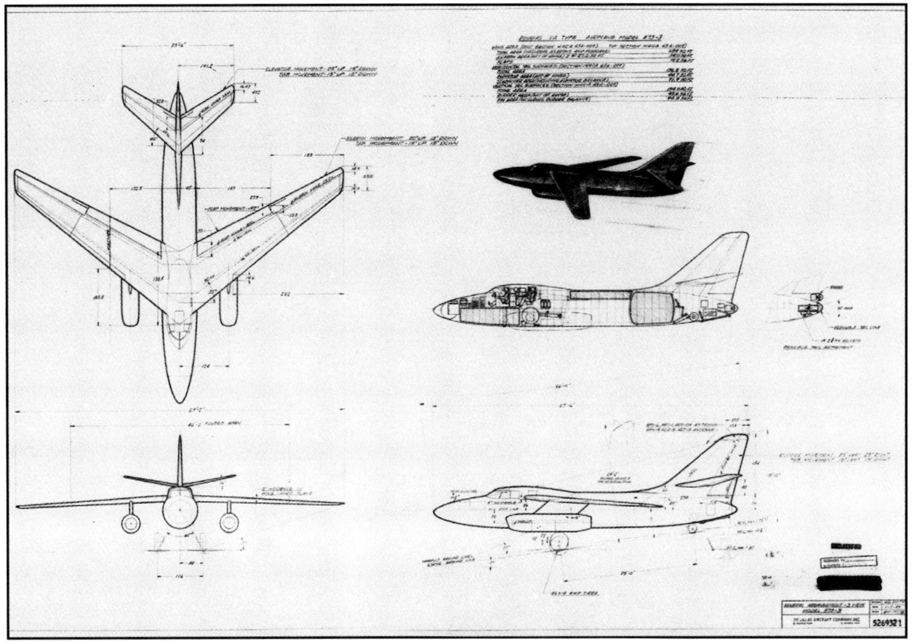

National Archives, RG 72

Above: General arrangement drawing of the Douglas Model 593-3, which appears to be a smaller and lighter version of the basic Model 593. However, unlike, the Model 593-2, the bomb load was carried completely internally. Surprisingly, it remained a tail dragger.

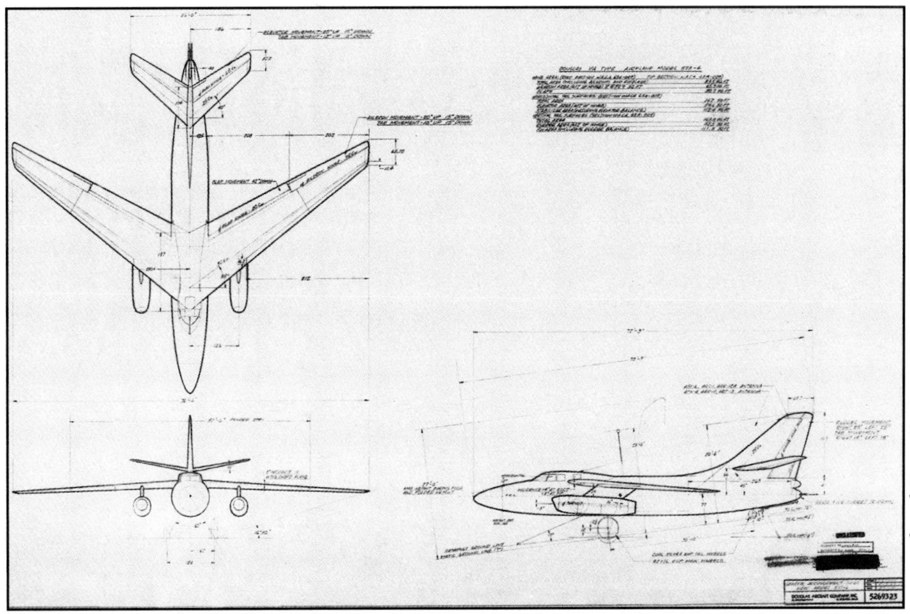

National Archives, RG 72

Above: General arrangement drawing of the Douglas Model 593-6, a larger aircraft than the Model 593-3 but still smaller than the original 593. Douglas and BuAer were still looking for the ideal trade-off between size and capability.

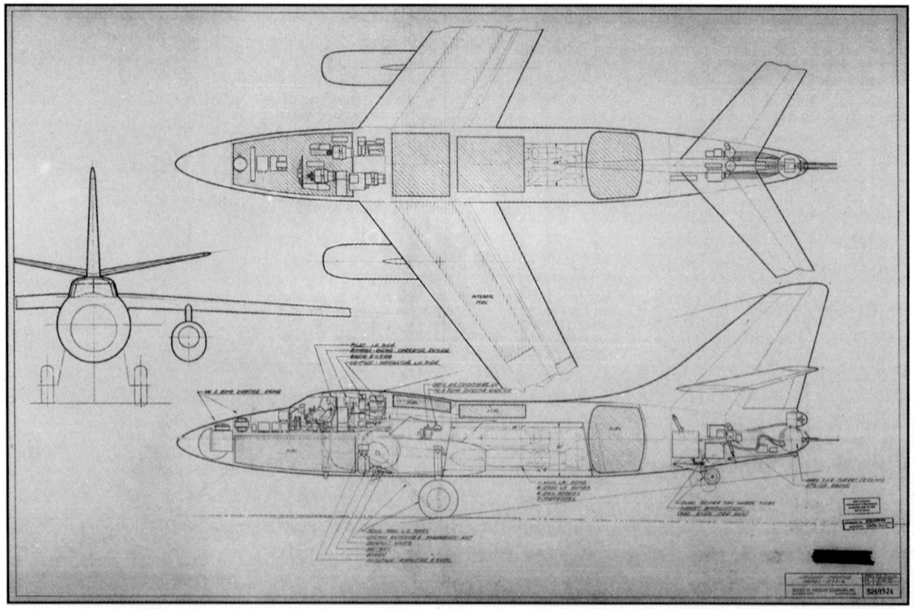

National Archives, RG 72

Above: Inboard profile of the Douglas Model 593-6; note the variety of stores that could be accommodated by the bomb bay.

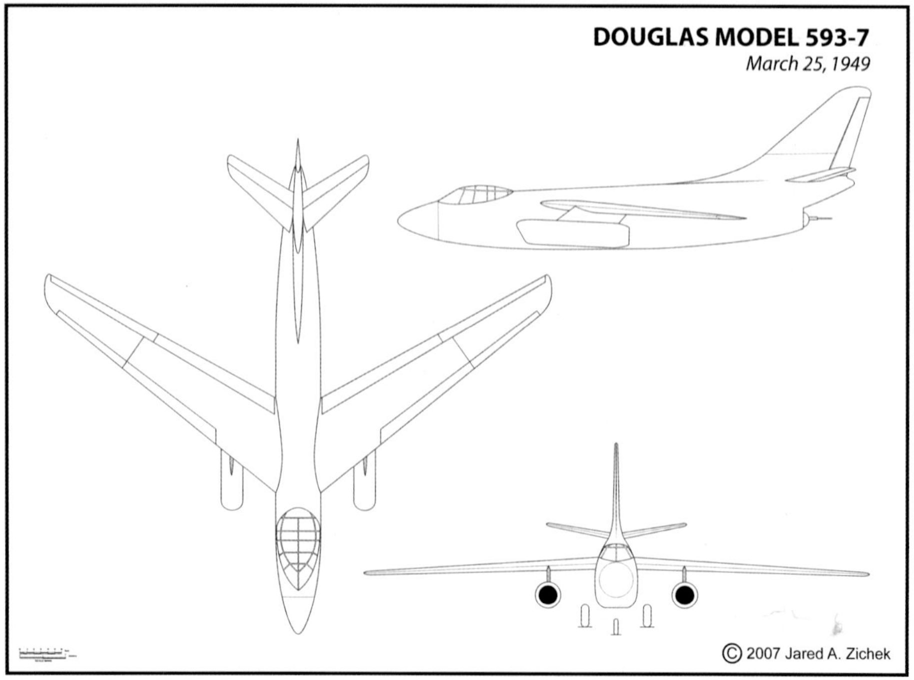

Above: General arrangement drawing of the Douglas Model 593-7; except for the design of the aft fuselage, it closely resembled the Model 593-8, which ultimately became the XA3D-1.

increasing the combat attitude or reducing the takeoff wing load by an amount sufficient to eliminate the JATO requirement for carrier operation.

The airplane configurations investigated by Curtiss were as follows:

1. BuAer evaluation of the P-558.
2. Curtiss-Wright analysis of P-558 proposal using BuAer drag and power plant data.
3. Curtiss-Wright analysis of P-558 proposal using BuAer drag, power plant and weight data.
4. Airplane with turret reduced in size for 6,000 lb bomb bay capacity and weight, with a combat radius nominally the same as that of Airplane 3. The landing stall speed was approximately 115 knots.
5. Airplane with turret, modified for 6,000 lb bomb bay capacity and weight with a combat radius of 1,700 nm. The landing stall speed was approximately 115 knots.
6. Airplane without turret, having a 6,000 lb bomb bay capacity and weight with a combat radius nominally equivalent to that of airplane 3. The landing stall speed was approximately 115 knots.
7. Airplane without turret, having a 6,000 lb bomb bay capacity and weight with a combat radius of 1,700 nm. The landing stall speed was approximately 115 knots.
8. This airplane had basically the same airframe as that of Airplane 7, in which the bomb was replaced by a rear tail turret and a cluster of Sparrow missiles for forward armament. The combat radius was 1,700 nm, which required the use of an auxiliary bomb bay fuel tank located above the missiles in the bomb bay. Due to the increase in weight empty from Airplane 7, the landing stall speed exceeded by a slight amount the desired value of 115 knots. Curtiss noted that the CG position of the airplane was approximately 3.0% MAC aft of that for Airplane 7. This was a necessary consequence of the addition of the rear turret though there was relocation of other equipment in order to minimize the CG movement. Thus, there was some deterioration of the flying qualities of the airplane.
9. Airplane with turret having a 6,000 lb bomb in a 10,000 lb capacity bomb bay and a combat radius of 1,700 nm. The landing stall speed was approximately 115 knots.
10. Airplane 9, in which the 6,000 lb bomb was replaced by the 10,000 lb bomb, which, by maintaining the same takeoff weight, required a reduction of 4,000 lbs in the fuel load.
11. Airplane with turret having the same fuselage and fuel load as Airplane 4 with a larger wing in an attempt to increase the combat altitude.
12. A modified version of Airplane 4 in which the wing area was increased and the fuel load decreased while maintaining the same takeoff gross weight in an attempt to increase the combat altitude.
13. An airplane without turret having a 6,000 lb bomb bay capacity and weight,

a combat radius of 1,700 nm and sufficient wing area to eliminate the JATO requirement for carrier operation.

It is not known which, if any, of these P-558 variants was seriously considered by BuAer before Curtiss's proposal was completely eliminated from consideration. No general arrangement drawings have been found illustrating the aforementioned derivatives of the basic P-558 design, though the table at right provides data on their general characteristics.

Cancellation of the USS United States

On April 23, 1949, the USS *United States* was abruptly cancelled; work on the Heavy Attack aircraft projects was suspended for 35 days shortly thereafter. To understand how this devastating turn of events came about, one must return to the world of politics and budgets. The latter half of 1948 proved to be a difficult one for the US Navy, which was fighting the other military services over the FY 1950 defense budget. The Navy's funding had been progressively cut by Truman and Congress for several years. For the FY 1947 budget, the Navy had asked for $6.325 billion to meet its basic requirements; it only received $4.1 billion. By FY 1949, the Navy's share of the defense budget had fallen to $3.511 billion, despite requiring a minimum of $5.393 billion to stay at current strength.

In July of 1948, President Truman capped the FY 1950 defense budget at $14.4 billion. This led to increased conflict among the military services over the limited funding available; the Navy's aircraft carriers came under particular attack from the Air Force and Army. The Navy received less support from Secretary of Defense James Forrestal than in years past, as the Navy's doctrine conflicted with the JCS's increased reliance on the strategic air offensive at the expense of conventional forces in its war planning. The Navy appeared to be fighting the completion of a unified defense budget, a perception strengthened by anti-Navy propaganda produced by the Air Force and its surrogates.

On March 28, 1949, James Forrestal was replaced by Louis A. Johnson as Secretary of Defense. This came about due to a perceived decline in Forrestal's job performance and rising friction between him and the President over foreign policy and budgetary matters. This would prove to be an unfortunate turn of events for the Navy, as Johnson was an ally of the Air Force, a relationship he had developed as Assistant Secretary of War under Roosevelt from 1937 to 1940 and subsequently as director of Consolidated Aircraft Corporation, which produced the B-36 Peacemaker strategic bomber.

In early 1949, the Air Force continued to believe that the Navy wanted to undertake a major role in the strategic air offensive, which reinforced Air Force opposition to both the flush-deck carrier and the Navy's existing fleet carriers. Forrestal had fended off the Air Force's attacks on the Navy's carriers, but Johnson offered no such support to the Navy. The Air Force began its campaign to cancel the USS *United States* in earnest, sending a memo on the supercarrier to Forrestal in his final days as Secretary of Defense, arguing that the probable military usefulness of a giant aircraft carrier remained unproven. It requested that the project be studied by committees in which all three services were represented.

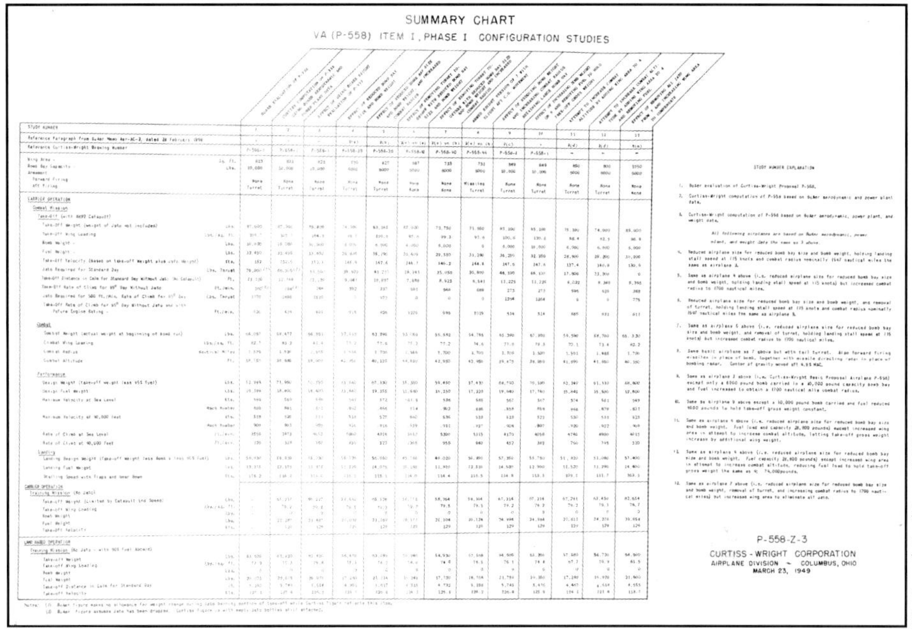
SUMMARY CHART
VA (P-558) ITEM I, PHASE I CONFIGURATION STUDIES
P-558-Z-3
CURTISS-WRIGHT CORPORATION
AIRPLANE DIVISION — COLUMBUS, OHIO
MARCH 23, 1949

National Archives, RG 72

Above: Table summarizing the performance characteristics of various modified versions of the Curtiss P-558 Class VA proposal, which was ultimately rejected by BuAer.

On April 15, 1949, Louis Johnson, having served less than a month as Secretary of Defense, sent a letter to General Eisenhower requesting the verdict of the JCS on the USS *United States* by April 22, a very short time frame. The Navy, represented by Admiral Denfeld, naturally argued for the continued funding of CVA-58. The Army, which had previously supported the Navy's position, switched to the Air Force camp, arguing that the USS *United States* was designed to employ heavy, long-range bombing aircraft, a role that belonged to the Air Force, which already was capable of performing this function. The Air Force concurred, asserting that the large carrier had minimal value compared to land-based aviation capabilities procured with the same resources.

The memoranda from the JCS were sent to Louis Johnson at 10:30 am on April 23. Half an hour later, the Secretary of Defense's office released a press release announcing the cancellation of the USS *United States*. Johnson simultaneously decided to increase funding for the B-36 program. Solicitation of the JCS's opinions had been a mere formality; Johnson had obviously decided to cancel CVA-58 well beforehand. Neither the CNO nor the Secretary of the Navy were consulted before Johnson made this devastating decision. To the public, it was presented as an economy measure in defense spending. In reality, Johnson held strong pro-Air Force sentiments and believed the Navy should not be allowed to participate in long range or strategic air warfare.

Fate of the Class VA, Long Range Heavy and Special Attack Aircraft

Of the two classes of attack aircraft conceived to operate from the Navy's supercarrier, only the Heavy Attack class survived its cancellation, doing so by becoming a smaller and lighter aircraft than initially planned. On April 29, the CNO instructed BuAer to modify the Heavy Attack project, requiring that the aircraft now be able to operate from the smaller CVB-41 class carrier. When work was resumed in May, Douglas had a clear advantage over Curtiss, having made its proposals substantially smaller and lighter from the outset. Douglas ultimately won the contract with the Model 593-8, receiving a contract in July 1949 providing $13,017,052 for the detail design and construction of two XA3D-1 prototypes and one static test airframe. The production A3D Skywarrior would go on to have a very successful career, serving over five decades with the US Navy in the attack, aerial refueling, electronic countermeasures, photographic reconnaissance, crew trainer and VIP transport roles. An Air Force version, designated the B-66 Destroyer, had a similarly successful and varied service life.

Despite extensive research in the National Archives, the author has been unable to determine if the Navy ever declared a formal winner to the Special Attack competition before the cancellation of CVA 58; in any case, there is no evidence that any of the proposals was selected for further development. The proposal charts in connection with the competition were distributed within BuAer on November 15, 1948. Fairchild did not submit the required charts, so Director Frisbie provided a brief summary in lieu thereof. A total of 14 designs, including alternates, was submitted by five contractors in

CONFIDENTIAL

PRICE AND TIME COMPARISONS

LONG RANGE SPECIAL ATTACK COMPETITION

MODEL	CVAC		DOUGLAS EL SEGUNDO 594		MARTIN 245-3	
PHASE I	16 mo. (Phases I–II)	927,629	10 mo.	474,923.70	7 mo.	256,894.43
PHASE II		220,713	14 mo.	569,120.60	12 mo.	402,148.22
PHASE III	38 mo. (Phases III–IV)	18,000,000 (Phases III–IV)	35 mo. (Phases III–IV)	2,585,602.10	23 mo.	2,794,982.05
PHASE IV				9,573,562.95	34 mo.	6,564,079.06
PHASE V	52 mo.	750,000	No. Est.	700,000.00	39 mo.	261,479.50
TOTAL CONTR. ESTIMATE		19,898,342		13,903,209.35		10,279,583.26

Douglas Santa Monica and Fairchild submitted no cost or time estimates.

Douglas, El Segundo cost and time estimates are applicable to all four proposals and the Phase V cost is approximate.

Martin estimates the hull and tip floats for Model 245-1 will cost $1,639,829.76 in addition to the quotation above.

Time estimates indicate total time in months after start of Phase I.

All proposals shown above are on a cost plus fixed fee basis but fee is not included.

CONFIDENTIAL

National Archives, RG 72

Above: In this chart prepared by BuAer comparing price and time estimates in the LRSA competition, Convair's proposal came out as the most expensive, while Martin's was the least.

National Archives, RG 72

Left: Photograph of the Douglas Model 593-8, better known as the XA3D-1 Skywarrior. While smaller and less capable than the Navy originally wanted, it ultimately proved to be a winning and durable design.

the competition. While OS-115 yielded no usable hardware, the Navy persevered with the concept of a large, supersonic carrier-based attack aircraft, ultimately developing the North American A3J (later A-5) Vigilante, which first flew in August of 1958. In hindsight, virtually any of the large and unconventional aircraft proposed to fulfill the Special Attack role would have been difficult and expensive to operate from a carrier, even one as large as the USS *United States*. Furthermore, rapid advances in long range missile and guidance technologies likely would have made the Special Attack aircraft obsolete within a few years of operational service, assuming that it would have made it past the testing and evaluation phase. Thus, however painful it was for the Navy at the time, the elimination of the Special Attack type in 1949 probably was for the best from the standpoint of economy.

The Aftermath

The cancellation of CVA-58 sent shock waves throughout the Navy, with Secretary of the Navy John Sullivan resigning in protest on April 26. This opened the way for even greater attacks by Johnson on the Navy in the spring of 1949, with the Air Force seeking to upset the balanced military establishment and becoming the dominant service. The Air Force had mastered public relations earlier than its rivals, managing to convince both Congress and the public that the strategic air offensive was the only effective way of combatting the Soviet threat.

Not satisfied with the elimination of the USS *United States*, the Air Force embarked on a campaign to strip the Navy of all its existing large aircraft carriers. It opposed Navy plans to modernize two Essex-class carriers, which was imperative given the loss of the Project 6A carrier and the ongoing need for carrier task forces to operate longer range attack aircraft against vital targets while remaining far enough from shore to reduce vulnerability to enemy air attack. Johnson ultimately overrode Air Force objections on June 21, approving $80 million to modernize the carriers. However, the decision was political in nature, with the Secretary of Defense demanding that the Navy be silent about anti-Navy actions by the other services, specifically the Air Force.

On May 25, 1949, Francis P. Matthews was appointed as the new Secretary of the Navy; his selection was strongly influenced by Johnson, who wanted a subservient appointee not inclined to fight strongly for Navy interests. By April 1949, the success of the Air Force's anti-Navy PR campaign and budget cuts in naval aviation prompted Cedric R. Worth, Special Assistant to the Under Secretary of the Navy, and Commander Thomas D. Davies, Special Assistant to the Assistant Secretary of the Navy for Air, to write what would later be known as the infamous "Anonymous Document." This report charged that the B-36 was a "billion dollar blunder" that resulted from the personal financial interest held by the Secretary of Defense and the Secretary of the Air Force in the continued production of the bomber. In addition, these men owed political and personal favors to Floyd Odlum, president of Convair's parent company. The Anonymous Document first found its way to Glenn L. Martin and later to several members of Congress.

In August 1949, the Housed Armed Services Committee (HASC) held what came to be known as the B-36 Hearings to examine the charges leveled in the Anonymous Document. Unfortunately for the Navy, the Air Force successfully defended itself and the B-36 program against the charges. It was revealed that this compilation of unfounded rumors had been drafted by Worth and Davies, publicly besmirching the Navy's reputation. However, the Navy was able to rebound in the late summer of 1949, defending its views in front of the Committee on national military strategy and the importance of strengthening naval aviation.

This was followed by the so-called "Revolt of the Admirals." In October of 1949, Senior Navy leadership delivered controversial testimony in the HASC's Unification and Strategy Hearings, challenging much of the accepted strategic wisdom regarding the effectiveness of the strategic air offensive, the employment of atomic weapons, the capability of the B-36, and the role of carrier aviation. Led by Admiral Radford and supported by Admiral Denfeld, both men made a compelling case for strengthening both naval aviation and the Navy as a whole. This testimony would provide the foundation for the subsequent restoration of the Navy's aircraft carrier program.

Secretary of Defense Louis Johnson fired Admiral Denfeld as CNO on October 27 in retaliation for his defiance. Johnson proceeded to cut the Navy budget further, reducing the number of Navy carrier air groups to 9 for FY 1951, in FY 1949, the number had been 24. Despite this setback, the Navy received increasing support from Congress due to its strong performance at the hearings. On March 1, 1950, the HASC issued its final report on Unification and Strategy, which concluded that intercontinental strategic bombing was not synonymous with strategic air power. US air power consisted of Air Force, Navy and Marine air power; of these, strategic air power was but one aspect. This was a stiff rebuke to the Air Force and its campaign to become the dominant service.

The Korean War broke out on June 25, 1950. Johnson had failed to adequately plan for US conventional force commitments or to properly budget for storage of surplus Army and Navy war-fighting materiel for future use, resulting in costly setbacks in the opening months of the war. As a result, Johnson was fired on September 19, being replaced by General George C. Marshall. With this formidable opponent of the aircraft carrier removed, Congressmen Carl Vinson and the HASC authorized construction of the CVB-59 *Forrestal* in March 1951, the first of several new 75,000 ton super carriers that could support an air wing of 80-100 jet aircraft. Among these was the A3D Skywarrior, which became the mainstay of Navy's long-range nuclear delivery capability from the mid to late 1950s. Much of the thinking that had gone into the USS *United States* was applied to the *Forrestal* design, though it retained the traditional island and had the added innovation of an angled flight deck. The *Forrestal* class carriers became the backbone of the service's power projection capabilities from the mid-1950s onward. In view of both Congress and the Navy, the carrier was the best weapon in the event of an international emergency. The large aircraft carrier remains the centerpiece of US Navy offensive power to this day, though the nuclear deterrent role has been largely assumed by the ballistic missile submarine (SSBN). While the 1949 congressional hearings saved the aircraft carrier, they did not reduce competition between the military services, which retain conflicting strategic doctrines resulting from their different operating environments, guaranteeing that they will continue to have competing views on roles and missions in the years to come.

APPENDIX — Northrop Class VA Studies

From August to October of 1949, Northrop produced a series of unconventional tailless studies for a Class VA Heavy Attack type aircraft. These were produced after the conclusion of the original competition, which was won by the Douglas Model 593-8. However, the author believes that Northrop was keen to land a Navy contract and produced these studies in hopes of derailing progress on the Douglas design or sparking the development of a more advanced alternative. At least 27 configuration studies were produced, designated Preliminary Design (P.D.) 1029 to P.D. 1049, along with six preliminary sketches. These studies were heavily influenced by Northrop's prior work on flying wings and tailless aircraft, such as the YB-49 bomber and X-4 research aircraft. A variety of jet- and turboprop-powered configurations was studied, though all were characterized by a tailless layout, tricycle landing gear, a crew of three, and similar dimensions due to the size restrictions imposed by the aircraft carrier elevator and the height of the hangar deck.

Whether Northrop submitted any of these studies to the Navy remains unknown, as official Navy reaction to these proposals, which were likely unsolicited, has not been located in BuAer records. It is unlikely, however, that any of these progressed beyond the design study stage. By October 1949, the tailless Vought XF7U-1 Cutlass had been flying for over a year, having first flown on September 29, 1948. Testing of this troubled aircraft revealed several problems in the operation of a carrier-based tailless aircraft. Foremost perhaps was the type's steep glide ratio and high angle of attack (AOA) during the carrier approach, which limited the forward visibility of the pilot and made landings hazardous. The high AOA also masked out airflow past the tailfins, reducing controllability, which was already mediocre due to the inherent difficulty of maintaining proper CG in a tailless aircraft. Any one of the Northrop Class VA studies would have likely suffered from the same problems. Digital fly-by-wire technology would largely solve these controllability issues in the 1970s, but the Navy's unpleasant experiences with tailless aircraft would compel the service to stick with more conventional aircraft for carrier operations.

These drawings on pages 215 to 222 originate from a roll of microfilm provided by collector Lowell Ford, who worked in the aerospace industry for several decades. They have been digitally traced by the author to improve quality and clarity and are reproduced here at 1/288 scale, with a table summarizing their known characteristics at the end of the appendix. The block of P.D. numbers assigned to the Class VA design effort has several gaps, as some of these were given to unrelated projects entirely, while others are missing. A few of these studies also received a separate "VA Type Carrier Based Airplane No.," which is indicated in the characteristics table when known.

Northrop Class VA Studies In Detail

Preliminary Sketches Six rough, fragmentary sketches from the early stages of Northrop's Class VA design effort have survived, none of which received an official designation; they are labelled here as *Sketch A* through *F* for sake of convenience. These are all side view drawings of tailless aircraft featuring a distinct fuselage, in contrast to the more elegant flying wing-type configurations that would appear later in the series. The nose and cockpit profiles are all quite similar, indicating perhaps that these may all be the work of a single designer. *Sketch A* appears to have a pair of podded turbojets attached directly to the undersurface of a low swept wing, a large external store located beneath the fuselage, a small vertical tail mounted on the aft fuselage, and a periscope for a remote-controlled tail turret, which is not actually shown in the drawing. *Sketch B* is a refinement of *Sketch A*, with the turbojets now mounted under the wing on forward canted struts, the large store recessed into the underside of the fuselage, a pair of small vertical surfaces placed mid span on the wing, and indications of a tail turret and gun laying radar in the aft fuselage. *Sketch C* depicts the most unusual configuration among the surviving sketches, with a pair of turbojets mounted on very large forward canted struts above a low swept wing; this impractical engine arrangement never reappeared in the succeeding studies. *Sketch D* is similar to *Sketch A*, except that the wing was now shoulder-mounted. *Sketch E* is the most fragmentary of the lot, showing a large recessed store under the fuselage, a mid-wing arrangement, and a small vertical tail. Finally, *Sketch F* appears to be along the lines of *Sketch A*, except that the recessed store has been moved forward, probably to improve CG; details of the engine mounting are missing and two distinct nose/fuselage contours are shown.

P.D. 1029 The first Northrop Class VA to receive a P.D. designation, this fragmentary design appears to be a refinement of *Sketch A*, with the pair of turbojets (identified as Westinghouse XJ40-WE-6s) now mounted on long, aftward swept struts. The external store is also mounted well away from the fuselage, towards the rear. The top view shows the seating arrangement, which likely placed the pilot and copilot/navigator side-by-side up front with the bombardier in the back, all housed under a large canopy providing good all-around vision. The engine arrangement necessitated a tall landing gear, which was heavier and more prone to collapse than more compact types.

P.D. 1030 resembles the original *Sketch A*, except that it incorporates the remote-controlled tail turret and gun laying radar of *Sketch B*. Note the vertical splitter in the air intake of the compact XJ-40 pod, which was mounted well away from the fuselage to reduce pressure losses and maintain undisturbed airflow. Also note the small area of the vertical tail - Northrop tended to favor minimal or no vertical tail surfaces to save weight in its tailless/flying wing designs, relying instead on wing reflex, wing tip-mounted drag devices, and elevons to provide stability and control. This is the first complete three-view in the Class VA series.

P.D. 1031 is powered by a single Allison 450-E-1 turbojet mounted high in the aft fuselage behind the crew; it is the only study to feature this power plant. The high engine position, along with the shoulder-mounted swept wing and deep fuselage, provided ample internal space for the bomb bay, fuel, avionics, etc. The wing position necessitated a tall main gear, which features two tandem wheels on each unit. Two installations were proposed for the main gear; the first folded inward and flat into the wing, while the second retracted upwards into a fairing under the wing that also carried a small vertical tail at its aft end. The air intakes were mounted above and behind the leading edge of the wing; this location would have likely suffered from boundary layer problems at high AOA, a phenomenon that was poorly understood at the time. The abbreviated aft fuselage housed a gun turret but no radar.

P.D. 1032 is the first known Class VA study to feature what would be described today as a Blended Wing Body (BWB) configuration, which combines high lift swept wings with a flattened, airfoil-shaped body. This enables the entire aircraft to generate lift and minimize drag, resulting in greater fuel economy and range. The wide fuselage also provides ample volume for engines, bombs, fuel, etc. BWB differs from a standard flying wing in that it has a distinct and separate wing structure, though the difference between the types can be quite subtle.

In addition to its handsome BWB planform, P.D. 1032 is also notable for its air intakes, which were placed well forward just behind the nose radome, resulting in long ducts to the jet engines in the aft fuselage. This ugly intake configuration would reappear in other studies later in the series. The canopy is long and narrow, indicating that the three crewmembers probably sat in line. Prominent vertical tails were mounted outboard of the fuselage-wing juncture to provide yaw. The rounded end of the aft fuselage protrudes from the trailing edge between the engines and could have housed a gun turret, though none is shown in the three-view, which is lacking in detail. Both the nose gear and main gear are fitted with dual wheels, implying a high gross weight.

P.D. 1033 reverts to a simpler unblended tailless arrangement, appearing to be a refinement of the original *Sketch B*. Interesting details of this study include the tandem wheel main gear, which first appeared on P.D. 1031; the bomb bay, which could be lowered to the ground for easy servicing and maintenance; and the asymmetric placement of the bombardier behind the pilot and copilot/navigator.

P.D. 1034 appears to be an evolution of P.D. 1032, featuring a more conventional fuselage and a higher aspect ratio wing with a span of 88 ft. The large air intakes were also placed further aft at the leading edge of the wing, reducing duct length. The wider canopy probably allowed the pilot and copilot/navigator to sit side-by-side, which provided for superior communication and was preferred by the Navy. The single wheel main gear retracted upwards into an aerodynamic housing that also supported a vertical tail. Note the slight outward cant of the XJ-40 turbojets, which was likely done to make single engine flight more feasible in the event the other engine failed or was damaged.

P.D. 1034-B is quite similar to P.D. 1034 except that the span has been reduced to 73 ft. The three-view drawing also features more detail of the internal structure; the crew arrangement was similar to the P.D. 1033. The design also incorporates wing folding, a necessity for carrier stowage.

P.D. 1035 returns to the BWB configuration of P.D. 1032, though the fuselage is less flattened and the wings are of shorter span. The more capacious fuselage allowed the bomb and additional fuel to be carried internally. The cockpit canopy is a much larger greenhouse type. The forward placement of the air intakes close to the radome is similar to the P.D. 1032. Overall, the drawing is more detailed than earlier ones, with fuselage cross sections and indications of radar and cockpit equipment.

P.D. 1036 eliminates most of the blending between the wing and fuselage, which now features a gun turret and radar to defend against attacks from the rear. The canopy has been substantially reduced in area while the air intakes have been redesigned, the ducts being flattened and snaking under the wing to feed air to the XJ-40 engines placed on the sides of the aft fuselage.

P.D. 1037 has a similar planform to the P.D. 1034-B but retains the nose section and canopy of the P.D. 1036.

P.D. 1046 The numbering skips to this design study, which features a thin high aspect ratio wing attached to a shallow, flat-bottomed fuselage. Prominent intake tunnels ran along the sides of the fuselage, feeding air to the pair of XJ-40 turbojets placed at the rear. The bomb load and a large portion of the fuel was moved to a large expendable store hung from the bottom of the fuselage on an aftward swept pylon, which also necessitated a somewhat taller landing gear than earlier studies. The pair of vertical tails were placed well behind the trailing edge of the wing on pods that also housed the main gear. The navigator was moved to the center line of the aircraft, probably due to the narrowness of the fuselage.

P.D. 1047 was essentially the same as P.D. 1046, except that the air intakes were moved to underneath the wing to reduce the length of the ducts. In practice, these "armpit" inlets could have suffered problems with boundary layer removal had the type been built.

P.D. 1048 was an evolution of the preceding design which retained the thin high aspect ratio wing but relocated the engines to large pods hung from forward swept pylons under the wings. These pods reduced the bending moment of the wing and provided undisturbed airflow for the engines, along with certain maintenance advantages. A single vertical tail was placed at the rear of the circular section fuselage, which featured a bicycle landing gear with small pogo type wheels extending from the engine pods. The expendable store was offset to the port wing, while the crew was seated in line under a very long braced canopy.

P.D. 1049 is virtually the same as the previous study, except that the fuselage cross section has been enlarged to accommodate the side-by-side crew arrangement of the P.D. 1033. The crew was housed under a large greenhouse canopy.

P.D. 1050 is reminiscent of P.D. 1047, though it differs in several important respects. The biggest change is in the carriage of the fuel and bomb load, which has now been separated into two droppable stores hanging from the port and starboard wings, respectively. The engines were placed in pods attached along the sides of the lower aft fuselage, with no blending between the intakes and the fuselage, unlike earlier studies. A single vertical tail was placed at the rear of the fuselage. The landing gear was shorter than the P.D. 1047 due to the shoulder wing and smaller stores/pylons.

P.D. 1051 is the first known Northrop Class VA study to be powered by a turboprop, in this case a Turbodyne XT-37-A. The high fuel consumption and unreliability of early turbojets compelled designers to seriously consider the turboprop as an alternative power plant, due to its greater efficiency and range. However, the propeller's loss of efficiency at higher speeds limited the aircraft's top speed; thus, the turboprop eventually found use mostly in transports, patrol aircraft, and other platforms for which range took precedence over speed. In this study, the XT-37-A is placed in a pusher configuration slightly offset to starboard to counteract the torque of the propeller. Also notable is the variable incidence wing, which was probably required to prevent the propeller from colliding with the deck during landings and to improve pilot visibility. A large pair of vertical tails were mounted on the wings with fairings that also housed the main gear. The landing gear was somewhat tall, necessitated by the large external store and propeller.

P.D. 1052 is nearly identical to P.D. 1049, except for the addition of an elegant wing-root fillet. This was likely done to reduce compressibility and improve overall aerodynamic fineness.

P.D. 1053 returned to the turboprop theme, being powered by two Allison XT-40s mounted in large nacelles in a pusher configuration under a swept high aspect ratio wing. Vertical tail surfaces were placed above and below the aft fuselage, the lower surface also acting as a bumper to prevent propeller damage during landings. The bomb and extra fuel would have likely been carried in the usual expendable store, not shown in the drawing.

P.D. 1054 reverted to a jet configuration, though it differed in several respects from the jet studies that preceded it. The bubble canopy was abandoned in this study for an arrangement similar to the Douglas A3D, with a step in the nose and the cockpit faired into the fuselage. This provided the pilot with superior forward vision, though the view to the rear was limited. The pilot and copilot/navigator operator sat side-by-side with the bombardier sitting in the back, offset to port. Two pods housing one Pratt and Whitney XJ-60 each hung from the shoulder-mounted swept wing; a bulbous fairing on the bottom of each pod housed a multi-bogey main gear. A separate detail drawing of this installation was prepared and is reproduced here. The aft fuselage carried a swept vertical tail, while the large expendable store was hung in an asymmetric position from the port wing.

P.D. 1055 Like the P.D. 1051, the P.D. 1055 was powered by the XT-37-A turboprop. However, instead of offsetting the engine a few degrees starboard to counteract torque, a large pod was added to the port wing tip, resulting in an asymmetric configuration. Two stores were carried underneath the variable incidence wing. Vertical fins were placed above and below the aft fuselage, the ventral surface protecting the propeller during landings. The tall landing gear was of very narrow track and probably would not have been acceptable to BuAer.

P.D. 1060 was a BWB study similar to the P.D. 1035, except that the fuselage is of shallower depth. An inboard profile and a loft line diagram were also drawn up for this design, indicating perhaps that it was the favored candidate for further development among Northrop's Class VA studies.

P.D. 1061 was another BWB configuration generally similar to the preceding study except for the addition of a large external store, which featured extendable "arms" to push it away from the fuselage when it was time to be dropped. This was likely added to minimize the chances of collision during separation.

P.D. 1067 was another variation in a configuration that first appeared with the P.D. 1034-B - a tailless twin engine aircraft with blending between the fuselage and wing. The P.D. 1067 was slightly larger than the P.D. 1034-B and featured a shallower fuselage and a curved trailing edge at the wing-fuselage juncture.

P.D. 1068 is basically variant of the P.D. 1060 in which each main gear folded upwards into a fairing that also supported a vertical tail, an arrangement used in the preceding P.D. 1067 and selected earlier studies.

P.D. 1071 was the first study in the Northrop Class VA study to be powered by four jets, which were labelled as "Allison composite fanjets" in the original drawing. This engine was likely an early form of turbofan, in which a low pressure compressor functions as a fan, supplying supercharged air to both the engine core and a bypass duct. The bypass airflow either passes to a separate 'cold nozzle' or mixes with low pressure turbine exhaust gases, before expanding through a 'mixed flow nozzle.' This produces an exhaust speed that is better matched to subsonic aircraft's flight speed, resulting in improved fuel consumption and much lower noise. Pairs of these were mounted side-by-side in large nacelles attached to the underside of the wings. These nacelles supported vertical tails and housed the main gear, which retracted forward and upward into a space between the intake ducts. The fuselage inboard profile was quite similar to the P.D. 1067.

P.D. 1073 was a variant of the P.D. 1049 powered by four Allison composite fanjets. These were housed in a pair of large nacelles hung from forward swept struts under the wing; except for these, the rest of the design was virtually identical to the earlier study.

P.D. 1074 is the final known Northrop Class VA study. It is essentially a four-jet derivative of the P.D. 1060 powered by the aforementioned fanjets. The additional pair of engines necessitated a wider air intake and changes to the aft fuselage; otherwise, the two studies were quite similar. Due to a lack of documentation from Northrop, it is not known whether these four-jet studies showed any appreciable performance gains over their twin-jet predecessors; in any case, reliable turbofan engines would not see widespread use until the early 1960s, making the question a theoretical one at best.

NORTHROP NAVY CLASS VA TYPE, CARRIER BASED, 1949

PRELIMINARY SKETCHES

SKETCH A

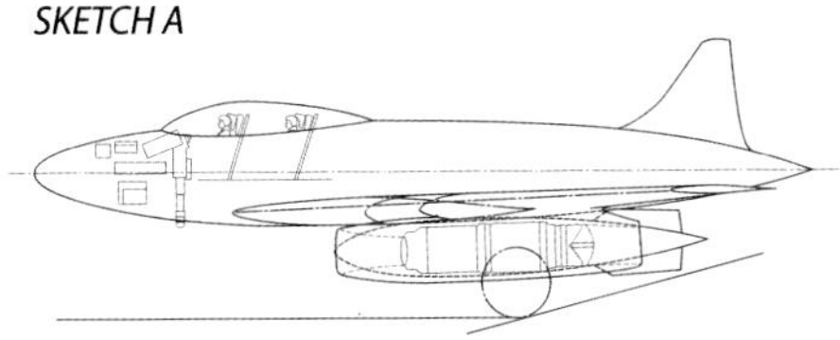

SKETCH B

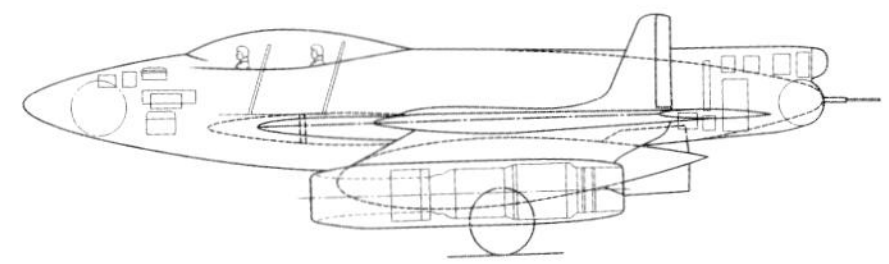

SKETCH C

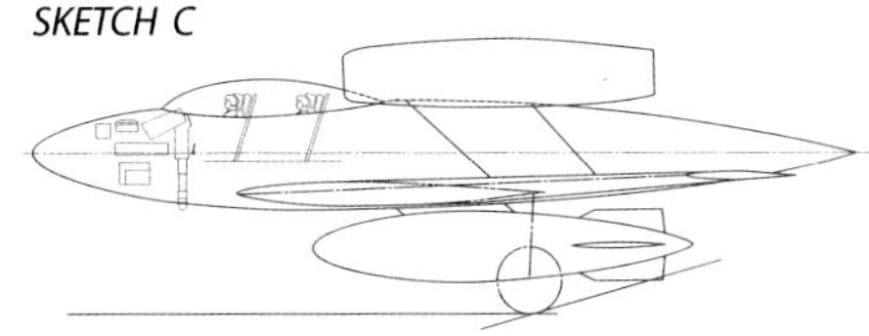

SKETCH D

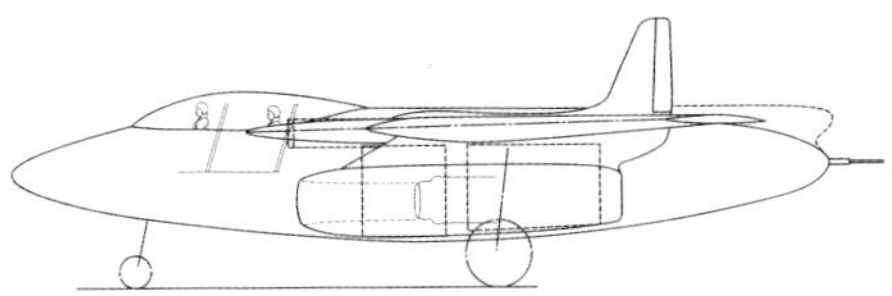

SKETCH E

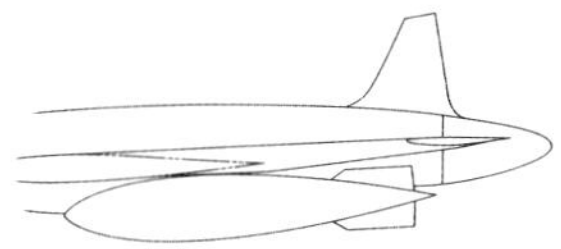

SKETCH F

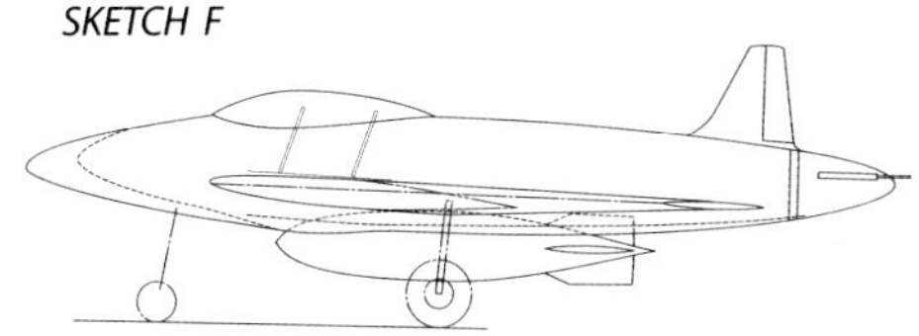

NORTHROP P.D. 1029

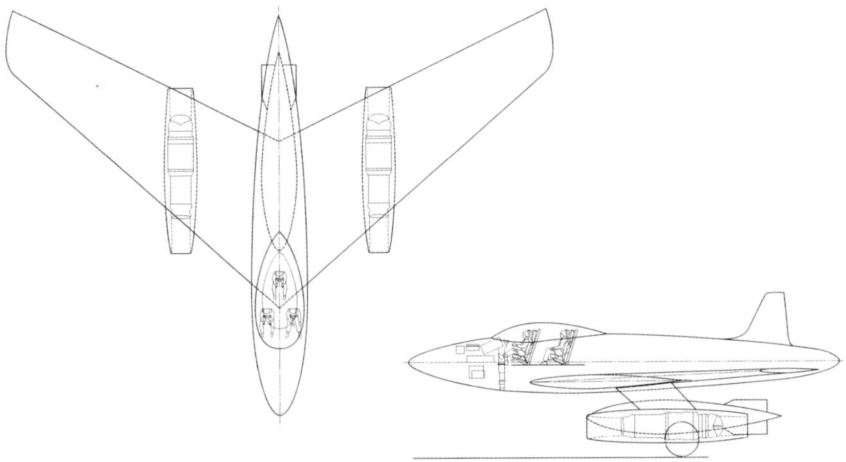

NORTHROP P.D. 1030

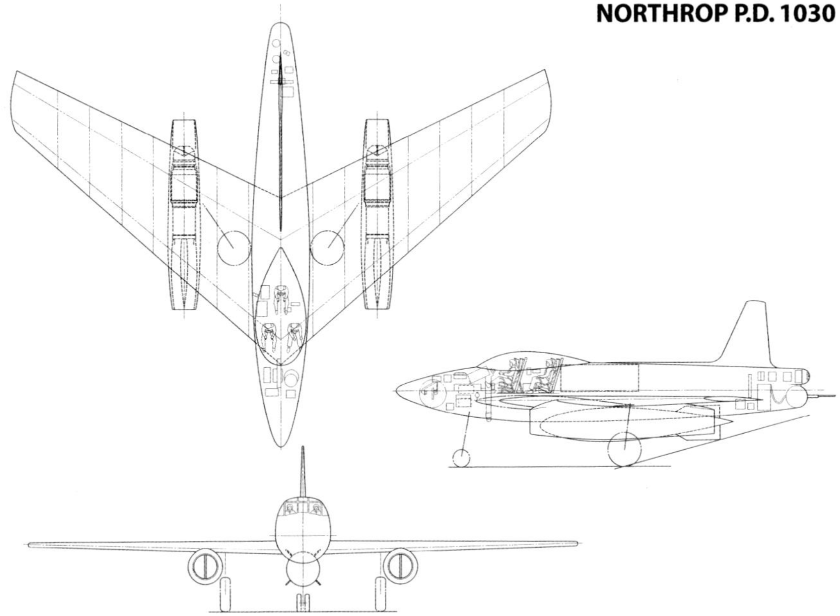

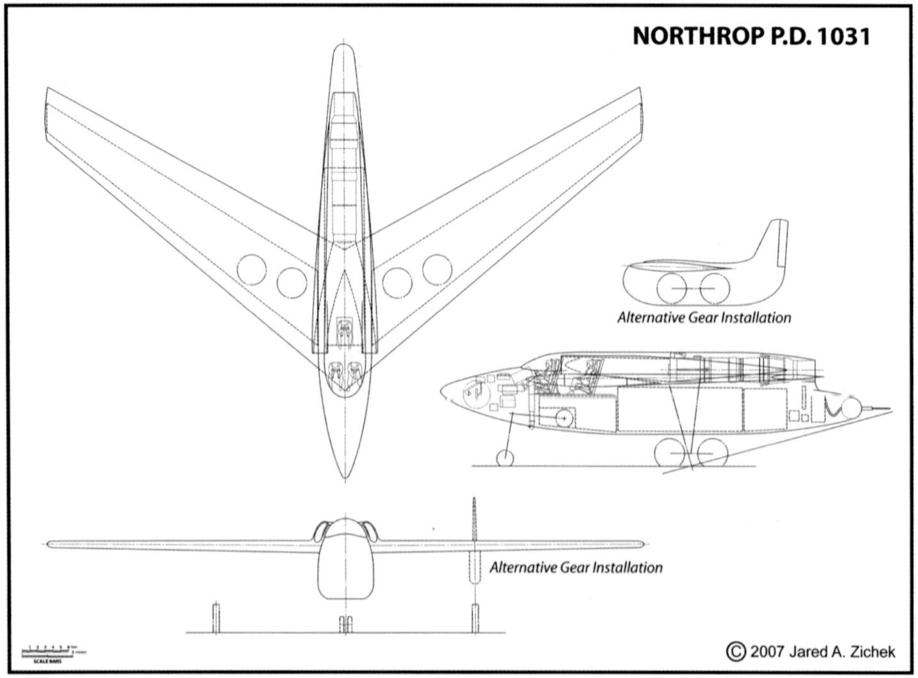
NORTHROP P.D. 1031
Alternative Gear Installation
Alternative Gear Installation
© 2007 Jared A. Zichek

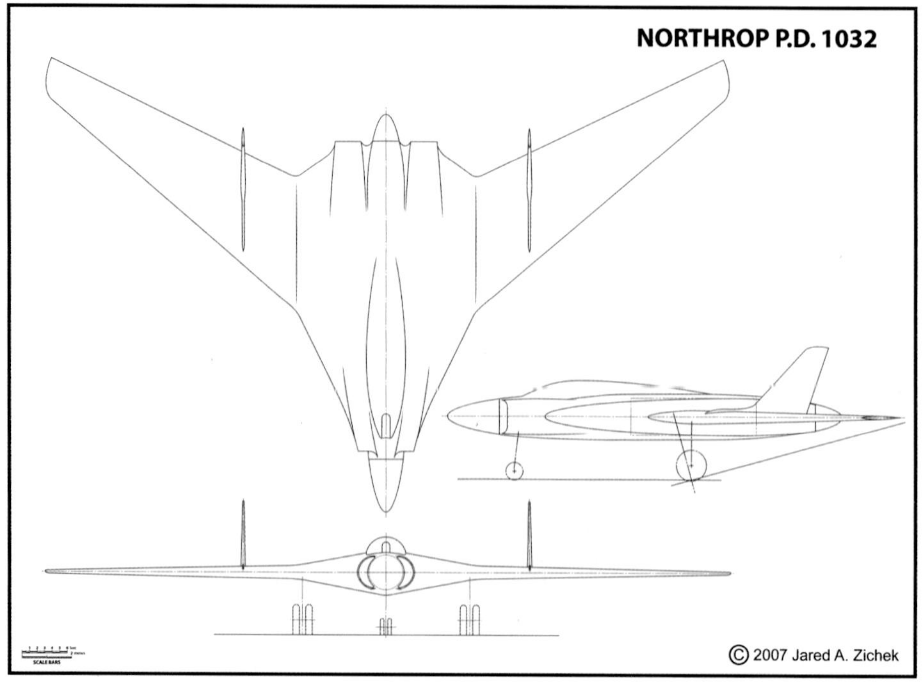
NORTHROP P.D. 1032
© 2007 Jared A. Zichek

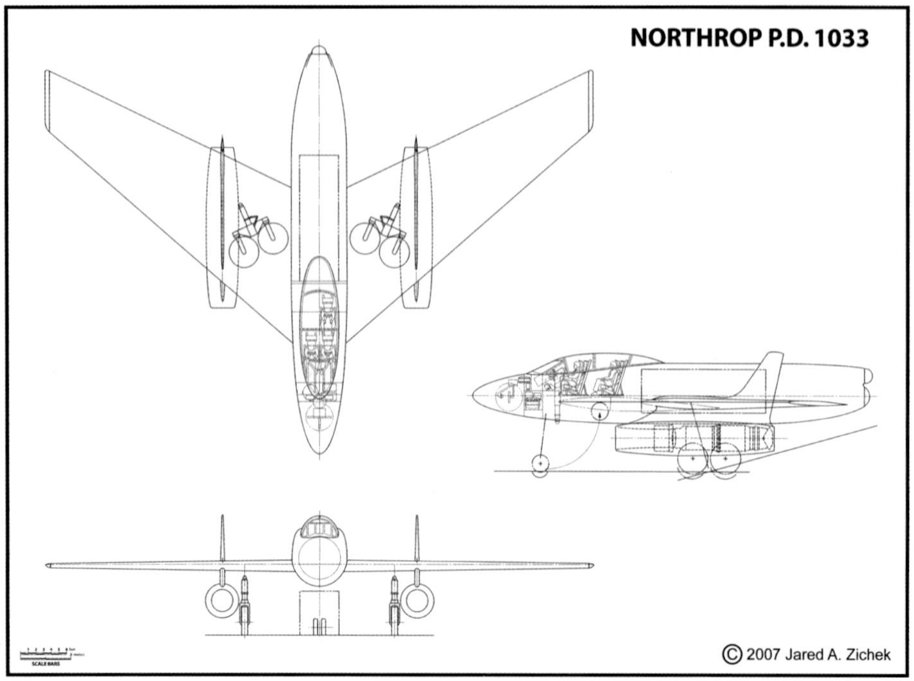
NORTHROP P.D. 1033
© 2007 Jared A. Zichek

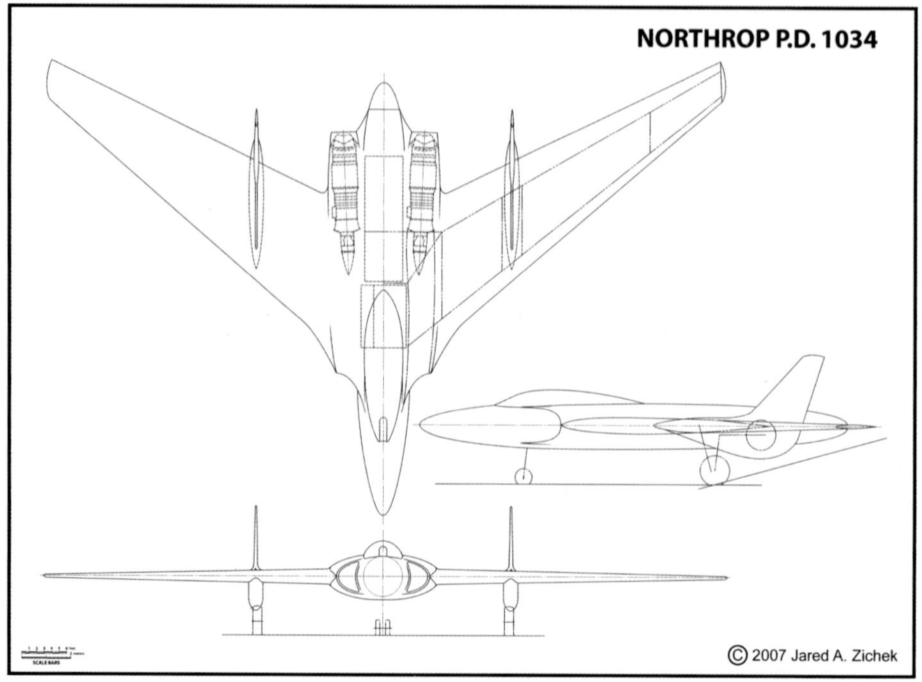
NORTHROP P.D. 1034
© 2007 Jared A. Zichek

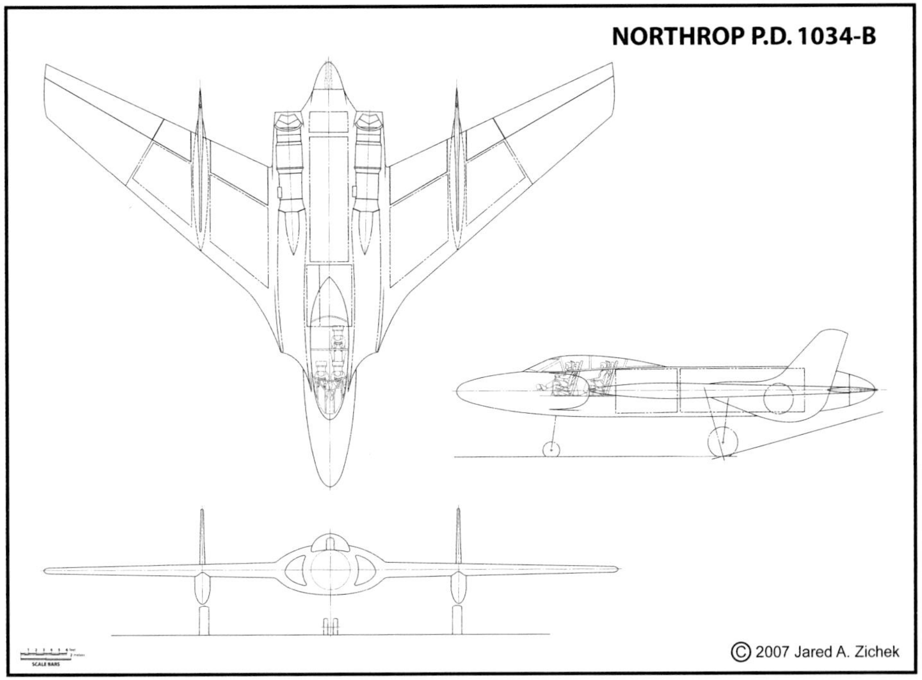
NORTHROP P.D. 1034-B
© 2007 Jared A. Zichek

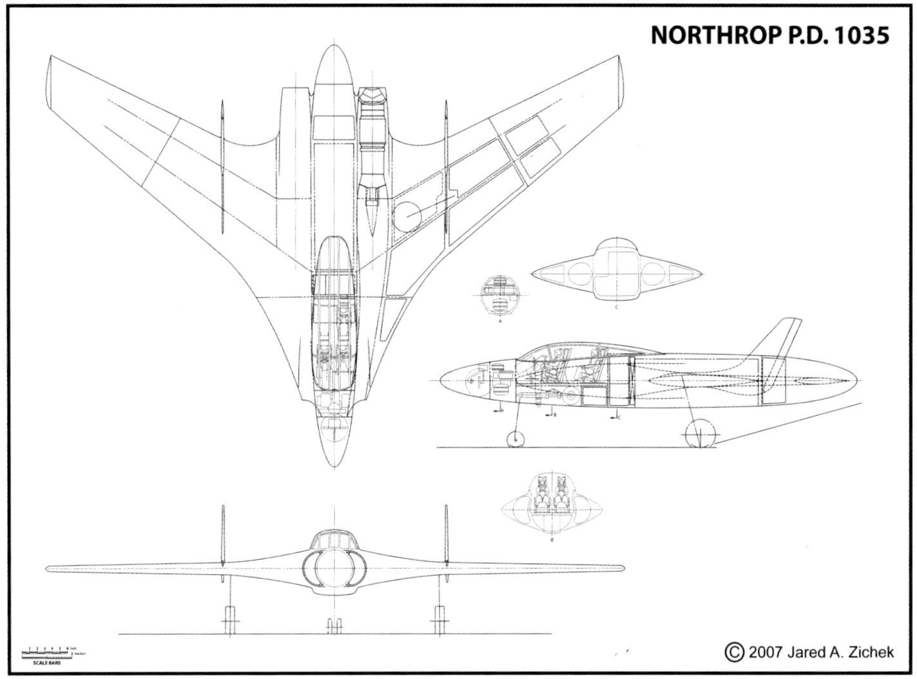
NORTHROP P.D. 1035
© 2007 Jared A. Zichek

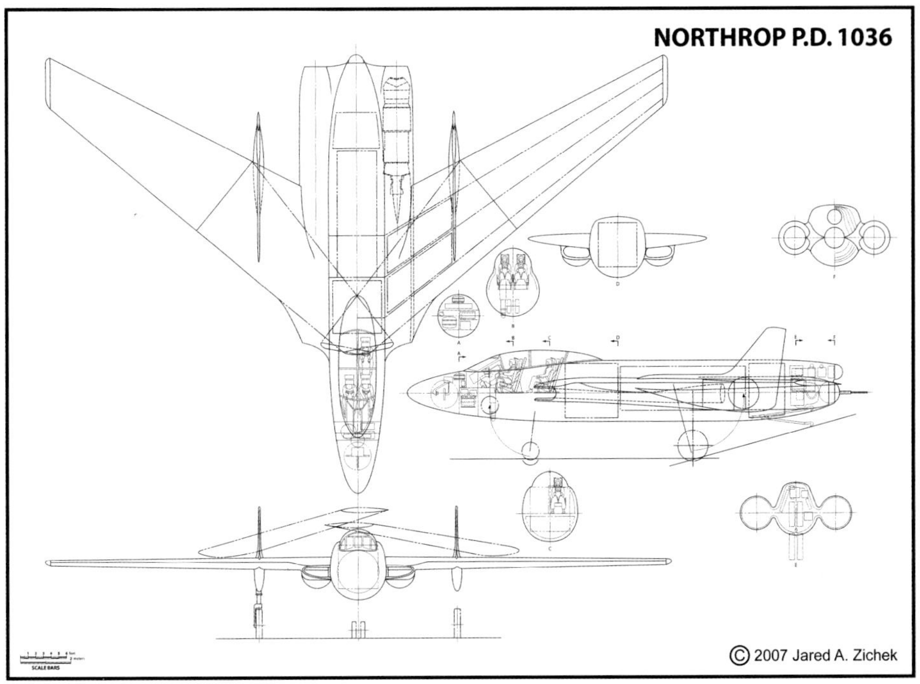
NORTHROP P.D. 1036
© 2007 Jared A. Zichek

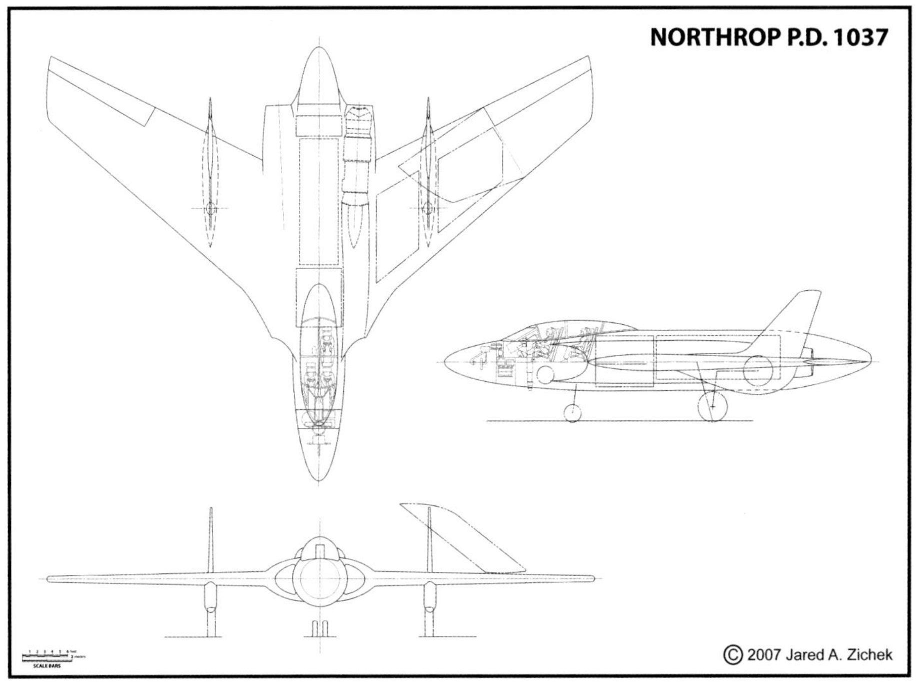
NORTHROP P.D. 1037
© 2007 Jared A. Zichek

NORTHROP P.D. 1046

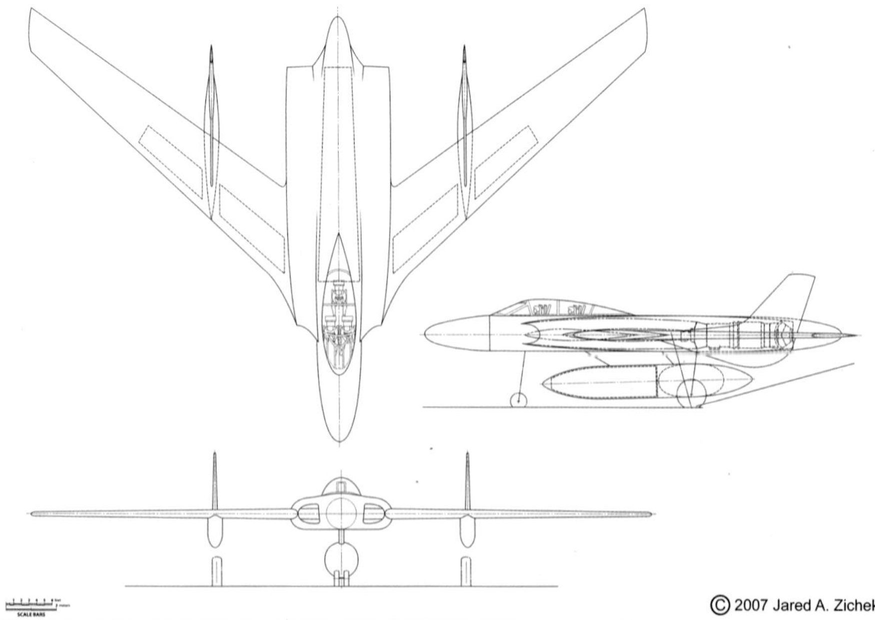

© 2007 Jared A. Zichek

NORTHROP P.D. 1047

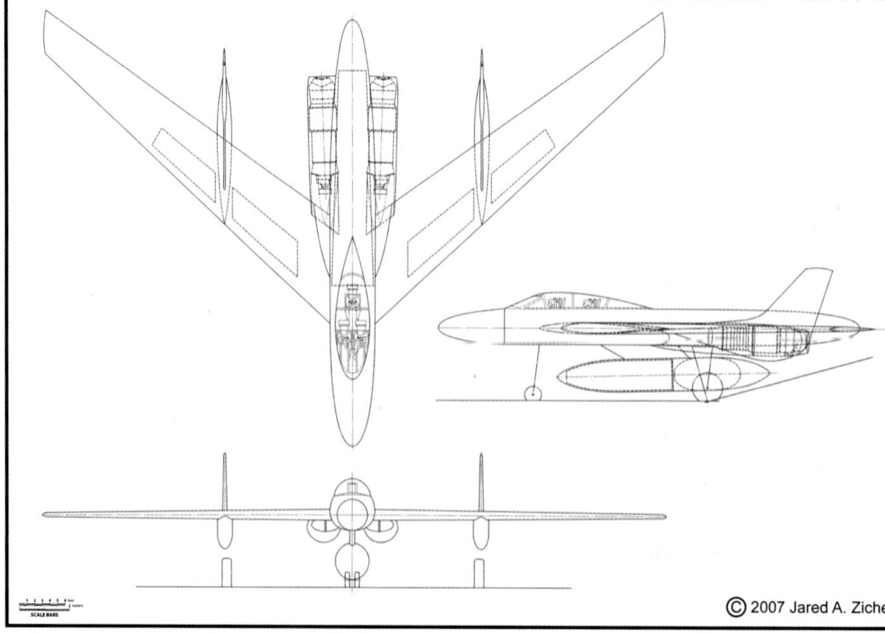

© 2007 Jared A. Zichek

NORTHROP P.D. 1048

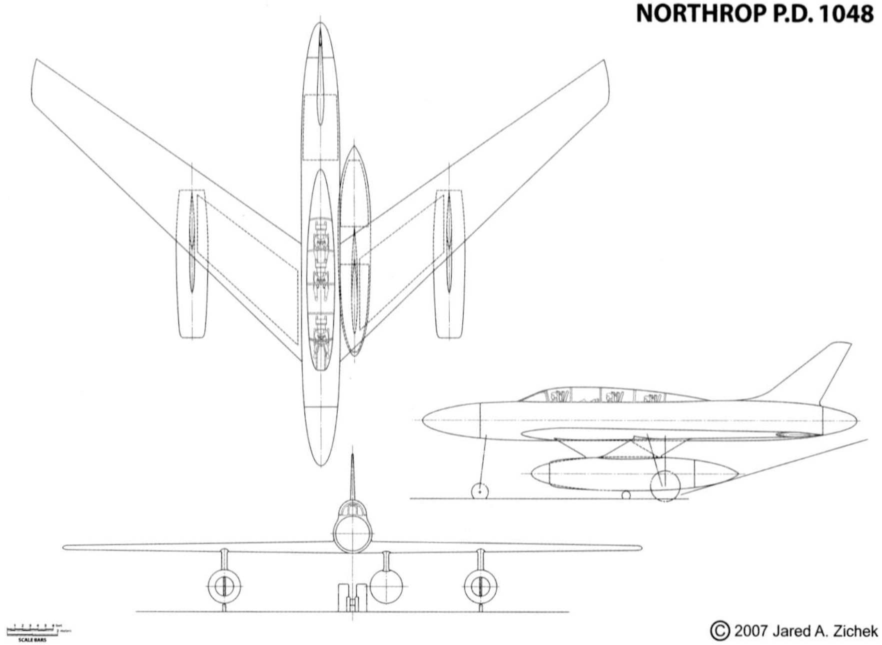

© 2007 Jared A. Zichek

NORTHROP P.D. 1049

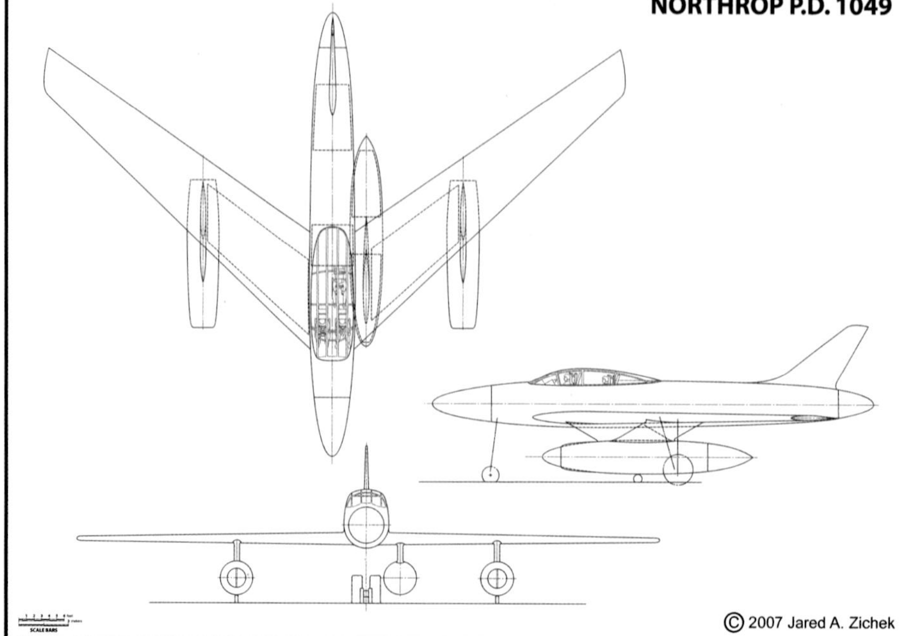

© 2007 Jared A. Zichek

NORTHROP P.D. 1050

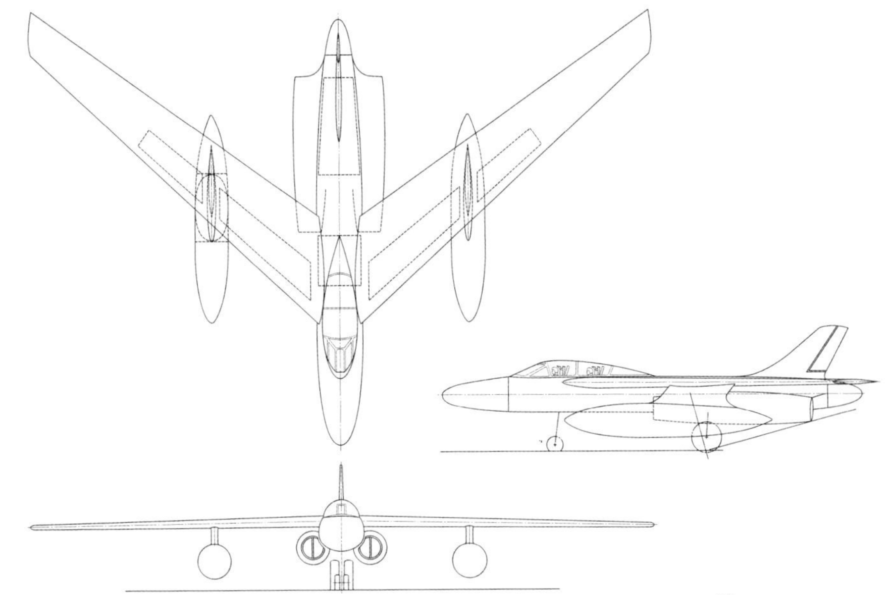

NORTHROP P.D. 1051

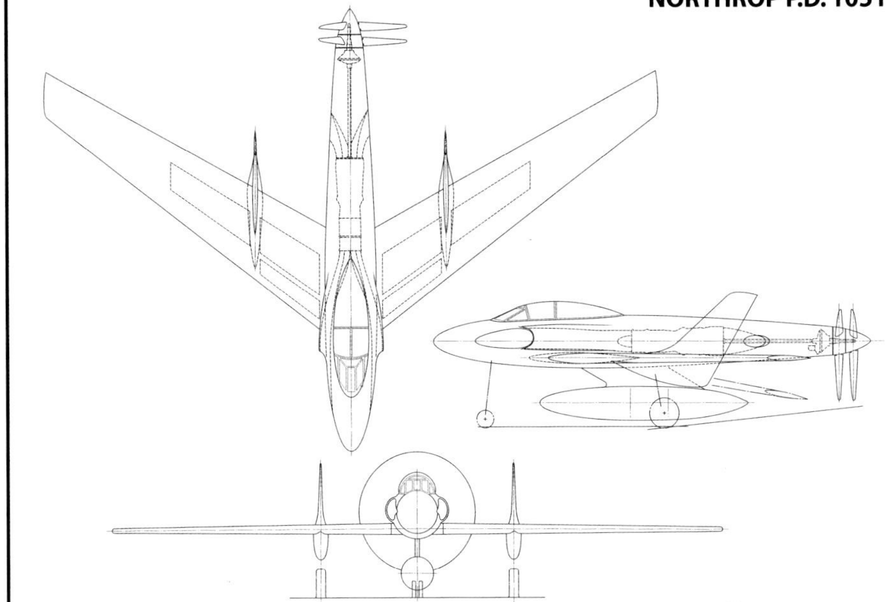

NORTHROP P.D. 1052

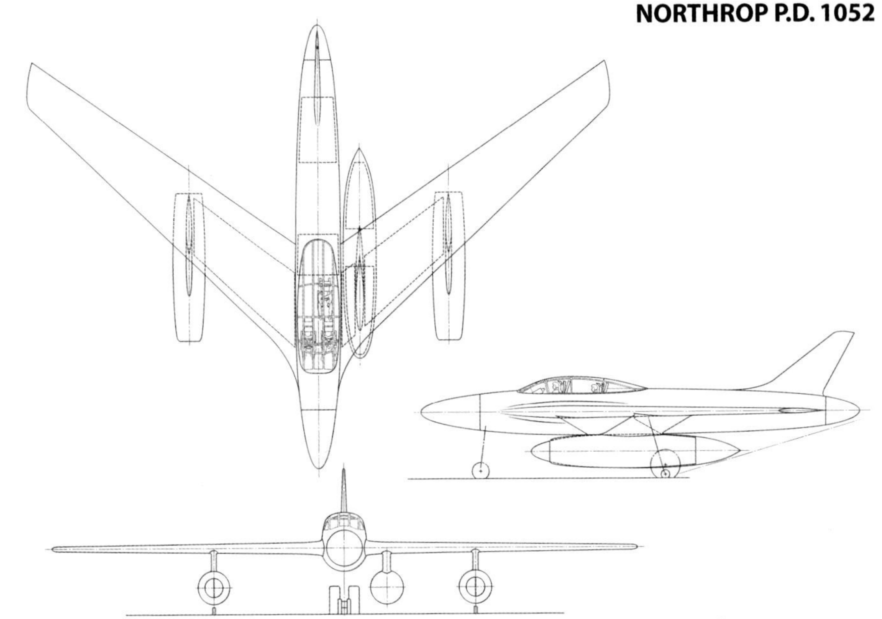

NORTHROP P.D. 1053

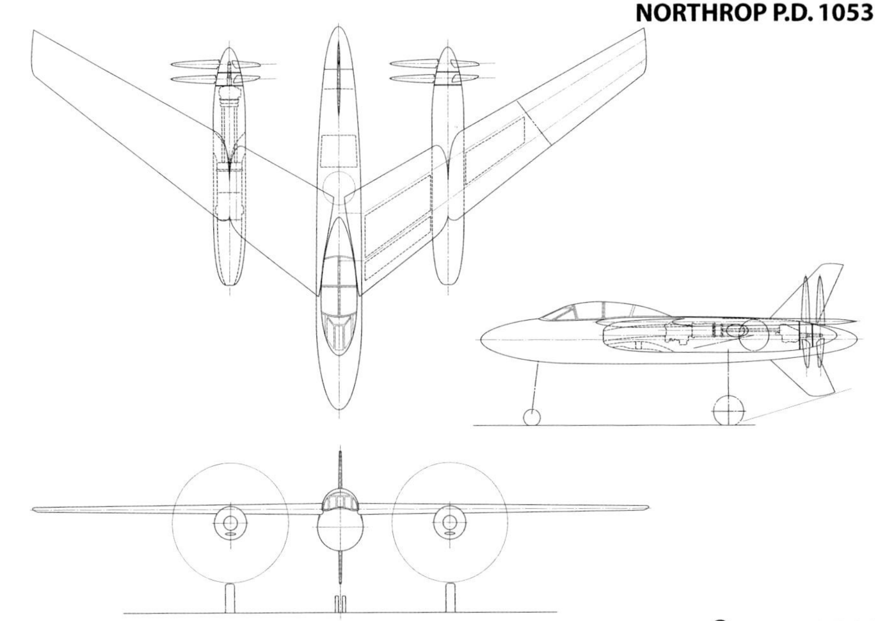

NORTHROP P.D. 1054

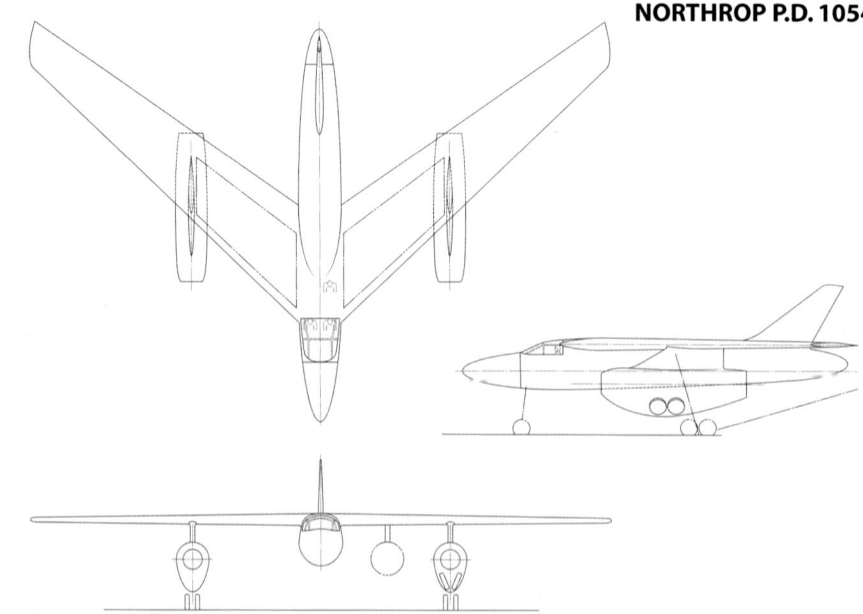

© 2007 Jared A. Zichek

NORTHROP P.D. 1054 DETAIL OF ENGINE NACELLE

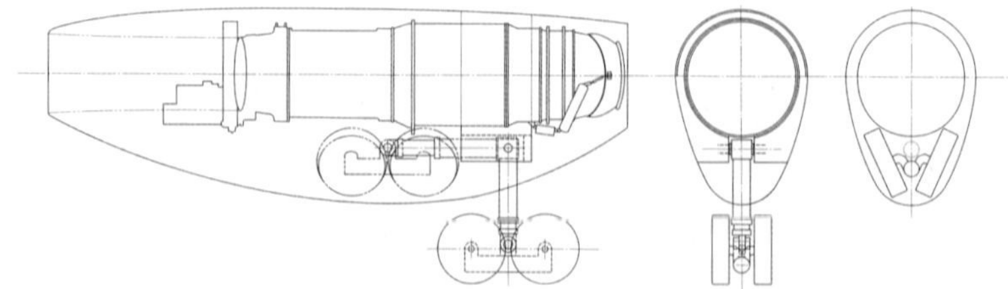

1 2 3 4 5 6 feet
2 meters
SCALE BARS

© 2007 Jared A. Zichek

NORTHROP P.D. 1055

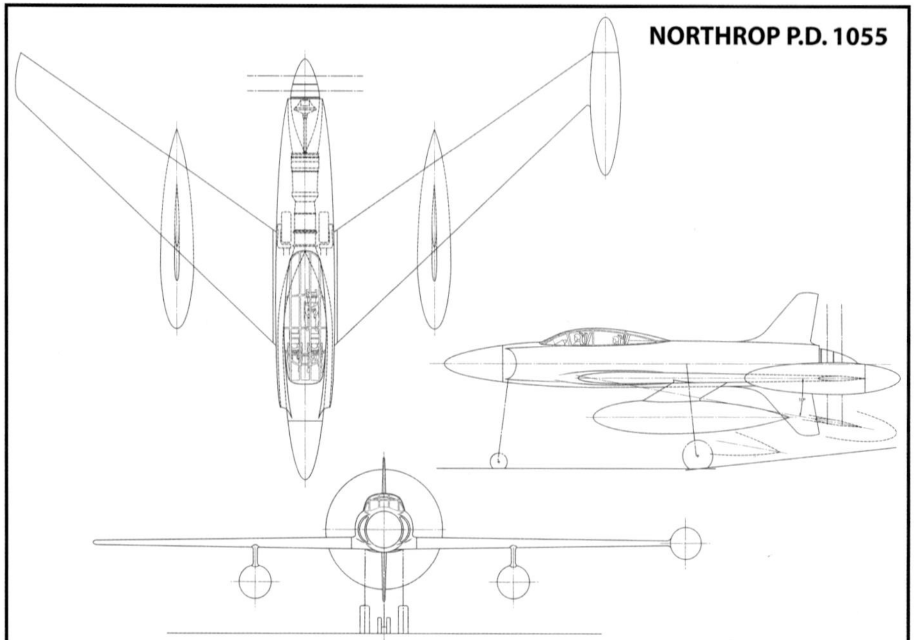

© 2007 Jared A. Zichek

NORTHROP P.D. 1060

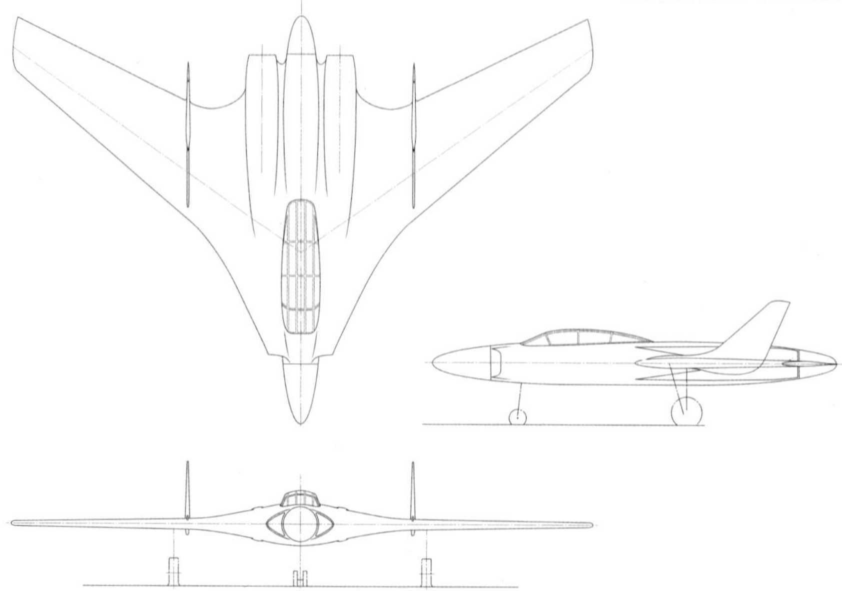

© 2007 Jared A. Zichek

NORTHROP P.D. 1060 INBOARD PROFILE

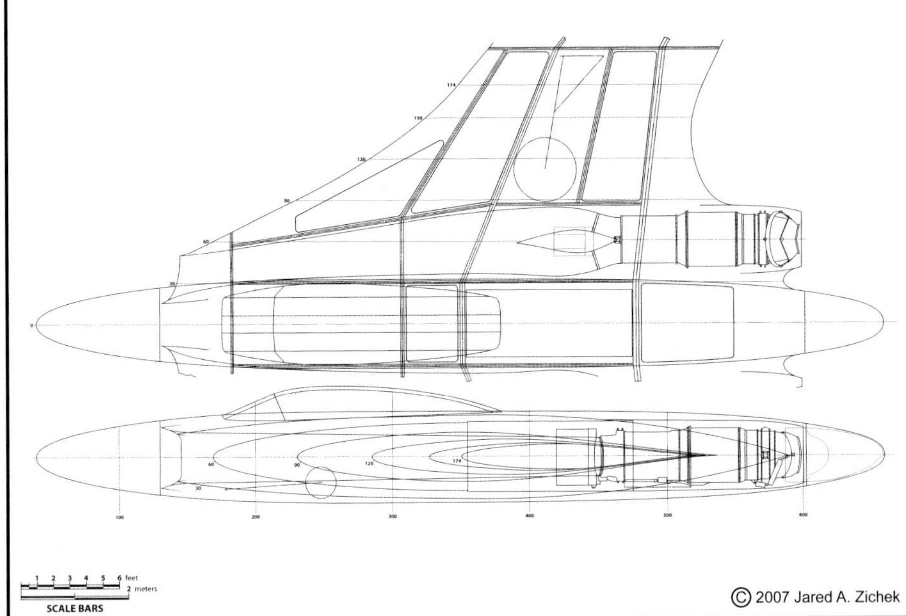

NORTHROP P.D. 1060 LOFT LINES

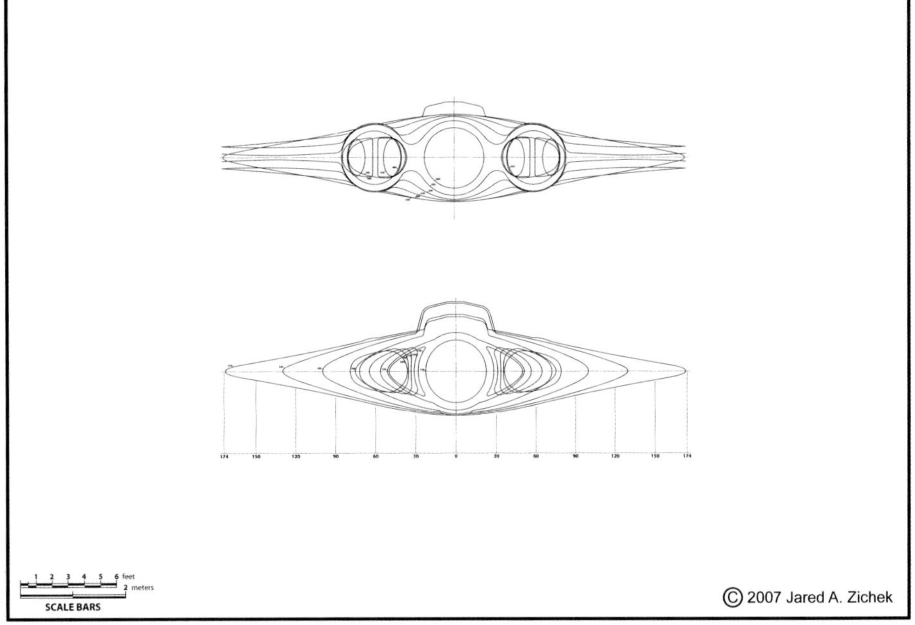

NORTHROP P.D. 1061

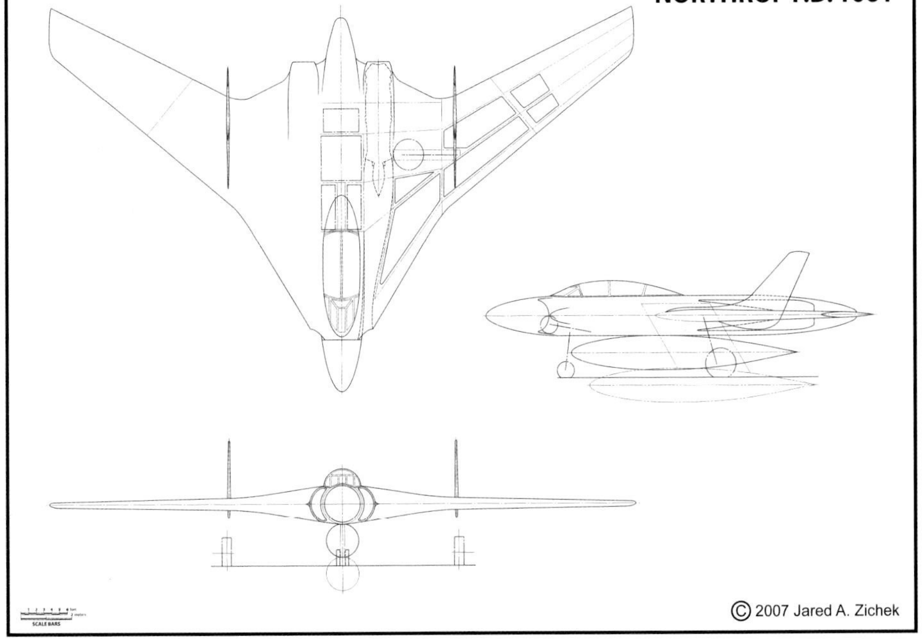

NORTHROP P.D. 1067

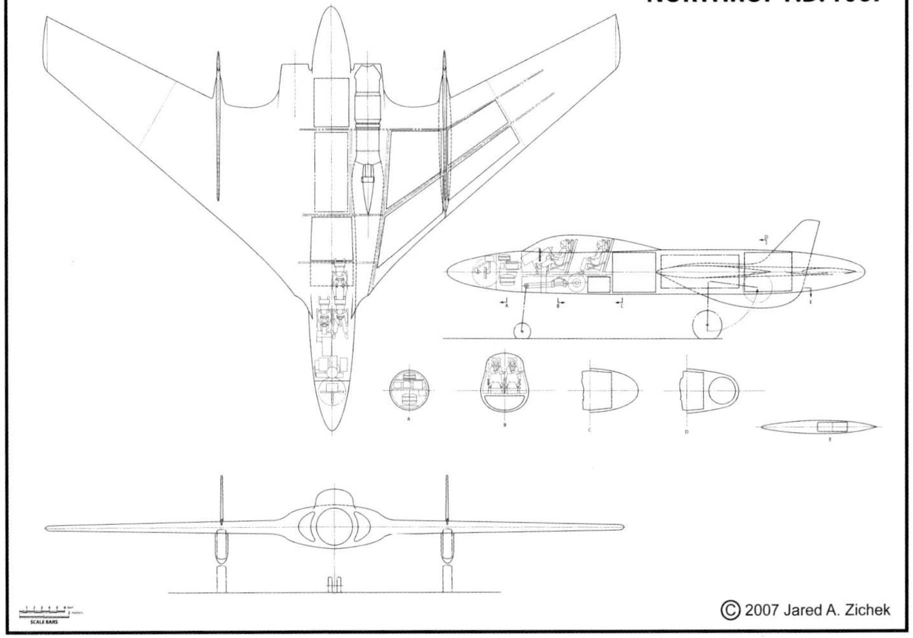

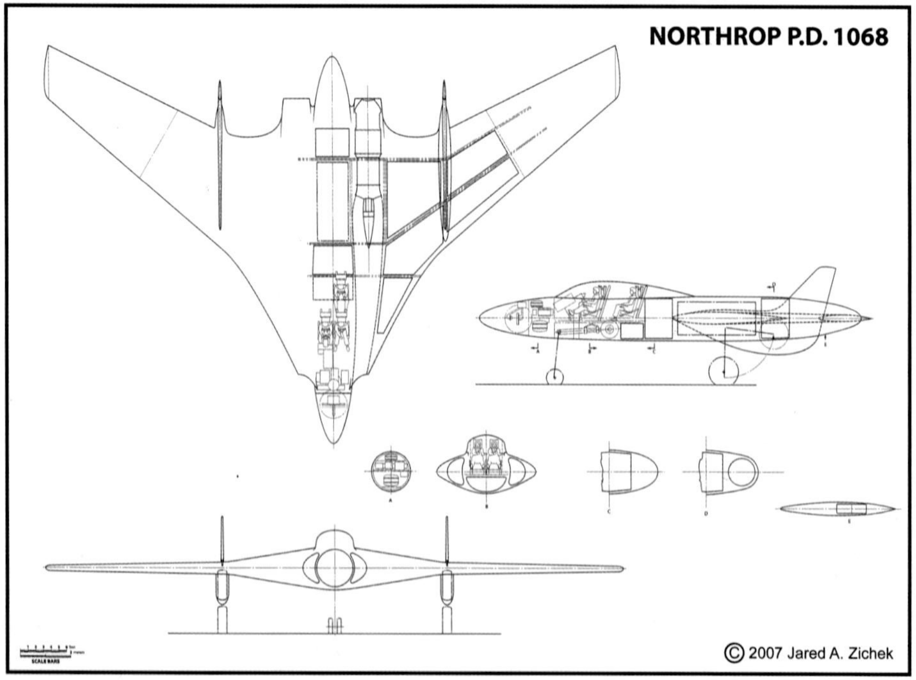
NORTHROP P.D. 1068
© 2007 Jared A. Zichek

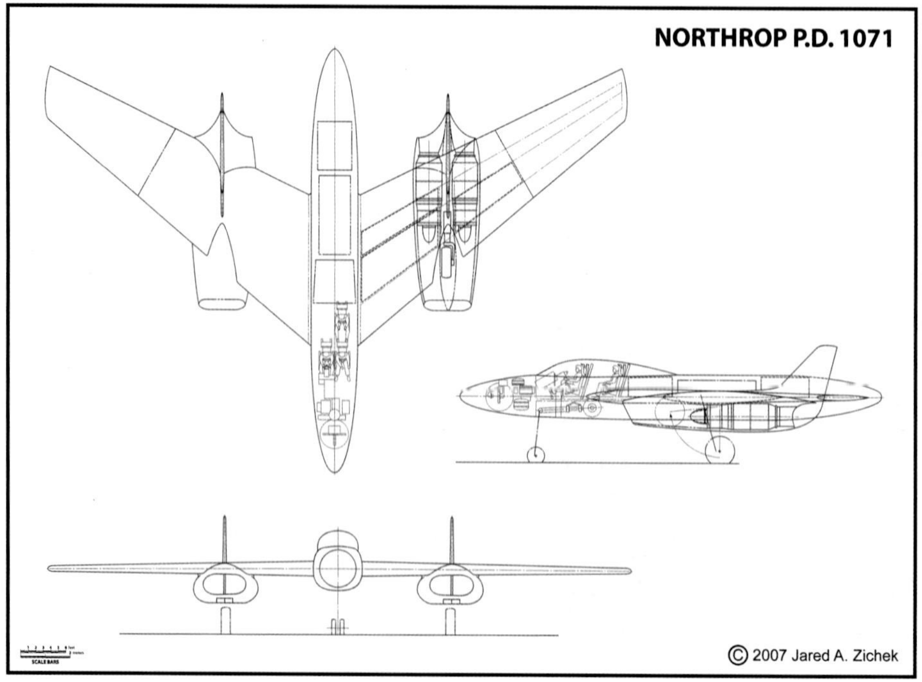
NORTHROP P.D. 1071
© 2007 Jared A. Zichek

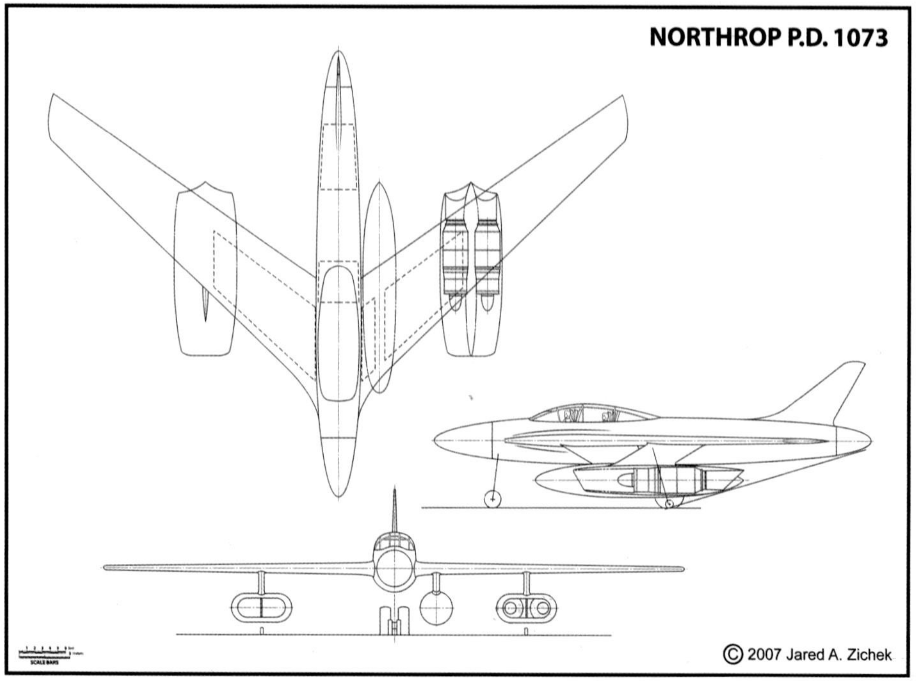
NORTHROP P.D. 1073
© 2007 Jared A. Zichek

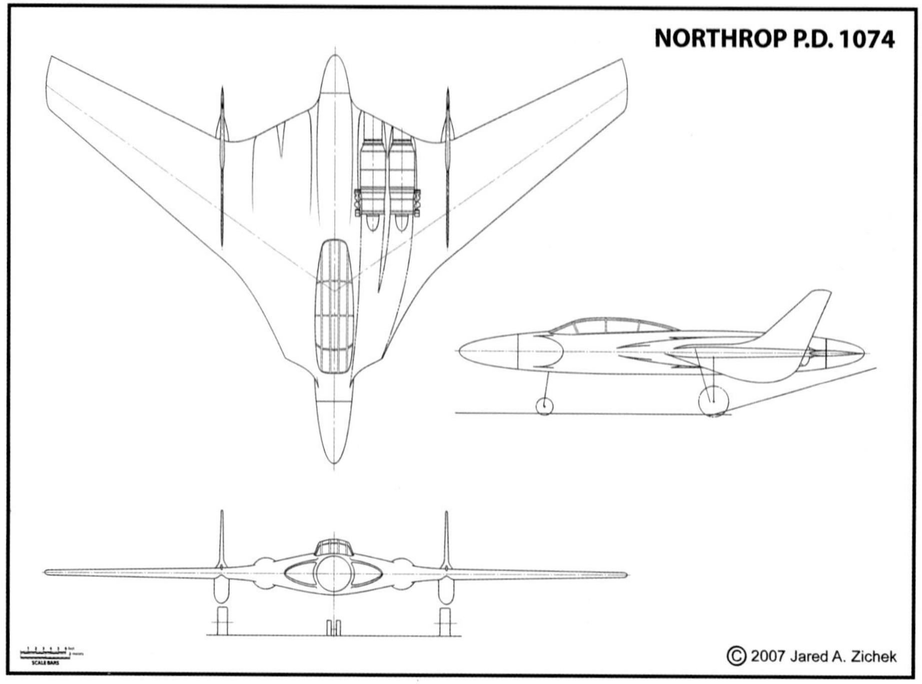
NORTHROP P.D. 1074
© 2007 Jared A. Zichek

Northrop Design Studies for Navy Class VA Type, Carrier Based, 1949 – Characteristics

Preliminary Design (P.D.) No.	VA Type Carrier Based Airplane No.	Engines	Wing Span	Wing Area	Aspect Ratio	Root Chord	Tip Chord	Airfoil/ Airfoil Thickness	Length	Height	Weight Empty	Gross Weight	Date	Designer
P.D. 1029*	2	2 x XJ40-WE-6	68' 2"						55' 4"	20' 7"			August 1949	C.L. Graham
P.D. 1030	3	2 x XJ40-WE-6	71' 3"						56' 10"	20' 8"			8/17/49	C.L. Graham
P.D. 1031		1 x Allison 450-E-1	78' 6"	880 ft^2	7.0			NACA 65 - 009			31,470 lbs	63,782 lbs	8/15/49	C.L. Graham
P.D. 1032*		2 x Turbojets	86' 2"						58' 1"	16' 9"				
P.D. 1033*	6	2 x XJ40-WE-6	70' 11"						51' 9"	15' 1"			8/28/49	Johnston
P.D. 1034		2 x XJ40-WE-6	88' 0"	1,217 ft^2	6.35			NACA 65 - 010	55' 6"		35,922 lbs	65,568 lbs	8/19/49	C.L. Graham
P.D. 1034-B		2 x XJ40-WE-6	73' 0"	1,020 ft^2	5.2			NACA 65 - 010	53' 7"				8/30/49	C.L. Graham
P.D. 1035		2 x XJ40-WE-6	75' 0"	1,063 ft^2	5.3	600"	80"				33,944 lbs	61,693 lbs	9/4/49	D. Smith
P.D. 1036		2 x XJ40-WE-6	56' 8"	1,000 ft^2		228"	74"			17' 0"			8/28/49	Johnston
P.D. 1037	10	2 x XJ40-WE-6	71' 0"	1,018 ft^2	4.96		94"	NACA 65 - 010	55' 2"				8/26/49	M.G. Huben
P.D. 1046		2 x XJ40-WE-6	80' 0"	800 ft^2	8.0			NACA 65 - 010	59' 7"				9/14/49	C.L. Graham
P.D. 1047		2 x XJ40-WE-6	80' 0"	800 ft^2	8.0			NACA 65 - 010	59' 7"				9/15/49	C.L. Graham
P.D. 1048		2 x XJ40-WE-6	75' 0"	810 ft^2	6.94	186"	72"		56' 3"			58,000 lbs	9/15/49	D. Smith
P.D. 1049		2 x XJ40-WE-6	75' 0"	810 ft^2	6.94	186"	72"						9/16/49	D. Smith
P.D. 1050		2 x XJ40-WE-6	80' 0"	800 ft^{28}	8.0			NACA 65 - 010	53' 7"				9/16/49	C.L. Graham
P.D. 1051		1 x XT-37-A Turboprop	75' 0"	800 ft^{28}										
P.D. 1052		2 x XJ40-WE-6	75' 0"	810 ft^2	6.94	186"	72"		56' 3"			62,000 lbs	9/21/49	D. Smith
P.D. 1053		2 x Allison XT-40 Turboprops	80' 0"	800 ft^2	8.0	171.5"	68.5"		58' 7"		38,881 lbs	58,081 lbs	10/3/49	Johnston
P.D. 1054*	18	2 x XJ-60	74' 10"						51' 1"	18' 11"				M.G. Huben
P.D. 1055		1 x XT-37-A Turboprop	75' 0"	810 ft^2	6.94	186"	72"		58' 10"			65,000 lbs	9/27/49	D. Smith
P.D. 1060		2 x XJ-60	75' 0"	1,063 ft^2	5.3	600"	80"		51' 8"	15' 8"	34,506 lbs	68,000 lbs	10/4/49	D. Smith
P.D. 1061		2 x XJ-60	75' 0"	1,037 ft^2	5.4	334.5"	73"		47' 8"		33,076 lbs	65,955 lbs		
P.D. 1067	23	2 x XJ-60	75' 0"	1,024 ft^2	5.5	259"	80"		53' 10"		40,451 lbs	66,671 lbs	10/6/49	M.G. Huben
P.D. 1068	24	2 x XJ-60	75' 0"	1,063 ft^2	5.3	600"	80"		49' 2"		40,315 lbs	66,571 lbs	10/7/49	M.G. Huben
P.D. 1071		4 x Composite Allison Fanjets	75' 0"	1,000 ft^2	5.64			10%	53' 10"		38,498 lbs	68,000 lbs	10/14/49	C.L. Graham
P.D. 1073		4 x Composite Allison Fanjets	75' 0"	810 ft^2	6.94	186"		10% to 8%	56' 3"		39,668 lbs	68,000 lbs	10/18/49	C.L. Graham
P.D. 1074		4 x Composite Allison Fanjets	75' 0"	1069 ft^2	5.3	600" (11% L/D)	80" (9% TR)		51' 8"	15' 8"	39,854 lbs	68,000 lbs		C.L. Graham & Unidentified Designer

*Dimensions are estimated

Bibliography

Primary Sources

National Archives and Records Administration, College Park, Maryland; Record Groups consulted: RG 72, 341, 428

Secondary Sources

Barlow, Jeffrey G. *Revolt of the Admirals: The Fight for Naval Aviation, 1945-1950.* Washington: Brassey's, 1998

Elliott, John M., Maj. USMC (Ret.), *Official Monogram U.S. Navy and Marine Corps Aircraft Color Guide, Volume 2: 1940 to 1949*, Monogram Aviation Publications, 1998

Friedman, Norman. *U.S. Aircraft Carriers: An Illustrated Design History.* Annapolis: US Naval Institute Press, 1983

Miller, Jay. *Convair B-58 Hustler: The World's First Supersonic Bomber.* Leicester: Midland Publishing Limited, 1997

Index

A

B

C

V

W

X

Y